Nelson

KT-513-092

A New Introduction to Sociology

THIRD EDITION

Mike O'Donnell

Senior Lecturer in Sociology and Education
Bath College of Higher Education

Thomas Nelson and Sons Ltd
Nelson House Mayfield Road
Walton-on-Thames Surrey
KT12 5PL UK

Nelson Blackie
Wester Cleddens Road
Bishopbriggs
Glasgow G64 2NZ UK

Thomas Nelson (Hong Kong) Ltd
Toppan Building 10/F
22A Westlands Road
Quarry Bay Hong Kong

Thomas Nelson Australia
102 Dodds Street
South Melbourne
Victoria 3205 Australia

Nelson Canada
1120 Birchmount Road
Scarborough Ontario
M1K 5G4 Canada

© Mike O'Donnell 1992

First edition published by Thomas Nelson and Sons Ltd
1992

I(T)P Thomas Nelson is an International
Thomson Publishing Company.

I(T)P is used under licence.

ISBN 0-17-448177-29
NPN 9 8 7 6 5

Printed in China

The author and publishers wish to thank the following for
permission to use copyright material:

Basil Blackwell Ltd for an extract from R Delmar, 'Looking
Again at Engel's 'Origins of the Family, Private Property
and the State' in J Mitchell and A Oakley, eds. *The Rights
and Wrongs of Women*, 1977;

The Guardian for Figs. 9.1, 11.7, 13.5, 13.6, 15.3 16.3 21.1 and
extract by Martin Woollacot, 25.3.91;

Kenneth Galbraith for an extract from *The Guardian*, 27.3.91;

Harvester Wheatsheaf for Table 6.4 from D N Ashton,
Unemployment Under Capitalism, 1986;

The Controller of Her Majesty's Stationery Office for Tables
4.6, 11.6, Figs. 3.3, 3.4, 4.3, 7.2, 8.2, 13.4, 15.1, 17.1 and short
extracts from *Employment Gazette*;

Hodder and Stoughton, Publishers, for an extract from A
Sampson, *Bankers in a Dangerous World*, 1981

Market & Opinion Research International Ltd. for data
included in Fig. 10.3;

New Statesman and Society for Fig. 15.4 and short text
extracts;

The Observer for Table 6.3 and a short text extract;

Penguin Books Ltd for Fig. 13.3 from J Lee and J Yang,
What is to be Done About Law and Order. Copyright © J Lee
and J Young, 1984;

Routledge for extracts from G D Mitchell, *A dictionary of
Sociology*, J Rex & S Tomlinson, *Colonial Immigrants in a
British City*, S Clegg & D Dunkerley, *Organisation, Class &
Control*, L Leghorn & K Parker, *Women's Worth*, Taylor-
Gooby, *Public Opinion, Idealogy and the Welfare State*, E
Durkheim, *Suicide*, G Marshall, *In Praise of Sociology*, Unwin
Hyman, P Cooke et al, *Localities*, Unwin Hyman, and P
Saunders, *Social Class and Stratification*;

Save the Children for Fig. 18.4, an advertisement;

Times Newspapers Ltd for Table 11.1, 11.5, Figs. 12.2,
16.4, 16.7 and short text extracts from various issues;

University of Cambridge Local Examinations Syndicate,
University of London Examinations and Assessment
Council, University of Oxford Delegacy of Local
Examinations for past examination questions;

Weidenfeld and Nicholson for extracts from R Miliband,
The State in Capitalist Society;

PHOTOGRAPHS

1.1 Topham Picture Source.
1.2 Rex Features.
    Topham Picture Source.
2.2 Mark Power/Network Photographers.
3.2 Homer Sykes/Network Photographers.
6.2 Times Newspapers Limited.
7.1 The Guardian Newspaper.
9.2 The Guardian Newspaper.
10.1 Mike Abrahams/Network Photographers.
10.2 Today Newspaper/Rex Features Limited.
15.2 Times Newspapers Limited.
16.2 Homer Sykes/Network Photographers.
18.1 Dave Hogan/Rex Features Limited.
    Alan Davidson/Alpha.
18.2 Tom Smith/Daily Express/Press Association.
18.4 Caroline Penn/Save The Children.
19.3 Ted Ditchburn/Northern News and Pictures.
19.5 The Guardian Newspaper.

Contents

Preface

The main purpose of the third edition of this book is to up-date it and to expand and re-write several chapters and sections. In doing so, I have particularly kept in mind the requirements of the AEB syllabus first examined in 1991.

Since I started writing this edition, the speed and scale of both national and global change has been almost unprecendented. Suddenly, what was initially intended mainly as an exercise in updating, developed into an attempt to describe and analyse profound and perhaps revolutionary and irreversible changes. Foremost among these has been the collapse of communism in the Soviet Union and Eastern Europe. Other changes at the global level such as a reversing of the arms race, the appearance of new patterns of work and organisation and of new financial and commercial systems, as well as developments in mass communications, seem to have brought us into a 'new age' – even if, as yet, it has not been satisfactorily named. These global developments have impacted highly on Britain and have become entangled with Britain's own unpredicted 'revolution' – Thatcherism. It has become virtually impossible to write about such matters as work and employment, regional development/under-development and the media in Britain without including a global dimension. The period towards the year 2000 will see a struggle to direct and control these powerful forces which at times seem almost out of control.

This edition has involved much more substantial re-writing than did the second one. Religion and media are now full chapters rather than brief sections and the chapters on sociological theory and method, gender, race and Ethnicity, and work and non-work are substantially new. All other chapters contain new material.

An innovation in this edition is the provision of a summary at the end of each chapter. A discussion of coursework issues also occurs at the end of most chapters. Because the bibliography is greatly extended in this edition, the 'Further Reading' sections are much shorter than previously. I have included questions at the end of most chapters but have not attempted to duplicate the stimulus questions which are a growing feature of 'A' level Sociology exams. However, I have included many lengthy quotations in the text and these could be used as stimulus material.

Readers of previous editions of this book may recall that I thought it desirable to state my own basic socio-political values in the preface. A well-known sociologist has attempted to turn this against me and charged me with 'bias' in the body of the book (a charge he also made against other sociology textbook authors). My critic misunderstands my motives in expressing my own values. I retain a strong commitment to both liberty and equality and I would like to think that this persuaded me to write the book in the first place. However, the purpose of telling you, the reader, 'where I'm coming from' is that should I fail in my efforts to be fair and objective, you will be fore-warned of the directions in which my values will take me.

Finally, I would like to encourage students to a healthy disrespect for this and other textbooks. In a world in which the ability to cope with and contribute to change rather than the capacity to remember large amounts of 'fixed' information is at a premium, what matters most is asking intelligent questions rather than remembering the 'right' answers. It is crucial always to relate the information presented in this book to the questions, issues and problems posed. If you don't like the questions I have asked, ask some of your own.

Mike O'Donnell, Ph.D., Senior Lecturer in Sociology and Education, Bath College of Higher Education.

ACKNOWLEDGEMENTS

The first edition of this book was typed mainly by Anne Vellender and Caroline Riddel who gave me much useful advice besides. Gina Garrett was the invaluable general reader. I am grateful for more specialist advice from Howard Newby, Stan Cohen, Tom Bottomore and James A Pey. Tony Marks, the former AEB Chief Examiner, also gave useful advice. My thanks also to Helen Huckle and Diana Grese for their editorial work. For the second edition, Sandra den Hertog, Karen Laws and Marie Brown efficiently met my typing needs. David Lee, Juliette Hunting and Pat Mayes gave useful advice and suggestions.

I have received substantial support in writing the third edition. Joan Garrod, as general reader, and Gordon Marshall, Bryn Jones and Rob Mears as specialist readers have been tremendously helpful. At Nelsons, Julia Cousins and Claire Gilman have seen me through. I thank all the above for their time, patience and assistance. Finally, however, the responsibility for what follows is entirely mine.

1 What is Sociology? Concepts & Perspectives

What is Sociology?

Sociology is the systematic study of societies. Societies may vary in size from a small tribe of Amazonian Indians to Western Society. A society consists of individuals belonging to groups which may vary in size, from, for instance, the family to the total population of a given area. Sociology studies interaction between the self (or individual) and groups, and interaction between groups. The self may both affect certain groups (and so society) and is also affected by groups. Social interaction between the self and others (or, at least, another) begins at birth and usually continues until death. Or to put it more poetically, 'from the rocking of the cradle to the rolling of the hearse', individuals are part of society.

Perhaps the main contribution of sociology is that it can help people better to understand their own lives. It does so by explaining the relationships between personal experience and 'external' events, between self and society. Thus, the loss of a job or the closure of a local school may be seen by a given individual as a purely personal problem or even tragedy, with perhaps little thought being given to the underlying causes of such occurrences. Sociology can help to explain such experience by exploring who is responsible for it – perhaps politicians, planners, investors or trade unionists – and, perhaps, whether what has happened is part of a wider social trend in, say, unemployment or school closures. Often, in making sense of society we begin to make more sense of our own lives.

Charles Wright Mills (1916–62) described the links between self and society in terms of 'personal troubles' – such as losing one's job or being wounded in combat – and 'public issues' – such as rising unemployment or war:

Perhaps the most fruitful distinction with which the sociological imagination works is between 'the personal troubles of milieux' and 'the public issues of social structure'. This distinction is an essential tool of the sociological imagination and a feature of all classic work in social science.

(Mills, 1959: 8)

Mills argued that it requires imagination to see that the immediate 'milieu' or social context of one's own life is often (perhaps always) linked to much wider developments. He urged that sociologists try to connect biography – personal life history – with social change and structure – history and sociology. He claimed that the 'classic' sociologists such as Marx, Durkheim and Weber – have always done this (see pp. 10–12). It remains true that a better understanding of the 'personal/public' axis is, as Mills put it, the purpose of 'the sociological imagination'.

Basic Sociological Concepts

SELF AND SOCIETY

This section further examines the relationship between self and society introduced above. It briefly describes how the self is socialised into a given culture or way of life and then examines the relationship between culture and social structure. Explanations of these key concepts are kept to a minimum here as they are all discussed in greater detail later.

SELF, SOCIALISATION AND CULTURE

SELF Manford Kuhn defines the concept of self as 'denoting the core of the personality system ... organised around its awareness of itself and its conscious and unconscious orientation toward its most vital interests and values, involving identity, status, commitment, and desire' (in J Gould and W Kolb eds. 1964: 628–9). Kuhn suggests that the term 'ego' is interchangeable with that of self within sociology. The important aspects to note from this definition is that the self is conscious of itself and has a sense of its own identity. In so far as personalities and identities are unique, we can speak of 'individuality'.

In considering the nature of the self, it is necessary to introduce a still more fundamental social scientific issue – the extent to which human beings are formed by biological inheritance, i.e. genetically, or through socialisation, i.e. culturally; the celebrated 'nature-nurture debate'. Another way of putting this is the difference between instinct and learned behaviour, the former being inherited, the latter being acquired through socialisation. In general, sociologists take a mininal view of what is instinctive behaviour (broader terms are 'drives' or 'needs'). Thus, most would accept that there are innate (inborn) needs of food, shelter and sex. Beyond this, sociologists prefer to explore the possibility that behaviour is shaped by social experience rather than that it is simply a biological 'given'. However, although the orientation of sociology is towards social explanation there is no contradiction between social and biological explanations of behaviour. It is a matter for empirical research by biologists, sociologists, social biologists and by other relevant subject specialists to establish explanations of human behaviour.

One approach to studying the role of society in forming human behaviour is to examine the development of individuals who were either wholly or largely excluded from social interaction for a period of their lives. Such cases include those who apparently spent much of their childhood isolated from others 'in the wild' and those who were cut off from others through confinement at a similarly early age. Examples of the former are the 'Wild boy of Aveyron' and two girls, the 'Wolf children of Bengal'. A case of the latter is the girl, Genie, who was locked in her room between the ages of one and a half and thirteen.

The effects of 'growing up' in such unsocial conditions in these and similar cases seem consistent. Immediately on emerging into society, the children were typically described by observers as 'primitive' and 'hardly human'. Despite efforts to resocialise them, none of the children developed social and communication skills beyond a rudimentary level. Above all, their limited ability to learn language prevented them from functioning fully in adult society.

The above examples of unsocialised childhood do not have the status of controlled scientific experiments (see pp. 21–5). However, collectively they do suggest that human development, including the acquisition of basic social and communication skills, requires substantial contact with others. It is only in a social context that the self can develop. Self and society are, therefore, complementary concepts rather than in opposition as they are sometimes presented. You cannot have individuals without society or society without individuals.

SOCIALISATION Socialisation is the process by which human behaviour is shaped through experience in social situations. Through socialisation the individual learns the values, norms (formal and informal 'rules'), and beliefs of a given society.

The American sociologist Charles Cooley (1864–1929) distinguished two types of socialisation: primary and secondary. These two forms of socialisation are defined partly in terms of the particular groups or 'agencies' in which they occur. Primary groups are small, involve face-to-face relationships and allow the individual to express the whole self, both feelings and intellect. The family, peer groups of close friends and closely-knit groups of neighbours are primary groups. Within these groups the individual learns, by personal experience, the primary values such as love, loyalty, justice, and sharing. Freud emphasised that the first few years of a person's life – those usually spent amongst primary groups – are the most important in forming the framework of his or her character. Secondary groups are larger, more impersonal, more formally organised, and exist for specific purposes. Secondary socialisation involves learning how to organise and conduct oneself in formal

◀

Figure 1.1(Far left)

The wild boy of

Aveyron

contexts and how to behave towards people who have different degrees of status and authority. The school is an important example of an agency of secondary socialisation, but all formal organisations influence their members to some degree and, to that extent, can be included within this category. Trade unions and professional associations are relevant examples: membership is granted to the individual on the assumption that s/he will conform to the beliefs, aims and regulations of the organisation. In allowing the organisation to affect his or her behaviour in this way, the individual necessarily accepts a socialising influence on his or her conduct. In addition to primary and secondary groups, the mass media – the press, radio, television, the cinema, records, tapes and various other forms of communication which comprise them – play a socialising role whose effects we will consider in more detail later.

The distinction between primary and secondary socialisation parallels that between informal and formal socialisation. Informal socialisation usually takes place as a part of everyday activity: it affects us unconsciously and must be distinguished from the formal acquisition of specific skills such as reading and writing. In primary socialisation, certain values and customs will be formally taught to a child (formal socialisation) but much else will be informally 'picked up' by imitating parents, siblings, and other children.

CULTURE Culture is the way of life of a particular society: it refers to all aspects of human behaviour that are learnt rather than genetically transmitted. It includes the values, norms and beliefs of a particular society as well as the way these are expressed through actions, words and symbols. Socialisation is the means through which cultural transmission occurs and, as we have seen, it is a continuous process. Cultures vary although cultural similarities also occur to a greater or lesser extent. Generally, the greatest cultural differences occur between non-industrial and non-literate societies such as the African pygmies and industrial (or perhaps now, post-industrial) and literate societies such as those of Western Europe. When two very different cultures come into significant contact one or both are invariably changed. Where change

is swift or great, it can be a disruptive and difficult process. This was (and still is) true of the impact of Western, capitalist, Christian culture on much of the rest of the world.

VALUES, NORMS, STATUS AND ROLE

VALUES Values are general but fundamental standards of a given society which have a wide influence on social conduct and organisation. Thus, the value of individualism has had greater influence in capitalist societies and that of collectivism (commitment to the community) more influence in communist societies. The values of hard work and achievement are often associated with capitalist societies and Mrs Thatcher's attempt to foster an 'enterprise culture' may be considered as an effort to reinforce this value orientation. It is not easy to clarify the fundamental values of a given society because of their sheer breadth. To do so is to define the basic nature of a particular culture. In attempting such a definition, it is worth considering whether certain cultural values clash – such as achievement and community or individualism and equality.

NORMS Norms are precepts or guidelines to behaviour. They may be formal – such as the written rules of an organisation – or highly informal such as what kind of dress it is more or less acceptable to wear on a very hot day. As with values, norms vary between cultures but, equally, they can change within a culture. You can probably think of a dozen ways in which norms in contemporary Britain differ from those of a more traditional society.

STATUS AND ROLE Values provide a general guide, and norms a rather more specific guide, to behaviour. The concepts of status and role describe aspects of behaviour itself. A status is a particular position in society. Thus, there are a range of statuses within the family, such as mother and daughter, and within the occupational system such as doctor or shop-assistant. A role is the behaviour expected of a person occupying a given status or social position. Thus, doctors play a role in relation to health and illness and shop-assistants in relation to selling goods. Roles are governed by certain norms or expectations (we 'know' how doctors are supposed to behave) but are also, to some extent, interpreted by the individuals playing them (no two doctors behave in exactly the same way). Robert Merton has suggested that where a status involves more than one social relationship, the term role-set be used rather than role. Thus, the role-set of a shop-assistant includes relationships with a manager, customers and perhaps other shop assistants.

Values, norms, statuses and roles can be thought of within the broader concepts of culture and socialisation. Their specific nature or 'content' is created within given cultures and they vary between cultures. Socialisation is the means by which specific values, norms, statuses and roles are learnt.

SOCIOLOGICAL CONCEPTS AND THEORIES

This chapter has so far examined a number of key sociological concepts: self, society,

socialisation, culture, values, norms, status and role. Other key sociological concepts examined in this book are structure, interaction, power and authority, ideology, community and alienation. These key concepts, or to adopt Robert Nisbet's phrase, 'unit ideas', are too limited to provide an adequate definition of sociology but they do clearly indicate its central concerns. This is even more the case when concepts are related in clusters such as 'self, socialisation and culture' and 'status and role'.

Like individual building bricks, sociological concepts are of limited usefulness in isolation. It is only when concepts are used in creating theories that they play a part in explaining as well as describing social processes. Thus, there are several theories of alienation and a variety of theories focusing on the concept of community. In the next section, we discuss some of the major theoretical issues of sociology.

Perspectives on Society: Sociological Theory

Sociology is an attempt to understand society: how it operates and the experiences and purposes of its members. One way of approaching sociology is to appreciate some of the key questions it raises. The questions and problems raised by the founders of sociology remain in essence those asked by sociologists and, indeed, other interested people today. Here I first briefly introduce the thought of the founders of sociology in order to give an idea of the framework and scope of the discipline. We then look at some key sociological questions. This prepares the way for consideration of the main sociological approaches or perspectives which can be seen as attempts to answer the fundamental questions of sociology. The chapter concludes with an examination of some of the main contemporary trends in sociology.

THE FOUNDING OF SOCIOLOGY: MARX, DURKHEIM AND WEBER

Marx (1818–1883), Durkheim (1858–1917), and Weber (1864–1920) have had a major and lasting impact on the discipline of sociology. They were among the first to look at society in what we have come to think of

as a specifically sociological way.

The continuing relevance of their work reflects two things. First, the general questions they asked are the same as, or similar to, those sociologists ask today. Second, the frameworks of social analysis and explanation or sociological perspectives they worked out have been developed and modified rather than replaced.

THE NINETEENTH CENTURY CONTEXT

The nineteenth century was a period of rapid change every bit as great as today's. Industrial and political revolutions, sometimes known as the 'dual revolutions', tore apart the fabric of society. The agricultural revolution forced peasants off the land, and the industrial revolution provided jobs for them in the cities. Often the new industrial workers – and at first these included women and children – lived and worked in conditions of squalid exploitation. By contrast, the manufacturing, commercial and financial middle class prospered in an industrial boom. The traditional landed aristocracy also generally

Figure 1.2

Karl Marx (1818–1883)

Max Weber

(1864–1920)

thrived, partly because of its great hereditary wealth and power, and partly because many of its members invested in industrial expansion.

Politically, the new middle class struggled successfully to share power with the aristocracy. In Britain, it managed to acquire the vote and other political rights without revolution, but France and other European countries experienced almost a century of political turmoil. As the century progressed, the claims of the working class for political rights and social justice were more and more strongly asserted. In 1848 Europe was swept by revolution. In this, the working class and its supporters played a prominent part. Marx himself participated in an unsuccessful uprising in Germany in that year.

Marx, Durkheim and Weber were interested in, and wanted to understand, the major changes that were occurring in Europe during their own time. Even though they were of different nationalities, Marx and Weber being German and Durkheim being French, the scale and scope of change was such that they were confronted by much the same problems. Our interest arises from the fact that our own period is a direct continuation of theirs, and society today can be partly explained by past events and developments. Ours is an industrial, urban society in which, at last, the working class and women have political rights, but in which class conflict is by no means dead. The nineteenth century was a battleground between the old regime and the new, the traditional and the modern. Along with the study of class relations, the contrast and

conflict between the traditional and the modern remains an axial consideration of sociology. Britain is still cloaked in tradition: witness the continuation of the monarchy and the House of Lords. Further, the conflict between traditional, rural society and modern, industrial society has been partly 'exported' from Europe to the wider world, in which the developing countries are the new battleground. Marx, Durkheim and Weber's writings are of relevance to all these matters.

But the founders of sociology wanted to do more than just tell the tale of their times and perhaps offer a few unsystematic interpretations of events. They went deeper than that in their search for explanations, and in doing so created the foundation of a new discipline, sociology. Separately, they attempted to develop ways of examining society and social change which would account not only for how their own societies functioned and changed but which would explain the nature and functioning of society itself. They believed that a scientific approach would assist them greatly in this enterprise. Indeed, perhaps they put too much faith in science, and many sociologists have since argued that, as well as being affected by society, people also help to create it – perhaps to a greater extent than Marx and Durkheim, though possibly not Weber, allowed. In their faith in science, the founders of sociology reflected the spirit of their period. Charles Darwin's exciting new scientific theory of evolution seemed to offer a biological explanation of the origin of humanity, and Marx, Weber and Durkheim sought to explain social life in similarly scientific terms. They were aware, however, that human consciousness and creativity raise issues that do not occur in the non-human sciences and we return to these later. Marx and Durkheim in particular built up distinctive perspectives or general models of how society works. Since their deaths, other perspectives have been developed within sociology, some of which address themselves more specifically to the problems of the individual in modern society. These are introduced later in this chapter.

The next section will tend to emphasise the differences rather than the similarities between the perspectives of Marx, Weber and Durkheim. However, we attempt to convey the common central concerns of sociology by examining their perspectives in the form of answers to a number of fundamental sociological questions. Sociology is better understood as a series of questions on the nature of society with no set answers, than as a set of agreed findings (although such findings do exist).

Sociological Theory: Structural and Interpretive Perspectives

At this stage, all that we mean by sociological theory is the body of ideas, tested and untested, making up sociological thought.

We can best understand the disagreements among contemporary sociologists, many of which have their roots in the thought of Durkheim, Marx and Weber, by examining some basic questions of sociological theory to which, in one way or another, all three gave answers. It would not be possible to construct an adequate sociological perspective without answering the following questions, although other major questions could also be asked:

1 How is society constructed?
2 How does society 'operate' or function?
3 Why are some groups in society more powerful than others?
4 What causes social change?
5 Is society normally in orderly balance or in conflict?
6 What is the relationship of the individual to society?
7 What is the primary purpose of sociological study?

The answers given to these questions by Durkheim, Marx and Weber helped to produce three distinct traditions of sociological thought or perspectives: functionalism which owes much to Durkheim, Marxism (Marx), and social action theory (Weber). We will examine separately these three traditions and the answers they give to the above questions of theory. All three of these sociological perspectives are structural in nature. Structural sociology is primarily concerned with how society affects individual and group behaviour, rather than with how individuals and groups create society. Thus, the sort of issue a structural sociologist would be interested in is how the class and family background of an individual (the individual's social-structural position) affect his or her chances of doing well at school and getting a good job. Functionalism is referred to as consensus structuralism because it emphasises the central role that agreement (consensus) between people on moral values has in maintaining social order. Marxism and social action theory, on the other hand, stress conflict in society rather than consensus. It is a further crucially important feature of the structuralist theories that they tend to seek scientific or positivist explanations of social behaviour.

Interpretive sociology, in contrast to structuralism, is primarily concerned with how individuals and groups create, find meaning in, and experience society, rather than in how society affects them. Examples of the kind of matters that have interested interpretive sociologists are what it 'feels like' to be labelled a 'criminal' or 'mad', or simply 'not very bright' at school work. Interpretive sociology is, in part, a reaction against the scientific or positivist approach associated with the structural perspectives. Interpretive sociology is further explained later in this chapter (see pp. 11–14). Immediately, the structural sociologies of functionalism, Marxism and social action theory are described by reference to the seven key questions stated above. It can be seen that the answers given to the questions by the various perspectives differ, sometimes to the point of contradiction. It needs to be stressed that the following section on functionalism reflects the work of later functionalists, besides Durkheim, particularly that of Talcott Parsons (1902–1979).

Structural Perspectives

Functionalism (Consensus Structuralism): Durkheim

1 How is society constructed?

Society or the social system is constructed of various institutions, the most basic of which is the family. A social institution is a group of people organised for a specific purpose (or purposes) – the nuclear family, for example, is organised in order to produce and rear children. As societies develop, the number and complexity of social institutions increases. This process is referred to as differentiation. The civil service and industrial corporations are examples of complex, modern institutions. They developed, respectively, from the King's adviser and small-scale cottage industries.

Institutions are grouped together into four sub-systems:-

- Economic (factories, offices)
- Political (political parties)
- Kinship (families)
- Cultural and community organisations (schools, churches)

2 How does society 'operate' or function?

Functionalists consider that society 'operates' in a way comparable to the functioning of a biological organism. This comparison is referred to as the organic analogy (or organismic analogy). So social institutions function in combination with one another and for the benefit of society as a whole, just as the various parts of the human body function in relation to one another and to the whole body. For example, schools function in relation to work because they prepare people for work. And, like the human body, society is more than the sum of its individual parts.

Although the structure and functioning of society can be separated for the purpose of theoretical consideration, in reality they are inseparable. Obviously, a society or organisation has to exist (have structure) before it can do anything (function).

3 Why are some groups in society more powerful than others?

The unequal possession of power in society has tended to interest Marxists and social action theorists more than functionalists. The latter tend to assume that it is practically necessary that some individuals and groups be more powerful than others, because only a limited number can take important decisions. Thus, they argue that there must be leaders in organisations and in society, otherwise there would be chaos.

4 What causes social change?

According to functionalists, social change occurs when it is functionally necessary for it to do so. For example, in modern societies educational systems tend to expand because such societies require a more literate and numerate population than less 'advanced' societies.

Change may occur through adaptation or integration. Adaptation occurs when an existing institution readjusts to meet new needs – as in the example given in the last paragraph. Integration occurs when a society adopts a new element and makes it part of itself. Thus, a society may successfully integrate (or fail to integrate) a group of immigrants. Functionalists tend to think of change as evolutionary (gradual), not revolutionary.

5 Is society normally in orderly balance or in conflict?

Functionalists consider that order and equilibrium (balance) are normal to society. Disequilibrium (civil war, for example), is an abnormal social state. They compare disequilibrium in society to sickness in a living organism.

The basis of social equilibrium is the existence of moral consensus. Moral consensus means that everybody, or nearly everybody in a society shares the same values. Thus, a high level of consumption of goods might be a value in American society, but not in many economically and technologically more 'primitive' societies. As we shall see in a later chapter, functionalists stress the importance of the effective teaching of social values in maintaining order and conformity. The role of parents and teachers in passing on values to the younger generation is stressed.

6 What is the relationship of the individual to society?

Functionalists regard the individual as formed by society through the influence of such institutions as the family, school and workplace. They leave little room for the view that the individual can significantly control his or her own life, let alone change society. Durkheim stated that, for him, the individual is the point of arrival, not of departure. In other words, in his view sociology is not about the individual. As we shall see, not all sociologists agree with this.

7 What is the primary purpose of sociological study?

The primary purpose of sociology is to analyse and explain the normal (and abnormal) functioning of society. This involves studying the relationship of the different parts of society to one another, and of the parts to the whole. Thus, the relationship between education and work is studied, but so too is the (necessary) contribution of both to the functioning of the social system as a whole. Durkheim insisted that sociologists should discover and explain the relationship between social facts, just as natural scientists do with physical facts.

Marxism (Conflict Structuralism 1)

1 How is society constructed?

According to Marx, society is constructed from classes. In all societies except the most simple, there are two major social classes. It is people's relationship to the means of production that determines which class they are in. The most powerful class is that which owns the means of production (land, factories) and the least powerful is that which has to sell its labour in order to make a living. In capitalist society (a society based on a private enterprise economy), the capitalist class or bourgeoisie as Marx called it, is the ruling class and the working class or proletariat, the subordinate class. In other words, in his view, business controls labour.

2 How does society 'operate' or function?

In Marx's view society operates mainly through class conflict. Each class normally pursues its own interest, and this brings it into conflict with other classes. In particular, he argued that in capitalist society the bourgeoisie and proletariat are fundamentally opposed. This point is developed and explained later.

3 Why are some groups in society more powerful than others?

For Marx, class is the basis of power. Some classes are more powerful than others because they own more property and wealth, and this gives them the means to defend and keep what they hold. Unlike functionalists, Marx did not consider that this state of affairs is inevitable and necessary. He believed that socialism could achieve a more equal sharing of power, property and wealth.

4 What causes social change?

Social change occurs as a result of class conflict. Class conflict is the dynamo of history. In the later middle ages, there was conflict between the landed aristocracy and the rising bourgeoisie, and in capitalist society the major conflict is between the bourgeoisie and the proletariat. The victory of a new class introduces a new historical period. Thus the rise of the bourgeoisie introduced the capitalist epoch.

5 Is society normally in orderly balance or in conflict?

Society is in a state of fundamental conflict between the classes. Marx recognised, however, that periods of social order and equilibrium can occur, in which class conflict is temporarily submerged. He argued that such periods benefit the rich and powerful more than others.

6 What is the relationship of the individual to society?

There are two major schools of thought amongst Marxists about the relationship of the individual to society, and these reflect an ambiguity in Marx's work itself. One tradition of Marxist thought tends to see the individual as powerless to affect either his or her own life or that of others. Those who hold this view regard class conflict and socialist revolution as inevitable regardless of what any single individual may do. Some Marxists, however, see a much greater role for the individual in society even though they still see the prime source of individual identity as coming from class membership (pp. 123–4).

7 What is the primary purpose of sociological study?

The purpose of sociology is to describe, analyse and explain class conflict. Marxists also want to change the world in a Marxist direction. However, in the late nineteen eighties and early nineties, the 'Marxist' Societies of Eastern Europe experienced crisis and change (see pp. 15–16). The main practical alternative model to capitalism began to fragment. Even so, this does not necessarily mean that Marxist sociological analysis of capitalism is wholly wrong.

Social Action Theory (Conflict Structuralism 2): Weber

1 How is society constructed?

Society is created through social interaction. Social interaction is the behaviour of people consciously relating to one another. In the process of interaction, people form institutions. Although people create institutions such as schools, factories and churches, these institutions in turn influence people. This is partly because pressure exists to observe the rules and procedures of institutions.

Weber felt that Marx overemphasised the importance of class groupings. He recognised that classes are important but considered political parties and status groups (social and friendship groups) to be further powerful and important forces in society, not necessarily dependent on class (as Marx contended they essentially were). This major point of difference between Marx and Weber is explained fully in chapter five. Weber also stressed the power of large organisations or bureaucracies over the life of the individual.

2 How does society 'operate' or function?

Again, Weber's answer to this question shows his keen awareness of both the individual's influence on society and of society's influence on the individual. On the one hand, he stresses that the ideas and feelings people have do sometimes inspire action and affect history. For example, he argued that certain powerful and dynamic figures, or charismatic leaders as he called them, such as Christ and Napoleon, really can change the course of events. On the other hand, he realised that most people's lives are formed and limited by the society they live in, and particularly by the immediate institutions they come in contact with, such as schools and places of work. He was personally concerned that large-scale institutions of modern societies (factories, government bureaucracies for example) would limit the scope of individual freedom and creativity. It seems to worry Weber more than it does the strict functionalists that many people may be only 'small cogs in large machines' as far as their work is concerned.

3 Why are some groups in society more powerful than others?

Power is one of Weber's central concepts. He combines elements of consensus and conflict sociology in his treatment of this matter. He agreed with the functionalists that for society to function efficiently some people have to have more power than others. He pointed out that in modern bureaucratic organisations (the civil service, for example) there are always more powerful people at the top, and less powerful people at the bottom; that is, bureaucracies are organised hierarchically. But Weber also accepted with Marx that those groups which do gain a powerful position in society tend to use it primarily in their own interest. Thus, in medieval society the king and nobility used power for their own ends, even though they may also have sometimes used it for the general good as well.

4 What causes social change?

Weber considered that social change can occur for many reasons, or, more technically, according to his analysis, social change is multifactoral. Ideas, new inventions, war, the rise and fall of power groups, influential individuals and other factors all contribute to, and are part of, historical change. In insisting on the possible variety of causes of change, Weber wished to distinguish his position from that of Marx, whom he thought overemphasised class conflict as an explanation for change.

5 Is society normally in orderly balance or in conflict?

The issue of equilibrium and conflict in society is posed to contrast functionalism and Marxism, and is of less central concern to social action theorists. Weber considered that society is not normally either in balance or in conflict – the state of society varies from case to case. A society may be untroubled for centuries and then be plunged into decades of turmoil. Weber preferred to study specific cases rather than make sweeping generalisations about what is 'normal'.

6 What is the relationship of the individual to society?

The relationship of the individual to society is of central importance in social action theory. Although Weber fully realised that individuals are affected by social institutions such as the family, school, the workplace and the mass media, he did not consider analysis of the operation and effect of these influences to be the only or primary purpose of sociology. It is more important, in his view, to understand the meanings that individuals experience in their own social lives than simply to analyse what 'causes' or 'influences' them to act as they do. Although Weber appreciated that individual social action is uniquely experienced by the social actor, he still felt able to generalise about social action, because in practice there are widely-shared patterns of social behaviour. For instance, people may act rationally, emotionally or idealistically, and it is possible to categorise and generalise their actions accordingly. Despite Weber's emphasis on interpreting the quality and potential variety of individual experience and meaning, he was committed to scientific sociology. Nevertheless, although we have termed him a conflict structuralist in this section, he was also a founding father of interpretive sociology.

The interpretive approach has become popular, and has developed in a number of forms in the twentieth century.

7 What is the primary purpose of sociological study?

The purpose of sociology is to understand and explain the meaning of social action and interaction.

Interpretive Perspectives

There have been other attempts besides Weber's to 'build in' individual meaning and intention into sociological theory. These include symbolic interactionism, ethnomethodology and the basically philosophical perspective of phenomenology. The most influential and easiest to understand of these is symbolic interactionism, or simply interactionism. This is dealt with first and at some length. Ethnomethodology is only briefly dealt with in this chapter and phenomenology is not presented until a later chapter.

Interactionism

The structural (or systems) theories so far examined tend to approach the relationship of self and society from the point of view of the influence of society on the self. Interactionists tend to work from the self 'outwards', stressing that people create society. The perspective is sometimes referred to as symbolic interactionism because of its emphasis on the importance of the symbolic means of communication;

including language, dress and gesture. Interactionists fully accept that society does constrain and form individuals although they consider that there is invariably opportunity for some 'creative' action – to use a favourite word of W I Thomas, an early interactionist. Interactionism developed mainly at the University of Chicago during the inter-war years. The social psychologist George Mead (1880–1949) was probably the most influential figure among interactionists.

Mead describes two general stages in the development of the self: the play and game stages. Prior to these stages the child's relationship to others is one of imitation without conscious awareness of the meaning of actions.

At the play stage, the child begins to try out certain familiar roles such as parent, teacher or doctor. The child's 'let's pretend to be ...' is a powerful in-built learning device. It is, however, limited. At this stage, the child does not see beyond individual roles to a more generalised view of social situations. He or she only attempts to perform the roles of certain 'significant others' seen at first hand or perhaps through the media. It is as if in the early stages of learning a play, the child 'gets to know' some leading parts but has little sense of the 'plot' as a whole.

The game stage involves virtually a double progression. Firstly, in Mead's words, 'the child must have the attitude of all the others involved in that game' or situation. Perhaps children play team games so badly because they have not fully developed an awareness of the various roles in the team or a competent way of fitting in with other roles. Gradually, the child becomes more socially aware, not only at games, of course, but in other group situations such as meals and outings. However, the full development of self depends not only on the awareness of all other roles in a situation but on the further ability to realise that the group,

community or society as a whole 'exercises control over the conduct of its individual members'. In this sense, Mead refers to the group as a whole as the 'generalised other'. Only in so far as the child learns to take the attitude of the other does s/he become a full member of society. Essentially, Mead is saying the same thing as Parsons. Both recognise the need for the child to learn 'the rules of the game' or of society. Crucially, Mead gives more emphasis to the capacity of the individual to 'play the game' actively and creatively. This is apparent in the aspect of his thought to which we now turn and which complements the above.

Mead divided the self into the 'I' and the 'me'. The 'I' is the active part of the self whereas the 'me' is passive, that is, the 'me' is the part that others (significant and generalised) act upon (see diagram below). Charles Cooley, a colleague of Mead's, used the term 'looking-glass self' to describe how we see an image or get an impression of ourselves through the responses of others. As the individual becomes aware of the 'me', he or she is also able to act upon him or herself, by controlling it. As Mead put it, the individual becomes an object to him or herself. More than Cooley, Mead wanted to stress that the 'I' can control or direct the self not only to conform but to act independently. As he put it: 'The 'I' gives the sense of freedom, of initiative'. Mead noted that the dynamic 'I' often dominates over the conformist 'me' in highly creative people such as artists and brilliant sportsmen but that we all have moments of originality (or, at least, moments that feel original). In providing a framework of analysis in which the social actor could indeed be conceived of as acting, often unpredictably and with uncertain consequences, Mead made an outstanding contribution to social science.

Mead's awareness of both the constraints on (controls and limits) and creativity of social interaction is apparent in his analysis of language – a central feature of symbolic interactionism. Language is the major vehicle of social communication. Its purpose is to express meaning. Of necessity, the young child is, at first, only the object of linguistic communication, but gradually begins to use language for his or her own purposes. Mead strenuously rejects the notion that language is simply a matter of imitation (except, he concedes, in the

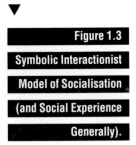

Figure 1.3

Symbolic Interactionist

Model of Socialisation

(and Social Experience

Generally).

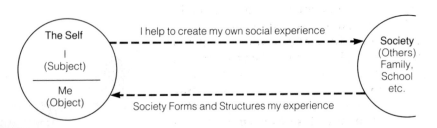

parrot). Nearly all the meanings that an individual could want to express are available in the stock of words of most languages, but even so, scientists and poets operating at the limits of available meaning and language do create new words and linguistic forms. This is what language is for: to provide meaningful symbolism. When necessary, new verbal symbols are created. Because the main concern of symbolic interactionists is with meaningful communication they have a primary interest in language. Interactionists frequently stress that (by means of language) people negotiate the various social roles they are expected to play. This means that they bargain with others, often those in authority, about how exactly they will perform them. This suggests the further concept of negotiated order. For example, certain students or workers may be able to 'get away with' doing less work than others because, over time, they have managed to establish or 'negotiate' a lower level of performance with whoever is in charge. Others may also try to do so but for some reason fail. Order exists but it reflects the complexities and negotiations of interaction. Similarly, interactionists note that different individuals interpret the same role in different ways. Roles are seen as less binding than functionalists suggest. Thus, as a glance around your classroom or lecture hall will verify, the role of student can be interpreted in many different and contrasting ways.

Before concluding this section, we need to be clear about how interactionists approach the analysis of social institutions. For them, an institution is not a 'thing' separate from the people that make up its structure, but is considered as the product of interaction; this is true of the family, the school, the peer group. Indeed, any institution can be viewed as the product of the interaction of the people of whom it is composed. As we shall see when we examine specific topics, such as education and work, this perspective is extremely fruitful.

The nature of modern symbolic interactionist theory is well illustrated by the metaphors interactionists use to describe social life. Erving Goffman has compared social interaction with the dramatic action of a play, and Eric Berne, the founder of transactional psychoanalysis, entitled one of his books *Games People Play*. For Goffman,

the main difference between acting in a play and 'acting' in life is that there is more scope for role interpretation in life itself; nor is the social actor tied to a formal script but can improvise freely. He recognises that social change greatly depends on such original and creative 'improvisation'. Yet, the essential similarity between drama and life remains and Goffman adopts a dramaturgical model of social interaction. Social life, like a play is 'made up': it is a human construction that has the meaning and 'reality' that human beings give it.

Two related criticisms of interactionism can be made at this point. Despite the perspective's emphasis on the interaction of self and society, it does not adequately deal with macro (large-scale) issues of power and structure. For instance, the question of which group or class controls society is not one that is central to interactionism. It is as though the approach of working out through the self via interaction with others loses direction before it reaches the issues of control and power that affect, perhaps, millions. Nevertheless, as we shall see, interactionism provides great insight into issues of power and control at the group or small organisation level. Thus, interactionism has become essential in understanding the detailed processes of teacher-pupil interaction and the 'labelling' of certain individuals as 'deviant'.

A second criticism of interactionism is that it suffers from a certain naive, liberal optimism. This criticism does not obviously emerge from the above account of Mead's key concepts, but Chicago interactionists tended to believe that given the 'freedom' to interact and learn through experience, people would reach rational and humane conclusions, and therefore create a rational, humane society. This view reflects both nineteenth century belief in progress and the American dream of self and societal achievement. Of course, this view of human nature is just as valid as the conservative emphasis of functionalism on the need for constraint and control and the more sombre view of Marxists that it is natural for people to act first and foremost in their own self (i.e. class) interest. However, post-second world war interactionists have not quite maintained the optimism of their precursors. For Goffman and the deviancy theorist Howard Becker, it is not the ordinary but the extraordinary person that is 'hero' – the 'outsider' who wittingly or otherwise challenges 'society'. If, in turn, this orientation has drawn the criticism of

romanticism it is, at least, an antidote to the conformism implicit in the structural perspectives.

Ethnomethodology

The Californian sociologist, Harold Garfinkel, founded ethnomethodology in the late nineteen fifties and early nineteen sixties. The cumbersome term ethnomethodology in fact accurately describes the approach.

'Ethnic' means 'people' or 'cultural group' and the term, therefore, means methods used by people – specifically, to create meaning and order in social life. Garfinkel considers that the basic method social actors use to create meaning is 'commonsense reasoning'. He argues that inter-subjective (i.e. personally shared) communication and reasoning can lead to shared interpretations of experience (i.e. people achieve a common understanding of things). Thus, typically, groups of people from, say, jurors to teachers develop their own ways of thinking and behaving and it is these that sociologists

should study.

Garfinkel stresses that social order is created and recreated by actors reasoning and communicating and is not the product of externally imposed norms. He has devised a number of 'natural' situations in which normal expectations of participants are not met and yet in which they continue to try to make orderly sense out of what is happening. Thus, he contrived a situation in which a student counsellor gave entirely arbitrary answers to clients. Nevertheless, the student-clients did struggle to make sense and order out of the nonsense. Garfinkel's view of order as a negotiated process rather than as 'something' externally imposed is a major contribution to sociology and, in particular, has greatly influenced organisational and institutional analysis.

Important Contemporary Influences on Sociology

In addition to the development of sociology through the major perspectives discussed above, there are a number of contemporary movements whose origin lies largely outside sociology, which nevertheless have greatly influenced the development of the discipline. Among the most influential of such movements are feminism, anti-racism, the new right ('Thatcherism') and the environmental or 'green' movement. These are briefly discussed below but they frequently recur in this book as strands of influence across specific sociological topics. The possible effects of the decline of communism on Marxist sociology and the emergence of a radical alternative perspective are also discussed.

FEMINISM

In the nineteen fifties women were, if not quite 'invisible' within sociology, certainly in a secondary and subordinate position to men. This was true both in terms of who had

power and prestige within the discipline – overwhelmingly men – and in terms of the presentation and content of the subject – 'masculinised' language and illustrations told about a world dominated by male concerns. Sociology has probably been more open to change than most areas of society in respect to gender (male/female relations). Today, the world is still largely dominated by males but there appears to have been a greater increase in the proportion of women in higher status positions within sociology than in other areas – although they are still in a minority even here. However, the presentation and content of the subject is undergoing radical change if not revolution because of the feminist movement. Certainly, most sociology textbooks and probably the majority of all sociology books are now written in gender neutral language (at least, their authors attempt to do so!). The content of sociology has been substantially 'feminised'. Gender relations;

including the (continuing) emancipation of women, is a topic in itself but the issue of patriarchy (male domination) and the problems and priorities of women have become part of every sociological topic. The research, redefining and theorising involved in this have made sociology a vastly more enlightening and potentially liberating discipline for both sexes.

ANTI-RACISM

Anti-racism is one of several terms which could be used to indicate the movements of opposition to racism and in favour of racial equality that have been a feature of the post-war world. Looked at in total, these movements have had both a cultural and structural dimension. Culturally, they have asserted the reality of black achievement – often missing from official syllabuses, including sociology ones – and have opposed racial prejudice by attacking racist stereo-types and 'humour'. Many sociologists have attempted to 'deracialise' the subject, and this has also happened in other academic areas, such as history. Black achievements and issues relating to black culture and its relations with white culture have been increasingly covered, although there remain large areas of inadequate understanding.

The structural dimension of anti-racism focuses on the lack of black power within institutions: business, educational or whatever. In this sense, institutional racism has been widely adopted as a concept within sociology. Whether sociologists have effectively applied anti-racist values to the organisation of their own discipline is more debatable. There appear to be as few black people in leading positions in sociology as in other professions. A partial exception to this is the sociology of race itself but perhaps this merely reinforces the stereotype.

THE NEW RIGHT

The new right is a more specifically political movement than feminism or anti-racism although it has had a very pervasive cultural influence. At the core of new right philosophy is a belief in a particular version of individualism and a converse scepticism about state control and interference. New right philosophers such as Roger Scruton, and politicians, such as Norman Tebbitt, are radical individualists in the sense that they believe in the maximum possible freedom for the individual. This ideology has had its most influential application in economics, where the 'free market' approach has had a world-wide impact in the last decade or so. However, the new right is equally a moral and cultural movement. Its rhetoric of individual enterprise and reward and its strictures against state 'meddling' (often identified with 'socialism') have, at times, had almost a revivalist fervour and, indeed, the extent to which this philosophy has revived from its low ebb in the nineteen sixties is remarkable. The new right strongly contends that capitalism is the only socio-economic system which adequately allows for individual freedom.

The impact of new right thinking on sociology has taken some time to develop. In the late nineteen eighties, David Marsland wrote highly critically about what he perceived as a distinct left-wing bias in sociology textbooks. However, he did not himself produce a general account of sociology which presumably would have incorporated new right perspectives. In his introductory text 'Social Class and Stratification' Peter Saunders does include precisely such analysis and leaves the distinct impression that he favours it over other accounts (see p. 163). However, it remains to be seen what the overall impact of new right thinking on sociology will be and whether a new right 'school' of sociology develops.

THE EFFECTS OF THE DECLINE OF COMMUNISM ON MARXIST SOCIOLOGY

At the time of writing in late 1991, it is too early to be sure what effects the apparent collapse of communism in the Soviet Union and Eastern Europe will have on Marxist sociology. The effects may be profound but it is unlikely that Marxist sociology will either be wholly discredited or abandoned. Marxist sociology is very different from communist political and social practice. Marxist sociology is a theory about how society 'works' and its most detailed application is to capitalist society. Marxist analysis of capitalism can be considered quite separately from the attempts to build communist societies. The Mexican writer Octavio Paz puts the point well: 'The failure of communism to provide a satisfactory answer to society's questions does not mean that the questions are wrong' (Quoted 'Times' October 1991). Marxism continues to offer explanation and comment on poverty and inequality, urban squalor, rising crime and consumer culture in capitalist society.

However, Marxist sociology cannot remain a purely critical perspective, unresponsive to historical events. I suggest that the failure of Soviet communism (perhaps of twentieth century communism) offers at least two main 'lessons' to Marxists who have not already learnt them. First, to be worthwhile at all, communism and/or socialism must be democratic. Totalitarianism is a human evil not to be risked again. The Marxist critique of capitalism might acquire greater bite and conviction if it had more to say about democracy and participation. Second, it is now virtually self-evident that in terms of both choice and efficiency 'free markets' must operate in respect to most goods and services (although, of course, cooperatives as well as capitalist enterprises can compete in free markets and, further, certain goods or services, such as health, might be provided on the basis of need rather than individual purchasing power). It may be that a 'communism' which is radically democratic and which broadly accepts economic markets won't be different to democratic socialism. Similarly, to the extent that Marxist sociology adopts these assumptions, it too may begin to lose its distinctive character and become absorbed within a more general radical sociological perspective or approach.

RADICAL SOCIOLOGY

It is highly arguable that, in practice, Marxism is no longer the main alternative sociology to 'functionalist/capitalist' sociology. As has already been indicated, a large body of sociology reflecting feminist and anti-racist perspectives has emerged since the nineteen sixties. Further, much sociological analysis of class inequality has not been based on precise Marxist assumptions (about which, in any case, Marxists disagree). Concern with the triple inequalities of gender, 'race' and class provides the focus for what can be referred to as a radical sociology of the left. Crucially,

in claiming the existence of a broad radical sociology, there is a clear tendency for sociologists concerned with one of these inequalities, also to be concerned, to a greater or lessor extent, with the other two.

Two of the main characteristics of radical sociology are that it is critical of the inequalities of present society and concerned to show that change is possible. Howard Sherman and James Wood make these points effectively in their book, *Sociology: Traditional and Radical Perspectives.*

Radical sociology attempts to view social arrangements from the perspective of oppressed groups – groups such as the poor, the unemployed, workers, blacks and other minorities, and women. From this point of view it carefully analyses the major institutions of capitalist society. It asks how these institutions – social, political and economic – evolved into their present forms. It asks who benefits by these institutions and if a major change in society is possible and necessary. Finally, radical sociology considers possible alternatives to present social organisation.
(1982: Preface)

It should be added that any radical sociology must be as concerned with human freedom as with achieving greater equality. The failure of Eastern European communism, particularly the oppression and denial of human and civil rights, should make it clear that attempts to bring about greater equality at the expense of basic freedom are likely to achieve neither. There needs to be careful analysis of the relationship between freedom and equality and of the desirable balance between the two.

Finally, the concern of radical sociologists with oppression and inequality is increasingly on a global rather than narrowly national scale. This reflects the increasingly inter-related nature of global society. This issue is briefly examined in the following section.

ENVIRONMENTALISM (AND INTERNATIONALISM)

Like the other movements discussed in this section, environmental awareness and concern occur outside of sociology. Indeed, sociology has been slower in incorporating an environmental perspective than, for instance, feminist and anti-racist perspectives. This may be because whereas the latter focus on specific social groups, the state of the environment is not the concern of any group in particular – although it affects everybody. Nevertheless, environmentalism has impinged on sociology in the area of economic and related social change. Thus, sociologists increasingly analyse economic investment and disinvestment both in Britain and internationally in terms not only of its effect on people but also on the environment. Community analysis now routinely locates people within environmental as well as social contexts. Both are related to economic development, or lack of it. Thus, the decline and possible revival of inner urban areas is envisaged as a complex economic, social and environmental issue. Urban decay has meant unemployment, a wasted industrial environment, and consequent lack of opportunity, demoralisation and discontent. What a revival will mean is not yet clear.

Integration of economic, social and environmental analysis similarly occurs in the area of international development and underdevelopment. For instance, it is increasingly appreciated that multi-national companies can make or break whole communities and that unless governments control them and hold them to account, they may do so irresponsibly. Further, there is a growing awareness of the environmental damage sometimes caused by economic 'development' in terms of both people and their planet and of the dangers of leaving this damage as a huge 'debt' to future generations.

Sociology is well suited to grapple with accelerating internationalisation. This phenomenon is occurring politically (for instance, in the moves to greater European co-operation); culturally, in the way both the media and religions cross international boundaries; and, of course, economically. Sociology has always sought to explain and make sense of change and is increasingly impelled to do so in the context of an interdependent world or, in Marshall McLuhan's words, 'a global village'.

◀

Figure 1.4

Sociology : Theoretical perspectives and influences

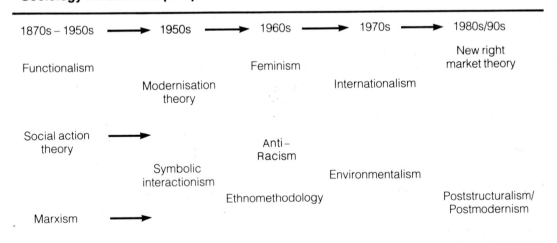

Note : The dates in the diagram are intended to give only an approximate idea of the growth and development of a particular perspective/influence.

SUMMARY

1 Sociology is the systematic study of societies. Society is made up of individuals and groups. Sociology can help the self or individual better to understand his or her life by explaining how 'external' events affect personal experience.

2 'Self, socialisation and culture' are a related 'cluster' of basic sociological concepts. Socialisation is the process by which the self learns the culture or way of life of his or her society.

3 'Values and norms' are a related pair of concepts. Values are standards which underlie the norms or rules of a society.

4 'Status and role' are a related pair of concepts. A status is a particular position in society and a role is the behaviour expected of a person in a particular status.

5 The sociology of Marx, Durkheim and Weber can be viewed as attempts to understand the great developments of their epoch: such as capitalism, industrialisation, urbanisation, and the emergence of new forms of social conflict. Their perspectives or models of society were structural in nature in that they mainly described how social forces and developments 'bear down on' or 'structure' the lives of individuals and groups.

6 Functionalism is based on the perspective that major social institutions and 'sub-systems' (such as the kinship and economic) exist to meet fundamental human needs (such as procreation and production/consumption). Modern functionalism is particularly associated with the American sociologist, Talcott Parsons, but Parsons himself was greatly influenced by Durkheim.

7 Marxism is based on the perspective that class conflict is the fundamental social force or dynamic. In capitalist society the main social classes are the capitalist class and the working class.

8 Weber's work cannot be categorised under a single label but is sometimes referred to as social action theory. Weber tried to integrate (bring together) both the structural perspective and what later came to be known as the interpretive perspective

9 Interactionism is the main interpretist perspective. George Mead considered that society forms and structures the self's experience but that the self also helps to create its own social experience.

10 Ethnomethodology is the study of the 'commonsense reasoning' of people by which they achieve a meaningful understanding of society and social events.

11 Several movements have recently influenced the development of sociology. These include:

■ Feminism
■ Anti-racism
■ The new right
■ Environmentalism and Internationalism

For further reading and questions, see the end of chapter 22.

2 Sociological Research: Theory & Methods

2

This chapter considers sociology's possible status as a 'science', and introduces the methods of primary and secondary research. It links the perspectives discussed in the previous chapter with the methods introduced in this one, and also discusses the extent to which the various perspectives are complementary or contradictory to each other.

Sociology and Science

There is a long-running debate on the nature of sociology as a discipline. Part of this debate is about whether or not sociology can be called a science. There are two main aspects to this question. The first is whether or not the subject matter of sociology – social interaction – is best understood by scientific methods. We will return to this in a later chapter. The second is the issue of whether the methods that sociologists use and the results they produce can be termed scientific. To make the comparison between social scientific and scientific methods, it is first necessary briefly to describe the latter.

NATURAL SCIENCE

This section offers a simple introduction to natural science. More problematic issues are considered later in the chapter.

Natural science describes those sciences concerned with researching and explaining the 'world of nature', the natural world. These include physics, chemistry and biology. Science is concerned with the accumulation of *verifiable* (capable of being proved true) knowledge. It has traditionally used two methods: observation and experimentation. For reasons outlined below, laboratory experimentation is often considered the most accurate and therefore the ideal method of testing an hypothesis. In practice, all the sciences also use observation. Biologists observe, record and attempt to explain aspects of organic life. The same applies to astronomers in respect of their field of enquiry. It is important that observations are precisely and accurately made. To establish the truth of an observation, it helps to repeat it. Sociologists make full use of observation but very little of the laboratory experiment. Instead, they have developed a battery of methods of their own. How these compare to the laboratory method we consider below. Invariably, experiment involves some observation but observation need not involve experiment.

Scientific research of an explanatory kind often involves establishing whether the scientist's initial idea or hypothesis is true or false. The research is the means by which the hypothesis becomes a proven theory. Thus, we can very simply present the process of explanatory scientific enquiry in several stages:

1 Observation of Phenomena ('facts').
2 Hypothesis (formulated so that it can be tested).
3 Collection of data using systematic method(s) (usually experiment or observation or both).
4 Analysis of data.
5 Test of hypothesis against data.
6 Confirmation or Refutation of Hypothesis (if the latter, 'return to 2' to reformulate or produce a new hypothesis).
7 Theory – a generalisation built upon a repeatedly confirmed hypothesis (or hypotheses).

In the natural sciences, a repeatedly confirmed hypothesis (or series of related hypotheses) is known as a theory or law. Two well known laws of natural science are Newton's law of gravity and Einstein's law of relativity. Laws state that given precisely the same conditions, specific factors or elements will interact in the same way. An important consequence of this is that natural science provides a basis of prediction, i.e. it provides a logical means of establishing what will happen to certain 'things' in given conditions (e.g. how two chemicals will react in given conditions). Few social scientists claim that their methods enable them to produce laws which provide precise predictions.

THE LABORATORY EXPERIMENT The most common method used by natural scientists such as chemists or physicists to test a hypothesis is the *laboratory-controlled experiment*. We discuss this method now because its ability to give precise findings and the relative lack of its use in sociology are often cited to undermine the claims of sociology to be scientific. Natural scientists, like social scientists, often want to measure the effect of one 'thing' on another. A biologist might want to measure the effect that being deprived of light has on the growth of a plant; a sociologist might want to measure the effect of class background on educational attainment. Let us see how a biologist might set up an experiment. S/he may hypothesise that light deprivation will slow growth, but is not sure by how much. S/he is likely to use two plants that for reasons of precise comparability are as similar as possible. One will be deprived of light and the other (the control) will not. Here we must introduce the concept of a variable, something that varies. Relevant variables that can affect plant growth are moisture, warmth, soil quality and, of course, light. All of the variables apart from light must be held constant between the two plants. This means that both plants must receive the same amount of moisture, warmth and so on, but not, of course, light. If this were not so, it would be impossible to tell whether light variation or some other variable accounted for the difference in growth. Another way of putting this point is that the conditions in which the experiment takes place must be controlled. In this experiment, light is referred to as the independent variable (because it is assumed to be the causal factor, not the affected factor, in the experiment) and growth is the dependent variable (because it is affected by the independent variable). The biologist can calculate the result of the experiment by measuring the difference between the plants. S/he will then be able to confirm, discard or reformulate the original hypothesis in more precise terms. A reliable and valid experiment is repeatable and so its findings are open to further verification (proof). A repeatedly verified experiment adds to the growing body of scientific knowledge.

THE IMPACT OF NATURAL SCIENCE ON SOCIOLOGY

The nineteenth and early twentieth century sociologists so far discussed were understandably greatly impressed by the achievements of natural science – physics, chemistry and biology – and wanted, as far as possible, to apply the same methods of research and analysis to society. Auguste Comte (1798–1857) arguably the founder of sociology, strongly reflected this influence and actually referred to sociology as 'social physics'. He advocated the use of experiment and systematic observation as the methods for the study of society and believed that by their use 'laws' of society could be established just as there are laws of physics or chemistry. He referred to sociology as a 'positive science' and sometimes used the term positivism to describe this approach. The positivist approach is based on the assumption that there are 'social facts' which interact with other social facts in ways which can be observed and measured. If it can be established that social facts repeatedly interact together in the same way then it becomes possible to predict that they will do so in the future. Within the positivist model, 'external' social facts are seen as causing human responses. On this basis, Comte anticipated that the 'science of society' would have important practical applications just as natural science has.

Few sociologists since Comte have believed that either the methods or precise aims of the natural sciences could be applied wholesale to sociology. In practice, sociologists have adapted some of the methods of natural science for their own use, as well as developing some that would rarely, if ever, be used in the natural sciences. A full discussion of whether sociology is a science is given at the end of this chapter (pp. 38–40).

THE COMPARATIVE-HISTORICAL METHOD: 'THE ONLY ALTERNATIVE TO EXPERIMENT'

It is rarely either practical or appropriate for sociologists to employ the laboratory experiment. Human beings cannot be treated like guinea pigs (see p. 39). This means that they have to adopt some other method for observing and measuring social relationships. Both Durkheim and the more contemporary sociologist Ronald Fletcher argue that the only way to do this is by employing what Durkheim termed the 'comparative historical method' and what Fletcher simply calls the 'comparative method':

In sciences dealing with inanimate subject-matter, and with organic, physiological facts, some inter-connections of which an explanation is sought can be artificially isolated from their normal contexts and examined in precisely measurable laboratory conditions. In sociology, except perhaps in the case of some small group interactions, this is completely impossible. We cannot put Great Britain, the Kwakiutl Indians, or the complex development of, say, Babylonian law, into laboratories. Furthermore, we know that any 'part' of a social system can only be understood in its essential inter-connectedness with others. Quite apart, then, from any ethical considerations (of which there are many) laboratory techniques are simply not appropriate to the nature and level of human associational facts.

We must, however, have some procedures for testing our theories, and the simple truth is that a careful formulation and use of the comparative method is sociology's only alternative to experimentation.

(Fletcher, 1981: 77)

The comparative method involves systematic comparison of apparently similar phenomena in separate social contexts such as the development of the family in two or more societies. To give another example, the apparent relationship between high social class origin and high educational attainment has been demonstrated by comparative research repeatedly to occur both within particular societies and between societies. Such a relationship is referred to as a concomitant variation or, more usually now, as a correlation which means there is some kind of relationship between the two factors – possibly a causal one. Thus, it may be that there is a causal relationship between high educational attainment and high social class origin.

Durkheim stressed the importance of systematic comparison. This could be done in terms of comparisons between similar types of society, comparisons within a society (e.g., between areas or groups) and comparisons between different types of society (e.g. between 'traditional' and 'modern' societies). Such comparisons help explain why a correlation does or does not occur in particular circumstances. Thus, research both within Britain and internationally has produced a number of explanations about the relationship between class and educational attainment (see pp. 76–86).

Durkheim himself attempted a major piece of comparative research on suicide partly to demonstrate the application of his methodological approach. He wanted to show that even so apparently personal an act as suicide is affected by 'external', social conditions. He argued that what he called the 'social suicide-rate' is the product of these 'collective' social 'forces' (see pp. 314–6).

THE 'IDEAL TYPE' AND THE COMPARATIVE METHOD Max Weber used the concept of ideal type particularly in the context of the comparative method. He used it to refer to concepts or models which attempt to describe the essential or main elements of a social phenomenon. Thus, in an ideal type description of capitalism as a system operating on the profit motive, Weber was then able to look at particular cases of capitalist societies to see what concrete forms profit-seeking took in each of them. Thus, the abstract or 'pure' ideal type description facilitates the analysis of individual cases. Another example of an ideal type is Weber's description of social action as rational, affective and traditional (see p. 10). This typology enabled Weber better to organise his examination of action in various societies in which action would differ to a greater or lesser extent from the ideal typology. By now it should be obvious that the concept of ideal type has nothing at all to do with 'perfection' in any religious or other sense.

THE COMPARATIVE METHOD AND CONTEMPORARY SOCIOLOGY The comparative method has not quite come to occupy the place in sociology which Durkheim and, more recently, Fletcher have advocated. This is partly because of the rise of interpretive sociology which does not seek to explain social action in terms of 'external' causes. In addition, sociologists have become much more aware of the problems of the comparability of statistics.

The comparative method has been presented here in some detail to exemplify the enormous influence on early sociologists of natural science method. Nevertheless, the meticulous methodology of Durkheim and Weber remains as an object lesson and much of the theory and concepts they employed in pursuing comparative research are still of great use.

In today's 'global village' of a world in which so many trends are international, the need for a comparative perspective – 'specialised generalists' as Stanislav Andreski put it – is indisputable, even if comparison is not always pursued with quite the same scientifically systematic intent of Durkheim. More systematic studies require sophisticated methodology, usually an international social survey of some kind. The social survey is presented in a later section of this chapter (pp. 26–31).

(pp. 26–31).

DISCUSSION ISSUES

Why are sociological research studies never 'repeatable' in the sense that laboratory studies are? Is it true to say that all laboratory experiments are, in fact, precisely 'repeatable'? Why or why not?

How effective do you consider the comparative method to be as an alternative to the laboratory experiment?

Sociological Methods

Before discussing sociological methods in detail, it will be useful to present some key general aspects of methodology. These can be conveniently listed into several pairs: descriptive and explanatory research; quantitative and qualitative research; subjectivity and objectivity; reliability and validity; and primary and secondary data. Finally, the relationship between the terms structural/interpretist and positivist/anti-positivist is briefly discussed.

DESCRIPTIVE AND EXPLANATORY RESEARCH

In general, sociological research may be descriptive or explanatory or both. Descriptive research is aimed at finding out and presenting 'facts' (for instance, the trend in the birth rate over a period of time) or at describing social processes (for example, how a gang operates). Explanatory research seeks to give sociological reasons why something happens. Thus, a possible sociological explanation for the downward trend in the birthrate for most of the nineteen seventies might be that more couples wanted to have a higher standard and quality of life rather than have a first or further child (like all hypotheses, this would have to be tested by research). 'Attitude surveys' are sometimes classified as a third type of survey. However, they can be regarded as descriptive, although what they attempt to describe are subjective states of mind rather than more concrete social facts.

QUANTITATIVE AND QUALITATIVE RESEARCH

Sociological methods are divided into two broad types: quantitative and qualitative. Quantitative methods are used to produce numerical or statistical data. They are usually employed in sociology in research into social relationships such as that between social class and social mobility. A now classic study in which a mainly quantitive approach was adopted was the *Oxford Social Mobility Survey* (1982). The study used a sample of 10,000 men from across the full range of social classes. The main quantitative techniques are questionnaires and structured interviews.

Qualitative methods are mainly used to produce data about the personal experience and meanings of social actors. They are usually based on the social actor's own words or on observations (sometimes filmed) of the actors behaviour. There are now many pieces of qualitative research which explore the experience of school pupils. These include several accounts of anti-school subcultures, including Stephen Ball's *Beachside Comprehensive*. The main qualitative methods are observation and unstructured interviews.

Later in this chapter, the relationship between quantitative and qualitative methods and the perspectives – structural and interpretist, discussed in chapter one, are explored. Broadly, quantitative methods are more suitable for structural research, and qualitative methods for interpretist research.

However, because sociologists often seek both types of information, there is considerable overlap in their usage. Many, probably the majority of sociologists, employ both types – often to provide complementary data.

OBJECTIVE AND SUBJECTIVE DATA IN SOCIOLOGY

Objective data refers to facts and information about 'social reality' 'outside' or 'beyond' the individual. Durkheim stated that the task of sociology is to establish how objective 'social facts' affect social behaviour. Thus, he argued that certain 'social facts' affect the suicide rate (see p. 314). Subjective data is information about the specific feelings and experience of individuals: it is less about how society affects the individual than about how the individual feels, thinks and acts towards society. In this sense, structural sociology deals more with objective data and interpretist sociology more with subjective data.

STRUCTURAL/INTERPRETIST THEORIES AND POSITIVIST/ ANTI-POSITIVIST METHODS

In many sociology books the mainly structural theories of functionalism, Marxism and Weber are described as positivist in their methodology. What is meant by this is that, like Comte (see p. 22), these theoretical approaches adopt the assumed methodological premise of natural science i.e., that there are factors external to social actors which determine their social behaviour. In contrast, interpretist theories are described as anti-positivist because they reject the positivist methodological premise and instead use methods aimed at describing and understanding the meanings of social actors. While these distinctions are helpful, it should be stressed that there are no rigid links between structural theories and quantitative methods and interpretive theories and qualitative methods. In general, the term structuralist rather than positivist will be used here to indicate the approach that there are factors or 'structures' external to social actors which influence their actions. One good reason for this, is that many sociologists described as positivist, including Durkheim and Parsons, reject the term as a description of their approach.

RELIABILITY AND VALIDITY

An experiment or piece of research is reliable if when replicated (repeated under exactly the same conditions) it produces the same result. Reliability in the social sciences is not as high as in the natural sciences. This is because it is not possible to control the conditions of sociological research to the extent of those of natural science. A laboratory experiment is generally more precisely repeatable, and so more reliable, than a piece of sociological research.

A piece of research is valid if it produces the type of data the researcher is seeking, i.e. if it measures or illustrates what the researcher intends. Thus, a researcher wanting to know the voting intentions of the national electorate will probably conduct a large-scale sample survey whereas a researcher wanting to understand teacher-pupil interaction will probably seek to observe particular examples. Both researchers have chosen valid approaches for what they want to find out.

It is sometimes argued that quantitative research is more likely to be reliable, and qualitative more likely to be valid. This is because the former tends to be highly structured and controlled whereas the latter is more open-ended and receptive to respondents' subjectivity. Structure and control are associated with reliability, whereas sensitivity to the subjects' own responses is considered more likely to produce a valid account of them.

Primary and Secondary Sources

Primary sources of information refer to data produced by the sociologist's original research. The use of observation, interviews and questionnaires produces primary data. Secondary sources of data are those which already exist, such as official statistics, newspapers, and research already carried out by other sociologists. Although these two sources of data are discussed separately, they are often used to complement each other.

Primary Sources

The Social Survey

Quantitative methods are virtually synonymous with the social survey. Sociologists who want to produce original statistical data, usually conduct a social survey. A social survey collects standardised data usually about a large population. Questionnaires and standardised (pre-set) interviews are the most frequent techniques used in implementing social surveys. The main purpose of a social survey is to produce data which provides a basis for generalising about the survey population or target group. This means that survey responses must be able to be turned into quantitative or numerical form. Social surveys – often of a simple, descriptive kind – regularly appear in the press, indicating that a certain percentage of people are 'for' or 'against' a given proposition.

CROSS-SECTIONAL AND LONGITUDINAL SURVEYS The two main types of survey are the cross-sectional and longitudinal. The cross-sectional survey gives information about a group (usually a sample) at a particular point in time. It is usually relatively cheap and quick to do. The longitudinal survey studies a selected group (or groups) over a period of time. It enables the effect of the variables to be studied over the longer term.

The famous television survey *Seven Up* is an example in point. A group of children from different social backgrounds have been interviewed at regular intervals of seven years (so far, the group has been interviewed at seven, and on four other occasions. It is quite clear that social class has had a great effect on the lives of these children and particularly on their educational career and cultural opportunities.

Social surveys, can, then, help to establish regularities or tendencies in human behaviour, but not social scientific laws. Taken together, established tendencies provide a basis for the cumulative (gradually increasing) development of social scientific theory and knowledge, just as scientific experiment and law provides a similar basis for science.

Sampling

The target population of a social survey is often very large. It may be working class families in East London, the electorate, or striking school teachers. Practicalities of time and money, therefore, usually require that only part of, or a sample of, the total population is surveyed – thus the term 'sample survey'.

It is important to select an accurate sample. If the sample is faulty in some way, it will not provide an adequate basis on which to draw conclusions about the target population. Often, sociologists test their chosen method of research by implementing a 'pilot study' prior to a full-scale survey. A pilot survey could show whether respondents fully understand or are comfortable with the questions in the survey, and may also provide practical insights on such matters as the time and expense involved.

The first stage in the sampling process requires identifying the relevant population for sampling, i.e. the target population referred to above. The term sampling unit refers to the individuals, groups or other phenomena (the survey may be of newspapers, households or whatever) which could provide part of a relevant sample for the survey.

The next stage is usually to obtain or produce a 'sampling frame' which is a list from which the sample will be taken (although this stage may not occur in less structured – and usually less accurate – sampling procedures). Examples of possible sampling frames are local electoral rolls, school rolls or the *National Census*. Although official records such as electoral rolls and the Census aim to be fully comprehensive they rarely completely achieve this. However, such inadequacies are not usually on a scale likely to affect the statistical significance of survey findings.

REPRESENTATIVE AND NON-REPRESEN-TATIVE SAMPLING The next stage in sampling – selecting the sample itself – involves the choice of a sampling technique or techniques. Usually, the function of these techniques is to ensure that the sample is as representative as possible of the members of the sampling frame and so of the relevant population, i.e. contains (or 'represents') their typical characteristics in the same proportion. Thus, a sample taken from a given school roll which is serving as the sampling frame should contain the same proportion of females and males and ethnic minority members as the roll itself if it is intended to be fully representative of these groups. Sample size is another factor which affects represen-tativeness. The right size for a sample varies according to the population being surveyed and the issue being researched – it is not always a case of the larger the better.

Non-representative sampling also occurs in sociology. The logic of this approach is that a non-representative sample may provide the most demanding and rigorous test of the researcher's hypothesis. Thus, Goldthorpe and Lockwood were sceptical of the view or hypothesis which was widely held in the late nineteen fifties that better-off members of the working class were becoming more middle class as a result of their affluence – the embourgeoisement hypothesis. To give the hypothesis every chance of being confirmed and their own doubts confounded, they tested it against an untypically affluent sample of workers in Luton. However, their findings did not confirm the embourgoisement hypothesis. They found that in a number of important ways the affluent workers could not be considered middle class (see pp. 141–3).

We now consider various types of sampling.

RANDOM AND SYSTEMATIC SAMPLING

A random sample or probability sample allows each member of the group being sampled a known and equal chance of being selected. Thus, a sample of fifty students from a total of five hundred could be randomly selected by putting the names of the whole group into a hat and drawing out fifty. It is more usual, however, to take a systematic sample. This involves selecting names at regular intervals, depending on how big the sample is to be. In the case of our 500 students a school or college list could be used from which every tenth name would be selected up to the five hundredth to get a sample of fifty. The same technique could be used in the case of electoral registers or other lists appropriate to particular areas of research. Usually, systematic sampling leads to greater precision than totally random sampling as it produces a more even sample spread over the population list.

It is important to appreciate the limits of random sampling. The technique depends on the mathematical probability that a number of members carefully selected from a larger group will be more or less representative of that group. Sometimes the improbable happens and the sample is unrepresentative of the target population. One way in which it is sometimes appropriate to increase the precision of sampling is through stratification.

STRATIFIED RANDOM SAMPLING

Stratification means that before any sample selection takes place, the population is divided into a number of mutually exclusive groups or 'strata'. Each stratum is then sampled – either randomly or systematically. Thus, a researcher wanting to select from a school list a sample which contained the same proportion of male and female pupils as the list itself would stratify the list according to sex and take two separate, proportionate sub-samples. Or the process of stratification could be carried further by dividing the male and female lists into black and white males and black and white females and then taking sub-samples of each of the four groups. In the example below a sample of 1 in 10 has been taken from each stratified group:

	Stratum size	Sub-sample
white male	60	6
black male	20	2
white female	80	8
black female	40	4

◄

Table 2.1

This example clearly shows that a stratified random sample has a greater chance of being representative of the total population than one which is merely random.

QUOTA SAMPLING

Moser and Kalton describe quota sampling as 'a method of stratified sampling in which selection within strata is non-random'. Thus, once the researcher has decided which groups or strata to survey, the required number (quota) of respondents within each group is then selected either by the researcher or an assistant. Moser and Kalton go on to emphasise that the 'essential difference between probability and quota samples lies in the selection of the final sampling units, say individuals'.

A quota sample replaces randomness with human judgement. A researcher seeking quotas of, say, six white male, two black male, eight white female, and four black female pupils would select them rather than draw them from a sampling frame. However, since the characteristics of a given quota are predetermined (e.g. black male pupil), the possibility of human error in sample selection can be limited. But not all quota controls (characteristics) can be clearly defined. Thus, deciding which class someone belongs to may be difficult, even with the help of guidelines.

CLUSTER AND MULTI-STAGE SAMPLING

A cluster sample is a sample drawn only from selected parts or clusters of the total target population. Cluster sampling design is sometimes adopted when the target population is too large for a random sample to be drawn (e.g. a sample of 20,000 from a population of 50,000,000) or where no satisfactory sampling frame exists (e.g. as in some undeveloped regions). In such circumstances, separate groups or clusters of urban, rural and, perhaps, suburban areas might be used to draw the sample from.

A multi-stage sample occurs when one sample is drawn from another. A cluster sample is a specific example. Thus, selected constituencies, wards and polling districts, could be, respectively, the second, third, and fourth stages of cluster sampling. Multi-stage sampling can save time and money, although in certain respects it increases the chances of the final sample being unrepresentative.

SNOWBALL SAMPLING

A snowball 'sample' is a sample of a particular group built up from an initial member (or 'contact') of that group. Research into youth gangs or criminal gangs may involve this technique. Snowball sampling lacks any statistical basis of randomness or representativeness but can make for interesting and illuminating reading. It perhaps better belongs to qualitative rather than quantitative research.

DISCUSSION ISSUES

What 'sampling frames' other than those suggested on p. 26 can you think of? What are their likely advantages and disadvantages?

Questionnaires

Questionnaires are the most frequent means by which a social survey is carried out. A questionnaire is a list of pre-set-questions asked by the researcher of members of the sample (the respondents).

CLOSED AND OPEN-ENDED QUESTIONS

Questions may be closed or fixed-choice, or open-ended. Figure 2.1 shows some examples of closed questions on the theme of gender treatment in school 'x':

Closed questions enable ease of quantification but they limit freedom of response. They can also lead to a false sense of precision when quantified: quantification only reflects the adequacy of the questions asked and of the response choices. How adequate do you think the above questions

Do you consider that female and male pupils are treated equally? Tick one of the boxes

☐   ☐
Yes   **No**

Score school x on the extent to which it has achieved gender equality between female and male pupils. Ring one number only.

1   2   3   4   5   6   7   8   9   10
Low   **High**

How would you rate school x on the achievement of gender equality between male and female pupils? Tick one of the boxes.

☐   ☐   ☐   ☐
Poor   **Satisfactory**   **Good**   **Excellent**

Figure 2.1 (Far left)

and response choices are?

Open-ended questions are designed to allow more freedom of response – sometimes complete freedom of response. Freer responses can vary greatly and can rarely be quantified with a high level of precision as closed ones. They are often primarily intended to provide depth and complexity – perhaps to complement numerical data. An example of an open-ended question is:

How do you think female pupils in school x are affected by the school's equal opportunity policies?

OPERATIONALISING CONCEPTS: CODIFICATION

Two further matters in relation to quantification require consideration: concept operationalisation and coding. Sociologists often seek to measure such abstractions as alienation or inequality. The first requirement in operationalising a concept is to define precisely what is meant by it. This may involve breaking it down into sub-concepts, termed components, as Blauner did with alienation (see p. 244). It is then necessary to establish concretely measurable characteristics or indicators of the concept. Thus, indicators of inequality may be considered to be differentials of income, health and education. These can be measured and compared.

Codification involves giving a symbolic – usually numerical – value to responses to questions. As we saw above, there is little practical difficulty in doing this in the case of closed questions which are often pre-coded

on the questionnaire. Coding open-ended questions is more complex. Responses have to be put into similar categories and these categories can then be numbered for statistical comparison. Thus, answers to the example of an open-ended question given above could be categorised as follows:

Question: How do you think female pupils in school x are affected by the school's equal opportunity policies:

(Categories Used by Researcher to Quantify Open-ended Responses)

1 More females now choose scientific subjects.
2 There has been less sexual harassment of female pupils.
3 The policies have had little effect.
4 The policies have made matters worse by making people over-conscious of gender issues.

Quantifying essentially qualitative responses is not only often difficult but sometimes inappropriate. Individuals may not want their free speech subjected to cumbersome quantification, and in any case such treatment may distract from appreciation of its personal meaning.

ADMINISTERING QUESTIONNAIRES

Questionnaires can be administered in a variety of ways including personally (by the researcher or an assistant), by post, by phone, or with a newspaper or magazine. Each of these methods has particular problems and advantages.

A questionnaire administered by an interviewer in which the latter merely reads out and, if necessary, clarifies questions for the respondent is the same as a completely structured interview (see p. 30). A personal approach of this kind usually achieves a better response rate than administering a questionnaire through the post. Difficulties in understanding the questionnaire, lack of interest, or forgetfulness mean that postal questionnaires often receive a low response rate. However, postal questionnaires have the advantages of being relatively cheap compared to interviews and, of being able easily to access a large sample who are perhaps geographically widely spread. Follow-up letters, or where possible visits, improve postal questionnaire response rate. A low-response rate can affect the representativeness of the final sample by making it less typical of the target population.

ADVANTAGES AND DISADVANTAGES OF QUESTIONNAIRES

The main advantage of questionnaires is that they provide a wide range of data on which to base generalisations. They are an essential part of the methodological tool-kit of structural sociology. Often, a questionnaire survey is used, in traditional social scientific fashion, specifically to test an hypothesisis. A celebrated example of a study which used questionnaires (as well as other techniques) has already been referred to: Goldthorpe and Lockwood's testing of the embourgeoisement hypothesis by means of their survey of affluent workers in Luton (p. 27).

The disadvantages of questionnaires partly reflect the limitation of the form itself and partly the nature of the structuralist assumptions underlying their use. The form of a questionnaire is such that the researcher 'imposes' questions on the respondent who may or may not answer them, or if s/he does, may or may not tell the truth. Low response rate, possible lies, 'jokes' and inaccuracies, can all undermine the reliability of a questionnaire survey. Even a well-designed questionnaire can fall foul of

these problems. The limitations of the questionnaire arguably reflect the limitations of the structural approach itself. Structuralists, sometimes by means of the use of questionnaires, attempt to build up explanations of behaviour largely in terms of external social factors. For interpretists, this misses out the most important aspect of people – their capacity to initiate meaningful and even original action. In practice most contemporary sociologists are well aware of the pitfalls of a rigidly structural approach and, even more of the limitations of research based exclusively on a questionnaire survey. Many combine both quantitative and qualitative methods as did Willmott and Young over 30 years ago, in carrying out their survey of family and kinship in East London:

But the statistical material [from mainly structured interviews], essential though it was, had its obvious limitations. We had set out from the beginning with the deliberate intention to combine statistical analysis with the kind of detailed description and individual illustration that could come only from fairly free and lengthy interviews and from personal observation, because we thought that this would give a more rounded – and more accurate – account than either method alone.

(Willmott and Young, 1969: 210)

Interviews

There are three types of interview: structured, semi-structured and unstructured. They vary according to the types of question asked and the data generated. A totally structured interview is a questionnaire by another name. Its main purpose is to provide quantifiable data. The semi-structured and unstructured interview produce progressively more qualitative data. In the case of the unstructured interview the researcher will invariably use only a schedule made up of general areas or topics to be covered which can serve as a checklist if responses become highly discursive. The schedule for a semi-structured interview gives more detail and direction but still allows considerable freedom of response. Two separate pieces of

research into the experience of housework used schedules of this kind: Hannah Gavron's *The Captive Wife*, and Ann Oakley's *The Sociology of Housework*. A practical aspect of conducting unstructured interviews is that the researcher cannot be sure how long each one will last. Ann Oakley's interviews in the above study varied from one and a quarter to three and a half hours.

CONDUCTING INTERVIEWS

In conducting interviews, it is important that the interviewer does not say or do anything that is likely to distort responses. Inadvertently intimidating or confusing the interviewee or seeming to imply that a particular answer is correct is likely to have an adverse effect on the data produced by the interview. In general, it is good practice politely to introduce oneself and the purpose of the research. In the case of long, unstructured interviews, considerable effort may be required to lay the ground for the interview – perhaps through using an intermediary-contact or by writing or phoning. In the interview situation itself, the brief, factual questions on such matters as the age and status of the respondent with which most interviews of whatever type usually begin provide a further opportunity to establish interviewer-interviewee rapport before more probing or demanding questions are asked. When possible, it is usually good practice to check responses with the interviewee, prior to concluding the interview. This is not only a check on accuracy but recognises that the data 'belong' first and foremost to the respondent.

RECORDING INTERVIEWS It is sometimes preferable to record an interview rather than attempt to take a written record during the course of the interview. The tape can be transcribed later prior to analysis. It can be particularly convenient to record unstructured and group interviews (i.e. interviews with two or more respondents) when the attention, sensitivity and skill of the interviewer is likely to be needed exclusively in conducting the interview. An interviewer who is busily writing in an attempt to 'keep up with' what is being said may well interfere with the natural flow of responses and so inhibit free and unself-conscious expression of feeling and opinion. It is easier for respondents to 'forget about' a tape-recorder or even a video-camera than a frantically scribbling interviewer. However, a film or video camera is potentially distracting – especially if respondents are tempted to 'play to the camera'. A visual recording can show gestures and expressions which may clarify respondents' meanings but the degree to which this is so may be be marginal.

During the nineteen seventies and eighties, a number of studies of secondary school pupils using tape-recorded unstructured interviews were conducted. These included Paul Willis's *Learning to Labour* – a study of a group of working class 'lads' and M Mac an Ghaill's *Young, Gifted and Black* – a study of several single-sex groups of black students.

What is noticeable in both cases in reading the transcribed texts of the group interviews is the brief and infrequent nature of the prompts and questions of the interviewers. Often, the respondents seem to 'take off' into their own conversation – which is precisely what an interviewer would generally hope for. Thus, in each of three transcripts with a group of young women referred to as 'the sisters', Mac an Ghaill makes only a single intervention – in each case further to prompt a line of thought already being pursued by a respondent. These are the interventions – all that occur in well over a thousand words of transcribed text:

1 'What do you mean? Compared to black women?'
2 'What about your brothers?'
3 'You changed your style and they didn't.'

A general indicator of a skilled in-depth interviewer is one who says little – effectively – and creates space for the respondent(s) to reply.

ADVANTAGES AND DISADVANTAGES OF INTERVIEWS

The advantages and disadvantages of interviews vary according to the type of interview. Those of the totally structured interview are the same as those of the questionnaire discussed above: it generates quantifiable data which provide a basis for generalisation. At the other extreme, the unstructured interview is potentially one of the most sensitive tools of qualitative research. By allowing such freedom of response, it enables the researcher to understand the feelings, motives and thinking of the respondent – always assuming that some form of misconception or miscommunication is not occurring. The nature of the data produced by unstructured interviews tends to be different in one significant way from that produced by participant observation, another key method of qualitative research (discussed below). Participant observation usually provides information about the research subject in natural, everyday action. The structured interview gives an opportunity for subjects to reflect on and explain action – their own or others. It is quite common, therefore, to

Observations

find the two methods used in a complementary way. Thus, in his study of homosexuals, Laud Humphreys first played the participant observational role of 'voyeur' (an accepted one within the homosexual community). He then went on to interview twelve of the group.

Observation can be divided into non-participant and participant observation. In both cases, the observation may be overt (open, not hidden) or covert (hidden, secret). These different circumstances raise different problems.

NON-PARTICIPANT OBSERVATION

Non-participant observation involves the sociologist in an exclusively observational role in relation to the subject of the research. At least that is the theory. In fact, however, one of the earliest examples of the use of observational technique showed how difficult it is for the researcher to remain entirely separate from the subject. This was in Elton Mayo's overt observation of the Hawthorne electricity plant in Chicago. Mayo and his team were asked to examine the effects of various changes in working conditions on the productivity of the work force at the Hawthorne factory. Mayo found that virtually any change in variables affecting working conditions – even those that made conditions worse than they were originally – seemed to result in an improvement in productivity! At last, he was forced to conclude that what caused the improvement in production was the presence of the research team itself. It had stimulated the workforce to greater efforts! The Hawthorne experiment provides a strong warning to sociologists to be aware of the effect they themselves can have on their findings. Researcher effect of this kind is sometimes referred to as 'Hawthorne effect'. Taking their cue from Mayo's experience, some sociologists have preferred to 'factor out' the effect of their own presence by observing their subject matter covertly.

One such recent piece of research is Valerie Yule's covert observation of adult-child interaction. Yule observed 85 adult-child pairs for three minutes each, all of them matched with another pair of people for comparison (the 'control' pairs were highly varied in terms of age and included male-female, all-female and all-male). Yule's interesting findings were that all-adult pairs tend to interact much more positively than adult-child pairs.

Non-participant observation often lends itself to a structured, quantitative analysis and presentation of findings, even though as in Yule's research the subject matter of the enquiry may be about the quality of human interaction. Yule observed that whereas four fifths of the all adult pairs 'had some speech together, or at least a glance or a smile', over half of the adults in the adult-child pairs 'took no notice of the children they were with' during the three minute period of observation. For two-fifths of the adult-child sample, the interaction was negative. She quantifies those interactions that did occur in a simple, descriptive way. Here are some examples:

Seven adults crossed roads telling their children to look out or hurry up, but none of them looked at the children they were speaking to. Five yanked the child by arm or hand.

Six children cried in pushers. Three were smacked, two given sweets round the side of the pusher without a glance at them, and one was ignored.

Four children in shops were told to behave themselves in varying degrees of severity, and one was then pacified with sweets.

Four children on buses were scolded or smacked for misbehaviour, following complete inattention.

Four children at bus stops were told to behave or keep still, and one was cuffed.

Four children tried to talk to adults who paid no attention.

Three children tried to talk to adults and were rejected.

(Yule, 1986: 445)

As far as achieving objectivity, non-participant observation, particularly covert, has certain advantages. The time and energy of the researcher can be devoted exclusively to precise observation (and recording). In contrast to participant observation, the judgement of the researcher cannot be biased or distorted by relationships with research subjects built up during the course of research. On the other hand, there is a limitation on the nature of explanation possible in research based exclusively on non-participant observation. This is that the views and feelings of the actors themselves about their actions cannot be systematically accessed by the researcher and may not be expressed at all unless they happen to come up during the course of observation. To acquire such qualitative information non-participant observation can usefully be supported by in-depth interviews, with at least a sub-sample of those observed, or by some other form of qualitative method.

PARTICIPANT OBSERVATION

Participant observation involves the sociologist taking part in the social action which s/he seeks to describe and understand. It is perhaps the most qualitative of all sociological methods but, as is always the case, it is possible to categorise, number and tabulate the data produced by this form of research. Participant observation has been particularly widely employed since the nineteen sixties by interactionists and ethnomethodologists.

ETHNOGRAPHY The origins of participant observation within social science go back at least to the early part of the twentieth century when anthropologists (researchers into non-literate societies) sometimes adopted it as part of the ethnographic approach. Ethnography is research based on closely observing and recording the way of life of a particular culture or subculture and participant observation was seen as a way of getting as close as possible to the subjects of the research. The method was notably employed by Bronislow Malinowski and Margaret Mead (see chapter 10 for further reference to Mead's work). One of the societies that Malinowski examined was the Trobriand Islanders of the Western Pacific. Malinowski used participant observation for the same purposes as more recent sociologists. He wanted to 'grasp the natives' point of view', to 'realise (their) vision of the world' and observe them 'acting naturally'. To do this he remained with them for over a year. In order for the participant observer to give people the opportunity to adjust to her or his presence and to show a typical range of behaviour, s/he must often be prepared to spend lengthy periods of time with them. It is crucial for the participant observer to win the confidence and acceptance of the people s/he is studying if they are to behave naturally. In the case of Margaret Mead, recent research suggests that she was not always taken entirely seriously by the subjects of her study, adolescent Samoan girls. In her book, *Coming of Age in Samoa*, first published during the nineteen twenties, she reports that women were sexually remarkably free by Western standards. Freeman (1983) now argues that the girls were largely 'having her on' in this matter.

PARTICIPANT OBSERVATION WITHIN SUB-CULTURES More recent participant observational studies have often been of specific subcultures. In particular, there has been a large number of participant observational studies of gangs and other youth subcultural groups. One of the earliest and most influential of these was William Foote Whyte's *Street Corner Society*. Whyte studied a gang in a poor, largely Italian immigrant part of Chicago. He described himself as 'seeking to build a sociology based on observed interpersonal events'. The following quotation from Whyte states a major justification for the participant observational approach:

As I sat and listened, I learned the answers to questions that I would not even have had the sense to ask if I had been getting my information solely on an interviewing basis.
(Whyte, 1955: 303)

In other words, participant observation teaches the social scientist what questions to ask as well as providing some of the answers.

In view of the apparent deception perpetrated on Margaret Mead, it is instructive that Whyte gained much of his information and insight from Doc, a gang leader with whom he struck up a friendship. Whyte confided overtly in Doc about the nature of his research although he was vague about it with others. Doc responded helpfully. This is a case when a strong subjective involvement of researcher and subject contributed positively to the research. Whyte suggests that he began his

▶

Figure 2.2 (far right)
'The gang of lads':
Deviant male
subcultures – a
popular area for
participant observation
among (male)
sociologists.

research as a participant observer and ended as an 'observing participant' and by doing so came to understand matters more deeply.

A more recent study of a gang is James Patrick's *A Glasgow gang Observed* (1973). Adopting a covert approach, Patrick joined a Glasgow gang. The result is a fascinating study of gang behaviour, and particularly of gang hierarchy and ritual. But was Patrick justified in keeping his identity secret? According to the author's own account, the members of the gang did not think so and would happily exact revenge on him for misleading them. No general moral rule can be laid down on this question of secrecy: each sociologist must make her or his own judgement on the matter. Patrick's study also raises another moral issue which can occur in the course of participant observation into areas of deviancy. Does 'the cause of research' justify the sociologist adopting a deviant identity and perhaps committing deviant acts?

Another study which was both covert (in part) and involved the adoption of a deviant role was Laud Humphreys' study of homosexuality in public toilets in the United States. Humphreys adopted the role of 'watcher' or 'voyeur' of the sexual activities of others. Only later, after he had become accepted, did he reveal his identity as a researcher and converse openly with some of the homosexuals. In this way he attempted to achieve the benefits of naturalistic observation and of direct questioning.

Ken Pryce's *Endless Pressure* (1979) – a study of the Afro-Caribbean community of the St Paul's area of Bristol – is now a classic of participant observation. Pryce adapted his approach to convenience and circumstances. Thus, he revealed his identity as a researcher to some but not to others. In an incidental but helpful meeting with a 'hustler', he concealed it 'not … to deceive, but merely to sustain … rapport'. However, with a more conventional group of contacts, he simply remarks that 'it was not necessary to be guarded about my true identity as a researcher'. Similarly, the precise focus of Pryce's study developed actively during the course of research. As he puts it, in terms similar to Whyte's: 'insights and hypotheses that later were to form the substance of the thesis, were developed in the actual process of investigation'.

ADVANTAGES AND DISADVANTAGES OF PARTICIPANT OBSERVATION The main advantage and disadvantage of participant observation are opposite sides of the same coin: the method can bring all the insight and understanding that comes with subjective involvement but also all the possible loss of objectivity. Ronald Frankenburg, himself the author of a participant observational study of life in a Welsh village, has usefully suggested three stages of research for the participant observer which offer some safeguard against excessive subjectivity. Each of these stages involves a different degree of involvement with the subject matter. Firstly, the research project must be set up – a relatively objective process. Secondly, the sociologist becomes subjectively (personally) involved with those s/he wishes to study. Thirdly, s/he withdraws to consider and assess his experience and findings.

Authors of participant observational studies are not uncommonly accused of sentimentalising and over-romanticising the deviants, criminals and youth groups which are typically the subjects of their research. Certainly, there is a strong suggestion of identification with 'the outsider' in a number of classic participant observational studies but on the credit side such studies often have an authenticity which could scarcely be achieved by survey work.

DISCUSSION ISSUES

What areas/topics of reseach can you think of which would lend themselves particularly to the use of participant observation and/or unstructured interviews? Why might quantitative methods produce less satisfactory results in such cases?

The Relationship Between Perspectives and Methods

There is a general, but by no means precise relationship between the theoretical perspectives described in Chapter two and the methods of primary research described above. This relationship is presented in figure 2.3.

It is worth summarising three ways in which the structural/quantitative and interpretive/ qualitative lines are frequently crossed. First, methods generally thought of as of a particular type can in fact often be used to produce data of the other type. Thus, Valerie Yule used observation ('normally' thought of as a qualitative method) to quantify adult-child interactions. Second, the two types of theory-methods are often used to complement each other. Thus, John Goldthorpe collected personal biographical data of a qualitative kind from a sub-sample of his main sample of 10,000 respondents to a questionnaire on social mobility (see pp. 150–1). Third, although well-aware of the important general linkages along structural/ quantitative and interpretive/qualitative lines, sociologists often adopt whatever approaches and techniques seem most effectively to meet the needs of their research. Partly to demonstrate this point, Colin Bell and Howard Newby edited a collection of researchers' accounts of their research, *Doing Sociological Research*, which generally show a considerable degree of methodological pragmatism and improvisation. In principle and in practice, they argue that methodological 'pluralism' (variety) is often more effective than an 'either/or' approach.

◄ **Figure 2.3**

Structural theories	Interpretive theories
Marxism, functionalism, Weber/social action,	Interactionism, Ethnomethodology
Quantitative methods	**Qualitative methods**
Social surveys questionnaires, comparative surveys, interviews	Unstructured interviews, observation (Non PO and PO)

Note: Max Weber's social action theory is presented as mainly structural but partly interpretive.

Secondary Sources

Secondary sources of data are those which already exist. This makes the field rather wide! Almost any data can be used in a study providing they are used relevantly and accurately.

OFFICIAL STATISTICS

The Census – a demographic survey of the whole population – was first conducted in 1801 and has been held at regular intervals ever since. From that time central government has been the major producer, user and disseminator of large-scale information. In addition to questions on 'established' areas such as occupation and residence, the 1991 Census was the first to ask a question about ethnic origin. Some were uneasy about this. What is your own view? Another issue in relation to the 1991 Census was the greater number of non-responses in inner-urban areas than elsewhere. This may have been because non-poll-tax payers in the inner-cities did not accept official assurances that census responses were wholly confidential, and feared that their returns might be accessed by local authorities to locate them. This matter could affect the overall reliability of the 1991 census data. Today each government department carries out its own research, which is coordinated by the Government Statistical Service. Two well-known annual digests of official statistics covering the main areas of public life are *Social Trends* and the *Annual Abstract of Statistics*. The former is designed for more popular consumption but each is based on the same sources.

There is lively debate among sociologists about the use of official statistics in research. Both interpretists and Marxists make radical criticisms of their validity and reliability. For instance, Cicourel and Garfinkel argue that, respectively, police and judicial stereotypes of offenders influence criminal statistics. Atkinson has made a similar case in relation to the taken-for-granted assumptions of coroners about what constitutes evidence of suicide. For their part Marxists argue that statistics collected by the capitalist state are generally framed and presented in a way which supports the capitalist system. In particular, they contend that there is a high degree of official tolerance to 'the crimes of the powerful'.

The accusation that official statistics were used in a biased, or at least suspect, fashion by government was made quite widely by opposition politicians and press in the nineteen eighties and early nineties. In particular, it was noted that nearly all of more than thirty changes in the way the official unemployment figures were computed resulted in a decrease in the total figure. In this case, part of the dispute centred on what constituted unemployment (being registered at a Job Centre? being unemployed for at least a month?), i.e. on how unemployment should be defined. The question of definition came to the fore even more sharply in a long-running debate on whether the numbers of those in poverty had increased or not under the Conservative government. Critics tended to argue that the numbers in relative poverty (i.e. allowing for changing standards) had increased whereas a number of Conservative politicians argued that precisely because standards of assessing poverty have changed, it is pointless to assess how many are 'in poverty'.

Issues relating to the use of official statistics are discussed in detail in relation to crime (pp. 292–7), suicide (pp. 313–6), and poverty (pp. 155–7).

OTHER SOURCES OF STATISTICS

In addition to the routine production of statistics, special government reports – often the work of 'Government commissions' – dealing with important areas of national interest or concern appear from time to time. Often these contain important statistical and other data. One such report was *Inequalities in Health*, sometimes referred to by the name of its chairman as the *Black Report*. The report provided a mine of information on social inequality and ill-health.

Many voluntary organisations and pressure groups regularly publish statistics in their specialist area. Unsurprisingly, their statistics often appear to be selected and presented to favour their own causes. Nevertheless, statistical data provided by for example the Low Pay Unit and National Society for the Prevention of Cruelty to Children frequently inform and enhance public awareness and debate on key social issues.

HISTORICAL SOURCES

Historical references are important in providing a basis of comparison in sociology, and also of course in establishing patterns of social change. Inevitably, there are often issues of reliability and interpretation in relation to historical evidence. For instance, Friedrich Engels' still influential *The Origin of the Family, Private Property and the State* (1884) was based on a secondary source, Lewis Morgan's *Ancient Society*, which recent scholarship has challenged in relation both to aspect of factual accuracy and interpretation. Peter Laslett's study, *Household and Family in Past Time* (1972) is generally accepted as authoritative. Laslett used statistical data from parish records which largely exploded the 'myth' of the predominance of the extended family in pre-industrial Britain – a highly significant contribution to the framework of family analysis.

Historical study provides much pictorial, artistic and other data of a non-statistical and also non-printed kind. The proportion of such data to statistical and printed material becomes greater the further one goes back in history: Philip Ariès *Centuries of Childhood* (1973) makes telling use of family portraits in pursuing his case that childhood was not conceived of as a separate 'age stage' in medieval Europe. Children are depicted in such portraits as 'little adults'. Such evidence usually requires corroboration. Thus, Ariès also draws on written materials to substantiate his argument.

Local historical sources have the advantage of accessibility to students. For example, an examination of disused factory or dock records and sites and, particularly, interviews with long-time inhabitants of an area (oral history) can provide the basis of lively social history/sociology. The former Open University course, *Popular Culture* effectively used three 'official' (Blackpool Corporation) holiday brochures, from the late nineteenth century, the nineteen twenties, and the current year to exemplify the changing nature of the seaside holiday in the cultural life of the North West, particularly for the working class. The 'story' was further brought up-to-date by student visits to five sites in Blackpool, including the Pleasure Beach and Coral Island, which were each subjected to cultural analysis. This kind of imaginative work can bring social science to light in a way that a textbook could not. For 'Blackpool', read 'Southend', 'Brighton', or 'Scarborough'!

PERSONAL DOCUMENTS

A personal document gives a participant's own view of particular experiences. Such sources are used in sociology to represent the opinions and meaning of actors involved in given social situations. Examples of personal documents are diaries, letters and informal life-histories. Published autobiographies are still personal documents but they may be filtered by consideration of others' feelings and by legal requirements, such as libel laws.

Sometimes, researchers who have conducted large-scale social surveys encourage a number of respondents to produce some form of personal document to give qualitative depth to their quantitative data. Both Young and Willmott in their survey of the family in Bethnal Green and John H Goldthorpe et al., in their survey of social mobility, did this. In the former case, some respondents kept personal diaries and in the latter some respondents provided life-histories. Goldthorpe and his colleagues provided eight questions for their respondents which were posed 'in an entirely open-ended form'. Here is a brief extract from the introductory 'Life-History Notes Leaflet' with which respondents were provided:

Below we have a list of questions. If you would write a paragaph or so in answer to each of these, this would give us the kind of notes that we want. On the other hand, you may wish to arrange what you write in your own way, taking these questions simply as a guide to the points which chiefly interest us.

(Goldthorpe et al., 1980: 219)

The more the sociologist tries to 'guide' or 'structure' responses, the less personally valid they are likely to be. Nevertheless, in general, personal documents tend to score high on validity, though there is no guarantee of their wider representativeness.

THE MASS MEDIA

The mass media provide an ever-growing potential source of material for sociologists. This material is of two types. First, is data routinely provided in programmes which may be supported by considerable research staff and resources. Thus, programmes such as *'Panorama'* and *'World In Action'* pour out a wealth of data which are often more up-to-date than anything else available. The problem is that the sociologist cannot be sure whether these data are accurate, so they need to be checked and the source clearly acknowledged in any published work.

More typically, sociologists use material from the printed and visual media for critical analysis. Thus, a variety of publications or broadcasts (more usually, a series of broadcasts) have been analysed for political or other ideological bias. The Glasgow Media Group has regularly published analyses of television news broadcasts in which the content has been scrutinised and quantified for bias (see pp. 420–1). This method is termed content analysis. Similar content analysis of sexism and racism in the media has also occurred. Another technique, often used in combination with content analysis, is semiological analysis. This involves working out or 'decoding' the meaning of mainly visual symbols and signs.

Like nearly all secondary source material, mass media material is not produced primarily for sociological use. It may, therefore, be incomplete or superficial from a sociologist's point of view. It may also be personally or politically biased and it is essential that the sociologist does not merely pass this on uncritically to readers.

Is Sociology a Science?

If science is defined broadly as the accumulation of verifiable knowledge, then sociology is a science. If it is defined narrowly as the testing of hypotheses by positivistic methodology, then sociology can hardly claim to be a science (See pp. 21–2). Such a definition would also exclude much observational work in other disciplines. It is true, however, that sociology rarely produces results that are as precise and repeatable as those produced by the natural sciences. Nevertheless, Durkheim, Marx and Weber never stopped trying to be as scientific as possible and their work laid a rich theoretical and methodological basis for the further development of the discipline along scientific lines. More recently, the complex and rigorous empirical research of professional sociologists, such as John Goldthorpe and A H Halsey, goes far beyond the competence and commonsense under-standing of lay people in its methodological basis and findings.

In contrast to self-consciously scientific approaches to sociology, interpretive sociology is often less concerned with causal explanation or factual description than with *human understanding*. Perhaps such work is closer to the humanities than to sciences. This does not make it unscientific but, perhaps, it is essentially non-scientific. Unlike functionalists and many Marxists, interpretive sociologists have often shown no great desire to have their work classified as scientific. C Wright Mills, a sociologist who does not admit to a simple label himself, refers disparagingly to the 'cook-book' appearance of some scientifically oriented sociological text-books. Erving Goffman compares traditional positivist methodology to the instructions on a child's chemistry set: 'follow the rules and you, too, can be a real scientist'.

Interpretive sociologists willingly embrace what embarrasses the positivists: the subjective element in society and in sociological research. Subjectivity cuts two ways. Firstly, researchers have their own values: secondly, those being studied behave individually and therefore in a way that cannot be precisely predicted. Ethnomethodologists, such as Cicourel and Garfinkel, claim that it is impossible for sociologists to be passive observers of 'truth'.

What they 'see' is bound, in some sense, to be the result of the interaction between themselves and what they study. Yet ethnomethodologists also claim to be in the business of discovering and describing how people act and interact. Given their emphasis upon the subjective element in perception, how can they be confident of the accuracy of their own observations and reports? Their answer is that they, at least, are aware of the problem and so better able to deal with it than positivists, who may naïvely believe that they can 'factor themselves out' of their work. On the matter of the individuality of the subject of social research, Schütz, the phenomenologist, is relevant, and goes further than the ethnomethodologists. He points out that, whereas the natural sciences have concepts about objects, the social sciences have concepts about objects which have concepts about objects (including, perhaps, the researcher). In other words, people can think and, we must add, choose. They may even decide deliberately to mislead the researcher. Because of this, the level of accurate prediction in the social sciences can never be as high as in the natural sciences. Schütz, however, also points out that groups of people share common patterns of thought and behaviour, and that the researcher is able to check his or her descriptions of these with those of other observers. If there is agreement about what is observed, this is perhaps as close to achieving objectivity as is possible.

So much for what sociologists themselves think about the nature of their discpline. We now examine the opinions of two major philosophers of science upon the same issue (a philosopher of science is somebody who systematically attempts to clarify the principles underlying science). On the whole, these commentators from outside sociology have tended to take a reproving tone. Karl Popper's particular 'bogey man' is Marx. It is, however, Marx 'the prophet of revolution' that Popper admonishes – not Marx the sociologist – although, in fairness, Popper's argument is that the two are inseparable. He says that in 'prophesying' proletarian revolution, Marx is essentially unscientific in taking as given something that has not yet happened. In Popper's view, 'prophecy', religion and ideology have no place in science and, therefore, he declares Marxism to be unscientific. We do not have to accept Popper's conclusion to agree that Marxists' sociological theory and concepts must be open to the same criticism and testing as those of other perspectives. The fact that Marxist sociologists are likely to be politically Marxist does not free them from the constraints of the discipline. No sensible Marxist sociologist would want the kind of illusory freedom in which mere assertion replaces argument based on reason and evidence. It is Popper's soundest and central point that social science, like natural science, must constantly test and re-test its theories. The most rigorous way to do this is for the researcher to attempt to falsify, rather than verify, his or her own hypothesis – Popper's famous principle of falsification. He argues that Marxism cannot be scientific because many of its major theories refer to the future and are not, therefore, open to falsification. It is impossible to prove definitely that there will not be a proletarian revolution because the future is unknown. The statement that there will be one is, therefore, unscientific. In their own defence, some modern Marxists would argue that their immediate concern is less with proving or falsifying propositions than with providing a theoretical critique of capitalist society and with developing theoretical alternatives to it. Most of them would also dissociate themselves from the supposed prophetic element in Marx's writing and, to that extent, Popper's criticisms become redundant.

A further point made by Popper is of particular interest to sociologists. It is that no hypothesis can be considered finally proven. For example, although thousands of white swans have been sighted, there remains the possibility of coming across a black one. Similarly, to do the same experiment 999 times with the same result may seem to prove something, but the thousandth experiment may produce a different result. The practice of science involves a sort of industrious scepticism and Popper would frankly like to see more evidence of it among social scientists. More research and less theorising seems to be his advice.

Ernest Gellner is a recent writer in the tradition of Popper. His particular objection is to Garfinkel's ethnomethodology. He condemns its obsession with subjectivism as mere romanticism and, like Popper, he advocates a staunchly empirical approach to the understanding of society. Although the Marxist Barry Hindess has little else in common with Popper and Gellner, he also attacks extreme ethnomethodological subjectivism in his critique of statistics (pp. 315–6).

There is much commonsense – if this is not too odd a word to use of such sophisticated work – in the thought of Popper and Gellner. Theoretical cloud castles in the sky must be brought to earth and examined for substance and content, a comment that applies to functionalism as much as to Marxism. Similarly, those who are so 'hung up' on subjectivism that they allow little hope of meaningful sociological discourse hardly help to further the development of the discipline as a collective enterprise. (For a further discussion of this point, see chapter 22, pp. 509–12).

WHAT IS SCIENCE?

Until now, we have tended to regard science as a standard by which to take the measure of social science. Apart from a simple distinction between a broad and narrow definition of science, we have assumed the concept of science itself to be unproblematic. In so doing, we are in danger of giving it the status of a sort of sacred cow, divine and inscrutable. The work of Thomas Kuhn, however, attempts to 'debunk' such a reverential view of science and to ask not only how true it is to its own professed principles of empiricism and objectivity, but also whether these principles are the ones by which the natural sciences actually operate. Subjectivity may be a spectre that haunts science as well as social science.

Kuhn dismisses the notion that science is merely a collection of theories, methods and factual findings. Instead, he suggests the view that scientists, like sociologists, make use of paradigms or perspectives about their specialist fields which influence the direction and nature of their experimental research. Thus, Einstein's theories can be said to have provided the basis of a new working paradigm for astro-physics. Many of his ideas were speculative, partial and unproven, but they have since inspired more detailed research into problems concerning space and time. To this extent, Einstein's thought seems to provide much the same function as a sociological perspective.

A central feature of Kuhn's argument is that scientific paradigms change radically at certain periods in history. Thus, his book is entitled 'The Structure of Scientific Revolutions'. This revolutionary change occurs when a discovery cannot be made to fit into the dominant paradigm. We need an example here. For centuries, it was believed that the earth was the centre of the universe and that the sun revolved around it. This paradigm survived despite the increasing difficulty of accommodating newly discovered facts to it. Eventually, Copernicus produced evidence that overturned it. A new paradigm, that the earth revolves around the sun, became accepted.

Given paradigmatic changes and revolutions within the sciences, similar disagreements in sociology, expressed through the perspectives, appear less crippling to the claims of the subject to respectability and even scientific status. It is true that the natural sciences generate a greater 'sense' of consensus about theoretical and methodological approach than sociology does, but it is still a young discipline and it is possible that greater 'paradigmatic unity' may yet develop.

A further criticism may be offered against the notion of science as a monument to objectivity. Science, too, is haunted by the problem of subjectivity. First, a relatively minor point. Heisenberg's uncertainty principle points out that the light required to observe tiny particles will affect the way they behave. Thus, to a small degree, the scientist causes the behaviour he observes! That is a classic example of the dilemma of subjectivity. Second, a serious ethical point.

Scientific research, like social research, takes place in society. Research provides knowledge which may be used constructively or destructively. Scientists who allow their skills to be used in a cause they believe to be morally wrong are in the same position as soldiers, administrators and others who do the same. Research findings do not exist in a social vacuum – some power is likely to use them. Einstein believed passionately that scientists should take responsibility for the work they do and its possible application to human life.

WHAT IS SOCIOLOGY?

By way of a long detour, we come again to this question. Sociology is the study of human social life by any means that are effective. These may be more or less scientific, depending on how that term is defined, or even non-scientific. All that is necessary is that their application contributes to our knowledge and understanding of social life. To do this, 'findings' must be presented sufficiently intelligibly to be communicable to the body of professional sociologists (and, ideally, via them to the interested public). C Wright Mills is surely correct when he argues that sociology is better practised with imagination and flexibility than with rigid adherence to the models of natural science. Sociology is a craft to be judged by its product: what works best is best. Whilst not rejecting the broadly scientific basis of sociology, Nisbet caps Mills in stressing the role of the creative imagination in sociology. This, he says, gives it the quality of an art form. Nisbet's observation brings the wheel full circle: sociology is both science and art. Given the complexity of its subject matter, it needs to be.

1   Natural science, particularly the laboratory experiment, provided a model which early sociologists tended to imitate. However, because the possibility of experimenting with humans is restricted, the comparative method was developed as an alternative to experiment. The comparative method involves systematic comparison of apparently similar phenomena in separate social contexts, e.g. the development of the family in two or more societies. Weber's concept of the ideal type can be useful in comparative analysis. An ideal type is a model of the essential elements of a social phenomenon.

2   A variety of 'contrasting pairs' was introduced to indicate the scope and variety of sociology. The discipline seeks to explain both society's effect on people and people's contribution to and interpretation of society. This difference in emphasis produces distinctions between quantitative and qualitative research; objective and subjective data; structural/interpretist theories and positivist/anti-positivist methods; and partly that between reliability and validity.

3   Primary Sources of information are produced by the sociologist's original research. Observation, interviews and questionnaires are major means of producing primary data.

4   A Social Survey collects standardised data usually about a large population. A social survey usually requires a sample to be taken.

5   A Sample is a part of a total population. Usually, every effort is made to select a sample which is as representative as possible of the total population but there are situations in which an unrepresentative sample can be effectively used. There are various

SUMMARY

types of samples, each with advantages and disadvantages.

6   Interviews are of three types: structured, semi-structured and unstructured. A structured interview asks 'closed' questions, an unstructured interview 'open' questions, and a semi-structured interview directs the respondent to address certain areas while allowing freedom as to how this is done. Some interviews use all the above techniques.

7   The advantages and disadvantages of the interview largely reflect the fact that it involves face to face interaction between the researcher (or representative) and respondent. Help and guidance can be given but bias can occur.

8   Observation can be divided into non-participant and participant observation. Non-participant observation has the potential advantage of greater objectivity as the researcher is not directly involved but for that reason lacks the benefit of subjective experience. The reverse is true of participant observation.

9   Structural sociology is associated particularly with the social survey and quantitative methods and particularly in the case of Marx, Durkheim and Weber with the comparative-historical method. Interpretive perspectives are strongly associated with qualitative methods. However, much sociological research and analysis freely draws on a variety of theory and method.

10   Secondary sources are data which already exist. There is a massive amount of secondary data and while some are of high quality, in general, they should be used critically.

RESEARCH AND COURSEWORK

Each topic area in this book is followed by a section titled 'Guide to Coursework and Research'. As a general guide to research the point by point description of the stages of scientific enquiry on page 21 should be useful. However, depending on whether the research inclines to the quantitative or qualitative, or both, the relevant later section(s) of the chapter should be read. An absolutely essential aspect of research beyond GCSE level is to link the theoretical and methodological aspects (see particularly p. 35, although this linkage is repeatedly explored throughout this book).

The overall design, implementation and writing up of a piece of research must be as methodologically rigorous as is possible. Examiners are not assessing 'a good idea' but award marks to the extent to which a piece of research meets given requirements or criteria (which, in this case, relate to good research practice). As well as using sound manuals of research method, it is wise to be armed with the relevant assessment criteria when doing a piece of coursework. These are published by examination boards which also often provide 'exemplars' of coursework and other guidance for research.

Having made the above essential points, it is worth briefly introducing a non-traditional type of research which may legitimately influence student researchers. This is action research. Action research is literally research which may provide findings which may guide future action. It has developed most strongly within education, where teachers have researched classroom, school, or school-community issues with a view to applying their findings to 'improving' matters. Students, as members of educational institutions, may also want to select a topic of research on which their findings may have practical relevance. There are many such issues including those involving gender, ethnicity and classroom interaction. However, these are sensitive areas and the choice of a topic will need to be negotiated with a tutor.

FURTHER READING

Murray Morison's *Methods in Sociology* (Longman, 1986) and Patrick McNeill's *Research Methods* (Routledge, 1989) are useful introductory texts. My recommendation is to access some original sources – perhaps most conveniently in the form of collected readings. The later sections of D Potter et al., eds., Society and the *Social Sciences* (Open University Press, 1981) contain some useful readings on theory and my *A New Introductory Reader in Sociology* (Nelson, 1988) has both theory and method sections.

3 Households, Families & Marriage

Great Britain	Percentages and numbers			
Household size	1961	1971	1981	1990–91
1 person	12	18	22	26
2 people	30	32	32	35
3 people	23	19	17	17
4 people	19	17	18	15
5 people	9	8	7	5
6 or more people	7	6	4	2
All households	100	100	100	100
Average household size (number of people)	3.09	2.89	2.71	2.51

(Source: Social trends 1992)

Great Britain	Percentages			
Type of household	1961	1971	1981	1990–91
Living alone	3.9	6.3	8.0	10.6
Married couple, no children	17.8	19.3	19.5	23.6
Married couple with dependent children	52.2	51.7	47.4	40.8
Married couple with non-dependent children only	11.6	10.0	10.3	10.3
Lone parent with dependent children	2.5	3.5	5.8	6.5
Other households	12.0	9.2	9.0	8.1
All people in private households	100	100	100	100

(Source: Social trends 1992)

▲

Table 3.1

Households:

by size

▶

Table 3.2 (Far right)

People in households:

by type of household

and family in which

they live

HOUSEHOLDS, FAMILIES AND MARRIAGE: TERMINOLOGY AND TRENDS

This section defines and gives some basic data on households, families and marriage. The statistics indicate great and rapid change in all these areas although whether this amounts to a 'crisis' or merely adaptation to the nature and demands of modern society is debatable.

A household is a person or group of people living in a given dwelling. In 'Social Trends 1990' it is remarked that:

One of the most notable features of the period since the Second World War has been the increase in people living alone: in 1988, over a quarter of households in Great Britain contained only one person, compared with about one-eighth in 1961.

(Social Trends, 1990).

If we add to the 26 per cent of single person households the 35 per cent in which only two people live, then, these account for three fifths of all households. Table 3.1 summarises this and related data.

While the circumstances and life-style of the small household majority must command increasing attention from sociologists, the above statistics could be misleading. If we consider people rather than households, then in 1991, 74.7 per cent lived in households headed by a married couple and a very large majority of these had children either dependent or non-dependent (see table 3.2). This indicates to the continuing popularity of marriage – although, as we shall see, the

pattern of marriage itself has significantly changed (p. 64).

The most common family systems are the nuclear family and the extended family. A nuclear family is comprised of mother, father and child or children, whether natural or adopted. The nuclear family is also sometimes referred to as the conjugal family. Usually, members of a nuclear family share the same household. The extended family consists of the nuclear family and at least one relative living in the same household. The extended family is also sometimes referred to as the stem family. The classic extended family in Britain was a couple, their eldest son, and his wife and children living in the same household. It is helpful, however, to broaden our conception of the extended family. Sometimes relatives such as grandparents or elderly aunts live near a given nuclear family and participate in fairly intense social interaction with it. It is useful to think of such a situation as an extended family type structure. We also include various communal structures within this broad description. Kinship is social relationship based on real or assumed (adopted) consanguinity (blood relationship).

A reconstituted family is a form of nuclear family in which one or both partners have had children from a previous relationship which become part of the 'new' family, i.e. there is at least one step relationship within the family. In a society in which at least one out of three marriages involves a partner who is remarrying – many of them with children – the reconstituted family is becoming increasingly common. Issues raised by the reconstituted family, including non-blood relationships, are in need of further research.

It is debated whether the single parent family is a distinct family type or an incomplete nuclear family. In any case, there are well over a million such families in Britain, and it is urgent both that sociologists adequately analyse the phenomenon and that society and politicians respond constructively to it.

Different forms of marriage affect family structure. Monogamy allows one wife to one husband and is usually the only legally permitted form of marriage in societies in which the Christian tradition has predominated. Polygamy, which allows a person to have more than one spouse is common in some traditional societies. Polygyny, where a man has more than one wife, is more common than polyandry, where a wife has more than one husband. The former is common in some tribes but is also practised by some modern Muslims. It also occurs as a result of Mormon religious belief, particularly in the North American State of Utah. Polyandry occurs as a matter of practicality in parts of Tibet. It operates as a form of birth control in poorer regions. However many husbands a woman has, she is limited by nature to a certain number of children.

Marriage patterns are becoming more varied in contemporary British society. Monogamy remains the only legally permitted form of marriage but a large and increasing number experience it more than once. About one in three marriages are remarriages for at least one of the partners. A minority pattern of serial monogamy in which a person marries two or more times – having divorced a previous spouse – is therefore developing.

Those who argue that continuity and conventionality characterise family and marriage patterns in Britain point to the fact that the majority are born into a nuclear family, marry and produce one themselves. Others are much more impressed by the variety and complexity of family and marriage practices. They perceive a pluralistic pattern rather than the dominance of the conventional or traditional nuclear family and marriage.

SINGLES AND COUPLES: NON-NUCLEAR FAMILY HOUSEHOLDS As table 3.1 showed, the majority of households contain only one or two residents. Yet, this 'group' has attracted relatively little attention from sociologists. This is perhaps because it is not truly a group at all, but an aggregate made up of a variety of different categories of people. Nevertheless, these people are a large and increasing part of the mosaic of domestic and social life and too much concentration on the nuclear family can obscure their lifestyles.

Who, then, are the single individuals who, in total, occupy more than a quarter of households? A small but growing minority are better-off young adults who are perhaps part of the trend to marrying slightly later and who buy a house for convenience or as an investment. Another group – at any one time, hundreds of thousands, if not millions, in number – are separated or divorced individuals who temporarily or permanently are living on their own. Unlike the former, younger, group, the social life of this group is relatively unstudied. Given the popularity of re-marriage, many in this situation are clearly highly concerned to find another partner. Where do they meet each other? Singles bars, over-30s nights, clubs and the personal sections of the classified 'ad' columns are all part of a communication network that has proliferated since the nineteen sixties to meet this group's needs.

In some contrast to the previous two categories, are the several million middle-aged or elderly individuals who live alone, most of them as a result of losing their partner. Personal health and wealth are often the key to quality of life in their situation which is discussed in a later chapter (pp. 229–32).

The rise in households of two people has been less spectacular than those of one, but at 35 per cent this is the largest category of all households. Their situation is fully considered in the following paragraphs.

What are the factors that have bought about this growth in small, non-family households? First, the rise of the individual and couple household has been accompanied by a reduction in the average number of children per family which is now less than two. The majority of couples have only one or two children. Assuming these are born within a few years of each other, the couple may have an extended period of less committed time either before the first child's birth or after the last child leaves home or both. Simply, children take up a smaller proportion of their parents' lives than they used to when the average family size was bigger. A second development complements this tendency. Average life expectancy has greatly increased during this century, creating what has been referred to as 'a third age' of relative freedom and choice, unhampered by dependent children. The creation of more 'free time' would be of dubious benefit, however, without a third development: the wealth to enjoy it. Wealth per capita in Britain has more than doubled since the Second World War, and with this a huge increase in leisure options has occurred. Single people, married couples without children, and the elderly have all become targetted as 'consumer' groups by advertisers and producers. Although 'the family market' is still the largest in terms of total people, the large minority groups mentioned above constitute lucrative leisure markets. Singles holidays, commercial coach trips for senior citizens, and even one-cup tea-bags and six-packs of small bottles of wine all attest to the growing commercial attention paid to Britain's 'solos' and couples.

In fact, the trends towards consumerism and privatisation, often considered to characterise the nuclear family, seem no less true of the groups under discussion. Certainly, they generally have more uncommitted income to spend on leisure consumption than most married couples who have young children and high mortgages or rent bills. It is not possible to generalise about the extent of privatised living patterns across so broad a group. However, older and middle-aged people mostly have less incentive than children and teenagers to indulge in out of doors activity. Even young single adults who have done a hard day's work may more often prefer the comfort and amenity of their own home to going out. These are areas which merit further research.

Perspectives on the Family

For many, the family seems a familiar and comfortable institution. It can be a 'haven in a heartless world', a refuge from the impersonality and stress of work or school.

Sociologists have never accepted as adequate this simple and romantic view of the family. They have always considered that the influence of society penetrates deeply into the family, and some have argued that the family, in turn, can substantially influence society. Nevertheless, until quite recently the sociology of the family was predominantly functionalist. Broadly speaking, the literature dealt with the functions of the family in relation to society as a whole or to the various social subsystems. The functionalist approach has now been challenged from various directions. Even so, functionalist analysis of the family provides perhaps the clearest and easiest to understand application of this perspective.

THE FUNCTIONALIST PERSPECTIVE

Functionalists regard the family as an important 'organ' in the 'body' of society. It is what the family 'does' or the functions of the family that most interest them. George Murdock, an early functionalist, considered the four basic functions of the family to be the sexual, the reproductive, the socialising and the economic. Although these functions can evolve, he considered them to be 'universal'.

We can take sex and reproduction together. According to functionalists, marriage and the nuclear family provide the best opportunity for the socially controlled expression of the sex drive. More importantly, they provide the necessary institutional stability for the reproduction and nurture (bringing up) of children. The bringing up of children requires considerable time and effort – human maturation takes longer than that of any other species relative to life-span. To be brought up effectively, children usually require the help of more than one person (for practical if not emotional reasons). In most societies the two people who produce a child are expected to take responsibility for its upbringing. Family work is usually divided into domestic and economic work. Practical commitment to children based on shared involvement and responsibility exists in polygamous as well as monogamous marriages. In polygamous

Muslim societies a man is not expected to marry more wives and produce more children than he can afford.

To argue that the nuclear family is a socially useful institution is not to say, as some functionalists do, that it is biologically necessary and inevitable. Margaret Mead seems correct in contending that the nuclear family is culturally created, not biologically given. Comparisons with similar species by no means provide conclusive evidence, but males of other primates often do not remain with the female they have made pregnant. The fact that the human male usually does so is probably because this arrangement conveniently provides a secure context for the lengthy child-rearing necessary to the species. Another pointer in this direction is the fact that whilst many societies have allowed considerable sexual freedom before marriage, the widespread tendency is to curtail or abolish it afterwards. This, again, is a question of practicality not biology: it focuses energy and attention on spouse and children and, in particular, prevents the male from having more children than he is able to look after. Historically, the taboo (social disapproval) on sex outside marriage is a protective device for children and, to that extent, the human species. This argument loses much of its practical, if not emotional, force, however, in this age of effective and easily available contraception. The family's role in laying down the basis of culture through socialisation is universally stressed by functionalists.

The basic economic function of the family is to provide food and shelter for its members. In pre-industrial societies many families produced much of what they consumed. Now, individuals work for wages but the family remains an important unit of consumption of industrially produced goods.

As explained in the first chapter, functionalists see each social institution in terms of its role within its own social subsystem and in terms of its relationship to society as a whole. The model below illustrates this point in respect of the modern family.

Figure 3.1 is very simple to interpret. It shows that the family gives 'something' to and gets 'something' from each sub-system. Take the example of the economy. The family provides labour for which its members get paid. Money is then 'recycled'

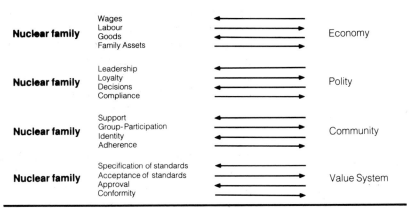

(Source: Adapted from Bell and Vogel (1960))

▲

Figure 3.1

The interchange

between the nuclear

family and the

traditional

subsystems of society

back into the economy through the purchase of goods which the family needs and through family savings. Thus, the family is seen as both dependent on and contributing to the economy. It is the same with the political system. In return for loyalty and obedience (compliance), family members get leadership from politicians (however confusing this may sometimes be!). From the community comes support and identity in return for participation and commitment (adherence). The only aspect of the model that might cause difficulty is calling the fourth sub-system the value system, rather than kinship. The family is, of course, part of the kinship system and reflects and passes on the values of society. Other institutions are involved in value socialisation, but the family's role is primary.

Despite great recent criticism of functionalist analysis, this model has a certain commonsense usefulness. However, as D H Morgan points out, Murdock's analysis suffers from a failure to consider whether other institutions could take over the functions he associates with the family, but later functionalists such as Parsons have explored this issue. Further, Murdock rather too readily assumes that the nuclear family functions harmoniously. More contemporary functionalists N W Bell and E F Vogel, as well as radical phenomenologists R D Laing and David Cooper, have shown that the modern family can contain frightening tensions. Recent functionalists, however, still tend to assume a 'fit' between the nuclear family and society as a whole, even though they may concede that it may be internally under stress. Arguably, they are overinfluenced by the harmony implicit in the organic analogy in making this assumption. We examine functionalist analysis of how the family has 'adapted' to the 'needs' of industrial society in a later section (Chapter 3 pp. 56–60).

MARXIST, OTHER CLASS-BASED AND FEMINIST FAMILY ANALYSIS

Marxists also adopt a structural perspective on the family. They do not, however, regard the nuclear family as a universal feature of human society, but put it in the particular context of capitalist society and, particularly, the class nature of that society.

Friedrich Engels' (1820–1895) *The Origin of the Family: Private Property and the State*, remains the starting point for most Marxist analysis of the family and of gender relations. Engels examines the emergence of the nuclear family and male dominance in an historical context. He hypothesised that in the nomadic stage of man's social development there was a substantial measure of sexual equality. Neither exclusive sexual possessiveness nor much private property existed. People and things were held in common although mothers had an immediate involvement with young children. Gradually, the male sphere of activity became more specialised and distinct: cattle breeding, mining and trade were added to their primary responsibility of hunting. This leads to the central point of Engels' argument. As men acquired greater control over wealth and property, they sought means to ensure that it stayed within their personal possession and was passed on to their offspring. To do this they had to know who their offspring were! This meant that the free sexual relations of the horde had to be replaced by monogamy, and a system of inheritance based on blood introduced. In a male-dominated society, the eldest male was established as inheritor. The state, also male-dominated, gave powerful legal support to male control over the family, women and private property. Thus, in Engels' analysis, the growth of private property and male dominance or patriarchy evolved together.

As Rosalind Delmar puts it, the major contribution of Engels was to assert 'women's oppression as a problem of history, rather than of biology.' She uses the word 'assert' rather than 'prove' because the details of Engels' historical account are thought to be wrong. The precise historical truth on this issue is probably beyond proof but the point to appreciate is that Engels concluded that as the monogamous nuclear family and female subordination had developed historically, it is possible to change them. This is the basis of Marxist and most socialist analyses of the family. The opposite view, that the sexual division of labour which consigns the woman primarily to the home and the man to economic labour, is founded on the analysis that such an arrangement is biologically rooted and virtually immutable (unchangeable). It is the basis of the more crude functionalist analysis of the nuclear family. Although the patriarchal (male-dominated) nuclear family predated capitalist society, Engels and Marx considered that it fitted the needs of capitalism particularly well. Capitalist society was based on the accumulation of private wealth and property mainly controlled by men. Accordingly, a patriarchal family structure linked to a system of primo-geniture (in which the eldest son inherits) suited it very well. Primogeniture was primarily of significance among the upper and middle classes: the working class had little to pass on anyway. Marx and Engels did argue, however, that capitalism provided a limited opportunity for women to escape domestic bondage by finding employment outside the home and thus acquiring an independent source of income. Even so, they considered that, ultimately, the liberation of women depended on a change of social system from capitalism to socialism. Private property would then be abolished and the organisation of child-rearing and socialisation would be a matter for the community as a whole to determine.

More recent Marxist and socialist writers – particularly Marxist feminists – have tended to be sceptical of the supposed improvement in the status of women that more direct involvement in the economy brings. Blackburn and Stewart point out that women often play the kind of 'service' role in the work situation which can be regarded as an extension of their low domestic status rather than an improvement on it. Further, Engels has been somewhat criticised for a 'waiting for the revolution' approach to the solution of gender exploitation. Contemporary Marxist and socialist feminists such as Juliet Mitchell and Ann Oakley tend to be much more diligent than he was in the search for immediate improvements in gender relations towards that larger end (see chapter 8, pp. 171–5 where non-Marxist feminist perspectives on gender are also discussed).

Some Marxists regard the sexual possessiveness of marital partners as just one expression of the possessive and, in their view, selfish individualism of capitalist society. Marx himself claimed that marriage 'is incontestably a form of exclusive private property'. The female 'gives' sex in return for the economic security her husband provides. She gets the worst of the arrangement because she is the more dependent. Engels suggested that her position is one of glorified prostitution. Perhaps the cultural stereotyping embodied in such phrases as 'she's a real gold-digger' and 'she's out to get her man' bear out the view that the economic dependency of women under capitalism can undermine their dignity.

Marxists consider that the family can socialise children to conform, even though, in the case of the working class, it is against their interests to do so (see chapter 8, pp. 172–3). On the other hand, experience of exploitation can produce feelings critical of the system among the proletariat (working class) and these may also be passed on through the family as well as through workmates and friends. As we shall see, Marxists generally consider that the socialising and other functions of the nuclear family could, at least, be pared down and done more effectively by other institutions such as state nurseries.

It would be wholly wrong to think that only Marxists are aware of the major influence of class on family life and, especially, of the way the family socialises children to 'belong' to a particular class. On the contrary, since the war a vast body of largely empirical work has contributed to our knowledge of the links between family and class. The writings of A H Halsey and J W Douglas are examples. Through the research of these and other scholars we later study the relationship between family, education and class, and that section (chapter 4 pp. 94–6) should be regarded as a direct continuation of this chapter. Indeed, class pervades not only the family but virtually all aspects of social life. The experience of class, however, begins in the family. (For an analysis of feminist family policy contributions, see chapter 15, pp. 370–2).

Is the Nuclear Family Universal or are Other Family Types Possible (and Functional)

THE TERMS OF THE DEBATE We now examine the functionalist claim that the nuclear family is universal. First, Murdock's definition of the family needs to be noted:

The family is a social group characterised by common residence, economic co-operation and reproduction. It includes adults of both sexes, at least two of whom maintain a socially approved sexual relationship, and one or more children, own or adopted, of sexually cohabiting adults (1949).

Murdock's claim that the nuclear family is universal has an empirical and theoretical aspect. He supported it empirically by examining 250 varied types of society and concluding that the nuclear family occurred in all of them. Theoretically, he argues that the nuclear family, with its shared division of labour between the sexes, is the most efficient and convenient instituion to accomplish the functions referred to above. This largely explains its universality. Functionalists, of course, recognise the widespread existence of the extended family but see the nuclear family as its essential core. Literally, the extended family is an extension of the nuclear family. The same argument is applied to polygamous families. One person may make several marriages but each separate coupling and offspring is regarded as a nuclear family.

Four categories of evidence can be cited against the functionalist position on the nuclear family. These are:

1 Comparative cultural evidence of non-nuclear families,
2 Deliberate attempts to produce collectively-based families,
3 Single parent families,
4 Lesbian and homosexual led families.

We will examine each of these categories in turn.

COMPARATIVE CULTURAL EVIDENCE OF NON-NUCLEAR FAMILIES

THE NAYAR CASE It can be argued that the Nayars of Malabar offer an example of a society in which the nuclear family did not exist. Until about the mid-nineteenth century, when their traditional social system began to break up under the impact of the British, the Nayar produced and reared children without the aid of the nuclear family. No direct institutional link existed between sex and reproduction and the rearing of children. Once a woman had undergone a sexual initiation ritual, she became free to take up to several sexual partners. As a result, paternity was often uncertain. In practical terms this did not matter, as the mother's brother, not the natural father, was responsible for her and her offspring. When this was not possible the next nearest male relative on the mother's side was responsible.

The Nayar case is surely an exception to the familiar nuclear family pattern. Kathleen Gough's point that a special and socially recognised tie existed between a woman and the man who first initiated her sexually does not affect the argument at all. The 'couple' certainly did not constitute the basis of a nuclear family in that the nuclear 'unit' had no continuous social existence. Further examination shows, however, that there was a sound functional reason for the Nayar form of child-rearing. The Nayars were a very warlike people. The women were able to assist each other during the frequent absences of the men, and in the event of one male relative being killed, there would still be others left to provide for the woman and her children. The Nayar system of child-rearing was, then, functionally well adapted to the needs of that particular society. Regarded thus, it is quite consistent with functionalist perspectives about the need of children for a stable social environment. Perhaps this is more significant than the literal fact that the Nayar case does represent a rare exception to the 'universality' of the nuclear family.

However, a separation of biological and social parenthood is not unique to the Nayar. It occurred, in similar circumstances, among the Ashanti of Ghana. In different circumstances, it is also increasingly common in modern societies.

DELIBERATE ATTEMPTS TO PRODUCE COLLECTIVELY-BASED FAMILIES

THE KIBBUTZIM There have been few attempts in modern society to abolish the nuclear family outright but many efforts to replace it partially by other institutions or to merge it within a larger extended family-type structure. Perhaps the best known attempt to supplement the family by providing alternative institutions to assist parents with childrearing is the Israeli kibbutzim. In the early days of the Jewish settlement in Israel, the kibbutzum stressed the collective values of the whole community against the more concentrated, limited, and it was thought sometimes selfish ties of the family. It was also part of the beliefs (or ideology) of the movement to release women from child-rearing and to enable them to have as much time for work and leisure as men. Young infants were taken to special children's houses after only a short time with their parents. They grew up together and were looked after by specially trained nurses (or metapalets) and teachers. They were allowed to see their parents for a few hours only each day, and slept in the children's houses and not their parents' residence. Women were therefore free to do any work on the same terms as men. Gradually, there has been a reversion to a traditional sexual division of labour and family form: the separation between parents and children is less complete; in many kibbutzim, children return to spend the night at their parents' flat, and women are more involved than men in traditionally feminine roles such as working in the communal kitchen or laundry.

Despite this partial return to nuclear family norms, some kibbutzim still thrive and are now well beyond the experimental phase. It is significant that children of the kibbutzim and adults from kibbutzim backgrounds are as psychologically well adjusted as others. Not unexpectedly, however, many have acquired values that express the importance of the group rather than individual achievement. The charge by Bruno Bettelheim that adults brought up in the kibbutzim lack the capacity for leadership has not been found to be true, however. It does seem, therefore, that the role of the family in rearing children can be successfully reduced, as long as other effective institutions exist to do the job.

THE SOVIET 'EXPERIMENT' There has been only one attempt by a government seriously to undermine the nuclear family. This happened in the Soviet Union in the period immediately following the revolution of 1917. Marriage, divorce and even abortion were made available on almost a casual basis. The ideological inspiration behind this attempt to undermine the family was the communist ideas of Marx, Engels and Lenin. They considered that in capitalist societies the family both expressed and helped to perpetuate the unequal and repressive nature of the system itself. In particular, they considered that the domination of husband over wife in the family reflected that of the capitalist manufacturer over the wage-labourer in economic and social life. But it was not simply ideology that motivated the Communist revolutionaries. Practically, they wanted to release more women from domestic toil to enable them to assist in reconstructing the country's economy which had been badly damaged by revolution and civil war. To help achieve this, communal facilities were established for bringing up children, though at first these were quite inadequate.

In the mid nineteen thirties, the government substantially changed major aspects of its policy towards the family. In 1935 a new law was passed, making parents legally responsible for the misbehaviour of their children. In 1936 much stricter marriage and divorce legislation was passed. This was partly because the previous approach had helped to produce considerable social problems, including a high rate of infant mortality and neglect and juvenile delinquency. In addition, the government was now keen to increase the birth rate and this was thought to require a stable family structure and fewer abortions. It is significant, however, that a progressively extending network of maternity homes, nurseries and kindergartens was also established both to assist population expansion and to allow women more freely to enter and remain in the labour force.

As Professor Bronfenbrenner says, conditions were so unstable in post-revolutionary Russia that it would be unwise to regard the Soviet experiment to undermine the family as a serious test of whether it is possible for a society to do without the family. Nevertheless, certain less general conclusions do suggest themselves. Firstly, the Soviet experiment again makes it obvious that the crucial functions concerning the reproduction, nurture and socialisation of children, traditionally fulfilled by the family, cannot just be left to chance. If the family does not perform them, then some other institution or institutions must. Secondly, where adequate alternative institutions are established, they can, at least in part, replace the family. The Soviet Union, and indeed other Communist countries, recognised the need for planned alternative facilities for child-rearing if the traditional functions of the family were to be reduced. The Soviet Union, East Germany and China were all much better equipped with nursery and pre-school facilities than Britain. In addition, the Soviet Union ran a state system of boarding schools which brought up millions of children and so freed their parents, particularly their mothers, from the need to do so.

THE SIXTIES COMMUNE MOVEMENT A much less organised effort to breach the limits of the nuclear family was the commune 'movement' of the late nineteen sixties. Communes of one kind or another have existed for thousands of years – religious communities are one example – and will no doubt continue to exist, although they have a tendency to be short-lived. An interesting example of communal idealism which illustrates the fragility of the movement was the plan of the poets Wordsworth, Coleridge and Southey to establish a utopia (perfect society) in miniature on the banks of the Susquehanna River in the United States. Like most people's dreams of returning to nature, this one remained a dream, although Wordsworth and Coleridge did go to live in the more accessible English Lake District.

The ideological theorising which inspired many of the communes of the nineteen sixties was rarely as well thought out as that of the Kibbutzim pioneers. Ideas of 'togetherness' and of 'sharing things, feelings and experience' were enough to persuade thousands of young people, at one time or another, to spend a few weeks or months in a commune. Others pursued the ideal of alternative living more rigorously and attempted to live self-sufficiently, practising communist principles in respect of property. In many communes nuclear families or, quite often, single-parent families simply fitted in – sometimes benefiting from the help that single adults or childless couples gave them with their children. In others, more organised attempts to bring up children communally occurred and in such cases these arrangements were often consciously thought of as alternatives to the nuclear family. Likewise, serious attempts were sometimes made to share the burden of domestic work equally between men and women. In other cases, as feminists have pointed out, the power-structure of communes was, in practice if not in theory, highly patriarchal.

Even at its peak in the late nineteen sixties the commune movement was never more than a marginal challenge to conventional family structures. The nature of modern society tends strongly to undermine the extended family type structure of communes. Geographical mobility – often caused by occupational change – is so great that the chances of the same group of people finding it convenient to stay together over a long period are small. Unless modern society itself breaks down and we return to a more localised agricultural pattern of living, communes seem likely to remain peripheral. Yet, for certain groups, especially students and young, unmarried adults, communal living can offer an enjoyable and practical social framework. It is also not uncommon for groups of one-parent families to live either together or close to one other in order to benefit from mutual cooperation and assistance.

SINGLE PARENT FAMILIES

The possibility that the single parent family is a distinct and viable family type requires discussion if for no other reason than that in 1990, one in six families in Britain were headed by a single parent, over ninety per cent of whom were women. Any adequate sociological discussion of this issue should not be influenced by the social stigma which some still attach to single parenthood. This taint is perhaps implicit in the functionalist

model which defines certain social institutions, such as the nuclear family, as 'the norm' and others as 'deviant' or even 'pathological' ('sick'). Given that there are tens of millions of single parent families throughout the world an attempt at sociologically neutral enquiry into the issue will be made here.

The majority of single parent families are headed by a divorced or separated female or by a female who is unmarried but 'ideally' might like to be. In other words, most single parents regard the nuclear family – roughly as defined by Murdock – as the most desirable type of family. Ellis Cashmore's study of over 250 single poorer parents demonstrates that for many in this group life can be hard and lonely (Cashmore, 1985). Yet, as the one parent family continues to grow it becomes increasingly necessary to understand it sociologically and to accommodate it in terms of social policy.

Some women do make a deliberate choice in favour of single parenthood. Jean Renvoize's *Single Mothers By Choice* (1985) examines 30 mothers of this kind. Significantly, however most of her sample are professionally qualified women who are able independently to afford a child. Cashmore's study finds few poorer women who regard single parenthood as in itself liberating although for some it is a better alternative to an oppressive relationship. Although the percentage of children born outside of marriage is increasing in all social class groups, the prevalence is much higher among lower social class groups and realistically must be considered generally to add to their problems.

The majority of British Afro-Caribbean children have been born within marriage. However, a relatively high number are born to unmarried mothers. According to the

1982 PSI survey, 31 per cent of Afro-Caribbean households with children under sixteen were headed by a single parent compared to ten per cent of white households and five per cent of Asian. More recently (1989), Charles Murray, citing government statistics, states that about 48 per cent of live births to black women born in the West Indies occur outside marriage and this is broadly in line with the general trend during the eighties (the overall figure in 1988 was 25 per cent).

Similar statistics to the above in the United States have caused some to argue that the single parent black family is a genuine adaptation to black experience and needs and so is merely a different type of family than the nuclear but just as 'normal' in its context. Evidence cited to support this analysis includes the polygamous nature of marriage among many black people's West African predecessors and the highly disruptive effect of slavery on marital and family relationships. The contemporary situation of many British, as well as American, black people also provides possible explanations for a high rate of one parent families. In particular, the high rate of unemployment among black males may deter some black females from marrying them on the grounds that they may be an economic deficit rather than asset. Instead, family support is sought from kin, particularly female kin although brothers, too, can be called upon. Indeed, it only seems possible to regard the one parent black family as an effective family type in the context of the wider kinship system. A higher percentage of British Afro-Caribbean than white women are in paid work and, given that a substantial minority are single parents, they could only achieve this on the basis of childcare offered by relatives. The lack of childcare facilities provided by local authorities in Britain reinforces this point. For those without such help, and given the high cost of private childcare, dependency on welfare might be the only alternative.

Ann Phoenix states that 'Afro-Caribbean families ... are represented in every possible category of family' and warns against representing the single parent family as typical of the black community or of negatively stereotyping 'the Afro-Caribbean family'. It is hoped that the above discussion avoids this. What it is intended to do is

explore whether the single parent family in general, and the Afro-Caribbean single parent family in particular, can be regarded as an alternative to the nuclear family and as an exception to its universality. The answer seems to be a qualified 'yes' to both these questions. In no modern society has the single parent family replaced the nuclear family as the dominant family form but it is becoming increasingly common throughout Western society and is clearly a functional (if minimal) unit, particularly in the context of wider kinship networks.

LESBIAN AND HOMOSEXUAL LED 'FAMILIES'

The number of lesbian and homosexual couples who bring up children is small but increasing. The following description of lesbian parenthood suggests that they can face much the same problems as heterosexual couples and some more besides:

Lesbian 'Parenthood'

Michelle G and Nancy S were lovers, lesbians who had been together for 11 years and wanted to fulfil their maternal instincts. They took a joint decision to have a baby, like a growing number of American lesbian couples. Ms G found a sperm donor and was present at the artificial insemination of Ms S and at the birth of their daughter in 1980.

There followed happy years of parenthood. A boy was born four years later. Both women were actively involved in bringing up their children – changing nappies, comforting them when ill or unhappy, exalting in their progress. That was until the partnership turned sour. Now they are fighting one another every inch of the way through the Californian courts for custody of the children they love.

It is a nasty battle, but one that is becoming increasingly common in the United States because of the number of gay couples having children, the ease with which they split up and the confusion surrounding the law on parenthood.

In the past year, courts in Maryland, New York and Los Angeles have had to confront the tricky issue of whether to give access rights to "mothers" who are not related by blood to their children, and who cannot legally marry the biological mother, but who have played the role of parent since the children were born.

So far the courts have ruled that such de facto parents are not parents in law and therefore have no right to see their children once relationships have ended. In contrast to what happens in most divorces between biological parents, the children's best interests are not even an issue. In the case of Ms G and Ms S (their names are being withheld by court order for the sake of the children) the Californian courts have decided that the children are not Ms G's and that she has no right of access, despite having helped to bring them up. This ruling is now being challenged in an appeal and a hearing is expected next spring.

(Lucy Hodges, 'When is a parent not a parent' The Independent, 28/9/90 1990: 19)

At about the same time as the above report was published, a British court of appeal reversed a decision which had given child custody to a man whose wife had declared herself a lesbian and from whom he was separated. Such cases are unlikely ever to be more than a small minority of those concerning 'the family' but they are common enough to require placing within 'the sociology of the family'.

Indeed, are such social units 'families'? They do not fulfil Murdoch's definition because they do not include 'adults of both sexes' and it is debatable whether the sexual relationships within them are 'socially approved'. As with the case of the single parent family, a more limited definition of the family is required if lesbian and homosexual families can, in fact, be defined as families. Such a definition would be that a family is a social group characterised by common residence and cooperation including at least one adult and child.

CONCLUSION: IS THE NUCLEAR FAMILY UNIVERSAL?

It is clear that a stable and happy nuclear family is outstandingly well-equipped to perform the basic functions of the reproduction and rearing of children although in many traditional societies it only functions efficiently as part of an extended kinship system. It is historical fact that in almost every society the nuclear family has been the basic social unit. However, it is not quite true that the nuclear family is universal to all societies. At least, it is strongly arguable that the Nayar and similar

cases are exceptions. It is certainly not true that the nuclear family is universal in all societies in the sense that it is the only type of family found.

The main exception is the single parent family. Murdock, of course, was aware of the single parent family 'exception' and the issue is really whether it should be regarded as a 'deviant' family form or simply as another family type of equal status to the nuclear family.

It is well worth noting that of those cases in which a child's biological father is not involved in its upbringing, those families which function best enjoy some other form of regular and routine assistance for the mother. In the cases of the Nayar and Ashanti, the mother relies on blood relatives. In the case of single parent families in modern societies – particularly, perhaps black single parent families – there may also be considerable reliance on kin. In lesbian families, a female couple provide mutual support.

A problem in most advanced societies is that many single parents do not have access to a significant network of kin support. There are two broad policy responses to this, not necessarily wholly contradictory. The first is to accept that modern family life is often unstable and fragmentary and for the state to ensure that the basic needs of children are met, above all, by ensuring an adequate national system of pre-school nurseries. This would meet the needs not only of single parents who want to do paid work but of the many married couples with children both of whom want to do paid work. The second policy response is to try to 'shore up' the nuclear family. For instance, divorce could be made more difficult to obtain, and absent fathers pursued and required to maintain their offspring. These issues recur throughout the remainder of this chapter.

The Family and Community in Britain from Pre-Industrial to Modern Times
••

It used to be thought that the extended family was typical in pre-industrial England and that the nuclear family became predominant as a result of industrialisation. It was argued by Goode and Parsons that the industrial economy requires a more mobile population and that this tends to break up

extended families; in particular, the urban, industrial areas drew in younger people. Historical and sociological research has shown this to be too simple a view. Nevertheless, as Edward Shorter and others argue, this new knowledge need not fundamentally change our perception of the difference between local community life in pre-industrial and modern times. Even though family structure has changed less than was thought, its relationship to the wider community has changed. We will divide our study of changes in the family into three historical phases: the pre-industrial, the early industrial and the modern.

1 THE PRE-INDUSTRIAL FAMILY

Peter Laslett has shown that, in fact, the nuclear family was the norm in pre-industrial Britain and other research strongly suggests that the same was true for North America. It is quite likely, however, that the extended family was more common in continental Europe, at least in the East. One important exception to the nuclear family norm existed in Britain. It was usual for the eldest and inheriting son and his family to remain in his parents' home. This was to mutual benefit: the ageing parents could receive help from their eldest son who was able to live in and look after the property he would eventually inherit. Although other children usually moved out of the parental home at marriage, they normally lived close by.

An interesting suggestion emerging from more recent research on the family further refutes the functionalist view that the predominance of the nuclear family occurred as a result of industrialisation. Harris argues that the very fact that non-inheriting children had to make their own way in the world helped to provide a mobile labour force and to foster the values of hard work and achievement necessary for capitalist activity. Seemingly, it was not necessary for the family to 'adapt' greatly to the early industrial society as functionalists maintain. On the contrary, the single inheritance system may have helped foster industrialisation. The same system of inheritance exists in Japan and may have had a similar effect.

Talcott Parsons has emphasised the multi-functional nature of the pre-industrial family. Whereas the modern nuclear family typically receives much assistance from the state in performing its basic functions, the pre-industrial family had to be more self-sufficient. At times of crisis, considerable help was often provided by kin and neighbours. If this help was essentially informal, it was also expected and needed.

Then, as now, the family was the major institution of sex, reproduction and nurture. As far as socialisation was concerned, the family, supported by church and community, taught traditional behaviour and morality. For the great majority there was no formal schooling and most could neither read nor write. Skills, including farming skills, were normally learnt through practical application, usually under the watchful eye of family or kin. The major economic function of most families was to produce enough for their members to survive – comfortably if possible. The better off and more successful produced a surplus which could then be sold in market towns – mainly for consumption by the urban minority. The function of job placement was more often performed by the family in pre-industrial times, than it is now. This means that older members of the family would frequently place younger members in work.

Whatever the precise size and structure of the pre-industrial family, Edward Shorter seems to be right to suggest that both kin and community had greater control and influence on individual and nuclear family life than now. This observation fits in with the view of some functionalists that family and community 'did' more for their members than today.

2 THE EARLY INDUSTRIAL FAMILY

With industrialisation and the movement of population to the towns, major changes began to take place in the functional relationship of the family to society. But just as sociologists have exaggerated the extent of the extended family in the pre-industrial past, so they have often overstressed the speed and extent of the change to the nuclear family in industrial, urban areas. Obviously, if the nuclear family was the predominant form before industrialisation, there could hardly have been a massive shift towards it after industrialisation. There is some evidence that in industrial working class areas the extended family was, in fact, more common than in rural areas. This was the pattern found by Anderson in his research into households in the cotton-manufacturing town of Preston and a rural area nearby, in the mid-nineteenth century. Peter Willmott and Michael Young's famous study of working class family life in Bethnal Green in the nineteen-fifties showed the strength of extended family type structures at that time and it is likely that this pattern had existed for several generations. The usefulness of extended family type structures to the working class in the nineteenth century is apparent. Older women could help out domestically when the younger married ones went out to work. People arriving from the rural areas would often stay with relatives, not only out of immediate necessity, but also in the hope of picking up tips about jobs, or even getting a specific recommendation and placement. Extended families in contemporary immigrant communities play much the same role.

There were also sound personal and social reasons for middle class families to stay close together in Victorian England. In particular, the old still depended on their kin for help and companionship, in the absence of a welfare state. Quite often, the large, three-floor Victorian middle class house was the home of three generations.

The pattern painted by modern scholarship is, then, of more continuity between pre-industrial and early industrial family structure and life than has been previously noted. The extended family and supportive community was often needed as much in industrial and dockland areas as it had been in rural areas. The real changes in family and community life occurred much closer to our own time, and these have more to do with family size and the break-up of families than with any marked change from the extended to the nuclear form.

3 THE 'MODERN' FAMILY

The twentieth century, our third period for consideration, has seen substantial changes in the size of the family and in its relationship to society. Largely because of improved methods of birth control and the resultant decrease in the fertility rate, families tend to be much smaller than in Victorian times. A family of four, parents and two children, has become typical of both the working and middle classes. Change in family size has probably had as much effect on family life as any supposed change in family structure. Nevertheless, it can be said

that the post-Second World War period is the one in which the nuclear family has overwhelmingly predominated over the extended. Indeed, as early as 1971, the majority of households contained only one or two people – a fact which suggests that even the nuclear family is suffering some fragmentation. According to functionalists such as Talcott Parsons, the modern nuclear family has adapted to fulfil more specialised functions. Further, the relationship of family to community has changed in certain respects, if perhaps less so than some authorities have previously thought.

Recent research by Peter Wilmott (1986) confirms that although Kin are now less likely to live close to each other, contact often remains quite frequent. He describes three types of Kinship arrangements in contemporary Britain:

1 The local extended family – two or three related nuclear families in separate but geographically close households (such as in 1950s Bethnal Green). This type of family pattern is on the decline (see pp. 61–3).
2 The dispersed extended family – two or more related nuclear families which are not localised and consequently see each other less than in the case of the local extended family. However, visits are still quite frequent, occurring perhaps on a weekly or fortnightly basis. This type accounts for about half of families, and is probably now typical of both the working and middle classes (despite other differences discussed below).
3 The attenuated extended family – this is like the dispersed extended family but contact is much less fequent. This accounts for about three eighths of families.

Overall, Willmott concludes that 'The most striking feature of British kinship, now and in the past, and in both rural and urban environments, is its resilience' (1988).

THE DEBATE ABOUT 'THE CHANGING FUNCTIONS OF THE FAMILY'

The classic functionalist 'position' on the changing functions of the family is that the state has largely taken over certain of its functions while the family has become more specialised in others. Talcott Parsons is perhaps the best known proponent of this view. Ronald Fletcher, a British functionalist, sharply disagrees with Parsons on this matter (as on others). Fletcher argues that the modern family is more involved across a wide range of functions – essential and non-essential – than previously. Marxists agree with functionalists that the family performs essential functions in capitalist societies but argue that it does so in a way that results in the exploitation of its members, particularly women. A view expressed from the new right is that inadequate family performance partly reflects a failure of individual responsibility, especially on the part of some male parents.

In general, functionalists consider that the basic functions of the modern nuclear family remain those that the family has traditionally fulfilled to a greater or lesser extent, but that all four functions have been modified. According to Murdock, these are: sex, reproduction, socialisation, and the economic. Talcott Parsons, in particular, argues that as the basic functions have tended to be reduced, the family has acquired a still greater role in personal and emotional life. There has been a parallel decline in the involvement of the local community with the individual. Often there is a wall of privacy between family and neighbourhood community.

For the majority, marriage is still the main outlet for sexual activity and some consider it to be the only morally acceptable one. Many people, however, no longer exclusively associate sex with marriage. Michael Schofield's work shows a growth in permissive attitudes to sex before marriage among young people. In the United States The Hite Report (1989) suggested that many women no longer regard sexual expression exclusively in terms of their marital relationship. If marriage is not as exclusively the outlet for sexual expression as in the past, it still provides the most popular basis of companionship and mutual assistance. The spread of AIDS does not appear to have greatly affected the above patterns of behaviour and it is not even clear whether it has bought about 'safer sex' among heterosexuals although this now appears to have widely occurred among the homosexual community (1991).

Reproduction still occurs predominantly within a two-parent family context despite a steep increase in births outside marriage in recent years. There has been a corresponding rise in the number of children taken into local authority care, but most of these still received early nurture and socialisation within some sort of family situation, however unstable.

The state has come increasingly to intervene in child socialisation, particularly from the age of five when children usually start school. Even infants (and for that matter unborn children) can benefit from a variety of advice and assistance available from central, and sometimes local, government sources. A state system of pre-school nurseries is not, however, provided in Britain and the responsibility for early child-care and socialisation falls more heavily on the family than in other European societies (see p. 69). Functionalists stress the continuing importance of 'the family' as the agency of primary socialisation. Here they are not merely referring to informal socialisation, which functionalists have always seen as necessary to passing on the values and norms of society but to formal teaching too. Fletcher suggests that more teaching and learning take place in the family now than in the past. We live in a complex world in which 'the three R's' are necessary rather than optional. Many parents play a large part in teaching these and other skills.

Although increasing numbers of individuals work wholly or partly from home, the family itself is rarely now a unit of economic production, although it is an important unit of consumption. Many goods, such as refrigerators, washing machines, and three piece suites are manufactured largely for the family market. It hardly needs to be said that without this market there would be economic collapse. In addition, families collectively produce and maintain the labour force. Finally, the investment of family money in banks, building societies, unit trusts and stocks and shares provides necessary loan capital for industrial investment.

The protection and assistance traditionally afforded by kin and community is now commonly provided by the state. The logic of welfare is that social security, not the family, must remain the final safety net for people faced with poverty. The National Health Service plays a major role here. So, too, do the contributory national insurance schemes covering sickness and unemployment payments, and the social security system, which is supposed to be the ultimate 'security' against poverty if all else fails. Some have seen the apparent loss of the family's welfare function and its assumption by the state as an example of the growing impersonality of the modern world. Even caring for one's fellows has been taken over by 'big brother', and strugglers are assisted by salaried social workers rather than friends. This is too simple a view. Firstly, the Welfare State provides many services, including necessary medical services to the poor, that people would not otherwise obtain. Secondly, help from family and friends does, and indeed should, supplement and overlap that provided by the welfare state. The state cannot usually supply the human and emotional support that people undergoing material or emotional crisis often need, although many social workers make remarkable efforts to do so. The administration of social security payments has, however, often been obtusely bureaucratic – hardly a bracing recipe for 'clients' often already dispirited and suffering.

Talcott Parsons emphasises the importance of the contemporary family in 'stabilising' the adult personality. It provides a relatively secure and personally meaningful context for self-fulfilment, in contrast with the frequently stressful and impersonal nature of work. Parsons considers that the family has shed some of its less necessary functions and has adapted to become more specialised in two tasks: that of socialisation, and 'tension' or emotional management.

Ronald Fletcher agrees that the nuclear family remains a functionally necessary social unit but disagrees that it has lost its non-essential functions. In *The Family and Marriage in Britain* (1962) Fletcher lists the non-essential functions of the family as political participation (e.g. voting), economic, education, health, religious, and recreation. It is largely the increased leisure time and wealth available to families that enables them to be more involved in these areas. However, Fletcher fully acknowledges that in some of these areas, particularly education and health, the state has also become much more involved. On balance, he considers that both family and state devote more time to 'non-essential' areas, and suggests that this reflects technological advance, greater leisure and more demanding standards. Although Fletcher recognises that the nuclear family is beset by a range of problems, these have intensified in the 30 or so years since he published his book. Although clearly a 'supporter' of the nuclear family it is likely that he would paint a less positive picture of its performance in the light of some of the trends discussed elsewhere in this chapter.

As David Morgan observes in his article *Socialisation and the Family: Change and Diversity* (1988) the various perspectives on how the functions of the family have developed in the past two hundred years are not easy entirely to reconcile. He himself takes the view that it is not particularly helpful to describe changes in the family in terms of a 'loss of functions'. He comments 'that there does not seem to be any evidence of an overall decline in the family in terms of its centrality in the lives of individuals or its importance in many areas of social life'. However, within this broad pattern of continuing importance, some specialisation has occurred: '(I)t is possible to talk of a shift in the range of uses to which family relationships are put ... with a particular sharper focus on the material relationship and with the business of childrearing. To this extent the family may be described as a more specialised institution' (40).

The issues of family relationships – particularly that of wife and husband – and of childrearing are fully discussed below (respectively pp. 59–60 and pp. 69–70).

MARXIST PERSPECTIVE ON THE FUNCTIONS OF 'THE FAMILY' Marxists agree that the family performs a range of functions within capitalist society. However, they evaluate these in a negatively critical way reflecting their overall view of capitalism. Marxists consider that in capitalist society, the working class family is subordinated to the needs of production. In early capitalism, high productivity could only be achieved if men, women and children were directly involved in industrial work. As machine productivity increased, it became economic and, in fact, potentially more productive to exclude children and women from industrial work. Children could then be educated and become more efficient producers, and women could better maintain male labour as full-time 'housewives'. Marxist-feminist Sue Sharpe (1972) has usefully conceptualised the role of women in industrial capitalist society in terms of 'reproduction'. They reproduce a labour force both by giving birth to it and by socialising it into the norms required to achieve working class acceptance of and conformity to capitalist society. They also help to reproduce the existing male labour force by meeting its maintenance and sexual needs. Of course, Sharpe challenges the inevitability of this structuring of the family and of the role of working class women, while recognising that it is apparently highly functional for capitalist society at a given stage of its development.

More recently, Juliette Mitchell has analysed the role of women, and by implication that of the family in capitalist society in its current stage of development, in which the service rather than the industrial sector predominates (Mitchell 1986). Once again, economic expansion has increased the demand for women in paid employment albeit typically in offices rather than factories. Mitchell points out that this development is not necessarily a wholly liberating one for women. They are on average less well paid than men, typically subject to male authority (frequently even when better qualified), and often overwhelmingly carry the burden of housework. In other words, women live within a patriarchal system. It is to the key issue of equality and democracy within the family that we now turn.

SYMMETRICAL OR PATRIARCHAL FAMILY? CONJUGAL ROLES

Peter Willmott and Michael Young make some interesting observations on changes in family roles and relationships in their book *The Symmetrical Family* (1973). Much of what they say continues and develops earlier British research on the family, including their own. In the nineteen fifties, for instance, Elizabeth Bott found that, on the basis of an admittedly small sample (twenty families), working class spouses tended to divide tasks sharply and pursue separate leisure activities whereas the opposite applied to the middle class. Thus, she describes these as, respectively, segregated and joint conjugal role relationships.

In *The Symmetrical Family*, Willmott and Young argue that 'the direction of change has, we believe, been from Bott's first to her second type' of family. By symmetrical, then, they mean a joint or shared approach to married life rather than one which is segregated into largely separate roles. The symmetrical family is not wholly egalitarian because a considerable degree of separate role allocation still occurs, but 'a measure of egalitarianism' does exist. They go on to say that 'In this context [egalitarianism] the essence of a symmetrical relationship is that it is opposite but similar'.

The data on which Willmott and Young developed their concept of the symmetrical family was a large-scale social survey of the adult population of the London Metropolitan Region. The interview responses show a large majority of husbands in all classes reporting that they help their wives at least once a week in a domestic task, although the majority is noticeably the smallest among the semi-skilled and unskilled category. Once a week is a very modest amount of help and as Willmott and Young themselves comment, 'most married couples were obviously still a long way from the state of unisex that some young people had arrived at'. Despite the qualifications with which Willmott and Young constantly hedge their symmetrical family analysis, they appear at times to strain their data to support what they see as an emerging trend to symmetry.

Willmott and Young consider that the pattern of economic development underlies the move towards symmetry. Firstly, as more women are doing paid work, there is practical logic and fairness in men becoming more involved with domestic work. Secondly, immense improvements in household technology are assumed to have reduced the time committed to housework, to have removed much of the drudgery from it, and to have simplified it to the point where any member of a household can do it. Within this context the development of the symmetrical family seems almost 'natural'.

Nevertheless, Mary Maynard represents the opinion of many feminists when she writes that 'despite the predominance of this view, a vast amount of empirical evidence suggests otherwise'. She goes on to cite two types of evidence which demonstrate that women still overwhelmingly carry the main burden and stress of housework: American time-budget surveys and mainly British sociological surveys and studies of housework and the housewife. These findings will be discussed in greater detail in a later chapter (p. 177) but need briefly to be referred to here. The time-budget studies measured time spent on housework and other activities, particularly paid work and leisure. They consistently show that although women tend to do less housework when they are also doing paid work, the overall length of their working week increases. In contrast, it is the husbands of wives who have the longest overall working weeks, that have the shortest working weeks themselves. The relatively little housework or childcare they do seems to be regarded as a form of back-up help.

Although the time-budget studies are American, table 3.3 provides data which suggests their findings might apply equally to Britain. The table contrasts how household tasks and child rearing were shared between men and women in 1983 and 1987. In the latter case, it provides data on how respondents thought the tasks ought to be shared, categorised for men and women. Unfortunately the data does not provide information on the paid-work status of respondents. The table merits close analysis, but, in general it shows that women do the more demanding household tasks and child rearing with men only approaching equal involvement in the lighter perhaps more 'symbolic' ones. The reality of sharing lags well behind what respondents tend to consider ought to happen although there is perhaps a very slight overall trend to greater sharing between 1983 and 1987.

The second type of research cited by Maynard – British studies of housework and the housewife – confirms the highly gendered organisation of housework (i.e. it is organised on the basis of sexual difference). Studies show that although modern household technology has changed the content of housework, it has had little effect on the amount women perform (although, as noted above, if they are also involved in paid work, some reduction in housework tends to occur). Whereas, in the past, basic housework took up more time, now the demands of quality childrearing,

and the selection, buying and other work involved in maintaining high standards of consumption and, in some cases, entertaining take up more time. Qualitative material on the experience of being a housewife shows what Maynard refers to as 'a series of contradictions and conflicts'. She cites several reasons for this including both that much of the work is routine, repetitive and boring – despite involving a degree of autonomy (independence) – and that men tend to underestimate and underappreciate it.

FAMILY PRIVATISATION AND CONSUMERISM

Both Young and Willmott and John Goldthorpe and David Lockwood in their 'affluent worker' study have noted a tendency towards family - rather than community - based social life both among their main sample of affluent manual workers and the smaller, control group of white collar employees. Spouses spent time together inside the home rather than in visiting friends and neighbours. Goldthorpe and Lockwood termed this trend the privatisation of family life (see pp. 142–3). It is a concept which chimes in well with Parson's notion of a more isolated, functionally-specialised nuclear family.

There are several reasons for the development of the privatised nuclear pattern of living. An underlying factor is the movement of population caused partly by the operation of a free labour market and government policy to disperse population from the declining inner city areas. This has undermined community and extended-family type social networks. Important, too, is the massive post-war boom in home-based, leisure consumer items such as televisions and hi-fi's. Many married people, as well as aspiring to a high material standard of living, have great expectations of their marital relationship as well. Unlike many Eastern societies in which marriages are arranged by parents, Western societies allow people to marry for love and romance. Even after the first flush is over, couples tend to expect and demand much of each other, both in terms of everyday companionship and deeper emotional and physical commitment. With this in mind some commentators have referred to modern

Percentages and numbers

| | Actual allocation of tasks | | | | | | How tasks should be allocated | | |
| | 1983 | | | 1987 | | | 1987 | | |
	Mainly man	Mainly woman	Shared equally	Mainly man	Mainly woman	Shared equally	Mainly man	Mainly woman	Shared equally
Household tasks (percentages)									
Household shopping	5	51	44	7	50	43	1	30	68
Makes evening meal	5	77	17	6	77	17	–	52	45
Does evening dishes	17	40	40	22	39	36	11	17	70
Does household cleaning	3	72	24	4	72	23	1	44	54
Does washing and ironing	1	89	10	2	88	9	–	69	30
Repairs household equipment	82	6	10	82	6	8	73	1	24
Organises household money and bills	29	39	32	32	38	30	22	15	61
Child rearing (percentages)									
Looks after sick children	1[2]	63[2]	35[2]	2	67	30	–	47	51
Teaches children discipline	10[2]	12[2]	77[2]	13	19	67	12	5	82
Household task base (= 100%) (numbers)		1,209[2]			983			1,391	
Child rearing base (= 100%) (numbers)		485[2]			422			1,391	

1 Married or living as married. 2 1984.
Source: Social Trends 1991

marriage as companionate marriage. There is 'another side' to the high expectations and emotional demands of modern marriage, however. They can contribute to disillusionment if the reality fails to match up to the ideal (see p. 65).

Christopher Lasch, a radical American intellectual, gives a depressing view of the nuclear family in capitalist society. He puts quite a different value on family consumerism and even on the marital relationship from that of functionalists. He argues, as do many Marxists, that the family market is manipulated by capitalist advertisers and producers. People are persuaded to buy the 'latest' item even when they neither need nor want it: this spending keeps the wheels of the capitalist economy turning. The stresses of a materialist society which lacks deeper spiritual or human values shows in marriage – and divorce. For Lasch the family in 'bourgeois' society has ceased to be a private refuge. In his view the privatisation of the family is breached by the consumerist ideology of the media. These observations are examined more closely later (Chapter 18).

Some quarter of a century after the publication of Goldthorpe and Lockwood's work, it is arguable that the developments which produced the privatised nuclear family now undermine it. The dedicated pursuit of private satisfaction may partly explain why so many marriages break-up and why twenty-six per cent of households now have only a single resident.

FAMILY, CLASS, CULTURE AND COMMUNITY

WORKING CLASS FAMILIES AND COMMUNITIES In this section we explore differences and similarities between working and middle class cultural and community life or 'social networks', to use Margaret Stacey's term.

Richard Hoggart's painstakingly detailed description of traditional working class life in 1950's Leeds now has an old fashioned snapshot quality. But the fact that traditional working class community is breaking up does not mean it never existed. Some recent commentators, failing to find thriving working class communities of the kind described thirty years ago by Young and Willmott and by Hoggart seem almost to assume that the whole phenomenon is a romantic fiction.

Coates and Silburn's late nineteen sixties study of the lower class St Anne's district of Nottingham falls a little into this trap. The fact that they find St Anne's to be a fragmented community does not mean it was always so. As they, in fact, well

▲

Table 3.3

Household division of labour of married couples[1]: by sex and task, 1983 and 1987

61

illustrate, the decline of community was due partly to urban renewal policies – a factor also emphasised by Young and Willmott in their Bethnal Green study well over a decade previously.

Apart from those working class people who have chosen to leave inner city areas, many had to leave because of compulsory clearance orders and were offered public housing elsewhere. This was part of a national plan (which had considerable local variations) to divert industry and population away from the inner cities, which could then be used as the location for office blocks, major shops and stores, and as the centre of the leisure and entertainment industry. Public housing makes up about a quarter of residential property, and generalisations need to be made carefully. However, a consensus has emerged, which includes even their original designer, that high rise flats have been a failure as a major means of providing cheap mass-accommodation. Incidents such as the collapse of the Rownan Point block, and the suicide jump of a depressed Birmingham mother, with her baby, from her high-storey flat have created the worst publicity, but myriad problems of design and functioning, such as block entrances leading out into garbage zones or lifts perpetually breaking down, have provided a daily diet of irritation and frustration for thousands. Nevertheless, it is, of course, a major contribution that the material conditions of living provided by many of these developments are vastly superior to that of the old-fashioned terraced houses they have often replaced. But this improvement can be achieved equally in smaller, low rise developments or still other kinds of accommodation at less cost to communal life. As potential communities high rise flats have limited possibilities. Living off the ground is not conducive to shared activity and most corridors in high rise flats do not provide an environment that encourages friendly conversations with neighbours. Even Frank Lloyd Wright's imaginative idea of high rise developments as 'vertical streets in the sky' with various shops, facilities and meeting places strategically scattered on all levels to facilitate interaction and communication seems expensive and artificial, though clearly the concept is better than the human filing cabinets that some blocks have become.

Working class housing estates make up most of the rest of public housing. These are often located on the outskirts of urban areas and replace traditional, more centrally situated housing. Living conditions on post-war, mainly working class housing estates vary from almost as bad as in the worst of the high rise flats to very good indeed. John Stedman's estate at Corby and the prize-winning Handley Green development at Laindon, near Basildon, are spacious, well-designed and attractive. But in general, people have to travel to work from public housing estates and shopping, too, can require a journey. The separation of these basic functions is not conducive to an integrated community life in the old style. A seldom remarked-on effect of the decrease in the fertility of working class mothers is that fewer children exist to establish inter-family social links and this must further reduce the numbers of friends within the neighbourhood. Community centres, which are a feature of some recently established estates, often fail to draw people together for leisure activities though teenagers do frequently use them. Even so, the streets and open areas of estates are often preferred by adolescents – especially by 'tougher' boys. Perhaps it is through their activity and that of younger children who still like to 'play out' that we see a glimpse of at least one continuous strand in the pattern of working class neighbourhood life.

As a result of the 'right to buy' policy of Mrs Thatcher, over 1.5 million council houses had been sold to former tenants by 1992. This policy has created or at least sharpened differences within the working class. Patrick Dunleavy goes so far as to argue that the differences between house-owners and non-house-owners can be as significant as those between people having 'middle' and 'working' class jobs. In particular, there is a correlation between house-ownership and voting Conservative. Critics of this view have pointed out that occupational status itself correlates with house-ownership and with characteristics associated with it (Marshall, 1988).

An important effect of the right to buy policy has been drastically to reduce the stock of public housing held by local councils. Partly because of cuts in support grants by central government, Councils were unable to build sufficient replacements to meet need. As a result, the number of families in temporary accommodation (e.g., bed and breakfast, cheap hotels) and the problem of homelessness visibly increased during the late eighties and around the turn of the decade. Whether the longer term homeless are now so detached or cut-off from the more 'solid' working class as better to be considered part of an 'underclass' is debatable. The matter is discussed in a later chapter (pp. 144–5).

MIDDLE CLASS FAMILIES AND COMMUNITIES Despite the complexity of the overall picture, most middle class owner occupiers still tend to live in suburban neighbourhoods. The term suburban neighbourhood can cover a wide spectrum from, for instance, areas of inter-war semi-detached property, with upper working as well as lower middle class residents, to areas of high status, often detached property occupied mainly by professional, managerial and business groups. Generalisations therefore need to be cautious.

In dormitory suburbs, the very fact that people live and work in separate places is not conducive to the development of integrated community life. As Elizabeth Bott shows, middle class friendship networks tend to be more extended than those in traditional working class communities (1957). For instance, the middle class are more ready to join clubs and associations requiring commitment to activity beyond the immediate neighbourhood. Middle class parents are more likely to participate in organisations and activities concerning their children's educational welfare such as Parent-Teachers Associations or school open days.

The privatisation of middle class family life is highly compatible with extended friendship networks and relative lack of involvement in the immediate neighbourhood. Social life is more organised and friends are not expected to 'pop in and out' as they might do in a traditional working class neighbourhood. A telephone call can courteously pave the way for a visit but it can as easily do instead if one of the parties is occupied. Privacy and control of time can be virtually a necessity if work brought home from the office and children's homework is to be properly done.

Mutual concern with children is what brings middle class people most readily together. In their book about the Canadian suburb of 'Crestwood Heights', Seeley and his co-authors argue that the major institutional focus of the community is on child-rearing. Interfamily social life is organised, mainly by mothers, around this central concern from the time when turns are taken to give children's tea parties, to when offspring depart for higher education. At this point the female parent often returns to paid work.

Despite the above contrasts, family and community life is more similar across the middle and working classes than, say, fifty years ago. Then, the majority of the working class was forced to live in rented accommodation. Now, the majority live in public housing or own their own houses. Indeed, over 65 per cent of families in Britain now own their own homes. This fact, in combination with the movement out of the urban areas means that the suburban ideal cuts across class lines to a considerable extent. A house of their own is what most families seem to want and many have already achieved it. Add to this the even more general processes of family privatisation, consumerism and, much more controversially, symmetrical gender role-playing already noted and a very real convergence in family life-style between, particularly, the lower middle and upper working class is apparent. The stable working class community networked by matrifocal extended families is an increasing rarity. Economic change and geographical and social mobility has reduced communal solidarity. Yet, as we shall see throughout the book, class and status differences still divide these groups and even more, those groups at the social extremes. In particular, although the family roles played mainly by females have adapted to the family changes described above (and below), gender inequality within the family and in paid work appears largely to continue.

Marriage and Families: Stress and Adaptation

A wide range of data and developments are often cited to demonstrate that the family as a basic social institution is under stress and is even in danger of 'breaking up'. In this section several factors relevant to this issue will be discussed critically. However, it is important at the outset to appreciate that many sociologists wholly or largely reject the thesis that the family is breaking up, and favour instead a different model of analysis and interpretation. They adopt a broadly pluralist model of families and life-cycles in which it is stated that individuals adopt or develop a variety of family types and situations and also non-family life-styles. The latter include living as a couple (married or unmarried) without children or as a single person. These sociologists criticise the 'family break-up' thesis as being based on a narrow view of families in which the nuclear family is considered the norm and sometimes specifically as the desirable norm both functionally and morally. Aspects of this debate have already been discussed in relation to the question of whether or not the nuclear family is universal as the most functional family type.

The key issues in relation to family change and adaptation discussed below are:

1 Divorce
2 Single Parent Families
3 Co-habitation
4 Child Neglect and Abuse
5 Generational Conflict: A Crisis of Authority?

DIVORCE

Arguably, the rise in the divorce rate is the most striking indicator of family stress, although it may also release married partners and their children from stress. Many thousands opt for separation rather than divorce, so the divorce figures underestimate the extent of marital breakdown. In 1961, 32,000 divorce petitions were filed and in 1988, 183,000. In the latter year, the proportion of marriages to divorces was about 3 to 1. Table 3.4 gives details of the rising divorce rate between 1961 and 1988. The figures suggest that the rise reached a stable plateau from the early nineteen eighties.

FACTORS UNDERLYING THE INCREASE IN THE DIVORCE RATE

THE DECLINE OF RELIGION AND CHANGES IN THE DIVORCE LAWS Changes in cultural attitudes towards marriage have created a climate of public opinion in which it has been possible to pass laws which have made it increasingly easy to opt out of marriage. The long-term background to the erosion of marriage as a permanent and binding commitment is the decline in formal religious belief. Marriage is less often seen as a sacred, spiritual union, but more as a personal and practical commitment which can be abandoned if it fails. This attitude to marriage has resulted in a series of changes in the law, making the grounds for divorce less strict and the administrative procedure for obtaining it less complicated and time-consuming (for instance, in 1977 it became possible to get divorced by post in some circumstances). The Divorce Law Reform Act of 1969 (actually implemented in 1971) established that it was enough merely to prove 'irretrievable breakdown of marriage' to obtain a divorce. The 'irretrievable breakdown of marriage' was made the sole cause. The phrase is general enough to be interpreted to include virtually all conceivable reasons for divorce. Although there was an increase in the divorce rate following the Act, it would be crude to think of the Act as 'causing' this increase. Deeper reasons for it must be sought in the broader cultural factors mentioned above. Viewed in longer perspective, the statistical trend is that of a gradual increase in divorce with occasional sharp jumps when enabling legislation was passed. In addition to the 1969 Act, another such instance was the 1949 Legal Aid Act which enabled women seeking divorce to obtain financial assistance in doing so.

Table 3.4 ▼

The divorce rate* 1961 – 1989										
1961	1971	1976	1981	1983	1984	1985	1986	1987	1988	1989
2.1	6.0	10.1	11.9	12.2	12.0	13.4	12.9	12.7	12.8	12.7

*The divorce rate is the number of persons divorcing per thousand married people

(Source: Social trends 1992)

CAPITALISM, THE RISE OF INDIVIDUALISM AND ROMANTIC LOVE Edward Shorter in his book *The Making of the Modern Family* (1975) argues that the onset of capitalism promoted individualistic and sexually freer or 'romantic' behaviour (Shorter's view of the 'romantic' behaviour is distinctly unrosy).

Capitalism broke up traditional communities and set their populations 'free', in the limited sense that they could come to towns and compete for work. But they were free also from traditional family and community control, freer to have personal and sexual relations with whom they wished. In the long-term, this freedom evolved into the virtual right to choose and, within ever more generous limits, get rid of one's spouse. The question of romantic marriage must be seen against the background of a steady decline in family and community control of choice of partner, courtship and marriage. Traditionally, couples married (or had their marriages arranged) for down-to-earth material reasons such as, to take a middle class example, joining two family estates or businesses together. Courtship was supervised closely, if more or less informally, within the community. For a period of about two hundred years, however, people have been increasingly marrying whom they want rather than whom they are told to. As Shorter points out, the danger in marrying for mainly romantic reasons is that when romantic love and attraction disappear, so too might marriage.

Although the sweep of Shorter's analysis covers several centuries of the influence of capitalism on cultural attitudes and behaviour, it is worth reading the following passage bearing in mind the free-market revival of the nineteen eighties and the accompanying pressures on families, all of which occurred after he had published his book:

How did capitalism help cause that powerful thrust of sentiment among the unmarried that I have called the romance revolution? To what extent may sleeping around before marriage and choosing partners on the basis of personal attraction rather than wealth be associated with economic change? The principal link here is the increased participation of young unmarried people, especially women, in the free-market labour force. The logic of the market-place positively demands individualism: the system will succeed only if each participant ruthlessly pursues his (sic) own self-interest, buying cheap, selling dear, and enhancing his own interests at the cost of his competitors (i.e., his fellow citizens. ... Thus, the free market engraves upon all who are caught up in it the attitude: 'Look out for number one.'
(Shorter, 1977: 253)

Improved birth control technology may have further contributed to sexual attitudes and behaviour based on personal gratification rather than any wider norms or morality. The spread of Aids has made it paramount that such behaviour should in any case be 'safe'.

PROBLEMS OF INTER-PERSONAL COMMUNICATION A cluster of other factors – most of which are fairly self-evident – correlate with divorce. Partners who are dissimilar in culture, social background, or religion, or who are of very different age are more prone to divorce, as are those who marry young and may still be developing personally and emotionally. Barbara Thomas and Jean Collard in *Who Divorces* (1984), suggest that for these and other divorced couples, a common underlying problem is often poor inter-personal communication. They agree with Young and Willmott that the small conjugal family has increasingly become the principal and sometimes sole source of deep emotional expression, and that this can put a strain on the marriages of those who have communication problems.

THE CHANGING STATUS OF WOMEN Some observers associate the increase in divorce with the changing status of women. The female share of divorce petitions has generally outnumbered that of men in both Britain and the United States in recent years. In Britain the female share was about seventy per cent in the early nineteen nineties. It may be that, as more women have entered the labour market, they have acquired the necessary economic independence to opt out of an unsatisfactory marriage if they choose to do so. Further, involvement in paid work also enables them to meet more prospective partners than if they remained full-time housewives. Interestingly, according to the US Bureau of Census Report (1972), better-

Table 3.5 (Far left) ▶

paid female divorcees are more likely to delay remarriage or remain single than are low-paid ones. Whether women will be able to maintain their limited gains in the contracting labour market of the early nineties remains to be seen.

However, perhaps the main effect on the divorce rate of the increasing involvement of women in paid work is a result of the dual burden of housework and paid work discussed by Maynard (above). In *When Marriage Ends* (1976), Nicky Hart argues that the contradictory demands of these two roles can produce tension between wife and husband and in particular, lead the former eventually to seek divorce.

THE RISE IN THE NUMBER OF SINGLE PARENT FAMILIES

This matter has been fully discussed elsewhere in this chapter (pp. 52–3) and is further dealt with in the context of the 'underclass' in chapter 6 (pp. 144–5). Two points can be stressed here in relation to single parenthood and family stress. First, the majority of single parent families occur because of divorce. To that extent, they are the product of stress on, or the failure of, what were originally nuclear families. Second, undoubtedly single parenthood is demanding and stressful for those many single parents without adequate income and resources. Policy issues relating to this are discussed on p. 52 and extensively on pp. 69–70.

THE RISE IN THE NUMBER OF COUPLES COHABITING

As table 3.5 shows, there has been a considerable rise in the percentage of couples cohabiting in the decade between 1979 and 1988. However, the percentage of 18 to 24 year olds cohabiting in Britain remains small when compared with that typical of the Scandinavian countries, which is over 40 per cent. Moreover, as the smaller figure for the 25–49 age group indicates, cohabiting couples in Britain tend later to get married whereas this is less the case in Scandinavia.

CHILD NEGLECT AND ABUSE

This issue is discussed fully in chapter 10 (pp.

Co-habitation in Britain		
Age-group	1979	1988
18–24	4.5	12.4
25–49	2.2	6.3
18–49	2.7	7.7

(Source: Social Trends 1991)

214–7) and the particular aspect of child care is given extensive treatment in this chapter (pp. 69–70). Essentially, contemporary sociological perspectives link the treatment of children, including child abuse, with general cultural attitudes to children rather than merely with individual mental pathology (illness). There is growing evidence in the late nineteen eighties and early nineties of a child-abuse problem of significant proportions. However more everyday problems receive less media attention – on a daily basis many young children and their mothers struggle to meet the practical demands of life. Poorer children are more likely to experience a variety of problems. At a wider level, Britain is at the bottom of the European league in terms of the provision of child care for 3 to 5 year olds. These facts offer a better starting point for analysis than moral panics about individuals characterised as 'monsters' or 'beasts'.

GENERATIONAL CONFLICT: A CRISIS OF AUTHORITY?

Again, the issue of generational conflict is one which is amply discussed elsewhere in this book (see chapter 10 pp. 227–9). In fact, surveys on the attitudes of teenagers repeatedly show that broadly they like their parents, get on reasonably well with them and are generally fairly satisfied with life. On the other hand, there has been a continuous and now highly destructive and expensive problem of juvenile delinquency and often related drunkenness since the Second World War, for which a supposed decline in parental authority is sometimes blamed.

Specifically, the charge made is that the family is failing to act as an effective agency of social control. This accusation, however, could equally be made against the schools and police. The causes of juvenile delinquency must therefore be sought in the wider society rather than in the failure of any single institution such as the family. This we do in chapter 10. Here, it need only be said that the more permissive and democratic ideals of the post-war period reduce the credibility of physical punishment as a means of maintaining control both within the family and within society. It is difficult to imagine a widespread reversion to more traditional forms of discipline within the family without some comparable broader change in society. Whether such a change would have much effect on juvenile delinquency is entirely debatable.

THE DYNAMICS OF FAMILY VIOLENCE: A VIEW FROM RADICAL PSYCHIATRY

One of the cult figures of the nineteen sixties was the radical psychiatrist Ronald Laing. His analysis of the family illustrates aspects of the phenomenological perspective. His primary concern is with the 'self' but he does not separate the life of the self from that of others. For him 'madness' is not a personal deficiency but must be interpreted as a way of making sense of experience. Thus, he spoke of schizophrenic families rather than schizophrenic individuals – if the self is forced into fantasy escape it is because there is something to escape from. Although Laing's primary focus on analysis is the micro level of group interaction, the tension and psychological 'violence' he sees in family life persuaded him to look at the wider world:

Concerned as I am with this inner world, observing day to day its devastation. I ask why this has happened.

If he finds an answer to this question it is that the violence of the outside world – the Vietnam war was particularly in his mind – fuses with and reinforces the potential for violence within us. Corpses on a dead television screen are unreal, but slowly we learn not to care about them or each other, or the human consequences of what we do. The family cannot cope with all this or give it meaning. He suggests that for some, personal madness is a retreat from 'madness out there.' This recalls the pained cry of poet Allen Ginsberg: 'I have seen the best minds of my generation driven mad.'

David Cooper, a colleague of Laing, goes beyond the latter in taking explicitly political attitudes. His approach owes much to Marx, but, unlike him, Cooper wants to abolish the family itself – at least, as a hard and fast biological unit. Cooper's basic criticism of the family in bourgeois society is the peculiarly limiting and constraining role it plays:

The child, in fact, is taught primarily now how to survive in society but how to submit to it. Surface rituals like etiquette, organised games, mechanical learning operations at school replace deep experiences of spontaneous creativity, inventive play, freely developing fantasies and dream.

That, perhaps, is the nub of Cooper and Laing. They want a freer, less repressive society – always provided that what is freely expressed is love rather than selfishness or hate. Cooper's belief that spontaneous, 'wanted' relationships should take preference over biological and legal bonds is what leads him to attack the traditional family.

In retrospect, Laing and Cooper's contributions have been less in the directly social and political dimension of their work than in nudging their sizeable audience, particularly among young, educated adults, further in the direction of experimental permissiveness in relationships, not only with children, but with each other. To that extent they are not entirely out of tune with the genial liberal adviser on childbearing of the fifties, Dr Benjamin Spock.

Another commentator on the family, anthropologist Edmund Leach, seems to capture the essence of the above criticisms of the family in his own description of it as 'a prison'. Although Leach intends the analogy to be derogatory there is a sense in which the family must inevitably constrain the individual. Society itself is also sometimes compared to a prison and for the same reason: it limits total freedom. If functionalists accept the need for social control too uncritically perhaps the radical psychiatrists underestimate the potentially dangerous as well as positive effects of its absence.

CONJUGAL CONFLICT: WIFE BATTERING

As is the case with child abuse, it is difficult to be sure whether the problem has become more widespread or whether it has merely come closer to public awareness. Dobash and

Dobash (1980) cite the police records of Edinburgh and Glasgow which show that the second most common form of violence is wife assault, making up 25 per cent of recorded violent crime.

In her introduction to '*Private Violence and Public Policy*' (1985), Jan Pahl, argues that wife battering should be seen as 'the extension of the domination and control of husbands over wifes'. Pahl rejects individualistic explanations of wife battering in favour of a structural analysis of patriarchy – one aspect of which can be violence by males against females, specifically in a couple relationship. She is able to cite an impressive array of historical and comparative cultural data to demonstrate that male violence against women is typically embedded in a patriarchal context.

CONCLUSION: IS 'THE FAMILY' BREAKING UP OR ADAPTING?

We have examined impressive evidence of stress on the nuclear family. This does *not* mean that the nuclear family is breaking up, or to use David Cooper's more dramatic work, 'dying.' Marriage remains highly popular and over ninety per cent of the population gets married. Moreover, the remarriage rates of divorcees are high, both in Britain and the United States, where three quarters of divorced women and five sixths of divorced men remarry. At current remarriage rates in Britain, nearly one in five people born around 1950 will have been married twice by the time they are fifty. True, statistics show that young people are living together for more lengthy periods than previously, but most established couples do eventually get married. So stress on the family does not result in either the family or marriage being unpopular – they are not.

When people divorce they are giving up a particular partner, not necessarily the idea of marriage. In any case, the majority of married people still do not get divorced but remain committed, more or less happily, to one partner for life. If present trends continue, however, a large minority will experience a different marital pattern from the traditional one. This pattern has been called serial monogamy. Less frequently, individuals have more than one family. These changes amount to a substantial adaptation of traditional marriage and the nuclear family and cannot be described as a pattern of simple continuity. Nevertheless, serial monogamy does not seem an especially functional social adaptation. Rather, it represents what a large number of people seem to want, or at least accept, as sometimes necessary regardless of considerable inconvenience. A United Kingdom survey in 1977 found that as many as sixty per cent of young people considered that divorce was something that might happen to them. So a recognition of the potential impermanence of marriage and even family commitment is now part of our cultural outlook.

Although the nuclear family survives and often flourishes still as the dominant family form, it is within the context of an increasingly pluralistic or varied pattern of family life. The single parent family is the most common exception to the nuclear family.

Part of the variety and complexity of private and domestic life comes from the fact that the majority of households now contain only one or two people – some of whom have deliberately opted out of having a conventional family life. In the light of such developments, Jaber Gubrium and James Holstein in *What is Family* (1990), answer the question in the title of their book by arguing that there is no longer a single answer. They suggest that a quasi-religious faith in a particular ideal of 'the family' can obscure the varied, complex and often difficult reality of creating families and relationships in which people are differently involved.

The above changes can give little obvious comfort to those who favour the extended family type structures. The modern family is typically small and second families especially so. No satisfactory general alternative to the nuclear family seems to exist. The nature of modern society works against extended family structures – attractive though these may be in principle. A less mobile, more localised society would no doubt produce a family system woven into kin and community but, for the moment, that is not the kind of society we have.

The Issue of Child Care and 'Women's' Work: A Policy Postscript

Just as in the nineteenth century women's labour was first required and then dispensed with in the factories and mines, there is an increasing demand for female labour in the service sector in the late twentieth century. However, as we have seen, this has not been accompanied by any significant decrease in the proportion of domestic work done by women compared to men. In terms of a more equal sharing of deomestic work, the 'symmetrical family' has largely not happened. Although there are obvious material advantages in both partners earning an income, the double load of work on the female partner can have adverse effects both for her and her children.

Figure 3.3 shows the upward trend in the percentage of women with children in paid work according to the age of the children.

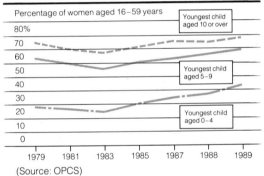

Mothers in paid work in Britain

Percentage of women aged 16–59 years

Youngest child aged 10 or over

Youngest child aged 5–9

Youngest child aged 0–4

1979 1981 1983 1985 1987 1988 1989

(Source: OPCS)

Of women with a child under five, 41 per cent were in employment in 1989, twelve per cent of these full-time, compared to 28 per cent in 1979. Overall, the percentage of women with dependent children in employment rose from 52 per cent in 1979 to 59 per cent in 1989 (having fallen to 46 per cent in 1983 as a result of a recession). 20 per cent of all women with dependent children are in full-time paid employment.

How well is Britain geared for the employment of women in terms of the needs of the women and children involved? Writing in *New Society* (5 February 1988), Judy Dunn gives the startling statistic that between 1948 and 1984, the proportion of pre-school children cared for in day nurseries fell from seventeen per cent to three per cent. 'Caring for children: the 1990 Report' states that public childcare for five to nine year-olds is available for 0.2 per cent in term time and 0.3 per cent during holidays (Family Policy Study Centre). However, during the second half of the nineteen eighties there was an increase in the numbers of childminders although some would not consider this as an equally effective form of care. Regional Trends, 1990, gives figures for registered childminders, playgroups and local authority nurseries in the form of the percentage of places available to the total of underfives in given regions. In England this varies from 14.7 in the North to 24.6 in the South West. By 1990, private and voluntary childcare provided more places than local authorities. In many areas, available places substantially fall short of meeting need. This must be made up by unregistered help including relatives and friends, or sometimes not made up at all.

The almost universally recognised inadequacy of childcare provision in Britain must greatly inconvenience many mothers and negatively affect their children – to put it mildly. For many – whether married or single parents – their only option is to

◀

Figure 3.3 (Far left)

◀

Figure 3.4

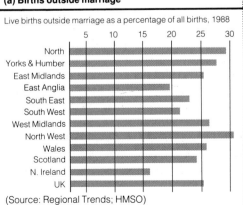

(a) Births outside marriage

Live births outside marriage as a percentage of all births, 1988

5 10 15 20 25 30

North
Yorks & Humber
East Midlands
East Anglia
South East
South West
West Midlands
North West
Wales
Scotland
N. Ireland
UK

(Source: Regional Trends; HMSO)

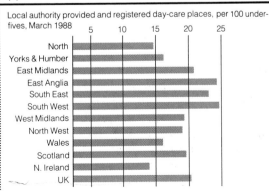

(b) Care for the under-fives

Local authority provided and registered day-care places, per 100 under-fives, March 1988

5 10 15 20 25

North
Yorks & Humber
East Midlands
East Anglia
South East
South West
West Midlands
North West
Wales
Scotland
N. Ireland
UK

manage as best they can. They 'juggle' their child or children with other domestic and employment commitments with energy and ingenuity – but at some risk to their health.

A group that is particularly hard hit by the cost and/or inadequacy of child care facilities is separated, divorced or single women with children. Many women on benefit would rather be in employment but the cost of child care plus employment related expenses often means that they are scarcely any better or even slightly worse off. This is largely because single parents can earn only fifteen pounds per week before a pound is deducted from benefit from each pound earned (1991). A clearer case of a poverty trap would be difficult to imagine. In 1990, two single parents took the British government to law on this issue on the grounds that it broke the European Community directives aimed at equalising access between the sexes to social security benefits and training facilities. The Court of Appeal referred the case to the European Court which could take around two years to hear it.

Given the increasing demand for female paid-labour, and the importance of producing well cared for and stimulated children, one is forced to wonder why a situation of inadequate childcare provision is allowed to persist. A possible reason may be ambivalence on the part of some politicians and members of the public about putting children under five in childcare at all. Mrs Thatcher herself seemed to see seeking informal help as the main solution to childcare in remarks made when answering a question about how she managed to combine a career with a family:

Yet no matter how hard you work or how capable you are, you can't do it all yourself. You have to seek reliable help – a relative, or what my mother would have called 'a treasure': someone who brought not only her work but her affections to the family.

Mrs Thatcher then went on to mention the role of voluntary agencies in helping with childcare and mentioned forthcoming government legislation aimed at fathers who failed to pay maintenance. It has also been Conservative government policy to encourage the private provision of childcare facilities and the cost of childcare to parents

was made exempt from tax in 1990. However, cuts in central government funding to local government has meant that public sector provision of childcare provision has often been cut itself. Some critics have suggested that the desire to cut public spending largely accounts for Conservative policy to childcare.

There is now a considerable body of academic opinion which should allay any fears that under fives are disadvantaged in day nurseries and 'would be better with their mothers'. Professor Bengt-Erik Andersson, head of developmental psychology at the Stockholm Institute of Education, went so far as to say that it 'seems the earlier children mix with others, the better'. He said that those who entered day care before the age of one performed better than other groups monitored at the age of thirteen – both academically and in terms of 'socio-emotional variables'. He suggested that a major reason for this was the amount of interaction they experienced with adults and peers. However, he added the proviso that:

The research was done in Sweden and ... it is a country with a very high-quality day care. If that situation differs, the findings might not be applicable.

Harriet Harman of the Labour Party has argued that there should be greater choice of childcare provision, more government resources for maintaining standards, and more community provision of childcare – especially for the less well off. This seems to accept that while the sources of funding for childcare may vary, ultimately central government in partnership with local government should ensure the right of childcare to all children. Currently, the country is a long way from achieving this.

In their book *For the Children's Sake*, Caroline New and Miriam David suggest that of the three main demands of the women's movement – control of their own fertility, equal pay for equal work and universal provision of childcare – it is the last one that remains conspicuously unachieved. The result is great difficulties for many women and disadvantage for many children. If it is true that educational standards in Britain lag behind those of most other advanced countries, perhaps the explanation for this begins with inadequate childcare.

SUMMARY

1   A household is a person or group of people living together. In the post-Second World War period, there has been an increase in the numbers of households with only one or two inhabitants. Nevertheless, a large majority of people experience a nuclear family at some stage in their lives. A nuclear family is comprised of mother, father and child or children, whether natural or adopted. The extended family consists of the nuclear family and at least one relative living in the same household.

2   There are various Perspectives on the Family. Functionalist perspective analyses the functions of the family in relation to society and the adaptation of the family to historical change. Marxist perspective analyses how the family helps to reproduce capitalist society by maintaining the current labour force and reproducing and socialising the next.

Feminist perspective stresses the subordination and oppression of women within the family and society.

3   Non-Nuclear Families:
Functionalists argue that the nuclear family is universal. However, there are several categories of evidence against this position. These are:

■ Comparative Cultural Evidence of Non-nuclear Families e.g. The Nayar Case
■ Deliberate Attempts to Produce Collectively-based Families e.g. The Kibbutzim; The Soviet 'Experiment'; Sixties Communes
■ Single Parent Families
■ Lesbian and Homosexual Led Families

Whether or not the above cases are considered as 'true' families, it is clear that in those cases in which a child's biological father is not involved in its upbringing, some other form of regular and routine assistance is usually available for the mother.

4   Historically, it helps to think of the development of the family in three phases.
The Pre-Industrial Family:
It is a 'myth' that the pre-industrial family was mainly extended. Laslett's research shows that it was mainly nuclear but it was often much bigger than the average contemporary family.

5   The Early Industrial Family:
The movement of population to towns often temporarily 'broke up' families but, once settled, working class families, in particular, were often extended in type.

6   The 'Modern' Family:
Functionalists and Marxists agree that the family performs a range of functions within capitalist society but whereas the former see these as 'necessary' the latter consider that they are often oppressive particularly in relation to working class families and to women. Another important debate centres on how 'symmetrical' male and female family roles have or have not become.

7   A key debate on the family is whether privatised patterns of family living have replaced previously more communal ones. As early as the nineteen fifties, Bott's work indicated that segregated (distinct) conjugal roles and more community-oriented living characterised working class life and that joint (more equal and shared) conjugal roles and wider spread friendship networks characterised middle class life. Much research and discussion has occurred about the extent to which working class families, indeed, most families are privatised and consumer oriented and much less involved in local community life.

8   There are a number of signs that marriage and the family can experience great stress in contemporary society. The most obvious is the high divorce rate. Edward Shorter suggests that one reason for the break-up of modern marriage is the high expectation that accompanies the romanticism which often surrounds it.

9   A range of other issues surround marriage and the family. Some such as the rise in single parent families and in cohabiting are open to differing sociological (and moral) interpretation. Others such as child abuse and wife-battering – although requiring careful analysis and understanding – belong to everybody's category of human misery.

10 Is the Family Breaking Up or Adapting?

Although this summary has used the term 'the family' for convenient 'short-hand', the chapter itself suggests that there are a plurality of households and families. An alternative to the view that 'the family' is breaking up is that people are adapting quite variously to small-scale living.

RESEARCH AND COURSEWORK

There are many possible research areas on households, families and marriage, including family roles, functions, change, and stresses on the family. It could be interesting, however, to probe one of the less well-researched areas. Why, for instance, are there more single person households than previously? Are there big differences among single person householders? Some will be elderly and have lost a partner, some will be younger and may have divorced a partner or never had one. Given the limits on your research of time and resources, you may only be able to research into one group. Research into younger divorcees living alone might produce interesting findings. Do they live alone out of necessity or choice? Do they prefer living alone to marriage? Do they intend to marry again? Are there differences between the females and males in your sample (both economically and in terms of how they manage their social lives)?

Locating a sample (perhaps a quota) of younger divorcees may not be easy. However, it is worth noting that large samples are often not practical or required. Five males and five females could be enough if the research is of a more qualitative kind – perhaps involving a semi-structured or unstructured interview with each respondent.

FURTHER READING

Current literature on households and families tends to have moved beyond rehearsing well worn arguments about 'the functions of the family'. David H J Morgan's article *Socialisation and the Family: Change and Diversity* in M Woodhead and J McGrath eds., (Open University, 1988) is a useful overview of established and more recent research on the family. Diana Gittins' *The Family in Question: Changing Households and Familiar Ideologies* (MacMillan 1985) brings a lively awareness of current issues to a staple topic. Adrian Wilson's *Family* (Routledge, 1991) remains a useful introduction to the topic.

QUESTIONS

1 Evaluate the contribution that feminists have made to the sociological understanding of family, kinship and marriage. (London, 1989) (See also chapter 8 for further information).

2 "Functionalist accounts of the family underestimate the extent of strain and exploitation in family life". Discuss. (AEB 1989)

3 "Functionalist accounts of family life fail to recognise the increasing variety of family structures in industrial society." Discuss. (AEB 1990)

4 Education: Ideology & Policy

4

96 *Gender in Education*

101 *'Race' and Ethnicity in Education*

107 *A Conservative Revolution in Education and Training?* **ERA** *(1988) and Beyond*

Educational Issues and Perspectives

This chapter should have personal relevance to all students who read it. The educational system claims a large portion of your life – a minimum of eleven years and probably thirteen or more, given that you are reading this book. It is certainly worth knowing what the educational system is 'doing' to you.

A major issue in the sociology of education is that of equality, particularly why working class children generally attain less (in terms of examinations) than middle class children of similar measured intelligence. This issue was hotly debated during the nineteen fifties and sixties. During the nineteen seventies, issues relating to gender and education and 'race' and education came more strongly to the fore both in terms of sociological theory and educational policy.

With the Conservative general election victory of 1979, a new educational agenda began to take shape largely focusing on educational standards and the relationship between education and industry.

There are several perspectives on the sociology of education of which five are particularly important:

- **Functionalist**
- **Marxist**
- **Liberal (Reformist)**
- **Free Market**
- **Interactionist**

Both functionalists and Marxists agree that education socialises people 'into' society by formal and informal processes. Because Marxists are opposed to capitalist society, however, they are highly critical of the ways in which young people are socialised to conform to it. Functionalists tend to take conformity for granted as normal. The liberal perspective reflects the reforming political orientation (inclination) which, as we noted in Chapter 1, characterises some sociologists. Liberal sociologists take their stand on the principle that everybody should have equal educational opportunity, even though they accept that fair competition will still result in inequality in examination results, and in career opportunities and rewards. They want equality at the starting line, not at the finishing tape. The attempt to achieve the limited goal of equal opportunity has involved much political campaigning and legal change. The abolition of the eleven-plus examination in many areas owed something to the analyses and efforts of liberal sociologists. Both Marxists and liberals see the source of inequality of educational opportunity in socio-economic background differences. Liberals tend to be much more optimistic that this inequality can be reduced by reform at the educational level itself, whereas Marxists argue that real change in the educational system requires a much more fundamental change in the structure of society. Thus, they contend that if there were more equality of income and if workers had more control of the places they work in, they would be able to afford to keep their children at school longer and also pass on greater confidence and experience to them.

The 'free market' approach to education is otherwise described as the new right or Thatcherite approach. The belief behind this approach is that by allowing parents of pupils choice in education and so forcing schools to compete against each other, standards will be pushed upwards. This philosophy dominated Conservative ideology and policy in the late nineteen eighties and early nineties.

Marxist, liberal and free market approaches to education are highly political although each cites social scientific data in support. The interactionist perspective is less obviously political. It focuses on classroom relationships and particularly on how classroom interaction can be affected by and in turn can affect external social factors.

The above perspectives should be regarded as 'ideal-type' descriptions rather than labels: reality is usually more complex than any description of it. Sociologists do not like being neatly labelled, any more than anyone else does. For instance, many functionalists take a liberal attitude to educational reform. Similarly, some Marxists carefully support certain educational reforms, even though these may not go as far as they might like. Both Marxists and liberals often adopt interactionist concepts and techniques in the process of research.

The Sociology of Education

There are three parts in this section: the first is on education and socialisation, the second is on the relationship of education to the economy, and the third examines the role of the school at the micro level in relation to cultural and economic reproduction.

1 Education, Socialisation and Cultural Reproduction

DURKHEIM AND MARX

Both Durkheim and Marx fully understood that in order to survive, societies need to socialise their young to accept dominant norms and values. If the existing culture is not passed on, it must die. The contemporary French Marxist, Pierre Bourdieu, has stressed the same point in referring to the need of capitalist society to 'culturally reproduce' itself. Reflecting the realities of his time, Marx himself concentrated relatively more on the role of religion in reinforcing cultural conformity whereas present day Marxists see a greater role for education. Interestingly, some of the major contemporary contributors to the sociology of education owe substantial debts to both Marx and Durkheim: this is particularly true of Althusser and Bourdieu.

We begin with Durkheim, partly because of the importance and detail of his work in this area and partly because of his continuing influence. The following quotation illustrates how great he considered the power of education over the individual to be:

... each society, considered at a given stage of development, has a system of education which exercises an influence upon individuals which is usually irresistible.

Although Durkheim considered that the individual can hardly resist the effect of the educational system, his own historical studies of educational systems show that he also regarded the educational system itself as open to wider social influences. Basically, it must pass on society's values. For example, he argued that the competitive examination system came about precisely because modern society is itself individualistic and competitive. He contended that such a system would have been positively dysfunctional (disruptive) in the middle ages, when people generally inherited their social status. For the aristocracy to have to compete with others to maintain their social position would have risked overthrowing the whole social order so such an idea was not entertained.

We need to give a more practical illustration of what Durkheim meant by the role of the educational system in producing conformity. Most obviously, teachers 'tell' pupils formally what to do. Formal socialisation can cover a great deal, such as telling pupils how to eat, dress and speak, as well as what values they should hold. Durkheim particularly emphasised the role of ritual in forming patterns of behaviour and in reinforcing values. Thus, school assemblies might involve rituals in which national patriotism is expressed and strengthened. He was also aware of the less obvious or 'unconscious' ways in which pupils are socialised. For example, schools are very hierarchical institutions (power is concentrated in the hands of given people), and it is precisely because hierarchy is assumed to be beyond question that children come to accept it as inevitable. They learn that some people, such as headteachers, can command more respect, politeness and obedience than others and, as a result, pupils are prepared to accept the same situation in society generally.

ALTHUSSER, BOURDIEU AND BERNSTEIN: MARXIST STRUCTURALISTS

The Marxist structuralists, Althusser and Bourdieu, have absorbed much of Durkheim's approach to analysing education, as well as that of Marx. It is worth explaining briefly how this dual influence has come about. Durkheim was French. His influence was passed on to Althusser and Bourdieu partly through a philosopher called Lévi-Strauss, the founder of a school of thought known as structuralism. An important aspect of structuralism is that by unconsciously (without conscious awareness) learning ways and structures of thought, feeling and behaviour, people 'automatically' carry on the culture into which they have been born. Really, this is to say little more than that people are socialised to conform, except that it emphasises the extent to which this process occurs unconsciously. Now, the socialisation of the unconscious mind has been stressed by Durkheim and, via Lévi-Strauss, it surfaces again in the work of Althusser and Bourdieu. It is to their work that we now turn.

It must be remembered that although Althusser and Bourdieu reflect the influence of their compatriots, Durkheim and Lévi-Strauss, they are also neo-Marxists. Marx's thought, therefore, figures prominently in their writings. Following him, Althusser considers that the functioning of the educational system is largely determined by the needs of the capitalist socio-economic system. As far as the working class is concerned, this means that it must also be socialised to accept its position in the class system and the kind of work it has to do. It is the second of these points which we concentrate on in this section – we examine the first in detail shortly. What must be grasped is that, to Althusser, the educational system serves the needs of capitalism. Bourdieu has made a specialist study of education in capitalist society, and particularly in France. It is in his writings that we see most clearly the convergence (coming together) of certain concepts of Marx and Durkheim.

Whereas Durkheim emphasised that certain aspects of a common culture (for example, patriotism) are passed on to all members of a society, Bourdieu concentrates on how middle and working class cultures are reproduced. He analyses particularly the role of the educational system in this process. Like Althusser, he argues that schools are middle class institutions, run by middle class people (teachers), in which, in general, middle class pupils succeed. Working class culture does not fit well into the demands of such an educational system. In support of his case, he is able to point to substantial empirical evidence to show that in the United States and the Western European countries, middle class children tend to achieve better qualifications and to get better jobs than working class children of equal measured intelligence. He explains this further by use of the term cultural capital. He argues that because the educational system is middle class, middle class children come into it better equipped to do well. Their values, attitudes and behaviour correspond more closely with teachers' expectations and the demands of the examination system than those of working class children who, in that sense, suffer a cultural deficit (see chapter 6 for a general view of class cultural differences). This observation does not mean that Bourdieu has a low opinion of working class culture, but that he regards it as largely non-academic. For instance, a working class novelist is a contradiction in terms because any such person who writes a novel employs middle class patterns of thought and expression and therefore starts to become middle class.

The work of Basil Bernstein on class culture is highly complementary to that of Bourdieu. Bernstein is particularly noted for his contribution to the analysis of the relationship between class and language. He has proposed a distinction between what he calls restricted and elaborated language codes. Restricted codes are everyday, informal speech patterns which everybody uses. People using restricted codes are usually familiar with each other and consequently these codes often use language short-cuts and expression which take a lot as understood. In contrast, elaborated codes fully express meanings and use more conceptual language in doing so. Bernstein describes restricted codes as context bound whereas elaborated codes are of more universal application. Whereas middle class children learn elaborated codes at home, working class children tend not to do so. As schools use elaborated codes, this gives middle class children an educational advantage. Thus, a working class child will understand from concrete experience what it means to be 'diddled' or 'done' by paying too high a price in a shop or supermarket, but s/he will be less prepared than the middle class child to understand and talk about, say, the concept of injustice raised by the situation. According to Bernstein, this is not just a matter of unfamiliarity with the relevant vocabulary – although this must play a part – but it is due, more fundamentally, to lack of practised competence in elaborated (or more conceptual) codes of thought.

Bernstein's hypothesis has been criticised by the American sociologist, William Labov, amongst others. Labov interviewed a number of black working class children and found that, once they felt confident and at ease with him, they were perfectly capable of expressing themselves in abstract conceptual terms, albeit in dialect rather than standard English. Interestingly, from the point of view of the effect of research method on findings, Labov stresses the importance of establishing an interview situation in which the subjects can behave normally. He suggests that formal interviews can sometimes have the opposite effect and produce misleading data. In defence of Bernstein, it still remains quite possible that middle class children have more practice in conceptual thought and expression. Further, to take Labov's point at face value, differences of dialect, whether based on race or class, would tend to disfavour working class children and to favour middle class children in communicating with middle class teachers. Both points are acceptable within Bourdieu's broad capital-deficit model of cultural reproduction. He himself relates his scheme to the whole range of cultural expression: it is not just the language and modes of thought but also the style and manners, sentiments and forms of emotional expression of teachers that accord better with those of middle class children. For example, behaviour that seems 'nice and well-mannered' to a middle class child may seem 'posh and snobby' to a working class child. Neither view is more correct than the other, but the middle class child is more likely to fit in with the middle class ethos of most schools.

Bourdieu regards the examination system primarily as a formal and ritual ('ceremonial') occasion, in which the already reproduced cultural ascendancy of the middle class child is ratified and legitimised (made to seem generally just and acceptable). The 'success' of middle class children and the 'failure' of working class children is certified. The examination system is not a fair competition although it seems to be as there is a surface appearance of neutrality. Because it is accepted as fair by the middle and working class alike, it serves to legitimise what Bourdieu regards as the fundamentally unequal process of cultural reproduction. As a result, the middle class is generally considered to have earned its superior rewards and status and the working class, likewise, to have gained its deserts. Bourdieu sums up the means by which this 'illusion' is achieved in the term symbolic violence. It is a powerful phrase and it means that the middle class cultural ascendancy and privilege is conserved and reproduced not by physical force but by a commanding superiority in the field of communication – particularly language. Thus, expertise in manipulating cultural symbols and forms such as literature, art and logic in a way acceptable to the middle class is a weapon in the class struggle, whether consciously used as such or not. Untrained and inexperienced in this skill, working class children are often overawed and 'mystified' by it. The almost physical sense of injury and loss undoubtedly suffered by many working class 'failures' perhaps justifies Bourdieu's savage metaphor of symbolic violence. At any rate, to him, it provides the answer to the question of how working class people are ideologically persuaded to fit into their often boring and relatively unrewarding roles.

Bourdieu has been criticised both by more orthodox Marxists and by liberals. Of the former, Raymond Boudon argues that Bourdieu overstresses the cultural or, as he calls them, the primary effects of stratification to the point of virtually ignoring the secondary, or material and practical effects. Boudon considers the secondary effects more important. These affect older working class pupils, who may find that they simply do not have enough money to stay on at school, or who may leave school just because their friends do. Boudon gets qualified support from the British sociologist, A H Halsey, whose refutation of Bourdieu we turn to shortly.

Bourdieu and his colleague Althusser, are also sometimes accused of a mechanical or deterministic view of cultural reproduction. Bourdieu in particular is arraigned as a 'cultural determinist.'

Basically, the charge of determinism means that Bourdieu is thought to believe that class culture is inevitably passed on from generation to generation, changing only in response to deeper developments in the economic substructure (or base) of society. Thus, he would recognise that changes in economic production, such as wide scale automation, might affect the way of life and the educational training of working people but, or so the accusation goes, he would not allow the possibility that working class people could change their own social position of cultural awareness outside the framework of such technological and socio-economic development. This charge seems broadly to be valid, although in defence of Bourdieu, he does allow that the educational system (and the cultural system generally) can operate in a 'relatively autonomous' (free) way. In other words, teachers, artists and other intellectuals and creative people have some freedom of thought and action. Bourdieu makes two major qualifications to this, however. First, such 'autonomy' does not ultimately change the class system; indeed, it may even provide a safety valve for tensions within it. Second, teachers and artists, like other people, are in any case socialised 'into' the class system and, consequently, most unlikely to think beyond it. Such freedom as exists is, therefore, very limited for most individuals. Althusser's position is similar to that of Bourdieu, although he uses different terminology to present it. We return to him in a later chapter (chapter 22).

HOW WORKING CLASS 'LADS' GET WORKING CLASS JOBS: A MARXIST ANALYSIS: PAUL WILLIS

Paul Willis' book is entitled *Learning to Labour*, but its real concern is manifested in its sub-title: 'How working class 'Lads' get working class jobs.' Willis describes a harsh collision between the tough working class 'lads' who are the subject of his study and the highly middle class world of the educational system. Willis's work provides concrete examples of some of the theoretical points made by Bourdieu. The lads seldom even begin to struggle for examination success which not only requires a kind of mental discipline foreign to their experience but is unlikely to be of much use in the kind of manual jobs most of them expect to get. The lads tend to find the conformist behaviour of the 'lobes', as they call more hard-working pupils, a matter for mockery and amusement.

The school experience of the lads fails significantly to alter the course of their lives. Schools are middle class institutions in that they are run by middle class people (teachers) and because success in them requires conformity to middle class values, such as academic commitment, and middle class goals, such as a career. Comparing the lads to the lobes, Spansky, one of the lads, says:

> *I mean, what will they remember of their school life? What will they have to look back on? Sitting in a classroom, sweating their bollocks off, you know, while we've been ... I mean look at the things we can look back on, fighting on the Pakis, fighting on the JA's (Jamaicans). Some of the things we've done on teachers, it'll be a laff when we look back on it.*
> *(Willis, 1977; 4)*

School seems to be good for a 'laff' and not much else. Judging by the following reactions of the lads to a lecture on the need for discipline at school and work, they obviously see little connection between school and the type of work they will do.

> *Spansky: He makes the same points all the time.*
> *Fuzz: He's always on about if you get a job, you've got to do this, you've got to do that. I've done it. You don't have to do none of that. Just go to a place, ask for a man in charge. nothing like what he says.*
> *Joey: It's ridiculous ...*
> *(92)*

Paul Willis notes that in later years, some of the lads do come to regret their failure to realise that education did offer a possible escape from life as a manual labourer. But to what extent does the school system give the lads a fair chance? Basically, Willis sympathises with their spirited rejection of the label of 'failures'. He appreciates, far more than Bourdieu seems to, that, in terms of their own class position, their way of life makes sense. It does so because most of them will, in fact, remain working class

YOUNG WOMEN FROM SCHOOL TO THE JOB MARKET: CHRISTINE GRIFFIN

Like many studies of young people of school age carried out in the nineteen sixties and seventies, Paul Willis's was exclusively about young males. Since then, there have been several about young females. One of the most interesting of these is Christine Griffin's *Typical Girls? Young Women from School to the Job Market* (1985). Griffin studied a group of young white working class women from Birmingham fifth forms into their first two years in the local employment market. The first stage involved interviewing 180 students and the second stage concentrated on 25 young women from five schools who had few or no qualifications. Like Willis, Griffin focuses primarily on the issue of cultural reproduction influentially explored by Bourdieu.

Griffin found that the young women differed significantly from the young males of Willis's study in their attitudes and behaviour. First, the female 'gang' did not occur among the young women – small friendship groups of two, three or four being much more common. Second, deviance for females was defined in terms of 'loose' sexuality rather than 'troublemaking'. Third, the strong identification the 'lads' made with factory work scarcely occurred among the females. A few referred to office work as 'snooty' but in practice most of them applied for jobs in the following order of preference: office, shop, factory. There was no clear division, therefore, of the kind that Willis found between the 'lads' and the 'ear 'olés' (or 'lobes'). The young working class women did not 'predestine' themselves to factory work as the 'lads' largely did.

The model Griffin offers to explain the situation and behaviour of the young women combines elements of gender and class analysis.' She suggests that they are simultaneously moving in three markets:

- the labour market
- the marriage market
- the sexual market.

To less qualified women the labour market offers either manual work or,

increasingly, routine office work – and this is what the young females sought. The relationship between the marriage and sexual markets is the key arena in which most of the young women negotiate their main future identity. To behave in a sexually loose manner could damage their 'marriage prospects'. Even though paid-work is becoming a larger part of women's lives, many young women still seek their identity chiefly through romance, marriage and, 'inevitably', a man. In a complementary study, Sue Lees examines the language of female sexual insult – particularly the use of the term 'slag' – which she describes as functioning 'to control the social and autonomous behaviour of girls and steer them into marriage'.

Angela McRobbie describes how 'girls magazines' spin an 'ideology of romance' which is the opposite side of the 'slag' stereotype but perhaps just as ensnaring (see p. 424). However, Griffin notes that a minority of the young women, particularly black females are sceptical of both 'mythologies' and seek more independent identities.

A H HALSEY'S CRITIQUE OF THE THEORY OF CULTURAL REPRODUCTION: A LIBERAL RESPONSE TO BOURDIEU

A H Halsey's approach is more liberal than those discussed above. His recent work draws heavily on a survey study of social change in Britain between 1913 and 1972, known as the Oxford Mobility Study. The original sample was of 10,000 men between the ages of 20 and 64.

Before describing the points on which Halsey differs from Bourdieu, it is important to be clear on their fundamental points of agreement. They are at one in stressing and lamenting the fact that many working class children do not reach anything approaching their full educational potential and, therefore, get jobs below their capacity. Both want to change this situation, although they have different views about how this might be done (see next chapter).

A substantial and important point of emphasis, rather than a total disagreement, divides Halsey from Bourdieu and other theorists of 'cultural reproduction'. To explain this, we need first to introduce the difference between material and cultural factors affecting educational attainment. Material factors are physical and environmental, such as the standard of housing, clothes and food. Virtually, they amount to 'the things money can buy.' Cultural factors refer to less tangible matters of values, norms and attitudes. We have already seen that Bourdieu argues that it is the possession of 'cultural capital' which accounts for the educational success of middle class children; school merely plays a part, albeit an important one, in the reproduction of cultural advantage. In his major work, *Origins and Destinations*, with A F Heath and J M Ridge (1980), Halsey tends to emphasise material rather than cultural factors in explaining class differences in educational attainment. He makes a number of points. Firstly, drawing on data from the Oxford study, he shows that there has been a substantial and progressive tendency for children to improve on the formal educational attainment of previous generations, and that even in state selective schools (mainly grammar schools selecting at eleven), the 'overwhelming feature' was that the majority of pupils came from social backgrounds in which neither parent had an education of grammar school quality. Clearly, therefore, these first generation 'selected-school' pupils could not have inherited their cultural advantage from parents who did not have it to pass on.

A second point in Halsey's case is his critique of Jackson and Marsden's *Education and the Working Class* (1962), a piece of research that seems to support Bourdieu's thesis. Out of a sample of 88 working class boys who went to grammar school, Jackson and Marsden found that a much higher number (34) than would have been expected purely on the basis of chance, came from 'sunken' middle class backgrounds. By 'sunken' middle class, they mean working class families with middle class relatives or families whose head had previously owned a small business. Halsey's data force him to work with a slightly different definition of sunken middle class; even so, his findings lead in the opposite direction from those of Jackson and Marsden. His evidence is that the relative chances of obtaining selective education declined for those from educated backgrounds, and that this was true of the sunken middle class as well as others. The group of middle class children that did benefit disproportionately from selective education did not have selectively educated parents, and so could not have inherited cultural capital in this way. Finally, although Halsey fully accepts that working class children are educationally disadvantaged, he makes much of the fact that those who did get places at grammar school and survived there to take 'O' levels did almost as well as children from middle class backgrounds. The problem, of course, as Halsey recognises, is that relatively few working class children got into grammar schools in the first place.

Although Halsey emphasises material rather than cultural factors in explaining the educational under-attainment of working class children, he is not conclusive on the issue. Indeed, he has to concede that class cultural, as well as material factors, may account for the fact that, under the tripartite system, a much higher proportion of middle class children sat 'O' levels. Disadvantage took effect particularly at the eleven-plus examination which prevented a large number of able working class children, as well as 'border-line' children from all classes, from obtaining an academic education.

Halsey is aware of the need to take into consideration the change in the secondary system from tripartite to comprehensive in explaining the relatively low attainment of working class children. In doing this, he uses the terminology of Raymond Boudon, who categorises the educational effects of class stratification into the primary and the secondary. As interpreted by Halsey and applied to British education, primary effects are cultural and material differences that hamper educational success in early schooling, and secondary effects are those that govern performance at secondary school level. Halsey suggests that, under the tripartite system, primary effects probably predominated, but that with the widespread abolition of the eleven-plus examination and the introduction of comprehensive education, secondary effects may be more potent. Their operation could well prevent the improvement in educational opportunity and attainment of working class children that comprehensivisation was widely expected to bring about (see pp. 91–4).

Halsey stresses that class is 'a major'

factor affecting educational attainment, but he avoids sweeping generalisation in favour of closely reasoned argument supported by detailed evidence. The following quotation, taken from one of his reviews, perhaps reveals his complex spirit:

Life, including the life of the ... examination room, is understood better by gamblers than by mechanistic theoreticians. The dice are loaded – by class, by sex, by date of birth and even, perhaps ... by genes. Among these, the force of class is a major one: it affects deeply the structure of opportunity. The force of stratification is still wider and deeper. But neither make it possible to deduce automatically the fate of particular individuals.

2 Education, The Economy and the Preparation of a Labour Force

The preparation of a labour force requires not only the teaching of specific skills, such as the three 'R's,' technology or computing, but also the more general socialisation of individuals to accept the discipline of work and, to some extent, their own likely place within the occupational structure. We will begin this section by presenting a functionalist perspective on these points, and then introduce other perspectives.

FUNCTIONALISM: OCCUPATIONAL SELECTION AND SOCIAL MOBILITY

Talcott Parsons gives a highly functionalist description of how he considers the educational system operates in relation to the occupational structure. He suggests that elementary (primary) schools sort out pupils according to their general level of ability (capacity), that secondary schools establish the more specific abilities and, accordingly, direct some to work and others on to further education:

Very broadly we may say that the elementary school phase is concerned with the internalisation in children of motivation to achievement. The focus is on the level of capacity ...
In approaching the question of the types of capacity differentiated, it should be kept in mind that secondary school is the principal springboard from which lower-status persons will enter the labour force, whereas those achieving higher status will continue their formal education in college, and some of them beyond.

Parsons, then, believes that the educational system actually does what is generally claimed for it – that is, selects people according to their ability and qualifies them accordingly. He and other functionalists tend to assume that there is a rough correspondence between individual intelligence, individual attainment (a pupil's measured performance) at school, and the job eventually obtained. Parsons sees the allocation of occupational status on the basis of 'achievement' as strongly characteristic of modern capitalist societies and particularly of the United States. More traditional societies allocated people to occupations on the basis of 'ascription' (by birth). Ralph Turner also considers that genuine and intense competition operates in the American educational system through comprehensive high schools, and he calls the resulting social mobility (movement up and down the social scale) 'contest' mobility. By contrast, he regards mobility of talented lower class children in Britain as 'sponsored' – through the grammar school system. This distinction, made in the nineteen fifties, has been blurred as a result of comprehensivisation in England and Wales. In any case, Turner's argument is severely weakened by the fact that he failed adequately to consider that lower social class membership substantially hinders social mobility in both countries.

THE RELATIONSHIP BETWEEN FUNCTIONALISM AND THE HEREDITARY VIEW OF INTELLIGENCE

It is clear that the functionalist case rests on whether intelligence, academic attainment and occupational position do in fact correlate strongly with one another. In particular, if intelligence and occupational status do not correlate strongly, then the functionalist model is largely discredited and the possibility must be examined that other factors are more relevant in determining occupational status. The functionalist position has recently acquired support from the work of a number of psychologists on both sides of the Atlantic though, as these scholars are not sociologists, it would be misleading to think of them as functionalists when their work merely complements the functionalist position. In Britain, Hans Eysenck is the foremost of these, and in the United States Arthur Jensen and Carl Bereiter have been prominent. Before briefly summarising their major points, something must be said about what is meant by intelligence. Intelligence refers to general cognitive ability, or the ability to reason, comprehend and make judgements. It is produced by heredity and environment. Psychologists do not agree on the precise relative importance of these two factors: some put the influence of heredity as low as 50 per cent, whilst others put it at 80 per cent, or even slightly higher.

As one might expect, those psychologists who consider that intelligence and occupational status strongly correlate estimate the hereditary element of intelligence at the high end. The 'high-estimate' viewpoint received a blow when it was demonstrated that the methodology of Sir Cyril Burt, on whose work the hereditarian case partly rested, was unscientific. Nevertheless, the debate continues. The psychologists who stress heredity – we may call them 'the hereditarians' – explain the fact that the children of parents of high occupational status also tend to achieve similar status in terms of their relatively higher level of inherited intelligence. The same applies, in reverse, to people of low social origin. Of course, although the hereditarians argue that there is a strong link between the level of intelligence of parents and children, they accept that this correspondence is not complete. For the minority of less intelligent middle class children and more intelligent working class children, the possibility of downward or upward mobility respectively, occurs by reason of the level of their intelligence. The hereditarians regard the fact that there is only a fairly small amount of long-range upward or downward mobility in both Britain and the United States as evidence for, not against, their argument. Like functionalists, the hereditarian psychologists consider that the educational system 'does its job'. It qualifies people according to their ability and directs them towards appropriate occupations.

FREE MARKET PERSPECTIVE, EDUCATION AND THE ECONOMY

Functionalist perspective on education has probably had no direct influence on the free market philosophy dominant in the Conservative Party in the nineteen eighties and early nineteen nineties. Nevertheless, there are substantial parallels between the two. First, the Conservatives have emphasised individual competition between pupils (testing), between teachers (appraisal – which may be related to promotion), and between schools (open enrolment) (see p. 109 for more detail on Conservative policy). Thus, competition is seen as the driving force behind individual and, ultimately, national achievement. Second, again like the Functionalists, Conservatives tend to set aside the evidence that class factors greatly distort fair competition partly on the basis that education can directly do little about class inequalities.

A third parallel between many Conservatives and Functionalists is the tendency to see the function of education as closely tied to the needs of the economy. Throughout the nineteen eighties, the government made a variety of attempts to increase the influence of the business world in education. More school governorships were allocated to businesspeople. The business-dominated Manpower Services Commission (MSC) took over much of the vocational training of young people, including the majority of Youth Training Schemes (YTSs) from further education colleges. Even within schools, the Technical and Vocational Educational Initiative (TVEI) was funded by the MSC There was a sustained attempt to spread the spirit of the 'enterprise culture' throughout the whole of the educational system. TVEI has become TVE – Technical and Vocational Extension – and vocational training is now controlled by the business dominated TECs (Training and Enterprise Councils) (1991).

MARXISM, OCCUPATIONAL SELECTION AND SOCIAL MOBILITY

A major refutation of the arguments of Functionalists and hereditarian psychologists comes from the American Marxists, Herbert Bowles and Samuel Gintis. We will present their refutation first and then describe the broader theoretical context of their position. On the basis of detailed statistical analysis, Bowles and Gintis show that, in the United States, the probability of obtaining economic success is considerably greater for those born of parents of high socio-economic status than for those of high intelligence. Put plainly, socio-economic background is generally a much more significant factor in obtaining economic success than is intelligence. They show that a man born in the bottom decile (tenth) in terms of socio-economic background has only 4.2 per cent probability of being in the top fifth of income distribution, whereas a person born in the top decile in terms of socio-economic background has a 43.9 per cent probability of being in the top fifth of income distribution as an adult. That this extreme inequality of outcome is due to socio-economic background and not to the differential distribution of intelligence is shown by a further sophisticated statistical calculation. This calculation is hypothetical (rests on supposition) and demonstrates how income would be distributed on the basis of measured intelligence only. Because the general level of measured intelligence is somewhat higher for those born into higher socio-economic backgrounds, those born into the top decile have, in this hypothetical model, a marginally better chance of reaching the top fifth of income distribution than those born into the bottom decile on the basis of 'the genetic inheritance of IQ' (Bowles and Gintis). Those born in the bottom decile would have an 18.7 per cent probability of being in the top fifth in income, and those born in the top decile a 21.4 per cent probability on the basis of differences in intelligence alone. These figures are so far from the actual patterns described above that we have to agree with Bowles and Gintis' insistence on the relative unimportance of IQ and the prime importance of socio-economic background

in explaining economic success. The best hope for obtaining high income, then, is to be born into a high socio-economic background. As Bowles and Gintis say succinctly: 'The power and privilege of the capitalist class are often inherited, but not through superior genes.'

Another American, Christopher Jencks, has also written with authority in this area. He sums up the matter effectively when he writes that although the heredity-environment argument is likely to rage indefinitely, the best evidence

... does not, however, suggest that variations in cognitive skill account for much of the inequality among American adults. There is nearly as much economic inequality among individuals with identical test scores as in the general population.

Jencks further points out that schools themselves cannot make an unequal and hierarchial society equal. For that to happen, income, wealth, cultural opportunity and status would have to be more equally distributed. This observation is obvious but nonetheless true.

It is a strength of Bowles and Gintis's case that they use their opponents' data on the relationship between heredity and intelligence. other authorities also see this relationship as less strong than Jensen and Eysenck do and point out that not only does the relative level of educational attainment of a child vary over time but so do scores in intelligence tests. Indeed, it is actually possible to prepare successfully for intelligence tests, so they can hardly be regarded as neutral instruments of measurement. J W B Douglas, whose work we refer to below, regards intelligence tests in this more sceptical light. He argues that scores achieved in them, as well as academic performance, are considerably influenced by social background.

A REFORMER'S RESPONSE TO MARXISTS AND FUNCTIONALISTS: A H HALSEY

Halsey rejects what he sees as the pessimism of Marxists and the conservatism of many functionalists. Yet, in arguing that educational reform can facilitate upward mobility from the working class, he has to work hard with the facts produced by his own research and that of his colleagues. The data he presents in *Origins and Destinations* largely confirm the established view that in Britain, as in America, the offspring of the middle class have a very much greater chance of remaining middle class than the offspring of the working class have of becoming middle class, (over six times greater, depending on precisely how middle and working class are defined). What is more, this situation did not substantially change between 1913 and 1972. What did happen is that because of the expansion of the service sector and the contraction of the industrial sector of the economy, more middle class jobs became available. All classes benefited, but the working class did not do so any more than others. Indeed, in the years following the immediate post-Second World War period, its members did relatively less well.

In the face of such evidence, Halsey is determinedly hopeful rather than optimistic. He conceded that so far the middle class has benefited proportionately more from the expansion of state education than the working class has, but he argues that this would be unlikely to continue if further expansion took place. Given that middle class youth is now largely catered for, an additional increase in educational opportunity would be bound to benefit the working class. He also hopes that as (and if) the comprehensive system becomes better established, it will reduce class inequalities in education. His own research, however, does not provide data on whether or not this is happening (see chapter 6). The section of Halsey's book on future educational policy is, inevitably, more speculative than the rest of *Origins and Destinations*. Perhaps its implied corollary is that in his view, there is, in any case, no practical alternative to reform.

MARXISM, ECONOMY, EDUCATION AND CLASS

Marxists do not consider that the educational systems of advanced capitalist societies effectively and fairly match people to jobs. They believe that education in capitalist society contributes to the continuance of the class system and class inequality; in particular, it reproduces a labour force which is socialised to accept its lot and has, in any case, no adequate alternative means of survival. By 'socialised' we mean that the majority of working class children who 'fail' academically tend to accept their own 'failure' and the 'success' of most middle class children as legitimate. The fact that a small minority of working class children do 'make it' helps to foster the illusion that the educational system is fair and 'neutral,' and a highly unequal society presupposes that most children will fail academically and fill the lower occupations. In a sense, these matters become 'facts of life' for them, although for many an underlying sense remains that circumstances could be different.

Like Bourdieu, Bowles and Gintis give many examples of how social relationships in the educational system echo those of the economic system and thus prepare children for working life. They stress especially that educational institutions, like factories and offices, are intensely hierarchical. Like workers, pupils are expected to obey authority and have little or no control over the content of their work. This results in a feeling of non-involvement in, or alienation from, work. Only a minority of mainly middle class children go on to experience relative freedom and responsibility in study: fewer still are educated for leadership.

The American Marxist, Harry Braverman, has expanded interestingly and controversially the analysis that, far from being primarily involved in teaching working class children specific occupational skills, it is one of the hidden functions of schools to prepare children for the tedium of work (by being tedious themselves!). Braverman's critique, however, is more complex than this suggests and deserves fuller presentation. He sees the educational system as subordinate to the economic, but not, perhaps, as might be anticipated. He makes a powerful argument that most unskilled, semi-skilled and even many so-called skilled manual and non-manual jobs can be done with little or no skill at all (see chapter 11). He therefore eliminates occupational training as a major function of education for the majority. Indeed, it is true that most jobs at these levels are learnt at work itself, not at school. He agrees that the three basic communication skills of reading, writing and arithmetic are learnt in schools, but he considers these to be necessary in the general context of modern life, rather than specifically at work (where, of course, they also help!) Braverman's thesis is supported by estimates that in Britain between two and five million adults are not fully literate; yet they obviously manage to do their jobs, despite this handicap. He also differentiates between the kind of work just described and professional, managerial and other work of a similar level, for which lengthy training is necessary. Some critics have suggested that even with these occupations, the length of time spent in studying in institutions could be profitably shortened. Thus, Robert Dore suggests that engineers could be well trained through a combination of supervised experience 'on-the-job' and part-time or short, full-time courses.

What, then, are the functions that Braverman thinks schools do perform? He considers that they socialise and 'child mind' whilst parents are at work. He points out that the raising of the minimum age for compulsory education has coincided with the increase in the number of working mothers. His comments on the relationship between educational expansion and the rate of unemployment are interesting and are echoed by the British social historian, Harold Silver. They both claim that in the nineteen thirties this relationship served to reduce unemployment amongst the young by removing large numbers of them from the job market. In addition, it provides jobs in teaching and administration for many thousands of middle class people. The increase in those staying on for further education in Britain during the late nineteen seventies and early eighties similarly 'mopped up' some of the unemployed. However useful or not qualifications may be, the pursuit of them occupies the time and energy of young people. Significantly, provision has been made increasingly for less qualified sixteen year olds, who are the weakest in the job market, to stay on in education. Braverman's rather exaggerated remark that 'there is no longer any place for the young in society than school' refers to the role of schools generally, but it has a particular application to those of school leaving age.

Braverman not only argues that few job-

specific skills are learnt in pre-sixteen education, but also that the 'qualification paper-chase' is in itself unnecessary and futile. Whilst there is empirical support for the first position, the second depends very much more on point of view. It is true, however, that pupils and the general public are sometimes unaware of the extent to which the job-market value of qualifications has become substantially less now that more people have them at all levels. To take two examples, teacher training and librarianship; the qualifications required for entry into both these courses have risen. This does not guarantee that the people now entering them will be better than in the past or that they will do the job more effectively, but they will appear more impressive on paper. Braverman suggests that employers use qualifications as a screening device to ensure a minimum quality of entrant and, to maintain the same standard over time, they tend to adjust their requirement upwards. He cites some interesting survey evidence from Berg that there is now chronic over-qualification in many areas of employment, particularly at the clerical level. Berg's data also showed that over-educated employees tended to do a worse job, and to be more dissatisfied than the less well qualified.

Although the functional relationship between the educational and economic systems in Britain and America is in some respects rather obscure, its importance should not be underestimated. Modern nations require, at least, a highly educated minority, particularly in the areas of scientific and technological research, and a generally literate and numerate population. Accordingly, education is a major item of government expenditure in all such societies. As we have seen, some argue that the educational system in Britain ought to be more closely directed to serve the needs of the economy. Japan is a country that has had a recent tradition of centralised planning in education: its 'economic miracle' would not have been possible without the efficiency of its educational system. Great emphasis is placed on the development of mathematical and scientific skills; although this has achieved results, it has often been at the price of putting extreme pressure on teenagers.

3 The Role of the School in Cultural and Economic Reproduction

Much has already been written in this chapter about the role of schools in socialising pupils (cultural reproduction) and the preparation of a labour force (economic reproduction). These two processes are intimately connected in that the way an individual is socialised greatly determines the job s/he will obtain.

This section briefly examines two aspects of the role of the school. First, a closer analysis is given of how teachers categorise or label pupils at the micro-level, i.e. the level of classroom interaction. Second, the question is asked whether, given the influence of external factors such as class and gender socialisation or educational performance, schools can 'make a difference' to the level of their pupils' achievements. The first sub-section tends to stress the extent to which schools reinforce external social factors whereas the second suggests that 'good' schools can make a significant difference despite social disadvantage.

1 SCHOOLS, 'LABELLING' AND CULTURAL REPRODUCTION

We have already seen how the Marxists, Bourdieu and Bernstein, see the educational system as a middle class agency which helps to reproduce middle class cultural ascendancy. A number of interactionists in Britain and America have reached similar conclusions. Their theoretical focus is, however, in some cases narrower than that of the Marxists, and their method of research is on a smaller scale and largely participant-observational.

A pioneering study in this area is David Hargreaves' *Social Relations in a Secondary School* (1968). The secondary school in question was an all boys' secondary modern school in which Hargreaves took on the participant observational role of teacher. His study was concerned with the factors within the school context which contribute to the creation of two sub-cultures, 'the academic and the delinquescent.' He emphasises how academic streaming greatly affects the membership of these two sub-cultures. Those who were placed in the lowest ('E') stream were the most likely to become part of the delinquescent (or delinquency-prone) sub-culture, whereas those in the 'A' stream tended to conform. Hargreaves attributes the formation of these peer-group sub-cultures directly to the school's policy of streaming which, he claims, results in an increasing feeling of inferiority on the part of the lower stream boys as they progress into the third and fourth forms. We can, then, conveniently think of the streaming process as a form of labelling which, in this instance and presumably often, has unintended consequences. It must be said that other sources show that social class factors mediated through the home and neighbourhood also contribute to the formation of youth peer-groups, although these were beyond the practical limits of Hargreaves' research.

Colin Lacey's *Hightown Grammar* (1971) is a parallel study to that of Hargreaves, concerned with the effect of streaming in a grammar school. His findings complement those of Hargreaves and he adds the observation that when frustrated expectations at school coincide with problems at home, 'the worst cases of emotional disturbance occur.'

Stephen Ball's study of polarised pupil sub-cultures in a comprehensive school completes a triology (*Beachside Comprehensive: a Case-study of Secondary Schooling*). Ball finds that 'banding' contributes to the formation of what he terms 'pro-school' and 'anti-school' sub-cultures. Interestingly, however, he found that when 'Beachside' did convert to mixed ability teaching, labelling of pupils largely on the basis of class stereotyping continued to occur. This suggests that a high level of skill and commitment is needed by teachers if they are to avoid stereotyping (see also Spender, pp. 98–9).

Ball's observations lead him to produce the following typology to explain the nature of pro and anti school groups.

Pro-School:
1 Supportive (Conformers because they believe they ought to be)
2 Manipulative (Conformers because it suits their self-interest)

Anti-school:
1 Passive ('Drifters' into noncomformist or apathetic behaviour)
2 Rejecting (Active nonconformers/rebels).

In Paul Willis' study, *Learning to Labour*, the role of the school, including the labelling of working class 'lads' and the formation of what he calls anti-school sub-cultures, is put in a wide socio-economic context. In pointing out that the academic failure of the 'lads' provides new recruits to manual labour, and so helps to maintain the capitalist system, Willis shows himself to be a structural sociologist as well as a detailed ethnographer (social scientist who studies cultural activity through detailed observation – see p. 79).

Like Willis, Nell Keddie draws on both interactionist and structural perspectives in her detailed examination of how cultural reproduction occurs in the classroom through the labelling process. She argues that sometimes intelligent working class children may be labelled, or mis-labelled, stupid because of 'troublesome' behaviour. This label can become a 'self-fulfilling prophecy,' if the child accepts it and loses the motivation to compete academically. Keddie distances herself, however, from Bourdieu and Bernstein by rejecting any implication that working class culture is inferior: she refers to this view as 'the myth of cultural deprivation'. She argues that the educational system should build on working class culture rather than ignore or repress it – a view that Bernstein himself accepts as having clarified his own position. One problem is that nobody has yet explained in detail what a curriculum based on, or even substantially reflecting, working class culture might be like, or how it would help working class children to function better in capitalist society (if, indeed, that were its aim). The way of life of the 'lads' seems to defy the limits of any curriculum outside that imposed by the experience and discipline of work.

2 THE QUALITY OF SCHOOLS

A piece of research which contrasts markedly with those described in the previous section is that of Michael Rutter et al., *Fifteen Thousand Hours*. Rutter's methods were highly empirical and statistical and both his methods and his findings have attracted strong criticism, but he has stood by his main conclusions. *Fifteen Thousand Hours*, published in 1979, summarised several years' research into the performance of twelve Inner London secondary schools. The aim of the research was to discover why some schools 'succeeded' and others did not. The team looked at four factors: attendance, academic achievement, behaviour in school, and the rate of delinquency outside it.

Rutter found that schools obtained very varied ratings on all the above counts, even when difference in social class background and intelligence in intake was allowed for. Those schools that scored well on one factor tended to do well on others. What, then, on Rutter's evidence, makes for a successful school? Pupil performance on the above four points is associated with a certain school 'ethos' of which sound teaching and professional behaviour is the keynote. Teachers who are punctual, well-organised and patient, who encourage pupils, share extracurricular activities with them, and can inspire by example, are likely to get the best from pupils. Whatever the teacher's style and values, consistency helps. This applies as much to senior staff as to juniors, and Rutter adds that an established system of rewards and punishments improves pupils' performance. Because some schools were successful on all four points, the researchers sought an underlying reason. These successful schools varied in their approach from the traditional to the progressive but the researchers concluded that what they had in common was a consistent commitment to their own values and rules. This consistency created an atmosphere or ethos that was secure and purposeful and in which effective work could take place and good human relationships prosper.

Fifteen Thousand Hours was initially well received both by the press and by many influential academics. Like many books that elicit such a response, it clarified and built upon a body of sentiment that had been growing for some time. In the mid-nineteen seventies, a concern for academic standards and quality in education, which had been simmering for some time, rose to the surface. The *Bennet Report* of 1976, comparing various kinds of teaching methods in primary schools, found amongst other things that whatever method of teaching was used, the ability, experience and commitment of the individual teacher was a crucial variable. Formal and informal teaching methods could both be successful –

provided that they were done well. Again, themes of consistency and commitment are stressed.

We can divide Rutter's critics into those who attack the quality of his research in its own terms and those who argue that, in addition to the limitations of his methodology, he also asks inadequate, if not wrong, questions. Of the former, several are especially concerned with the limitations of his statistical method. Amongst these are Anthony Heath and Peter Clifford of Oxford University, who argue that the effect on performance which Rutter attributes to secondary school factors might well have been caused by the carry-over effect of primary schooling or by the interest of parents. In brief, Rutter has not controlled for the various non-school factors that are known to affect children's school attainment.

The second group of Rutter's critics put their criticisms of his methodology within a broad critique of his whole theoretical approach. Michael Young rejects the assumption that social relations in school can be adequately understood on the basis of a model that assumes value consensus within the school. He finds it inconceivable that a school could 'function' or be properly analysed without reference to class, gender and racial divisions. To him, it is ludicrous to applaud consistency without raising the question of 'consistency in the pursuit of

what purposes?' Rutter's answer to Young was that his research was only concerned with school performance in relation to the four factors mentioned above.

A further criticism of the report is that it tells us nothing about the fate of the children when they leave school. Rutter does not even present data on the question of whether, because children in some schools do better in public examinations than others, their occupational prospects are improved – a point which cannot be assumed, given that most of the children in the study were highly disadvantaged and that even 'the examination successes' were moderate by national standards.

Perhaps Rutter cannot be condemned for asking a particular set of questions, but clearly these questions are limited in scope and context and, to judge by the current state of debate, the answers to them need to be treated with caution. Even so, it is worth recalling in the heat of argument that, if interpreted cautiously and in the light of other relevant data, Rutter's findings appear neither startling nor particularly original. Writing in 1968 of lower manual working class pupils, J W Douglas said:

Although (they) ... are at a disadvantage relative to the middle class in all types of school, those at schools with a good record are far less handicapped.

Educational Issues and Policy: 1944–1991

INTRODUCTION A period of almost 50 years is a long one to cover in relation to an area as controversial and subject to change as education. Yet, conveniently the post-war period falls into two clearly identifiable parts with a brief time of uncertainty and transition inbetween. The first period is from 1944 to 1976, the second from 1979 to the present (1991) and perhaps beyond, and the transition was roughly between 1976 and 1979. All these dates must, of course, be regarded as approximate, particularly the last (the new government of 1992 may begin a new epoch in educational policy and reform).

The key theme of the first period was

that of equality of opportunity in relation particularly to class disadvantage and later gender and 'race'/ethnicity. It was initiated by the Butler Education Act of 1944 and partly brought to a close by Prime Minister James Callaghan's Ruskin College speech of 1976 when new priorities were signalled at the top of the educational agenda. These priorities were the relationship of education to industry and the standards attained by pupils and students in the state sector. Callaghan's brief premiership, 1976–79 – our 'transitional' period – saw these problems discussed rather than acted upon. They became the main points in the educational agenda of 'Thatcherism', along with the issue of curriculum content –

1940s/1950s	1960s/1970s	1970s/1980s	1980s/1990s
Market Liberalism	Reformist Liberalism	'Equality' for Minorities	Market Liberalism (and central curricular control)
'Meritocracy'? by Competitive Selection	Increased Equality of Opportunity/Status within the Educational System	Liberal Radical Socialist Strands	Quality and Selection through Market Mechanics
Tripartite System Private Education	Comprehensive System Compensatory Education (Sole Quasi-socialist Measure)	Impacted on the Whole of the Educational System Feminism Multii-Culturalism/Anti-Rascism Special Needs	1988 Educational Reform Act National Curriculum Competing Schools

▲

Figure 4.1

Educational Ideologies

and policies: 1944-90s

particularly what is culturally appropriate for 'British' pupils to learn. Even so, it was not until Mrs Thatcher's third period in office that the main Conservative educational reforms were passed in law via the Educational Reform Act ('ERA') of 1988.

Class and Equality

Much of the earlier part of this chapter examined the effect of social class on educational attainment. Both the Butler Education Act of 1944 and the systematic introduction of comprehensive education from 1965 were attempts to widen equality of opportunity albeit very different in kind. They were both essentially liberal measures although, for reasons discussed below, supporters of the comprehensive system regarded it as much more egalitarian than the tripartite system introduced by the 1944 Act (see below). A third measure discussed below is compensatory education. This policy, which only affected a small percentage of the school population, was more genuinely socialist than comprehensivisation as it attempted to compensate for the material and cultural disadvantages experienced by working class children by enriching their home and community experience.

Before discussing various policy measures it is worth briefly examining again the issue they were largely concerned with – the underachievement of working class children. In the nineteen sixties, J W Douglas compared the attainment level of high ability students from different social backgrounds and found that success at 'O'

level and staying on at school after the fifth year were strongly correlated with class (see table 4.1).

Douglas found the difference between intelligence and attainment was even greater among pupils of less measured intelligence from a similar wide range of social backgrounds. According to Anthony Heath (1987), and despite the reforms we are about to discuss, much the same pattern of working class underachievement persisted into the nineteen eighties (see p. 92). Social class, then, makes a substantial contribution to academic attainment. A number of sociologists, including the American Jencks, have raised another important question of educational inequality. They argue that even when children of different social backgrounds do achieve similar levels of attainment, their life-chances, in terms of careers and acquiring wealth, are not equalised as a result: higher classes still do better. Research by Gordon Marshall demonstrates that this is also true in Britain (1988).

THE TRIPARTITE SYSTEM

There was a sizeable political and public consensus behind the Butler Act. It stated the government's commitment in principle to providing an educational system suited to each child's 'age, aptitude and ability'. In pursuit of this objective, local authorities were required to organise education in three progressive stages; primary, secondary and further (most post-school education excluding higher education, which was based mainly in universities). Although it was not specifically laid down in the Act, most local authorities divided secondary education into grammar, secondary modern and technical schools. This threefold division became known as the tripartite system. Grammar schools were for more 'academic' children and secondary modern schools for virtually all the rest. Nationally, only a very small percentage of students went to technical schools which provided practical, vocationally-oriented courses. Most local authorities used an eleven-plus examination to select pupils for specific types of schools. Very few offered grammar school places to even as much as thirty per cent of their secondary intake and many offered far fewer. Critics of the tripartite system soon began to argue that it was inadequate to meet the aptitudes and abilities of all children.

The problems and related policy debates which we deal with below must be understood in the above educational context. Of course, the broader social context is also relevant, particularly the class nature of British society. It became clear in the nineteen fifties and early sixties that the educational system as it had developed under the 1944 Act was not ensuring equality of opportunity between social classes and was failing to bring out the potential of many children, particularly those from disadvantaged backgrounds. Halsey's early work with Floud and Martin, and Jackson and Marsden's, and J W B Douglas's studies already referred to were significant sociological contributions to this growing awareness. The major issue at secondary level focused on the eleven-plus exam and the system to which it paved the way.

THE COMPREHENSIVE SYSTEM

The major criticism against the tripartite system, put forward particularly by the Labour party, was that the eleven-plus

	Upper-middle class	Lower-middle class	Upper-working class	Lower-working class
%Gaining good GCEs	77	60	53	37
%Leaving school in their 5th year	10	22	33	50

(Source; adapted from J.W.B. Douglas, *All Our Future*, 1968)

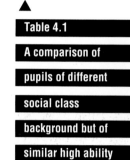

▲

Table 4.1

A comparison of

pupils of different

social class

background but of

similar high ability

examination discriminated against working class children. Details of the examination results were kept secret and relatively few working class children were offered grammar school places even among those who were of comparable intelligence to successful middle class children. However, shortage of places meant disappointment for some middle class families too (thirteen per cent of eleven year olds were offered places in London, 29 per cent in Wales). Unless their families could afford to send them to private school, unsuccessful middle class children, too, had to share the common fate of 'failures' – and 'failure' was the term used. An educational system that had many more 'losers' than 'winners' was likely to cause widespread resentment. It was not long before specific and detailed arguments against the tripartite system began to be presented. Criticism also focused on the content of the exam itself, as well as on the divisive effects of the tripartite system. Some authorities cast doubts on the validity of the aptitude and attainment tests frequently used in the exam. In local authorities in which teachers' reports were also used as a basis of selection, it was an easy matter to suggest that unfair and subjective judgement might decide a child's future. 'Deciding a child's future at eleven' was at the nub of the debate: eleven was widely considered to be too early to determine this issue. A child might have an 'off day' during the eleven-plus examination period; might not realise the importance of the exam, or be a 'late developer'. For those who accepted them, these arguments suggested the alternative to tripartite of a non-selective or comprehensive system of secondary schooling. Those who favoured comprehensivisation did so because they believed that it would remove the damaging and unfair stigma of eleven-plus 'failure.'

Further, by enabling pupils of different social backgrounds to mix with each other, it was thought that a cultural 'rub-off' effect would occur, of particular benefit to working class children. The Labour government elected in 1964 issued Circular 10.65 inviting those local authorities which had not yet done so – still, in 1965, the large majority – to draw up schemes for comprehensive education. By the end of 1978, just over eighty per cent of state secondary education was organised along comprehensive lines, although some observers seriously doubt whether much more than sixty per cent are 'genuinely' comprehensive.

In assessing the performance of the comprehensive system, it must be realised that the term comprehensive covers many different types of school. The Leicestershire system, for instance, involves separate institutions for the 11 to 14 age group and for the 14 to 18 age group. More typically, South East Essex has 10 schools for 11 to 16 year olds which 'feed into' a single-site sixth form college. Despite the growing popularity of the sixth form college and of other 'sixteen-plus' colleges, the most common form of comprehensive is still the school for 11 to 18 year olds.

HAS THE COMPREHENSIVE SYSTEM IMPROVED THE ATTAINMENT LEVELS OF WORKING CLASS CHILDREN? A H HEATH

Supporters of comprehensivisation argued that the eleven-plus exam discriminated particularly against working class children. They believed that effective comprehensive education might partly reverse social class disadvantage so that by 16 the public examination results of working class children might be better than under the tripartite system. Early comparisons of the overall performance of comprehensive schools and grammar/secondary schools in similar socio-economic situations showed little difference between the two (Eggleston 1975, National Children's Bureau, 1980). More recently (1987), Anthony Heath concludes that 'one of the most widespread myths in contemporary education is that comprehensive schools have sacrificed standards on the altar of equality' ('Class in the Classroom', *New Society*, July 17, 1987)

Heath specifically examines the issue of whether the attainment level of working class children has improved under the comprehensive system. Using data from three different studies (including, most recently, his own) he compares the attainment level of the children of the 'salariat' (higher class), intermediate class and working class from the beginning of the century to the early eighties (see figure 4.2). The left hand side of the figure (a) compares the findings of the 1949 (Glass) on class origin and selective schooling with these of the 1972 (Halsey) study. The right hand side of the figure (b) compares the findings of the 1972 study on social class and 'O' levels obtained with those of the 1982 study (Heath). The figure looks somewhat complicated but its main message is simple. It is in Heath's words that

'class inequalities first in access to selective secondary schools, then at O

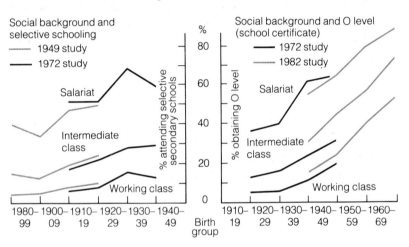

Figure 4.2

(a) Social background and selective schooling

(b) Social background and O level (school certificate)

NOTES FOR INTERPRETING THE TABLES

1 The reason why the lines for the 1949 and 1972 and the 1972 and 1982 studies are not continuous is that the studies used slightly different definitions of class.

2 The decade dates in the figure refer to birth groups – their examination results come 11 years (eleven-plus (a)) or 16 years ('O' level (b)) later.

3 Each social class is given a percentage score to indicate the overall performance of its members in eleven-plus and 'O' level (in the case of each class grouping, the score has progressively improved but the difference in performance between class groupings has remained roughly the same).

and next perhaps at A-level, have shown no overall tendency to decline ... (T)hey seem to reappear in a new guise but fundamentally unchanged as the educational environment changes around them'.

According to Heath's analysis first the 1944 Act and then comprehensivisation has failed to shift the relative inequalities of attainment according to class:

'The evidence of the 1972 study showed that the social engineering of the 1944 Act had no measurable impact on class inequalities' ... *and in the mainly comprehensive period, the 1982 study showed that the 'inequalities in examination success are very similar to those already documented in access to selective schools'.*

Heath offers two explanations for the stubbornness of relative educational inequalities. First, the reforms were not as radical as they were sometimes presented. Second, educationally ambitious families are generally able to 'play the system', whatever it happens to be, especially those who are able to afford private education for their children.

It is worth elaborating on the first point. The 1944 Act did nothing directly to equalise class inequalities except require all children to remain in full-time education until fifteen. Indeed, the eleven-plus represented a built-in disadvantage for working class children. Often, too, comprehensive reform was too mild to affect class disadvantage.

Very important in judging whether a school is genuinely comprehensive is its internal system of academic organisation. These vary widely. Some schools 'stream' pupils rigidly – 'tripartite under the same roof' as their critics would say – whilst others use mixed ability teaching for most, if not all, classes. Many would say the former are not really comprehensive. Similarly, pastoral or tutor systems (concerned with general pupil welfare and discipline) can vary greatly in quality. Tutor groups which contain children from a variety of social and, where relevant, racial backgrounds are closest to the comprehensive spirit. However, a study of Julienne Ford suggested that children are more likely to make friends on the basis of academic rather than pastoral groupings. Middle class children, who were a majority in the upper academic groupings, tended to associate with each other, and the same applied to the working class children in the lower academic groupings.

A REFUTATION OF HEATH: A MCPHERSON AND J WILLMS On the basis of their own separate research, Andrew McPherson and J Douglas Willms disagree with Heath's conclusion about the ineffectiveness of the comprehensive system in equalising attainment between working and middle class children:

Anthony Heath says that research has shown that comprehensive reorganisation, in common with other educational reforms this century, has made little impact on social-class inequalities in British education (New Society, 17 July 1987). He is not correct to say this about comprehensive reorganisation, nor to conclude that, 'in the face of this remarkable resilience of class inequalities, educational reforms seem powerless, whether for good or ill'.
(A McPherson and J Willms, 1988)

McPherson and Willms carried out their research in Scotland. They state that although social class differences in attainment remained roughly stable in Scotland (as well as England) for several decades after 1945 their own more recent research (1987) 'has a different and more up-to-date story to tell about comprehensive schooling'. If anything, the statistical aspects of their study are more complex than those of Heath's, but, again, their findings are straightforward and can be listed as follows:

1 Average attainment between 1976 and 1984 increased across all social-class groups.
2 There are still large social class differences in attainment.
3 Attainment has been rising faster among lower groups – For example:
(i) The skilled manual improved their performance in relation to the intermediate by roughly half an ordinary grade.
(ii) Overall, working class pupils improved their performance in relation to middle class schools by about half an ordinary grade.
(iii) Pupils of average socio-economic background attained higher, the longer the school had been an all-through comprehensive.

Importantly, McPherson and Willms also argue that Heath's data can also be interpreted as showing the beginnings of an improvement at 'O' level in the performance of working class children in relation to the children of the salariat. What is clear, therefore, is the need for further research on the effects of established comprehensive schools and local comprehensive systems on pupils' attainment.

THE COMPREHENSIVE SYSTEM AND ATTAINMENT: CONCLUSION The following points can be made reflecting current research on the comprehensive system:

1 Average attainment across all social classes has continued to improve under the comprehensive system as it did prior to comprehensivisation (since 1945).

2 The rate of improvement in pupil attainment in other industrialised nations (e.g. Germany, France, Japan) has tended to be greater than in Britain (see p. 108).

3 It is possible, even likely, that the relative attainment of working class to middle class children has recently begun to improve as a result of comprehensivisation.

4 Attempts radically to change the comprehensive system or reverse further progress towards it *may* occur just as it appears to be beginning to increase its effectiveness.

COMPENSATORY EDUCATION: AN EXAMPLE OF POSITIVE DISCRIMINATION

The principle behind compensatory education is to provide additional educational or education-related help to those who are socially disadvantaged.

Like many recent progressive initiatives in post-war education and social work, compensatory education was first tried in the United States. There, the major motive was to compensate those who had been deprived for racial reasons, whereas in Britain, the focus has been on compensating for general social disadvantage (though in the inner cities this has included large numbers of black people). Compensatory education was often justified by cultural deprivation theory. Some who put forward this view, such as Charlotte K Brooks seem to assume the inferiority of working class

culture and not surprisingly have been criticised.

As early as 1956, a 'demonstration guidance project' was established in New York, to provide extra educational support for intelligent children of the deprived racial minorities. It seemed a success and similar programmes followed, but with the difference that they included the whole ability range. In 1965, the Johnson government included a 'Head Start' programme in its policies of social reform. As its name suggests, the purpose of 'Head Start' was mainly to prepare disadvantaged minority children for school by giving them special pre-school help.

Assessments of Head Start vary. The principle criteria used in the follow-up studies in evaluating success were gains in IQ and improvement in academic performance. On both counts the results of the initial follow-up studies were disappointing. IQ gains tended to be short-term, and there was little difference in attainment between the Head Start children and others of similar background. The hereditarians in the nature-nurture debate have cited this as evidence that intelligence and even educational performance cannot be significantly improved by 'environmental engineering'. Others have viewed the matter differently. Hunt argues that some schemes in the Head Start programme were inappropriate to the needs of the children they were supposed to help. Apparently, the curricula adopted often assumed considerable competence in the verbal and numerical skills that it was the object of the programmes to teach! This was because available curriculum material reflected the needs and attainment of middle class children who normally had virtually exclusive access to pre-school education. Several better designed pre-school programmes have, in fact, achieved lasting gains. A prominent feature of some of these has been the close involvement of the children's mothers, but Bereiter and Engelmann report several successful projects not involving direct maternal participation. Frequently, these involved a special stress on developing linguistic skills. A later (1976–77) and more comprehensive follow-up of Head Start by Lazar and Darlington showed an average reduction of academic failure in project children of 36.4

per cent. It must be noted, however, that their findings were based on better pre-school projects, and not from a random sample of Head Start projects. They are not, therefore, representative of the whole original Head Start population.

In a useful review of the evidence relating to Head Start, Harry McGurk adds a cautionary note. He points out that both mothers and children often got considerable pleasure out of Head Start schemes and increased their confidence as a result of being involved in the programmes. This is important in itself. As McGurk says, there are other values than that of improving IQ scores.

The Educational Priority Area (EPA) programme, has been Britain's major effort in the field of compensatory education. The EPA's embodied the principle of positive discrimination (that extra help should be given to the socially disadvantaged) advocated by the Plowden Report of 1967. The EPA projects were set up by the Labour Secretary of State for Education and Science, Anthony Crossland. They were located in London, Birmingham, Liverpool and the West Riding of Yorkshire. On the basis of their exploratory work, they recommended positive discrimination, especially in the form of pre-schooling, in their report to government in 1971. Plowden aside, the main propagandist and theorist of positive discrimination in Britain has been A H Halsey. The policy of positive discrimination has not been short of critics however and we will briefly review their comments before returning to Halsey's defence.

CRITICISM AND DEFENCE OF COMPENSATORY EDUCATION First is a powerful criticism of the limited scope of positive discrimination based on analysis initially put forward by Barnes and Lucas, but later reiterated by Peter Townsend. They correctly point out that although particular areas of geographical concentration of poverty do exist, the majority of the poor are scattered throughout the country and outside these areas. As a result, positive discrimination can miss the needs of the majority and serve as a smokescreen for penny-pinching by government. Barnes and Lucas refer to the 'ecological fallacy' underlying the EPA

approach: a policy that is generated through area analysis rather than the needs of specific social groups.

The above observations partly provide the basis for a more fundamental criticism by Townsend. He argues that policies of positive discrimination tend to be merely cosmetic whilst the real causes of disadvantage and poverty remain untouched. In his view, these causes are national in scope and structural in nature. He demands industrial, employment, housing and land policies which will radically redistribute wealth and systematically reduce, if not abolish, poverty. In order to illustrate his point, he draws on the experience of an exercise in positive discrimination outside education, the Community Development Project. In particular, the Coventry CDP group argued that in the face of national or even international factors which affected the local context in which they worked, they could do relatively little. For example, a few community workers could not deal with the consequences of thousands being thrown out of work as a result of a recession in car production. They contended that only a national policy of economic redevelopment and social justice could cope. This kind of analysis has received support from the American Christopher Jencks, in his book *Inequality*.

Basil Bernstein's controversial article, *Education Cannot Compensate for Society* (1970), was concerned with the cultural aspects rather than socio-economics of positive discrimination. The essence of his criticism is that compensatory education implies that working class culture is in some sense inferior. The policy implications of this are to direct attention away from the quality of schools and curricula towards supposed inadequacies in working class families. Bernstein suggests that is the wrong emphasis. He argues that it is more important to put right the mainstream of the educational system than to over-concentrate on marginal 'compensatory' reforms. He argues that curriculum reform is needed to take into account the way working class children live their lives – the 'conditions' and 'contexts' of their culture should affect everyday education as much as do those of the middle class. Bernstein is surely correct in this central point.

Educational change that does not affect the central curriculum is likely to be of only peripheral influence. On the other hand, there is no reason why both major reform and special help for the acutely disadvantaged should not occur.

A H Halsey has consistently defended compensatory education against its critics. The starkly assertive title of an article he published in 1980 is *Education Can Compensate*, and it is clearly intended as a reply to Bernstein's piece of ten years before. He especially emphasises the reassuring American evidence of Lazar and

Darlington. He stresses that, given enthusiasm and careful organisation, a pre-school programme of compensatory education can be a 'crucial weapon' of government policy. He fully accepts, however, that the mainstream of the educational system must also be fair and effective as well. Thus, he continues passionately to support comprehensive education. For their part, his Marxist critics continue to wonder whether educational reform can significantly help the disadvantaged in the absence of fundamental social and economic change.

Gender in Education

This section is divided into two parts. First, the academic attainment of females and males is compared and explanations for the differences briefly discussed. Second, the main perspectives on gender and education are introduced and discussed. Each perspective is based on a particular ideological approach which is reflected in both analysis of the current situation and policy suggestions for change.

GENDER AND EDUCATIONAL ATTAINMENT

Concern about gender and educational attainment focuses mainly on the extent to

which females and males perform differently in different subjects and their tendency to study different subjects, given the choice. However, it is not true that males generally attain more qualifications or higher grades than females at school. In fact, the reverse is the case. In 1987/88 62 per cent of females left school in the United Kingdom with at least one GCSE grade A–C or equivalent whereas the figure for males was 54 per cent. On the basis of similar measures, females also perform slightly better at 'A' level.

Figure 4.3 shows the percentage of school leavers with grade A–C at GCSE by subject and sex in 1987–88. The stronger performance of females in languages, including English, and Biology and the stronger performance of males in Maths, Physics and Chemistry has been long entrenched and overall changed little during the nineteen eighties.

Figure 4.4 gives the break-down of subjects studied at university by sex. A comparison with figure 4.3 shows that differential subject specialisation is actually greater at university than school level. Females make up about 15 per cent of those studying engineering, 22 per cent of those studying mathematical sciences and 25 per cent of those studying physical sciences. In contrast, they represent over 60 per cent of students in languages, librarianship, biological sciences, creative arts, studies allied to medicine and about 80 per cent of those in education.

The subject specialisms in which females

Figure 4.3

Percentage of school leavers with grades A - C at GCSE[1]: by subject and sex, 1987/88

▼

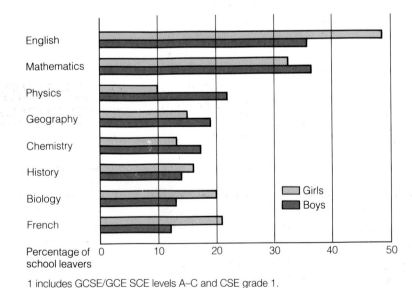

Percentage of school leavers

1 includes GCSE/GCE SCE levels A–C and CSE grade 1.

Source: social trends, 1991.   Source: Department of Education and Science

predominate, especially the more vocational ones such as education and librarianship, parallel the tendency of better qualified women to enter the lower professions rather than the better paid higher professions (see p. 96).This is by no means always because they are not qualified to study subjects likely to lead to higher paid occupations. To what extent the educational and vocational paths typical of better qualified females reflect the way they are socialised and so the way they think of themselves is discussed below. It is also relevant to consider whether a country short of engineers and scientists can afford to 'lose' able females to these areas (see table 4.2).

Note: In some professions, current recruitment to training (see figure 4.4) suggests a somewhat more equal gender balance will gradually develop e.g. in architecture, and medicine and dentistry.

It is not only better qualified females who experience occupational stereotyping. Females with minimal or no qualifications are likely to do unskilled manual work in particular occupational areas and those somewhat better qualified are likely to do routine office work (see p. 186). How education can contribute to occupational sex stereotyping is a major theme in the following pages.

GENDER, EDUCATION AND THE CURRICULUM: PERSPECTIVES

Sandra Acker usefully suggests that there are three main Western feminist theoretical frameworks – liberal, radical and socialist – each of which have an application to education. However, this typology does not include some traditional and/or politically Conservative thinking on gender and education which, for convenience, will be referred to here simply as 'conservative' – with a small 'c'.

The four theoretical areas to be considered are, then:

- **liberal**
- **radical**
- **socialist**
- **conservative**

Gaby Weiner and Madeleine Arnot have suggested that as far as teacher's practice is concerned a simple polarity between an

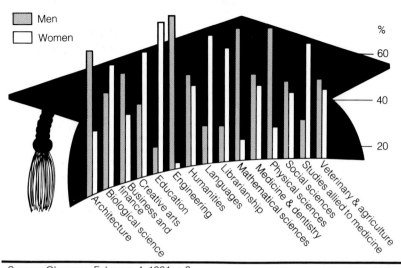

Source: Observer, February 4, 1991, p.9.

equal opportunities/girl friendly approach and an anti-sexist/girl centred approach occurs. However, as we shall see later, Weiner and Arnot do not consider their own and Acker's typology to be mutually exclusive.

LIBERAL FEMINISM AND EDUCATION

The basis of liberal feminism is a commitment to equal opportunities for males and females. The Sex Discrimination Act of 1975 has generally been interpreted to mean that females are entitled to the same treatment as males in the main areas of public life including education. The Equal Opportunities Commission (EOC) has responsibility for implementing the Sex Discrimination Act, including taking relevant cases to law.

With the passing of the 1975 Act, it was made clear for the first time that the formal, public and legal position in Britain was opposed to sex discrimination just as the

▲

Figure 4.4

Degrees of difference:

How the gender divide

affected subjects

studied by full-time

university

undergraduates in

1989-90

Table 4.2

Women in Professions

▼

	Men %	Women %		Men %	Women %
Accountants	90.3	9.7	Engineers	99.5	0.5
Architects	92.2	7.8	Solicitors	78.6	21.4
Barristers	79.8	21.2	Surveyors	94.3	5.7
Dentists	76.8	23.2	Vets	73.5	26.5
Doctors (GPs)	77.6	22.4			
(Surgeons)	96.8	3.2			

(Source: UK Inter-Professional Group, 1990)

Race Relations Acts had done so in respect to racial discrimination (sport and single sex schools were exempt from the terms of the Sex Discrimination Act). Since the Act was passed, the previously widespread practice whereby schools required females to study certain subjects and males to study others became illegal and virtually ceased. The Act not only banned sexual discrimination (direct and indirect or unintended) but also encouraged the active promotion of equal opportunity. Some commentators such as A Dora (1985) have stressed the potential of the Act to legitimate strong policies of equal opportunity.

Others have been more critical of what they consider to be the limited practical effect of the Act on gender equality in schools. Thus, Madeleine Arnot considers that while the EOC has often effectively intervened with local education authorities to prevent curriculum differentiation between the sexes, it has done relatively little to promote anti-sexist projects and has been 'disappointing for those who wish to see greater evidence of sex equality in schooling – i.e., improvements in the quality of schooling for girls and in the experience of women teachers' ('Political lip-service or radical reform' in M Arnot and G Weiner ed., Gender and the Politics of Schooling (Hutchinson, 1987)). As we shall see, these kind of initiatives have occurred more through individual teachers, groups, schools and sometimes Local Education Authorities.

The terms of the Sex Discrimination Act applicable to education did represent an important clarification of principle and guide to practice. Previous major pronouncements by government on gender and education had been at best ambiguous and, at worst, reinforced a highly traditional version of roles and expectations. Ann Marie Wolpe's analysis of the 'gender content' of three government reports on aspects of secondary education – *The Norwood Report* (1943), *The Crowther Report* (1959) and the *Newson Report* (1963) – makes this point strongly:

In conclusion it can be said that none of the three reports considered the reality of the situation which applies to such a large proportion of women, viz as workers outside the home. Their focus on women and marriage provides them with a means of extricating themselves from this situation. The stated overriding concern of girls with their future marriages provides them with the means of legitimation for this omission. Having established this dichotomy between the world of work and marriage all three reports are able to provide an ideological basis for the perpetuation of an education system which does not open up new vistas or possibilities to the majority of girls.

Wolpe in Flude and Ahier, 1976: 141

RADICAL-FEMINISM AND EDUCATION

Radical-feminists consider that patriarchy – the system of domination of females by males – is the central issue for women. In their view, patriarchy permeates the whole of society and the whole of the educational system. They therefore address and attempt to confront sex-bias not only in the allocation of the subject curriculum to females and males but in all aspects of the educational system. It will be helpful to look at this in terms of the cultural reproduction of patriarchy and the structure of patriarchy in each case both within education and society.

Dale Spender has analysed the cultural reproduction of patriarchy in several publications of which perhaps the most relevant to education is *Invisible Women: The Schooling Scandal* (Writers and Readers Cooperative, 1982). She finds patriarchal assumptions in both the formal and hidden curriculum. About the former, she writes:

What is considered inherently interesting is knowledge about men. Because men control the records, and the value system, it is generally believed that it is men who have done all the exciting things: it is men who have made history, made discoveries, made inventions and performed feats of skill and courage – according to men. These are the important activities and only men have engaged in them, so we are led to believe. And so it is that the activities of men become the curriculum.

Spender, 1982: 58

Spender is equally concerned to uncover the processes within the hidden or informal curriculum that maintain and reproduce patriarchy. She finds that teachers, often unconsciously, behave towards males and females in ways which reinforce the self-concepts of the former as dominant and the latter as submissive. Thus, her video-tapes of lessons frequently show teachers paying substantially more attention to boys (partly in response to boys demands) even when boys are in a minority in the class.

Radical-feminists seek to raise girls' awareness of the structure of patriarchy in schools, the workplace and within families. One strategy for doing this is establishing female discussion and support groups in which patriarchy can be examined and the confidence and skills of females to combat it developed. Support groups and also less formal networking among female teachers can be helpful in dealing with such matters as female career advancement in male dominated institutions, 'routine' sexism and sexual harrassment.

Some radical feminists, including Dale Spender, have argued that single-sex schools or classes can be beneficial to girls as they remove the negative influence of boys referred to above. There is some debated evidence that more females chose to study scientific subjects in single sex institutions and that their attainment is better (however, the EOC cites data to suggest that other factors – such as selection – account for these trends). Others argue that separating females from males is hardly a good preparation for dealing with them after leaving school. They contend that raising teachers' awareness, changing the 'male-centred' nature of science curricula and other measures can be effective in improving the performance of females in scientific subjects in a co-educational environment. The *Girls into Science and Technology project* (GIST) achieved promising results on the basis of such strategies.

SOCIALIST-FEMINISM AND EDUCATION

Socialist-feminists consider that gender inequality is deeply linked to the class nature of capitalist society and that for female liberation to be achieved both inequalities must effectively be dealt with.

However, socialist-feminists have increasingly tended to adopt the same kind of immediate reforms as those favoured by radical-feminists except that they consistently seek to raise class as well as gender issues and particularly to link the two. They see the educational system as reproducing gender inequalities in a way that broadly suits the needs of capitalism. Thus, Christine Griffin attempted to show how it is that working class girls get working class jobs – if routine office as well as factory work is assumed to be working class (see p. 88).

Certainly, socialist-feminists have been able convincingly to show that gender identity is greatly affected by the class experience of a particular female or male i.e. that gender identity is mediated by class. In this respect a telling study is Katherine Clarricoates' *The Importance of Being Ernest ... Emma ... Tom ... Jane: The Perception and Categorisation of Gender Conformity and Gender Deviation in Primary Schools.*

Clarricoates examined gender socialisation in four different types of school of which two will be considered here:

- **A traditional working class school, 'Dock Side',**
- **A modern suburban 'rural' middle class school 'Apple gate'.**

In Dock Side the behaviour and norms considered 'typical' of the two sexes were 'sharply differentiated'. 'Toughness' and 'masculinity' were expected of the boys (as described by Willis p. 88) whereas the girls were expected to be cooperative and helpful. When girls did do well academically this tended to be 'explained away' and seen as 'wanting to please rather than being intelligent'. Separation and even segregation was imposed on the two sexes – emphasising difference, polarity and even opposition – 'separate playgrounds, separate toilets, separate games, even separate lists on registers'.

Whereas in Dock Side high academic achievement was 'neither highly valued nor expected', the opposite applied at Applegate – for both sexes. Sex-separation was considerably less rigid at Applegate although not to the point where complete role symmetry occurred. Thus, when a male pupil dressed-up as a female, the ridicule of his peers went unchecked by the teacher.

Equal opportunities/girl friendly	Anti-sexist/girl-centred
Persuading girls into science and technology	Recognizing the importance of girl-centred study; for example, what is 'herstory', or girl- and woman-centred science or technology.
Providing a compulsory common core of subject, to include 'hard' sciences for girls and humanities for boys	Providing girls with skills and knowledge to challenge the male system in the workplace and the home
Rearranging option blocks to reduce stereotyped choices	Giving girls a sense of solidarity with other members of their sex, and hence greater confidence and motivation.
Analysing sexism in textbooks, readers and resources	Widening girls' horizons while not denigrating the lives and work of their mothers, female friends and women in the community.
Reviewing school organisation – for example, registers, assemblies, uniform, discipline	Changing the nature of schooling: replacing hierarchy, competitiveness, authoritarianism and selection with co-operation, democracy, egalitarianism and community.
Producing in-service courses and policy guidelines	Exploring the relationship between sexuality, women's oppression and sexual harassment in school and the workplace
Establishing mixed-sex working parties to develop and monitor school policy	Establishing schoolgirls' and women's support groups
Creating posts for equal opportunities	Decision-making through wide consultation and collective working

(Source: Arnot and Weiner 1987: 356)

▲

Table 4.3

Liberal and

Radical/Socialist

Feminist Educational

Strategies

Aggression was not approved of for either sex but more tolerated in the case of boys. Clarricoate's findings appear to complement Elizabeth Bott's much earlier (1957) in which she found that conjugal roles in middle class families tended to be joint (more similar) and those in working class families to be more segregated. Already, in primary school differential class and gender influences seem to be shaping future patterns of behaviour.

The very scope of socialist-feminist analysis, embracing patriarchy, capitalism and their inter-relations, makes the task of describing, let alone producing, an alternative education for females all the more daunting. Sheila Miles and Chris Middleton argue that much more than equal opportunities is needed and that 'education to make children aware of their

social and political environment, including anti-sexist and anti-racist work, has to be built into the foundations of the curriculum, not added as an afterthought' in (M Hammer and M Flude: 1988, p. 204).

At a more preliminary level, the right-hand column of table 4.3 contains some socialist influenced strategies of an egalitarian and participatory kind.

CONSERVATIVE PERSPECTIVES ON FEMINISM IN EDUCATION

At the time of writing (1991), Conservative administrations have been in power for twelve consecutive years. Until the Education Reform Act of 1988, Conservative central government intervened little in gender matters in education. Thus local authorities and individual teachers and schools were largely left to pursue their own policies within the existing framework of legislation. To that extent, Conservative administrations accepted the liberal framework of equal opportunities set up by the 1975 Sex Discrimination Act.

The establishing of a legally compulsory national curriculum did have profound implications for gender and education. Hence forward girls (as well as boys) would be required to take science to 16 and boys would be required to take a foreign language as well as English to 16. These requirements remained in place even when the compulsory national curriculum for the years 14 to 16 was trimmed back to five subjects in 1991. Ironically, these reforms could be interpreted as a move in the direction of the firm action demanded of central government by many socialist feminists to establish a compulsory curriculum in which girls could not 'opt out of' the 'hard' sciences and maths. However, there is a proviso in the Act referring to science which allows students to study this area of the curriculum for either 20 per cent or 12.5 per cent of their timetable, with only the former providing an adequate route to 'A' level. Miles and Middleton have commented on the 12.5 per cent route that 'pupils taking this option, the majority of whom will undoubtedly be girls, will face severe constraints on their choice of jobs'. However, Miles and Middleton themselves make the point that there is no basis for devaluing or undervaluing the subjects in which females currently out perform males.

It remains to be seen how the science provisions of the national curriculum evolve. However, it may be that the government introduced them less in a spirit of sex equality and more because it perceived a 'national economic need' to do so. It may have decided that the reduction in the number of young people (due to low birth rates in the nineteen seventies/eighties) and the shortage of scientists and engineers has made it necessary to foster latent female scientific talent. This interpretation is lent plausibility by the absence of any more general concern about sexism in the Act.

Some traditionalists have attacked the awareness (of partiarchy and sexism)

raising and other activities of radical and socialist feminists referred to above. Mervyn Hiskett suggests that these feminists are attempting to 'hi-jack' the minds of young people whose parents would often not approve if they were really aware of what was happening ('Should Sons and Daughters be Brought Up Differently?: Radical Feminism in Schools in D Anderson, 'Full Circle?' (The Social Affairs Unit, 1988)). Hiskett argues that girls should be allowed to decide for themselves how they want to balance domestic and paid-work commitments. Perhaps Hiskett is being a little simplistic. The national curriculum itself massively prescribes what the young should learn. That said, all education should be critical.

'Race' and Ethnicity in Education

Two main issues have emerged in the context of 'race' and ethnicity in education. The first concerns the attainment level of the children of more recent immigrant minorities, particularly of black minorities. The second concerns the nature of the curriculum in a society in which a number of minorities live.

BLACK MINORITIES AND EDUCATIONAL ATTAINMENT

In the nineteen sixties and seventies, the most frequently expressed educational concern in relation to black minorities was about the low average attainment level of children of Afro-Carribbean origin. Although this concern continues, it has developed into a more general awareness of the variety of levels of attainment of the children of various minorities. Differences between the performances of ethnic groups is shown in the research of Florisse Kysel into the 'O' level and CSE results in 1985 of children from twelve groups (including 'other') in the former Inner London Education Authority. As can be seen from table 4.4 the performance of the children of certain minorities, notably Indian and African Asian, exceeds that of English, Scottish, Welsh and Irish (ESWI) while that of others, notably Bangladeshi and Turkish, is considerably worse. The performance

score is arrived at by giving a specific number of points for each grade from 7 for an 'O' level to 1 for a CSE5. Before attempting any explanation of the performance differences between groups, it will be helpful to compare the rate of improvement between groupings over time.

It is noticeable that whereas the improvement rate of ESWI pupils and Asian pupils has slowed that of 'Caribbean' and pupils of other minority groups has been substantial.

A considerable range of sociological explanations has been put forward for why some minority groups perform well academically and others do not. We discuss these below. First, however, it needs to be stated that for those who consider that black people are genetically less intelligent than Caucasian (Indo-European) people, no problem is presented by the evidence of their comparatively low achievement. Jensen, for instance, believes that the fact that 'negroes' (sic) score, on average, 12 to 15 points less on general intelligence tests than whites is a clear indication that they are innately substantially less intelligent. From his point of view, the kindest course would be to accept this and to cease trying to make them achieve levels of academic attainment that are generally beyond them. A variety of arguments can be cited against Jensen's view, but here we will concentrate

	Average performance score	Number of pupils
African	16.9	426.
African Asian	22.7	162
Arab	14.0	91
Bangladeshi	8.7	333
Caribbean	13.6	2,981
ESWI*	15.2	10,685
Greek	17.6	243
Indian	24.5	398
Pakistani	21.3	231
SE Asian	19.1	300
Turkish	11.9	268
Other	21.3	940

(Source: Florisse Kysel, 'Ethnic Background and Examination Results', Educational Research, Vol 30, No. 1, June, 1988.)

* ESWI = English, Scottish, Welsh and Irish.

		Performance score	Number of pupils
Asian [1]	1976	18.4	389
	1985	18.9	1,124
Caribbean	1976	10.3	2,382
	1985	13.6	2,981
ESWI	1976	14.0	19,820
	1985	15.2	10,685
Other [2]	1976	14.5	1,808
	1985	18.4	2,268
All	1976	13.7	24,398
	1985	15.6	17,058

1 Includes African Asian, Bangladeshi, Indian and Pakistani pupils

2 Includes all groups other than Asian, Caribbean and ESWI

▲

Table 4.4

Average performance

scores

▶

Table 4.5 (Far right)

exclusively on the social factors which might affect the performance of blacks in attainment and in intelligence tests. In view of the exploitation and racism experienced by Afro-Caribbean people, it is perhaps ill-judged if not highly racist, to suggest they are intellectually inferior when convincing social explanations for their educational performance, including the effects of white racism, have not yet been fully explored. We consider these explanations now. In doing so, a comparison is frequently made between Afro-Caribbean and Indian Children as there is a wide gap between their average levels of attainment. The discussion occurs under the following headings:

- **Class and Minority Attainment**
- **Family (Class and Gender)**
- **Racism in Society and Minority Group Responses**
- **Racism in the Educational System**

CLASS AND MINORITY ATTAINMENT

Part of the explanation for the high average attainment level of Indian minority children is that the Indian minority is a relatively middle class group. The same is true of African Asians – many of whom were businesspeople prior to their expulsion from Kenya and Uganda in the late nineteen sixties. During the nineteen fifties and early nineteen sixties, thousands of Indian

doctors, chemists and nurses answered the call of the National Health Service. Others set up small businesses – shops and restaurants – sometimes as a response to being passed over for promotion by white employees. In time, some of these businesses have become medium and even large-scale. In contrast, many more immigrants from Bangladesh and parts of Pakistan were rural peasants and this is reflected particularly in the educational performance of the children of the former group, most of whom are relatively recent immigrants.

Most Afro-Caribbean male immigrants took up manual jobs, mostly skilled or semi-skilled, on immigrating to Britain. Females, who tended to come later, were typically employed in unskilled manual work and, increasingly, routine office work. Their children were, therefore, overwhelmingly working class. Some commentators (Mabey, 1981), argue that this fact alone largely explains why the educational performance of Afro-Caribbean children tends to lag behind that of Indian and white children (both of which groups contain more children from middle class families), Marxists and socialists certainly incline to favour this explanation. However, research by Craft and Craft (1983) does seem to show that Afro-Caribbean working class children attain significantly less than white working class children and that the same is true of middle class children of the two groups. So, while class may explain some of

Examination Performance	White (%)		Asian (%)		West Indian (%)		Other (%)		All (%)		Totals (%)
	MC[a]	WC	MC	WC	MC	WC	MC	WC	MC	WC	
High [b]	31	18	32	16	20	9	26	16	30	16	21
Medium	55	62	58	64	49	51	59	63	56	61	59
Low	14	20	10	21	31	41	16	21	14	23	20

[a]MC = Middle Class, WC = Working Class. These categories are based on OPCS classification. See original paper for further details.

[b]High, Medium, Low. These categories are based on number of GCE 'O' level and/or CSE passes.
(Source: Craft and Craft (1983) in *The Swan Report* 1985: 60)

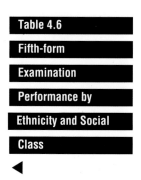

Table 4.6
Fifth-form
Examination
Performance by
Ethnicity and Social
Class
◀

the under-attainment of Afro-Caribbean children, we are still left with the need for further explanation.

FAMILY (CLASS AND GENDER)

The high value put on educational achievement in the Asian community and the active support given by families to children in their studies, partly accounts for the high attainment levels of certain Asian minorities, including Indian. Again, however, the class factor may be relevant in that effective support seems to come particularly from more middle class families. There is a long established higher education network in Indian and middle class (or higher caste) females as well as males are often motivated by family expectation to compete academically.

There is also great enthusiasm for educational achievement in the Afro-Caribbean community (Tizzard, 1988). However, relatively few Afro-Caribbean families have the experience and tradition of seeking higher education and once more this largely reflects their class. Their concern tends to be focused on problems of primary and secondary education. Further, for the large minority of lone parent families in the Afro-Caribbean community, there are inevitable practical problems of time and money in supporting their children's education (see pp. 52–3). However, perhaps the main contrast between the Indian and Afro-Caribbean experience of British education is that there appears to have been a relatively easy 'cultural fit' in the first case but not in the second (see below). Something of a vicious circle of mutual near-rejection has occurred between some Afro-Caribbean children and the educational system. In frustration, many Afro-Caribbean parents have sought extra education for their children outside the state system:

'In every city with a sizeable black population, Saturday schools exist, organised by black community activists, educationalists and parents, running them with a great deal of energy, inspiration and very little else. Parents pay what they can.

(Reva Klein, 'Saturday is the only alternative', Times Educational Supplement, March 15 1991: p. 26).

It is relevant at this point to refer to some limited evidence that Afro-Caribbean females tend to perform better academically than males. Barbara Tizzard et al.'s *Young Children At School In The Inner City* (1988) addresses both the issue of the influence of the home on educational attainment and the relative performance of black (Afro-Caribbean) and white girls and boys. Tizzard et al. tested 343 children, of whom 171 were white and 106 were black, across 30 schools. The study was longitudinal and was carried out between 1982 and 1985. The children were mainly working class.

The study found that parents of both black and white children were interested in and practically supportive of their children's education and that this was especially true of black parents. These findings are reported emphatically:

There is another widely held belief amongst teachers, that black parents are particularly likely to fail to provide adequate educational support for their children. This, too, proved to be a myth. We found that black parents gave their children even more help with school work than white parents, and had a more positive atittude towards giving this help ...

Both black and white parents read aloud to their children with equal frequency – during the reception year 40 per cent said that they read to them every day. The great majority of parents provided their children with books – at school entry, as we saw for ourselves, only a quarter of the children had as few as ten or less books – and similar proportions of black and white parents said that they borrowed children's books from the public library, and attended school meetings.

(Tizzard et al., 1988: 176)

On the matter of the relative performance of black and white girls and boys, it is again worth quoting Tizzard at length:

One of the main aims of our study was to look for factors that might account for differences in the school attainments of boys and girls, and black and white children. At the pre-school stage, we found no significant ethnic differences in early reading, writing and maths skills, or in scores on the WPPSI vocabulary test. The only sex differences at this stage was that both black and white girls were superior to boys in writing. This superiority continued throughout the infant school. At the end of infant school, there was still no overall ethnic difference in attainment, but the black girls had emerged as ahead of all other groups in both reading and writing, whilst black boys were doing worst. Both black and white boys made more progress than girls at maths, with white boys making the most progress. When we retested the children at the end of the first year of junior school, there were still no significant overall ethnic differences in attainment. By now there was a significant sex difference in reading, with girls definitely ahead of boys.

(Tizzard et al., 1988: 180–1)

Tizzard goes on to suggest that racism might play an increased role in the underachievement of Afro-Caribbean children in later schooling and this is discussed below. Even so, there is fragmentary evidence that black girls may continue to maintain an edge over black boys into secondary school. Geoffrey Driver's survey of school leavers in five multi-racial inner-city schools showed that Afro-Caribbean pupils and, especially, the girls achieved results that were generally better than those of English boys and girls. Driver attributes the success of the girls to the strength derived from the matrifocal family tradition in Jamaica and carried over, out of practical necessity, to England. A major problem with Driver's research is that he does not control for social class variables and it may be that he is comparing groups of white and black children of different socio-economic background.

Another limited piece of evidence that Afro-Caribbean females attain at higher educational levels than Afro-Caribbean males is provided by Mary Fuller (1982) who in a single case study found that in the 'academic' band of the fifth form of a mixed comprehensive school, black girls averaged 7.6 'O' level and CSE exam passes as against 5.6 for the black boys. Fuller's study is full of illuminating detail. She observes that the girls 'formed a discernible subculture within the school' which emerged 'from the girls' positive acceptance of the fact of being black and female'. They were committed to achieving academic success but were not pro-school. Acadamic and ultimately career success were necessary both materially and psychologically: the first because many black women have to be major breadwinners, the second to give them a sense of self-worth. However, they had no normative commitment to general conformity at school. There are three aspects to this attitude. First, to appear too keen might attract the ridicule of black boys with whom they saw themselves as partly in competition. Second, their self-image tended to be that of fun-lovers not 'goody-goodies'. Third, they realised that public examinations were not assessed by their teachers so there was no undue need to please them.

On the basis of her data, Tizzard is able to offer no explanation for the apparent difference between the attainment of Afro-Caribbean females and males. However, both Driver and Fuller hypothesise that the relatively independent and central role of women in the Afro-Caribbean community both domestically and in paid work may act as a motivation to achievement. They are particularly accustomed to hard work and coping. What, then, explains the underachievement of Afro-Caribbean males? Several studies suggest that the process of rejection of Afro-Caribbean males by white society and their response to rejection may, among other effects, result in educational underachievement. The next two sections are largely concerned with this issue.

RACISM IN SOCIETY AND MINORITY YOUTH RESPONSES

Chapter 9 presents evidence that substantial racism occurs against black minorities in Britain. Indian and Afro-Caribbean minorities have coped with racism in some ways similarly and in others quite differently. A common reaction in both communities, especially among the second and third generations since immigration, is anger. This seems a psychologically healthy response to prejudice and discrimination. As far as Afro-Caribbean youth is concerned anger seems a less self-damaging reaction than the low self-esteem reported in earlier research among black children in both the United States and Britain. In the course of research in the Southern United States, Robert Coles noted that the drawings of black children contained some strange features. They tended to picture themselves as small, dowdy and, sometimes, with various features missing, whereas they portrayed white children in a large and positive way. Even the weather and landscape on the pictures depicting the white children were better! More recently, Bernard Coard came across a similar phenomenon in Britain (*Urban education*, 1971). However, since the nineteen sixties positive images of 'black power' and 'black is beautiful' have been readily available to black youth and judging from black youth culture, these are the ones that have been imitated.

It is arguable that the response of Afro-Caribbean youth, especially males, to racism differs from that of Indian youth in the way and perhaps the extent to which they reject white institutions, including education, and pursue alternative means of opportunity and expression (see pp. 204–5 and p. 297).

Stuart Hall goes so far as to refer to a culture of resistance to dominant power structures among Afro-Caribbean youth. Indian middle class youth, despite common resentment at racism and a willingness to defend themselves against intimidation, are able to use the professional and business resources of their own community and their own qualifications to make socio-economic progress. Because of different circumstances, they have tended to 'negotiate' a different 'solution' to the problems posed by British society.

RACISM IN THE EDUCATIONAL SYSTEM

A distinction must be made here between individual and institutional racism although these terms are discussed at greater length in a later chapter (p. 192). Individual racism refers to the racial prejudice or discrimination of one person against another. Institutional racism occurs when a set of rules or an organisational system operates in a racist way. Both individual and institutional racism may be intentional or unintentional although some definitions of institutional racism assume it to be unintentional. How far is the educational system characterised by individual or institutional racism?

The analysis that the British educational system is institutionally racist is as much a political as a sociological one in that it is aimed at changing the system in an anti-racist direction. Chris Mullard argues that the relatively small number of black Head Teachers and other more senior teachers, the relatively high number of Afro-Caribbean children in lower streams and designated educationally sub-normal and the racially biased (in his view) curriculum demonstrate that the British educational system is structurally racist. What Mullard suggests should be done about this is discussed shortly.

There are no nationally representative social surveys which quantify the extent of individual racism among teachers. However, a relatively large scale study by P A Green (unpublished Phd thesis) is reported by Cohen and Manion. Green observed and recorded 70 white British teachers in multi-ethnic teaching situations. He then asked them to complete an attitude inventory in which a scale designed to measure their prejudice had been 'hidden'. Twelve highly prejudiced teachers, and twelve who scored low on prejudice were identified. Cohen and Manion summarise Green's findings on the differences between these two groups in classroom interaction – established through analysis of his recordings:

1 Highly intolerant teachers gave significantly less time to accepting the feelings of children of West Indian origin.

2 Highly intolerant teachers gave only minimal praise to children of West Indian origin.

3 Highly intolerant teachers gave significantly less attention to the ideas contributed by children of West Indian origin.

4 Highly intolerant teachers used direct teaching of individual children significantly less with pupils of West Indian origin.

5 Highly intolerant teachers gave significantly more authoritative directions to children of West Indian origin.

6 Highly intolerant teachers gave significantly less time to children of West Indian origin to initiate contribution to class discussions.

Cohen and Manion comment that what is now needed is qualitative data on teacher-pupil interaction in the multi-ethnic classroom to complement Green's more quantitative approach.

Mac an Ghaill's *Young, Gifted and Black* (1988) provides qualitative data on this issue not in the form of observed classroom interaction but in the form of interviews with members of various pupil peer groups, including an anti-school group of Afro-Caribbean males calling itself the 'Rasta-Heads'. The interviews clearly show that the Rasta-Heads feel they are negatively labelled by teachers. Interestingly, the Rasta-Heads are supported in their view by members of a mainly Indian working class peer group, the Warriors:

MM: Do you think that West Indians cause more trouble than Asians?

Ashwin: No, don't be stupid, that's what teachers think. The Indians cause just as much trouble.

Raj: The West Indians are more obvious some'ow. They're seen more easily ...

MM: Do you think they are more dumber?

Raj: No I don't.

Iqbal: No, because they can do as well as Indian kids, better than a lot of them. The ones who have been in most trouble were the brainy ones, like Kevin and Michael, in the first year they were the brainy ones, really brainy.

(Mac an Ghaill, 1988: 122–3)

Although something is clearly going badly wrong for many young Afro-Caribbeans in school, it may not be the educational system alone or primarily that is causing it. Tizzard (1988) leaves open the possibility that it is factors in the wider society that may be decisive in alienating many young Afro-Caribbeans, especially males. A highly statistical analysis by David Drew and John Gray questions whether schools have a major negative effect on the attainment of Afro-Caribbean children arguing that their performance at sixteen can be roughly predicted at twelve without reference to any 'racist factor' (*The Black-White Gap in Exam Achievement* (Sheffield University, 1990)).

CONCLUSION The average attainment of children of minority groups varies greatly. It seems likely that class is a more important variable than ethnicity or racism in explaining average levels of attainment. However, the tradition and resources of an ethnic group may play a part in how its members negotiate the educational system. The attainment levels of Afro-Caribbean children, especially males, continue to give cause for concern, despite improvement. Whether the cause of their relatively strong resistance to the educational system lies within education or the wider society or both is open to debate.

MINORITIES AND THE CURRICULUM: PERSPECTIVES

What is the appropriate curriculum for a society which is multi-ethnic and in which substantial racism occurs. We will briefly review four approaches:

■ **The Assimilationist**
■ **The Multi-cultural (Pluralist)**
■ **The Anti-Racist (Radical/Marxist)**
■ **Educational Needs**

The assimilationist approach was the general 'commonsense' of the nineteen fifties and early nineteen sixties. It was widely assumed that black immigrants and their children would eventually learn to behave like white Britons. This applied to education as to other matters. A more sophisticated version of this approach was put forward by the new right in the nineteen eighties. Thus, Ray Honeyford, a head teacher in Bradford, argued that it is the role of the schools to teach a common national culture – whatever particular minorities might wish to do privately. A modified version of this approach is apparent in some aspects of the national curriculum as it has been developed under Conservative governments. The emphasis on British history, English literature, the Christian religion in the curriculum exemplifies this. However, the Educational Reform Act (1988) also requires the multicultural nature of British society to be recognised across the curriculum – although some have doubted the strength of this commitment.

The multicultural approach argues that minorities are part of British society and culture and that this should be fully reflected in the curriculum, which should therefore be multicultural. The multicultural movement has helped to broaden and enliven the curriculum but has been criticised as superficial and 'merely' concerned with culture – 'saris, samosas and steel bands'! In particular, anti-racists have argued that multiculturalism fails to address the central problem of racism.

Anti-racists want to rid the British educational system, including the curriculum, of racism (see p. 105). Given that they consider that the educational system is 'structured' in a racist way, this is a sizeable task. It would require the appointment of many more black teachers and educational administrators, particularly at a senior level, and confrontation of the 'racist' nature of much of British imperial history and contemporary society. When the borough of Brent attempted to embark on such a policy, it attracted massive negative coverage from the popular media and a visit from the national educational inspectorate.

Maureen Stone's *The Education of the Black Child in Britain* (Fontana, 1981) argues that the priority of black parents is that the educational system should meet the educational needs of their children, particularly the three 'r's'. Multiculturalism, especially if incompetently handled by white liberals, could detract from this. Black children respond best to straightforward teaching and discipline, not lax progressivism. Smith and Tomlinson's study of 20 urban comprehensive schools between 1981–1988 can be interpreted to support Stone (Policy Studies Institute, 1988). They conclude that schools which are effective for white children are also effective for black children. In other words, both benefit from good teaching. Of course, multiculturalism and anti-racism are compatible with good teaching but should not occur at its expense.

A Conservative Revolution in Education and Training? ERA (1988) and Beyond

The Educational Reform Act (ERA) of 1988 is widely regarded as the most significant piece of legislation since the Butler Act of 1944. The main points of the Act are summarised below. However, a variety of measures and policies have occurred both before and after the Act which relate to these main points. The following list, therefore, will provide a basis for discussing these as well as the content of the Act.

- The establishment of a national core curriculum (subjects that must be studied by all pupils).

- The introduction of national standardised tests in certain key subjects at ages seven, eleven, fourteen and sixteen.
- Local management of schools (LMS) – headteachers and governors allowed greater control of budgets and to decide how much to spend on such matters as heating, books and teachers.
- Open enrolment: this means that schools will be able to expand their numbers if there is the demand

without the local authority being able to stop them.

■ **Opting out: parents and governors will be given the right to receive money directly from the Government and so 'opt out' of local authority control. 'Opted out' schools will run their own affairs, including the hiring and firing of teachers and hiring certain services e.g. catering.**

■ **Inner London Education Authority to be abolished.**

The above points can be divided into two. The first two deal with curriculum and the remainder deal with establishing a form of 'free market' in schools. In reading what follows it should be remembered that the precise shape and outcome of the above reforms is still in the 'making'. It is not possible to make any real judgement yet.

THE NATIONAL CURRICULUM AND TESTING

The principle of a national curriculum has become relatively uncontentious particularly in its milder form established in 1991 which required only English, Maths, Science, Technology and a Foreign Language to be studied to 16. However, as was discussed above, the content of and balance between various subjects has been a matter of intense disagreement. A main criticism is that the national curriculum is developing as too nationalistic and fails adequately to reflect Britain's own multi-cultural identity, or to embrace 'Europe 92', the emerging 'Third World', and the post cold war era.

The debate on testing is likely to remain lively. The government sees testing as a way of monitoring standards and of letting parents know how well their children (and the school they attend) are doing. Critics point out that schools differ greatly in their socio-economic intake and the publication of test results (compulsory, except for the tests at 7) may lead to grossly unfair comparisons. In addition, the arguments against eleven-plus have also been raised against the new, extended system of testing – although it is not clear yet whether tests will be used for selection.

Much of the concern with raising educational standards reflects an unease at

Britain's relative economic decline. By most measures, general educational standards in Britain have declined relative to those of other major industrialised nations, notably Germany, France and Japan. While it is highly questionable whether Conservative politicians were right to blame educationalists so severely for Britain's decline, it is generally agreed that to halt it, educational standards must be improved, and the numbers of young people remaining in education or training to eighteen be substantially increased. The three main parties agree that vocational education must be expanded and improved in quality. The Conservative government put the burden and responsibility of training mainly in the hands of business people who dominate the Training and Enterprise Councils (TECs).

As an editorial in the *Times Educational Supplement* observed:

> *The TECs will be a critical test-bed of the Government ideology that a skilled workforce should be trained according to the ideas and cash of local businessmen, rather than through government agencies or education departments.*
> *(TES, 22 March 1991: 23)*

As in the case of the TECs, throughout the nineteen eighties central government tended to remove vocationally oriented curricula and, to some extent, technological harming, out of the Department of Education. Both the Youth Training Scheme (YTS) and the Technical and Vocational Education Initiative (TVEI) were funded by the Manpower Services Commission (MSC) which was run for several years by the former businessman, David Young. In this way, the government, and particularly Mrs Thatcher hoped to effect a 'cultural revolution' in the education system in which the status of business would be enhanced and interest in technical and business careers increased.

While the need for improved technical and vocational education is undoubted, many educationalists felt that their professional independence and judgement was being threatened by the above reforms. In particular, they wanted to maintain as a clear priority that – once a pupil has acquired basic skills – education is primarily about learning to think critically (i.e. for oneself), including about the role and performance of business in society. The perhaps mythical story of one inspector 'fleeing' the Department of Education and Science in the early days of Thatcherism with the words 'The mechanics are taking over' illustrates the concern.

THE 'FREE MARKET' PACKAGE

The 'free market' aspects of the 1988 Act are far-reaching in their implications. Open enrolment allowed parents – or, 'customers' as official jargon sometimes has it – to choose which school their children should attend, subject to the school's physical capacity. Local Management of Schools gives schools more freedom from local authority control, particularly budgetary, thus, enabling more choice in expenditure. The much more radical 'opting out' provision allows schools, under certain conditions and procedures, to apply to the Secretary of State to leave local authority control entirely. 'Opted Out' schools are then maintained by a grant from central government. In 1991, the Secretary of State for Education, Kenneth Clarke, stated that he hoped that within five years a majority of schools would have 'opted out'. He also removed an original provision of the Act requiring schools to retain their character (e.g. grammar, comprehensive) at the time

of opting out for at least five years. The abolition of the Inner London Education Authority was part of the general move towards decentralising educational provision.

The 1988 Act increased the financial and planning powers of individual schools at the expense of local education authorities. The argument for retaining local education authority power is that it can plan on the basis of the needs of the area as a whole. Thus, it can ensure that the requirements of special needs children are met within the local system (which may not happen in a largely 'opted out area'). Most crucially, local authorities have been the agents for introducing and managing local comprehensive systems. The purpose of the comprehensive system is to increase equality of opportunity and to provide a generally egalitarian educational and social environment within a sound educational context. If, presumably on the basis of self-interest, large numbers of comprehensive schools opt out and become selective, then, this system will be gravely weakened. Those who favour an increase in grammar school type education see this as a good thing. Critics envisage that such a process will involve the exclusion of millions of individuals and thousands of schools, thus again creating a two-tier educational system of winners and losers.

SUMMARY

1   The main educational issues in the post-war period have been concerned with class, gender, race/ethnicity and attainment, and more recently with educational standards and the relationship between education and industry. The main educational perspectives are functionalist, Marxist, liberal (reformist), 'free market', and interactionist.

2   One of the main functions of education is the socialisation of the young and thus the reproduction of a society's culture. Durkheim stresses the necessity of such socialisation for a society's effective continuation and Marxists emphasise that intentionally or not working and middle class children are largely socialised differently within the educational system. Paul Willis describes how 'working class lads get working class jobs' and Christine Griffin describes how gender crucially effects class in the context of educational socialisation. Liberals recognise the importance of class in educational socialisation but stress that, partly as a result of education, a person's class of origin may not be their class of destination, i.e., education can enable

social mobility to occur.

3 The perspectives on the relationship of education to the economy are in each case closely linked to what they say about socialisation. What occurs through educational socialisation greatly affects job prospects. Functionalists and hereditarian psychologists argue that the educational system is broadly effective in selecting people for appropriate roles. Marxists argue that, on the contrary, the educational system helps to reproduce and legitimate the class structure of capitalist society. Liberal, A H Halsey disagrees with both, arguing that the educational system has the potential more effectively to reach disadvantaged groups.

4 Two aspects of the role of schools are specifically considered. First is the process of labelling and stereotyping which can reinforce class (and gender and racial) disadvantage. Second is the issue of whether, regardless of the social origins of pupils, a 'good' school can significantly help them. The answer is that it can but schools alone cannot wholly compensate for wider social inequality and disadvantage.

5 The first major area of educational policy in the post-war period concerned class and equality of opportunity. Both the tripartite system and the comprehensive system were initially conceived as attempts to bring about greater equality of opportunity and to tap previously 'wasted' sources of talent and ability. Compensatory education was relatively a more socialist policy in that it attempted to reverse disadvantage in homes and communities.

6 Gender is a second area of educational policy in which issues of equality arise. Average attainment of males and females is now roughly equal, but differential subject specialisation remains an issue. Actual reform such as that embodied in the Sex Discrimination Act largely reflected liberal views of equality of opportunity. Radical feminists and socialist feminists would go further. Both seek to challenge patriarchy in all its aspects within education and by implication in society. This involves a variety of forms of 'consciousness raising'.

7 Race/ethnicity is a third area of educational policy in which issues of inequality arise. The education attainment level of children of given minority groups is highly varied. Although the attainment level of Afro-Caribbean children seems to be improving, there are a variety of factors which may still disadvantage them educationally.

8 There are a number of perspectives on race/ethnicity in education. Assimilationists consider that the educational system should be used to enable minority groups to adapt to British culture. Multiculturalists believe that schools and the curriculum should reflect the variety of ethnic culture. Anti-racists argue that racism within education – individual and structural – should be opposed. The 'basic needs' approach is not incompatible with the other perspectives but stresses that the prime purpose of education for black and white children is the teaching of necessary skills.

9 The 1988 Educational Reform Act inaugurated a potential conservative revolution in education. Its key aspects are a centrally prescribed national curriculum and system of testing and the creation of a 'free market' in schools – at the expense of local education authorities. The former has been criticised as rigid, cumbersome and even authoritarian, and the latter as likely to produce greater inequalities in the provision of education between areas and social groups.

Gender and education is an area in which both a substantial amount of theoretical analysis and a good deal of practical reform has occured. A piece of research which linked the two would be demanding but potentially rewarding. You could attempt to analyse the 'gender equality' reforms and activities in your own institution in terms of the leading feminist positions: liberal, radical and socialist – and perhaps also establish the basis of any opposition to them. You might well find differences in the views of 'leading players'. Thus, a head teacher may take a different view of matters than, let us say, a sociology teacher.

It would be essential precisely to define the focus of such a piece of research. Essentially, it is about the relationship between theories and practice. Does belief by certain individuals in a particular theory explain why particular changes have

RESEARCH AND COURSEWORK°

occurred in your institution? Or is there little apparent connection between theory and practice? You need to decide which issues you want to explore and how you. Are likely to need copies of the institution's key policy statements on 'gender equality' and to require to interview leading policy-makers within the instituion. There are easier subjects to research in this area – such as the relationship between gender and subject choice or performance or between ethnicity and educational performance, but these too would have to be adequately 'theorised'. A current issue is the introduction of National Curriculum testing in schools. Do the views of parents and teachers contrast with 'official' statements?

FURTHER READING

Stephen Ball's *Education* (Longman, 1986) is a good basic, if slightly dating, introduction. It needs to be supplemented by something post-ERA (1988). Leslie Bash and David Coulby eds., *The Education Reform Act* (Cassell, 1989) is a useful though quite demanding collection of readings. On education and gender M Arnot and G Weiner eds., *Gender and the Politics of*

Schooling (Hutchinson, 1987) is recommended. On education and race M Mac An Ghail's *Young, Gifted and Black* (Open University Press, 1988) combines gender, race and class perspectives.

QUESTIONS

1 'Schools reinforce social class, ethnic and sexual divisions'. Discuss. (London, 1989)
2 To what extent are schools responsible for the production of deviant subcultures (London, 1990)
3 'Differences in educational achievement are influenced more by

processes within schools than factors outside them.' Examine this view.
(AEB, 1990)

5 Stratification: An Introduction

DEFINITION AND IMPORTANCE OF STRATIFICATION

Stratification is the division of a society or group into hierarchically ordered layers. Members of each layer are considered broadly equal but there is inequality between the layers. Among the main criteria by which people tend to be stratified are: class, gender, race/ethnicity and age. However, the relevant criterion for stratification can vary greatly according to context: speed for sprinters, dexterity for conjurors, or (among other things) oratorical skills for politicians.

The division of society into layers, or strata (stratum – singular), as they are more frequently called, is often compared to geological formation. But to compare social stratification to layers of rocks, one on top of each other, suggests more rigidity in social structure than is usually found. If we remind ourselves that the relationship between geological strata can shift and change, the simile begins to tell us more about the dynamic relationship between social strata. Further, just as in certain cases, where there is extreme tension between geological strata an earthquake can erupt and change the structure of the land, so too, extreme social conflict, in the form of revolution or invasion, can overturn a given social structure.

It would be a small-minded contemporary sociologist who failed to recognise wider units of stratification than those within the nation-state: most conspicuous is the division of the world into richer and poorer nations. As we will see in chapter 21, the wealthy nations have vied for influence in the poorer or 'Third' World, using as their means 'aid', and in some cases military intervention.

Stratification on the bases of the important criteria mentioned above – class, gender, race/ethnicity, and age – should be analysed in an international as well as a national context. The capitalist class, whether seen in individual terms (e.g. Rupert Murdoch, the late Robert Maxwell) or institutional terms (e.g. International Publishing Corporation, Maxwell Communications) is increasingly international in scope. Different patterns of gender stratification throughout the world provide challenging comparisons with Western practice (see pp. 484–6). International migration has long meant that race/ethnicity can only be properly understood in an international context. Age provides perhaps the most contrasting international comparison of all with Europe and the United States increasingly 'aging' and most of the rest of the world struggling to maintain young, largely dependent populations.

The term social differentiation is closely associated with that of stratification, although it has even broader application. Differentiation refers to that which makes an individual or group separate and distinct: thus differentiation can provide a basis for categorisation and comparison. For instance, within class strata, occupation, income and education provide criteria for differentiation, classification and comparison. Where differences on the basis of a given criterion, say, class or age are ranked *hierarchically* (e.g. the old being regarded as more important than the young), stratification occurs. The extent to which differentiation inevitably leads to stratification is a matter of debate (see pp. 162–6).

We will introduce the concept of social mobility only briefly here, as a full section will be devoted to it in the next chapter. Social mobility refers to movement either up or down the social scale to a different social status or position. In industrial society this is usually brought about by occupational change.

Theories of Social Stratification

This section is mainly concerned with describing the theories of stratification put forward by Marx and Weber. Influential though these theories have been, neither has been fully adopted as the 'official' basis for presenting class in Britain. The Registrar Generals' social class scale is based on classification according to occupation and a rather simple division of all occupations into manual and non-manual. John Goldthorpe's class schema is also based on occupation but greatly reflects Weber's influence.

Feminists have found all the above theories and classificatory schemes deficient in their tendency to assume that the class position of women is derived from that of men: either husband or father. This issue is discussed at some length below. The relationships between race/ethnicity and class and age and class are analysed in later chapters.

MARX'S THEORY OF STRATIFICATION (CLASS CONFLICT)

THE ORIGIN AND SCOPE OF CLASS CONFLICT

Marx argued that conflict between social classes is inevitable because of their different relationship to the means of production (see pp. 116–17). There is always a dominant and a subordinate class: the former is the class which owns the means of production (e.g. land or machinery) and the latter sells its labour to survive. There are two exceptions to this: the primitive communism of hunting and gathering societies and the mature communism that Marx believed would eventually replace capitalist society. Marx's historical typology of societies is described later (pp. 474–5) and is summarised schematically here:

Primitive Communism	Non-class Society (Simple Equality)
Asiatic Mode of Production Ancient Form of Society Feudalism Capitalism	Class societies
Communism	Non-class Society

Whereas Weber considered that in some societies stratification is based primarily on status (honour/prestige) rather than class differences, Marx considered that class is always the over-riding basis of social stratification. Thus, Weber considered that status differences embodied in the law and supported by military might predominated in feudal or estate societies. Similarly, in caste societies, such as Hindu India, status differences, sanctified by religion, predominate. In contrast, Marx considered that it was the economic control and power of the feudal nobility and of the Hindu upper class/castes that was the basis of their dominant position in society. Marx viewed as mere ideological convenience the claim that such wealth and power was sanctioned by law or religion – whether or not this was recognised within these societies.

We now consider in detail Marx's analysis of class conflict in capitalist society. He argued that in capitalist society the two major antagonistic classes are the capitalist, or bourgeoisie, and the industrial working class, or proleteriat. In the following quotation, Marx briefly reviews the history of class conflict up to the capitalist 'epoch':

The history of all hitherto existing society is the history of class struggles.

Freeman and slave, patrician and plebeian, lord and serf, guild-master and journeyman, in a word, oppressor and oppressed, stood in constant opposition to one another, carried on an uninterrupted, now hidden, now open fight that each time ended, either in a revolutionary reconstitution of society at large, or in the common ruin of the contending classes.

The modern bourgeois society that has sprouted from the ruins of feudal society has not done away with class antagonisms. It has but established new classes, new conditions of oppression, new forms of struggle in place of the old ones.

Our epoch, the epoch of the bourgeoisie, possesses, however, this distinctive feature. It has simplified the class antagonisms. Society as a whole is more and more splitting up into two great hostile camps, into two great classes directly facing each other – bourgeoisie and proletariat.

(Marx and Engels, 'The Communist Manifesto': 79).

In Marx's view, class conflict, rooted in the economic realities of differential relations to the means of production, flowed into every aspect of social life, including work, politics, education, family and religion. With particular reference to capitalist society, let us discuss what he meant by conflict in the economic context before describing how it operates in other areas. Marx contended that those who own the means of production always try to make a profit on the commodities (goods, services) produced by those who work for them. The lower the wages paid, the higher the profits made by the capitalist. The difference between the wages and the price of commodities (goods, services) produced by those who work for the capitalist class Marx called surplus value. The interest of the capitalist class is to maximise surplus value and thus increase profits. Marx's contention that the economic relations of production produce the framework for social relations, is aptly illustrated by the startling facts of economic inequality. Even in our own day, the richest one per cent own over 17 per cent of personal wealth and the bottom 50 per cent about six per cent (1988). In Marx's time inequality was even greater. He and his friend Engels commented bitterly on the low wages, poor housing, insanitary living conditions, and lack of medical care of the working class (see Engels' *The condition of the English working class*, 1844).

THE BASE AND SUPERSTRUCTURE In order to explain how Marx considered class conflict operates, it will be helpful to introduce the simple, two part classification of the social system which he put forward – the division of society into the base or infrastructure, and superstructure. We have already described what Marx meant by the base: it is the economic system and the bi-polar (two part) class system that economic relations produce. The superstructure refers to all other major aspects of society, such as politics, education, intellectual and religious life and so on. Marx argued that the base greatly influences and even determines the nature of the superstructure, although there is much argument about how complete he considered this determination to be. He

certainly thought that class relations are lived out in all major areas of social activity. The superstructure can be roughly divided into the state (government, civil service, judiciary) and ideological institutions (e.g. the educational system, the church, the media). Marx's model of society can be presented in dragrammatic form (figure 5.1).

Marx considered that, in a capitalist society, control of the state is in the hands of the economically most powerful class, the bourgeoisie. The following quotation, again from *The Communist Manifesto* was meant for political rather than academic consumption but is a very clear statement of Marx's analysis:

Each step in the development of the bourgeoisie was accompanied by a corresponding political advance of that class ... the bourgeois has at last, since the establishment of modern industry and of the world market, conquered for itself, in the modern representative state, exclusive political sway. The executive of the modern state is but a committee for managing the common affairs of the whole bourgeoisie ...

(From The Communist Manifesto: 80.)

Marx and Engels' statement does not mean that they thought that capitalists and businessmen held all, or most, of the top positions in politics, civil service, or in the legal profession themselves. They meant that the power of the bourgeoisie as controllers of wealth and production is so great that it limits the power of other groups effectively to act against the capitalist system and the capitalist class. For Marx, therefore, economic power is the key to political power: the economically most powerful class

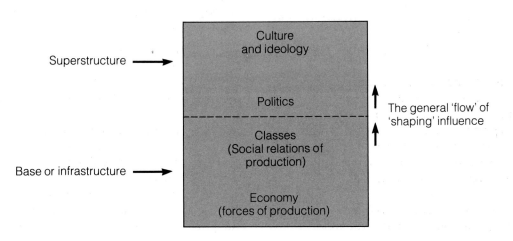

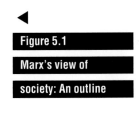

Figure 5.1

Marx's view of

society: An outline

is also the ruling class. We will examine in detail later, Marx's controversial analysis of the relationship between economic and political power (Chapter 14, 338–42).

Marx is as clear and consistent, within the terms of his own analysis, about the relationship between class and ideology as he is about that between class and state. He believed that, in any age, the ruling ideas (those predominant and most generally accepted) are those of the ruling class. For example, in the feudal period most people believed that the monarchy was, in some sense, divinely ordained. A Marxist would argue that this idea became widespread because it suited the practical interests of the monarchy that it should be. If people believed that the monarchy was 'hedged in with divinity' they would be more likely to respect and accept it. Today, when the monarchy is no longer powerful, few believe that it is a divinely inspired, rather than a purely human, institution. The same analysis is applicable to 'bourgeois' ideology. Marx described the ideology of the capitalist class as bourgeois liberalism or bourgeois individualism. As far as he was concerned, this meant little more than the liberty of the bourgeoisie to pursue private gain and wealth. Bourgeois ideology, like bourgois society, emerged out of feudalism. In feudal society people were expected to keep to their station and there was legal restraint on individual initiative, particularly in the area where the bourgeoisie most resented it – the economic. The bourgeoisie achieved their aims through parliamentary pressure, refusing to pay certain taxes, and by civil war. Marx pointed to communism, which emphasised collective action and greater material equality, as an alternative to bourgeois liberalism. In his analysis of the spread of bourgeois ideology to other sections of the population besides the capitalist class, he was particularly concerned to explain how some sections of the working class came to adopt a bourgeois liberal ideology rather than communism, which he considered to be more in their interests. How modern Marxists consider people are socialised to conform has already been referred to in chapters 1 and 4, and we examine this issue further in chapters 14 and 18.

CONFLICT AND CHANGE So far, our account has tended to stress Marx's analysis of how

the ruling class establishes and maintains its position. We know, however, that he considered change and conflict to be at the heart of the social process. He argued that the position of the working class in the economic structure placed it in conflict with the capitalist class. Trade unions are the organisational means by which the working class seek higher wages and better working conditions. Marx also stressed the need to establish a revolutionary party of the working class, with socialist and communist ideals. He observed several contradictions and developments in the capitalist system which, he felt, would promote the rise of revolutionary class consciousness. He suggested that a major contradiction in the capitalist system was that, in order to make as much profit as they could, the bourgeoisie would pay as low wages as possible to the working class and thus immiserate them (make their situation miserable). The precise meaning of Marx's so-called immiseration hypothesis is the subject of scholarly debate, but we can take it that he expected the working class to suffer increasing economic exploitation, and that this would provide a stimulus to revolutionary discontent. Critics of Marx argue that, in fact, working people have become much better off under capitalism and that therefore this 'scenario' for revolution was wrong.

In retrospect, Marx's analysis of the contradiction that can develop between the relations of production (the formal and legal framework governing the relations of workers and capitalists) and the forces or means of production (machinery/ technology), seems a more important and lasting contribution to sociological theory. He meant that technological developments can make obsolete, and so help change, the relationships of social classes to one another, even to the point where the established system breaks down. (A clear example of technological change producing profound, if not 'break-down' social effects, is apparent in our own time in the impact of the micro-chip 'revolution'.) Marx argued that the capitalist class itself rose to power because it controlled capital (money) and productive machinery, and that these became even more important than the old basis of wealth and power – land. A revolution in both the forces and relations of production constituted a change in the mode of production, a term encompassing both concepts. Marx believed that the development of large-scale production would eventually make it a reasonably simple matter for the working class to take over control of industry, if they were to consciously organise to do so.

Marx stressed the need for the working class to become conscious of its collective power as a pre-condition of revolution. In this respect he distinguished between the working class as a class in itself (i.e. its members had a certain objective relationship to the means of production) and as a class for itself (i.e. a class conscious of its own power and potential, and therefore willing to act for itself).

A factor that facilitated the development of working class consciousness of its own power and interests was that its members were increasingly crowded together in urban areas and factories. This gave them the opportunity to react collectively to collective grievances and to organise against them. Marx expected that the factors promoting the creation of revolutionary consciousness among the working class would prove stronger than those persuading them to accept capitalist society. He did not, however, assume that this would happen without the conscious efforts of committed individuals and groups to bring about change and revolution.

OTHER SOCIAL GROUPS (PETIT-BOURGEOISIE, PEASANTRY, LUMPEN PROLETARIAT) So far, our analysis of Marx's account of social class in capitalist society has referred to only two social classes: the bourgeoisie and the proletariat. This fairly reflects Marx's own emphasis. Nevertheless, he recognised the existence of other groups which he envisaged would be transitional while polarisation into two classes became virtually complete. He referred to small businessmen and, sometimes, to professionals as petit-bourgeois. He considered that, as the conflict between the bourgeoisie and the proletariat developed, the petit-bourgeoisie would be forced into one side or the other of the class struggle. At the bottom of the social stratum are two further groups: the peasantry and the so called lumpen proletariat. Marx considered that, in an industrial and urban society, the peasantry would become smaller, less powerful and less relevant to the central class conflict of the capitalist order. The

lumpen proletariat refers mainly to the unorganised working class: it includes those in low-paid and irregular employment and those who, for one reason or another, are virtually unemployable. Many of these are poor. Marx rightly considered that the lumpen proletariat was much less powerful than the industrial proletariat.

MARX AND STRATIFICATION: CONCLUSION
We will deal with various criticisms and revisions of the above aspects of Marx's class analysis in the appropriate parts of this book. However, some major general criticisms of Marx's class analysis may be briefly referred to here.

First, Marx's class analysis is seen as too simplistic. Critics argue that even in Marx's own time the class structure of capitalist societies was becoming more complex rather than resolving itself into a bi-polar system. Second, Marx is criticised for exaggerating the importance of class and particularly class conflict. His historical analysis and prediction of future society ultimately depends on a total antagonism between classes that many find unlikely. Third, and relatedly, frequently the consciousness and behaviour of the working class has proved much more 'moderate' and open to compromise than Marx envisaged. Fourth, Marx's class analysis is sometimes seen as a mixture of political and ideological bias and quasi-religious wishful-thinking purporting to be scientific analysis. We will return to the view of Marxism as 'the God that failed' later.

Conveniently, Max Weber addressed himself fully to several important issues raised by Marx, and it is to Weber's analysis of stratification that we next turn.

MAX WEBER: POWER AND STRATIFICATION

CLASS, STATUS AND PARTY For Weber, as for Marx, the public life of a society is largely concerned with power conflict. Whereas Marx saw stratification and power conflict in terms of an exclusively class-model of society, Weber defined two additional dimensions of stratification – party and status. Weber used these terms to refer to three separately distinguishable but greatly overlapping areas of stratification: the economic (class), the political (party), and the social (status). It is much easier to differentiate these factors in theory than in practice, but Weber was keen to distance himself from Marx's view that party and status are merely functions of class.

CLASS Although Weber did not attach the absolute importance to class that Marx did, he still considered it to be a most important aspect of stratification. He differed from Marx, however, on the precise definition of class, making a distinction between economic class and social class. He defined economic class as a person's situation in the economic market; both the commodity market (buying/selling) and the employment market (providing or seeking jobs). Qualifications and experience largely determine a person's situation in the economic market, and the better qualified and experienced can usually command greater rewards. Social class includes economic class but, in addition, members of the same social class share similar chances of social mobility (thus people from a low social background would tend to have a poor chance of upward mobility). Members of a given social class, therefore, share a common socio-economic situation. This difference in the definition of class led to a fundamental disagreement between Weber and Marx about the class structure of capitalist society.

Depending on how finely an individual's market position is differentiated, Weber's definition allows for any number of class gradations. However, he indicated four main classes: upper; petit bourgeois; middle and working class. He agreed with Marx that the most powerful class in capitalist society is that of the owners of property and wealth – the upper class. Again, like Marx, he recognised that, in rare cases, education could provide entry to the upper class from lower down the stratification hierarchy. He also agreed with Marx that a second class, the petit bourgeoisie, was likely to become of less importance and that the growing strength of the third group, the manual working class, gave it great potential importance. Contrary to Marx, however, Weber gave great emphasis to what he considered was a distinct and numerically expanding class: propertyless white-collar employees. He referred to them as 'technicians, various kinds of white-collar employees, civil servants – possibly with considerable social differences depending on the cost of their training.' It is Weber's view of the role and importance in capitalist society of

this class that fundamentally distinguishes his class analysis from that of Marx who was far more interested in the industrial proletariat. Weber regards white-collar employees as middle class. What distinguishes their market situation is that they sell mental or intellectual labour and skill rather than manual. In general, these skills are rarer than manual skills; thus the market situation of the middle class tends to be stronger than that of the working class. Obviously, this applies to some more than to others: it is more true of a top civil servant than of a clerk.

STATUS Weber defined a 'status situation' as any aspect of social life 'determined by a specific, positive or negative, social estimation of honour'. He went on to state that any factor might be the basis of shared honour or status – religious, taste, ethnic group membership or whatever. The main expression of status group membership is style of life or lifestyle. Membership of a status group gives exclusive right to certain privileges and opportunities, as in the estate and caste systems discussed below. Ascribed status is the status a person is born with, and achieved status is acquired during the course of life. Weber argues that ascribed status has rapidly declined as a means of access to economic and political power in modern societies. In the political area, for example, the titles and functions of royalty and aristocracy have generally become of symbolic significance only – they are certainly no longer an automatic passport to national or local leadership. Similarly, he regards economic and career opportunities as increasingly open to competition in modern society.

As mentioned above, according to Weber, estate and caste social systems are two main types of society, mainly determined by status. The former is a system of reciprocal rights and duties sanctioned by law, and the latter is a social system reflecting a particular religious world-view. It is worth describing these further in Weberian terms. Estate systems date back to the Roman Empire, but the European feudal system is a more recent example of this form of stratification. In an estate system, the people of the various strata were identified by the rights they had and the duties they were expected to perform. These rights and duties were enforceable by law or by military might. At the top of the feudal hierarchy in medieval England were the king, nobility and clergy. The gentry, free tenants, and serfs followed in order of descent. Each of these groups was a separate status group within an overall status system. A most important right, from the king's point of view, was that of being able to summon the nobility to provide soldiers for him. This was established when they took their oath of allegiance to him. It was generally believed that the feudal system was 'sanctioned by Almighty God'.

In general, there were therefore strong legal barriers against social mobility in estate systems. Exceptions could occur, however. The king could ennoble a given individual. The church provided an avenue of social ascent for some able individuals – as, indeed, it was intended to do. The growth of a powerful commercial and industrial class, and with it the increasing demand for economic and political rights, contrary to feudal law and practice, eventually undermined the feudal system in Europe. Even so, its influence lingers on – perhaps most conspiciously in the survival of the House of Lords in Britain.

Another form of stratification is the caste system. A pure caste system is a form of stratification rooted in religious belief, involving rigid ranking according to birth, and restrictions on occupation and marriage. The Hindu caste system of India comes closest to matching this definition. The term 'caste' has also come to be used more widely to refer to any hereditary and exclusive social group. In caste societies, social mobility is open to groups but not to individuals. This is because every individual, from the highest to the lowest, is considered to be divinely predestined to fulfil the role into which s/he has been born. In India, the caste system has been undermined, but by no means destroyed, by Western influence: caste and class exist uncomfortably side by side. An example of the deep-rooted nature of caste affiliation occurred in 1990. Indian Prime Minister Singh, announced his determination to pursue reforms which would enable India's tens of millions of untouchables (literally, 'out castes') to have access to the society's institutions on a basis of equality rather than continue to suffer the exclusion legitimated by the caste system. Among the widespread protests against this was the suicide of over 60 high-caste youths by self-immolation.

Weber argued that particularly extreme forms of status stratification can occur when different ethnic groups live in close proximity. When such stratification involves a dominant and subordinate ethnic group, a caste situation occurs. Weber gives the example of the Jews as an historically subordinate caste throughout Europe. Modern Weberians, such as John Rex, argue that the apartheid system in South Africa was a caste system, and it is possible it may remain so despite the formal abolition of apartheid.

Weber's concept of status is of especially interesting application in relation to generational stratification. Berger and Berger, for instance, considered that membership of the sixties youth movement crossed class (but seldom age) lines, thus creating a form of status based on age stratification. The concept of status group or status sphere – whether membership be based on youthful lifestyle or some other criterion – does seem to have relevance to the late twentieth century when 'style groups' form and evaporate with apparent ease and regularity.

Weber's difference with Marx on the nature of status is worth stressing again. Marx regarded status distinctions primarily as a product of class stratification. Certainly, the overlap between the three dimensions of stratification – which Weber himself stressed – is particularly obvious in the case of status. In modern societies, an individual's status is usually derived from his economic or class situation. The wealthy generally adopt the status symbols they can afford, as do other groups. Even though Weber accepted this, he also believed that the chain of causation can operate in the other direction: status group membership can give access to economic and political power and advantage, as he argued it did in the caste system. Later, we further examine Weber and Marx's disagreement about the importance of the concept of status in the context of our analysis of race and youth.

Finally, in a telling contrast between status group and class membership, Weber states that whereas status groups are 'communities' classes are usually not. By 'community' he meant that members 'Know each other' and have a degree of common consciousness and identity and exclude those unlike themselves. On the other hand, class membership is determined by economic criteria and members of the same class will usually have no knowledge of each other, let alone belong to the same community. Marx dealt with this issue by distinguishing between class membership in simple economic terms – a class in itself – and a class that had become conscious of itself or developed into a 'class community' – a class for itself. Whereas Weber argued that classes are 'not naturally' communities, it has been a central problem of Marxism that the working class as a whole has not become an active, ultimately political, community.

PARTY According to Weber, parties 'live in a house of "power"'. Their 'actions are always directed towards a goal which is striven for in a planned manner'. Party membership may be based on a single social group or on many: Weber suggests that '(i)n most cases they are partly class parties and partly status parties, but sometimes they are neither'. Thus, to take contemporary examples, the Labour party is partly a working class party, the Ulster Unionists are largely a status (Protestant religious) party, and, according to its own members' claims, the Liberal Democrats appeal beyond the lines of class and group interest.

For Weber, then, parties are a further and distinct dimension of stratification adding to the complexity of the total picture. He did not regard political power as a function of economic factors as Marx did. In further contrast to Marx, Weber did not regard liberal political democracy as mere 'window dressing', designed to obscure the fact that the capitalist class had the real decision making power and influence. He felt that once the working class had won the vote, it could be used as a powerful level to achieve social change. He considered that policies such as nationalisation, redistributive taxation, expansion of the welfare state and public education, adopted by political parties supported by the working class, could help to provide new economic and social opportunities for the working class. For Marx, of course, these policies were no substitute for socialist revolution and 'real' change.

Weber insisted that, although economic factors could certainly affect political ones, the reverse was also true. For instance, the policy of nationalisation favoured, in some degree, by most European Socialist parties of

Weber's own day, was likely to have profound economic consequences. In the chapter on political sociology (chapter 14), we will look much more closely at the relationship between economic and political power. For the moment, it is enough to be aware of the major issues involved in Marx and Weber's 'great debate' on power.

WEBER AND STRATIFICATION: CONCLUSION

In conclusion, Weber's overall model of society – if, indeed, such a precise description is appropriate – is both more pluralistic and more voluntaristic than Marx's base/superstructure model described above. He considered that a variety of groups, based on class, status or whatever (pluralism), form and by their judgement and action genuinely influence (voluntarism) society. He also argued that the relationship between culture (Marx's 'superstructure') and class (part of Marx's 'base') is 'looser', more 'two-way', and less predictable than did Marx.

Although Weber is rightly seen as a conflict theorist, he deliberately set out to qualify Marx's extreme emphasis on conflict. He argued that party and status identities could cut across class lines and thus blur the edges of class conflict. In rejecting Marx's polarised analysis of the class structure and replacing it with a more finely graded version, he attempted to undermine further Marx's theory of stratification. Yet, the basis of Weber's perspective is power-conflict. He sees throughout society individuals and groups competing for power and control and the wealth and prestige that often accompanies them. On this fundamental point, he and Marx were in agreement.

THE REGISTRAR-GENERAL'S CLASS CATEGORIES

Since 1921, social class in the United Kingdom has been officially described in terms of the Registrar General's social classes. These are the class categories used by the Office of Population Censuses and Surveys, and also widely used in sociology and public life. As Marshall et al. put it, the 'Registrar-General's class schema rests on the assumption that society is a graded hierarchy of occupations ranked according to skill' (18). Occupations are put into five social classes on the basis of how skilful they are considered to be.

Class		%
1	Professional, etc.,	3.7
2	Intermediate occupations	24.9
3N	Skilled occupations, nonmanual	22.4
3M	Skilled occupations, manual	27.2
4	Partly skilled occupations	16.1
5	Unskilled occupations	5.1
(6	Armed forces	0.7)
		100.0

(Note: The percentages in each class are taken from the Essex Survey Findings)

The Registrar-General's class categorisation is given above (table 5.1).

The schema has been extensively criticised. Firstly, the theoretical principle of the schema was changed in 1981 when the classificatory basis of occupations was changed from 'standing within the community' to occupational skill. However, the principles behind this reconceptualisation were not explained by the Office of Population Censuses and Surveys. Secondly, the occupations going into given social class categories have been changed so often as to cause doubt about the basis of the categorisation. Thirdly, feminists are critical of the Registrar-General's schema, as they are of other 'mainstream' or 'male-stream' approaches because it was designed with mainly 'male' occupations in mind and cannot be very effectively used for studying the class position of females as individuals (i.e. as distinct from their husband's class position, see pp. 124–6).

A number of class schemas have been developed which attempt to be both theoretically more explicit and consistent and empirically more reliable than that of the Registrar General.

THE GOLDTHORPE SOCIAL CLASS SCHEMA

John Goldthorpe's social class schema, devised for the Oxford Social Mobility Inquiry, is used widely by academics in studies of social mobility. Goldthorpe observes that all capitalist societies have a roughly similar social division of labour in which some employees enjoy better working conditions than others. A class is a group or,

more precisely, an aggregate of individuals and their families who occupy similar locations in the social division of labour over time. Goldthorpe defined these class locations on the basis of two criteria: 'market situation' and 'work situation'.

'Market situation' is defined in terms of how an individual earns income from a job (e.g. self-employment, selling labour); how much is earned from a job; and the prospects for promotion and wage increments. Work situation describes the degree of control and autonomy (freedom) characteristic of a particular occupation and, thus, its place within the overall structure of authority. The influence of Weber on the Goldthorpe schema is obvious.

Table 5.2 presents the Goldthorpe Social Classes. The percentages in each social class given in the table are based on a sample of 10,000 adult males living in England and Wales (see pp. 147–9). The larger class categories of service, intermediate and working, are used as short-hand referral points to describe the British class structure. The Goldthorpe schema is neither hierarchical nor static. Individuals are constantly upwardly and downwardly mobile.

Two main sources of criticism of Goldthorpe's class schema are the Marxist and the feminist.

Marxists define class not on the basis of market position but on that of an individual's relationship to the means of production. Given this different starting point, it is not surprising that disagreement follows. In particular, Marxists argue that for Goldthorpe to classify major capitalists, such as Lord Hanson and Richard Branson in the same category as higher professionals and top managers greatly understates their wealth and power as a class. This categorisation occurs because large-scale capitalists record occupational statuses such as company director – though these do not indicate their great economic power and wealth. Goldthorpe defends his approach on the technical grounds that the sample of 10,000 who formed the basis of the Oxford Study would have produced very few large-scale capitalists and on the theoretical grounds that the Oxford Study is about mass rather than elite social mobility. However, Marxists continue to argue that a social class scheme which provides a separate category

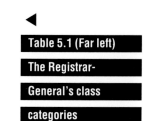

Table 5.1 (Far left)
The Registrar-
General's class
categories

Table 5.2

Goldthorpe class categories, and distribution of respondents to Oxford Social Mobility Inquiry, 1972

Class				%
SERVICE	I	Higher-grade professionals, self employed or salaried; higher-grade administrators and officials in central and local government and in public and private enterprises (including company directors); managers in large industrial establishments; and large proprietors.		13.6
	II	Lower-grade professionals and higher-grade technicians; lower-grade administrators and officials; managers in small business and industrial establishments and in services; and supervisors of nonmanual employees.		11.5
INTERMEDIATE	III	Routine nonmanual – largely clerical – employees in administration and commerce; sales personnel; and other rank-and-file employees in services.		9.2
	IV	Small proprietors, including farmers and smallholders; self-employed artisans; and all other 'own account' workers apart from professionals.		9.4
	V	Lower-grade technicians whose work is to some extent of a manual character; and supervisors of manual workers.		11.6
WORKING	VI	Skilled mannual workers in all branches of industry, including all who have served apprenticeships and also those who have acquired a relatively high degree of skill through other forms of training.		21.2
	VII	All manual wage-workers in industry in semi- and unskilled grades; and agricultural workers.		23.5
Total				100.0

(N = 9,434) Source: Social mobility and Class Structure in Modern Britain, Table 2.1.

for the 'petit-bourgeoisie' (small business people) but not large-scale capitalists seriously misrepresents the class structure.

Feminists such as Michelle Stanworth and Sarah Arber contend that Goldthorpe's class schema inadequately represents the class position of women. Goldthorpe's sample of 10,000 were all men and he argues that an all-male sample effectively demonstrates the class position of families because, in general, men earn substantially more than women, that wives careers tend to reflect family convenience and so are regarded as secondary to those of their husband's, and that roughly forty per cent of women are not in paid employment at any given time. Goldthorpe further argues that contemporary marriages tend to be homogeneous in class terms i.e. members of families share common experiences and attitudes. In support of this position he cites empirical evidence that married women tend to adopt class identities and voting behaviour derived from their husband's occupational position rather than their own separately considered. Further, on the question of social mobility, his particular

concern, his analysis of data from the *British General Election Survey* of 1983, leads him to conclude that the relative rates of mobility within the sexes are virtually the same. This confirms him in his view that separate consideration of male and female class positions is not required. In doing so, he believes he is partly accepting feminist argument that women are disadvantaged in paid work because of being stereotyped into domestic-type roles.

Goldthorpe's initial position, then, was that the family is the appropriate unit for class analysis and that the class position of families is best determined by locating the occupation of the male breadwinner (which he later termed the 'dominance principle'). Importantly, however, he has been persuaded by Robert Erickson that in female-led single parent families (the large majority), the occupation of the female head of household should be considered to define the class position of the family. This concession, however, has not been sufficient to satisfy critics who want a much fuller location and consideration of females in the class structure.

CRITICS OF GOLDTHORPE Two forms of classification have been put forward more adequately to deal with the class position of women (as their proponents see it). One is a system of joint classification of husband and wife and the other is a system of classification based entirely on individuals. Both are dealt with in the section 'Feminist classificatory schemas' (pp. 124–6). Proponents of the system of joint classification Anthony Heath and Nicky Britten argue that many differences between families (e.g. in voting behaviour and fertility patterns) can be better explained if data about wives as well as husbands is used. In principle, this seems a modest and likely claim. A system of individual classification has been advocated by Michelle Stanworth and by Sarah Arber and her colleagues at Surrey University (see p. 125).

Stanworth's position is that considered independently the majority of women are in a very different class position than the majority of men. Generally, they are in inferior class positions and she suggests that this is fundamentally because of the discriminatory way the class system itself operates, rather than because of negotiation between married couples about 'who would do what'. The class system is gendered to the disadvantage of women. In order therefore to understand the total structure of class the occupational position of women must be separately considered (see p. 125 and, in bar chart form, p. 180). Marshall et al., succinctly summarise the basis of Stanworth's radical opposition to Goldthorpe:

Stanworth in fact challenges all three of Goldthorpe's principal claims: namely that, within families, husbands have the major commitment to labour market participation; that wives' employment is conditioned by husbands' class positions; and that contemporary marriages are largely homogeneous in social class terms (66).

The above debate leaves unresolved 'the unit of analysis' problem in class investigation. Even if a joint or individual classification schema is adopted, it is not clear how to 'average' or otherwise analyse two individual and often different class position in a household. However, the complexities of how class and gender stratification may operate do appear to be emerging into better focus.

Perhaps Gordon Marshall is a little kind to Goldthorpe when he states, in his review of the latter's book, that Goldthorpe and his feminist critics are 'in large measure talking at cross purposes' – and, therefore, presumably both right in their own way (In Praise of Sociology Unwin Hyman, 1990). It is certainly true that Goldthorpe tells us much about patterns of social mobility and class formation within families. However, even within Goldthorpe's own terms, in not providing data about females within families, and, in particular, in excluding information about females, he seems to risk an incomplete account of class structure. The nub of the feminist criticism of Goldthorpe's class schema is that it is yet another patriarchal account of a patriarchal class structure and, as a result, fails even to address why the class system is patriarchal.

MODERN MARXIST CLASS SCHEMAS

Modern Marxists continue to define the basic class division as that between those who own and those who do not own the means of production. The framework of Marxist analysis of class structure, therefore, continues to be the division between the bourgeoisie and the proletariat.

'The problem' for modern Marxists has been to locate in their analysis of the class structure the many new or greatly expanded occupations which are not traditional proletarian (manual employment) that have developed during the twentieth century. These range from managerial and professional jobs on the one hand to routine clerical on the other. In general, Marxists have pursued a two-fold solution to this issue. First, higher white-collar groups have usually been seen as in 'intermediate' or 'contradictory' class locations. 'Intermediate' in the Marxist sense means that these class locations have features in common with both the bourgeoisie and the proletariat. Thus, as a group they enjoy higher wages and more freedom at work, but on the other hand they sell their labour for wages and are subject, to some extent to the authority and control of others. Second, Marxists now widely regard routine white-collar employees as working class although they recognise that this group's involvement with the process of production is somewhat different from those involved in manual work.

Writing in the early nineteen seventies, Harry Braverman employed the above framework of analysis to class in the United States. A schematic summary of his analysis of the class structure of that country is given in figure 5.2.

Another American Marxist who has also written influentially in the area of class analysis is Eric Olin Wright. Wright has reformulated Marx's concept of capitalist economic control. He states that capitalist control includes: control over the physical means of production, mainly, land, factories and offices; control over investment capital; and control over labour-power. This conceptualisation of control brings into focus for Marxist analysis the financial and service sectors of the economy in addition to the industrial sector which so concerned Marx himself.

Recognising the importance of the financial and service sectors also enables Wright to reconceptualise the proletariat (see p. 125) and to develop a Marxist analysis of a range of higher non-manual employees whom he describes as being in contradictory class locations.

Wright argues that there are a range of contradictory class locations in capitalist society 'which are exploiting along one dimension of exploitation relations, while on another are exploited'. What enables certain non members of the bourgeoisie to 'exploit' others (whilst themselves being exploited by the bourgeoisie) is that they have 'assets' of skill, credentials (qualifications) or

organisational control. So, they benefit from subsidiary and lesser systems of exploitation within the overal exploitative capitalist system of production. Table 5.3 divides vertically into owners of the means of production (1, 2, and 3) and non owners (4–12). Read horizontally, the figure divides into three groups with different degrees of organisation assets.

Critics of Wright argue that there is little difference between his analysis of contradictory class locations and Weber's analysis of the new white collar classes. However, Wright argues that in locating contradictory class positions within an overall structure of exploitation he is distinctly Marxist rather than Weberian.

FEMINIST CLASSIFICATORY SCHEMAS

Two types of class schemas have been suggested by feminists: individual classification and joint classification.

Individual classification is more radical in that it discards the view that the head of household and family should be the basis of class analysis and replaces it with the individual as the basic unit. One of the most useful of such schemas has been produced by a group from Surrey University: S Arber, A Dale and G Gilbert. The Surrey Occupational Scale (see table 5.4) is devised to discriminate as precisely as possible between occupations in which females are concentrated but can also be used for classifying males. In fact, such comparison is particularly instructive in that it confirms the dominance of males in higher occupational areas.

Arber et al. are not equally happy with

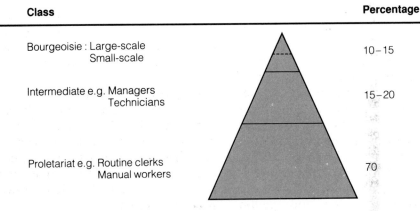

Figure 5.2	Class		Percentage
	Bourgeoisie : Large-scale Small-scale		10–15
	Intermediate e.g. Managers Technicians		15–20
	Proletariat e.g. Routine clerks Manual workers		70

◄

Table 5.3

Owners		Non-owners (wage labourers)			
1 Bourgeoisie	4 Expert managers	7 Semi-credentialled managers	10 Uncredentialled managers	+ Managers	
2.0%	5.6%	7.9%	3.2%		
2 Small employers	5 Expert supervisors	8 Semi-credentialled supervisors	11 Uncredentialled supervisors	>0 Supervisors	Organization assets
4.5%	2.2%	3.8%	3.4%		
3 Petit bourgeoisie	6 Expert non-managers	9 Semi-credentialled workers	12 Proletarians	− Non-management	
6.0%	4.1%	14.4%	42.9%		
	+ Experts	>0 Skilled	− Non-skilled		
		Skill/credential assets			

(Note: The percentages are taken from the Essex Class project)

◄

Table 5.4

Surrey

Occupational

Class

Surrey Occupational Class by Employment Status and Sex

Surrey Occupational Class	Men Full-time	Women Full-time	Women Part-time	Women Unwaged
1. Higher Professionals	6.1	1.2	0.4	0.6
2. Employers and Managers	13.4	5.3	1.7	2.5
3. Lower Professionals	5.3	13.3	9.2	8.1
4. Secretarial and clerical	9.1	39.4	19.8	29.2
5. Foremen, Self-employed Manual	12.0	3.5	3.8	1.6
6. Sales and	3.2	13.8	35.2	25.2
Skilled Manual	32.3	5.1	3.0	6.3
7. Semi-Skilled	15.2	16.2	9.7	20.3
8. Unskilled	3.4	2.1	17.2	6.0
Total	100%	100%	100%	100%
N =	(7498)	(2967)	(2379)	(3418)

(Source 'The Measurement of Social Class' (Social Research Association, 1986), p. 84.)

the bases of classification for the four groups given in the table: men, full-time; women, full-time; women part-time; and women unwaged. They see little problem in respect to the first two categories, classifying them according to current full-time occupation. Although they classify women in part-time work on the same basis, the latter are more likely to change jobs frequently and their paid-work may be an indifferent indicator of their overall socio-economic situation. For unwaged women, the best indicator of individual class position is the occupation held prior to their first child's birth, but unfortunately this information can be difficult to obtain. For this group, the most recent occupation is a poorer indicator of class position.

Despite the above classificatory problems, the Surrey Occupational Scale does successfully highlight occupational areas in which females (and males) are concentrated and it also shows up a significant difference in the areas of concentration between full-time and part-time female employees. As Arber et al. claim:

The two main advantages of SOC for women are, first, it provides a distinction, blurred in ... RG class ..., between employers and managers (SOC 2) and lower professionals (SOC 3). SOC 2 is predominantly male, containing thirteen per cent of full-time men compared to five per cent of full-time women and under two per cent of part-time working women, and SOC 3 is predominantly female, containing thirteen per cent of full-time women compared to only five per cent of men. Second, it separates shop work (SOC 6) from secretarial/ clerical work and sales representatives (SOC 4), and separates personal service workers (SOC 6) from semi-skilled factory workers (SOC 8). These two changes highlight the concentration of part-time women in shop and personal service work, 35 per cent, compared to fourteen per cent of full-time women and a bare three per cent of men. They also show clearly the smaller proportion of part-time women in clerical and secretarial occupations, which is masked in other classifications. Under 20 per cent of part-time working women are in SOC 4, compared with 33 per cent in RG class IIIN and 44 per cent in collapsed SEG 3.

(From 'The Measurement of Social Class' p. 68.)

Joint classification is based on the premise that the class position of household is derived from both partners' occupations. Only on this basis, can a fuller picture of a household's class position be established. This is especially so in the case of cross-class families i.e. families in which husband and wife are in different class positions. Thus, A Heath and N Britten argue in *Women's jobs do make a*

difference: a reply to Goldthorpe (1984) that joint classification can produce useful data not afforded by simply classifying according to husband's occupation. For example, families in which the wife is a white-collar employee and the husband a blue-collar employee tend to have different fertility and voting patterns from those families in which both partners are blue-collar.

GOLDTHORPE AND WRIGHT EMPIRICALLY APPLIED: THE ESSEX UNIVERSITY CLASS PROJECT In 1988 G Marshall, H Newby, and D Rose of Essex University and C Vogler of Oxford University published 'Social Class in Modern Britain' which reported a wide-ranging survey on that topic. Their data was produced from structured interviews with 1770 men and women.

A useful aspect of their work is that they analyse their data in terms of both Goldthorpe's and Wright's definitions of social classes and, within each, in terms of females as well as males. Understandably, the results are complex. In general, they judge that Goldthorpe's classificatory schema makes better sense of their data than Wright's. They do, indeed, point out some apparently odd 'anomalies' which result from using Wright's definitions. Thus, in Wright's schema the following, who are allocated service class status in Goldthorpe's schema, appear as proletarian: a lawyer, a chartered accountant, a couple of electrical engineers, one lecturer in higher education and others of similar occupation.

The Essex data will be used in the next chapter to help resolve some key issues of debate on social class, mainly between Marxists and Weberians. However, their data and conclusions require critical handling – not least, because the Essex team is strongly Weberian.

SUMMARY

1   Stratification is the division of a society into hierarchically ordered layers. Members of each layer are considered broadly equal but there is inequality between the layers.

Differentiation refers to that which makes an individual or group separate and distinct (e.g. income/wealth): thus, differentiation can provide a basis for categorisation and comparison.

2   The theoretical frameworks of Marx and Weber still inform current debates on stratification including attempts to

categorise people on the basis of class.

3 Marx stated that class is determined by a person's relationship to the means of production (i.e. whether they own, say, agricultural implements/ land or productive machinery) or, on the contrary, have to sell their labour to survive. The former is the dominant class and the latter, the subordinate class. The two major classes in any society are in conflict. In capitalist society, the two main antagonistic classes are the capitalist, or bourgeoisie, and the working class or proletariat.

4 Marx divided society into the base and the superstructure. The base is the economic system and the bi-polar (two part) class system that economic relations produce. The superstructure refers to all other major aspects of society, such as politics, education, intellectual and religious life and so on. Marx argued that the base greatly influences and even determines the nature of the super-structure. The relationship between the base and superstructure has been a matter of considerable debate among later Marxists.

5 Weber described stratification in terms of social divisions of class, status and party. Although these forms of stratification are distinct, they are also connected (e.g. a person's class affects their status (prestige) in society and, possibly, the party (political) they support). Importantly, Weber defined class differently to Marx, making a distinction between economic and social class. Economic class is a person's situation in the economic market and social class (which is related to economic class) refers to a person's chances of social mobility – members of the same social class share similar chances of social mobility. Qualifications and experience largely determine a person's situation in the economic market and the better qualified and experienced can usually command greater rewards.

6 Weber's overall model of society – if, indeed, it can be called that – is both more pluralistic and more voluntaristic than Marx's base/superstructure model described above. He considers that a variety of groups (pluralism) form and by

their action genuinely influence (voluntarism) society. He also argued that the relationship between culture (the superstructure) and class (the base) is 'looser', more 'two-way', and less predictable than did Marx. Both Weber and Marx are conflict theorists but Weber's group conflict approach implies generally less intense and concentrated conflict than Marx's class conflict approach.

7 The Registrar General's class categorisation of occupations is the most widely used official class schema but has been criticised for a variety of inadequacies.

8 John Goldthorpe's social class schema is widely used by academic sociologists. He defines a class as a group or, more precisely, an aggregate of individuals and their families who occupy similar locations in the social division of labour over time: these locations are determined by 'market situation' and 'work situation'. Goldthorpe's class schema has been criticised by both Marxists and feminists.

9 Contemporary Marxist class analysis has been faced with the central problem of where to locate in the class structure many new or greatly expanded service sector occupations. Generally, routine white collar employees have been classified by Marxists as working class and higher white-collar groups as in 'intermediate' or 'contradictory' class locations.

10 Feminist classificatory schemas reject what they regard as the 'male-biased' view the 'head' of household should be the basis of class categorisation. Two types of alternative classification are suggested: individual and joint. The former, in particular, results in a very different model of class structure than traditional schemas.

11 The Essex University Class Project analyses data on social class from a sample of 1770 men and women and in terms of both Goldthorpe and Wright's social class schemas and, in respect to some issues, the Registrar General's as well.

See the end of chapter six for 'Research and Coursework', 'Further reading', and 'Questions'.

6 Class Stratification in Britain

PERSPECTIVES ON THE CHANGING BRITISH CLASS STRUCTURE

The purpose of this section is to outline four perspectives on the mass of data about social class given later in this chapter. Their respective claims to provide the best account of the British class structure are discussed below. With the exception of the Marxist approach, there are obvious points of overlap between the perspectives. All of the perspectives apart from the marxist are essentially 'liberal'.

A LIBERAL PERSPECTIVE: AND THE 'EMBOURGOISEMENT' THESIS A common view among certain sociologists of the post-war period is that social class has become less important both subjectively, in terms of its perceived significance to individuals and families, and, objectively, in terms of social structure. Thus, individuals are thought to have other preoccupations than class – often centred on consumption – and, objectively, the general increase in wealth is considered to have reduced the significance of remaining inequalities. American sociologist, Clerk Kerr, saw these developments as part of the 'logic of industrialism' which would eventually make extreme industrial and social conflict redundant. Daniel Bell agreed with him, declaring an 'end of ideology' in the sense of radically conflicting social and political systems of belief. In the nineteen eighties, there was a revival of the view that the importance of social class in Britain has declined.

Gordon Marshall et al. – although disagreeing with this view – have conveniently summarised the Key themes which characterise the 'decline of class' interpretation in relation to Britain. These can be briefly listed, then explained:

- **the restructuring of capital and labour**
- **the growing complexity of class processes**
- **the emergence of instrumental collectivism and sectionalism**
- **the privatisation of individuals and families**
- **the fatalistic acceptance of structural inequality – allied to an inability to conceive of an alternative**

The main factor in the 'restructuring of capital and labour' is the decline of manufacturing industry and the rise of service industries with the consequent numerical decline of the manual or traditional working class. Capitalists are considered to have used the changing economic situation to have reasserted control over labour. Second, greater variety and difference is considered to occur within the major class grouping than in the past (a view discussed separately below, p. 130). Third, instrumental collectivism describes the tendency of workers in a particular industry (sector) or members of a union to pursue their own advantage rather than that of the working class as a whole. Fourthly, a corollary to this is that individuals and families are seen as becoming increasingly home-centred and privatised and as often enjoying relatively affluent consumer lifestyles. Finally, against the background of these developments, 'remaining' issues of inequality are either obscured or seen as less pressing. It is important to add that liberals consider that, as a result of these developments, a more classless culture and less consciousness of class identity and difference are characteristic of modern Britain.

The 'embourgeoisement' thesis was associated with liberal thinking. It was applied to the affluent manual working class who were described by some as 'becoming more middle class' (embourgoisement, see pp. 141–3). Although specific to this group, the embourgeoisement thesis reflects a more general belief in the decline of class. The thesis had wide currency in the nineteen fifties and sixties and was revived in somewhat different form during the nineteen eighties.

A MARXIST PERSPECTIVE: PROLETARIANISATION The main Marxist response to the 'embourgeoisement' thesis is the 'proletarianisation' thesis. This is the view that, far from better-off manual workers becoming 'middle class', service sector employees have been progressively 'deskilled' in their work and are becoming members of the working class i.e. proleterianised. The proletarianisation thesis is most notably associated with Harry Braverman who developed it in relation to class structure in the United States but others have argued its application to Britain.

In addition to their work on proletarianisation, Braverman and fellow American, Eric Oln Wright have each produced full and somewhat similar analyses of the total American class structure. Again, these approaches are applicable to the class structures of other advanced capitalist societies, including Britain. In addition, there has been substantial Marxist and radical analysis of the British class system by British sociologists.

The importance of culture and consciousness must be noted in relation to Marxist as well as liberal class interpretation. It is of limited usefulness for Marxists to demonstrate the continued 'objective' existence of a large proletariat if, in practice, its members do not live and think like members of the same class and community or, at least, show some signs of doing so.

TWO WEBERIAN VIEWS

1 A FRAGMENTARY CLASS STRUCTURE It has already been suggested that, taken to its extreme, Weber's analysis of class implies that every individual has a more or less distinct position in the employment market and, therefore, a unique class position. Few Weberians find it constructive to push matters so far, but some greatly stress the increasing differentiation and even fragmentation of the British class structure. Fragmentation is said to be occurring not only between classes but within them. Thus, Ralf Dahrendorf uses the telling term 'decomposition' to describe the processes of change which he argues have affected both the capitalist and the working classes (see p. 135).

A specific study of 'the middle class' argues that 'decomposition' or, to use the authors term, 'fragmentation' is occurring to this group also. Roberts et al. examine the 'class images' (roughly, 'consciousness' of class) of a wide range of male white collar employees. They conclude that a variety of class images occur and that this is indicative of the fragmentation of the middle class into various strata. Accordingly, it is no longer accurate to talk of *the* middle class.

There are considerable similarities between the above view and the liberal view. 'Fragmentation' and 'embourgoise-ment' are compatible tendencies. However,

there is less emphasis on generalised affluence and more on continued inequality in Dahrendorf's work. To this extent, he has more in common with the Weberians discussed next than with the liberals.

2 CONTINUING CLASS INEQUALITY IN THE CONTEXT OF GREATER AFFLUENCE The authors of the Essex Class Project – Marshall, Newby, Rose and Vogler – produced results that largely support and extend those of John Goldthorpe. They readily agree that there has been an increase in wealth and mass consumption in the post-war period and considerable social mobility, especially upwards. However, they also find substantial relative inequalities in wealth and consumption, together with substantial cultural differences between the classes, including those of political orientation. They also reiterate Goldthorpe's observation that the relative chances of social mobility have remained remarkably constant between the classes over a period of about fifty years. For them, therefore, class structure, class attitudes, and class relations have changed less fundamentally than the 'embourgeoisement' liberals and Dahrendorf contend.

While Marshall et al. accept that instrumental collectivism (acting in group self-interest, see p. 143) is typical of all the classes, they refute the analysis that this is particularly new among the working class. On the other hand, they also reject the view that people, including working class people, act collectively exclusively on the basis of self-interest and suggest that an appeal to social justice might still be a powerful motivating force.

THE ECONOMIC CONTEXT OF CLASS CHANGE: FROM A MANUFACTURING TO A SERVICE ECONOMY

The most striking change in the British economy in the post second world war period has been the decline in the numbers employed in the manufacturing sector and the increase of those employed in the service sector. There has been much less change in the numbers employed in the tertiary sector – mainly agriculture and extraction – which in 1986 accounted for less than five per cent of the total labour force. The point at which less than 50 per cent of the labour force was employed in manufacturing was passed in 1956 although the process of decline relative to the service sector began long before then. The decline in manufacturing jobs during the recession of 1979–81 is particularly notable (see figure 6.1). In 1990, less than 25 per cent of the labour force was employed in manufacturing. Figure 6.1 graphically illustrates the comparative trends in employment in the manufacturing and non-manufacturing sectors between 1971 and 1986 – with the former declining from 8 to 5 million employees and the latter rising from 12.5 to 16.5 million.

The most notable trend within employment in the service sector has been the numerical 'rise and rise' of female employment. Between 1960 and 1980 the numbers of women employed in the service sector increased by over 2 million. By 1986 the number of females employed in services outnumbered the number of males by almost 1.5 million (see table 6.1). However,

Figure 6.1

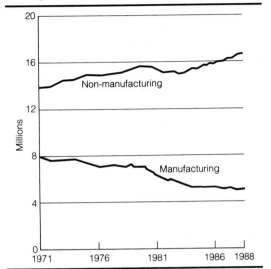

Manufacturing and non-manufacturing employees in employment in Great Britain

Source: Social trends, 1989

Table 6.1

Employees in

employment: by

industry[1]

United Kingdom								Thousands
	Standard Industrial Classification 1980	1971	1979	1981	1986	1988		
						Males	Females	Total
Manufacturing								
Extraction of minerals and ores other than fuels, manufacture of metal, mineral products, and chemicals	2	1,282	1,147	939	778	592	179	771
Metal goods, engineering and vehicle industries	3	3,709	3,374	2,923	2,334	1,751	468	2,219
Other	4	3,074	2,732	2,360	2,125	1,214	893	2,108
Total manufacturing	2–4	8,065	7,253	6,222	5,236	3,557	1,541	5,097
Services								
Distribution, hotels, catering, and repairs	6	3,686	4,257	4,172	4,403	2,043	2,509	4,551
Transport and communication	7	1,556	1,479	1,425	1,340	1,080	293	1,372
Banking, finance, insurance, business services and leasing	8	1,336	1,647	1,739	2,202	1,239	1,229	2,468
Other	9	5,049	6,197	6,132	6,541	2,509	4,311	6,820
Total services	6–9	11,627	13,580	13,468	14,486	6,870	8,342	15,212
Agriculture, forestry, and fishing	0	450	380	363	329	230	83	313
Energy and water supply industries	1	798	722	710	539	387	72	459
Construction	5	1,198	1,239	1,130	991	901	121	1,022
All industries and services	0–9	22,139	23,173	21,892	21,581	11,946	10,158	22,104

[1] As at June each year. (Source: Social trends 1989)

A Comparison of Occupational class: including and excluding female employees.

		men and women	men
Higher Grade Professionals etc.	I	9.4	13.1
Lower Grade Professionals etc.	II	17.9	17.1
Routine Non-manual – Clerical etc.	III	19.5	6.0
Small Proprietors etc.	IV	8.7	11.4
Lower-grade Technicians etc.	V	8.1	11.4
Skilled Manual Workers etc.	VI	12.5	17.4
Other Manual Workers	VII	23.9	23.6
	Total	10.0	100.0

(Source: Marshall *et al.*, p. 86.)

Note: The Goldthorpe class categories are used with data from the Essex Class Project Survey.

▲

Table 6.2

it is important to remember that a very much larger proportion of women than men are in part-time and/or temporary work.

The effect on the occupational structure of the expansion of the service sector and the related increase in female employment has been large and significant. In terms of understanding occupational structure and the nature of work in contemporary society, it has become increasingly necessary to record and consider female occupational status as distinct from that of male occupational status and to reject the view that it is adequate to locate females within their husband's occupational category. Table 6.2 shows clearly why this is so. It provides two descriptions of class structure – the first based on male and female occupations and the second based on male occupations only. As Marshall et al. comment:

a concentration on males only tends to inflate the proportions within classes I, IV, V and VI, while decreasing (rather spectacularly) the relative importance of class III. These differences are entirely what one would expect given the sexual segregation of occupations ...
(Marshall et al., 1988: 87)

Any relevant discussion of class and work in contemporary Britain must, then, engage firmly with 'the gender question'.

British Class Structure and Culture

THE UPPER CLASS AND THE MANAGERIAL ELITE

The upper class consists of the few thousand wealthiest and most culturally privileged businessmen and property owners in the country. We also consider top managers and professionals in this section because they often work closely with the upper class and are highly privileged themselves. By this group is meant people like managing directors of large companies rather than middle level management; chiefs of staff rather than high ranking officers; top rather than middle level civil servants, and so on. The important issue is whether the wealth and opportunities of the upper class also give much greater power and control over industrial, political, and cultural life than other groups.

UPPER CLASS CULTURE A common culture is an essential aspect of a fully developed class. During the twentieth century, traditional landed and newer commercial wealth have, perhaps until recently, increasingly shared a similar background and cultural outlook. Their way of life is substantially different from that of most of the rest of the population. Writing about upper class culture, Anthony Giddens says:

The most striking characteristic of the British upper class in the latter half of the nineteenth century is the mutual penetration of aristocracy and those in commerce and industry ... Certainly the dominant ethos [cultural tone] remained a 'gentlemanly' one, facilitated by the entitlement of industrialists, or at least of their offspring; but the very creation of the notion of the 'gentleman' was in substantial degree the product of the nineteenth century, and the rise of the public schools was the milieu [cultural context] for effecting this peculiar fusion of the old and the new. In this manner there came about that 'blend of a crude plutocratic [power based on money] reality with the sentimental aroma of an aristocratic legend' which R H Tawney described as the feature of the British upper class.
(Giddens, 1979)

David Carradine's *The Decline and Fall of The British Aristocracy* (1990) charts the gradual loss of 'senior-partner' status by land owners to industrialists in the aristocratic-business coalition. Other authors have argued that the 'Thatcher revolution' has accelerated the dominance of newer, business wealth within the upper class. The partial decline of the major public school both as a cultural status symbol and as a means to success in a top career seems to be at the heart of the apparent change. Thus, Jeremy Paxman cites as evidence of a 'change to the meritocrats' that 17 out of 19 of Mrs Thatcher's 1979 Cabinet had attended public schools whereas the 1990 Cabinet contained several members who had been to grammar schools, only half the number of old Etonians as the 1979 Cabinet, and a preponderance of members who had been to 'second division' public schools rather than major ones. Paxman describes this as 'not quite the supremacy of the self-made man that the party (Conservative) likes to pretend, but a distinct shift none the less' (Paxman: 1990).

It may be that the 'Thatcher revolution' most notably occurred where one might expect – in business. The following extract from a newspaper report, which draws on academic research, certainly suggests their has been rapid change in this area with those of grammar rather than public school background gaining an increasing role in corporate leadership.

Educational Background and Corporate Leadership

Executives spurring Britain's top companies to success in Europe are now more likely to have been educated by the state than by public schools.

Britain provides 20 of the top 30 corporate performers in Europe. Yet only one has a chairman who went to a major public school.

Eleven years after Margaret Thatcher, herself a product of Kesteven and Grantham Girls' grammar school, became prime minister, evidence is emerging that the grip of public schools on British life is being broken.

The revolution has been bloodless, but rapid. In 1979 the old-boy network still opened boardroom doors. Now seven of the top 20 UK firms in Europe have chairmen who went to a grammar school ....

Separate research by the London School of Economics also shows a sudden shift away from public schools in Britain's top 50 industrial companies.

In 1979, nine chairmen of these companies went to Charterhouse, Eton, Rugby, Shrewsbury or Winchester, 20 to other public schools and only nine to grammar schools. Last year, however, only one of the chairmen surveyed attended a top public school. Lord Prior, chairman of GEC, is an old boy of Charterhouse. Of his fellow chairmen, 20 are now past pupils of grammar schools.

Sir Denys Henderson, chairman of ICI, went to Aberdeen grammar school; Sir Michael Angus, chairman of Unilever, was a pupil at Marling grammar school in Stroud; Sir Jeffrey Stirling, chairman of P&O, is from Reigate grammar school.

In all, 70 per cent went either to a grammar school or to other state-maintained schools.

Professor Leslie Hannah of the LSE has described the changes in the class and educational background of industrial leaders as "astonishing" ....

Sir Philip Harris, who left Streatham grammar school at 15 with one O-level after the death of his father and now chairs the Harris Ventures chain of carpet and furniture shops, said: "I think grammar school gives you more of a basic education and is more linked to the needs of industry. Eton is more for scholars."

Lord Tombs, chairman of Rolls-Royce, said companies were no longer appointing chairmen from within the family ...

(From M Chittenden and A Davidson Sunday Times, 1990: 1).

The above developments can be interpreted to support rather than undermine Marxist analysis of capitalist society. They can certainly be presented as showing the emergence of a bourgeois or pro-bourgeois group over the more traditional aristocracy – roughly what Marx foresaw. It may be that in a decade or so, increasing numbers of people from comprehensive school backgrounds will acquire top business positions. It is possible

▶

Figure 6.2

Is the Grammar

School 'Type'

Replacing the Public

School 'Type'? If so,

what difference will

it make?

that what is occuring is not particularly the 'Thatcher revolution' but first, the effects of the tripartite educational reforms, and perhaps next, the effects of the comprehensive system. In both cases, the capitalist system is left intact. Indeed, Marxists see upward social mobility as strengthening capitalism. By contrast, reforming liberals favour the opening of opportunity suggested by the data cited above while remaining concerned at continuing inequality and poverty.

UPPER CLASS WEALTH AND ECONOMIC POWER We now consider the wealth and economic and industrial power of the upper class. The wealth of the upper class has diminished as a percentage of total wealth but remains formidably large. Wealth is much more unequally distributed than income, mainly because of the importance of inherited wealth. According to Lord Diamond's commission, in 1923 the top one per cent owned 61 per cent of all private wealth. In 1974, this had dropped to 22 per cent but, by 1976, had risen to 25 per cent. The increase between 1974 and 1976 was due mainly to the rises in share prices during that period. Under the first Thatcher administration, the top ten per cent became relatively slightly wealthier and the bottom 50 per cent relatively slightly poorer – a trend which sharpened in 1983/4.

Not unexpectedly, the wealth of the very rich tends to be made up differently from that of other people. Despite the increase in share ownership in the 1980s they are disproportionately likely to own shares, often in quantity. Frequently they own exclusive property, including land. They are also more than likely others to own art treasures, precious metals and jewels. The preservation and creation of substantial wealth gives the upper class a shared material basis for class identity and sets them apart from the majority. Upper class exclusiveness can be partly explained as an attempt to maintain and defend its common interest.

Few of the wealthy depend on earned income as a major source of their wealth. The share of all national incomes of the top one per cent of income earners in 1981/82 was 4.6 per cent – a small figure compared to the percentage of wealth owned by the most wealthy one per cent. Many major shareholders draw salaries as directors of the company or companies in which they have holdings. Usually, however, the day-to-day running of large companies is in the hands of paid managers who are not usually extremely wealthy people in their own right. This raises the crucial issue of where industrial power lies in contemporary capitalism – with owners (or, at least, large shareholders) as Marx argues, or with managers. It should be noted that the new managerial class is just as well established in central and local government and in nationalised industries as in private enterprise.

The Weberian, Ralf Dahrendorf has made a significant contribution to the debate about where power lies in modern societies. He argues that with the development of large scale joint stock companies which enable the general public to buy shares in a company, much control is exercised by top salaried managers and less by capitalist owners. He refers to this process as the decomposition of capital. Following Weber rather than Marx, he goes on to argue that in advanced industrial societies, power operates through large organisations rather than through a few very rich individuals (those who make up the capitalist class). Managers of organisations, unlike old-style capitalists, cannot pursue their own interest alone, but must answer to shareholders, perhaps to government, and even to the general public. According to Dahrendorf, this applies especially to the managers of publicly owned companies and to top civil servants. Dahrendorf, therefore, sees modern societies as 'managed' societies. To understand modern societies, 'capitalist' or socialist, it is necessary, therefore, to come to terms with their institutional (organisational) nature (see chapter 16 for the development of this point). He further contends that the rise of managers has produced considerable potential for conflict within the economic elite (that is, between owners and management). He considers that whereas owners tend to be interested in profit, managers are more concerned with the long-term productivity and security of the corporation which they see both as in their own interest, and in that of its shareholders, small and large. Again, managers are regarded as more constrained (controlled) by the rules of the large organisations of which they are a small part than the tycoons of early capitalism ever were. It is part of Dahrendorf's thesis that management is also constrained by the powerful organisations of the working class, mainly unions, as well as, to some extent, by government.

Anthony Giddens criticises Dahrendorf sharply on two counts. First he points out that, even though the growth of joint stock companies has broadened the basis of ownership, profit remains the purpose of capitalist enterprise: thus, the system is still a capitalist one. In addition, only a minority still gains substantial profit from shareholdings. There is a huge difference between multi-millionaires, like Sir James Goldsmith, with majority holdings in several major companies and somebody who owns, perhaps, a few hundred pounds of shares. Giddens's second point is related to his first. He suggests that far from there being a conflict of interest between capitalists and top managers, there is more likely to be a close identity of interest. This is intensified by the fact that many managers are themselves large share-holders in the companies they work in. They are both primarily concerned with the success and profitability of the company. As far as companies having a public 'conscience' is concerned, there is no guarantee of this, although some do. We examine in chapter nineteen several examples in which companies put their own welfare before that of the general public, if the latter is considered to include workers (made redundant) and local communities (variously neglected or abused).

John Scott also sees the economic structure of contemporary Western societies as no less capitalistic than in the recent past. He considers that capitalist business methods are dominant throughout these societies – in agriculture as well as manufacture, commerce and finance. Scott divides capitalists into three groups: entrepreneurial capitalists; internal capitalists; and finance capitalists. Entrepeneurial capitalists tend substantially to own and control 'their own' business. They are closest to the nineteenth century model of individualistic and family capitalism but are now a less significant group (see the decline in individual ownership of share equities, table 6.3). Internal capitalists are the top career managers discussed above, but whom Scott considers to be rather less important than a third group, finance capitalists. Finance capitalists are the representatives of banks, insurance companies, pension funds and similar institutions who, to a greater or lesser extent, own, manage and finance big business. Table 6.3 shows the extent to which such institutions have become the main owners of equities in British industry.

Although Scott particularly emphasises the rising power and control of finance

Who owns UK equities

	1963	1975	1981	1989
Institutions	%	%	%	%
Pension funds	6.5	16.9	26.7	32.0
Insurance (life and general)	10.1	15.9	20.5	20.0
Unit and investment trusts	12.6	14.6	10.3	8.0
Total	29.2	47.4	57.5	60.0
Personal sector	%	%	%	%
Individuals	53.8	37.5	28.2	20.0
Government	1.5	3.6	3.0	3.0
Other UK	8.6	5.9	7.7	8.0
Overseas	6.9	5.6	3.6	9.0
Total	70.8	52.6	42.5	40.0

(Source: Observer, Sunday 21 October 1990, p. 35.)

▲

Table 6.3

capital, he contends that the three groups referred to above form a 'constellation of interests' and together run capitalism. In this respect, he is in broad agreement with Giddens. Scott argues that as far as Britain is concerned, the dominant interest is probably finance capital, although he concedes that in Japan and the United States internal or managerial capitalists may be more powerful. He describes the trend in Britain from individual and family control of the capitalist system to institutional control as the 'depersonalisation' of property.

UPPER CLASS SOCIO-ECONOMIC AND POLITICAL POWER Giddens' contention that owners and top management – the economic elite – share common goals, leads to the important and wider question of whether the upper and middle class dominate the other major institutional elites, as well as the economic elite, of the country. Drawing on a study of elites, carried out at Cambridge, he concludes that at least half the top positions in all major institutional sectors in Britain, including the economic, the military, the armed forces, the judiciary and the church, are filled by people from public school backgrounds (see chapter 14 for details). In other words, a majority of those in top positions in this country come from a privileged and, more or less, wealthy upper or middle class background. Whether these people can be called a ruling class is also discussed in chapter 14 pp. 337–8.

The importance of the Dahrendorf-Giddens disagreement needs emphasising. It is, after all, about who controls our society, how they do so and in whose interest. This must surely matter to all of us. Do capitalists manipulate our world in their own interest or is power mainly located in large organisations which, almost impersonally, run our lives? We can agree with Dahrendorf that we live in a society of large organisations run by 'experts', and with Giddens that there is still a rich and powerful upper class with a distinctive culture. How and to what extent these two points can be reconciled we leave for further consideration (see especially chapters 14 and 18).

THE 'MIDDLE' CLASSES

The word 'middle' in the title of this section is put into inverted commas because the precise position of both managerial, administrative and professional groups and of routine white collar employees is hotly debated. There is certainly no consensus among sociologists that they are middle class.

MANAGERIAL, ADMINISTRATIVE AND PROFESSIONAL The Registrar General's and John Goldthorpe's class scales locate managerial, administrative and professional groups in high social class categories – which can be thought of as broadly upper middle class. However, although these groups form the basis of Goldthorpe top class category, the service class, he divides them into higher and lower grade – recognising, for instance, a difference in class location between lawyers and nurses, and between managers in large and small companies. Those allocated to service class are considered to be in a better employment market position and to enjoy better work situations than those allocated to lower class categories.

A number of Weberians have examined the way in which professions operate, particularly in defending the power and rewards of their position. Frank Parkin has employed Weber's concept of social closure in this respect. Parkin distinguishes between two forms of social closure: exclusion, which is aimed at keeping social subordinates out of the profession and usurpation, which is aimed at advancing a group's position at the expense of another dominant group. Exclusion is achieved mainly on the basis of credentialism: the use of qualifications to control and restrict entry to a profession. The hoped-for effect of exclusion is to secure or improve the market value of the services offered by a profession. Parry and Parry take a similar approach to that of Weber and particularly examine the role of self-governing professional associations in effecting exclusion.

As has already been explained, the massive expansion of managerial, professional and administrative employment has presented Marxist class theorists with a problem. Does this group belong with the capitalist or working class or should it be categorised in some other way (see p. 138)? In fact, most Marxists describe this as being in some way in a contradictory class location. Both Marxist and Weberian views on this issue are discussed at greater length later (see pp. 139–44).

WHITE COLLAR EMPLOYEES: 'LOWER MIDDLE' OR 'WORKING CLASS'? There is lively debate over the class position of routine non-manual employees – mainly clerks and sales personnel. Most Weberians would describe this group as lower middle class but, in the view of Marxists, Wright and Braverman, they are mainly 'new' working class. The latter view is referred to as the 'proleterianisation' thesis. For Marxists, the importance of establishing that routine white collar employees are working class is obvious. According to the Standard Occupational Classification 17.9 per cent of all employees in 1988 were clerks, 7.6 per cent personal service and 6.8 per cent sales: a group of about the same size as manual employees. Further, whereas this white collar group is increasing in size, the numerical decline of manual employees continues. It is only on the basis that routine non-manual employees can be considered working class that the Marxist model of capitalism, class conflict, and change can plausibly survive. However, there has been no shortage of work by Weberians, notably David Lockwood, to demonstrate that the class position of lower white-collar employees is distinct from that of manual employees.

WHITE COLLAR EMPLOYEES: CHARLES WRIGHT MILLS C Wright Mills published *White Collar: the American Middle Classes*, the first major post-war analysis of the white collar employee, in 1951. He draws almost exclusively on American data but the basic

developments he comments on are also a feature of British society. His work reflects the influence of both Marx and Weber. The influence of Marx is apparent in Mills' distinction between the old, property owning and self-employed middle class and the new, salaried white collar class. He includes in the latter group managers, paid professionals, sales people, and office workers (a wider but comparable definition to our own). Even in 1940, this group outnumbered the old middle class and now does so overwhelmingly. Thus, the United States has gone from a nation of small capitalists to a nation of hired employees. A similar process has occurred in most advanced industrial countries. In this sense, what Zweig calls debourgeoisement has certainly taken place. Whatever we call the 'new class' it is certainly not identical with the old bourgeoisie and petit-bourgeoisie.

Mills recognised that, in terms of their class situation, source and size of income (often relatively small), the white collar group could be considered working class – but he hesitated to classify them as such. In fact, he tended to refer to them as the new middle class for reasons which recall Weberian stratification theory. He claimed that the white collar group had higher status than manual workers among all sections of the public. Historically, this was largely because of the 'borrowed prestige' they acquired from working in close proximity to ownership and management. This 'reflected' status has become less common with the growth of separate, often relatively large-scale 'office areas', many of which seem closer to the factory floor than the boss's room. More recently, it is the better 'perks' associated with white collar work and the continuing belief that non-manual work is more prestigious than manual work that gives the white collar class a status edge over manual workers.

Mills observed that the white collar class is uncertain of itself and insecure about its future position relative to that of well paid manual workers. The high wages and comfortable standard of living of the affluent manual workers challenged the white-collar group's marginal superiority, sometimes causing what Mills referred to as 'status panic'. He saw several possible directions of development for the white collar class. These were:

1 It might become part of the working class or proletariat.

2 It might establish itself more securely as part of the middle class.

3 As it increases in number and power, it might form a buffer between labour and capital and so blunt class conflict.

4 It might become a distinctive class, separate from others.

Thus, over 40 years ago, Mills sketched out the main possible directions of class development for white collar employees. One possibility he does not mention is that it might itself become a fragmented sector. This view is actually proposed in relation to British white collar employees by Roberts, Cook et al., below.

WHITE COLLAR EMPLOYEES: DAVID LOCKWOOD; HOWARD DAVIS In contrast to Mills, David Lockwood's 1958 study of clerical work in Britain, does come to a firm conclusion about their class position. He rejects the proletarianisation thesis and argues that in most respects they are in a better class situation than manual workers. Lockwood examined the social position of clerks broadly under the model of stratification presented by Weber. He analysed their market position, work situation and status situation. It will be remembered that, according to Weber, the major indicator of class is market position. Lockwood was in no doubt that the market situation of clerks is substantially better than that of manual workers, even though the average wage of skilled workers was higher than that of clerks. Clerks have more job security, better prospects of occupational mobility (into management) and, generally, better pension rights and fringe benefits, such as cleaner, more comfortable work conditions and longer holidays. More recent data come from Lord Diamond's *Commission on the Distribution of Income and Wealth*. In 1977, employee benefits added the equivalent of 20 per cent of the value of their pay for white collar workers, compared to only 14 per cent for the blue collar workers. The value of these benefits is, however, increasing fast for both groups. Lockwood also emphasises the higher wages of clerks as compared to manual workers although this is now less true than at the time he wrote.

Lockwood extends Weber's conceptual-isation of class to include the work situation of clerks. Again, he argues that, historically, clerks have tended to be closer to, and more influenced by, management than labour. He concedes, however, that in large, modern mechanised offices, separated from management, identification with 'the boss' is less apparent. Developments since Lockwood wrote show a continuation of this trend. In particular, a rapid unionisation among white collar employees hardly suggests deferential attitudes to employers. In 1970, white collar union membership as a percentage of all white-collar employees was 38 per cent, a increase of one third since 1964. Despite the overall sharp decline in union membership during the nineteen eighties, unionisation among white collar employees has remained relatively high (see p. 253).

Finally, Lockwood argues that although the status position of clerks has declined somewhat in the post-war period it is still distinctly higher than that of manual workers. On the other hand it is lower than that of managers and professionals. On this basis, Lockwood describes the situation of clerks as characterised by 'status ambiguity'.

Most of Lockwood's observations and arguments about the class situation of clerks were supported by Goldthorpe et al., in *'Social Mobility and Class Structure in Modern Britain'* published in 1980. Goldthorpe locates routine non-manual employees at the top of an intermediate class grouping which is below the service class and above the working class. Generally, they have more job security and higher status – partly reflected from their association with the service class – than the working class. However, Goldthorpe does not consider that they have or are likely to develop a strong class consciousness largely because their considerable horizontal and vertical occupational mobility militates against this developing.

Howard Davis's study of the 'class images' of nineteen senior clerks supports the view that this occupational group has not developed a strong, distinctive class consciousness. Although the clerks invariably call themselves 'middle class' they are, nevertheless, reluctant to define themselves as 'not working class' because many of them 'came up' from the working class and consider that opportunities of mobility still exist. To a much greater extent than the traditional working class they believe in the effectiveness of individual action in career terms and also in making social relationships not necessarily bound by ties of class. The following quotation from one of the respondents makes the latter point quite eloquently:

I don't like to try and put people in compartments. I've always tended to take people as I find them ... I don't think class is a valid way to describe ... Someone from the poorest slum can be a hell of a nice person and a person from the top drawer can be a so and so.
(Davis, 1979: 168).

Marxists would typically regard such sentiments as showing an extremely limited level of 'class consciousness'. However, affiliations based on individual preference or felt status rather than class commonly occur and present one of the biggest barriers to the development of 'mature' class consciousness as envisaged by Marx.

WHITE COLLAR EMPLOYEES: THE PROLETARIANISATION THESIS

Marxist analysis of the class position of white collar employees occurs within a different theoretical framework from neo-Weberian. Whereas the latter define class mainly in terms of market position, Marxists define it in terms of relations to the means of production. The French sociologist Serge Mallet in an influential article titled *The New Working Class* (1963) suggested a reconceptualisation of productive relations to accommodate the realities of modern capitalist industrial organisation. He argued that occupations which perform 'a productive function' even though they are separate from the physical process of production should be classified as working class. In particular, he contended that 'white-collar' technicians in large research units 'in which working conditions grow increasingly similar to those of a modern workshop, but devoid of physical strain, dirt and stink' should be categorised as working class along with traditional working class occupations.

Perhaps the best known application and development of the proleterianisation thesis is Harry Braverman's *Labor and Monopoly Capital* in which he analyses white collar employment in the United States and the position of this group in the class structure. Braverman extends the view that a large number of non-manual employees are in a working class relationship to the means of production and applies it not only to routine non-manual employees such as clerks but to some professional and semi-professional groups such as teachers and nurses. Typically, these groups work either in large capitalist organisations or for the capitalist state. Importantly, Braverman emphasises the creation of millions of low-level service jobs which people used either to do for themselves (or their mothers/wives/sisters used to do) or, in the case of the wealthy, servants used to do. Thus, cleaning, washing, cooking (cheap, quick meals), and child care are rapidly expanded occupational areas. Braverman argues that the genuine service element has virtually disappeared from these jobs and the relevant work is produced as a 'commodity' just as physical commodities are produced by the traditional working class. Most employees of this kind work for large capitalist or state organisations. These relatively unskilled occupations can, then, also be considered as working class, and Braverman emphasises the fact that in order for the jobs to be done, women have been increasingly drawn into the paid labour force.

Braverman controversially argues that, in general, 'working class' occupations, including some professional and most routine white-collar occupations, have been subject to a process of 'deskilling'. The main cause of this is that, largely to impose their own control, employers have divided up the process of work into specialised functions requiring little skill. For example, whereas in the late nineteenth century, clerks carried out a wide range of tasks, they now carry out only a limited, specialised number. Braverman argues that modern technology, notably office technology, has intensified rather than reduced specialisation. Lack of control over the work process and possible low levels of work-satisfaction could produce alienation. Braverman draws heavily on his deskilling argument to support the proletarianisation thesis:

Does the proletarianisation thesis apply to Britain? Not surprisingly, Braverman's wide-ranging hypotheses have sparked empirical work aimed at testing them as well as further theoretical elaboration. A Stewart, K Prandy and R M Blackburn (1980) studied a sample of male white-collar employees in large firms (i.e. with a minimum of 500 employees). They conclude that for their respondents the issue of proletarianisation is largely an irrelevance because 81 per cent are no longer clerks by the age of 30 and that of these 51 per cent have been promoted. They support Goldthorpe in seeing the occupation of clerk as intermediate not only in the class structure but in the additional sense that it is transitional in the career of most males who hold it and, therefore, not conducive to the development of consciousness, working class or otherwise.

An obvious criticism of Stewart et al.'s study is that it ignores females – to whom Braverman's proletarianisation thesis particularly applies. This criticism was made by R Crompton and G Jones (1984) who themselves made a study of 887 white-collar employees from three institutions, one from the public sector and two from the private sector. 70 per cent of the clerks in their sample were female, of these 82 per cent were on clerical grades compared to 30 per cent of males sampled which suggests deskilling in relation to females in the sense that they experienced poorer promotional prospects. In examining the work done by the clerks they found that only a low level of skill was required and that computerisation seemed to accentuate this tendency. Further, they argue that the occupations into which some of their sample (mainly males) had been promoted had also been subject to deskilling. Overall, then, Crompton and Jones's findings tend to support the proletarianisation thesis.

THE PROLETARIANISATION THESIS: A CRITICAL EXAMINATION: MARSHALL ET AL.

G Marshall et al. give extensive consideration to the proletarianisation thesis in *Social Class in Modern Britain*. Because their sample of 1770 contains both men and women, they are able to compare the relevance of the thesis to both sexes. They do not claim to make an exhaustive study of the issue but they examine the following important areas:

1 skill as technique (the level of skill required in doing the job).
2 skill as autonomy (the degree of freedom available in doing the job).
3 rates of occupational mobility.
4 'cultural' proletarianisation.

Even in respect to areas 1 and 2, Marshall et al., concede that more definitive conclusions would require direct observation over a long period of time. In fact, given that Braverman is arguing that deskilling has occurred during a period of over 100 years, historical data would seem to be necessary to examine the issue.

In true Weberian mode, Marshall et al. approach the questions of deskilling in respect to technique and autonomy by asking respondents to state their own view of what has happened: specifically, they were asked to report on whether their present jobs required more, less, or approximately the same skill as when they started them (technique). On the issue of autonomy a range of questions was asked covering control and freedom in relation to the design, pace and routine of work were asked. In relation to both areas, they feel able broadly to dismiss the poletarianisation thesis on the basis of their data. In particular, the responses of category III (a crucial group for the proletarianisation debate and which contains clerks), show that the perceptions of both females and males about skill and autonomy to be similar and not supportive of the proletarianisation thesis. However, Marshall et al. do produce considerable evidence in relation to the III N group – personal service workers such as receptionists, check-out operators, and shop assistants – which suggests that their perception of their work situation, particularly in relation to lack of autonomy, 'is similar to that of the manual working class' (117). Notwithstanding Marshall et al.'s tendency to dismiss the proletarianisation thesis, here is some support for it, albeit in relation to only one group. However, as this group contains a large majority of female employees – about whom the proletarianisation thesis is considered particularly to apply – this finding is clearly important.

Marshall et al.'s data on occupational mobility again do not lead them to support proletarianisation. In general, there has been more upward than downward social mobility in the post-war period even if personal service work is considered as a working class occupational category – which it is in Marshall et al.'s calculations. Although proportionately more women than men from the service-class are downwardly mobile into other forms of employment and fewer are upwardly mobile into the service-class from clerical or working class occupations, there is significant upward mobility among females from routine clerical work to professional occupations. Overall, Marshall et al. conclude that 'it is not the case that their relative mobility rates are different from those found among men'. However, as some Marxists consider that 'professions' such as teaching and nursing, into which women are typically mobile, are themselves being proletarianised, these findings can be subject to different interpretation.

We now turn to the issue of 'cultural' proletarianisation. Throughout our discussion of proletarianisation, the importance of subjective or self-assigned class consciousness has been emphasised. People tend to think and act on the basis of their own perception of their class identity, rather than on the basis of some 'objective' classification. In this respect, Marshall et al. corroborate the previous work of Lockwood and others in reporting that their 'evidence is that routine clerical employees will more probably describe themselves as 'middle class' than 'working class', if they are males, and are almost as likely to do so if they are females.' An examination of their data (table 5.14) bears this out in respect to men in IIIa (clerks) but not in respect to women in the same category who are more likely to self-assign themselves to the working class. Again, those seeking evidence for proletarianisation could actually find some support in Marshall et al.'s figures. Matters are further complicated by the fact reported by Marshall et al. that the majority of married women self-classify themselves and vote according to their husband's occupation – whatever 'their own' class.

THE MANUAL WORKING CLASS

The most obvious fact about the British manual working class has been its decline in size. This parallels the increase in white collar employment discussed above into which a sizeable minority of the manual working class moved. In the decade between 1961 and 1971, Britain employed 12.5 per cent fewer people in the manufacturing sector. By contrast, Japan employed 21 per cent more and Germany two per cent more.

Table 6.4

	1973 %	1979 %	1983 %
Agriculture, forestry and fishing	2	2	2
Manufacturing	34	31	26
Coal, oil and gas extraction	2	2	2
Construction	6	5	5
Total industry	42	38	33
Wholesale, retail, hotel, catering	18	18	20
Transport, postal, tele-communications, electricity and gas	8	8	8
Banking and finance	5	7	9
Public administration	19	21	22
Other services	6	6	6
Total services	56	60	65

(Source: DN Ashton, *Unemployment under Capitalism*, Wheatsheaf Books, 1986.)

Table 6.4 shows that the decline in percentage employment in manufacturing industry continued into the nineteen eighties.

Two features of the optimistic liberal view of industrial society should be noted. First, relatively high rates of social mobility, including mobility out of the working class, were seen as increasing prospects for affluence and success. Second, the more affluent sections of the working class were thought of, by some commentators as becoming, in a variety of ways, more 'middle class': the embourgoisement thesis.

The embourgoisement thesis is described and criticised below. An equally strong area of criticism of liberal optimism about class development focuses on the emergence in the nineteen eighties of what some have termed a new underclass (see pp. 144–5).

THE AFFLUENT WORKER: EMBOURGOISE-MENT OR WHITE-COLLAR CONVERGENCE?
The 'embourgoisement' hypothesis, first presented in the late nineteen fifties, sparked off one of sociology's classic debates. The issue is about what is happening economically, socially, politically and culturally to the upper end of the working class. Are its members, as Zweig suggested, becoming more middle class – that is, experiencing 'embourgeoisement'? Or, is what is happening more complex than this term suggests?

The 'embourgeoisement' hypothesis

seemed particularly persuasive in the aftermath of the decisive defeat of Labour in the 1959 general election. As with the 1979 election, twenty years later, there was a swing against Labour among the working class. D E Butler and R Rose suggested that Labour might be experiencing particular trouble in holding the affluent working class vote. The response of A R Crosland, a leading Labour politician, was to suggest that Labour should try to widen the basis of its political support to include as many middle class people as possible, rather than rely too exclusively on its traditional working class support.

In this atmosphere of rather speculative and politically charged debate, John Goldthorpe, David Lockwood and their collaborators decided to put the embourgeoisement hypothesis to empirical test. Their inquiry, which spanned several years in the early nineteen sixties, is considered something of a model of sociological research, but has also attracted criticism.

Their initial assessment was that the embourgeoisement thesis was probably an oversimplification. In order to avoid bias, however, they followed the scientific procedure advocated by Karl Popper and sought to disprove their own expectations. This meant choosing an area and sample as favourable as possible for the validation of the embourgeoisement thesis. (A selected sample of this kind is termed a purposive sample.) Luton, a prosperous and expanding town, qualified well as a suitable locale. It had the particular advantages of having a substantially migrant labour force – clearly willing to move to find better paid work – and of being without a strong Labour tradition. The research was based primarily on 229 manual workers and, for comparison, 54 clerks of various grades. The former were drawn from three high wage paying local manufacturing firms. The sample consisted of married men, as the researchers had a particular interest in examining family life-style, although this meant that the sample was not representative in terms of marital status and age.

Goldthorpe and Lockwood questioned their respondents within three broad areas: economic, relational (family/community relationships and social attitudes); and normative (mainly political orientation).

ECONOMIC Goldthorpe and Lockwood did not consider that wages alone determined class – several other factors are also relevant. Nevertheless, they found that the high wages of the men in the sample did put a 'middle class' standard of living within their reach. They shared many of the consumer items enjoyed by the middle class, such as televisions, refrigerators and automatic washing machines. Apart from this, their economic situation was largely different from that of the middle class. Firstly, their high wages were usually gained only at the cost of overtime: the average working week was 40 to 50 hours. Moreover, 75 per cent of the sample were on shift work. A 'normal' background of overtime and shift work could put pressure on family and social life of a kind rarely experienced by the lower middle class. Secondly, promotional prospects were appreciably worse than for non-manual workers and this was fully realised by the majority of both groups sampled. The manual workers appreciated that any economic advances they made were likely to be on the basis of their present economic role and through collective bargaining, with the help of their trade unions. The non-manual sample typically entertained more hope of personal progress. Thirdly, as already mentioned, white collar employees generally benefit from greatly superior fringe benefits. Fourthly, and perhaps more importantly, most of the manual workers expressed much lower levels of intrinsic satisfaction (pleasure in the job for itself) than did the white collar sample.

RELATIONAL Goldthorpe and Lockwood's second category, relational aspects, may be thought of as cultural and community life. Not surprisingly, given the nature of the sample, few of the men studied shared the traditional pattern of community life often found among urban industrial workers and their families. Equally lacking, however, was any evidence that middle class company and life-style was sought, as might have been expected if 'embourgeoisement' had taken place. Kin still played a relatively prominent part in the social lives of the couples studied. This was particularly true of the (approximately) 50 per cent of the sample whose kin lived mainly within a fifty mile radius of London, but it still applied to many of the rest. 41 per cent of the former and 22 per cent of the latter named kin in response to the question 'who would you say are the three people that you spend most of your spare time with?' (apart from spouse and children). Otherwise, close neighbours, rather than selected individuals from within the larger community, provided most friends. Interestingly, white collar couples had more contact with friends who were not neighbours, even though they also spent still more time with kin (probably because their kin were generally nearer).

Only seven per cent of the couples sampled deviated from the above relational pattern to the extent of having predominantly and unambiguously middle class friendship networks. Generally, affluent working class couples associated with those whose presence in their lives was largely 'given', such as kin, close neighbours and workmates. Relations were usually informal. They were, for instance, much less likely to have people round for dinner than the white collar groups. They were also far less likely to belong to formal organisations and those they did participate in, such as working men's clubs, tended to be solidly working class.

The changes in relational patterns that did typify the sample were not in the direction of embourgeoisement. The difference between them and the traditional working class could be explained by reference to major objective factors of their existence, such as work and geographical and residential mobility. Their relatively high level of consumption was explicable in terms of their hard work and relatively high pay. Their family centredness or privatisation can partly be explained in terms of new leisure facilities in the home and lack of traditional community links. In these limited aspects the life-style of the affluent worker converges with that of the lower middle class.

POLITICAL Goldthorpe and Lockwood's findings under their third heading, the political aspect, are dealt with in chapter 14, and are summarised only briefly here. They concentrated particularly on the voting behaviour of the main sample. On the basis of what they admit is limited data, they found a negative correlation between working class affluence and Conservative voting. In other words, the affluent worker is less likely to vote Conservative than less affluent workers. Again, they explain this by reference to the social, and not merely economic, realities of the affluent worker's life. Employment in large-scale industry, high union membership (87 per cent) and frequent life-long membership of the working class are factors cited. It is interesting, however, that Goldthorpe and Lockwood note a marginal trend away from Labour among affluent workers. This trend was apparent in their own data, assessed on the basis of the way members of the sample had voted in 1959 compared to their intended votes for 1964. Certainly, the long-term tendency since 1945 has been for the Labour vote to drop as a percentage of the total vote, and much more recent data than that available to Goldthorpe and Lockwood suggests that 'defections' among affluent workers have contributed to this trend. They themselves comment that the strong Labour vote among affluent workers was based on instrumental (practical self-interest) thinking rather than traditional emotional solidarity (identification) with the party. This important finding left open the possibility that they would change their vote if it seemed to suit their interests to do so.

MIDDLE AND WORKING CLASS CONVERGENCE? In place of the 'embourgeoisement' hypothesis, Goldthorpe and Lockwood offered the observation that some convergence was occurring between the upper working and lower middle class. Instead of the upper working class becoming more like the middle class, both classes are in some respects developing a number of common characteristics. As we have seen, convergence is not much apparent in the political and social relational areas. It is, however, occurring in the field of economic consumption. Both groups seek a good standard of living, particularly in furnishing their homes with modern amenities. Given this, it is logical that home and family centredness should be a feature of members of both groups. Outside the family, their patterns of social life continue to be distinct. Money is the basis on which the consumer-family life style exists and it is not surprising that, in pursuit of it, collectivisation in the form of unionisation has been increasingly adopted by the salaried middle class as well as by the working class. The areas of convergence are, then, economic consumption, family centredness and privatisation, and instrumental collectivism. A H Halsey adds the observation that, in addition, status distinction between the middle and working classes has become less obvious and less important during this century and especially since the last war. He attributes this primarily to increased rates of social mobility. With so many more first generation middle class people about, spotting the 'right' accent or the 'right' dress becomes a more precarious way of identifying status. But Halsey is aware of the relative superficiality of this. Just as important for him in the making of a fairer and more equal society are the political and legal rights (mainly of association, such as the right to join a union) only acquired or consolidated by the majority during this century and discussed elsewhere in this book (see, especially chapter 14). Even so, he cannot be accused of underestimating the extent of continuing inequality. The middle sections of society may have converged but the vestiges of status no longer cover the continuing huge discrepancies of wealth and poverty at the social extremes (see next chapter).

THE 'UNDERCLASS'

Although widely used, the term 'underclass' still requires to be introduced in inverted commas as its meaning remains somewhat imprecise and its usage is controversial and politicised. Nevertheless, the rise of the term both within sociology and in social commentary reflects a need to identify and examine a substantial but ill-defined number of people for whom poverty has somehow become a way of life. The term was first used in this way by Ralf Dahrendorf who felt that this group had substantially increased as a result of 'Thatcherism'.

Frank Field, the Labour politician and author identifies the underclass as follows:

The underclass is drawn from the long-term unemployed, single mothers on welfare with no hope of escaping and very frail old pensioners

This does not conflict with the rather fuller statement of the right-wing sociologist Peter Saunders, that the underclass can be thought of as:

a stratum of people who are generally poor, unqualified and irregularly or never employed. This underclass is disproportionately recruited today from among Afro-Caribbeans, people living in the north, those who are trapped in run-down council estates or in decaying inner cities, and young single people and single-parent families.

(Saunders, 1990: 121)

Saunders goes on to enumerate what he considers are 'four key features' of the underclass: multiple deprivation; social marginality; almost entire dependence upon state welfare provisions and a culture of fatalism. Few would disagree with the first two of these. The third seems slightly overstated given that, like other social groups, some members of the underclass benefit from the informal economy and an unquantified and probably unquantifiable number of single parents receive some officially unrecorded material help from partners and others. Saunders' fourth alleged feature of the underclass, a culture of fatalism, is highly debatable. Rather like the notion of a 'culture of poverty' it lacks convincing empirical support. For instance, although the percentage of children born out of marriage is substantially higher among Afro-Caribbean than white women, the former are more likely to be in paid-work than the latter. In no way does this suggest an attitude of passive, indifference to work or life in general. Indeed, if we are operating at the level of impression or unsystematic observation the opposite seems to be the case as far as this group is concerned.

Charles Murray, an American social policy expert of right-wing inclination, has also commented on the possible emergence of a British underclass. His comments on its supposed salient characteristics can be added to those of Saunders:

There are many ways to identify an underclass. I will concentrate on three phenomena that have turned out to be early-warning signals in the United States: illegitimacy, violent crime, and drop-out from the labour force
(Sunday Times 26/11/89).

Murray concedes that his remarks about a British underclass are hypothetical but he speculates on a possible tissue of connection between the lack of stable masculine role models for illegitimate male children. When they become teenagers, some seem to prefer crime, particularly violent crime, as a way of life and as a way of making a living to paid work – even when the work is reasonably well paid.

If, then, through the observations of Field, Saunders and Murray, we can identify what may be meant by an underclass, what has caused its emergence? Left and Right differ profoundly on this matter. Frank Field holds Thatcherism responsible. The decline of the welfare state and of government commitment to policies to achieve full employment removed, in his view, the framework of support and opportunity that both reduced poverty and kept those who were poor in touch with the rest of the community. Field illustrates how each of the three groups he mentions above have been undermined by Thatcherite policies.

The long-term unemployed increased in size as a group during the nineteen eighties and yet were offered a series of training schemes which were criticised as underfunded, inadequate and demeaning. In particular, young people not in full-time education or work were faced with the option of the Youth Training Scheme or with surviving as best they could – once the right to social security had been removed from them. The quality of YTS schemes varied greatly. As far as single parents were concerned, one reform which would have made a substantial difference to most of them – a cheap or free national nursery system – was consistently denied on Thatcherite ideological grounds of non-interference in the free market. The freezing of child benefit also hit this group particularly hard. Poorer old age pensioners were adversely affected both by the erosion in real terms of the old age pension and by the decline in public services, especially health.

Charles Murray is circumspect in his speculations about the cause of the emergence of a British underclass but his conclusions lead in rather the opposite direction to those of Frank Field. He considers that as the welfare state has made it increasingly less uncomfortable to be a single parent, more women have opted to become one. As far as crime among young males is concerned, he links its rise to the tendency to more lenient sentencing. Similarly, he considers that the disinclination of a minority of young working class males to work reflects the relative ease of survival in unemployment in present as compared to past society. In fairness, however, he does not conclude that lower state benefits, harsher sentencing and 'workfare' (welfare payment in return for 'community' work), are the relevant policies to deal with the underclass. In fact, his solution – that 'communities' should be enabled to deal with 'their own' problems – seems to bear little obvious connection to his diagnosis. However, his recommendation does contrast with Field's emphasis on a centrally funded welfare state and macro-economic policies to achieve fuller employment.

Those who favour the use of the term 'underclass' argue that is not just another word for 'the poor'. They describe the underclass as a section of society cut off from or with only limited access to the mainstream. Those on the political left give structural reasons for this, especially the rise in long term unemployment and the limitations of welfare and training programmes. However, Marxist and most radical sociologists prefer the term 'sub-proletariat' or, simply, 'the poor' to describe this miscellaneous 'group'. Commentators on the right are more likely to stress cultural factors in their explanations of the emergence of the underclass: at the macro level, the decline of the family and increased violent crime, and at the individual level, workshy and 'fatalistic' attitudes. Despite attempts to 'theorise' the underclass many critics argue that the concept confuses rather than clarifies our understanding of inequality. They also suggest that the term has offensive overtones and lends itself to being turned against the people it describes. In particular, Marxist critics prefer to focus on the causes of inequality which they argue lie within the capitalist system (see pp. 160–1).

CLASS CULTURE AND IDEOLOGY

The concept of culture has already been introduced as meaning 'way of life'. As Nicholas Abercrombie suggests, there are two broad Marxist interpretations of working class culture (1980). First is the approach which sees working class (and bourgeois) culture as based on class *membership* and *interest*. In this perspective, shared interest is seen as likely to produce shared culture and consciousness. Second, the working class is seen as sometimes misled by 'bourgeois ideology' and as a result some of its members develop 'false consciousness' and may break from working class cultural values. Abercrombie has described the latter interpretation as the 'dominant ideology thesis'. Many, probably the vast majority of Marxists draw on both interpretations, and regard the first situation as desirable and the second as undesirable.

In contrast to Marx, Weber considered culture to be much more loosely associated with class. He did not regard it as unlikely, still less as 'false', that members of different classes should have common cultural interests and perhaps belong to the same groups, such as religious or leisure groups. For Weber, the class dimensions of culture are just one aspect of cultural diversity.

Contemporary Marxism tends to give great emphasis to cultural and ideological analysis. In general, the tendency has been to conceptualise culture as a contested area between the working and capitalist classes. Gramsci's concept of hegemony has been fully influential. 'Hegemony' refers to the cultural ascendancy that a given class may achieve. Typically, this is 'won' through ideological power and influence, particularly through education and the media. Many

Marxists argued that 'Thatcherism' attained a hegemonic influence in Britain during the nineteen eighties. Gramsci makes the central point that hegemony is a 'moving equilibrium', it can always be challenged.

French Marxist Louis Althusser divides the capitalist state into the *repressive state apparatus* and the *ideological state apparatus*. The former includes the army and police and the latter, the educational system (see p. 77) and the media. He stresses the power of the capitalist state in ideologically reproducing capitalism. However, his concept of 'the relative autonomy of the superstructure' embodies the notion that some cultural opposition to the dominant order is possible. Overall, though, he is less optimistic about the likely effectiveness of cultural challenge to capitalism than is Gramsci.

In Britain, E P Thompson, Raymond Williams, and more recently Stuart Hall and Paul Willis have attempted to present working class culture as vital and resilient and as potentially alternative and socialist. *'Common Culture'* (1990), a recent contribution by Willis is discussed at length in chapter ten. In this book, Willis appears to argue that cultural activity offers more immediate potential for progressive change than political action.

It is arguable that the trend among some Marxists to regard culture as a crucial (perhaps, as the central) area in which capitalism can be contested, brings them closer to Weber and liberal thought in general.

Social Mobility

TERMINOLOGY AND FACTORS ASSOCIATED WITH SOCIAL MOBILITY We have already defined the concept of social mobility as movement up or down the social class hierarchy. Mobility may be long-range (e.g. from manual working class to professional/higher managerial) or, much more commonly, short-range. Individual and stratum mobility can occur and the former is considered to be generally more possible in modern than in traditional societies. Ascribed status refers to social position which is predetermined by others and is usually acquired at birth on the basis of the social standing of the individual's

parents. Achieved status refers to the social position individuals acquire in their own lifetime, whether higher or lower than the one they had at birth. Again, the possibility of achieving a change in social status is considered to be greater in modern than in traditional societies, although most people remain in the class of their birth. The word 'achieved' is slightly misleading in this context, because merit is not necessarily implied in a change of social status.

The terms class of origin and class of destination provide a more neutral alternative to describe the same phenomenon. Class of origin refers to the class into which a person is born and class of destination to the one he or she acquires. Intragenerational mobility describes the situation when an individual acquires a different social status from the one which he or she previously held. Intergenerational mobility describes social mobility between generations and it is our main concern here. Finally, the terms vertical and horizontal mobility are frequently used. Vertical mobility is simply another way of referring to upward or downward mobility and horizontal mobility involves a change from one occupation to another of equal status. Strictly speaking, horizontal mobility refers to occupational rather than social mobility as it involves no change of social status.

Status and class differences usually coincide, but rapid social mobility can cause them to be 'out of joint'. For example, a public school 'type' who finds himself having to do, say, a manual job may find the symbols of middle class status, such as accent and dress, something of an embarrassment. The same can happen to the working class 'lad' who suddenly 'makes it': he may appear to lack the polish of the more established rich. Status dissonance is the term used to describe this kind of occurrence.

It should be remembered that most people remain in the class into which they are born. This can be partly because their life-style effectively cuts them off from other groups. For example, the traditional working class were often culturally very 'inbred' i.e. its members had little cultural experience beyond their own class. Parker has referred to this as social closure.

We now give a list of the major factors associated with social mobility – simply as a checkpoint: they are explained later in the section. It is scarcely possible to separate the overlapping factors affecting group and individual mobility. Broadly speaking, however, those affecting groups come first:

1 Substantial Change in Occupational Structure
2 Differential Fertility
3 Educational Opportunity (Qualifications)
4 Social and Cultural Factors
5 Intelligence and Talent
6 Marriage

All these are explained and illustrated below in our detailed analysis of social mobility in England and Wales.

SOCIAL MOBILITY IN ENGLAND AND WALES: A TEST OF THE LIBERAL IDEAL OF EQUALITY OF OPPORTUNITY

There have been few more important public issues in twentieth century Britain than that of equality of opportunity. For Britain to be the 'open society' of liberal ideals, a society in which equality of opportunity exists, a good deal of social mobility must take place. More precisely, people must be able to compete for occupational position, on equal terms, regardless of their social class background. Many liberals of various political persuasions have regarded equality of opportunity as a pre-condition of a fair society. Of course, equality of opportunity does not guarantee equality of outcome: it means that people will achieve jobs suitable to their intelligence and talents, regardless of social background. As we have seen, Marxists want a different kind of equality from this: they want resources to be distributed in terms of need rather than competition. Others, again, are influenced by both views. Here, however, we examine how far the classic liberal ideal of equal opportunity is achieved in Britain. To do this, we must analyse the extent of social mobility in this country.

STUDIES OF SOCIAL MOBILITY IN BRITAIN
There have been two major studies of social mobility in England and Wales, the first led by David Glass in 1949 and the second conducted by a team of sociologists at Nuffield College in 1972. The latter is known as the Oxford Mobility Study. Like most mobility studies prior to the Essex one, these two argued that trends in female social mobility could be derived from data about males.

Ideally, the findings of the two surveys would be directly comparable, and it was certainly the intention of the Oxford group to achieve this as far as possible. In fact, they do not attempt precisely to replicate Glass's methodology partly because of a number of criticisms that have been convincingly made against it. The major effect of the flaws in Glass's methodology is that he may have underestimated the rate of social mobility, particularly long-range upward mobility. As one of his important findings was that there was little long-range mobility, either upwards or downwards, the methodological criticisms are significant. Glass also found that family and social background had a major effect on social status and that most people remained at a similar level to their fathers.

Our analysis of the 1972 study will be assisted by reference to table 6.5 which presents the main findings. The top half of the table – (a) – gives data about the class origin of respondents in 'Outflow' terms, and the bottom half – (b) – in 'inflow' terms. Thus (reading across), in table (a), 45 per cent of those with a class I father were themselves in class I, whereas only six per cent were in class VII. In table (b), the total percentage inflow into the various classes is given. Thus (reading down), of the total percentage inflowing into Class I, 24 per cent had a Class I father, whereas thirteen per cent had a class VII father. It is notable that of these 'inflowing' into Class VII only two per cent were from Class I whereas 39 per cent were from Class VII.

Broadly, the findings of the Oxford Study confirm two popular clichés. The first is that the chances of improving one's social status got better in the post-war period, and the second – perhaps more a sociologist's than a layman's cliché – is that is is still much easier to retain high social status once born to it than it is to achieve it in the first place. Let us take these points in order.

Because of the expansion of the middle or service class since the war, there has been more opportunity for the lower middle and working class to move upwards. John H Goldthorpe, a major contributor to the Oxford Study, rejects the thesis that a significant degree of 'closure' exists at the higher occupational levels of British society. Writing of the upper end of the middle class (the top seven per cent occupationally) he argues that the survey data shows 'a very wide basis of recruitment and a very low degree of homogeneity in its composition'. In other words, people from a great variety of social origins are members of this class (recruitment), and by that very fact its members are in many ways dissimilar (lack homogeneity). Another interesting illustration of lack of homogeneity

▶

Table 6.5

Intergenerational class mobility among men in England and Wales

(a) Class distribution of respondents by class of father at respondent's age 14 (% by row)

			Class of Respondent								
			I	II	III	IV	V	VI	VII	(N)	Total %
	S {	I	45	19	12	8	5	5	6	(688)	7
		II	29	23	12	7	10	11	9	(554)	6
Class of Father	I {	III	18	16	13	8	13	15	17	(694)	7
		IV	13	11	8	24	9	14	21	(1329)	14
		V	14	14	10	8	16	21	18	(1082)	12
	W {	VI	8	9	8	7	12	30	26	(2594)	28
		VII	6	8	8	7	12	24	35	(2493)	25
		(N)	(1285)	(1087)	(870)	(887)	(1091)	(2000)	(2214)	(9434)	
Total	%		14	12	9	9	12	21	23		100

(b) Class composition by class of father at respondent's age 14 (5 by column)

			Class of Respondent								
			I	II	III	IV	V	VI	VII	(N)	Total %
	S {	I	24	12	9	6	3	2	2	(688)	7
		II	13	12	8	4	5	3	2	(554)	6
Class of Father	I {	III	10	10	10	6	8	5	5	(694)	7
		IV	13	14	12	37	11	10	12	(1329)	14
		V	12	13	12	9	15	11	9	(1082)	12
	W {	VI	15	21	25	19	29	39	30	(2594)	28
		VII	13	18	24	19	29	29	39	(2493)	25
		(N)	(1285)	(1087)	(870)	(887)	(1091)	(2000)	(2214)	(9434)	
Total	%		14	12	9	9	12	21	23		100

Note: Percentages may not add up exactly because of rounding.
(Source: Adapted from Marshall, 1990: 19, from the Oxford Mobility Study)

is that in 1972, marginally more members of social class I originated in social class VI than in social class II. Generally, the data shows a very much higher rate of long-range upward mobility than Glass found. Perhaps most notable, however, is the large percentage of people of working class origin achieving intermediate occupations i.e. the large amount of short-range mobility.

Concluding this point, then, opportunity for upward mobility substantially increased in post-war Britain. There is, however, quite another way of looking at the findings of the Oxford Study and we must adopt this perspective now.

The chances of a class I son remaining in class I compared to the changes that a working class son has of reaching class I have changed little over recent generations. Again, summarising from the table, the proportion of sons of middle class origin who retained middle class status is more than one in two, whereas only about one in seven working class sons achieved this status. What has happened is that increased opportunities have been shared more or less equally between the classes: there have been rather more opportunities for all. But if the chances of upward mobility for working class sons have improved, the shrinkage of working class jobs and the expansion of middle class ones has protected the middle class against downward mobility. Overall, therefore, relative mobility rates or the odds ratio (7:1, class I/VII) have changed remarkably little. Goldthorpe concludes that the pattern of inter-generational mobility in recent decades has been one of stability or even marginally increasing relative inequality.

It needs to be said that the Oxford Study does not address itself directly to the Marxist concern with the upper class. Other data shows that there is much more self-recruitment to this group than to the much larger class I as a whole. It is also quite probable that those of non-upper class origins who do become members of it tend to adopt the values and attitudes of that class. Marxists are also able to interpret what is happening to the working class in a way quite consistent with their perspective. The working class is the most closed class and despite the differences between them, its members remain relatively disadvantaged. These factors may provide a sound basis for solidarity and collective action.

FACTORS EXPLAINING THE RECENT PATTERN OF SOCIAL MOBILITY IN BRITAIN We now turn to discuss the factors that account for the pattern of social mobility described above. First, the increase in upward mobility has been largely due to a substantial shift in employment from the industrial to the service sector. Men have particularly benefited because lower status white collar jobs have been filled mainly by women, and men have been able to fill most of the new professional, technical, administrative and managerial posts. The increase has had little, if anything, to do with government policy. Indeed, in so far as the relative class rates of mobility have not changed, government policy to achieve greater equality of opportunity can be said to have failed.

Historically, differential fertility rates between the middle and working classes (that is, middle class families have produced fewer children) has created 'space' into which some working class people could move. Quite simply, the middle class did not produce enough children to fill all the middle class jobs available. This has been especially true in the rapid expansion of the service sector in the post-war period. Since the mid-nineteen sixties, there has been a tendency for family size to fall throughout the social classes, and although differences remain, differential fertility is now less important in explaining upward social mobility. The slight general increase in the birth rate in 1978 and 1979, even if sustained, is not likely to change this.

We have already examined the effect of educational expansion on social mobility and there is no need to rehearse the contents of this lengthy section here (see chapter 4). In summary, Halsey et al.'s research on the tripartite system and various less extensive studies of the comprehensive system show little relative change in the educational success and career achievements of children of different class origins in the post-war period. The middle class has taken as much, if not more, advantage of state education as the working class and has virtually sole access to the privileged private sector. Gamely, but not entirely convincingly, Halsey argues that a further expansion of educational opportunity must, by deduction, disproportionately benefit the working class. There may be no liberal alternative than but to try this, but history warns against excessive optimism about the likely results.

The influence of social and cultural factors on both educational and career opportunities does not need to be laboured here. It has been a constant theme in earlier chapters. The material disadvantages of a lower working class background are obvious, but the cultural disadvantages, if any, remain open to debate despite Halsey's sophisticated statistically-based attempt to show that they are much less than Bernstein and Bourdieu have argued.

However much intelligence may be helped or hindered by social environment, there is no doubt that the possession of high intelligence can be of assistance in upward mobility, and that low intelligence is a near fatal bar to it. Obviously, this factor applies virtually exclusively to the lower classes. It requires no intelligence at all to be born into the upper classes (although it usually requires, at least, the intelligence to appoint a good accountant to stay there). Lipset and Bendix have suggested that high intelligence may help working class children to recognise middle class attitudes and norms and to see the advantage of imitating them.

Traditionally, exceptional talent in either entertainment or sport has been an avenue to the top for a few working class people and, particularly in the United States, for some black people. But for most, this possibility is just a dream. There are not many Madonnas or Paul Gascoignes. A further miscellaneous group of factors, such as character, looks and luck can no doubt play a part in mobility but they are too unpredictable and personal to require more than brief acknowledgement here.

Of more sociological importance is the fact that women achieve upward mobility by marriage more often than men. This is a result of their generally inferior economic position and earning power. 'She's a gold digger' can be understood more sympathetically in the context of a society in which women depend heavily on men for material comfort and social status. This dependency is not the fault of individual women but lies in the nature of our sexually unequal society (see chapter 12).

If the recent past is a good guide, the prospects for upward mobility in Britain depend on the further expansion of the service sector. In the early nineteen eighties, the medium term prospects are for less employment in this area. Clearly, expansion cannot go on for ever. If higher status and better paid jobs are not available, a better academically qualified population will go to waste at the dole queues.

CONCLUSION: STRATIFICATION IN BRITAIN

Britain is still a class divided society. Wealth remains concentrated and relative poverty persists. Social mobility out of the working class has increased but middle class children have as good a chance as ever of maintaining the status inherited from their parents. Both of these factors are due to the expansion of the service sector and not to the success of government policies aimed at bringing about greater equality of opportunity. There is more 'room at the top' (or, more precisely, in the middle) but the class origins of those who 'make it' are roughly in the same proportion that they were fifty years ago. And in the future, it is quite possible that upward access will become more difficult. During the nineteen eighties, the most rapidly expanding 'occupational' group in British society was the unemployed! When, in 1991, unemployment reached 2.5 million for the second time in a decade, more middle class people were affected than in the recession of the early nineteen eighties. It was possible that the great expansion of opportunity in the post-war period was faltering.

1 In the welter of detail about the British class structure, it is helpful to bear in mind four perspectives/ interpretations of Britain's changing class structure. These are:

Liberal Perspective: and Embourgoisement

Marxist Perspective: Proletarianisation

Two Weberian Views –

1) A Fragmentary Class Structure

2) Continuing Class Inequality in the Context of Greater Affluence

2 A liberal perspective. The term liberal is a broad one but in this context it is intended to indicate the view that class has become less important in British life largely because of the general increase in wealth.

3 Marxist perspective on class requires to deal with the substantial numerical reduction in the size of the manual working class and the corresponding rise in numbers of non-manual workers. A large part of 'the answer' is Harry Braverman's 'proletarianisation thesis' which argues that most of the latter group are working class.

4 Two Weberian Views.

i) The view that the British class structure is fragmenting or 'decomposing' is basically as simple as it sounds – the British class structure is considered to be 'breaking up' partly due to the increasing complexity of the occupational system.

ii) Continuing Class Inequality in the Context of Greater Affluence is a view propounded by more 'hard-nosed' Weberians such as John Goldthorpe. They reject the progressive optimism of the liberal perspective described above in the light of substantial evidence of continuing and even increasing inequality.

SUMMARY

5 The economic context of class change, particularly the rise of the service sector and the decline of manufacturing employment, is relevant to class analysis both because of the relative increase in white-collar employees and in female employment.

6 The Upper Class. The key issue in relation to the upper class is whether its power and influence has declined or not. In Marxist terms, is the upper class (still) a 'ruling class'?

7 The 'Middle' Classes. The key issue in relation to lower white collar employees is whether they are best categorised as middle class as David Lockwood argues in his study of clerks or whether they are mainly working class as Braverman contends.

8 The Working Class. The key issue in relation to the working class is whether it is in some sense declining and losing its identity (or perhaps 'converging' with the middle class), or whether it remains a distinct, potentially powerful, social grouping.

9 The 'underclass' is not a class at all in the sense that its members share a common occupational location or relationship to the means of production. The term describes people who, for various reasons, are 'cut-off' from the relative affluence of the rest of society.

10 Social mobility is movement up or down the social hierarchy. Although there has arguably been an increase in higher status jobs in post-war Britain the relative chances of achieving high status jobs between middle and working class people has hardly changed.

RESEARCH AND COURSEWORK

Several of the studies of class cited in this chapter are large-scale social surveys such as the Oxford Study and the Essex Project. It would be quite impossible to attempt anything of this scope. However, some of the issues raised by these studies are open to exploration on a smaller scale. The Essex Project, for instance, opens up a number of class/gender matters. A hypothesis that could be tested is whether when a married couple are both in paid work, the female tends to derive her view of her own (and perhaps her family's) class position from her own occupation, her husband's or both. Another matter which could be explored in this piece of research is whether female married partners' political views are more likely to be influenced by their husband's occupational status than their own. If you include a question on whether or not female respondents would describe themselves as 'feminist' you might find that those answering 'yes' emerge as a sub-group with distinctive views. Again, however, be wary of allowing your research to get out of hand. A study of ten couples might require say, 20 in-depth interviews and even this might be too much in practical terms.

FURTHER READING

For those who want to do project work on class or simply to study the questions relating to it more deeply, it is worth emphasising that method-ological appendices – though they may look technical – can be the most useful part of a book. It is in appendices that you can sometimes learn how to conceptualise problems and formulate questions. Two examples occur in, respectively, G Marshall et al., *Social Class in Modern Britain* (Hutchinson, 1988) and Howard H Davis *Beyond Class Images* (Croom Helm, 1979).

QUESTIONS

1 Explain the relative neglect of women in studies of either social stratification or work (London, 1987).
2 Outline the major studies of social mobility in Britain and examine the criticisms of them (AEB 1989).
3 'In the past Britain was divided into two classes, but we have now reached a position where the class structure is fragmented.' Assess the arguments and evidence for and against this view (AEB 1990).

7 Wealth, Poverty & Inequality

INTRODUCTION Poverty and inequality are not the same thing. A wealthy businessperson and a 'comfortably-off' teacher are materially unequal but the teacher is not poor. Social inequality means that certain individuals or groups have more material or cultural resources than others.

Poverty implies some *insufficiency* in the material or, arguably, cultural resources of an individual or group. There is considerable disagreement about what constitutes poverty in modern societies. Is not being able to afford a coloured television set poverty? Or not being able to afford a family holiday away from home? Some have defined poverty to include such situations. Others consider that these situations involve inequality rather than poverty. Taking this view, former Chancellor of the Exchequer Nigel Lawson stated that he saw no reason to limit inequality but that he was concerned about poverty. Critics of this view argue that poverty is more likely to occur in a society which accepts extreme inequality.

Definition and Extent of Poverty and Inequality

ABSOLUTE POVERTY

Poverty may be defined as either absolute or relative. Absolute poverty is insufficiency in the basic necessities of existence: in practical terms, this usually means being without adequate food, clothing or shelter. In 1899, Seebohm Rowntree carried out a survey into poverty in York and attempted to define poverty in absolute or subsistence terms in order to establish eligibility for state help. He stated that in order to qualify for such help 'nothing must be bought but that which is absolutely necessary for the maintenance of physical health and what is bought must be of the plainest and most economical description'. Thus, Rowntree introduced the notion of a 'poverty line' which in its first conception was thought of as minimal. In practice, Rowntree himself revised his definition of a subsistence standard upwards in later surveys of poverty in York in 1936 and 1950.

More recent attempts to establish what absolute poverty means in practice have also met problems in defining and operationalising the concept. Drewnowski and Scott attempted to operationalise the concept of absolute poverty by suggesting measures of both basic physical and cultural needs (e.g. security, education). The admitted fact that such needs, especially cultural ones, vary between individuals, between societies, and within the same society over time, ironically means that absolute standards of poverty are unlikely to be other than approximate and tentative. It would appear unwise to put much reliance on them except in cases of extreme scarcity and necessity.

Although Britain became an increasingly unequal society in the late nineteen eighties and early nineties, *absolute* poverty remains rare and exceptional. In parts of the so-called 'Third World', however, it is commonplace. The relationship between the West and the 'Third World' is itself one of great inequality and, some would argue, exploitation. Chapters 20 and 21 examine inequality and poverty in the 'Third World', broadly in an international context (see especially pp. 468–9).

RELATIVE POVERTY

A second type of poverty is *relative* poverty. Peter Townsend has argued that those who have 'resources so seriously below those commanded by the average individual or family that they are, in effect, excluded from ordinary living patterns, customs and activities' are relatively poor. Similarly, Joanna Mack and Stewart Lansley consider that relative poverty exists in the absence of 'a minimum standard of living on socially established criteria and not just the criteria of survival or subsistence'.

Critics of relative definitions of poverty argue that those who adopt this approach tend consistently to move the poverty line upwards – thus obscuring the fact that in Britain, as in other wealthier countries, those at the bottom of society have tended to become better off – as have other groups. In 1988, the Department of Health and Social Security stated that measuring poverty on the basis of the numbers receiving means tested benefits, as is commonly done, can make it appear that more become poor when benefits are increased – because more become eligible for them. Speaking on the same theme, the then Social Security Secretary, John Moore argued that in advanced societies such as Britain, some people were 'less equal' but not in poverty.

MEASURING POVERTY

OFFICIAL MEASURES Although there has never been an official poverty line in Britain, figures based on those receiving benefits have provided a gauge for measuring poverty. Thus, until 1985, the numbers receiving supplementary benefit (replaced in 1988 by income support) provided a quasi-official measure. However, the government stopped producing this calculation from 1987 and instead introduced a new statistical series based on the number of households with below average or half average income. In order to maintain the two-yearly comparison of the numbers (of families) on supplementary benefit, the Institute for Fiscal Studies calculated the relevant figures for 1987. In practice, both the calculations based on supplementary benefit and those based on household income showed a sharp increase in poverty between 1979–1987 (i.e. relative poverty – given the real increase in the value of supplementary benefit and of average income).

In addition to the 4.3 million families living on supplementary benefit in 1987, another 1.9 million families were living on income lower than the safety-net level of social security and of these over 800,000 failed to claim the state benefits to which they were entitled (table 7.1). Between 1985 and 1987, there was a four per cent increase in families not receiving benefit but having an income on or below benefit level. According to the House of Commons Social Security Committee, lack of take-up of

Number of Low-income Families

	Supp. benefit	Equivalent or less	Total
1979	2,590	1,420	4,010
1981	3,010	1,610	4,620
1983	3,640	1,880	5,520
1985	4,110	1,830	5,940
1987	4,330	1,910	6,240

(Source: Department of Social Security 1981–83). IFS (1985/87)

benefits increased after the implementation of the 1988 Social Security Act.

Official statistics on both households with below half average earnings and on supplementary benefit/income support as a percentage of average earnings show a clear increase in relative poverty (table 7.2).

Households with below half average earnings (figures in thousands)

	1979	1987
Before allowance for housing costs	3.7	7.7
After allowance for housing costs	4.9	10.5

(Source: Department of Social Security)

The Department of Social Security argued that the continuing decrease in the benefit rates as a percentage of average income demonstrated that work incentives – a main aspect of government policy – were increasingly effective. Others might see them as further evidence that an underclass has developed in Britain, significantly adrift from the majority in terms of its standard of living.

PETER TOWNSEND The numbers of those on supplementary benefit/income support (whether measured individually or as families) show a sharp increase in relative poverty over the decade of the nineteen eighties – an increase that is likely to have accelerated during the economic recession of 1990. However, there have long been those who argue that the 'official' measure of those in poverty is inadequate. Peter Townsend has argued this case for over three decades. In 1979, he published his huge empirical survey *Poverty in the United Kingdom*, in which, on an admittedly much 'higher poverty line' than the government's, he found 14 million people (or 22.9 per cent of the population) in poverty.

More recently, Townsend has led a research team from Bristol University which concluded that government rates for income support were about 50 per cent too low. The team reached this conclusion on the basis of both subjective and objective measures. The research is based on surveys in Greater London and separate studies in Islington, Hackney and Bromley but, possibly with minor qualifications, its conclusion should be nationally and even internationally applicable.

The subjective measure of poverty was

◄ **Table 7.2**

◄ **Table 7.1 (Far left)**

Supplementary benefit/Income support as a percentage of average earnings

	July 1986	April 1987	April 1988
Single person	20.8	19.,5	19.1
Couple	32.1	30.3	28.3
Couple + 1 child	38.5	36.4	32.9
Couple + 2 children	43.1	40.8	37.1
Couple + 3 children	47.2	44.8	41.1
Couple + 4 children	51.0	48.5	44.8

(Source: Department of Social Security)

▲

Table 7.3

obtained by asking people, in Townsend's words 'their opinions on the meaning of poverty, its presumed causes, how the household managed on its income and how much was needed in weekly income to stay out of poverty' and 'whether household income was much above or below this level' (The Guardian). The survey covered ten different types of households, and nearly all respondents put the basic income needed much higher than that payable under social security rules, with the average at 61 per cent higher.

The objective evidence, supporting the above perceived need, was obtained by giving the same respondents 'a long list of questions about their diet, clothing, housing, home facilities, environment, location, work, rights in employment, family activity, community integration, participation in social institutions, recreation and education … The intention was to cover every possible major aspect of material and social life.' The research team established that there was a level of income below which multiple-deprivation almost certainly occurred. This level was 57 per cent above government rates of means-tested assistance for couples under pensionable age; 51 per cent for couples with two children; and 68 per cent for single parent families.

Townsend comments on the closeness of the subjective and objective measures of poverty produced by the research team: both indicating that Government rates for income support fall short of need by over 50 per cent. Townsend concludes his article by asking whether these rates are so low that they are 'simply perpetuating … poverty'.

JOANNA MACK AND STEWART LANSLEY In their book, *Poor Britain* (1985), Joanna Mack and Stewart Lansley attempt to establish a relative definition of poverty by questioning

members of the public on the matter and, on that basis, attempt to measure degrees of poverty in the country.

They establish that there is a considerable degree of consensus among the British public on the necessities required to maintain 'a minimum standard of living on socially established criteria and not just the criteria of survival or subsistence'. Over 90 per cent of people (from a representative quota sample of 1174 respondents) agree on the importance of the following for basic living in the home: heating, an indoor toilet (not shared), a damp-free home, a bath (not shared), and beds for everyone. A further 21 items – from having enough money for public transport to possessing a warm waterproof coat – were regarded as necessities by more than one-half of respondents. This list of 26 necessities, established by the majority of respondents, is the basis on which Mack and Lansley measure poverty. They find that 'all those with an enforced lack of three or more necessities are in poverty. … All fall below the minimum way of life laid down by society as a whole.' On this measure, 5 million adults and 2.5 million children were in poverty. The table below shows the varying depths of poverty in Britain as measured by lack of necessities. The authors comment on those in intense poverty: 'their lives are diminished and demeaned in every way, so far do they fall below the minimum standards of society today'.

Mack and Lansley find five main groups whose living standards are too low: the unemployed, single parents, the sick and disabled, pensioners and the low paid. There are roughly as many in poverty who are in low-paid work as there are unemployed, but the unemployed are almost twice as likely to suffer intense poverty. The authors argue that the impact of the 1981 recession – particularly the very high level of unemployment – and government social policy which has resulted in an increase in income for the super-rich and a decrease for the poor are the main causes of current renewed concern about poverty. Their survey also noted, however, a waning in the backlash against 'welfarism' which partly swept Margaret Thatcher to power and they found a majority (57 per cent) who thought the government was doing too little to help those lacking necessities.

SOME MISSING NECESSITIES

■ approximately 3 million people in Britain today cannot afford to heat the living areas of their home

■ around 6 million go without some essential aspect of clothing – such as a warm waterproof coat – because of lack of money

■ some 1.5 million children go without toys or, for older children, leisure and sports equipment because their parents do not have enough money

■ nearly 3.5 million people do not have consumer durables such as carpets, a washing machine or a fridge because of lack of money

■ around 3 million people cannot afford celebrations at Christmas or presents for the family once a year

■ at least 5.5 million people cannot afford basic items of food such as meat or fish

every other day, a roast joint once a week or two hot meals a day

■ nearly half a million children do not have three meals a day because their parents are so short of money

(Source: Adapted from J Mack and S Lansley 1985: 184 and 90)

The Depths of Poverty (in millions)

	In or on the margins	In Poverty	Sinking deeper	In intense poverty
Adults	7.9	5.0	3.3	1.7
Children	4.2	2.5	1.4	0.9
Total (millions)	12.1	7.5	4.7	2.6
Percentage of the population	22.2	13.8	8.6	4.8
Lack of necessities (number of)	1/2	3	5/6	7+

▲

Table 7.4

Theoretical Perspectives on the Causes of Poverty

Four theoretical perspectives on poverty are discussed below. The controversial concept of the underclass is considered by some to be a further perspective on Contemporary Poverty (see pp. 144–6).

INDIVIDUAL INADEQUACY: CONSERVATIVE PERSPECTIVE 1

Nineteenth and early twentieth century writers on social problems, including poverty, in both Britain and the United States commonly sought their causes in individual pathology or weakness of either a physical, mental or moral kind. Belief in self-help and the survival of the fittest gave support to the view that the deserving succeed and the weak and worthless fail. This philosophy is indicated in the title of Charles Henderson's textbook on social problems published in 1906: *An Introduction to the Study of Defective, Dependent and Delinquent Classes*. Religious and moralistic motives were common among those who helped the poor and the urge to uplift them spiritually was as strong or stronger than the desire to assist them materially. At this time few envisaged that the state would largely

take over 'charitable' activities from the churches.

Individualistic explanations of social problems flourished again in the nineteen seventies and eighties. Such approaches have always had some popular currency but in this period they gained substantial political and academic support. Both Ronald Reagan, the former American President and Republican Party leader, and Margaret Thatcher, the former British Prime Minister and Conservative Party leader, vigorously adopted philosophies of individual enterprise and reward, and cut back on many welfare programmes. Thus, Thatcher stated 'Let our children grow tall, and some grow taller than others'. More down to earth was her then Minister of Employment, Norman Tebbit's advice to the unemployed to 'get on your bike'.

To those who argue that poverty in modern capitalist society is largely social structural in nature, such comments misleadingly individualise poverty and inequality. In their view welfare dependents are more likely to be the 'victims' rather than the 'villains' of capitalism – typically offered jobs so lowly paid that some might find there is little incentive. Their solution lies in a higher wage economy and, generally, a more equal distribution of wealth.

THE CULTURE OF POVERTY THESIS: CONSERVATIVE PERSPECTIVE 2

Another explanation of poverty popular among conservative thinkers is that it is generated and regenerated by the cultural attitudes and life style of the poor. This is the 'culture of poverty' theory. It often involves 'trait analysis' of the life style of the poor. These traits, or characteristics, are said to include present-centredness, a sense of resignation and fatalism, and a strong predisposition to authoritarianism. At its most extreme, this interpretation sees the poor as inadequate and pathological. Edward Banfield describes the 'lower class individual' as follows:

> *Although he has more 'leisure' than almost anyone, the indifference ('apathy' if one prefers) of the lower class person is such that he seldom makes even the simplest repairs to the place that he lives in. He is not troubled by dirt and dilapidation and he does not mind the inadequacy of public facilities such as schools, parks, hospitals and libraries; indeed, where such things exist he may destroy them by carelessness or even by vandalism. Conditions that make the slum repellent to others are serviceable to him.*
>
> *(Cited in Raynor and Harris eds., 1977: 234)*

Given that Banfield regards the cause of poverty as rooted in psychological attitudes, he is dubious about easy solutions aimed at changing the way in which people live. Cultural attitudes tend to undermine imposed reform.

An earlier study by Oscar Lewis puts the concept of the culture of poverty in a wider context. The conditions in which it flourishes include a low-wage, profit-oriented economy and inadequate government assistance for the poor. These are frequently to be found in Third World areas which are under-going 'development' by foreign capital and, more locally, in inner-city areas almost anywhere in the world. Given this wider context, the culture of poverty thesis loses its conservatism and becomes, generally, more useful.

Sir Keith Joseph's concept of the 'cycle of deprivation' had some similarity to the 'class culture' approach but it lays greater stress on the effect of material factors, such as poor housing and low income, in undermining prospects for self-improvement from generation to generation. Among cultural factors, he particularly emphasises the inadequacy of parental upbringing and the home background. The logical answer to this is to help and strengthen the family. Whether this can be done on a piecemeal basis is highly debatable. In any case, research led by Michael Rutter has shown that most poverty is not intergenerational.

The notion of 'the dependency culture', popular among Conservative politicians and ideologies in the late nineteen eighties, is essentially a version of the culture of poverty thesis. According to Charles Murray, there are broadly two types of poverty that of the 'deserving' and 'undeserving' poor. It is the latter who have created for themselves a 'culture of dependency' and they have been able to do this by living off welfare. A one-time adviser to President Reagan, Murray attempts in his book *Losing Ground, American Social Policy 1950–1980* to provide intellectual and empirical support for the above philosophy and related policies. Murray argues that in the post-war period in the United States, the most marked improvement in the condition of the poor occurred throughout the 1950s and early 1960s before the War on Poverty of the Johnson administration and the continued massive welfare programmes of his successors prior to Reagan. Ironically, after two decades of relatively steady progress, improvements in the condition of the poor, as measured by a number of indicators, slowed in the late 1960s and stopped altogether in the late nineteen seventies. In other words, poverty got relatively worse as programmes to reduce it increased. According to Murray, this is because many found it preferable to be 'on welfare' (i.e. in poverty) than to work: they took advantage of what he calls 'the generous (welfare) revolution'. This view, of course, has also frequently been voiced on this side of the Atlantic. In fact, Murray himself, had access to leading British Conservative politicians in

1989 and, as we have seen, applied his ideas to the British context (pp. 144–5).

It may not be coincidence that two of the three most important measures announced by the Conservative government for the 1989–90 session related to issues identified by Murray as central to the dependent underclass: single parent families and rising crime. The government proposed to set up a child support agency which would trace absent fathers and secure maintenance payments from them. Among its planned legislation on crime were measures to make parents take greater responsibility for offences committed by their children, and tougher community penalties.

In practice, notions of individual irresponsibility and cultural deficiency easily blend together. It is the 'inadequate' individuals who are considered to create the 'inadequate' culture. Whether the measures mentioned in the previous paragraph will be effective in dealing with this 'syndrome' remains to be seen. There is perhaps a pessimistic parallel in the Conservative government's earlier attempt to make school leavers join the Youth Training Scheme if they were unable to obtain employment. The mechanism for achieving this was to withdraw eligibility for social security from those who refused to join what authorities regarded as a 'suitable' scheme. The unintended consequence of this was that many youngsters had opted out of the system altogether – sporadically living rough or participating in the black economy. It does not require much imagination to conceive of negative unintended consequences of requiring less well off absent fathers to pay maintenance or of requiring families under pressure and perhaps in conflict to be responsible for the crimes of their children.

POVERTY AS SITUATIONAL: LIBERAL REFORMIST PERSPECTIVE

An analysis of poverty developed in the United States is that it is frequently the result of the situation an individual or group experiences. Thus, illness; unemployment, low pay and loss of income in old age can be immediate causes of poverty yet these are rarely the 'fault' of the people concerned. This approach tends to stop short of 'blaming capitalism' for poverty but seeks to help

people to cope with the particular misfortune that has afflicted them. Nevertheless, many non-Marxists who adopt this approach are well aware that the capitalist system can operate in a way that can cause or exacerbate poverty.

This perspective on poverty is associated with progressive liberal or social democratic political ideas, and it inspired much of the reforming legislation that set up the framework of the twentieth century Welfare State. First, contributory old age pensions and then insurance for employees against sickness and unemployment were introduced by government. The Welfare State was consolidated and extended by the first post Second World War Labour government. Two important measures were the setting up of the National Health Service, and of the National Assistance Board. The purpose of the latter was to provide help for those who remained unemployed after their unemployment benefit had been exhausted, or who were otherwise without income. The role of the NAB has since been taken over by the Supplementary Benefits Commission.

The reformer's view that poverty 'hits' certain identifiable groups, who must therefore be helped, is enticingly simple, yet poverty stubbornly persists despite the Welfare State. It is a severe disappointment to the many politicians and intellectuals, who hoped that the Welfare state would virtually abolish poverty, that millions are in receipt of social security in the early nineteen nineties. Such was certainly not the intention of Lord Beveridge whose official report was largely responsible for the structure of the NAB. He hoped that a low unemployment and high wage economy, coupled with a better system of unemployment insurance, would mean that the supplementary function of the NAB would substantially decrease rather than increase. There are other concerns about the way the Welfare State operates. One is that it fails significantly to redistribute wealth from the better off to the poor. This is because the middle class make more use of the Welfare State than the poor. Thus, they keep their children in education for longer, and, often, use the health service more. Further, as middle class people, from clerks to Principal Secretaries (top civil servants), run the Welfare State, it is in a sense, an employment subsidy for them. Often, the bureaucratic way in which welfare is administered confuses or 'mystifies' those who need help. Long waits, form-filling and questioning may or may not be the norm, but they happen frequently enough – particularly in the administration of social security – to intimidate some.

Despite the above reservations, the extent of poverty at the beginning of the nineteen nineties ensured both widespread public support for the Welfare State and heavy demand for its services. An ageing population, high long-term unemployment, and increasing numbers of one parent families required massive expenditure on social welfare.

'THE CAPITALIST SYSTEM' AS THE CAUSE OF POVERTY: RADICAL STRUCTURAL AND MARXIST PERSPECTIVES

As understood here, radical structural and Marxist perspectives agree on one central point: that capitalism produces fundamental social problems. The classic free enterprise system, so praised by conservative individualists, is seen as inherently incapable of producing social justice and stability. The pursuit of profit and the exploitation of labour results in severe inequality. Radical structural and Marxist theorists tend to regard inequality not so much as a social problem but as the core social issue of capitalism, out of which other problems and issues are generated. Thus, Marxists in particular consider that problems relating to freedom of expression cannot be solved adequately unless the issue of inequality is first dealt with. People cannot enjoy freedom if their fundamental needs are not first met. J C Kincaid puts the Marxist point of view particularly strongly: 'Poverty cannot be abolished within capitalist society, but only in socialist society under workers' control, in which human needs, and not profits, determine the allocation of resources'.

The above approach is, of course, more than a perspective on poverty, it is an analysis of a system – the capitalist system. Though theorists adopting this broad analysis agree on the basic cause of social problems in capitalist society, they do not necessarily agree on the solution. Some argue that social justice, equality and freedom can be achieved by the reform of capitalism whereas others consider that these goals cannot be attained unless the system is abolished. I refer to the former as radical structural theorists and the latter as Marxists. The disagreements between the two groups become more apparent in the section on policy in a later chapter, though not all writers take a clear position (see chapter 15).

The Marxists, John Westergaard and Henrietta Resler adopt a structural analysis of inequality in *Class in Capitalist Society: A Study of Contemporary Britain'* (1976). They prefer the term inequality to poverty because the latter can so easily be (mis) explained as an individual or group problem. They wish to focus on inequality as a product of the capitalist system. Inequality cannot be dealt with simply by making efforts to get certain groups above the poverty line. Reforms gained in times of expansion may be lost during a recession, or economic and technological developments may put new groups into poverty. For them, poverty or rather inequality is a class rather than an individual or group issue. All wage-workers, employed or unemployed, are potential victims of the capitalist system. Like Kincaid, their solution lies in collective action to change the system, not in supporting piece-meal 'remedies' which are not designed to produce wholesale change in the general structure of inequality'.

Marxists argue that capitalist politicians and the media typically obscure the real cause of poverty and inequality in capitalist society, sometimes by scapegoating the poor or other minority groups. Thus, Stuart Hall and his co-authors argue in *Policing the Crisis, Mugging the State and Law and Order* (1979), that blacks in Britain have frequently been made the scapegoats of economic crisis, particularly rising unemployment. Political and media attention on the race issue whipped up a series of moral panics which distracted attention from the failure of capital to generate economic growth and high employment. The 'mugger' was a particularly negative stereotype of young, black urban males which aggravated racial tension and hampered the development of class solidarity across racial lines.

Michael Harrington's *The New American Poverty* (1984) makes a structural analysis of poverty in that country which is almost equally applicable to poverty in Britain. A reforming socialist rather than a Marxist,

Harrington nevertheless offers an analysis that would be broadly acceptable to many Marxists. He begins by locating 'a deep structural source of a new poverty that could persist into the indefinite future' – the 'internationalisation of the economy (and) of poverty' by the multinational corporations. The power of the multinationals to switch investment and production around the globe has weakened the bargaining power of labour in developed capitalist societies and has tended to lower wages and increase unemployment. Labour itself has become internationalised and far more disorganised and weak as a result. He refers to the millions of undocumented migrant labourers in the United States who are very low-paid and who may also depress the wages of indigenous workers by their willingness to work for so little. We examine the same process in relation to European migrant and many black workers in Britain in chapter 9. As Harrington puts it, '(t)he Third World is ... not simply out there, it is within and at the gates'. He points out that most of the service jobs that are replacing those in heavy manufacture in both Britain and America are relatively low-paid. He also dispels the myth that there will be many 'high-tech' jobs available. In fact, far more routine 'low-tech' than high-tech jobs are being produced and far more non-technical jobs in the low paid sector, such as fast-food and janitoring, than either.

Partly as a result of the above trends, Harrington sees a new 'underclass' developing, largely cut off from the materially good life available in various degrees to other Americans. The use of the term underclass will not recommend Harrington's analysis to Marxists, most of whom prefer that of lower working class, but there is little doubt that he has located an empirically real phenomenon however we conceptualise it. He uses the term underclass primarily to indicate those in long-term structural poverty among whom are disproportionate numbers of the unemployed, the low-paid, ethnic minorities, the 'rootless' mentally ill or retarded, the less educated young, and one parent families. The rise in the number of one parent families – most of whom are headed by women – living in or at the margin of poverty, and of low-paid working women leads Harrington to refer to the 'feminisation' of poverty. In 1960, 65 per cent of poor families were headed by men under 65 years of age, and 21 per cent by women, whereas in 1979 the respective figures were 42.4 per cent and 43.7 per cent – a profound change and an ironic commentary on the position of women in the supposed age of female emancipation. This figure also explains why 20 per cent of America's children are in poverty according to the estimate cited by Harrington.

Britain is even more vulnerable to international economic trends than the United States. Indeed, André Gunder Frank has suggested that Britain may be the first advanced capitalist country to 'underdevelop' (see p. 477). This would happen if, in the context of the international division of labour, Britain were to become a mainly low-wage rather than mainly high-wage economy. This might happen if, for instance, large sections of the labour force were engaged in assembling and manufacturing goods developed and designed in, say, Japan or Germany.

It will be clear that radicals see the causes of most poverty as structural rather than individual in nature. However, they do appreciate that there are cultural as well as material consequences of economic change or 'restructuring'. Thus, in an earlier book, *The Other America* (1963), Harrington wrote of the 'low levels of aspiration and high levels of mental stress' among the poor. Similarly, Coates and Silburn wrote of 'the hopelessness and despair of slum in life in Nottingham' (*Poverty, the Forgotten Englishmen* 1970). For them, the main solutions as well as causes of poverty are structural and their implementation requires a social system based on greater equality.

CONCLUSION: THE CAUSES OF POVERTY An examination of the groups that make up the lowest quintile (fifth) group of household income – one measure of poverty – may help the reader reach some conclusion about which of the above theoretical explanations of poverty is more convincing (see figure 7.1). The case of the unemployed can be best considered in relation to figure 11.6.

Few would argue that either pensioners or the sick or disabled are responsible for their own low income. Together, these made up 30 per cent of the lowest quintile group of household income in 1981 and 30 per cent

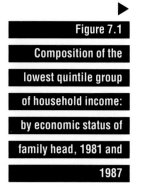

▶

Figure 7.1

Composition of the lowest quintile group of household income: by economic status of family head, 1981 and 1987

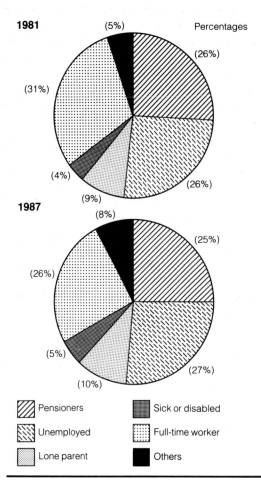

(Source: Social trends 1991)

which are beyond their control? There is perhaps a clue to the answer in the trend to greater unemployment from 1981 to 1987 (see figure 7.1) and the trend by which the unemployed increased as a percentage of those in poverty between 1981 and 1985 (from 26 per cent to 33 per cent) and again in 1990. It seems clear that more people became unemployed and more of the unemployed entered the lowest income group because of the economic recession, not because of personal laziness – in other words, for structural rather than personal reasons. As figure 11.6 shows unemployment increased as job vacancies decreases – pointing to economic rather than personal explanation. Similarly, low-pay as a cause of poverty for full-time workers actually increases when there is fuller employment. Again, to blame low-paid workers for their poverty seems unfounded. A national minimum wage of an adequate level would take them out of poverty at a stroke.

Single parents accounted for only one in 11 and one in 10 in the lowest quintile household group in 1981 and 1985 respectively. Although the figure is likely to be somewhat larger by 1992, it is surprisingly small given the political targetting of this group as a drain on public expenditure at the turn of the last decade (p. 158). A national system of pre-school nurseries might be a more positive way of releasing the productivity of this group and enabling them to contribute to the national exchequer.

A brief overview of who the poor are provides one way of testing the theories of poverty against realities. It is worth remembering, however, that the majority of the poor are children to whom no blame can be attached.

in 1987. In their case, poverty is structural in the sense that they can do little about it and 'political' in the sense that the public and government have 'decided' not to take the steps necessary to remove them from poverty.

Together, unemployed and low-paid full-time workers make up well over fifty per cent of the total group. Is their poverty 'their own fault' or, again, are there social, economic, or political factors causing it

Social Equality and Freedom: Four Views. Is Stratification Inevitable?

This chapter and the previous two have presented and discussed a mass of empirical data on class and inequality. This section examines the underlying social philosophical issues behind such data. What is the relationship between equality and freedom? What are the implications for the ideal of equality of the failure of Soviet and Eastern European communism. Is social inequality

part of the 'nature of things' or is it possible greatly to diminish if not wholly to abolish it?

This section discusses four perspectives on the issue of equality and the relationship between equality and freedom. These are:

■ **Classical liberal**
■ **Functionalist**
■ **Marxist**

■ Social democratic (or 'reforming' liberal)

The classical liberal and functionalist perspectives on equality are broadly complementary, although they have distinct roots – the former in economics, the latter in sociology. The social democratic or modern liberal reformist perspective draws from both Marxism and the classical liberal tradition but is manifestly different from both.

CLASSICAL LIBERAL PERSPECTIVE

Classical eighteenth and nineteenth century liberals emphasised economic liberty or freedom rather than material equality. Adam Smith (1723–1790) considered that a 'free' economy i.e. a capitalist economy, was the basis of a free society. The 'free market' was the basis of freedom to travel, to meet others of all kinds, and to make ones own individual wealth and happiness. Nineteenth century and modern free market thinkers also often argue that a free market is a pre-condition for democracy. In the early nineteenth century, the only equality that such freedom implied was the equal right in law to protection and to compete economically. However, limited equality under the law in no way implied that the state should help those with fewer resources. Rather, people were considered to have the right to succeed or fail on the basis of their own resources. In the late nineteen seventies, when the first edition of this book was being written, it would have occurred to few people that nineteenth century liberalism would be revived – in the form of Thatcherism and Reaganism – and become the dominant political ideology of the nineteen eighties. Contemporary free-market theorists, such as Frederich Hayek and Milton Friedman, have reiterated the points made two centuries ago by Adam Smith. Already, their views have had considerable practical application although widespread criticism of them increased in the late nineteen eighties and early nineties.

The implications of the classic liberal position for social equality have been well summarised by Peter Saunders, a sociologist who has some sympathy for this perspective. Saunders points out that writers such as Hayek:

argue that inequality is the necessary price to be paid for economic growth in market societies. In this view, individuals pursuing their own self-interest indirectly benefit everybody else at the same time as they benefit themselves. This is because, in a capitalist society, some individuals will try to make money by innovating, setting up business, or investing in other people's business to enable them to expand ... Thus, a few entrepreneurs become rich, some others fail and go bust, and meanwhile the rest of society grows more affluent as it gains by their efforts ... Capitalism is dynamic because it is unequal, and any attempt to equalise wealth and income will succeed only at the expense of stifling initiative, innovation and social and economic development.

(Saunders, 1990:53)

Saunders' arguments are admirably clear. Not only is capitalism an unequal system but it has to be in order to work effectively. However, as capitalism is a system devoted to the creation of wealth, 'the rest of society grows more affluent' as a result of the efforts of 'a few entrepreneurs'.

FUNCTIONALIST PERSPECTIVE

Within sociology, the view that stratification is inevitable has always been associated with functionalist theory. The definitive functionalist presentation of this issue was by Davis and Moore (1956), but the roots of the functionalist position can be traced to Durkheim and Herbert Spencer. Both of them considered that as societies evolve and grow more complex a greater variety of social roles and functions develop. One of the first examples of role differentiation in the evolution of most societies is that of tribe or band 'leader' or 'priest', or perhaps a combination of both. Now differentiation need not lead to stratification if equal power, status and rewards are attached to all roles but, in practice, this rarely, if ever, occurs. Indeed, Durkheim and Spencer assumed the opposite – that key or particularly demanding roles, such as leader or chief, would be recognised as having more status than functionally less important and demanding ones. Since role differentiation, in a factory or bureaucracy, for instance, is so much a part of modern life, so must stratification be. A complex system of stratification is seen by functionalists as a necessary product of a complex society.

Davis and Moore extend some of the arguments of earlier functionalists and add a number of their own. They contend that some positions in the social system are more important than others for the functioning and stability of society. Thus, the position of 'chief' or managing director are both relatively crucial in these respects. Functionally important positions require talented people to fill them and there are only a limited number of such people in a given population. Even talented people must undergo long periods of training if they are to execute such key roles as surgeon, air pilot or research scientist. In return for undergoing lengthy training and for the qualifications and skills thus acquired, they require more pay and 'perks' than less able and less well trained people. In addition, they would also expect their occupations to carry high status. The existence of a group with greater access to material and status rewards than others means, in effect, that a system of stratification also exists. As such a group is necessary to all societies, it follows that stratification must be inevitable as well as functional.

Marxist scholars have been notably energetic in revealing and attacking the assumptions behind the arguments of Davis and Moore. Recently, Bowles and Gintis have pointed out that, in the United States, economic success (and thus career success) is less associated with intelligence than with the socio-economic status of a person's parents (see chapter 4 for details of this argument).

Tom Bottomore, writing several years before Bowles and Gintis, firmly refutes the contention that the occupational hierarchy is a true reflection of innate 'talent' or ability:

The major inequalities in society are in the main social products, created and maintained by the institutions of property and inheritance, of political and military power, and supported by particular beliefs and doctrines, even though they are never entirely resistant to the ambitions of outstanding individuals (Bottomore, 1991).

Bottomore has further argued that this state of affairs is only mitigated, not abolished, by increased educational opportunity and more open competition in

the job market.

Davis and Moore have also been attacked by Tumin for failing to appreciate the great wastage of talent and potential amongst the lower classes that stratification can cause. Because of social background disadvantages there is not, in his view, equal opportunity. Tumin also stresses the human cost of stratification in terms of the frustration and sense of failure that quite able, but less privileged, members of society can feel.

MARXIST PERSPECTIVE

Marxists argue that stratification exists because of the unequal ownership of private property. They consider that if private property is abolished and communism established, class stratification will cease to exist. Marx argued that capitalism is characterised by certain inherent contradictions which make it prone to self-destruction. In particular, he contended that capitalism creates increasing inequality and involves the 'immiseration' (increased impoverishment) of the proletariat. On this point, the evidence seems, to say the least, strongly to favour the classic literal view – that capitalism has increased the wealth of the majority as well as the minority. However, this in itself by no means destroys the Marxist critique of capitalism or the argument for a different kind of society. Whether the working class has been becoming increasingly poor or not, many of its members have undoubtedly been 'exploited' in respect to their working conditions and pay. This is especially so, if capitalism is examined as a world system. To cite the extreme case, there are examples where capitalists have treated labour as little better than cattle, providing unhealthy and even dangerous working and living conditions, no job security, and wages at around subsistence level. Examples of this kind have been and continue to be so numerous that it is entirely reasonable to pose the possibility of a less 'exploitative', more equal socio-economic system.

The difficulty for Marxism has not been in criticising capitalism but in producing theoretically and practically a convincing alternative. Marx's own descriptions of what communist society would be like are fairly skimpy. The main practical attempt to produce a communist society – in Soviet

Russia appears, at the time of writing (1992) effectively to have been abandoned. Similarly, the Soviet 'satellite' countries of Eastern Europe have, to a greater or lesser extent, adopted mixed (i.e. partly capitalist) economics. Former communist East Germany has capped all this by unifying with former West Germany – perhaps Europe's most successful post-war capitalist economy.

As a practical example of equality, then, communism has lost much credibility. First, the above societies did not even approximate to social equality and did not appear to be developing towards it before introducing capitalism. However, material equality was probably rather greater in the societies than in the capitalist West even though their general level of wealth was lower. Second, none of these societies achieved a high level of political, cultural and social freedom compared to Western European and North American societies. This provides some evidence for the view of Hayek and Friedmann that communism and freedom do not mix. In summary, the record of these communist societies compared to the capitalist Western ones was slightly more material equality; substantially less wealth; and substantially less freedom. That this is perhaps a fair summary is supported by the abandonment of authoritarian communism by the Eastern European former communist countries.

Marxists seem able to cite enough evidence to demonstrate that stratification benefits some at the expense of others and that it persists, not merely because it is useful, but at least partly because the rich and powerful wish it to. However, they tend to overlook the possibility that as well as benefiting the rich and powerful at the expense of the less advantaged (as most systems of stratification certainly do), stratification may exist for other, more necessary reasons.

The essence of the functionalist position is precisely that somebody must do the more difficult and skilful tasks and will, as a result, expect higher rewards and status. This argument could still be true, whatever the social origins of those who came to occupy the top occupational positions. It would be sustainable even if children of lower class origins were disproportionately successful (instead of the opposite). The Marxist reply to this would be that, if people were rewarded according to need rather than on the basis of the nature of work they performed, no material or status inequality would result from differences in occupation. In a communist society, all property would be held in common and the product of all human labour would be shared on a rough basis of equality, with variations depending on individual circumstances and requirements. In addition, as far as possible, jobs would rotate so that more people had an opportunity to do interesting work and escape being permanently trapped in boring and unhealthy occupations.

In an ideal sense, Marx's vision – for it is a visionary's dream – of a classless society is 'better' (if we may speak for a moment in moral terms) than the stratified societies that we are more familiar with. But whether such a society is possible is another matter.

SOCIAL DEMOCRATIC (OR 'REFORMIST' LIBERAL) PERSPECTIVE

The social democratic (or modern liberal reformist) tradition can be considered as an 'intermediate' position between classical liberalism and Marxism, although it has roots partly independent of both. Social democrats accept that the free enterprise system is the most effective means of producing, distributing and exchanging goods. Probably most now agree that political freedom largely depends on the existence of economic freedom. They accept, too, that a mainly capitalist economy produces great social inequality. It is at this point they differ from both classic liberals and Marxists. They differ from the former in that they consider the extent of the inequality typically produced by capitalism to be unacceptable. For instance, the general widening of the gap between rich and poor under Thatcherism is the reverse of what most social democrats regard as fair and just. This presents social democrats or modern liberals with the problem of achieving greater equality within a fundamentally capitalist economy.

There are at least three ways in which social democrats seek to bring about greater equality. They seek to ensure equality of opportunity; to redistribute wealth through taxation, the Welfare State and the provision of public services; and, where necessary, they are prepared to control or regulate the economy in the public interest. The concept of equality of opportunity is at the heart of modern liberalism and social democracy just as the equal right to individual protection under the law and free competition is central to classical liberalism. Throughout the thirty years following the end of the second world war, a series of measures designed to reduce class, racial and, finally, gender disadvantage or discrimination and to increase equality of opportunity were passed (these are discussed in the relevant sections of this book).

The second great aim of social democracy in relation to equality is to reduce the 'excessive' inequality of outcome (i.e. income and wealth) that may occur despite or even because of attempts to increase equality of opportunity. The main mechanism through which they have sought to do this has been the Welfare State. Social democrats can reasonably claim that the improvements in the material conditions of the mass of the people which classical liberals attribute to capitalism are partly if not mainly the result of the Welfare State. It is certainly a defensible reading of history to argue that capitalists do not significantly distribute wealth downwards unless required to do so by the state or pressured to do so by workers' organisations – usually, both. However, the arguable success of the Welfare State has been tarnished by waste, inefficiency and by the bureaucratic and undemocratic way in which welfare agencies have often operated. These rather large areas of weakness provided opportunity for the 'new broom' of Thatcherism to sweep in, although Thatcherite reforms, too, are now mature enough for criticism. In particular, massive unemployment; widespread low-pay and the development of what has been termed a new underclass provides ample scope for social-democrats to counter-attack with reformulated ideas and policies.

The control and regulation of the economy (where deemed necessary) in the public interest is the third aspect of social democracy chosen for discussion here. Opinion is fast-changing on how this might be best achieved and, in any case, different circumstances require different strategies. Nationalisation of an industry can be effective in ensuring supply of a particular commodity or service to the public and in maintaining necessary investment. However, some now consider nationalisation rather a blunt instrument of control and associate it with the bureaucratic and undemocratic aspects of welfarism referred to above. Regulatory bodies, inspectorates, and taxation are now more popular instruments of regulation. An example of the latter would be an environmental tax which would require polluters to repay the cost of pollution to the community.

CONCLUSION The above interpretations of the relationship between equality and freedom offer very different visions of society. Classical liberalism offers an extreme commitment to economic freedom whereas Marxism aspires to socio-economic equality. Social democracy accepts that neither full economic freedom nor total social equality are possible but seeks an effective and humane balance between the two.

SUMMARY

1 A distinction must be made between social inequality and poverty. Social inequality means that certain individuals or groups have more material or cultural resources than others. Poverty means that an individual or group has insufficient of some material (or cultural) necessity.

2 Absolute poverty is insufficiency in the basic necessities of existence e.g. in food or shelter. Relative poverty is existence below a minimum standard of living on socially established criteria.

3 There is considerable debate about how best to measure poverty. In particular, Peter Townsend argues that government rates for income support are about 50 per cent below what is required to achieve a decent standard of life.

4 There are four main theories of the

causes of poverty:

Individual inadequacy: conservative perspective I

The culture of poverty thesis: conservative perspective II

Radical structural and marxist perspective

Poverty as situational: liberal reformist perspective

5 Poverty is sometimes seen as caused by individual pathology or weakness of either a physical, mental or moral kind.

6 Poverty is sometimes seen, usually by more conservative thinkers, as generated and regenerated by the cultural attitudes and lifestyle of the poor.

7 Radical structural and marxist perspectives agree that, whatever its benefits, capitalism also produces fundamental social problems. The pursuit of profit and the exploitation of labour results in severe inequality and poverty.

8 A more liberal view of poverty is that it is often situational i.e. the result of particular circumstances, such as illness or unemployment, for which the victim may not be to blame.

9 Is stratification inevitable? Or, put another way, how much social equality is possible? How can equality be best balanced with freedom. Four views are discussed in the text:

Classical liberal perspective
Functionalist perspective
Marxist perspective
Social democratic (or 'reformist liberal') perspective

10 Classical liberals regard inequality as the inevitable price of the freedom provided by 'the free market' system. Classic free-market liberals are much less inclined than reformist liberals to 'interfere' with the free market to reduce its inegalitarian effects.

11 The functionalist perspective regards stratification as functional, inevitable and, therefore, as universal.

12 Marxists argue that stratification exists because of the unequal ownership of private property, the main example of which is unequal relations to the means of production.

13 Social democrats accept the economic advantages of the free market but seek in various ways to reduce the inequalities it creates.

'Research and Coursework' – see the end of the previous chapter.

FURTHER READING

The relevant theoretical sections in Peter *Saunders' Social Class and Stratification* (Routledge, 1990) are particularly good on the classical liberal and Functionalist perspectives on stratification. For balance, T B Bottomore's *Classes in Modern Society* (Allen and Unwin, 1991) is comprehensive on Marxist perspective. Poverty is not a very easy matter to remain up to date about but the annually published *Social Trends* and publications from the Child Poverty Action Group help in this respect.

QUESTIONS

1 Examine the view that social stratification and social inequality are permanent, necessary and inevitable features of human society. (AEB, 1983)

2 To what extent have sociological explanations of poverty helped us to understand poverty in Britain in the 1980s? (AEB, Nov. 1989)

3 Discuss the difficulties sociologists face in attempting to define and measure poverty. (AEB, 1990)

8 Gender

Theories of Sex and Gender

Three perspectives on sex and gender will be discussed below. These are the sex differences approach, the cultural (or sex roles) approach and the integrated approach.

THE SEX DIFFERENCES PERSPECTIVE

The sex differences approach is based on the theory that the main social differences between males and females are caused by and are reflections of biological differences. Thus, in this view, 'biology is destiny', in the sense that women are considered biologically programmed for childrearing and related domestic work whereas men are regarded as 'naturally' breadwinners. Tiger and Fox present a particular radical version of this thesis, arguing that the two sexes have different 'biogrammars' which determine their conduct. Several psychologists have posited a biologically-based maternal instinct matched by a mother-need in babies. This analysis is particularly associated with John Bowlby who, however, modified his position to the extent that he allowed that a 'mother substitute' could meet a child's need for love and affection.

Functionalist explanations of gender differences allow for greater cultural flexibility on the biological base. George Murdock sees the sexual division of labour with women bearing and rearing children and men doing tasks involving strength as a matter of practicality and convenience. Each sex is *biologically* best suited to these respective tasks. Talcott Parsons is more culturally relative in his analysis of the sexual division of labour. He considers that it is functional in the context of capitalist society that women should fulfil the expressive (nurturing, caring) role and men the instrumental (competitive, acquisitive) role. In this way, a married couple complement rather than compete with each other. Parsons reflects something of Freud's view of the 'naturalness' of sex-gender differences. However, Parsons did recognise that women might not be entirely fulfilled as housewives and mothers. Writing in the late nineteen forties he suggested that 'any attempt to force or persuade an overwhelming majority of American women to accept a role of pure and virtuous domesticity alone is probably doomed to failure' (*The Social Structure of the Family*). In view of the avalanche of feminist criticism to come, he might be thought to have understated the case!

THE CULTURAL PERSPECTIVE

The cultural perspective explains gender differences – roles and related behaviour and attitudes – as the product of cultural socialisation. Ann Oakley's explanation of the difference between sex and gender has been basic to the cultural approach. She states that sexual differences are biological in nature, whereas gender differences are culturally produced. This distinction has the further implication that sex differences are more or less unchangeable, whereas gender differences are very much open to variation, change and adaptation. The definitive sexual difference between males and females is based on the parts of the body concerned with sex, procreation and nurture: the genitals and breasts. An example of a difference in gender behaviour occurs in Muslim society. Frequently women veil their faces, whereas men do not. Clearly, there is nothing 'natural' about this. Due to the greater cultural influence of the West in Kuwait than in Saudi Arabia, this custom is somewhat less prevalent there.

Many cross-cultural studies show a wide range of gender behaviour. In particular, Margaret Mead's work seeks to demonstrate that there is no universal 'masculine' or 'feminine' personality. For example, in her fieldwork in the South Pacific she found that both sexes of the Arapesh conform roughly to our traditional stereotype of 'feminity', and both those of the Mundugumor to our 'masculine' stereotype.

A society which provides evidence to support the cultural approach is that of the Wahiba, a Bedouin tribe of central Oman in the Persian Gulf. Gender relations bear little similarity to what would be regarded as 'normal' in Western society:

'The men live with their mothers, apart from their wives, whose huts may be as much as 50 miles away, and just visit them occasionally. Both men and women share the work of making the home but wives then have sole ownership.

In general, work is equally divided, with

goats and sheep being the responsibility of the women while the men tend the camels ...

One of the traditional tasks of the men is the cooking ...'

(Observer, 19/11/78)

The term 'gendered' is particularly associated with the cultural approach. Male and female roles learnt through socialisation are considered to be 'gendered'. Thus, for the Wahiba, domestic cooking is gendered as a male activity, whereas in Britain and the United States it still tends to be gendered as a female activity.

AN INTEGRATED PERSPECTIVE

A third approach to understanding gender is increasingly adopted. For simplicity, I will refer to it here as an integrated perspective. It is integrated in that it draws on both biology and culture and thus avoids the 'either/or' approach of cruder versions of the other two perspectives. It is also an historical approach and, for the reasons below, this is sometimes identified as its main feature.

R C Lewontin and his co-authors argue in *Not In Our Genes: Biology, Ideology and Human Nature* (1984) for 'an integrated understanding of the relationship between the biological and social' rather than either biological or cultural determinism. Such an approach recognises that biological differences occur between individuals and between the two sexes but that interpretations of their significance and meaning can substantially vary. Emily Martin's *The Woman in the Body* (1987) illustrates the main aspects of the integrated approach. Martin examines three specifically female biological experiences – menstruation, childbirth, and the menopause (which have no precise male parallel). She compares the way women undergoing these experiences tend to be dealt with by scientific medicine with the way the women respond to these experiences and to medical management of them. She argues that male dominated medical science treats these female biological processes as a form of production: menstruation is 'failed' production; childbirth, a form of labour – 'managed' by the medical team; and the menopause is the end of productivity.

Martin finds more resentment and opposition to the practice of scientific and managed medicine among working class than middle class women. Here are some brief statements of 'resistance' (188):

'He did an episiotomy without asking or telling me, he just did it. By that time I was his as far as he was concerned'
(Carol Gleason).

'They didn't let me stay in labour too long. My doctor said he didn't want me to go through pain ... I wanted to go through it all, it wasn't hurting that bad'
(Juliet Cook).

'I remember when I went to the hospital. Considering I'm not in a good financial position, not being married and having a baby, she said to me, "Oh, you're going to put the baby up for adoption?" I really, really was angry ... I felt like saying, "How dare you talk to me that way! I'm not some sleazo or some piece of shit or something!"'
(Elizabeth Larson).

Martin is well aware that the above type of statement does not represent a developed feminist position or consciousness. But such statements could be understood as a step on the way to a wider understanding of oppression. The psychology of oppression and of liberation remain part of much current feminist analysis: the key questions being 'how can the oppressed become aware of the source and nature of their oppression' and 'what will prompt them to do something about it'. By making use of frequent historical and cross-cultural references, Martin shows that females can take much greater control of these three basic biological processes and experience them much more positively and creatively than under 'modern' medicine. Martin also contends that in attempting to empower themselves in stereotypically female areas such as the 'health and domestic', females may begin to draw parallels with their lack of power in paid employment. They may become aware that their roles in the latter area are similar to those they play in the domestic and child production/care areas.

A word of caution may be needed about the integrated approach to gender described above. It is certainly not a perspective which states that biology determines gender differences – indeed, it is radically opposed to such an approach. Those who adopt an integrated approach tend to stress how biological differences are differently interpreted historically and across cultures and to be highly conservative in drawing social consequences from biology. Finally, it needs to be said that the integrated approach is really not so new. In practice, much of the work of cultural socialisation theorists, including Ann Oakley, recognised the reality of biological differences between the sexes and took these into account in analysing the gendering process. Ann Oakley's own analysis of scientific medicine (pp. 390–1) and Ross Gill's study of the objectification of the female body in some media (p. 424) stress the impact of patriarchal ideology on the way women are treated but each assumes that things could be very different. What the integrated perspective does is clarify a theoretical approach which was already becoming established.

The remainder of this chapter will have cause to refer to each of the perspectives described above. My own preference is for the integrated perspective although much useful research has been carried out from the cultural approach and this is fully utilised below.

PATRIARCHY; SEXISM; CAPITALISM AND STRATIFICATION

Patriarchy is the system and practice by which males dominate and exploit females. The patriarchal system refers to the principles, regulations and structures of male domination (such as that men are 'naturally' superior to women, or that only men should have certain rights or hold given offices) and to the power and control of men over organisations, institutions and other practical areas of life. The practice of patriarchy refers to the everyday gender relationships which reflect and reproduce the system of patriarchy.

Sexism is discrimination against someone on the basis of their sex. Women rather than men have been systematically discriminated against as a sex, although as individuals men too may be victims of sexual discrimination. Patriarchy is a system based on sexual discrimination.

As we shall shortly see, Marxist feminists link patriarchy with capitalism. Class stratification is seen as the basic context in which patriarchal oppression is structured. Similarly, a number of black feminists have insisted that patriarchy as experienced by black women has been 'mediated' (or structured) by racism. They then attempt to explain the relationship between gender, class and racial stratification.

Feminist Perspectives on Gender

In an essay entitled 'What is feminism', Rosalind Delmar helpfully constructs a 'base-line definition of feminism and the feminist' which most people, feminist or otherwise could probably agree on. She suggests that

At the very least a feminist is someone who holds that women suffer discrimination because of their sex, that they have specific needs which remain negated and unsatisfied, and that satisfaction of these needs would require a radical change (some would say a revolution even) in the social, economic and political order.

(Delmar in J Mitchell and A Oakley eds., 1986:8)

There are three aspects to this definition:
A feminist is someone concerned with:
1 Discrimination against women.
2 Unsatisfied needs of women.
3 The necessity for radical change (or revolution) if these unsatisfied needs are to be met.

These points offer an outline agenda for describing and explaining the position and aspirations of feminists and women in general. However, they will not be pursued sequentially here but will be used as a reference point throughout the chapter. Thus, discrimination against women, their unsatisfied needs, and policy solutions (i.e. ways of meeting these needs) are all more or less explicitly discussed in the context of gender and the family, gender and education and gender and work. Delmar defines a feminist as 'someone' concerned with the above issues. Whether 'someone' can include males as well as females i.e. Can males be feminists, you may wish to consider further.

Having provided a basic definition of

feminism, Delmar goes on to remark – with good reason – that beyond this 'things immediately become more complicated'. They do so because while feminists can probably agree on a broad description of 'the problem', they differ in their explanations of it and in the solutions they offer. The main feminist perspectives are now discussed in detail.

MARXIST-FEMINISM: FEMINIST-MARXISM

In the 1970s, a number of feminists began to draw on Marxist theory in order to explain the oppression of women. There were frequent references in their writings to Engels' *The Origin of the Family, Private Property and the State* which attempted to explain how the legal status of a woman had evolved into that of the private property of her husband (see p. 48). In an article published in 1972 titled *The Role of the Family in the Oppression of Women*, Sue Sharpe analysed the function many women have in reproducing and sustaining the labour force – at great cost to their freedom, potential for development, and often mental health (New Edinburgh Review Seminar, 1972). She suggests that women are thoroughly taken for granted in both the home and the workplace:

What are the consequences of ... work in the home? A woman frequently sinks her identity in that of her man, becoming a mirror image of his successes and failures and a receptacle for his joys, sorrows and angers ...

Employers ... frequently regard women as mere temporary labour, and consider that they should be thought lucky to have the opportunity to earn some money for themselves. They can be used as a surplus labour force, to be employed or laid off at will.

(Sharpe: 1972)

Juliet Mitchell's *Women's Estate* (1971) is a Marxist-feminist attempt to analyse the nature of female oppression, particularly in capitalist society, and to explore how to combat it. She rejects a simple biological explanation of the sexual division of labour in the sense that women 'have to' bear and produce children. Instead, she points to the superior physical power and ability to coerce, of men. The point is that men have been able to make women do almost whatever they wanted. In her words 'Women have been forced to do women's work.' And 'women's work' can be almost anything. Thus, in many zones of tropical Africa women still perform many heavy 'customary' duties, such as carrying loads. The richness of Mitchell's analysis is, however, that she does not exclusively emphasise any one factor in explaining male domination. She considers that repression can operate in any of the three interconnected 'structures' of the family – the sexual, the reproductive, and the socialising – and also in the sphere of economic production.

Accordingly, she urges that the 'fight' for liberation must be directed at all these structural levels, with particular reference to whichever is weakest at a given time.

Like other Marxist-feminists, Mitchell sees women's oppression within the family and in economic production as closely related: women's lack of power in the economic sphere is 'explained' in capitalist society by the supposed 'need' for them to be housewives. She is particularly interested in the psychological aspects of female oppression both in terms of how adult women come to accept their oppression as 'normal' and 'natural' and in terms of how young females are socialised into inferiority. Mitchell sees the oppressed mentality of women as a product of their structural position within the family and society.

What does our oppression within the family do to us women? It produces a tendency to small-mindedness, petty jealousy, irrational emotionality and random violence, dependency, competitive selfishness and possessiveness, passivity, a lack of vision and conservatism. These qualities are not the simple product of male chauvinism, nor are they falsely ascribed to women by a sexist society that uses 'old woman' as a dirty term. They are the result of the woman's objective conditions within the family – itself embedded in a sexist society. You cannot inhabit a small and backward world without it doing something to you.

(Mitchell, 1971: 162)

Like a number of Marxists writing in the nineteen sixties and early seventies, Mitchell drew upon the work of Sigmund Freud in trying to explain the psychological aspects of oppression. In particular she cites Freud's interpretation of the Oedipal situation to explain why '[t]he girl will grow up like her mother but the boy will grow up to be another father'. The Oedipal situation is that a son loves his mother and sees his father as a rival for her, whereas a daughter loves her father and experiences her mother as a rival. In brief, the male rivalry is 'buried' rather than resolved whereas the female rivalry tends to settle down. The difference is that according to Freud, whereas the young male feels his penis to be dwarfed by his father's and so initially opts out of the contest, the young female compares herself more equally with her mother who, like her, has not got a penis at all. In puberty, the young male reasserts himself. All this appears to leave females in a passive role.

Nancy Chodorow offers a very different explanation of how young males and females learn gender identity and rules in which the latter play a more active role (1978). She argues that initially both females and males identify with their mother and that it is fairly straightforward for females to continue to do so. Males have the specific problem of detaching themselves from the identification and developing a male identity. According to Chodorow, young females 'draw in' males later when they are needed as mates. As a model for explaining the reproduction of female identity this is simpler and perhaps more plausible than the Freudian one adopted by Mitchell. In any case, Mitchell's synthesis of Marx and Freud has been rejected by many Marxist-feminists and certainly does not seem necessary to explain the oppression of women.

Mary Maynard adopts a distinction between Marxist-feminists and feminist-Marxists. The former emphasise the economic subordination of women and the latter their ideological subordination. Thus, she classifies Veronica Beechey as a Marxist-feminist. Beechey argues that women are a source of cheap labour for capitalism both domestically and in paid work (Beechey 1987). Michele Barrett is classified as a feminist-Marxist, as she contends that the explanation of why women accept social arrangements which clearly oppress and disadvantage them is that they are ideologically mystified into doing so. They come to believe that the way things are,

including their own subordination, is the only way things can be (Barrett 1980). The different emphasis of these two groups implies a different analysis of the route to women's liberation: Marxist-feminists stress the need to overthrow the capitalist economic system and feminist-Marxists argue that before this can happen, an ideological change must occur in the consciousness of both sexes, but particularly females which frees them from dependence on traditional gender roles. Juliet Mitchell's view that the relationship between economic and ideological oppression can vary but that both have to be dealt with, partly reconciles the two approaches.

RADICAL-FEMINISM

Radical feminism is based on the analysis that patriarchy – the domination of females by males – is the central issue to be faced by feminists.

Two books that can be classified as early radical feminist are Kate Millett's *Sexual Politics* (1970) and Shulamith Firestone's *The Dialectic of Sex* (1972). Millett describes but does not account for the widespread nature of patriarchy. She concentrates particularly on the ideological reproduction of patriarchy by which many females become willing collaborators in their own oppression. Firestone argues that the core of male domination of females is their control of females' roles in reproduction and child-rearing, which has its origins in a biological 'inequality' between the two sexes and is expressed through the nuclear family. The result of bearing and rearing children is to make women dependent on men for the material necessities of life and protection. She, therefore, writes of 'sex class' as an additional category to 'economic class.' She argues that the liberation of women depends on the abolition of the family and the 'power' relationships and psychology that its unequal structure breeds. It is probably true to say that, as a result of Firestone's work, many feminists recognise more clearly the issues that can result for women from their reproductive roles. However, rather than the abolition of the family, they look for other solutions, including much more available and better child care facilities and a redefinition or even abolition of gender roles.

During the nineteen seventies, the focus

Offences involving violence reported to selected police departments in Edinburgh and Glasgow in 1974

Offence	Total number of offences	Percentage of offences
Violent: Family		
Wife assault	776	24.14
Alleged wife assault	32	1.00
Husband assault	13	0.40
Child assault	110	3.42
Parent assault	70	2.18
Sibling assault	50	1.56
	(1051)	(32.70)
Violent: Non-family		
Male against male	1196	37.20
Male against female	292	9.08
Male against police	452	14.06
Female against female	142	4.42
Female against male	53	1.65
Female against police	29	0.90
	(2164)	(67.31)
Total	3215	100.00

(Source: Dobash and Dobash; 1980)

▲

Table 8.1

of radical feminism moved to female-male relationships and, in particular, to the issue of male violence against females. The matters of female socialisation and their stereotyping as 'sex objects' or 'helpmates' to men are dealt with in later sections of this chapter. These have become common concerns not only within feminism but within the media, education and elsewhere. Here we will briefly concentrate on the issue of male violence against females.

Official statistics on violent crime show men to be overwhelmingly the more violent sex. A study by Dobash and Dobash of offences involving violence in parts of Edinburgh and Glasgow showed that the largest category of such offences was 'male against male' with 'wife assault' being the second largest (see Table 8.1).

In analysing the above and related data, Jan Pahl adds that many women comment that 'the mental battering was worse than the physical battering'. She also points out that the more accurate presentation of the issue is as 'the problem of violent husbands' rather than as a problem of women.

Pahl interprets male battering of their spouses as 'the extension of the domination and control of husbands over wives' i.e. as a logical, if brutal, aspect of patriarchy. She suggests that part of a solution to the

problem of violent husbands would be a general recognition that the problem is not a private or personal one but a major public issue. Dobash and Dobash estimated that only about two per cent of assaults against wives are reported to the police, which does suggest that society is far from adopting a frank and open perspective on the issue – let alone finding a solution to it.

CAPITALISM AND PATRIARCHY

The feminist perspectives so far considered have given the greatest emphasis either to class (Marxist/socialist feminist) or to patriarchy (radical feminist). Another perspective is to argue that both capitalism and patriarchy must be taken into consideration when explaining the oppression of women. Some analysts, such as Zillah Eisenstein, see capitalism and patriarchy as highly interwoven, whereas others such as Magrit Eichler regard them as separate systems. Eichler's analysis is considered later (p. 183).

LIBERAL-FEMINISM

Liberal-feminism is less a current of social thought and more a movement of political practice than Marxist-feminism and radical-feminism. However, to ignore it here would be to give a misleading impression of the nature and impact of feminism during the last quarter of a century.

Whereas both Marxist and radical feminists stress the need for structural change, liberal-feminism is a reformist and incrementalist ('brick by brick') approach. Its promise is that there should be equal opportunity for women and men. The Equal Pay Act (1970) and the Sex Discrimination Act (1975) are the fruits of a widely supported effort to achieve liberal equality between the sexes (see pp. 184–5). Although a leading member of the Labour Party, and inclined robustly to describe herself as a socialist, Barbara Castle was a liberal feminist in this sense and an influential supporter of these measures. Liberal feminism has been particularly effective in the sphere of education where the right of females to compete on equal terms with males has increasingly come to be accepted both in principle and practice (see pp. 97–8).

Marxist-feminists consider that the liberal approach merely encourages females to

Perspectives on Gender: A Summary		Table 8.2
PERSPECTIVE	**SUMMARY-DEFINITION**	
MARXIST-FEMINISM	Patriarchy in capitalist society reinforces and complements capitalism. The fundamental nature of female oppression is economic	
FEMINIST-MARXISM	Patriarchy in capitalist society reinforces and complements capitalism. The fundamental nature of female oppression is ideological	
RADICAL-FEMINISM	The fundamental inequality and injustice faced by females is the domination of females by males	
CAPITALISM AND PATRIARCHY	This catch-all phrase describes feminist perspectives (distinct from the above) which regard capitalism and patriarchy as separate systems. Disagreement occurs on how far the two systems are interwoven	
LIBERAL-FEMINISM	Liberal-feminists seek equal opportunity for women and men	
BIOLOGICAL-DETERMINISM	Males and females are 'naturally different' and this explains their traditionally different roles	
FUNCTIONALIST-PERSPECTIVE	Differentiated gender roles (traditional) are practical and functional for society	

compete in an unequal and class-divided world. Radical-feminists find that liberalism does not sufficiently address the psychological, relational and institutional aspects of patriarchy. Nevertheless, most feminists supported liberal gender reforms as a modest step on the way to creating a society less oppressive to females.

Gender Socialisation: The Ideological Reproduction of Patriarchy

FAMILY (EDUCATION AND MEDIA)

Gender behaviour is first learnt through primary or basic socialisation within the family and is reinforced later in practically every sphere of social life and particularly at school and work. Socialisation refers to the various ways in which a child learns to act in a manner acceptable to a given society. Gender socialisation is part of this process. Traditional patterns of socialisation in most Western countries distinguish sharply between male and female, although this has begun to change in the wake of the women's liberation movement. It is probably still true that by the time they are sixteen, the majority of young men and women have been socialised into an ideology of male supremacy even if the forces of resistance to this ideology are stronger than they were and patterns of socialisation based on gender equality occur more frequent.

Table 3.3 suggests that a substantial minority retain stereotypical attitudes to job roles and it is worth remembering that people's behaviour may be substantially less 'liberated' than their attitudes.

There is a considerable body of British and American research which claims to demonstrate substantial differences in the socialisation of baby and infant boys and girls. H Moss observed that in the early months of life boys received more attention than girls. Later boys were encouraged to display more active and exploratory behaviour whereas mothers interacted more closely with girl babies and were more likely to comfort them. Ann Oakley argues that the differences in the types of toy given to infant males and females can greatly affect their concept of gender appropriate roles. She suggests that differences in behaviour caused by differential gender socialisation are often cited to 'prove' that the sexes are 'naturally' different. Boys and girls are socialised towards future gender roles in a variety of ways. Boys are often given presents of cowboy suits, doctors' outfits and meccano sets, whereas girls are given dolls, nurses' uniforms and cookery kits. The message could hardly be stronger. Jobs involving leadership and construction skills are for boys, whereas girls are expected to care for, assist and give service to others, either at home or at work. The basis of this division of labour is clearly laid down in childhood. This is most obviously so in families in which the jobs children are given to do around the house are based on gender – say, cleaning and sewing for the girls, and mending broken plugs or furniture for the boys.

Children's literature often reinforces gender stereotypes. This is especially true of traditional fairy tales in which helpless damsels in distress are forever being rescued by handsome and dynamic princes. More recently written stories often reproduce gender stereotypes. Thus, in the 'Janet and John' series, John is frequently at the centre of the action while Janet hovers admiringly in the background only coming into her own when refreshments are served. Birthday cards and Christmas cards also frequently perpetuate gender stereotypes. Sue Sharpe quotes two classic examples of the gender stereotyping of males and females from birth congratulation messages:

Bet she's sugar and spice
And everything nice.
A pink and petite little treasure
Your new little 'she'
Who's certain to be
A wonderful bundle of pleasure!

A Son is Fun!
He'll keep you busy
With blankets an' pins
And charm your hearts
With his boyish grins!
What's more he'll make you
Proud and glad
Congratulations mother and dad!

Probably an increasing number of contemporary parents deliberately try to avoid socialising their children into traditional gender roles. One enterprising group of mothers in Liverpool, finding that the images of gender portrayed in available children's story books were too traditional, set about writing their own material. They rejected stereotypes in which the female is always weak and dependent and the male strong and dominant. Why shouldn't

princesses sometimes rescue princes? If Little Red Riding Hood had been trained in basic self-defence, perhaps she could have dealt with the wolf on her own account. Such notions may strike many as odd, but recorded interviews with some of the children who heard or read the stories showed they understood the point behind them. In small ways like this, social change can perhaps take place.

Gender socialisation occurs in the educational system and via the media despite considerable attempts to mitigate the process, particularly within education. Partly because of the selling power of traditional sexual and romantic images, gender stereotyping has proved especially difficult to combat and reduce in the commercial media. There is, however, considerable consensus among feminists of all perspectives that such imagery should not dominate the portrayal of gender. The sections in this book which deal with gender socialisation in education and in the media are pp. 96–101 and pp. 423–4 respectively.

GENDER ROLES: SYMMETRY OR CONTINUING INEQUALITY?

There are two main areas in which inequality of gender roles occurs: in the family and in the economy. We have already extensively discussed the former in chapter 3 so a brief treatment is appropriate here.

As we have seen, Young and Willmott interpret their survey into the matter to suggest that symmetrical gender roles are replacing segregated ones. By this they mean that there is more democracy, equality and sharing between partners, not necessarily that partners do similar amounts of given roles (such as household repair or cooking). This pattern initially developed among middle class couples, and particularly when both husband and wife worked as professionals. As Rhona and Robert Rapoport, (a dual-career couple themselves), point out it is still among dual career families that symmetrical roles most frequently occur. With more women of all classes in paid work, however, role symmetry may be becoming rather more common among working class couples. One survey, by Hannah Gavron, actually found that working class husbands shared housework more than middle class husbands, though this goes against other findings. Ann Oakley is, in any case, sceptical about whether there has been a marked recent trend for couples to share housework and child rearing (see below). Mary Maynard has also robustly refuted the symmetry thesis (see pp. 59–60).

Most of the remainder of this chapter illustrates that different and unequal gender roles persist throughout the economy. Indeed, women employees form a majority in each of the ten worst-paid occupations. In the light of this, it is perhaps surprising that figure 8.2 does not indicate an even greater preponderance of stereotypical attitude among the public (although, significantly, males show more stereotyped attitudes to job roles than females).

Only the job of car mechanic is seen by a majority as more suitable for men, although several other occupations are seen in terms of traditional gender stereotypes by a significant minority. It is important to remember that people's behaviour may be considerably different from – and more rigid than – their expressed attitudes.

Gender Inequality and the Sexual Division of Labour

GENDER, THE FAMILY AND WORK

So far we have described how gender identity is culturally created in advanced Western societies through socialisation and role-allocation. The question must now be asked why gender differentiation occurs at all. Mitchell and Oakley argue that a division of labour has developed in capitalist society by which women tend to be primarily involved in child nurture and domestic work and men in acquiring the basic means of livelihood. Socialisation prepares girls and boys for their future roles in the socio-economic system. Now, the only biologically inevitable feature of this particular form of sexual division of labour is that women give birth to children. The rest is open to gender adaptation. What follows, therefore, more closely reflects the perspective adopted by Mitchell and Oakley, rather than that of Firestone, that the sexual division of labour in capitalist society has taken a 'severe' form because this has been convenient for the capitalist system. The fact that in the last hundred years women have become increasingly involved in paid employment illustrates rather than refutes the point – they have been needed in the expanding service sector. Nevertheless, the sexually based division of labour as described above is still powerfully entrenched in contemporary capitalist society, as was shown in the two recent recessions when female labour was widely treated as more expendable than male. The sexual division of labour in capitalist society has resulted in a large degree of female dependency on males. This dependency has resulted in lower social status for women and correspondingly higher social status for men. As well as having less economic power and social status than men, women have also tended to be politically less powerful, because they are isolated and not organised e.g. through trade unions. In short, although the social consequences of the sexual division of labour in capitalist society have tended to be disadvantageous to women and advantageous to men, this state of affairs is not inevitable. Both cross-cultural comparison and historical analysis of gender roles in Britain show that change is possible. We adopt the historical perspective next.

Changing Gender Roles Within the Family and Economy: Historical and Contemporary Perspective

PRE-INDUSTRIAL One of the few generalisations supported by recent research into the pre-industrial family in Britain is that it was patriarchal at all social levels. Fathers had decisive power over their daughters and husbands over their wives. Young and Willmott suggest that brutalising their wives can rarely have been in the interests of husbands but wife-beating was an accepted way of asserting domination and, sometimes no doubt, mere ill temper. Most peasant families were units of agricultural production in which women took a full part. Women matched men in work if not in power. Ann Oakley states that 'in their role as agriculturalists, women produced the bulk of the family's food supply'. They managed dairy production, grew flax and hemp, milled corn and cared for the poultry, pigs, orchards and gardens. Men were primarily responsible for planting, cultivating and harvesting crops and for maintenance. Women allocated tasks, including household ones, to daughters, and men to sons. Textile work was second in national importance to agriculture and was shared between men, women and children: men doing the weaving, and women the spinning and allocating minor tasks such as picking and cleaning to the children.

Many better-off households had servants. Laslett calculates that 40 per cent of children spent part of their lives as servants and 20 per cent were raised in households with servants. As Harris puts it, the majority of members of such households were 'the dependents of some senior or more powerful person, usually of the male gender'. Laslett's thesis, endorsed by Harris, is that industrialisation broke up not the extended family (which was not, anyway the dominant family form) but the patriarchal family/household. For many modern feminists, however, the patriarchal family is a long time in dying!

THE NINETEENTH CENTURY Industrialisation disrupted traditional patterns of gender behaviour as it disrupted so much else. For a time, working class men, women and children worked together in industrial production and mining. Between 1802 and 1898, however, a series of Acts abolished child labour and gradually reduced female labour in these areas. Though many women found other work, often in the low-paid domestic service sector, a woman's place was increasingly considered to be in the home. In some ways the position of the working class woman in industrial society was worse than that of the peasant wife. In pre-industrial society most families produced some of their own food and clothes – largely under the wife's organisation – whereas in industrial society the wife was often wholly dependent on what money her husband chose to give

her to buy these things. This was a position of striking inferiority. No doubt some of the above legislation was passed in a spirit of paternalistic protectiveness but it was also notably convenient to have the labour force adequately catered for domestically (for a specifically Marxist interpretation of this point see chapter 3, p. 48). In this way, the workers were both healthier and more productive.

Although the economic situation of middle-class women was much better than that of working-class women, they were similarly dependent on their husbands for money. In a wealthy family, servants might free 'the mistress of the house' from domestic toil and child-care, but there were limits to what she could then do with her time. Most professions, apart from teaching, were barred to women. In practice, middle-class women were likely to spend their often ample leisure time in socialising, improving the decor of their homes and sometimes in charitable works.

The law put the lid firmly on the trap of female subordination. As we have already observed women were debarred from the best-paying working-class and middle-class jobs. Worse than that, women had no legal existence at all in early nineteenth century Britain. Before marriage a woman was the responsibility of her father, and afterwards she and her possessions belonged to her husband.

By the end of the nineteenth century a series of Acts had partly improved this situation. One of these, the Married Women's Property Act of 1882, gave a wife the right to own property and to dispose of it to whom she wished.

THE EARLY TWENTIETH CENTURY: THE GROWTH OF FEMINIST CONSCIOUSNESS

The decline of the Victorian patriarchal family has been a major feature of twentieth century social history. Contraception (the control of fertility) undermined the Victorian family and the position of male as patriarch as much as anything else. Given the choice, most women preferred to have two or three children rather than six or seven. Traditional taboos against contraception did not die overnight, and in addition some socialist women were suspicious that population control might be used as an alternative to social reform. Even so, the practical advantages of birth control were too obvious to miss. 'Having a family' of six or seven was a lifetime's work for many women, and could be physically ruinous as well as intellectually severely limiting. In any case, the beginning of a steady fall in the birth rate occurred in the late eighteen seventies and this correlates with an increase in propaganda in favour of birth control. Certainly, in the long run, women have overwhelmingly accepted that family planning is a precondition of their own independence. Decrease in family size, coupled with the development of efficient time-saving household technology, enabled many women to spend much longer as part of the paid labour force. In turn, experience of work widened women's horizons, boosted their confidence and whetted the appetite of some for more freedom and equality. The massive involvement of women in production, service industries and administration during the First World War strengthened this new mood.

The fight for female political and civil rights was substantially a middle class led movement, although as historian Sheila Rowbotham says, the tendency of accounts of the suffragette movement to concentrate on the Pankhursts as personalities has meant a lack of detailed work on the social compo-sition of the movement. There were certainly many working class women participants, including the doughty Hannah Mitchell, who criticised the 'talk' of some of the middle class radicals whom she found better preachers than practitioners of sexual equality:

Even my Sunday leisure was gone for I soon found that a lot of the socialist talk about freedom was only talk and these socialist young men expected Sunday dinners and huge teas with home-made cakes, potted meat and pies, exactly like their reactionary fellows.

It would be absurd to underestimate the importance of the acquisition of the vote for women. The vote is a basic right of modern citizenship. Nevertheless, merely having the vote in no way solved the problem of sexual inequality at work and domestically. More recent legislation has, with limited success, attempted to deal with the former (see this chapter, pp. 184–5) but the latter, perhaps because it concerns the 'private area of life' has not been seriously dealt with by legislation and government policy in Britain. In Sweden and the major communist societies, however, legislatively supported policies in this area have been both pursued and enforced more effectively (chapter 3, p. 51).

Women in the Contemporary Labour Market

So far, we have considered domestic and directly economic labour together because they are two sides of the same coin: one would not be possible without the other. It is necessary, however, to give a more detailed analysis of women's position in the employment market. Generally, increased job opportunities for women have been seen as part of their assumed 'liberation' and work has certainly often provided individual women with an escape from the tedium of domestic toil. Marxists and socialists point out, however, that there is considerable evidence of female 'exploitation' and accompanying under-achievement in employment, and that female employment and unemployment has varied with the economic need for it. Women have been the most expendable of workers. First, we will look at some of the main facts relating to female employment and then we will examine some theoretical explanations.

Even in the mid-Victorian era, when working-class women were legally banned from working in heavy industry and mining, and middle-class women were denied the right to qualify for most professions, women were by no means entirely excluded from the labour market. Working class women were 'needed' as domestic servants and a certain number of middle class women worked in lower status professions. Working class women often had to find work to supplement the wages of their husbands. They frequently did so as full- or part-time domestic servants of whom there were well

Figure 8.1

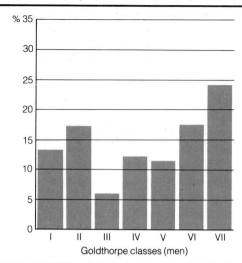

Goldthorpe class distribution for men

Goldthorpe classes (men)

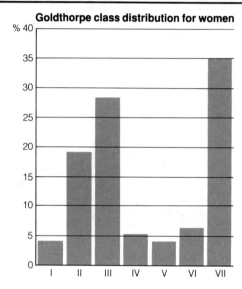

Goldthorpe class distribution for women

(Data: Marshall *et al.*, 1989)

Table 8.3

The make-up of the judiciary

Judges	Total	Women	%	Ethnic Minorities	%
House of Lords	10	0	0%	0	0%
Court of appeal	27	2	0.54%	0	0%
High Court	83	2	1.66%	0	0%
Circuit Judges	429	19	4.4%	1	0.2%
Recorders (part-time)	744	42	5.7%	3	0.4%
Assistant recorders	433	27	6.0%	2	0.4%
The Candidates					
Practising barristers	5,994	1,246	21.0%	376	6.0%
Practising solicitors	54,734	12,683	23.2%	709*	1.3%

*16,622 respondents to the latest Law Society survey declined to specify their racial group
(Source: Lord Chancellor's Department 1991, Law Society 1989–90; Bar Council 1989–90)

over half a million at this time. Hundreds of thousands of others were employed in textile production, an area of traditionally high female employment and low wages. Middle-class women who needed to work, perhaps because they were spinsters or widows, could earn a living as elementary school teachers. By the 1890s, there were almost 150,000 female teachers. Nursing was also a major area of female employment. The 'semi-professions' of teaching and nursing were of much lower status and pay than the major professions of law and medicine (for instance) from which women were excluded.

The situation of women at work began to change towards the end of the nineteenth century and even more so in the twentieth century. Even allowing for population expansion, the increase in the numbers of women in paid work has been massive. Between 1911 and 1989 six million more women were added to the total labour force of about twenty eight million. Of the six million people in part time work well over half are women.

Although most women who do paid work probably want to, it would be a mistake to assume that the increase in female labour has been an unmitigated boon for them. Women in full time work have for a long time been paid less than men, even though the gap has narrowed substantially in recent years. Yet even though the Equal Pay Act of 1970 established the legal principle of equal pay for equal work, the average wage of women in manual jobs is only 72 per cent of men's pay and that of women in non-manual jobs only 63 per cent of the male wage. This is largely because, historically, women have been concentrated in low paid jobs. Clerical and secretarial work which became increasingly available to women from the latter half of the nineteenth century is often poorly paid.

A comparison of the occupational concentration of males and females amply illustrates the overall difference in status and rewards enjoyed by the two sexes.

One of the most notable comparisons in the two figures is the much larger percentage of males than females in class 1, top professional, administrative and managerial. This is illustrated in respect to one specific profession – the law – in table 8.3.

About two thirds of all female employees do either routine non-manual work or semi-

or unskilled manual work. This is a formidably large concentration of women in lower paid, lower status, and probably less intrinsically satisfying jobs. Women's work situation is often directly subordinate to men for whom they act as assistants. Even women in social class II – nearly 20 per cent – are often thought of as in the 'caring' professions. It is almost as if the domestic role of looking after others is transferred into the work situation. Like domestic labour itself, work in these areas is comparatively poorly paid. The

Figure 8.2

Percentage distribution of persons in employment by occupational grouping and sex, 1987

Great Britain

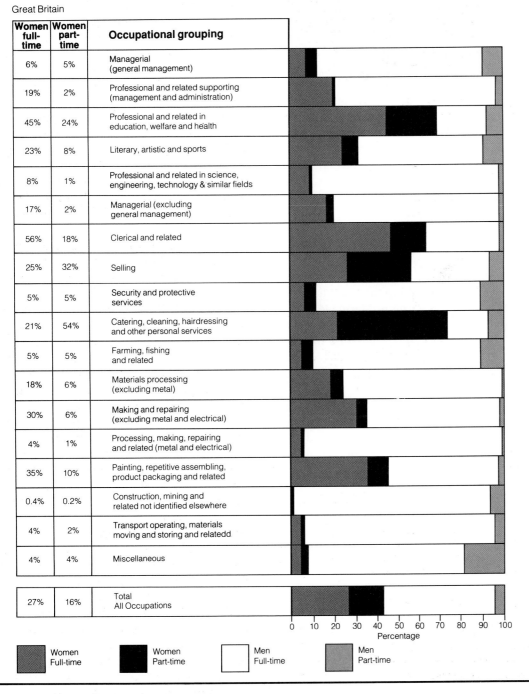

Women full-time	Women part-time	Occupational grouping
6%	5%	Managerial (general management)
19%	2%	Professional and related supporting (management and administration)
45%	24%	Professional and related in education, welfare and health
23%	8%	Literary, artistic and sports
8%	1%	Professional and related in science, engineering, technology & similar fields
17%	2%	Managerial (excluding general management)
56%	18%	Clerical and related
25%	32%	Selling
5%	5%	Security and protective services
21%	54%	Catering, cleaning, hairdressing and other personal services
5%	5%	Farming, fishing and related
18%	6%	Materials processing (excluding metal)
30%	6%	Making and repairing (excluding metal and electrical)
4%	1%	Processing, making, repairing and related (metal and electrical)
35%	10%	Painting, repetitive assembling, product packaging and related
0.4%	0.2%	Construction, mining and related not identified elsewhere
4%	2%	Transport operating, materials moving and storing and relatedd
4%	4%	Miscellaneous
27%	16%	Total All Occupations

Women Full-time   Women Part-time   Men Full-time   Men Part-time

(Source: New earnings survey)

fact that teaching is sometimes said to be 'not badly paid for women' is perhaps more a reflection on the historically low wages of women generally, than on the great financial rewards offered by that profession. In any case, in teaching as in all professions, women tend to occupy lower scale, less well-paid posts. Figure 8.2 gives a clear and detailed picture of the paid work men and women do – and merits close study.

In addition to enjoying less authority, status and wages at work than men, women also tend to have less security. Although about 40 per cent of female workers are unionised, the majority still lack the strength and protection union membership gives. Part-time workers are in an especially weak position in the labour market. Of Britain's six million part-time workers, three and a half million are women. Part-time workers employed for fewer than sixteen hours a week are not entitled to redundancy payment, nor most other benefits under the Employment Protection Act. In effect, they can be hired and fired at the employer's wish.

Homeworkers or 'outworkers' are particularly disadvantaged in terms of pay and conditions. These workers are overwhelmingly women and dispropor-tionately of Asian origin. Many work in the textile industry in the Midlands and North. It is estimated that there are over a million of them in Britain (*Observer* 5, June, 1988). When classified as self-employed, home-workers have no statutory rights to protection under the 1978 Employment Act. The requirement that employers should register them with the Local Authority seems widely ignored by the former and unenforced by the latter. Pay of around 50 pence an hour is not uncommon. A survey (1990) by the National Homeworking Unit found that homeworkers typically had virtually no guaranteed conditions of work at all either in relation to health, safety of contract, let alone entitlement to maternity leave, redundancy pay or pension. Why, then, do they do it? Kabron Phillips of the NHU suggests, reasonably enough, that they need the money – little though it may be.

She goes on to argue:

'Homeworkers need basic employment rights, a decent wage, a contract of employment, a right to a payslip and holiday and sick pay ...'

(Guardian)

Employers might reply that they could not afford this and would have to lay off homeworkers, and some of the latter might prefer even low-paid work in poor conditions to no work. Fundamentally, however, a rich society has to determine what are the minimum standards acceptable for its workforce and then allocate resources to ensure these are met. Employers, government, trade unions and public opinion need to reach a realistic and caring consensus on this matter.

A fundamental weakness of most women as independent wage-earners lies in the fact that they also produce and are expected to bring up children. This means that they are not usually consistently involved in a career between the ages of approximately twenty-five to thirty-five, which is a crucial period for gaining experience and promotion. Highly qualified as well as less qualified women are disadvantaged. Female recruitment to the professions is almost equal to male recruitment but as figure 8.2 shows, many leave professional work and few occupy high status positions. In practice, because of their dual commitments as housewives and workers, many women do not seriously attempt to complete effectively with men in the labour market. Many find 'temping' or part-time work fits in best with their domestic responsibilities. In addition, it is well established that large numbers of women welcome an 'escape' from the home, even into work that does not seem particularly fulfilling. Further, women who restart their careers at, say, thirty-five sometimes do not have quite the same expectations as a similarly qualified man of the same age. In time of high unemploy-ment, they are frequently glad to be able to get a reasonably suitable job at all. Those who have families and try simultaneously to develop careers often put immense pressure on themselves – despite sometimes succeeding. A society which presents half its population with the above range of options seems deeply flawed. The basic problem is that, as Hannah Mitchell put it, women compete 'with one hand tied behind their back' – the hand that 'holds the baby' and does the housework. That problem can only be solved either by relieving women of much domestic work or by rewarding them more substantially and securely for it. We deal with this issue in the next section.

EXPLANATIONS OF THE POSITION OF WOMEN IN THE LABOUR MARKET

A RESERVE ARMY OF LABOUR? NEO-MARXIST PERSPECTIVE The term 'reserve army of labour' refers to a section of the labour force which can be easily and cheaply hired and easily fired and so can be used to facilitate the functioning of capitalism. Black minority workers and female workers are considered to be a disproportionate and, in the latter case, growing proportion of this reserve army. Clearly, if employers can use female labour in this way it would be profitable for them to do so. Further, Veronica Beechey has argued that because females' wages often represent a second source of family income, employers are therefore able to depress male wages.

Irene Breugel's 1982 review of the above thesis in relation to the experience of female labour from 1974–78, provides only mixed support for it. She did find that the rate of unemployment of women rose three times more quickly than that of men and that the decline in female employment in industries experiencing increased unemployment exceeded that of men. Part-time female employees were particularly hard hit. On the other hand, the rapid expansion of the service sector to some extent protected the market position and employment security of women. More recently, Marxist-feminist Juliet Mitchell has speculated that microchip technology and the demand for jobs of males displaced from manufacturing industry may weaken the position of women in the service sector. Pessimistically Breugel suggests that women's best protection is the low-pay they receive.

DUAL LABOUR MARKET THEORY We will discuss in detail the concept of a 'dual labour market' when considering the Fordist/post-Fordist debate (chapter 11, pp. 238–9). Barron and Norris argue that there are two distinct labour markets, the primary and secondary (1978). The former is characterised by well-paid, secure work with good promotion prospects and in a pleasant environment whereas the latter is characterised by the opposite. Women are considered overwhelmingly to be located in the secondary labour market.

Like the reserve army of labour theorists, dual labour market theorists emphasise the profitability for capital of having access to a pool of easily expendable labour. In terms of the Fordist/post-Fordist debate, the existence of such a group adds to business 'flexibility'. The mechanisms by which women remain in the secondary labour force include not putting them on promotion tracks and failing to plan institutionally to ensure women are not disadvantaged because their pattern of paid work may be disrupted by maternity. Indeed, it seems likely that until the issue of child care is dealt with at a national level, the fact of maternity will continue to be used directly or indirectly as justification for disadvantaging women (see Chapter 3, pp. 69–70)

RADICAL FEMINIST PERSPECTIVE: PATRIARCHY AND CAPITALISM The 'pure' radical-feminist position on the domination of women by men in the area of paid-work is that it is another example of patriarchy. As we have seen, radical-feminists tend to stress male exploitation of women's biological functioning, particularly child bearing. The logic of this analysis is that there should be much more adequate public funding of child care facilities to off-set female disadvantage.

A number of feminists see patriarchy and capitalism as separate but interlocking and largely complementary structures. Thus, Eichler (1980) acknowledges that women are exploited in the economic sphere, but unlike Marxists she sees the source of their inequality within the family rather than in relations to the means of production (i.e. the economy). She sees the family not as a capitalist but as a 'quasi-feudal institution' within which women are virtually serfs, uncertain of what, if any, economic reward they may receive from their husbands. Married women as a group, across class lines, are in this position which as well as disadvantaging them within the family, radically reduces their chances of success in paid work and may even affect their control of their own wages. Eichler considers that single women in paid work are in a different structural position to married women. Their exploitation is essentially based on their position in paid work. However, she does see a basis for common cause between the two groups.

WOMEN AND THE LABOUR MARKET: CONCLUSION There are a number of important comments that need to be made about the above theoretical explanations of female oppression in the labour market. In general, what these theories have in common is perhaps more significant than what divides them. First, they all offer a structural rather than an individualistic explanation of the position of women in the labour market and of their place in the occupational structure. Each theory avoids 'blaming' individual employers or politicians, men or women (blaming the victim!) to explain gender inequality, and instead concentrates on the structural relations between the family and the economy and the roles of females and males within them. Patriarchal ideology – belief in male supremacy by either or both men and women – is seen as the product of

experience within patriarchal (and capitalist) structures rather than as the result of a male conspiracy.

Second, there are obvious similarities between the reserve army of labour theory and dual labour market theory. Indeed, the reserve army and the secondary labour force appear to be virtually synonymous (although the way they function within the capitalist system is open to different explanation).

Finally, however, it would be misleading totally to homogenise the theories of female exploitation in the labour market. It is clearly necessary for feminists to debate to what extent and in what ways female emancipation can occur in a capitalist society. A number of serious differences of perspective and policy among feminists are discussed elsewhere (see pp. 171–5).

Women's Liberation: Policy and Continuing Problems

We have seen the extent of gender inequality. We now ask what governments have tried to do about it. The main measures of the 'equality package', as Ann Oakley calls it, are as follows. The Equal Pay Act (operative from 1975); the Sex Discrimination Act (1975); and the Employment Protection and Social Security Pensions Acts (1975). The 1967 Abortion Act and the Divorce Law Reform Act (implemented in 1971) also have profound implications for women, though they are not specifically part of the 'package'. The first two focus largely on employment. None of this legislation has resulted in a reduction of the concentration of women in low-paid occupations. A more interventionist policy might, for instance, involve guaranteeing women a minimum quota of top and middle level positions in business companies and professional establishments. Sometimes, what is required is to achieve actual equality more than legal equality, after all, we are all legally entitled to eat at the Savoy Grill ... The terms of the Sex Discrimination Act are more easily enforceable in education, and there are more signs of greater quality of achievement in that area, though the gap remains wide.

The Employment Protection Act contains the first legal entitlement to maternity leave for women in Britain. It bans dismissal on grounds of pregnancy and guarantees

mothers their jobs for up to 29 weeks from childbirth. Circumstances (and there are potentially many: the death of the child is one) in which paternity leave rather than maternity leave might be desirable are not recognised by the Act, and to this extent it has an element of chauvinistic protectionism about it. Still, 29 weeks 'grace' is better than nothing, although it could hardly have been much less. Further, the Social Security Pensions Act puts women's sickness and unemployment pay and pension rights on an equal basis to those of men.

Despite the above legislation and the seemingly not very effective Equal Opportunities Commission, women's status at work relative to that of men did not much improve during the nineteen eighties and early nineteen nineties.

Relatively few cases are taken to the Employment Appeals Tribunals under the Equal Pay and Sex Discrimination Acts. Thus, in 1988/89 only 368 cases were heard under the former (of which complainants were successful in 14), and 300 under the latter (of which 78 were successful). Proof of discrimination can be difficult, but such a record is unlikely to encourage those who believe they have got a grievance even to attempt redress. In addition to the prospect of failure, there is also the cost (if this is not borne by the Equal Opportunities

Commission), and the possibility of later victimisation by employers. Like the comparable legislation covering racial discrimination in employment (p. 207), this legislation or, at least, its implementation is in danger of being impaired because of inadequate funding.

Little legislation was passed during the Thatcher administrations specifically to improve the position of women in society. Indeed, the freezing between 1986 and 1990 of child benefit which is paid directly to women may be considered to have disadvantaged them. The exception was the new tax ruling by which from 1990 the earnings of husband and wife were automatically taxed separately without the husband having to forfeit the married man's tax allowance (which had previously been the case if separate taxation had been opted for). As Martyn Denscombe puts it the move allows women 'privacy and control over their own financial affairs for the first time since the income tax system was introduced some 200 years ago' (Denscombe, 1991).

The extent of women's participation in politics may be taken as one measure of their influence on national life. On this basis their influence is low – notwithstanding Mrs Thatcher. In January 1991, only five per cent of MP's were women, and not one was a member of John Major's first cabinet.

Education is often thought of as the key to the further advancement of women. As we have seen, in many ways females have already closed 'the achievement gap' between males and females. While differential subject choice persists, this may be further eroded by the implementation of the National Curriculum. However, the education successes of women have not yet been substantially reflected in career success. Without again rehearsing why this is so, it is worth quoting Joanna Forster, Chairwoman of the Equal Opportunities Commission that it is the 'pitiful' lack of childcare facilities 'which confines most women to part-time, marginalised, low-paid work'. (EOC Report, 1990)

Gender Liberation: Directions, Images and Issues

It is fairly clear what feminism opposes. It opposes the oppression of women by men and the resulting inequality of the sexes. Despite the differences between various feminist perspectives, most feminists welcome the reforms of the 'equality legislation package' even if some would doubt its effectiveness in the absence of more radical change.

However, many feminists want more than merely an end to the oppression of females by males. They want a world in which gender relations are freer, more equal and more fulfilling. What do these fine phrases mean? In this section, we look at some interpretations – variously complementary and contradictory.

RE-EVALUATING THE HISTORICAL ROLES OF WOMEN Recently, an interesting strand of opinion has become more noticeable in the feminist movement. It cannot easily be labelled but it involves a re-assessment and upgrading of the historical roles of women, and a better appreciation of their variety and

necessity. While insisting on policies of equal opportunity in the job-market, those who share this emerging perspective reject the notion that the success of women should be judged merely or even mainly by their achievements in traditionally male dominated areas (such as warfare or banking). Instead, three things are stressed. Firstly, that some domestic and child-rearing work can be creative and humanly very rewarding – this carries the rider that men could beneficially involve themselves in it more. Secondly, historically, in any case, women have borne a heavy and necessary burden of labour. Of course, such labour has often been oppressive and it is worth repeating Sheila Rowbotham's warning that attempts to idealise 'women's work' are invariably 'reactionary.' Ideals of motherhood tend to collapse before the distasteful reality of changing nappies and scouring toilets. Third, as feminist researchers increasingly examine the historic contribution of women to literature, science and ideas, they are finding it was much more substantial than (men) previously thought.

Feminists have constantly stressed the skill and caring that goes into much domestic work while also recognising the long hours, elements of drudgery, and typical thanklessness that characterise it. Ann Oakley virtually despairs that men will ever recognise that qualities traditionally associated with women but which can occur in either sex – such as caring, gentleness and sharing – might provide a better moral blueprint for human conduct and survival than such traditionally 'masculine' characteristics as ambition, aggression and competitiveness. Ann Oakley, in the article quoted from above, cites a variety of feminist science fiction which speculates on precisely this possibility. Men are sometimes missing from this hypothetical future – their destructiveness is implicitly seen as both undesirable and dangerous. In the spirit of this literature, perhaps the nuclear bomb can be seen as a symbol of the male contribution historically: an achievement heavy with destructive potential. If so, it is perhaps time that the 'other' sex had a turn at, or at least more involvement in, the creation of a new social reality based on more positive and life-enhancing principles.

Ann Oakley severely questions whether the way towards women's liberation is simply to compete with men in the employment market. Yet she despairs that men will ever recognise or allow proper reward for the work women do. As long as this is so, the prospects are that women will continue to depend materially and psychologically (for security and identity) on men. As she says:

Men and women cannot be equal outside the home if they are not equal partners inside it.
(Oakley, 1979: New Society, 22/8/79)

Paid housework, or a guaranteed right to a proportion of the main breadwinner's salary, are possible solutions to material dependency (although they do not appear to have much support). In reality, however, Oakley is thinking mainly of the need for a change, indeed, a revolution in attitudes – of both sexes – to the quality, dignity and humanity of child rearing and domestic labour – whoever does it.

Second, the massive contribution of female labour – physical and mental – has typically been underestimated. Virginia Novarra's book *Women's Work, Men's Work* forcefully asserts that women's work has made a vital contribution to the survival of the race. It has done so in the following major ways.

Through
1 Reproduction
2 Agricultural Production (globally, more women are involved in agricultural production than men)
3 Clothing the Family (often making or mending clothes)
4 Tending the Family and others
5 Cultural Transmission
6 Caring for the Home and Home Environment (unpaid or lowly-paid work)

Of course, a re-evaluation of work traditionally done by women does not guarantee them more of the power and resources largely monopolised by men.

The third point refers to the rediscovery, or perhaps, discovery – mainly by women – of a vast, disregarded body of creative and intellectual work done by women. Novels, diaries and contemporary accounts of 'forgotten' female writers have been published and there has also been an outpouring of work by current female writers.

BECOMING LIKE MEN: ASSIMILATION In undermining patriarchy, it is possible that females may adopt traditional 'masculine' attitudes themselves. Aggression, personal ambitions, the desire for power and control are functional characteristics in 'a man's world' and in attempting to 'beat them', some women may have ended up 'joining them'. This approach to female progress may be referred to as the assimilationist model although those who adopt it may not always have formally thought it through.

Uneasy about accepting a patriarchal world on its own terms, a number of feminists have stressed that to achieve equality on 'male' terms may be a 'hollow' victory.

FEMALE ALTERNATIVES: SEPARATION AND PLURALISM The previous section presents the argument that there is much of value and therefore much worth preserving in female practice and achievement – even though women have worked within oppressive structures. One feminist response to this perception has been that what has developed as distinctly female is so in need of nurture and so threatened by men that women need to adopt a separatist strategy of development. Some feminists have gone further and regarded separation from men as an ultimate goal. In particular some lesbian feminists feel that they can better develop their relationships and way of living by excluding males. Separatism has also been adopted in a much more limited way in specific institutional contexts such as education and politics. Thus, Dale Spender has argued that females achieve more in sexually segregated than in mixed schools (see pp. 98–9). Beyond education, however, Spender accepts that the sexes will mix freely.

Perhaps the best known example of separatism was the women's peace camp at Greenham Common. It was, in part, an experiment in what a society of liberated women might be like. The women organised the camp along participatory, egalitarian and organic lines, doing jobs because they needed to be done and not for power, status or reward. Specifically, the camp was a peace protest, and many feminists do feel an overriding commitment to preventing nuclear holocaust and have little confidence that men of power will do what is necessary to achieve this.

A gender pluralist world would be one in which, although different gender roles would be distinguishable, there would be equality between them. Thus, women might still make up the majority of housepersons but would have comparable independence, status and rewards to men. Simply to describe gender pluralism in the abstract is to indicate that it is probably not fully achievable. Historically, domestic work, including child care and rearing, has been of such low status and power that it is likely to continue to be so as long as women do most of it. In any case, a growing majority of women want work in the main economy. They will, therefore, need more public, commercial or male-partner help with child care and other domestic work. This leads to a final alternative.

A NON-GENDERED SOCIETY: AN END TO GENDER ROLES? What practical progress there has been towards women's liberation has probably been mainly in the slow and partial breaking down of traditional gender stereotypes and roles. Economically, women appear to be more empowered than in the recent past both as a result of increased earnings and because legislation has partly established a more effective framework of financial independence and security. In terms of qualifications, females already match males up to and including 'A' levels and should reach parity at degree level around the year 2000. If and when equality of qualifications is ever reflected in equal occupational status and rewards, and equality of domestic effort between the sexes, then unequal gender roles would cease to exist. We are a long way from this point.

CHANGING MODELS OF MASCULINITY

What is masculinity? At the beginning of this chapter, a distinction was drawn between biological differences between the sexes and differences of gender which are culturally structured. The nature-nurture argument in relation to masculinity cannot be further pursued here but it can be safely stated that many men do not conform to the model of masculinity as 'dominance' and being 'macho'. This clearly suggests that the 'macho' version of masculinity is not inevitable. Nevertheless, as David D Gilmore shows in his comparative cultural study *Manhood in the Making: Cultural Concepts of Masculinity* (1991), males tend to dominate females in most (but not all) societies. According to Gilmore, the almost universal practice of masculinity is 'Man the Impregnator – Protector – Provider'. He argues that manhood involves productive and often competitive activity to achieve these goals. What Gilmore does not discuss, however, is the extent to which these 'male' functions may be under challenge and declining in the West in ways that may be undermining traditional concepts of masculinity.

John H Moore in *But What About Men* (1989) does discuss the contemporary challenge and 'threat' to traditional masculinity. Traditional masculinity is based on power and this power has been contested, questioned and, in some cases actually diminished, in all areas of society. The increase in the numbers of women in paid work has bought them more resources, power and independence and for many this has carried over into personal and family life. Women are increasingly as well educated and qualified as men and, slowly, this is beginning to be reflected in the numbers achieving higher status employment. Further, if we examine how far Gilmore's description of masculinity as 'man the impregnator – protector – provider' applies to Western Europe and the United States, these functions are in each case undergoing change.

'Man the impregnator' may appear to be one of the great biological givens but for over half a century, females have been gaining greater control over their fertility and sexuality. This is largely due to improved methods of contraception. In those poorer parts of the world where for whatever reasons contraception is little used, males tend to want large families both as status symbols (a proof of 'virility-masculinity') and as a means of controlling their wives (ditto). 'Man the protector' of women and children is a notion that needs to be put into context. To the extent that historically men have protected their families and communities it has been against the threats and violence of other men. We are also increasingly discovering that within relationships and families male violence against females is no rarity (see p. 174). In Western societies, women increasingly depend for their protection on the effective enforcement of the law and, to a considerable extent, on their own mutual cooperation and organisation (see p. 187) Finally, in the West the basis on which men are the exclusive or even 'main' providers is increasingly eroding as more females do paid work. In any case, the concept of 'man the provider' verges arrogantly on a stereotype which grossly underestimates the work women have done, particularly domestic and agricultural.

In the light of the above developments and under sustained feminist criticism, it is not surprising that some men, individually or in groups, have begun to revise their ideas about and practice of 'masculinity'. In the nineteen sixties and seventies men's 'consciousness raising' groups were formed by some radical males, partly at the suggestion of feminists, to explore masculinity. Traditional stereotypes of masculinity have long been questioned in the male homosexual community. Many male

homosexuals seek freer emotional and stylistic expression than allowed by 'tough', repressed masculine roles. Yet, homosexual men themselves have often been subject to severe stereotyping, including the 'butch' and the 'passive' stereotypes. It is highly unlikely that more than a small minority of homosexual men conform to these stereotypes either in appearance or behaviour. Male homosexuals are more likely to look like 'the boy next door' than, say, John Inman in his 'Are You Being Served' incarnation. Nevertheless, in so far as they are freed from having to be traditionally 'masculine', male homosexuals can explore and express 'masculinity' differently.

New, or at least less stereotyped, patterns of male behaviour have also been developed by some heterosexual males. Perhaps, the arrival and persistence of unisex fashions symbolises a lowering of resistance on the part of both sexes to behaving more like the other. A feminist and, perhaps more generally, a female demand of males is that they show more sensitivity and 'open up' more emotionally. It is a central thesis of Victor Seidler's writings that historically males have been thought of as 'rational' and females as 'emotional'. He suggests that males need to explore their 'emotional side' much more and that females need them to (Seidler 1991). It may not be entirely frivolous to suggest that 'Gazza' made his own start in his celebrated crying episode in Italy in 1990. It seems to be an aspect of traditional masculinity that men cannot or will not cry.

CONCLUSION It would be misleading to suggest that gender relations have entered or are about to enter a new phase in which males express a new sensitivity towards and sense of equality with females. The 'new man' remains illusive as a large-scale phenomenon. It is true that the basis of working class male dominance over females has been eroded with the massive decline of employment in the manufacturing and extractive industries. However, mainly male-dominated hierachies proliferate in the white collar and professional sectors and most of the very rich are, as they have always been, men. Perhaps what this chapter shows is that many women have taken some steps towards their own emancipation and that some men are beginning to respond and may take steps towards their own emancipation.

1 There are both biological and cultural explanations of gender differences. More recently attempts to understand the biological in relation to the cultural in a more integrated way have occurred.

2 Patriarchy is the system and practice by which males dominate and exploit females. Sexism is discrimination against someone on the basis of their sex.

3 There are a number of key perspectives on gender. The most important of these are feminist perspectives in that they reflect the prime concern of women for emancipation (i.e. freedom from domination and equality with males). A full summary of gender perspectives is given on page 175.

4 The ideological reproduction of patriarchy occurs initially through family socialisation and also through education and the media. Whether or not stereotypical gender roles are breaking down is debatable.

5 The sexual division of labour refers to how work, both domestic and non-domestic, is organised between the sexes. This has changed considerably through history with women by no means being involved only in 'housework'. Indeed, worldwide they have probably carried the majority of certain kinds of agricultural labour such as planting and harvesting crops. Most of the world's food (3/4) is grown by women!

6 Women increasingly returned to paid work during the twentieth century, having been excluded from large areas of the economy during the nineteenth century. This paralleled a growth in the political consciousness of many women and the rise of feminism.

SUMMARY

7 The position of women in the contemporary labour market is one of sharp disadvantage in terms of status and rewards. Women tend to be concentrated in low status occupations and within these at the lower levels of the hierarchy. The fact that 'the qualification gap between males and females has been greatly reduced has not yet produced an obvious 'pay-off' in women achieving higher status jobs.

8 There are a number of explanations of why females are occupationally disadvantaged. One theory is that, along with certain other groups, females constitute a reserve army of labour: easily hired and easily fired. Rather similarly, dual labour market, theory argues that there is a well paid, secure labour force and less well-paid, easily-shed labour force – with women being predominantly in the latter. Radical-feminists stress that patriarchy structures work both within the family and the economy.

9 Mainly during the nineteen seventies a number of reforms were implemented – the equality package – aimed at establishing equality of opportunity and rights between men and women. Despite this, actual economic inequality stubbornly persists.

10 There are several possible outcomes of the women's movement. Assimilation would involve becoming like men in terms of attitudes and behaviour. Separatism would mean cutting off from men. Pluralism implies equal but different roles. A non-gendered society would not link roles with sexual differences.

RESEARCH AND COURSEWORK

There are many areas of social life immediately accessible to students in which gender issues occur: the family, education, leisure, paid work and others. A more ambitious piece of coursework might try to find a relationship between two or more areas. Thus, an enquiry into the occupations and work patterns of a group of younger women (say, 20 to 30 years old) could include questions on their educational qualifications/ experience, the domestic division of labour in their households and perhaps a question or two on their attitudes to their sons and daughters education and career prospects. The expected level of theoretical sophistication could come through probing the effect of class on the women's situations (Marxist-feminist perspective) and the ways in which patriarchy structured their lives (this would involve reference to radical-feminist perspective).

Relatively little has been said in this chapter about gender in relation to males except in the context of patriarchy and class. However, there is much scope for examining the basis of male power and control of people and resources in a number of contexts. Images related to and the experience of traditional 'masculinity' could be explored and explained as could that illusive phenomenon 'the new man'.

FURTHER READING

The continuing explosion of women's studies is apparent in that most large bookshops now have a section devoted to the area. Indeed there are some bookshops entirely devoted to it. There is plenty, therefore, to choose from. Pat Mayes, *Gender* (Longman, 1986) is a lively and wide-ranging starter and Stephanie Garrett's 'Gender' is thorough and comprehensive. Sue Sharpe's *Just like a Girl* (Penguin, 1976) and *Double identity* (Penguin, 1984) cover a wide-area of younger women's experience. For these who want to explore *masculine Identity*, Antony Easthope's *What a man's gotta do* (Paladin, 1986) is a stimulating, if speculative, read.

QUESTIONS

1   'It's a girl!' 'It's a boy!' To what extent do such gender definitions determine life chances in different societies? (London, 1984)

2   'The idea of a universal division of labour by sex is but a patriarchal myth.' Discuss. (London, 1984)

3   'In talking of the division of labour between men and women, we are talking almost exclusively of gender roles rather than sex roles, determined by culture rather than biology.' (Rogers: *The Domestication of Women*). Explain and discuss this statement with reference to gender roles in the workplace. (AEB, 1989)

4   To what extent is there now more role sharing in the contemporary British family? (London, 1990)

9 Race & Ethnicity

TERMINOLOGY AND PERSPECTIVES

'RACE' AND ETHNICITY: MINORITIES

'Race', in the sense of certain innate biological differences existing between given groups of people, has proved a vague and unconvincing basis for explaining differences of attitude and behaviour. Indeed, it has proved dangerous and destructive as demonstrated by Nazi theories of Jewish inborn moral corruption used to justify genocide and American and European theories of African inhumaness used to justify slavery. Following the Second World War, the United Nations commissioned a number of leading biologists and social scientists to analyse and define the meaning of race. The biologists concluded that the human species had a single origin and that so-called races were distinguishable by the greater statistical likelihood of individuals having certain physical characteristics such as hair type or skin colour but that these characteristics overlapped between groups. They did not consider that psychological and behavioural differences correlated with the physical differences.

Sociologists are primarily interested in why and how concepts of biological 'race' are frequently used so oppressively. Frequently, in the relations between groups, one group's 'theory of race' about the other is essentially a form of oppressive ideology (a body of interconnected sentiments and ideas) as the above theories about Jews and Africans indicate. It is 'race' as ideology that is of concern to sociologists, and for that reason the term is used in inverted commas here.

Whereas 'race' refers to ideologies of superiority/inferiority based on (mis)interpretations of biology, ethnicity refers to cultural differences between groups. Duncan Mitchell defines ethnicity as denoting membership of a distinct group of people possessing their own customary ways or culture. He illustrates this as follows:

The Germans, the Jews, the Gypsies are all ethnic groups, so also are Congo pygmies and Trobrianders. It will be observed that the characteristics identifying an ethnic group or aggregate may include a common language, common customs and beliefs and certainly a cultural tradition ...

(Mitchell, 1979.)

It is important to note that aspects of ethnicity can change and develop (such as language) but that ethnicity also provides a sense of group continuity and identity as, for instance, in the area of religion and 'folk' mythology. Thus, cultural heroines and heroes (real or imagined) provide role models and foci of communal feeling and unity. Churchill is an example from British culture and perhaps Crocodile Dundee from Australia.

In everyday life the above distinction between 'race' and ethnicity is seldom made. In particular, those discriminating against another group may do so on ground of 'race' or ethnicity or both. John Stone therefore suggests that rather than 'race' or ethnic group, 'the concept of "minority" is a better tool to use in the analysis of race and ethnic relations' (Stone, 1985:42). The term minority will be used here unless a specific reference to 'race' or ethnicity is required. For instance, we will refer to Afro-Caribbean, Jewish, and Greek and other minorities. A minority assumes a majority and this term will be used to describe the most numerous and usually most powerful 'racial'/ethnic group in a particular community or society.

RACISM, RACIALISATION AND INSTITUTIONAL RACISM

In defining racism it is helpful to distinguish between narrow and broad definitions. Narrow definitions limit the use of the term racism to describe belief systems based on the premise that there are certain biological or 'natural' differences between 'racial' groups on the basis of which cultural differences supposedly develop. The Marxist, Robert Miles, has robustly adopted such a definition:

We can ... define racism as any set of claims or arguments which signify some aspect of the physical features of an individual or group as a sign of permanent distinctiveness and which attribute additional, negative characteristics and for consequences to the individual's or group's presence.

(Miles, 1990: 49)

Miles goes on to suggest the use of the term racialisation to describe the discriminatory categorisation of a given individual or group on the basis of supposed 'racial' criteria. He argues that British politics has been continually 'racialised' since the nineteen sixties as black people have been 'scapegoated' for a variety of 'ills' such as unemployment and rising crime rates.

Broader definitions of racism include deterministic belief systems in which supposed 'superiority' and 'inferiority' may be based on cultural as well as biological criteria. John Rex, a leading Weberian, adopts this broader approach to racism.

Rex also employs the term 'institutional racism' to describe what he sees as a particular type of racism. It describes institutional rules and procedures which discriminate against one group but not another. Some use the term particularly to describe unintentional and indirect discrimination of this kind. Rex cites the procedures governing the way public rented accommodation was allocated in the nineteen sixties as an example of institutional discrimination:

There were ... rules about overcrowding, which prevented the allocation of houses to large families. The first of these sets of rules, but the second to some extent, had the effect of preventing the allocation of houses to black families. The problem then was one of indirect discrimination. Quite essential to fighting institutional racism then was the task of combating such indirect discrimination.

(Rex, 1986: 112)

Table 9.1 summarises some aspects of individual and institutional racism. The reader might find it useful to think of examples of the various factors indicated.

Racial Harassment

It is difficult to estimate the number of cases of racial harassment but there are many tens of thousands of incidents every year (the PSI Survey, 1984, estimates about 70,000). Racial harassment can be brutal and vary in its effects from creating inconvenience to disabling or murdering people. Here are some examples of 'routine' racism in Britain.

Mrs Zerbanoo Gifford, who is standing

Definitions/measures of racism

	Attitudinal	Behavioural
Individual	Personal attributes, Opinions, Values	Personal acts Behaviours, Chocies or
Institutional	Organisation/Societal Norms, Symbols, Fashions, Myths	Organisational/Societal Procedures, Programmes, Mechanisms

(Source: Adapted from Chester and Delgado, 1987:185)

Table 9.1

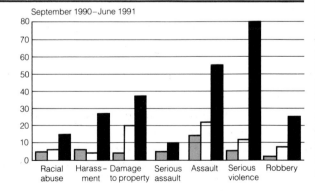

Type of racial incidents on the Teviot estate

September 1990–June 1991

Racial abuse · Harass-ment · Damage to property · Serious assault · Assault · Serious violence · Robbery

■ Police figures (grey)

□ Housing Dept

■ Homeless Families Campaign, Tower Hamlets, Law-Centre

'There is a gang who hang around, some are black boys and some white and when they see an Asian kid they chase him. The children want to go out. It's very painful to see them crying'.

'One day my husband went out shopping when they started banging on the door with a wooden stave. I just sit at home, I'm scared to let the children out and I can't go out and see people'.

Figure 9.1

Ten months of racial violence on an East London housing estate. Is a new law making specifically racial violence a criminal offence required?

as a parliamentary candidate (1992) was warned by a National Front supporter that her home would be fire bombed if she stood. Her home was broken into and a death threat left there.

Eugene Sutton, a building site worker, was subjected to racist taunts which a member of the management contributed to. In the court case, his employees said that such language was 'common parlance' on building sites.

A youth was slashed with a knife by an older white boy as he walked along a school corridor between classes.

A family was burned out of their home and a pregnant woman and her three children killed.

Note: The first two of the above cases were reported in The Times, *June 13, 1991, and the others are cited by Paul Gordon in* Citizenship for Some. *(Runnymede Trust, 1989)*

The Historical and Economic Background of Racism in Britain and The West

Race is a crucial contemporary issue both in Britain and internationally. South Africa remains a major focus of racial tension in the world, because until recently racial differentiation was openly proclaimed there as the very basis of stratification. That system was known as apartheid, although it was also presented as 'separate development'. Apartheid involved the legally enforceable separation of whites and blacks in a way that ensured far higher material and status rewards for the former. Due partly to the efforts of Nelson Mandela of the African National Congress and of President de Klerk, apartheid has been formally abolished, but its effects will last a long time (see p. 113). In certain other countries, the lines of racial stratification are less sharply drawn than in South Africa but are still quite clear. In Britain and the United States, black minorities tend to hold low-paid, low-status jobs, to live in poor housing and to be less well-educated than the white majority.

A THE HISTORICAL BACKGROUND OF RACE RELATIONS The roots of contemporary racial division lie in the expansion of European empires, particularly during the eighteenth and nineteenth centuries when these empires straddled the world. The British Empire extended to the Far East, but more significant from our point of view was the occupation of India, Pakistan, large parts of Africa, and several islands in the West Indies. A key factor in laying the foundations for later racial conflict in Britain, the United States, and parts of Africa was the exploitation of Africans, especially West Africans. The major element in this exploitation was the slave trade. Slave traders, mainly from Britain, France, Spain and Portugal, bought and kidnapped Africans, and transported them to the southern United States and the West Indies, where they were sold to work on plantations. In the southern states, a social structure based on slave labour developed, which left a legacy of bitterness, bigotry and exploitation, even after the formal abolition of slavery in the United States in 1863.

Between the two world wars, Britain and other European imperial powers sought to hold down discontent in conquered territories. By the early nineteen sixties, most British colonies had acquired independence, and already immigration into Britain from the former colonies had begun. The focus of conflict shifted from the struggle for independence in the colonies to problems associated with the settlement of black immigrants in Britain itself. As early as 1958, 'race riots' occurred in the Notting Hill area of London. After 1980, when Zimbabwe (formerly Rhodesia) became independent under majority rule, the only African country in which a minority of European extraction (in this case a large one) continued directly to dominate the black majority was South Africa.

The desire for economic gain is certainly a major motive for imperial expansion. The hope of acquiring political power and prestige, and of converting the conquered to, for example, Christianity or Marxism, are others. Economic realities clearly underlie much twentieth century racial conflict – the spread of racial conflict in the United States is an example. From the late nineteenth century, there was a strong demand from northern industrialists for cheap, black labour from the south. Later, this demand also occurred on the West Coast. As well as being cheap, black labour could be used to undermine the power of trade unions and to divide black and white working class people along racial lines. For their part, many black people were glad to leave the South, still darkened by the shadow of slavery, even though they encountered resentment and sometimes violence from the white working class in the urban areas of the North and West. In the mid-nineteen sixties, the big cities of the North and West USA were as torn by racial conflict and riots as the South.

B THE ECONOMIC BACKGROUND OF RACE RELATIONS (WITH PARTICULAR REFERENCE TO BRITAIN) Economic factors also provide the major explanation for the pattern of black immigration in Britain and, to some extent, for the 'panic' about immigration in the late nineteen sixties and nineteen seventies.

Migration can be explained in terms of 'push' and 'pull' factors. The 'push' factors refer to conditions in the country of origin, such as unemployment and poverty, which persuade people to leave: the 'pull' factor is the demand for labour in the country of immigration. The economic motive is considered by Peach and others to be the dynamic influence behind British post-war immigration. A major personal motive for migration is sometimes to rejoin family and kin.

Immigrants to Britain went mainly into unskilled and semi-skilled jobs in industrial production. This enabled more of the indigenous population to move up into the expanding service sector – a fact which, at first, certainly sweetened acceptance of immigration. Not all immigrants, however, started at the bottom of the social hierarchy. Many thousands of doctors and nurses from India, Pakistan and the West Indies were needed to support Britain's overstrained health system: even so, they tended to get the toughest and least prestigious posts, often in large metropolitan hospitals.

In some areas where a shortage of labour existed, active recruitment occurred. London Transport recruited drivers directly in the West Indies and the Health Service also advertised widely. Official figures show that, in 1965 alone, Britain took 1,015 doctors from India, 529 from Pakistan and 182 from other Commonwealth countries. The Health

Service is a striking, though not unique, example of Britain's dependence on the work of immigrants. In 1975, 35 per cent of hospital doctors and 18 per cent of family doctors came from outside Britain.

It is useful to draw a parallel between migrant workers in Europe and British immigrants. In the post-war period, the expanding economies of Western Europe needed foreign labour to increase production. Those countries which had colonies or former colonies, such as Britain or France, first recruited labour from these. Other countries which were without colonies, particularly West Germany, Luxembourg and Switzerland, had to recruit from elsewhere. They did so mainly from the poorer, less-industrialised countries of Eastern and Southern Europe – Greece, Turkey, Yugoslavia, Italy, Spain and Portugal. In 1974 it was estimated that 15 million immigrant workers and their families were living in Western Europe. A Common Market report for 1974 gave the proportion of immigrant workers in the labour force of the Western European countries as follows:

Luxembourg	35%
Switzerland	25%
France	11%
Germany	10%
UK	7%
Belgium	7%
Denmark	2%
Netherlands	3%

(Source: EEC Report, 1974)

These workers were overwhelmingly concentrated in low-paid jobs with unpleasant and sometimes quite dangerous conditions (such as asbestos processing) and long hours (like the restaurant trade). They were also particularly vulnerable to redundancy during recession.

A vital difference, however, exists between Britain's immigrants and migrant workers in some other European countries. Immigrants to Britain who were Commonwealth citizens had a right to settle here with their families and to exercise full civil and political liberties, including voting. Most came believing that they would receive fair and equal treatment with white citizens. For many, these hopes have not been fulfilled.

stirring of ethnic nationalism occurred throughout the Soviet Empire both before and after the collapse of Soviet Communism. Estonia, Latvia and Lithuania were the first Soviet republics to declare independent nationhood in 1991. The other republics of the Soviet Union became sovereign and independent following the failed communist 'coup'. Some joined a new voluntary federation but others remain reluctant. Tension exists between some of the states, including Christian Armenia and Muslim Azerbaijan. The area most affected by ethnic tension following the sharp decline of the Soviet Empire has been Yugoslavia, where Serbs and Croats entered upon a bloody civil war.

The spread of liberal free market and democratic ideals within the former Soviet Empire has had a destabilising as well as an

Figure 9.2

Ethnic nationalism was a major force in breaking up the Soviet Union

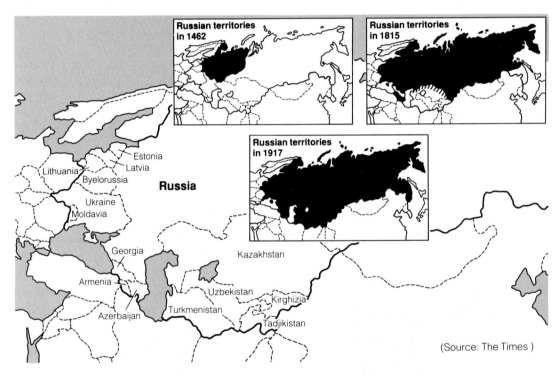

Russian territories in 1462

Russian territories in 1815

Russian territories in 1917

Estonia
Lithuania
Latvia
Byelorussia
Russia
Ukraine
Moldavia
Georgia
Kazakhstan
Armenia
Uzbekistan
Kirghizia
Azerbaijan
Turkmenistan
Tadjikistan

(Source: The Times)

Figure 9.3

The states of the former Soviet Union

ETHNIC NATIONALISM AND INTERNATIONALISM AND THE DECLINE OF COMMUNISM

In modern history and contemporary society, ethnic groups concentrated in particular geographical areas often perceive themselves as 'nations'. For instance, a strong sense of religious and cultural identity fed a sense of nationhood in Ireland despite centuries of subjugation to England. To take another example, a widespread

invigorating effect. Now that the grip of Soviet totalitarianism has been removed, regions and states are freer to express their sometimes substantial differences and disagreements. Ironically, Marxists have long argued that when the masses reject socialism, they frequently turn to nationalism. In the case of stronger states, nationalism can take the form of assertiveness internationally and/or imperialism.

Internationally, the most expansionist ethnic movement in the past two decades has been Islam. For many people in poorer parts of the world, Islam has replaced Marxism as a focus of identity and source of hope. However, Islam does not always coexist easily with Western liberalism – the other ideological success story of the post-war era. The Rushdie matter and the Gulf War have sharply and tragically demonstrated the massive potential for conflict between these two ideologies.

There are some signs that international solutions are being increasingly sought to ethnic conflict and national aggression. The Western European nations exercised a major role in the ethnic conflict in Yugoslavia. Iraq was defeated by an alliance authorised by the United Nations albeit one dominated by the United States. Communism itself was touted by its adherents as an ideology of international solidarity which would transcend and make redundant 'petty' ethnic and national conflicts. It failed to do this. However, the collapse of communism has left a power vacuum which is likely to require a strong, benign and constructive internationalism to achieve greater global peace and justice. These issues are further discussed in chapter 21.

Race and Ethnicity in Employment

This section will first present the facts – as provided by official surveys – about the occupational distribution of various groups, particularly black ones. It will then examine a number of explanations about why, in general, black people occupy lower positions in the occupational hierarchy than white people. We will then briefly examine the distribution of housing in a similar context.

DATA ON EMPLOYMENT BY ETHNIC ORIGIN
The data provided in figure 9.4 gives the occupational pattern for different ethnic groups (based on employed people of 16 and over). The chart combines data for both males and females.

Figure 9.4 presents employment (according to ethnic origin) by broad occupational group. Using more detailed

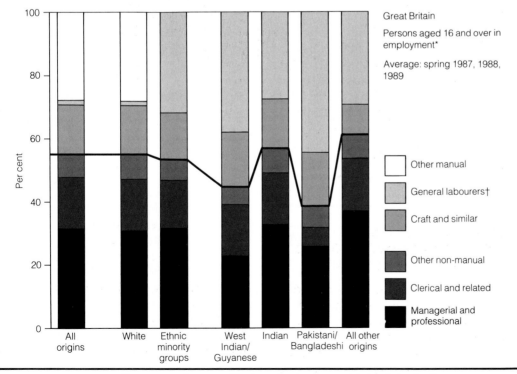

Great Britain

Persons aged 16 and over in employment*

Average: spring 1987, 1988, 1989

Key:
- Other manual
- General labourers†
- Craft and similar
- Other non-manual
- Clerical and related
- Managerial and professional

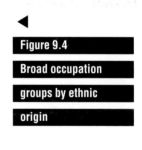

Figure 9.4
Broad occupation
groups by ethnic
origin

*Excluding those on Government schemes   †Too few to be shown separately for ethnic minority groups
(Source: LFS estimates, in *Employment Gazette* February 1991: 64)

data than the LF surveys, we will separately analyse the occupational positions of males and females. The overall percentages of male minority workers and male white workers in both non-manual and manual employment were the same, 47 per cent and 53 per cent respectively. However, this picture of similarity is superficial and needs to be qualified in two ways. First, certain minority groups are significantly under-represented in in non-manual employment. Only about a third of West Indian/Guyanese males are in non-manual occupations with the 'shortfall' being particularly marked in the area of managerial and professional employment. Similarly, only about a third of Pakistani/ Bangladeshi males are in non-manual employment. These two groupings together make up about 60 per cent of black minority males in employment and a large majority of them are in manual employment, much of it low paid and low status. A considerably larger percentage of black minority than white employees are concentrated in the retail and hotels and catering sectors. In contrast, a slightly higher proportion of Indian than white employees are in non-manual employment.

A second point to be borne in mind when interpreting male minority employment patterns is that within occupations black men tend to receive lower wages. Table 9.2 shows that Asian/West Indian males receive lower wages than white males in the same occupational grouping at all levels from professional to unskilled manual. The data derives from a survey carried out several years earlier than that which figure 9.4 is based on but the basic pattern it shows is unlikely greatly to have changed.

Thirdly, as figure 9.5 shows, unemployment is higher among black minority males than among white males. Whereas white male unemployment is given at nine per cent Pakistani/Bangladeshi male unemployment is twenty five per cent, and West Indian/ Guyanese eighteen per cent. These differences are substantial and represent one of the major areas of inequality between ethnic groups. It is particularly young males in the above groups that are likely to be unemployed – with potentially disastrous effects.

Around two thirds of all employed women are in non-manual occupations in the case of both white and black minority women. However, economic activity rates vary greatly among women of different ethnic groups. They are highest for women of West Indian origin at 76 per cent and lowest for those of Pakistani or Bangladeshi origin at 21 per cent (although it is possible that the Labour Force Surveys under-represent the latter group by failing to reach many homeworkers – see p. 182). Although there are some differences in the pattern of employment between white and black minority women – notably, more of the latter being employed in health services and parts of manufacturing, the Labour Force Survey finds that the overall pattern of employment between the two groups is very similar.

Contrary to expectation perhaps, black women's average earnings are higher than those of white women (see table 9.3).

▶

Table 9.2

Gross earnings of full-time employees by job level (£ median weekly earnings): Male

Job Level	Male	
	White	Asian/West Indian
Professional Employer Manager	184.70	151.80
Other non-manual	135.80	130.40
Skilled manual	121.70	112.20
Semi-skilled manual	111.20	101.00
Unskilled manual	(99.90)	97.80
All	129.00	110.20

(Source: Colin Brown, 1984)

▶

Table 9.3 (Far right)

Gross earnings of full-time employees by job level (£ median weekly earnings): Female

Job Level	Female	
	White	Asian/West Indian
Professional Employer Manager	106.80	122.10
Other non-manual	81.70	86.00
Skilled manual	(66.90)	(74.40)
Semi-skilled manual	66.50*	72.40*
Unskilled manual		
All	77.50	78.50

*This figure is semi-skilled and unskilled manual.
(Source: Colin Brown, 1984)

Further, black women's wages are a higher percentage of black men's wages (71 per cent) than are white women's wages of

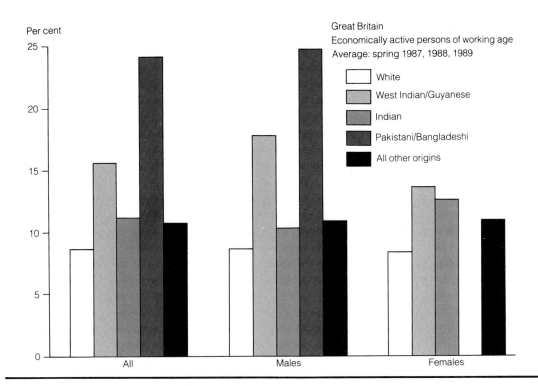

Per cent

Great Britain
Economically active persons of working age
Average: spring 1987, 1988, 1989

☐ White
▨ West Indian/Guyanese
▨ Indian
▨ Pakistani/Bangladeshi
■ All other origins

All   Males   Females

Figure 9.5

Unemployment rates

by ethnic origin and

sex

(Source: LFS estimates, in *Employment Gazette* February 1991: 67)

white men's (60 per cent). Contrary also to stereotype the formal qualifications of women of West Indian origin (though not those of Pakistani/Bangladeshi origin) are on a par with those of white women.

Despite the above considerations, Irene Breugel has argued that 'in terms of the "total employment package", black women can be seen to be considerably worse off than white women' (Breugel, 1986). She points out that black women work longer hours in both full-time and part-time work, that they are concentrated in London (where wages are higher but so is the cost of living); and that their younger 'and hence better qualified profile' has not yet fully resulted in the corresponding rewards. Black women earn less per hour on average than white women and black women graduates earn 71 per cent of what white women graduates earn. Both black women and men are much more likely than white people to be overqualified for the job they are doing: twenty per cent in both cases, compared to ten per cent of white women and one per cent of white men. Breugel suggests that the 'overqualification phenomenon' is probably due to racism. It is to the issue of racial discrimination in the labour market that we now turn.

EXPLANATIONS OF THE POSITION OF BLACK MINORITIES IN THE EMPLOYMENT MARKET

There are few, if any, more important preconditions of a racially harmonious and tolerant society than fairness and justice in employment. There are various explanations of the continuing substantial inequalities experienced by black minorities in the employment market and in employment. Some of these explanations overlap, but they are distinct enough to require separate analysis. The explanations examined below are:

■ Ethnic Adjustment (Liberal Perspective);
■ Racism and the Dual Labour Market: A Black Underclass;
■ Marxist Perspectives
  i) Reserve Army of Labour: Castles and Kosack
  (ii) Class Fractions: Robert Miles
■ Marxist feminist and Black feminist Interpretations.

Before evaluating these explanations, however, it will be helpful to examine some empirical evidence of racism in the employment market.

EVIDENCE OF RACISM IN THE EMPLOYMENT MARKET

The most convincing evidence that extensive racial discrimination occurs in the employment market, comes from the research of the Policy Studies Institute (formerly Political and Economic Planning – PEP). There have been three major PSI studies of this issue – in 1973-74, 1977-79, and 1984-85. The method adopted by the PSI team was for black and white 'candidates' (some were actors) to apply for specific jobs. The candidates were precisely matched in qualifications, experience and other relevant criteria. A substantially larger percentage of white candidates received positive responses and roughly the same percentage of black people were discriminated against throughout the studies. In 1973-74, 27 per cent of West Indians and 28 per cent of Asians were discriminated against and in 1984-85, the percentages were 27 per cent and 27 per cent respectively.

A very different and less formal piece of research – a piece of television journalism ('Black and White') – also demonstrated high levels of discrimination in the employment market and other areas. Geoff Small, a black journalist, and Tim Marshall, a white journalist, tested the extent of racism in various situations by each approaching, in turn, for example, an employer or landlord as applicants for an advertised job or room. Small appeared to be discriminated against on numerous occasions including 4 out of 10 occasions when applying for a job (the figure for bed and breakfast was 5 out of 15).

The following section presents more theoretical interpretation of the position of black minorities in the employment market each perspective addressing the issue of racism differently.

ETHNIC ADJUSTMENT (LIBERAL PERSPECTIVE)

When the first post-war black immigrants came to Britain, it was a commonly expressed view, especially among more liberal politicians, that as the new immigrants adjusted to British life, increasing numbers would move up the occupational hierarchy. It was assumed that language, educational and cultural adjustment problems experienced by the first generation which affected their position in the labour market would less strongly affect their children and grandchildren. Even when it became clear that white racism might impede black advancement, optimists felt that a continuation of anti-discrimination legislation and immigration control would secure generally fair conditions for black Britons.

The ethnic adjustment perspective is derived partly from the experience of immigrant groups in the United States. Each wave of ethnic immigrants into the United States took its place in turn on the bottom of the ladder and began to clamber up – sometimes on the shoulders of the next in-coming group. The British, Italians and Eastern Europeans have all done this. A version of the same process has happened to black Americans who have edged significantly beyond the Hispanic elements (those of mainly Mexican and Puerto Rican origin) in the population. A problem in applying this model to black Britons is that no further wave of immigrants is likely to replace them on the bottom rung of society's ladder. Nevertheless, those who take the ethnic adjustment perspective are able to point to considerable black progress in employment and housing to support their view.

RACISM AND DUAL LABOUR MARKET THEORY: A BLACK UNDERCLASS?

We have already discussed dual labour market theory in relation to female labour and, more generally, in the context of 'post-Fordism'. The essence of the theory is that there are two labour markets, the primary and secondary. The first recruits to well-paid, secure and more crucial jobs and the latter to generally less well paid, less secure and perhaps occasional jobs. John Rex and Sally Tomlinson have argued that black employees are substantially more likely than white employees to be in the secondary labour market. The following is an extract from their mid nineteen seventies study of Handsworth, Birmingham, *Colonial Immigrants in a British City: A Class Analysis*:

In Handsworth it is fair to say that about half of the non-white population are employed in semi-skilled and unskilled manual work and less than ten per cent in white-collar jobs, whereas only about a quarter of whites are in the low-skill groups and a third in white collar jobs. That already suggests a considerable difference despite the overlap. If one then looks at industrial and occupational differences, one finds that the West Indian and Asian populations are more concentrated in labouring jobs and in hot and dirty industries, and are poorly represented in professional, scientific and administrative jobs. Both West Indian and Asian workers had to work extra hours to earn the same as white British workers, and were more also likely to be on shift work ...

These figures may not confirm that there is a completely dual labour market situation with whites gaining internal appointments and promotions in protected jobs and the immigrants getting what jobs they can in the open market. But they are consistent with the notion of two kinds of job situations with whites predominant in one and blacks in the other. In fact, the degree of apparent overlap may be deceptive and case studies of actual employment might well show that in each industrial, occupational, skill and social class category, the actual job situation of the black is less desirable and secure than that of the white ...

(Rex and Tomlinson 1979: 279).

Rex has gone on to argue that due mainly to racism, black disadvantage and segregation in employment (and housing, see p. 204) is such that a black underclass has been created in Britain. He felt strengthened in his analysis when often irregularly employed black youth prominently participated in the urban disorders of 1981 and 1985. Nevertheless, many commentators, both liberal and Marxist, have argued that Rex overinterprets the evidence in developing dual labour market/underclass theory. Indeed, in the above passage, there is some degree of tentativeness about whether black employees are fully in a dual labour market situation. If there was a degree of overlap between the situation of black and white employees in the late nineteen seventies, the Labour Force Surveys of the late nineteen eighties suggest considerably more (see p. 197) and it is doubtful whether Rex would find them generally supportive of his theoretical approach.

MARXIST PERSPECTIVES ON THE EMPLOYMENT OF BLACK PEOPLE

S Castles and G Kosack give an analysis of black immigrants into Britain in which their situation is seen as essentially similar to that of migrant workers in Western Europe (*Immigrant Workers and Class Structure in Western Europe* (Oxford University Press, 1973)). Both immigrant and migrant workers are seen as part of the working class but as a particularly disadvantaged group or 'bottom stratum' within it. They function as 'a reserve army' of labour which can be drawn on during periods of capitalist expansion and relatively easily laid off during periods of contraction.

Castles and Kosack argue that the use of black immigrant labour provides a further advantage to the capitalist class in addition to flexibility – its presence divides the working class by allowing indigenous workers to move into employment with better pay and conditions from which they typically seek to exclude the 'newcomers'. They stress the deep and stubborn nature of this division and argue that 'it can only disappear when it is supplanted not merely by a correct understanding of the position of immigrant workers, but by a class consciousness which reflects the true position of all workers in society' (Castles and Kosack, 1973:482).

Robert Miles also regards class stratification as more fundamental than 'racial' or ethnic division but recognises that due partly to racism the British working class is 'fractionalised' i.e. divided within and, in his view, against itself. Miles further makes the point that black people are by no means all in the working class or, as he puts it, they occupy 'all the main economic sites in the relations of production' (Miles, 1989: 121). He points out that there is 'a small, but increasing, Asian and Caribbean petit bourgeoisie'; that they represent a significant part of the 'surplus population' (i.e. unemployed); and that there are significant differences between black workers, not least, according to sex and nationality'.

On the basis of the above observations, Miles specifically discusses underclass theory:

The view that Asian and Caribbean people in Britain collectively constitute a 'black' underclass, a collectivity homogeneous in its poverty and economic disadvantage relative to 'white' people as a result of racism and systematic exclusionary practices, is therefore mistaken.

(Miles, 1989: 123)

However, he does recognise that 'the economic position occupied by a large proportion of Asian and Caribbean people is inferior to that of the indigenous population'. Racism plays a part in producing an inferior class situation for many black people but it does not, as Rex contends, create a black underclass.

MARXIST-FEMINIST AND BLACK-FEMINIST INTERPRETATIONS Marxist-Feminists tend to argue that the position of white and black women in the labour market is much more similar than that of white and black men. For instance, there is less difference between white and black women in terms of earnings and job levels. Sheila Allen suggests that this is because the exploitation both white and black women experience as women leaves limited scope for black women to be still further exploited as black:

The position of black women in the labour market can be understood only by relating it to women more generally. Briefly the sexual division of labour segregates women into very few industrial sectors and within these they are usually in the lower segments of occupational hierarchies. They are in the main found in service industries, in jobs designated as semi-skilled, and they earn less than men. In the professions, they either constitute a very small percentage relative to men, for instance in law, medicine or university teaching, or where they are a higher percentage, such as in

school-teaching, they are found disproportionately in the lower grades. A suggested explanation of the similarity between the wages of black and white women which was reported in 1974, was 'that the enormous disparity between men and women ... left little scope for racial disadvantage to have a further, additive effect' (Brown, 1984: 169).

(From Allen, in C. Husband, 1987: 182)

As we have already seen, Irene Breugel illustrates a degree of inequality in employment between black and white women despite apparent comparability (see p. 199). Hazel Carby puts the matter in broader historical context by arguing that British employers have been inclined to view black women as more 'normally' in paid work than white women. While black and white women are part of a reserve army of labour, black women are more routinely and frequently exploited.

BLACK MINORITIES, THE EMPLOYMENT MARKET AND STRATIFICATION Table 9.4 links explanations of the position of black people in the employment market with parallel theories of how they are stratified in the social structure. The diagram is intended to clarify the stratificational aspects of the particular perspectives.

It can be debated whether the differences between John Rex and Robert Miles are as sharp as Miles himself presents. Putting it simply Rex is saying that due to racism the situation of black people within the class structure tends to be worse than that of white people to the extent that the majority of black people form an underclass in danger of becoming separated from the rest of the working class. Miles argues that while black

Table 9.4

Source	Labour market theory	Main casual factor	Type of stratification
Liberal/ Social Democrat	Equal opportunity- but initial difficulties	Adjustment Problems	Pluralist
Weber John Rex	Dual labour market	Racism	Black underclass
Marxist	(Part of) reserve army of labour	Class exploitation	Class-fractionalised by racism. Emergent black middle class

people are increasingly distributed throughout the class structure, the majority are working class and their situation is further disadvantaged by racism. Both Rex and Miles are much more pessimistic about the effects of racism than liberals who incline to the view that ultimately the class profile of black minorities will not be greatly different from the national class profile.

Perhaps the main point on which Rex and American underclass theorist, Douglas Glasgow (1981), differ from Miles is the extent to which they consider black people, particularly young black people, to be cut off from upward social mobility by racism. This tends to make the black underclass intergenerational. Although a higher percentage of black workers are members of trade unions than white workers, Rex argues that the trade union movement has done little to promote the cause of black people or black workers within it. He finds it unsurprising, then, that given little assistance from dominant 'white' institutions and often victimised by racism, a number of black people, including younger ones, have turned inwards toward their own ethnic communities. This process can take many forms, including family self-help in business, ethnic politics, and a less organised 'dropping out of the system'.

Minority and Majority Culture and Class

The debate about the relative effect of class and racial/ethnic factors on forming the lives of black minorities will now be briefly examined in the context of majority and minority cultures. This will prepare the way for a later discussion on politics, class and ethnicity. First, however, it is necessary to describe the possible range of adaptation/ rejection that a minority group might experience in relation to the majority culture. This process is a two-way one involving members of both a given minority and of the majority. In this sense, it is a negotiated process although power and coercion may be involved.

The possible relationships between a minority and majority can be presented in the form of the following model which should be regarded as indicating points in a continuum.

Possible Relationships between Ethnic
Minority and Majority Cultures

Assimilation   Pluralism   Separatism

The assimilation of a minority occurs when it becomes fully absorbed into a majority culture. Thus, the descendants of French Huguenots (who fled from persecution to Britain) now appear to have little or no distinct ethnic identity. Ethnic pluralism occurs when a minority group retains its own customs and identity but also fully participates in the 'mainstream' life of a society. For instance, Jews frequently maintain their own religious and cultural practices while playing a full part in 'mainstream' society's economic, political and social life. Total minority separatism is virtually impossible in highly inter-connected modern societies. Certain groups of Asian origin, particularly Bangladeshis, appear to fall between pluralism and separatism, on the model. Whole groups may have few English speakers and participate relatively little in life outside their own families and ethnic community.

There are some problems with the above model as applying it to Britain makes clear. Can we usefully use the concept of 'British culture' (or 'English culture') as a basis for analysis. What is it? Does it change over time? If so, are there parts that remain stable and perhaps fundamental and parts that change? It would take too long a detour adequately to answer these questions here. What can be said is that culture as a sociological concept refers to 'a way of life' and that this is expressed in a group's norms, customs and values, and in its language and shared experience (history). In this way, and obviously at a high level of generality, we can refer to British or German or other national cultures in which the majority of members of these societies participate. Minority groups immigrating or migrating to a society interact with it both adapting to and, to a greater or lesser extent, changing the majority culture. It is not only ethnic groups that form subcultures within a majority culture but also regional, class and other subgroups.

PERSPECTIVES ON MINORITY/MAJORITY RELATIONS

The following perspectives on minority/ majority group relations are as much ideological as sociological. Issues of 'race', ethnicity and nationality are more fraught with emotion and subjectivity than most.

ASSIMILATIONIST The assimilationist view is that incoming ethnic minorities should fully conform in major public areas to what they take to be the established British way of life. This approach is particularly associated with the new right (i.e., the rightwing of what used to be referred to as 'Thatcherism'). Thus, Roger Scruton argues that the prime purpose of education in Britain is to facilitate the participation of the individual in British culture and that 'there can be no real argument for a "multi-cultural" curriculum' (Scruton, 1986). Similarly, assimilationists do not consider that other institutional areas of British society should adapt to minority groups but contend that the latter should do the adapting. However, perhaps few would insist on assimilation in the area of private life and personal taste. Norman Tebbitt is an exception. His 'cricket test' was that a true 'English' person would support the English cricket team rather than, say, the West Indies.

PLURALIST The pluralist or liberal-pluralist view is that a variety of cultural groups can and do exist in Britain within a common legal and democratic framework. Again, this approach can be illustrated in the area of education where liberal-pluralists argue that the curriculum ought fully to reflect the multicultural nature of contemporary Britain while also educating in basic skills and fundamental values. Pluralists also consider that in other institutional areas of British life, such as the welfare state and social services, accommodation to and awareness of specific cultural needs is desirable.

MARXIST Marxists argue that ethnic culture is of secondary importance to class culture. They use the concepts of dominant and subordinate class cultures rather those of majority and minority cultures. Writing about the notion of a majority culture, Charles Husband has argued that 'there is no single monolithic ideology' of nation 'shared by all Britons' but that people have varying 'images' of Britain which do 'not necessarily have the same range of meaning' (Husband, 1982). Thus, for some, British Imperial history embodies the essence of British 'greatness' whereas for others it may seem a national disgrace. Further, Marxists contend that ethnic and nationalistic identification tends to be reactionary and to create a false unity among groups who, at a deeper level, are divided by social class.

UNDERCLASS John Rex's analysis that a black underclass may have emerged in Britain, has an application to culture. A group that is racially and economically oppressed is likely to have a common awareness and resentment of its oppression and to develop a culture that reflects this. This is particularly true of young unemployed or irregularly employed Afro-Caribbeans whose music, religion (i.e. in the case of Rastafarians), and politics often express an opposition to racism. As Rex has noted, during the nineteen eighties (and early nineties) there was also evidence of increased militancy against racism among young Asians.

CULTURE: CLASS AND ETHNIC INFLUENCES: THE AFRO-CARIBBEAN CASE As we saw above, the precise effect of class and ethnic influences on the culture or way of life of a given group is the subject of theoretical debate. Ken Pryce's study of the Afro-Caribbean community of St. Paul's, Bristol in 1979 attempts to describe the combined effects of class and ethnicity on lifestyle. The righthand column of the diagram includes both class and ethnic aspects of culture.

Pryce describes Afro-Caribbeans who have white-collar jobs as 'mainliners', that is, as conforming, stable, law-abiding citizens. The same is true of the majority of the manual working class whom Pryce divides into religious ('saints') and non-religious – partly in recognition of the importance of religion in Afro-Caribbean culture. Some white-collar and manual employees enjoy an expressive (extrovert, pleasure-seeking) leisure life-style which may bring them into contact with the 'disreputable' life-style of part of the

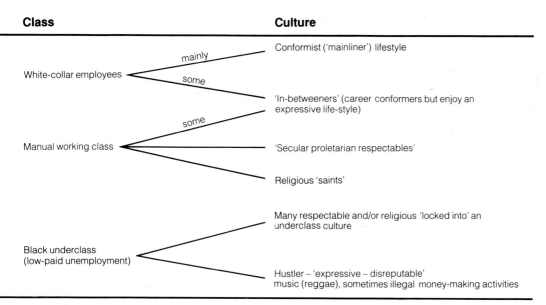

Class	Culture
White-collar employees	Conformist ('mainliner') lifestyle (mainly)
	'In-betweeners' (career conformers but enjoy an expressive life-style) (some)
Manual working class	'Secular proletarian respectables' (some)
	Religious 'saints'
Black underclass (low-paid unemployment)	Many respectable and/or religious 'locked into' an underclass culture
	Hustler – 'expressive – disreputable' music (reggae), sometimes illegal money-making activities

(Source: Derived and adapted from Pryce, 1979)

▲

Figure 9.6

Class and cultural

variety within the

Afro-Caribbean

community

underclass. The latter is itself divided into those who manage to maintain a legal living and those who adapt by creating a largely alternative lifestyle (see also p. 224).

Pryce's model is presented descriptively and uncritically here simply to illustrate class and ethnic influence on culture or, as Pryce puts it, 'life-style'.

Ethnic and/or Class Politics

In the 1970s and 1980s, John Rex frequently argued that it was likely that black minority groups would organise on a communal basis to confront issues such as black unemployment, the educational underattainment of black youth, and racial victimisation by the police and other authorities. He thought that such action was likely to be locally based but he did not preclude the possibility of national action. In contrast to Rex, the major political parties have tended to assume that the bulk of black political action would occur within the party system. In practice, as we shall see, the black vote is strongly for Labour. Marxists argue that black people should organise on the basis of class politics but of a much more radical kind than is likely to occur within the Labour Party.

ETHNIC POLITICS John Rex suggested that three types of black political movements occur: issue-oriented, personality-oriented and ideologically-oriented. A major example of an issue-oriented movement was the protest against the number of black youths arrested on

suspicion ('sus'). This was a charge under the 1824 Vagrancy Act which allows the police to arrest, without warrant, a person whom they reasonably suspect to be 'loitering with intent to commit a felonious offence'. Police evidence alone could be sufficient to convict. Estimates of the percentage of black people making up 'sus' arrests vary from 44 per cent (Home Office) to 80 per cent for certain inner urban areas (Law Centres Working Group). The 'sus' law and the manner of its application caused widespread concern within and beyond the black community. The 'sus' law has now been abolished but police relations with parts of the black community have remained fragile. Urban disorders in Brixton in 1981 and in Handsworth and Tottenham in 1985 were triggered by incidents involving black people and the police although deeper socio-economic causes lay behind the conflict.

Education is another quite different issue, which has provoked black action. In Redbridge and elsewhere, black parents and teachers have very positively involved themselves in supporting the school curriculum, with additional schooling in the evenings or at weekends.

We now consider Rex's second type of movement, the personality-oriented. An example of a nationally-known (though sparsely supported) personality-oriented movement in Britain was the Black power Group led by Michael X during the nineteen-sixties. He was a mere shadow of the much better known Malcolm X who led the Black Muslim movement in the United States. Rex has in mind, however, local personalities who can manipulate incidents sometimes to further a cause but often for maximum personal publicity.

A more reliable basis for a political movement than the merely personal is ideological belief – Rex's third category. The founding of an Islamic Party in Bradford in 1990 is an example of this kind of movement. Within the British black community, there are a number of groups which are as much cultural as political, and which have distinctive ideologies. One example is the Rastafarian movement. Members of the group are disciples of the late former Emperor of Ethiopia, Haile Selassie, whom they believe to be divine. With varying degrees of conviction, Rastafarians subscribe to black separatism and some wed socialism to their religious beliefs. It has been said of this and of other 'back to Africa' movements that they represent an extreme defensive reaction by blacks against a white society which has already rejected them. A return to Africa is not, however, a realistic option, particularly as the majority of black immigrants have never been there in the first place. But the identity, confidence and expression that such movements provide should not be dismissed or underestimated. We develop this point further when discussing black youth (p. 223–4).

CLASS POLITICS Community politics alone are unlikely ever to be enough radically to change the position of Britain's black population. John Rex may virtually despair of an effective black and white working class alliance but he still recognises its ultimate desirability, if the massive governmental resources needed by inner city ethnic groups are ever to materialise. Community politics are necessary both to 'defend' and develop the community, but only government (arguably in combination with industry) can provide the means to lift 'ghetto' conditions – economic, housing and educational – much nearer to the acceptable national norm. In getting political support for such a programme blacks are not without some political muscle. At the lowest level, political parties need black votes just as unions require members.

Historically, black people who vote have overwhelmingly supported Labour although this is now somewhat less true of the Indian community. Surveys show that the issues which most concern black voters are generally those that most concern white voters: unemployment, the cost of living, and education. However, black people, particularly those of Asian origin additionally express great concern over immigration control. The number of black local and national political candidates has increased in recent years. For instance, in the 1979 general election, five black candidates stood unsuccessfully, whereas in the 1987 general election twenty-seven stood, four successfully (all Labour). In all four cases, the Labour candidates were helped by a large black vote in their constituencies. It still remains to be seen whether black candidates will be able to run for office across the whole country without experiencing a racist backlash. The difficulties the black barrister John Taylor met in Cheltenham in 1990–91 after he had been adopted as prospective Conservative parliamentary candidate suggest others may face problems of this kind. However, Marion Fitzgerald's analysis of the results of black candidates in the 1983 general election suggests that they lost few votes because of their colour (Fitzgerald, 1983).

POLITICS, POLICY AND THE LAW Has the support of the large majority of black voters for the Labour party been justified by that party's policies when in office? On the credit side, it can be said that the three major Race Relations Acts aimed at preventing racial discrimination in key areas of public life were all passed under Labour governments and that only one of the Immigration/ Nationality Acts (that of 1968) aimed at controlling immigration was passed by a Labour government (see figure 9.7).

Immigration/nationality and race relations legislation: the 'liberal compromise'

N.B. The letters 'L' and 'C' given in brackets after the title of an Act indicate whether it was passed under a Labour or Conservative administration

1948 British Nationality Act (L)
Commonwealth citizens allowed freely to enter and settle in Britain.

Immigration/nationality laws

1962 Commonwealth Immigrants Act (C)

removed the rights of the 1948 Act for most New (black) Commonwealth citizens. Instead a limited number of *employment vouchers* were issued.

1968 Commonwealth Immigrants Act (L)

restricted the entry to East African Asians who held U.K. passports issued by the British Government.

1971 Immigrant Act (C)

made a distinction between patrials (those born in Britain or with a parent/ grandparent born in Britain) who kept full British citizens' rights, and non-patrials (mainly black, new Commonwealth) who were required to obtain work permits prior to entry.

1981 British Nationality Act (C)
Restricted forms of British nationality provided for those whose entry rights had been removed by previous laws – by this time the entry of blacks for settlement is highly controlled and virtually limited to close relatives.

1988 Immigration Act (C)

An immigrant husband who wants his wife and children to join him in Britain has to prove he can house and support them.

Race relations laws

1965 Race Relations Act (L)

(i) made discrimination illegal in certain places – *but* the means of enforcing the Act were very weak.
(ii) made incitement to racial hatred illegal.

1968 Race Relations Act (L)

enlarged the scope of the 1965 Act (discrimination being made illegal in employment and housing, for the first time) *but* enforcement still weak – relying on the new *Community Relations Council* to take up *individual complaints*.

1976 Race Relations Act (L)

extended the anti-discrimination laws to *UNINTENDED* as well as intended discrimination – a very important principle.

This record provides a basis for the Labour Party's claim that it has long had an active commitment to the creation of a society characterised by equality of racial opportunity. Critics, particularly from the left, argue that the Race Relations legislation and the institutions it established have lacked 'the teeth' to enforce anti-discrimination and, indeed, evidence can be cited to support the view that there has been little, if any reduction in racism and racial discrimination in Britain since the nineteen fifties (see, for instance, p. 200). Ironically, such evidence can also be used to support the view of some Conservatives that legislative tinkering in race relations is unlikely greatly to affect actual behaviour. However, it must be said, that on the issue of immigration, Conservatives have been the opposite of non-interventionist and have passed legislation which has had the effect of tightly controlling black immigration but much less so white immigration. In 1990, the Commission for Racial Equality demanded that employers should be required to keep and publish annually records of the ethnic make-up of their workforce and that 'targets' (but not compulsory quotas) be introduced for the recruitment of non-whites.

Those who continue to believe that the law can be used as an effective instrument in the creation of a racially equal society have generally shifted their emphasis from anti-discrimination to the setting of more positive goals, the attainment of which would clearly indicate the achievement of fairness and equality. Two examples of this occur commonly in the United States but not in Britain: establishing quotas and contract compliance. Quotas refer to specific numbers of black people required to be employed in a given organisation, say, a local police force, frequently by a target date. Contract compliance involves the granting of a contract, usually by central or local government, to a business provided that it employs a given number of black people – possibly at specified job levels and again sometimes subject to timing. Such techniques are considered by their supporters to have more 'teeth' than generalised anti-discriminatory legislation and to be particularly effective in combating institutional racism (see p. 192). However, it is arguable that, at the very least, anti-discriminatory legislation remains valid as a statement of a society's commitment and intent in the area of racial equality.

SUMMARY

1 The term 'race' in sociology refers to people's often imprecise notions or theories of 'race' rather than any precisely established biological reality. Ethnicity denotes the membership of a distinct people possessing their own culture. Racism narrowly defined, refers to prejudice and discriminate based on a view of a group's supposed biological inferiority. More broadly defined, it includes views based on a group's supposed cultural inferiority.

2 Contemporary racism in Britain has important roots in British imperial and economic expansions, particularly slavery. In present-day Europe inequality between people is largely based on international flows of labour. World-wide, and despite some reform, apartheid remains perhaps the most overtly racist ideology and practice.

3 Data on ethnic employment and unemployment for the late nineteen eighties generally continues to show inequalities between whites and others, especially Afro-Caribbeans and Pakistani/Bangladeshis. The position of black and white women appears more similar but Breugel cites data to suggest that significantly greater inequalities are still experienced by black women.

4 Several explanations are offered for the position of black minorities in the employment market. The ethnic adjustment perspective argues that black minorities like other ethnic groups can progress in Britain. The underclass perspective contends that racism may well cut large numbers of black people off from advancement, thus creating an underclass. Marxist analysis presents black people *primarily in class terms with the majority of them being seen as working class but particularly disadvantaged by racism. Feminist analysis stresses the additional gender disadvantage experienced by women in the labour market with different emphases occurring in respect of the relative importance of the links between class inequality and gender and racial inequality and gender.*

5 Several perspectives also occur on the relations between black minorities and the majority group. Assimilationists take the view that black people should wholly or largely forsake their own cultures and 'become British' (despite problems in defining precisely what 'British culture' is). Marxists argue that the concepts of dominant and subordinate class cultures have more explanatory value than those of minority and majority cultures, although they recognise that ethnic and national cultural identities cut across and complicate class culture. The

cultural dimension of underclass theory is that some young blacks, marginalised from occupational success, create their own alternative sub-culture.

6 Ken Pryce's study of Afro-Caribbean life-styles is used to illustrate cultural variety within a single community and particularly to show the interplay of class and ethnic factors on culture.

7 John Rex's underclass analysis leads him towards the view that the politics of ethnic self-defence and self-interest (ethnic politics) is likely to be a major feature of black minority political behaviour. Marxists argue that ultimately class is a sounder basis of action than ethnicity. The political parties appear to assume that black minorities will act within the party political system although the Labour Party has made some adaptations to meet requirements of black groups.

8 The Conservatives have been mainly responsible for introducing the immigration control of black people and the Labour Party for the Race Relations Acts.

The two main themes of this chapter have been about ethnic culture and racism. Obviously, it will be easier to research into ethnic culture if you live in an area in which there is a sizeable minority group or groups. In studying an ethnic group it would not be sufficient to be merely descriptive. It would be necessary to concentrate on some specifically sociological aspect of cultural processes such as how and to what extent a given group adapts to the majority culture. The Pakistani Muslim community in Bradford would provide an interesting case of both cultural continuity and change and of examples of both harmony and conflict with aspects of the majority culture. Possible research might include observation (participant, if appropriate), social surveys, and use of the local press.

Racism needs to be treated as the

RESEARCH AND COURSEWORK

sensitive subject for research that it clearly is. Attempts to observe racial harassment could involve risk and should be avoided. Content analysis of the presentation of racial issues in the press or in broadcasting (possibly using tapes) should generate useful data (see pp. 423–4 for a description of how to go about content analysis in relation to gender bias in the media – this could be adapted for race). A comparison between certain types of publications or programmes would add point and interest.

Concealment in the Study of Racism: A Brief Discussion
One of the main practical problems concerning research into racism is that many are reluctant to admit to it. There

is widespread disapproval of racist beliefs and attitudes (at least, formally) and much racist behaviour is illegal and so is hidden or denied.

Miles and Phizahlea (1979) adopted an indirect approach to researching racist beliefs among white working class people in Willesden, London. They asked no specific questions on race at all! However, they noted such references to race that respondents did make which were *assumed to be genuine* because they were not prompted (75 per cent did make negative comments about black people). Another study of racist attitudes and behaviour which contained an element of concealment was carried out by P A Green (1982) (see p. 105). Green wanted to establish whether teachers with more prejudiced racial attitudes also behaved in a less tolerant way towards black pupils. Part of the research involved the 70 participating teachers in completing an attitude inventory in which a 25-item prejudice scale had been 'buried' (he did find that teachers with less tolerant

attitudes behaved less tolerantly).

The justification for concealment in studying racism is similar to that given for using a 'covert' or 'hidden' approach to participant observation. other things being equal, and if the concealment is successful, the subject of study should behave as normal. The ethical objection against concealment in the study of racism is perhaps less strong than in the case of most covert participant observational studies. The ethical objection is to deceiving people about what is actually happening, specifically what is happening to them. Do they not have a right to know (and perhaps to decide whether or not they wish to be involved in the research)? Against this, in the case of racist behaviour, it can be argued that, they should not be behaving in a racist way and would be unlikely openly to admit to their behaviour. Further, it is arguable that it is in the public interest, as well as in the interest of black people, that an accurate measure and account of discrimination should be available.

FURTHER READING

There is a wide range of material in this area. My own *Race and Ethnicity* (Longman 1991) takes further many of the issues raised in this chapter although it is written at an introductory level. John Rex's *Race and Ethnicity* (Open University Press, 1986) written from a Neo-Weberian perspective, and Robert Miles *Racism* (Routledge, 1989) written from a Marxist perspective are introductory but quite demanding. More 'grassroots' is Ken Pryce's *Endless Pressure* republished in a revised edition 1986 by the Bristol Writer's Press.

QUESTIONS

1 'Racial inequalities in contemporary societies are the direct consequences of those societies exploiting colonised peoples as cheap labour.' Discuss. (London, 1984)

2 To what extent do the concepts of an 'underclass' or 'reserve army of labour' help to explain the high rate of unemployment amongst certain minorities in industrial societies? (Adapted, AEB, 1985)

3 Either (a) What is meant by racism? Can modern Britain be properly described as a 'racist' society. Or (b) It is argued by many sociologists that 'race' as a biological category, has no useful role in social analysis. To what extent do you think this is true? How useful a replacement for the concept of 'race' is 'ethnicity'? (Welsh J E C, 1989)

10 Age & Generation

Terminology and Overview

I have occasionally asked groups of students which form of stratification they regard as the most important: class, gender, race or age. As often as not, the majority reply age. Perhaps this reflects the particular importance of the peer group and age relations to adolescents. However, most people, regardless of age would probably agree with S N Eisenstadt's remark that 'Age and differences of age are among the most basic and crucial aspects of human life and determinants of human destiny.'

The term age group refers to a group of people differentiated from others according to age. The term age grade is commonly used to describe age groups which are clearly and formally established, especially in relation to those primitive societies stratified according to age. For instance, male aborigines pass through the age grades of hunter, warrior and elder. Age is best conceptualised in terms of the life-cycle. The life-cycle refers to those stages through which all who survive a full life-span pass. There is not complete agreement on the precise length and nature

of the age-stages but Erik Erickson's eight-stage model is widely, if critically, used (see the table below). His model is a developmental one and attempts to present the maturational relationship between biological/chronological, psychosocial and social aspects of development (columns 1, 2 and 3 respectively). As Eisenstadt suggests, the basic biological processes are probably more or less similar in all human societies although crucially the rate and quality of biological change is subject to wide individual variation for both genetic and environmental reasons. Freud was the first systematically to explore the notion that psychological development occurs in childhood partly through the resolution of certain tasks or crises – the first one of which is to establish a trusting relationship with the mother or mother substitute. Erickson extended the concept of central crisis to every stage in the life-cycle (see table 10.1).

The third aspect of Erickson's model describes the typical social context – in terms of relationships and institutions – in which

▶

Table 10.1

Eight Stages of

Psycho-social

Development

Stages	Psycho-social crises	Significant social relations	Favourable outcome
1 First year of life	Trust versus mistrust	Mother or mother substitute	Trust and optimism
2 Second year	Autonomy versus doubt	Parents	Sense of self-control and adequacy
3 Third through fifth years	Initiative versus guilt	Basic family	Purpose and direction; ability to initiate one's own activities
4 Sixth year to puberty	Industry versus inferiority	Neighbourhood; school	Competence in intellectual, social and physical skills
5 Adolescence	Identity versus confusion	Peer groups and outgroups; models of leadership	An integrated image of oneself as a unique person
6 Early adulthood	Intimacy versus isolation	Partners in friendship; sex, competition, co-operation	Ability to form close and lasting relationships; to make career commitments
7 Middle adulthood	Generactivity versus self-absorption	Divided labour and shared household	Concern for family, society, and future generations
8 The ageing years	Integrity versus despair	'Mankind'; 'my kind'	A sense of fulfilment and satisfaction with one's life; willingness to face death

(Source: Erik Erickson, *Childhood and Society*, W. W. Norton, 1963, as modified in S R Hilgard et.al., *Introduction to Psychology*, Harcourt Brace Jovanovitch, 1979.)

development at given stages occurs. These contexts are very general and allow for great cultural variations. Even so, Erickson has been widely criticised for over-universalising the social and psycho-social aspects of his model. Judith Stevens-Long suggests that his enthusiasm for the institutions of monogamy and the nuclear family is somewhat ethno-centric, reflecting his own Western rather than any truly universal values and reality.

Childhood, youth and old age will be dealt with in detail here. It may seem that young adulthood and middle age are neglected stages of the life-cycle. This is partly so, although most sociology focuses on the family, work and leisure lives of mature adults. For young adults, the task is often to establish a career or family (or to decide not to) and for the middle aged it is to develop or perhaps change what has been established. There is a substantial body of social psychology which examines the various stresses and challenges of adulthood, including the imprecisely defined 'middle age crisis'.

The concept of generation occurs frequently in age group analysis although Erickson gives it scant attention. Mannheim distinguishes between generation as location and as actuality. The former refers to a group of similar age but the latter only applies when a generation shares a community of feeling or experience. Perhaps the world wars and the Vietnam war stimulated such communal identity for the youth of those times. Such widely shared experiences are rare and Mannheim used the term generational unit to describe a group within a generation which has a common view of events. Thus, there were pro and anti-war units among the 'Vietnam war generation'. Other social factors that affect given generations are structural change, such as that causing a big rise in unemployment (see p. 250) and the size of a

The social structuring of age in contemporary Britain

Age Stage	Structure	Contemporary issues
Childhood	Parents State (law)	Neglect Pre-schooling Abuse, Poverty
Youth	Parents School Peers — relationships / sex Work/training	[Dis]order Authority Control Commitment 'Resource'
Young adulthood	Commited relationship/ or not Children? Career	Stability/Divorce Responsibility Equality (Gender)

Middle age – Continued parental role, but commitments/responsibilities
reducing
Key theme: Achievement/failure

Early old age – Retirement 'Leisure' Late old age – Retirement Single living		Irrelevance wealth (or not) Gender Community Care Cost

The above issues are discussed in the context of each age stage. You might want to add issues under the age staged or disagree with the ones I have selected.

generational cohort itself (see p. 454).

Although Erickson's model remains a useful outline 'map', much historical, anthropological and sociological research and theory tends rather to stress the different ways age is perceived and structured between cultures. The works referred to in the following section describes and illustrates how this occurs in the particular context of Britain. Table 10.2 provides a reference point for checking some main factors which structure age stages in Britain and lists some key contemporary issues in relation to each. It is a more sociological model than that provided by Erickson. You may wish to add to the table.

▲

Table 10.2

Childhood

THE SOCIAL CONSTRUCTION OF CHILDHOOD: HISTORICAL AND COMPARATIVE PERSPECTIVE

Ariès' Centuries of Childhood argues that 'in medieval society the idea of childhood did not exist' and that it developed from the fifteenth century as part of the modern

preoccupation with family. In the middle ages the child was 'absorbed into the world of adults, soon after infancy'. The development of schooling was the factor that separated children and eventually adolescents from other age groups and provided them with their own age-specific experience (see p. 217). Something of a romantic traditionalist, Ariès extols what he sees as the community-based sociability of medieval society into which the young were expected to fit and deplores the obsession of the modern family with its younger members. Not surprisingly, de Mause and others have criticised him for minimising the evidence of neglect and brutality towards children in the medieval period as well as of a general indifference to children's welfare. Nevertheless, Ariès does introduce what has become a central feature of much contemporary social scientific analysis of age – that it is substantially a socially constructed phenomenon rather than simply a biological given.

The anthropological studies of Malinowski provide comparative data which further demonstrate that much of what we take for granted in the West about given age groups need not occur universally. Writing in the inter-war period, Malinowski describes the life of Trobriand children and adolescents as considerably freer and more open than that of similarly aged British contemporaries in terms of taking responsibility for their own activities, relations with parents and in sexual exploration. He contrasts the relationship of father to child in the two cultures: 'At the time when our father makes himself pleasant at best by his entire absence from the nursery, the Trobriand father is first a nurse and then a companion'. The prime responsibility for exercising authority over children lay not with the father but with the mother's brother. The paternal role in contemporary Britain is less rigid than it was, but other formidable structures of social control over children and adolescents still exist. Thus, the easy paced initiation of Trobriand youth into adult work contrasts sharply with the bureaucratically controlled and hierarchically administered Youth Training programme.

CHILDHOOD: CONTEMPORARY ISSUES AND POLICY

Reading through the vast literature on the family, it is not easy to get a sense of what it is like to be a child. Adolescents seem to speak much more clearly for themselves but the voices of young children come from a different world. Perhaps the long period of human maturation makes childhood dependency, powerlessness and vulnerability inevitable. What follows

certainly demonstrates the power and control – for good and ill – of adults over children.

Ariès suggests that children were not so clearly differentiated from others until separated off by the system of compulsory education (see below p. 217). In traditional society they had worked with their parents, mainly in agriculture, and even in the early stages of the industrial revolution many young children were workers. Ronald Fletcher's insightful comment that both parents and the state have come to take an increasing interest in children suggests the framework within which modern childhood has been moulded. Let us take the involvement of the state with children first.

Throughout the nineteenth century a steady flow of legislation first restricted and then prohibited certain forms of child labour – notably in mines and factories – and the age limitation was steadily raised. In parallel, the state increasingly encouraged and financed the education of children until finally compulsory education was enacted. Why did the state take such a growing interest in children? First, as both Marxist and functionalist commentators have observed, basic education was seen as likely to contribute to the efficiency of the labour force. In addition, as the comments of some of the late nineteenth century educational inspectorate show, the teaching of moral conformity was also officially regarded as a goal of education. Second, more productive technology meant that child labour was not really needed. Third, some of the concern for children's education, health and moral welfare was undoubtedly motivated by philanthropic feeling of the kind expressed in literature by Charles Dickens and in politics by the Earl of Shaftesbury.

Modern families are often said to be 'child-centred'. Two trends – both well established since the start of this century – have contributed to this: first, parents have generally had fewer children and, second, the increase in leisure has given them more time to spend with those they do have. A considerable amount of time and concern is spent by parents, especially among the middle class, on their children's education. The fact that modern society is seen as open to talent and ability encourages this tendency. Parental relations with children must, of course, be seen within the context of the sexual division of labour. Historically, women have done most of the domestic work, including rearing children. As women moved back into the paid labour force from the late nineteenth century, the education system expanded to accommodate children for longer periods of time.

Despite the greater scope for child-centredness in the twentieth century, other developments potentially militate against the welfare of children. The fragmentation of many families is a major relevant factor (see Chapter 3, pp. 64–8). Many concerned commentators, notably Neil Postman, criticise the use of television as a device of busy parents to 'keep the children occupied'. Postman argues that 'blanket' viewing by children is threatening literacy and the quality of the experience of childhood itself. Indeed, in exposing children fully and uncensored to 'the adult world' it destroys childhood itself (1985).

Arguably, state and parental interest in children has intensified in the post Second World War period although again it needs to be emphasised that this statement is not without qualification, and the reality can often be quite different. Whatever the outcome, the needs and protection of children rather than the right of parents over children emerge as the dominant theme of post-war legislation in relation to children although the 1989 Children Act seeks to reconcile the two (see below). Children benefited from the introduction of the National Health Service and other welfare measures, particularly child benefit. An important initiative was taken in 1948 with the formation of a child care service under the Home Office. The period of just over a decade between 1969 and 1980 was very significant in the field of child care legislation. B I Slomnicka describes the Children and Young Persons' Act of 1969 as 'a brave attempt to revolutionise the law relating to young people' by treating children in difficulty equally on the basis of need. This applied to delinquents as well as others with problems (such as the threat of physical or moral danger). Making the needs of the child paramount meant a parallel increase in the involvement of social workers and probation officers with children in difficulty. However, it can seldom be an easy decision to remove a child from her or his family to care, and understandably, social

workers can find such a decision hard to make. Child abuse can occur in public institutions as well as in the family, as several cases made public in 1991 demonstrated. It is worth quoting a key section of the 1980 Child Care Act to show the principles guiding local authorities when considering applying for a care order:

In reaching any decision relating to a child in their care, local authorities shall give first consideration to the need to safeguard and promote the welfare of the child throughout his childhood; and so far as practicable ascertain the wishes and feelings of the child regarding the decision and give due consideration to them, having regard to his age and understanding.

The Children Act of 1989 (implemented 1991) re-emphasised the fundamental principle that the prime concern of the state should be the welfare of the child. Fresh stress was put on the importance of authorities listening to what children themselves say about their experiences and needs. The second main principle embodied in the Act is that there should be a partnership between local authorities and parents to protect the welfare of children – if possible without compulsory powers against parents. Parents themselves are encouraged to work out a framework of shared responsibility to children rather than seek exclusive rights and protection over them. If necessary, the Courts can make an order for parent-child contact.

The Act reflects the immediate concern that in the recent past local authorities and particularly certain professions with child-welfare responsibilities have misguidedly acted insensitively and divisively towards families (in, for instance, the Cleveland and Orkney cases). More widely, the Act embodies the view that the Courts and local authorities should work to counterbalance and compensate for those powerful trends, such as the increase in divorce and single-parenthood, which have tended to fragment larger, potentially more protective family structures. A problem anticipated in implementing the Act is a familiar one in relation to several key social reforms of the nineteen eighties – lack of resources (see p. 367).

These considerations provide a useful background against which to consider the problem of child abuse. Ruth and Henry Kempe divide child abuse into the following four types: physical violence, physical and emotional neglect, emotional abuse and sexual exploitation. Reliable statistics on the extent of child abuse do not appear to exist – reflecting perhaps, the hidden and shaming nature of the problem, the importance attached to family privacy and parental rights, and the relative powerlessness of most children to alert others to what is happening. According to the National Society for the Prevention of Cruelty to Children, 7,000 children were physically abused by their parents in 1984, 70 per cent more than in 1979. There were similar apparently huge increases in child abuse in the early nineteen nineties. However, such 'increases' probably reflect greater public awareness of abuse and increased reporting of suspected abuse, rather than a real growth in the crime. On the matter of sexual abuse, a Mori Poll conducted in 1985 indicated that one in ten children is victimised, often by a parent, sibling or other relative. Although cases of child abuse involving working class families come more often to law, it cannot be concluded that they are any less common among the middle class.

Sometimes children are killed as a result of abuse. Two cases may be mentioned. Jasmine Beckford died in July 1984 and Gemma Hartwell in March 1985, both killed by their fathers. The Blom-Cooper enquiry into Jasmine Beckford's death and the court reports on the Gemma Hartwell case show certain parallels. First, both fathers had substantial records of cruelty to their children. Second, and especially in the Beckford case, the judgement of the social workers involved tended to be sensitive to the parents' rights rather than children's rights and needs. The Blom-Cooper report provides a strong, clear directive to the contrary: 'Put the child first and if that means doing something that is disliked by the parents, that's what has got to be done.' Third, the question of adequacy of the training of many social workers is raised by these and other cases. Blom-Cooper recommends three rather than the usual two years' training for social workers, with more time spent on developing skills in specialist areas such as child abuse. This recommendation has only partially been implemented. Not all authorities consider

that the best approach to child abuse lies in the direction indicated above. In separate articles in the same edition of *New Society* (13 December 1985), both Bill Jordan and Tailgunner Parkinson express concern that the Blom-Cooper report may turn social workers into a frightened breed who live by the book. Jordan argues that 'social workers, like the police ... bear the stigma of an unjust social order' and that more should be done to equalise the hard and squalid circumstances with which they often have to deal. Parkinson and Jordan may well consider that a number of fiercely disputed cases of alleged abuse in the late eighties and early nineties bore out their premonition. In Cleveland and in Orkney, doctors and social workers were severely criticised for interventions which they saw as protecting children but which others perceived as 'breaking up families' on the basis of flimsy evidence.

The matter of child abuse raises profound issues of social policy and sociology. Policy is concerned with solutions and some relevant suggestions are referred to in the previous paragraph. Sociology seeks a profounder understanding of phenomena and can feed back into social policy, making it better informed and more effective. Sociologically, what causes child abuse? A variety of factors, including stress and alcohol, have been found to be associated with it. Ruth and Henry Kempe claim that child abuse is less common in extended that in nuclear families – presumably because the chance of protective adult intervention is increased and because the strain of childcare can be more widely shared. From a macro perspective, it is probable that certain widespread cultural attitudes, particularly related to child rearing, may produce a climate more or less conducive to child abuse. In her article 'Why are Parents Tough On Children?', Valerie Yule enquires whether there is a pattern of behaviour among many British parents which begins with brusqueness towards their children and which can end in brutality. She observed 85 adult-child pairs each for a few minutes and found that for two-fifths of the sample, interactions were negative and in most of the other cases the adults took no notice of the child at all. Yule suggests that the freer expression of physical affection, on the part of parents for their children might make for greater happiness all round. Certainly, her small piece of research is thought provoking.

Another large-scale issue for consideration, is the relationship between child abuse (and general child welfare) and poverty. There is evidence that in both Britain and the United States children have replaced the old as the age group most at risk from poverty. Norman Fowler's green paper of 1985, *The Reform of Social Security*, commented that it is families with children that face the most difficult problems, but his reforms have not reversed the trend by which a greater proportion of the poor are made up of children. It is perhaps significant that in the nineteen eighties and early nineties there have been several moral panics in both the United States and Britain about child abuse, but not about child poverty. As Nigel Parton points out (1986), the very repugnance felt against the perpetrators of child abusers may distract from the contribution that poverty can make to neglect and abuse. Is a society that tolerates widespread poverty among children blameless of abuse itself? When we talk of child neglect and abuse, we are not just talking about how they – the 'monsters' of the popular press – treat children, but about how we as a community treat them (see pp. 69–70 for a discussion of child care facilities). This argument is even more uncomfortable if we apply it to the international responsibility for the condition of children in the Third World (see, pp. 462–3).

A H Halsey is highly critical of the view that the twentieth century has been the century of the child. On the contrary, he considers that a greatly strengthened network of support for children and parents needs to be put into place to prevent a substantial minority getting into serious difficulties. He suggests a threefold policy initiative – greatly increasing child allowance; strengthening community support (pre-school and extended school hours); and the provision of 'a future of opportunity ... for children' (education training and full employment). However, such an approach goes against the individualistic view that parents are responsible for their children – unless major problems occur.

Youth: Terminology and Perspectives

Four major perspectives on youth can be noted. These are social constructionist, functionalist, generational 'unit' and class-structural. It is predominantly the first and last of these perspectives that will be drawn on during this chapter. There are, of course, variations of each. Talcott Parsons and S N Eisenstadt present functionalist models. For them, youth is a period of training and preparation for adulthood. Personal difficulties in 'growing up' and even group rebellion are seen as dysfunctional, if predictable. Even so, they note that most young people do in fact successfully negotiate the transitional phase of adolescence. This functionalist model is not ahistorical (it does not lack historical awareness). Functionalists fully recognise that in modern society the period of youthful socialisation tends to be longer and that particular stresses accompany it. Weber's concept of the status group is also sometimes used in functionalist analyses of youth. Young people are considered to share the same pre-adult status and also to share similar problems of adjustment. Identity, security and much personal 'problem solving', as well as leisure activity, are based on the peer group.

Karl Mannheim's concept of the generational 'unit' has elements of functionalist perspective and the concept of separate generational consciousness that was popular in the nineteen sixties. Mannheim appreciated, as functionalists do, that the educational system cuts young people off from the work-centred life of adults. Within generational groups, particular units sometimes form. Thus, in higher education, under certain circumstances student movements emerge. This is because students are frequently together and, as a result, are able to discuss and organise their response to major issues such as wars and racial discrimination. Sometimes their response takes the form of protest. No doubt because the nineteen sixties was a period of exceptional student activism, some commentators tended to overstress the separateness of the generations and the extent of generational conflict. Charles Reich in his book, *The Greening of America*, wrote as if a 'new consciousness', inspired by youthful imagination and idealism, was about to engulf America. He forgot that this radical consciousness was largely confined to middle class students in higher education, and was by no means adopted even by all of them.

More recently, British sociologists, particularly the mainly Marxist group at the Centre for Cultural Studies in Birmingham, have argued that youth should be analysed in the specific class context of particular youth groups. Thus, student protest movements should be seen not just as the action of young people, but of young middle class people. Again, 'slum' gangs should be analysed not merely as 'young delinquents', but in relation to their class, neighbourhood and family environments, including the culture of working class adults. This approach, therefore, allows for the operation of generational factors within a broad framework of class, and we use it more than any other in this chapter.

Although we have already explained the meaning of the terms culture and sub-culture (see chapter 1), it is appropriate to expand the definition here. Culture refers to the way of life of a given group, for instance, of a particular society or class. Sub-culture refers to those aspects of the life of a group which distinguish it from the main or dominant culture. Thus, we can speak of Afro-Caribbean or Jewish sub-culture in Britain. A counter-culture or contra-culture describes a sub-culture which is opposed to the dominant culture. The term was widely used of the new radical life-style of the nineteen sixties.

The Social Construction of Modern Youth

The view that childhood is socially constructed can be extended to youth and, indeed, to any age stage. Generally, the factors discussed below illustrate this point although, in some instances, the argument is raised that, for whatever reason (biological, psychological or social) certain character-istics of youth are virtually universal. A point you might care to consider before reading on is when, sociologically speaking, childhood ends and youth begins. Does the 'transition' occur at the same point in the life-cycle and in the same way in all societies?

UNIVERSAL EDUCATION

Universal education helps to shape the experience of modern youth just as much as it does childhood. At first, education was mainly an upper and middle class male privilege – as described fictionally in Tom Brown's Schooldays – but it is now a universal right and legal requirement. Sharing a common structural situation for the purpose of formal socialisation, young people naturally develop a sense of shared interest. Yet, it is in the informal peer groups that intra-generational interaction is most free to flourish. As S N Eisenstadt observes, the peer group provides a means for experimentation and experience in roles, status and romance, and is generally an effective vehicle for transition between childhood and the complex demands of modern adulthood. In much the same way as universal education, though to a lesser extent, national service also provided a basis of collective experience and identity for many young men. Sometimes, generational peer groups and even whole units turn against dominant norms and adopt delinquent and/or culturally deviant life-styles. Geoffrey Pearson points out that riotous behaviour by young people not constrained and motivated by either education or work, long predates the nineteen eighties. Peer groups can form and operate on the streets – sometimes in a disorderly and criminal way. Finally, peer groups generated largely within the educational context or on neighbourhood streets reflect the influence of class, race, gender and individuality.

MODERN YOUTH CULTURE OR SUB-CULTURES?

In his pamphlet *The Teenage Consumer* (1959), Mark Abrams was one of the first to suggest that a new youth culture had been created in post-war Britain. As the title of the pamphlet suggests, the new culture was based on increased affluence enabling the purchase of such items as records, motorcycles, cosmetics and other recreational goods. Berger and Berger argued that '… international mass youth consumption and culture expanded further in the nineteen sixties', cutting, in their view to a considerable extent '… across class lines'. This is almost an embourgeoisement theory of youth culture, and British Marxist sub-cultural theorists, in particular, disagree with it. They argue that the Bergers' concept of almost classless 'status spheres' of the young is belied by the continued impact of class, race and gender on youth subcultures which often survive and even undermine the powerful homogenising forces of 'international capitalism'. However, with the apparent decline of highly distinctive youth subcultures in the nineteen eighties and nineties, Marxists have broadened their analyses to include youth as a whole (see pp. 220–2).

YOUTH AND 'PREFIGURATIVE CULTURE'

In her essay '*Culture and Commitment: a Study of the Generation Gap*', Margaret Mead focuses on the problems of youth by distinguishing between three kinds of culture: postfigurative, configurative and prefigurative. A postfigurative culture gains its authority from the past and little change occurs. The young learn and apply traditional wisdom. A configurative culture is one in which change is occurring and the model of behaviour is that of contemporaries rather than elders. A prefigurative culture is one in which the speed of change is so rapid that culture must become anticipatory; the future of the child, rather than the knowledge of the parent or wisdom of the elder must become its guiding light. Undoubtedly. Mead's concept of prefigurative culture was affected by the idealisation of youth of the nineteen sixties and is perhaps tinged a little with bias. However, it suggests two concrete observations. One, that the mental flexibility of young people may enable them better to cope with a rapidly changing world. This is apparent in the skill many young show in manipulating information technology but it may also apply to ideas and principles, (perhaps science fiction stories – widely popular among the young – are 'fairy tales' of the future). Second, the survival of the young is in the balance because of the urgency of the environmental, population and particularly the nuclear issue. Their future depends on the present solution to these problems. As Mead puts it, the future is now. However, in the period of conservative reaction of the nineteen eighties, it was clear that even if the young did envisage the future more clearly than adults, they possessed limited power to do much about it. Perhaps the example of Band Aid suggests that this is too pessimistic a conclusion.

THE PSYCHOLOGY AND 'PROBLEMS' OF YOUTH

In the Western world, crime and suicide rates are relatively high among the young. A variety of mental disorders shows a sharp upwards incline during the teenage years. According to data assembled by Michael Rutter, these include alcoholism, schizophrenia, anorexia nervosa and depression – although only a minority actually suffer from these illnesses. No single sociological explanation would precisely cover all these phenomena but, in general, the sociological perspective is that the complexities and pressures of modern adolescence are such that signs of difficulty and instability are to be expected. Poverty and joblessness can make matters worse. A contrary argument, put forward by Anna Freud and others, is that adolescence is naturally and universally a period of rebellion. Margaret Mead's *Coming of Age in Samoa* was an attempt to refute such theories by demonstrating that in Samoa 'adolescence represented no period of crisis or stress, but was instead an orderly developing of a set of slowly maturing interests and activities'. However, Derek Freeman's formidable critique of Mead's methodology in this study undermines her claim to have found a crucial 'negative instance' of the universalist view. Mead believed that her study of 50 Samoan adolescent girls showed that in general their adolescence was orderly and constructive thus providing a 'negative instance' to invalidate the proposition that adolescence is universally problematic. However, Freeman finds that of the 25 girls Mead studied in greatest detail, 4 were delinquent and 3 at odds with their kin: a percentage total of 28. His point that this suggests quite a high level of stress and conflict seems well taken.

Youth Conformity and Sub-Cultural Non-Conformity: The Importance of Class

Most young people conform, more or less, to society's norms. For them, peer group identity complements more than conflicts with their roles in the family and at school or work. We explore conformity among youth shortly. Immediately, we examine the minority sub-cultures of non- or less conformist young people. The only reason for preferring the term non-conformity to deviance here is that much youthful sub-cultural activity only borders on the deviant. (The explicitly deviant we examine in chapter 13.) We have already explained how young people tend to be 'set apart' from the rest of society and we have mentioned some of the influences and stresses upon them. This section is more interpretist in that it analyses how certain minority groups of young people respond to their own experience, including the pressures of the media and the educational systems and, in doing so, often create original and interesting life-styles. We can roughly categorise these responses into three types: delinquent, pleasure seeking or political. Response is, however, mediated or influenced by social context – to express it crudely, either middle class, working class and/or ethnic culture. Differences in family, neighbourhood and educational experience as well as gender deeply divide young people. We can put the above points in simple, diagrammatical form:

Table 10.3 ▼

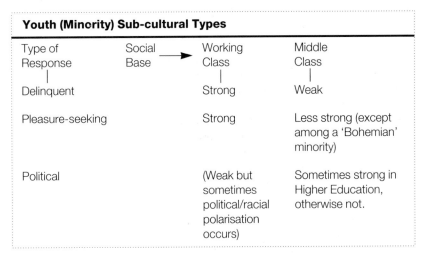

Youth (Minority) Sub-cultural Types

Type of Response	Social Base →	Working Class	Middle Class
Delinquent		Strong	Weak
Pleasure-seeking		Strong	Less strong (except among a 'Bohemian' minority)
Political		(Weak but sometimes political/racial polarisation occurs)	Sometimes strong in Higher Education, otherwise not.

We will use these three types of sub-cultural response as a general guide (but no more than that), first to examine working class youth, then middle class youth. It must be noted that many young people opt in and out of sub-cultural activity and that between conformity and non-conformity there is a considerable 'grey' area.

WORKING CLASS YOUTH CULTURE AND SUB-CULTURES: THE NINETEEN SIXTIES AND SEVENTIES

Working class youth culture is concentrated in areas such as the inner city and, more recently, public housing estates. It is a field of research that has been well studied both in Britain and the United States. The Chicago School of urban sociologists began the serious sociological study of this topic (see chapter 19), but much interesting material has been published in Britain. It will be helpful to list some of the main values underlying working class youth subculture as a reference point for what follows. These are: anti-authoritarianism; pleasure-seeking ('fun'); a strong sense of territory; masculinity and an admiration of physical strength and skill.

Annoying 'authority' is often seen as a good way of 'having fun'. The bating of authority is a constant theme in the now vast literature on the activities of working class youth. Teachers, the police and youth club leaders are the frequent butt of their ridicule and, less often, of their practical jokes. In an observational survey of a group of working class youths, Paul Corrigan found that a large number thought of teachers as 'big-heads'. We saw similar antagonism reported by Hargreaves and Willis (chapter 4). Social workers and probation officers possibly escape more lightly because they usually work on a one to one basis with 'clients' rather than as obvious representatives of large and dominant institutions such as schools or the police force. At school, fun often takes the form of a rearguard action against being bored. The ultimate resort is to 'bunk off'. In all inner city areas, there are always some working class 'kids' on the streets or at home during school time. They might be playing football, listening to music or just 'waiting for something to turn up'. In more official jargon, they might be referred to as 'at risk'.

It would be misleading to suggest that working class youth culture is exclusively or even mainly concerned with mocking authority. Much of it is positively motivated and energetically pursued. Mending, painting and decorating motor-bikes and cars, playing football and being a football supporter, 'chatting up girls' can all involve great commitment and skill. There are many middle class teenagers relatively deficient in these areas compared with the working class. A minority of working class 'kids' play music and write songs, and many more take an intelligent interest in music, although the research of Murdoch and Phelps suggest that, for the boys, music is largely a matter of background noise or 'aural wallpaper'.

It is obvious that young working class people like spending time together away from adults. Nevertheless, they are working class and this shows in their activity. The skinheads of the middle and late nineteen sixties exemplify this point. Like other groups of young lads, no doubt the aggressive and occasionally violent behaviour of the skinheads can be explained in terms of a pursuit of excitement, but John Clarke, in a contribution to the collection of writings, *Resistance Through Rituals* (edited by Hall and Jefferson, 1976), offers additionally a more thought-provoking explanation. He suggests that the behaviour and style of the skinheads, far from being random and irrational, closely reflects the realities of their lives. He points out that many features of the skinhead style – the short haircut, the wearing of braces over shirts, turning trousers up inches above the ankles, the wearing of cheap, heavy boots – were only slightly exaggerated and dramatised versions of traditional working class dress. Clarke suggests that, by dressing this way, the skinheads were, perhaps unconsciously, reasserting traditional class and community identity. This interpretation gains credibility when we remember that East End working class communities have been damaged and destroyed in the post-war period. Decline in employment opportunities, housing clearance programmes, near-chaos in parts of the London educational service must have caused disorientation, anger and despair in many lives, not least in those of the young. It is perhaps not surprising – although deplorable in itself – that the skinheads frequently turned their aggression against immigrants rather than on the investors, developers and planners who were more responsible for their grievances and fears. Clarke, therefore, sees skinhead aggression and violence as largely defensive. He explains their behaviour as 'a symbolic defence of (threatened) territory' and as 'a magical attempt to recover community'. There was a resurgence of racism among 'skinhead types', more or less closely associated with the British National Party, during the recession of the early nineteen nineties.

Even in the nineteen sixties and seventies, sociologists could not locate all youth subcultures so convincingly in a class context as Clarke did the skinheads. This is partly because the media tends quickly to take up and popularise stylistic and creative sub-cultural aspects – a process referred to by Dick Hebdige as 'incorporation'. Thus it may be that punk music and style of dress was originally the product of unemployed, working class youth but, within a few months, the movement was being commercially exploited in the youth market generally. The punk clothes worth hundreds of pounds which were advertised in Vogue magazine illustrate the point. In adopting sub-cultural forms such as Punk music for mass consumption, the commercial enterprises involved, and the media, attempt to adapt the product for maximum acceptability and consumption. Thus the attempt to 'devulgarise' the Sex Pistols was seen by the group as an attack on their freedom to produce and perform the material they wanted. When a sub-cultural symbol, like punk rock music, is commercialised, instead of providing a long-term focus on which the movement can coalesce and identify, the symbol is 'stolen' by the pop industry, reprocessed and presented to a wider audience which does not seriously associate it with the protest and rebellion it may have originally represented. In contrast to the punks, the skinheads did not produce anything saleable on the mass market, although some London and fashionable provincial boutiques attempted to market skinhead style clothes.

As well as providing ideas for the pop industry and media, youth sub-cultures also borrow freely from them and from other sources. The Teddy Boys of the nineteen fifties combined features of the style of London upper-class 'toffs' and American 'movie' gangsters to produce their own distinctive, swash-buckling, rather status-conscious style.

Underlying the above rituals is the desire to assert masculinity, often in a physical way. This is not exclusive to the working class, but it is chiefly in manual labour that working class males have expressed themselves and physical toughness is particularly respected among them.

In the hard world of working class youth sub-cultures, the position of the female is very much that of pillion-passenger. Motor-bike 'burn-ups' and gang fights (real or mock) are forms of display, and all the better if girls are there to observe closely. As a Sunday Times newspaper analysis of a gang fight wryly states: 'excitement is heightened if police, press, TV – and girls – are in attendance'. In the nineteen sixties and now, however, it would be a mistake to see the girls as mere status symbols and prizes in the social game-playing of the boys: the female peer-group has a distinct and important existence within the larger teenage peer group itself. Girls share much leisure activity. They are more likely than the boys to know details of the top twenty, to read teenage magazines, and to be familiar with the latest dance routines – which they perform, usually in protective togetherness, at discos. A serious relationship with a male may temporarily detach working class girls from the single-sex peer group. If they can, they tend to marry earlier and have lower career aspirations than middle class girls. We reviewed these matters in our chapter on education.

Working class youth sub-cultures are not usually overtly political. Nevertheless, when an issue affects their own interest closely, working class youth sometimes respond in a more or less political way. One such issue is unemployment. In the late nineteen seventies and early eighties and again in the early nineteen nineties, unemployment was experienced by increasing numbers of young people, black and white. More and more sixteen year olds left school for their first year of 'non-work'. 'Dole-queue rock' – full of strident protest and youthful disillusion – was one response in the earlier period.

MIDDLE CLASS YOUTH CULTURE AND SUB-CULTURES

Most middle class young people, like most working class people, more or less conform. They do not, however, conform to the same way of life. After all, they come from different backgrounds. Middle class youth are still more likely to receive post-compulsory education than working class youth from sixteen although increasing numbers of the latter are involved in training. Homework takes up much of the time of young middle class people. Even if they had the inclination, they would seldom have the opportunity to 'mess about' on the streets of their neighbourhood. Research by Murdoch and Phelps, on the other hand, shows that by no means all middle class teenagers spend most of their out-of-school time doing homework. In addition to the more academic ones, Murdoch and Phelps observed a group of young, middle class males who, as well as doing their academic work adequately, found time to pursue an interest in 'progressive' pop music. Their taste was much more likely than that of working class youth to include some folk and pop music protest songs.

We will defer until a later chapter our consideration of delinquency among middle class youth and concentrate here on pleasure seeking and political sub-cultural activity. Their pleasure seeking is rather different from that of working class youth. It needs to be understood in the context of higher education because it often occurs on or near college or university campuses. These campuses, particularly the residential ones, concentrate students, relatively free from financial worries, in a cloistered and tolerant situation. In Kenneth Kenniston's phrase, they are allowed a 'period of extended youth' which enables them to experiment with, and test, various values, attitudes and life-styles, as well as to acquire advanced formal education and training. Kenniston refers to this further as 'youth as a stage of life' which, for some, can continue into their late twenties. During these years, a minority of students sometimes adopt life-styles which may involve certain modes of dress, drug-taking, 'getting into' music, a freer attitude to relationships and other behaviour less common to the majority of the population. It is true that under the climate of Thatcherism, the campuses became, at least superficially, more conventional and quieter places in the nineteen eighties and early nineties. However, many students continue to enjoy a lifestyle of greater freedom and options than readily occurs elsewhere.

We will examine a study by Jock Young of

psychedelic drug-taking as an example of a minority mainly middle class youth sub-cultural form of activity. Although Young's observations, now made a quarter of a century ago, may seem of interest mainly to 'ageing hippies', in fact they provide excellent data for a 'then and now' comparison. It is also a minor classic study of a type of subculture which, like the skinheads, keeps recurring. Clearly, hippies provide a model for some! Of course, from a legal point of view, psychedelic drug-taking is delinquent. Here, however, we are viewing it from the perspective of those involved, who saw it as a way of acquiring desired experience. Over the years, members of such groups have been described as 'bohemians', 'beatniks' (or just 'beats'), 'hippies', or simply 'student-types'. We will use the term bohemian for general reference. Following Matza, Young describes the pleasure-seeking, bohemian life-style in terms of subterranean values, although he is careful to point out that the use of psychedelic drugs is only one aspect of this way of life. Other subterranean values are short-term hedonism, spontaneity, excitement, and dislike of conventionally organised work. These contrast with formal values such as deferred gratification, planning future action, predictability and acceptance of productive work as virtuous. Broadly, subterranean values are concerned with pleasure and self-fulfilment for its own sake, and formal values with work and the necessary control that goes with it. Herbert Marcuse has seen the same contrast between subterranean values and formal work values in Freud's pleasure and reality principles. He expresses this as follows:

Pleasure Principle Values	Reality Principle Values
Immediate Satisfaction	Delayed Satisfaction
Pleasure	Restraint of Pleasure
Joy (play)	Toil (work)
Receptiveness (to stimuli and experience)	Productiveness (in work)
Absence of Repression	Security (in return for self-repression/ control)

Source: Marcuse: 1956: 12

We will not argue the merits of the pleasure and reality principles here, but simply note that the former rules in the bohemian world, and the latter in the world of organised work.

Bohemians sometimes take psychedelic drugs, such as cannabis and LSD, because they believe that these improve their moods, and even enhance their perception of the world. Cannabis is a relatively mild psychedelic and is taken for its relaxing 'mellowing' effect. LSD is stronger, and some claim that under its influence new insights may be realised and joyful and profound states of awareness achieved. We must add that any psychedelic drug may also produce the opposite effect, especially amongst inexperienced or 'naive' users. Young suggests, however, that experienced users can often exercise considerable control over the effects of psychedelics, and the drug then becomes part of the whole way of life of the sub-culture rather than its main dominating influence. Psychedelic drug-taking may fit in with the kind of music, literature, leisure style and even personal relations preferred by this type of group. To get a 'feel' for bohemian sub-culture, it is best to read the novels of, say, the American 'beat' of the fifties, Jack Kerouac, or to listen to the 'sixties' music of the Grateful Dead or Jefferson Airplane. Of course, these artists belong to different 'moments' in the history of 'bohemia', but they are, nevertheless, part of the same broad tradition. It is likely that the drug 'ecstasy' has similar subcultural associations.

BLACK YOUTH

Although most black youths are working class as measured by parental occupation, it is not appropriate to treat them exclusively under the heading of working class youth because of the important of racial and cultural (ethnic) factors. As we saw in chapter 9, the same argument applies to black adults. All young people have the problem of forging a workable identity, but for black youth it is particularly acute. They are presented with two potentially conflicting adult models. First is that of the British citizen, sharing equal rights and duties with whites; second is that of the black person, visibly distinct and with a cultural heritage that goes back to the Punjab, Nigeria, Barbados or Hong Kong. Achieving a workable balance between these identities is possible but often difficult. There are two major reasons for this. Firstly, as we have just mentioned, it is bound to be difficult to bring into focus two separate national, historical identities. Secondly, the problem is made much worse by the experience of prejudice or rejection, since self-identity partly depends on what others think of you. Black immigrants and their children cannot avoid seeing themselves in the mirror of white people's eyes. What they often see there is suspicion and resentment, if not downright hatred. (We studied this more empirically in chapter 9.) The cultural life of immigrant groups, and particularly of the young, cannot be properly understood without bearing in mind the hurt and anger that racism can provoke. Equally, it must be remembered that Britain's minorities, including second and third generation 'immigrants' are proud of, and attached to, their ethnic cultural heritage. This is obvious in many areas such as literature, language, dress, food, religion, family tradition and so on. The phrase 'black is beautiful' captures both the pride and defensive self-assertion that has notably characterised ethnic groups in America and Britain since the nineteen sixties.

We will take Afro-Caribbean youth sub-culture for more detailed analysis here. Love of music, religion and a liking for street based social activity are well known aspects of West Indian culture. Unemployment, or irregular employment, is also part of the familiar background of life, and young black people, both here and in the Caribbean, are accustomed to dealing with it. The Afro-Caribbean hustler in Britain has his parallel in the Jamaican 'rude boy' or 'rudie'. Rudies cope with the indifference of the job market by 'hustling' a living out of dealing in drugs, gambling, pimping or stealing. As a last resort, some hustlers may 'play the welfare system', but they have little taste for the bureaucratic 'hassle' this can involve. Often they live in some style, sporting smart cars

and well-cut clothes with an easy air. Not altogether surprisingly, some prefer this life-style to the lower-level manual work that might occasionally be offered them. Still, we must be careful not to suggest that the hustler is the typical figure of Afro-Caribbean youth sub-culture. Many young blacks look hard for work and are demoralised and embittered if they do not find it. We simply do not have the empirical data available to say what is typical. All that we are doing here is describing some options available to West Indian youth.

The cool, worldly image of the hustler contrasts sharply with the religious fervour of another major West Indian youth sub-cultural figure, the Rastafarian. The 'Rasta' movement illustrates the defensive, retreatist trend which is an almost inevitable part of the cultural tradition of a group actually or potentially oppressed. Rastafarians trace their spiritual roots back to Africa; their plaited hair and sometimes their style of dress imitate African originals. They believe that the late Emperor Haile Selassie of Ethiopia will be reincarnated and will lead them out of 'Babylon' – a biblical reference to capitalistic society. From Kingston to Brixton, Reggae is the music of Rastafarianism. Reggae lyrics are heavy with biblical references, and the music's slow, moody rhythms reflect the influence of the 'sacred' drug, ganja (a type of marijuana).

Stuart Hall has described the ways of life of many young black people, which brings them into conflict with 'white' power structures as 'cultural resistance' (*The Empire Strikes Back* (Hutchinson, 1978)). Certainly, the simmering resentment of many young black people helped to fuel the urban disorders of 1981 and 1985 as well as more routine conflict with the police. However, as Hall would agree, the cause of cultural resistance lies in racism and class inequality.

Youth in the Nineteen Eighties and Nineties: 'Ordinary Youth'?

To an extent, the sociology of youth itself 'grew up' or came to maturity in the nineteen eighties. Instead of concentrating almost exclusively on what Bob Coles has referred to as the 'glamorous fringe' of subcultures, research tended to be wider and more

representative of youth as a whole. There are two main ways in which this has occurred. First, young females and young black people have figured more prominently in the research – not only in specific studies but also as part of samples typical of a broad section of youth. For instance, two studies already referred to which have helped undermine negative stereotypes about young black women are Mary Fuller's *Young Female and Black* (1982) and Mac an Ghaill's *Young, Gifted and Black* (1988). In both cases, the authors selected for study groups of academically high achieving young black females. In Mac an Ghaill's case, the group was mixed Afro-Caribbean and Asian, and was part of a wider study of young black peer groups. Christine Griffin's *Typical Girls* is also a salutory corrective to the 'gang of lads' model of working class youth (see pp. 79-80). It is worth reflecting again on the Fuller and Griffin studies in the light of their challenge to sexist, and in the former case, racist assumptions. The second way in which the sociology of youth has become more widely representative of the age group has been in a greater concentration on the 'ordinary' majority of youth. Within this, there has been a particular emphasis on 'ordinary' working class youth. This has been stimulated partly out of concern for many less well qualified young people in facing what a respondent in one study refers to as 'shit jobs and govvy schemes' during (and after) the Thatcher years. A third alternative, 'the dole', disappeared for many, at least as an immediate option, when the government removed the right of social security from those

who refused a placement on a 'suitable' YTS scheme. Bob Coles and Robert MacDonald's research into the responses of young people to local labour market conditions stresses that variety not uniformity of response occurs, making generalisations difficult:

Thus whilst the collapse of the labour market in one of our areas, Whitby, has resulted in a swelling of the ranks of male 'swots' (getting on in Whitby means getting qualified and getting out – of the area) twenty miles down the road in Malton 'swots' still form only a small minority of the boys as most of them leave school in droves willing to risk their fortunes in a more buoyant local labour market

(reported by Bob Coles in 'The Social Science Teacher', Vol 15, No. 3)

While it is necessary to be cautious about generalisations, it is safe to say that the social environment of 'sixties youth' was very different from that experienced by 'eighties' youth. The social climate of the sixties was liberal and even permissive – and many young people were very much a part of this – whereas the nineteen eighties were dominated by economic anxiety and a conservative cultural backlash. YTS and, longer term, the National Curriculum were in part attempts to control youth and to exploit its economic value. It appeared that 'the country' could

◀

Figure 10.1

Reality for some

youth in the eighties

and nineties.

► Figure 10.2
Style and meaning.

Figure 10.2
Style and meaning.

no longer afford a 'wayward' younger generation. While many young people did conform to the new 'realities', a growing minority of the less privileged found a fourth alternative to 'shit work, govvy schemes and the dole' – leaving home and living rough as urban 'street kids'. No doubt this was an unintended but perhaps forseeable consequence of government policy.

Youth styles in the nineteen eighties and early nineties appeared to become both more individual and more fragmentary. Perhaps, the 'Casuals', symbolising the more affluent side of the mid-nineteen eighties, were the last clearly identifiable stylistic subculture (apart from the continuing fleeting presence of the 'Goths'). The so-called post-modern idiom is towards personal idiosyncrasy and cultural fragmentation.

EVERYDAY YOUTH CULTURES IN THE NINETIES: FAREWELL TO SUBCULTURES?

One group of radical critics appear relatively unperturbed by the diverse trends indicated above. Paul Willis and his co-authors of *Common Culture: Symbolic Work at Play in the Everyday Cultures of the Young* (1990) suggest that cultural variety and individualism has superseded subcultural conspicuousness. Willis et al. now find that the symbolic creativity they once associated particularly with subcultural types is characteristic of many young people. Most – perhaps all – young people create meaning in one way or another – if they cannot make music, they can make their own interpretations of it; if

they cannot buy an expensive wardrobe of clothes, they might make their own.

Willis sees evidence of cultural democracy and power in this hive of cultural busyness. He argues that the commercial market in fashion and culture does not necessarily control how individuals actually use, say, tapes, records, posters, clothes etc. Consumption can itself be a productive activity, if done with a degree of individuality. Moreover grass roots cultural activity can influence commercial production as well as vice-versa. For instance, reggae and rap started 'on the street' before being commercially mass-produced. Willis goes so far as to suggest that cultural activity, not only of the young but also of other age groups, is the main dynamo for change in contemporary society. He would prefer that the direction of change be towards socialism but does not assume that this will be so. Controversially, however, he does find evidence of incipient socialism in what he refers to as the 'proto-communities' which people create in responding to certain widely and deeply felt issues. He gives as examples Live-Aid, Comic Relief, and the public response to the Hillsborough tragedy in which 95 Liverpool football club fans died. He sees these events as a merging of cultural style and social concern, although whether this can be thought of as nascent socialism is highly debatable.

'Common culture' is a challenging book which provokes comment. First, it is suffused with a kind of cultural populism which, despite Willis' Marxist pedigree, curiously echoes Thatcherism. Both Willis and Thatcher invest their 'faith' in the thinking consumer (or consumer-producer), although for Willis the communal and social aspects of consumption are substantially more pronounced. Willis' thinking consumer is certainly potentially more subversive than Thatcher's. Second, 'Common Culture' is largely atheoretical. Again, this is partly the result of Willis' determination not to attribute meanings to people's activities that they do not attribute themselves. Third, and relatedly, this book verges on being apolitical. Willis implies that 'the people', not Paul Willis, will define socialism by their own activity (or perhaps they will not define it at all). All this rather begs the larger question of whether or not the direction of modern culture, youth or otherwise, is towards a greater degree of personal and communal liberation. Willis seems to be suggesting that it is but he does not really address this key issue.

Finally, the matter of whether the 'age of youth subcultures' is over can be briefly addressed. Willis seems to imply that stylistic creativity is now so widespread that particular subcultures are unlikely to stand out as quite so spectacular or bizarre. While this may be so, it is also true that considerable scope for peer group subcultures reflecting specific aspects of, for example, ethnicity or class remains.

Even as I write, I am aware of a group in the West country whose members dress in old and shabby clothes and are often accompanied by rather savage looking dogs. I have heard them referred to as 'hippies' – although they do not greatly resemble the hippies of the sixties. They are also sometimes referred to as the 'Crusties'. What do they 'stand for'? Are there many such groups? Are there any Crusties in your neighbourhood?

Is There a Generation Gap?

Survey data over a period of some twenty years going back to the early nineteen seventies indicates no profound gap in attitudes and values between parents and their teenage children. However, tension and conflict can occur around issues of leisure behaviour and cultural expression such as drinking alcohol, dress, and staying out times. There is no evidence that any but a small minority of either younger teenagers or those in their late teens and twenties are more politically radical than the rest of the population. We will first examine the survey data in more detail and then attempt to explain it.

SURVEY DATA ON TEENAGERS AND YOUNG ADULTS

In 1974, the National Children's Bureau conducted a survey of more than 13,000 sixteen year olds (members of an age cohort not quite old enough to be the parents of current readers of this book). Respondents were all those still able to be contacted who were born in a single week of March, 1958. Questions were asked on a wide variety of aspects of behaviour and attitude, but sex and drugs were excluded as topics, because answers were considered likely to be evasive. On questions relating to marriage and the family, mid-seventies teenagers emerged as thoroughly traditional in their attitudes and values. Only three per cent rejected the idea of marriage and most wanted to have children. Four out of five respondents said that they got on well with both their parents. The main areas of conflict with them were over dress and

hair, although in only eleven per cent of homes was this a frequent source of friction.

In the early nineteen nineties, several surveys of teenagers and, usefully from the point of view of comparison, of that of parents of teenagers, were conducted. These surveys concentrated mainly on *matters of behaviour* rather than attitudes and values, and particularly on behaviour in relation to sex, alcohol and drugs. They clearly showed a difference between parental demands and expectations of teenagers and the actual behaviour of teenagers. Thus, a nationwide survey of people born in 1970 carried out in 1990 found that 32 per cent of young men and 46 per cent of young women said that they had had sexual intercourse before their sixteenth birthday. In contrast, the National Opinion Poll survey (1991) of parents of eleven to sixteen year olds found that only five per cent expected that their own children would lose their virginity before the age of sixteen. As far as alcohol consumption is concerned, there is also a substantial gap between teenage reality and parental aspiration. Over half of sixteen to seventeen year olds claim to go to pubs to drink alcohol at least once a week, yet the NOP survey found that only fourteen per cent of parents intended to allow their offspring to drink alcohol regularly before the age of eighteen.

The findings of the above surveys are not surprising. It is hardly news that many teenagers, including some under-age, indulge in sex and alcohol and that their parents worry about this and tell them not to. It was ever thus! It may be that the AIDS epidemic and the injury contemporary teenagers can inflict on themselves and others through drunken-driving has added an edge of anxiety to parental warnings. Parents may also feel ineffectual given the relative affluence and freedom of many young people. The huge gap between the behaviour parents want of their off-spring and many of the latter's actual behaviour does suggest that many teenagers are 'out of their parents' control' in these two areas.

The survey data on the drug-taking habits other than alcohol teenagers suggests rather more of a meeting of minds between the two generations, though not completely so. A survey in 1990 of the Health Education Authority suggested that fifteen per cent of sixteen to nineteen year olds were occasional or regular cannabis smokers – hardly more than a significant minority. Even so, the NOP survey of parents found that only three per cent thought it likely that their young would experiment with soft-drugs while still teenagers. Over ten per cent of parents, therefore, would appear to be living under an illusion about what their children are 'up to' in relation to cannabis and perhaps other illegal substances.

While some teenagers behave contrary to their parents wishes on matters of life-style, there is little evidence to suggest significant political radicalism or cultural alienation among school-age teenagers. If anything, young adults are even more likely fundamentally to conform in these areas. A *Reader's Digest* (1991) survey of a rather older age group – 18 to 34 year olds suggested little

radicalism. The three main figures of influence cited were teachers, Members of Parliament and managing directors of large companies (see figure 10.3). The majority said they were satisfied with and committed to their work and as many as three-quarters had turned up to work when feeling unwell. Although respondents did not appear radical, their view of 'important issues facing Britain' perhaps has what Margaret Mead would call a 'prefigurative' flavour about it. Thus, 46 per cent saw pollution/ environment emerging as a most important issue. Further, as many as 55 per cent expected that Britain would become part of a United States of Europe by the year 2000.

INTERPRETING THE SURVEY DATA IN A WIDER SOCIAL CONTEXT: PERSPECTIVES ON YOUTH

In British society young people are generally not 'revolutionary' in their values and attitudes to the family, society and politics. A significant number, however, do appear routinely in conflict with their parents on leisure behaviour matters. In this respect, Peter Kellner refers to early nineteen-nineties teenagers as 'rebellious' in a review of the data presented in the previous section (The Independent August 1991). However, it is doubtful whether these generational 'style wars' are much more intense now than throughout the post-war period – and perhaps for much longer. To say that generational conflict is generally limited to the area of life-style, is not to underestimate it. As Paul Willis

Figure 10.3

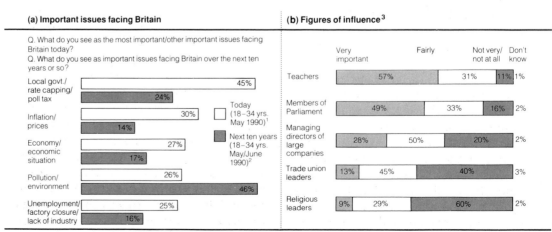

(a) Important issues facing Britain

Q. What do you see as the most important/other important issues facing Britain today?
Q. What do you see as important issues facing Britain over the next ten years or so?

Local govt./ rate capping/ poll tax	45% / 24%
Inflation/ prices	30% / 14%
Economy/ economic situation	27% / 17%
Pollution/ environment	26% / 46%
Unemployment/ factory closure/ lack of industry	25% / 16%

Today (18–34 yrs. May 1990)[1]

Next ten years (18–34 yrs. May/June 1990)[2]

(b) Figures of influence[3]

	Very important	Fairly	Not very/ not at all	Don't know
Teachers	57%	31%	11%	1%
Members of Parliament	49%	33%	16%	2%
Managing directors of large companies	28%	50%	20%	2%
Trade union leaders	13%	45%	40%	3%
Religious leaders	9%	29%	60%	2%

Source: [1]MORI/*Reader's Digest* [2]MORI/*Sunday Times*, [3]Mori/*Guardian*)

(1990) has argued, for many people, particularly the young, leisure culture is their main area of self-expression and identity.

Functionalists such as Eisenstadt tend to see youthful 'deviance' and conflict as part of adjustment to growing up and, therefore, as transitional. Young people make mistakes and misjudgements in the process of learning to become adults, but they generally behave more 'acceptably' as they get older. There does seem to be some truth in this analysis. However, I prefer to put functionalist insight within a broader power-conflict perspective. Young people conspicuously lack power in the 'real', i.e. instrumental world of work (whether school or economic) and, to a large extent also within the family. In these areas they are dependent on adults and largely controlled by them. Further, young people have little power in the area in which rules are made – the political – legal area. Indeed, adults have created a large body of rules which constrain (as well as protect) specifically young people, encompassing the whole of their lives, including sex, drink, and driving. Young people may or may not 'battle' with adult power and authority at school or at work, but their easiest and most complete escape from it is in their own leisure lives.

Generally, the trend in the nineteen eighties and early nineties has been towards tighter control of young people at school and work. The movement in favour of traditional discipline and teaching methods in schools, social control exerted through youth training schemes, and the strengthening of management at the expense of labour, especially young employees, have created a more controlled framework of youth than previously – even though power and control may be contested in these areas.

Several factors may have weakened the position of young people born in the seventies. First, due to a fall in the birth-rate, there are much fewer of them than were born in the nineteen forties, fifties and early sixties (see p. 456). Second, any advantage 'scarcity' might have given young people in the job-market was severely reduced by the economic downturn of the late eighties and early nineties. Third, although widely welcomed in itself, the increasing numbers of adult females remaining in or returning to paid employment has put further pressure on younger job-seekers. A piece of research apparently finding that a store which hired only workers over 50 (B and Q in Macclesfield) was on average eighteen per cent more profitable and experienced 39 per cent lower absenteeism and less than 50 per cent of the thefts than five stores with conventional employment recruitment policies must have made grim reading to youthful job-seekers (*The Guardian* 16/8/91).

The general data on youth from the surveys supplements rather than replaces the specific analysis of class, ethnic and gender factors on youth. There may yet occur further instances of youth subcultures reflecting specific social circumstances. However, the survey data and Willis' recent work suggest that 'ordinary kids', too, are busily 'doing their own thing' in whatever cultural space they can create and is allowed to them.

Perspectives on Old Age: Ageism

There are several perspectives on old age. Here we will briefly examine insights from comparative and historical perspectives, interactionist and Marxist perspectives. This should help both in interpreting and summarising later sections on old age in this book (see pp. 454–6). One of the main advantages of the comparative perspective is that it can indicate what is a universal social fact and what is subject to cultural variation. Cowgill and Holmes found a number of universals and variations in their wide survey of old age. Among the universals are that old age is a separate social category in all societies; that some old people always continue to act as political, judicial and civil leaders; and that mutual responsibility between the old and their adult children exists. Among the important variations between traditional and modern societies are that in the former, the old tend to have higher status, more power, and do not retire merely because they are old. Historical perspective helps to explain why the old in modern society have become comparatively marginalised. One factor was the policy of removing the old from paid work. Another was the way the old have become targeted as a client group for practice (and profit) by professions such as medicine and social work – interestingly explored in Carole Haber's *Beyond Sixty-five: the Dilemma of Old Age in America's Past* (1983).

Ageism is negatively to regard or behave towards someone merely because they are of a particular age. Like sexism and racism it is easy to be unconsciously ageist. Interactionist concepts such as stigma and stereotype are helpful in understanding ageist interactions. More broadly, as Christopher Lasch points out, to regard 'the old' as a problem group is itself implicitly ageist. Interestingly, a Harris poll on the so-called problem of old age, found that on every count the general public had a grimmer view of the problems of the old than did the old themselves (USA, 1975).

As its title suggests, Chris Phillipson's *Capitalism and the Construction of Old Age* (1982) supports Marxist analysis with insight from phenomenology. Phillipson argues that capitalism 'is irreconcilable with meeting the needs of elderly people' – largely because as non-producers, they are marginal to its needs.

He further contends that the old are particularly vulnerable to government cuts during economic recessions. Phillipson published well before the announcement in 1985 of the government's intention radically to cut back the State Earnings Related Pensions Scheme (SERPS) and encourage private and occupational pensions. Whatever the eventual results for the old, this policy does seem as much a matter of financial economy as of social policy.

Two main theoretical approaches attempt to explain the social stratification of the elderly: proletarianisation theory and labour market continuity theory. The former presents the elderly as homogeneous, disadvantaged group. The latter emphasises inequalities within the elderly due to previous labour market position. In a review of relevent evidence, Sara Arber (1990) concludes that, on balance, the latter theory more closely fits the facts. Those who had enjoyed a middle class income tend to remain better off after retirement although often not as well off as previously.

Old Age, Population and Social Policy

So far in this century, there has been a steady increase in the number of old people, both absolutely and as a percentage of the total population. In 1921, the number of men and women over 65 was under three million, and in 1991 it was over nine million. Those over 65 now make up more than fifteen per cent of the total population. For a variety of reasons, mainly relating to the birth rate at particular times, the number of older people is projected to continue to increase after a slight decrease in the early nineteen nineties. As a result, the working population must expect to have to maintain, for the foreseeable future, a largely dependent retired population of fifteen to twenty per cent of the total population. Within this group, it is projected that the very old, those aged 75 or over, will grow as a total percentage of the retired. For instance, the number of 85 year olds is expected to increase by 50 per cent to 700,000 by 1995 (See figure 10.4). Indeed, it is helpful in understanding the situations of older people to think in term of early old age

(65–75) and late old age (75 onwards).

Concern for the elderly tends to be intermingled with an uncomfortable awareness of cost: care of the very elderly is the most costly. Inevitably, the old have been allocated a growing proportion of public expenditure, despite the claims of other needy groups. Yet the standard of living of pensioners as a group has declined relative to the rest of the population. Nicholas Bosanquet gives impressive evidence of this in his book, *A Future for Old Age*. As real incomes rise, people spend relatively more on transport, services and leisure, and less on food, shelter and heating. More is also spent acquiring cars and certain other consumer durables. Apart from a minority of old people who do have quite a high standard of living, the expenditure patterns of the elderly do not reflect these changes. In fact, they are much as they were twenty years ago. A proportion of 43.4 per cent of income is spent on food, housing and heat by all households, whereas married pensioner couples spend 52.8 per cent of

(a) changes in the dependency population

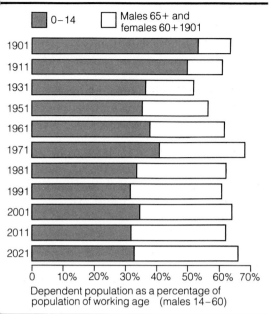

(b) An aging population   Population projections

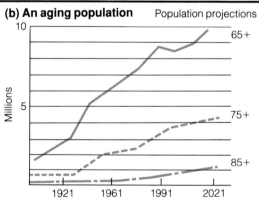

with just a spouse and 28 per cent living with others. The fact that over 70 per cent do not live with their children reflects the dominance of the nuclear family. In practice, this means that many old people are often lonely, even if they are seldom genuinely neglected.

Yet, in addition to relationships, and activity based on the family, old people, like other age groups, seem to prefer the company of their own generation. Many churches have old age pensioner clubs or other associations or activities, such as whist evenings, 'suitable' for old people. Most local political clubs and working men's clubs make similar provisions. Small groups of old people appear to meet frequently and informally at times of day when most of the rest of the population are at work. Women are preponderant in these groups since women outlive men, on average, by about five years. In the post-75 year old population, the proportion of women to men is about two to one. In addition, women are able to retire on a state pension at 60, whereas men work to 65. Amongst these facts is, perhaps, the basis of a case for an old men's liberation movement.

It is, perhaps, because modern societies value work so highly that the retired population suffers in status. Traditionally, a person's social identity has been derived mainly from his or her work and, implicitly, the old often seem to be regarded primarily as 'spent' workers. It is possible that if, as a result of unemployment, enforced leisure increases further, assumptions about the relationship between work and leisure and their relative value will change – and the status of worker, non-worker and past worker will change with them. These changes would, in turn, depend on the continuing substitution of machine labour for human labour, not only in the production of goods but also of services. Possibly, the working positions of the old and other generations will not be so different if more people experience periods of non-work, enjoy even shorter working weeks and generally perhaps come to regard work less and less as the centre of their lives.

It is debatable, however, whether even a change in cultural attitudes of this kind would mean that 'the wisdom of the aged' would be more appreciated in contemporary society. By contrast, the old of 30 or 40 years

Figure 10.4 (Far left)

their income on these three necessities, and single women pensioners 60.3 per cent. Bosanquet gives a detailed picture of the relative poverty suffered by the old which reflects this basic inequality.

The economic situation of many of the old suggests the low social status they have in our society. Yet, contrary to the still popular myth, the British are not flagrantly neglectful of their elderly. Surveys by Townsend and others show that the majority of them are actively involved with relatives and friends; even among the bedridden, over half are looked after outside hospitals. In fact, only five per cent of all old people are in residential institutions – about the same figure as in the early 1900's. Arguably, however, this is not the most telling statistic. An Age Concern survey of old people outside institutions found 38 per cent living hence will all have experienced mass education and will have been brought up in a technological society. Margaret Mead's statement, that in a post-figurative or fast-changing, future-oriented society, the knowledge and skills of the old become quickly dated, may no longer apply so forcibly to the old of 2020. All this is speculative and, for the present, the immediate issue is to help the elderly to deal with their material and human problems without patronising them, or seeming to regard them as a 'problem' in themselves. Christopher Lasch has suggested that the tendency of America to regard old age as a 'problem' reflects the selfish individualism or narcissism, as he calls it, of American society. We can entertain the same possibility of Britain. Lasch argues that the decline of belief in an after life and the identification of youth with beauty and success makes us dread old age. We push the thought of it to the back of our minds, just as we push old

people into the sidings of society. When we do confront it, we often try to explain it away. Some pretend old age is exclusively a social category when clearly it has its roots in biological decline; others try to arrest the biological process itself by pills, potions or jogging. The refusal to face old age is a refusal to come to terms with our own mortality. Lasch, a radical and severe critic of American culture, offers no easy solution to what amounts to a national neurosis about old age. He insists that nothing but a re-ordering of work, education, the family and other major institutions will bring the old out of their redundancy and isolation back into the mainstream of society. For this to happen, we would need to believe that it is valuable for the old to be involved with us, and we with them. This would have to include a willingness to face with them the problem that ultimately comes to all – our own deaths.

SUMMARY

1   The term age group refers to a group of people differentiated from others according to age. Age groups can be effectively studied in the context of the life-cycle which refers to these stages through which all who survive a full life-span pass. In modern societies the main age stages are childhood, youth, adulthood, and old age. It is important to remember that age stratification occurs along with other forms of stratification, particularly class, gender and race/ethnicity.

2   Childhood: according to Philip Ariès 'in medieval society the idea of childhood did not exist'. Modern childhood was socially constructed largely through schooling. The two institutions which form and control modern childhood are the state and the family.

3   Child abuse can best be understood in terms of general cultural attitudes and behaviour towards children and particular stress factors such as poverty rather than in simple tabloid – like terms of 'sick' or 'animal-like' individuals.

4   Youth: modern youth is socially constructed by universal education and cultural images purveyed through the media. Margaret Mead suggests that the culture of contemporary youth is anticipatory or prefigurative. Another issue in relation to modern youth – and perhaps youth more generally – is the extent to which the young 'have problems' or are merely portrayed by the media as 'problematic'.

5   Class greatly affects youth culture and particular subcultures. A classic example of a working class youth subculture is the skinheads. Their tough, 'macho', territorial, and anti-authoritarian attitudes reflect similar strains in male working class culture. Working class youth subcultures have tended to be male-dominated.

6   Middle class youth culture also reflects the norms and values of its class. This is true of the partly campus-

based hippie movement which nevertheless also revolted against conventional values, exploring a subterranean world of pleasure and 'alternative', idealistic values.

7   Race-ethnicity is a distinctive 'ingredient' in youth subcultures. Two examples of Afro-Caribbean youth subcultures are the rudies of the nineteen sixties and the Rastafarians. As with other youth subcultures, semiology (the interpretation of signs, including dress and music styles) is useful in understanding Afro-Caribbean youth subcultures. The hustler and Rastafarian lifestyles are more associated with adult as well as youth roles than is the case with other youth subcultural lifestyles.

8   Is there a generation gap? The answer to this question is that generally young people do not greatly differ from their parents in their attitudes to key social and political matters. However, young people in modern societies are in a different structural position to adults – they have less power and authority. They are also in a situation of learning and transition. These factors can lead to some tension and conflict between some young people and parents, teachers, the police and other 'authority figures'.

9   There is a variety of perspectives on old age and ageism (negatively regarding or behaving towards someone merely because they are of a particular age). Cowgill and Holmes usefully divide the factors associated with age into two categories: cultural universals and variations. Contrastingly but compatibly Chris Phillipson analyses old age in the British context with a keen edge to class differences.

10   The association of old age with 'problems' is itself problematic. There is evidence that others tend to see 'the old' as having more problems than they do themselves. However, for some old people real issues of poverty, status, power and isolation do occur.

11   The chapter concludes with a model framework illustration of the social construction of age and some key contemporary issues in relation to given age stages.

RESEARCH AND COURSEWORK

This area offers many research possibilities both relative to a single age stage or cross-generational. Childhood lends itself to cross-generational analysis, particularly in relation to the role of adult males and females in child care and socialisation (there is substantial relevant material in chapter three on this topic). Contemporary material such as newspaper reports and analysis can be useful in studying cultural attitudes and behaviour towards children. Children are not easy to interview successfully but observation can be effective (see Valerie Yule pp. 216–7).

For obvious reasons youth is an interesting area for many students to study but it is important to avoid simplistic and subjective judgements and analysis. An element of contrast within a study should lead to it being adequately theoretical and sophisticated. Thus, a comparison of the experience of males with females, black youth with white youth, working with middle class youth, should involve consideration of respectively, gender, race/ethnicity, and class theory. In fact, it is likely that any project on youth will involve some consideration of all these theoretical areas although the amount and 'blend' will vary according to the topic. Similarly, a comparison of the 'ordinary' majority of young people in a given class with an 'extraordinary' or spectacular subculture (e.g. conformist working class youth with skinheads) should encourage theoretical development (including the use of some semiology). A particularly wide range of secondary sources and contemporary data is available on this topic and a rich variety of methods is appropriate for original research. What must be avoided is the merely descriptive and anecdotal.

Given that the habits of older people may partly be designed to avoid frequent contact with young people, there may be problems producing a well selected sample of this age group. It is never sufficient merely to interview one's own or a friend's 'granny' unless such an interview is part of a properly designed quota sample or merely a minor piece of biographical illustration in a larger study. Again, an in-built comparative element – middle compared to working class old, older males compared to older females – should move the research away from the merely descriptive towards the explanatory and theoretical.

FURTHER READING

My *Age and Generation* (Tavistock, 1985) covers the full life-cycle with the emphasis on youth and, to a lesser extent, old age. On childhood, P Ariès *Centuries of Childhood* (Jonathan Cape, 1962) is a standard work. Stuart Hall and Tony Jefferson's *Resistance Through Rituals* (Hutchinson, 1976) remains a seminal collection of readings on youth subcultures from a Marxist phenomenological perspective. Dick Hebdige's *Subculture: The Meaning of Style* (Methuen, 1979) uses semiology effectively and covers the subcultural ground to the punks. John Williams' 'In Search of the Hooligan Solution', *Social Studies Review*, Vol. 1 No. 2, examines football hooliganism.

M Hepworth and M Featherstone's *Surviving Middle Age* (Blackwell, 1982) and Chris Phillipson's *Capitalism and the Construction of Old Age* (Macmillan, 1982) are recommended.

QUESTIONS

1   Why do societies differ in the social significance they attach to age differentials? (London, 1984)

2   'Being elderly, a teenager or a child is more a matter of social construction than biology'. Explain and Discuss. (AEB 1989)

11 Work, Unemployment & Non-work

INTRODUCTION

It is almost a truism of sociology that developments in the economy and the workplace greatly affect the rest of society. On the other hand, the impact of Thatcherism – first economically then more widely – lends support to those who argue that ideas and ideology can influence society. This chapter starts with the changing structure and organisation of work and then briefly deals with how this affects people in terms of gender, 'race' and age. There follows a long section on the experience of work, which along with family remains central to the life of most people. The following section deals with unemployment which is seen as a varying experience, though devastating for some. The sections on industrial interest groups and the professions cover the 'nitty gritty' of industrial organisations and relations. The final section on work and non-work explores the question of whether the relationship of work to leisure has radically changed.

The Changing Context of Work

THE CHANGING INTERNATIONAL, NATIONAL AND REGIONAL CONTEXT OF WORK

Economic internationalisation means that in certain crucial respects, national economies are increasingly becoming part of a global or world economy. The key feature of economic globalisation is that more money is transferred more easily across national boundaries. Money is transferred in this way for the purpose of investment, i.e. to make more money. Much of this money is simply invested in foreign currencies – which may strengthen (increase in value) – and government bonds or bank accounts which pay interest. However, money is also invested more directly in business either through buying shares in a foreign company or by wholesale takeover of a foreign company (i.e. by purchasing enough shares to control it). This process has increased greatly over the past decade. It was made easier by the so-called financial 'big bang' of 1987 which 'deregulated' or reduced government regulation of the financial functions of the City of London. It is notable that in the period following 'big bang' European takeovers in Britain have increased in total value by about twentyfold (from 1985 to 1988, see table 11.1). According to one estimate, half of the British workforce will be employed by foreign owned companies by the year 2000.

Britain is a major focal point of global economic change. It is not possible to understand work in contemporary Britain without having at least a basic appreciation of how and why this is so. A preliminary distinction must be made between financial and industrial capitalism. Financial capitalism refers to the management of money by banks investment houses, firms of stockbrokers and other financial companies. Industrial capitalism refers to the production of goods and services for the market. Clearly, industrial capitalism requires investment loans from the financial sector.

London has been and remains a major world financial centre and although now relatively declining, Britain remains a major industrial power. The role of London as a world financial centre can be readily appreciated by the fact that the annual worth of European, Japanese and United States financial business done in London (often involving companies, banks, governments from all three – and elsewhere – may be involved) dwarfs the value of

Figure 11.1 (below)

▼

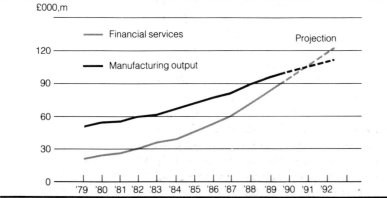

A nation of bankers The changing relative value of manufacturing and financial services

£000,m

Financial services

Projection

Manufacturing output

120

90

60

30

0

'79 '80 '81 '82 '83 '84 '85 '86 '87 '88 '89 '90 '91 '92

(Source: CSO)

exclusively British financial business. The financial services sector generates a large number of high status and well-paid jobs as does the fact that London is the location of central government and much of the civil service. Professional, administrative and business people are supported by a vast army of lower white collar employees which tends to keep employment relatively bouyant in the capital and the South East.

The tendency for business investment and ownership to become more international is well exemplified by Britain. The flow of capital investment both into and out of Britain has greatly increased since the mid nineteen eighties. As table 11.1 shows, since 1985 European companies have invested much more in takeovers in Britain than British companies have invested on takeovers in continental Europe.

The above trend seems set to increase after 1992. However, the gap with Europe has been somewhat offset by massive takeover action by British companies in the United States, where in the second half of the nineteen eighties, they took over £30 billion worth of corporate America. Further, British international companies generally enjoy powerful if not dominant positions in relation to less developed economies (see chapter 21). What we are witnessing, therefore, is a genuine internationalisation of the economy, not simply an increase in 'foreign' investment in British industry – although it may sometimes appear like the latter within Britain.

The internationalisation of the British economy has affected different regions differently. As described above, London as a world financial centre (and as the seat of central government) has been the main beneficiary from internationalisation. The South East and much of the rest of the South has enjoyed a 'Knock-on' effect from the wealth and prosperity of London. The North (and West) have been more peripheral to international wealth and investment. In addition, the decline of manufacturing industry has adversely affected the North much more than the South. The result of these factors are that the North, by most measures, is at a substantial economic and social disadvantage to the South. Figure 19.2 gives two bases of

BRITAIN'S LOOMING TAKEOVER GAP

Year	UK deals in Europe, £m	European deals in Britain, £m	Balance £m
1984	348	145	203
1985	228	260	−32
1986	477	1,343	−866
1987	1,312	1,683	−371
1988	2,788	5,821	−3,033
1989*	2,382	4,038	−1,656

* First 11 months

FOREIGN FIRMS' ACQUISITIONS IN BRITAIN, 1988–9

Target	Bidder	Nationality	Value, £m
Rowntree	Nestlé	Swiss	2,622
Jaguar	Ford Motor	American	1,560
Inter-Continental Hotels	Seibu Saison	Japanese	1,350
Pearl Group	AMP	Australian	1,243
Morgan Grenfell	Deutsche Bank	West German	950

NOTE: table includes deals that are still pending 29.35%

UK FIRMS' ACQUISITIONS ON CONTINENT, 1988–9

Target	Nationality	Bidder	Value, £m
Center Parcs (65%)	Dutch	Scottish & Newcastle	518
Carat (50%)	French	WCRS	202
Banque de l'Union Européenne	French	National Westminster	180
Elsevier (15,4%)	Dutch	Pearson (6.7%)	143
Newmont Mining (Oil & Gas)	Dutch	Clyde Petroleum	139

(Source: Acquisitions Monthly (Sunday Times, 3 December 1989, D11))

▲

Table 11.1 (a, b, c)

comparison although many more could have been selected. They show the South at an advantage, respectively, in average income and in its lower unemployment rate. Even the 1991–2 recession which 'bit' first in the South has not greatly affected this pattern.

It is possible to exaggerate the differences between South and North. The average differences between the two areas such as those given above are far less than the extent of the differences that occur within each. There has been Japanese investment in the North East and Wales as well as the South; there is poverty in London as well as Liverpool and millionaires in both cities. Nevertheless, there are substantial and increasing regional differences reflecting the uneven development of the British capitalist economy. Whether these differences will continue to increase or decrease as a result of the recession of the early nineteen nineties is not yet clear.

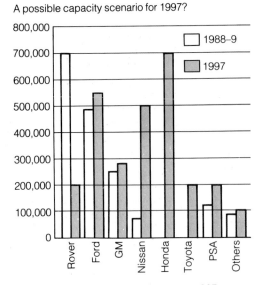

A possible capacity scenario for 1997?

Potential British car Production Capacity, 1997
(overwhelmingly Japanese and American Owned)

Source: Adapted from D.G. Rhys (Cardiff Business School, 1990) reprinted in 'Running The Country' (O.U., 1992, Unit 12:133)

Figure 11.2
Britain is part of the
global capitalist
system

THE FORDISM AND POST-FORDISM DEBATE

The analysis that capitalist production is moving from a 'Fordist' to a 'post-Fordist' era is an interesting but much challenged one. The analysis was popularised by M J Piore and C F Sabel *The Second Industrial Divide: Possibilities for Prosperity* (1984). They argue that capitalism is undergoing a process of 'restructuring' and becoming in a number of ways less rigid and more 'flexible'. As we shall see, although most commentators on technological and economic change recognise that some fundamental developments in capitalism have been occurring, many do not agree that the Fordism/post-Fordism polarisation is the best way of describing them.

Philip Cooke gives a useful description of Fordism: 'Fordism was associated with large-scale, mass production methods as pioneered by Henry Ford in Detroit and extended even to the factory building of mass housing in the 1960s. 'Fordism' is a shorthand for the method of social, political and economic regulation which linked, by making interdependent, mass production and mass consumption'.
(1989, 8–9)

The prototype of Fordist production is, of course, the original Ford car itself – coming off the production line as it did in standardised millions. The organisation and experience of mass assembly-line production at a much later date was well described in Huw Beynon's *Working for Ford* (1973): 'They [management] decide on their measured day how fast we will work. They seem to forget that we're not machines'.

Such highly controlled and precisely measured work is associated with the management techniques developed by Frederick Taylor (see below, p. 272) which complemented mass production methods.

Fordist mass production depends upon and helps to foster mass consumption. Without the mass consumption of mass produced products, companies would quickly go bankrupt. Indeed, thousands of Ford cars remained unsold when the mass car market collapsed following the 1929 Wall Street Crash. Governmental support for large-scale Fordist-type industries takes the form of grants, tax concessions, government-industry partnership schemes, and planning and development cooperation and assistance. More important perhaps, governments also undertook to stabilise demand for products through 'full' employment and income support schemes i.e. to ensure people could buy products.

The key concept of post-Fordist analysis is 'flexibility'. Piore and Sabel argue that 'flexible specialisation' is a growing feature of capitalist production. As a result greater variety and variation of products occurs.

Specialisation can occur in several ways but commonly involves higher skilled, more cooperative work to produce small, sometimes customised batches. One example of specialised production is the emergence of smaller, specialised firms which may adopt quasi-craft production processes, aided by high-tech equipment to produce individualised, high quality, and sometimes customised products. According to Piore and Sabel, the causal driving force behind these developments is the increased demand from the consumer market for more varied and different products.

J Atkinson, in a series of publications, has discussed the management of labour in terms broadly complementary to post-Fordist theory. He has developed a model of the flexible firm which contrasts strongly with the Fordist mass production monolith. According to Atkinson, the flexible firm concentrates chiefly on ensuring a flexible labour force. There are two main aspects to this:

1 numerical flexibility
2 functional flexibility

Numerical flexibility involves having a somewhat smaller core of permanent full-time workers than in the traditional industrial firm and the use of more temporary, part-time, and sub-contracted workers. Functional flexibility involves employing and often training a labour force that is more multi-skilled and using it in a variety of work which might well cross the demarcations traditionally insisted on by unions. Implicit, therefore, in the development of the flexible firm is the decline of traditional unionism and the individualisation of the work force and/or the emergence of unions willing to negotiate more 'flexible' working conditions. Not surprisingly, some have seen this as a threat to the strength of unions and to job security. Certainly, in Britain it is a process that has been facilitated by the 'Thatcherite' legislation on the unions (see p. 254).

Atkinson's flexibility model substantially draws from the longer established dual labour force theory. This theory argues that due largely to the strategy of capitalists, the labour force has become increasingly divided into a core (or primary) group and a peripheral (or secondary) group (see figure 11.2). The core labour force is appointed to give reliable, full-time service in meeting the essential and predictable needs of a firm, for which it is relatively highly rewarded in terms of pay and job security. It tends to be overwhelmingly male and disproportionately white. The peripheral labour force is employed, as far as possible, when and how a firm's management requires. It tends to be largely female and disproportionately black. This latter group is sometimes referred to as a 'reserve army of labour' – easily hired in a time of economic expansion and redundant during contraction.

By no means all occupational groups indicated by Atkinson fit into the core/peripheral model. Indeed, as figure 11.3 indicates, a growing number of self-employed (e.g. business consultants) and sub-contractors, usually enjoying high pay and status are outside the primary labour market. However, employers expect quality and reliability of service from such groups.

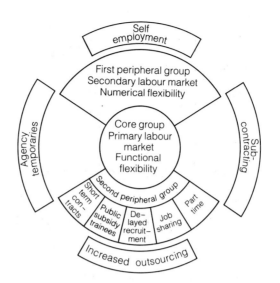

Figure 11.3
The flexible firm

FORDIST AND POST-FORDIST PRODUCTION SUMMARISED

	FORDIST	POST-FORDIST
Technology	Dedicated, Fixed Machinery	Micro-electronically, Controlled, Flexible, Multi-Purpose Machinery
	Economies of Scale Vertical Integration Mass Production	Economies of Scope Sub-Contracting Batch Production
Product	Mass-consumption Relatively Cheap	Varied and 'Niche' Products Varied/High Price Varied/High Quality
Labour Process	Highly Fragmented Few Tasks Little Autonomy Hierarchical Authority and Technical Control	More Integrated Many Tasks Greater Autonomy Group (e.g. 'Task-Group' Control)
Contract	Collectively Negotiated Rate for the Job Secure	Varied (Individually) Negotiated Performance Related Pay Varied Dual Labour Force

NOTE: The points under'Technology' and 'Product' roughly summarise Piore's analysis and those under 'Labour Process' and 'Contract' Atkinson's.

EXTENDING POST-FORDIST ANALYSIS

Table 11.2

The application of the Fordist/post-Fordist framework to economics, industrial organisation and relations, and, by implication, to class is highly significant in itself. However, this theoretical model has been extended to apply to developments in politics, education and culture as well. These applications are taken up at the appropriate points in this book. However, it is relevant to give here M Rustin's ideal type summary model of Fordism/Post-Fordism along with brief, necessary explanations in order to demonstrate the scope of this theoretical approach.

The ideal types of Fordist and post-Fordist modes of production and regulation can be summarised (with some sectoral applications) as follows:

AREA OF SOCIETY	FORDISM	POST-FORDISM
INDUSTRY	low technological innovation fixed product lines, long runs mass marketing	accelerated innovation high variety of product, shorter runs market diversification and niche-ing
	steep hierarchy, vertical chains of command mechanistic organisation	flat hierarchy, more lateral communications organismic organisation
	vertical and horizontal integration central planning	autonomous profit centres; network systems; internal markers within firm; out-sourcing
	bureaurcray	professionalism, entre-preneurialism
	mass unions, generalised wage-bargaining	localised bargaining: care and periphery; workforce divided; no corporation
CLASS	unified class formations; dualistic political systems	pluralised class formations; multi-party systems
	institutionalised class compromises	fragmented political markets
WELFARE STATE/ EDUCATION	standardized forms of welfare prescibed 'courses' in education	consumer choice in welfare, credit transfer, modularity, self-guided instruction; 'independent' study
POLITICS	class parties, nationwide	social movements; multi-parties; regional diversification
PRIVATE CONSUMPTION/ STYLE	standarised consumption (cars, houses, dress); styles	more varied consumption and personalised styles

(Source: Rustin 'The politics of post-Fordism' in New Left Review, No. 175 (1989))
Adapted and extended

▲

Table 11.3

Most of the content of Rustin's summary should be clear from what has already been said. However, the model does highlight an aspect of post-Fordist analysis not so far specifically emphasised: the less hierarchical,

decentralised modes of management supposedly characteristic of the post-Fordist 'era'. Again, this is to allow more flexibility for local managers or managers within large firms dealing with particular work teams to deal with problems specific to their own situation. The section of the summary model on management is from 'steep hierarchy …/flat hierarchy' to 'bureaucracy/professionalism'. The model also suggests that the traditional 'dualistic' mould (middle versus working class) of politics is fragmenting and that the Welfare State, too, is being remoulded to respond to the different demands of various consumer groups. The model further presents education as becoming increasingly flexible in terms of skills and courses taught, methods of access and delivery, and of assessment. Finally, the model suggests that the basis of politics is becoming significantly more decentralised and regionally based and focused around issues which give rise to social movements distinct from the traditional class parties (e.g. the feminist movement, see chapter 8).

Even Rustin's broad summary model does not give the full scope of the Fordist/post-Fordist analysis. The analysis of post-Fordist production links easily with the post-modern emphasis on consumption and style. Thus, consumption, like production, is seen as more individualised, less 'massified' and less predictable.

CRITICISMS OF POST-FORDIST ANALYSIS It is not uncommon for proponents of a new theory to exaggerate the possible extent of its application. Stephen Wood (1989) suggests as much in respect to Fiore and Sabel and their Fordist/post-Fordist analysis. He argues that in some cases, they consider what, in his view, are relatively minor changes in the organisation of production to be examples of flexible specialisation. Thus, he contends that the modifications to traditional Fordist production adopted by Japanese firms such as the introduction of quality circles, flatter management structures (and, more recently, project managers), do not amount to a radical transformation of work. Indeed, he dubs such approaches 'neo-Fordist' – emphasising that they are incorporated within Fordism. Further, the success of Japanese firms has been based mainly on the production of the 'niche' markets (although there have been some recent moves in the latter direction).

A number of commentators have been highly critical of the limited empirical basis of claims that a full transition to post-Fordism has occurred in Britain. Bryn Jones' examination of the British engineering industry failed to establish a systematic trend towards flexible specialisation (1988). As a technologically advanced industry, such a trend might have been expected in engineering if it is, in fact, occurring in Britain. Christabe Lane's comparison of the extent of flexible specialisation in Britain and Germany finds substantial evidence in the case of the latter but little in the case of the former. Jones further observes that labour market segmentation appears to have occurred more in the public than in the private sector (e.g. the creation of more part-time and temporary posts in education) where Conservative governments have been able to enforce Thatcherite policies.

Anna Pollert (1988) has strongly criticised post-Fordist theory, and particularly the work of Atkinson. In general, her arguments and interpretation of empirical data lead her to emphasise variety and complexity rather than any single overarching trend such as post-Fordism. Thus, she argues that Fordism was never so overwhelmingly dominant a method of production nor have new methods replaced Fordism to the extent that some analysis suggests. For instance, batch production continued alongside Fordist production and currently many smaller firms cannot afford to invest in flexible, computerised technology. Second, she rejects the implication that flexibility generally requires a more skilled workforce. Actual practice again suggests a complex picture with both skilling and deskilling occurring in different situations. Third, Pollert is also unconvinced that there has been an increase in the numbers of 'peripheral' workers. She points to a decline in proportion to full-time workers in manufacturing although there is no doubt that there has been a sharp increase in part-time female workers in the service sector.

Marxists differ in the extent to which they consider that neo-Fordism has taken over from Fordism. However, they are agreed that neo-Fordism is an adaptation within capitalism and, therefore, offers at best only limited gains for workers. Workers are still managed – perhaps, even more managed – and 'exploited' by capitalism for profit. Nor do Marxists consider that under neo-Fordism workers regain significant power and control over their own work, the workplace or what they produce. For this, the kind of changes discussed later in this and the next chapter would be required (see p. 258 and pp. 278–83).

POST-FORDISM: FOR AND AGAINST: A SUMMARY

Areas of General Agreement:

1 Advanced technology (especially micro-chip) has increased flexibility – more machine than labour intensive, greater product variety.

2 The globalisation of capital (though Marxists refute the notion of a fundamentally changed or 'restructured' capitalism and free-market theorists note the complementary rise of small-business).

3 Changes in the organisation of the work force e.g. removal of job demarcation lines more individualised contracts (post-Fordists see this as flexibility, Marxists as a potential strategy for capitalists better to exploit labour).

4 The production of a greater variety of consumer products.

Areas of General Disagreement:

Economic

1 No consensus that the labour force is organised in a fundamentally different way than in the 'Fordist' phase of capitalism or that labour militancy is 'dead' (Marxists disagree on both counts).

2 Empirical data on some key aspects of post-Fordism is inconclusive e.g. the relationship between full-time and part-time employees.

Political and Cultural

3 There is not agreement that the class basis of politics is over.

4 'Consumerism' is seen as a sign of progress by some but as a form of capitalistic control and manipulation by others.

THE CHANGING LABOUR MARKET: GENDER, RACE AND AGE

The economic developments and changes in the workplace and working practices so far described in this chapter have resulted in changes in the labour market. The particular effect of these changes on women, black people and youth will be discussed in the relevant chapters but a brief overview is appropriate here.

By no means all, but a disproportionate number of women, black people and youth are disadvantaged in the labour market. It can be argued that in each case there is an element of discrimination in the disadvantage. Women have tended to fill the more routine office jobs and many positions (usually lower status) in the educational and welfare professions that the massive expansion of the service sector has provided. The crux of disadvantage in the case of women lies in the fact that the time and work they put into childcare and the household frequently damages their career prospects. Patriarchy is the system that tolerates and fosters gender inequality, i.e. it is a system which discriminates against women.

Black people tended to do low paid jobs in manufacturing or other manual work during the nineteen fifties and sixties. There is ample evidence that racial discrimination has been a major factor barring their progress up the occupational hierarchy (pp. 199–200). The labour market position of many black people has been made acutely worse by the fact that it is in the areas in which the employment of black people has been concentrated – manufacturing and manual work generally – that large-scale job losses have occurred. During the recession of the early nineteen eighties job losses in these areas were massive as was unemployment among black people. Black youth was particularly severely affected. A similar pattern appears to be developing in the recession of the early nineteen nineties.

The position of contemporary young people in the labour market is not so obviously characterised by disadvantage and discrimination as is that of women and black people. The majority of young people move into work, training or further education at sixteen. However, during the nineteen eighties and early nineteen nineties, unemployment has varied in a range from about 1.5 to three million, which is extremely high compared to the rest of the post-war period. Quite simply, this has weakened the bargaining power of young people in the employment market and for a substantial number made getting a job more difficult – particularly for the less well qualified in areas of high unemployment. The average wage of young people as a proportion of the national wage has declined. Some young people have had to take places on training schemes or face unemployment without access to social security. However, both the quantity and quality of training schemes in Britain have been criticised compared to those of several other European countries (see figure 11.5). Overall, the position of young people relative to other age groups has weakened, particularly when compared to that of 'sixties youth' although this is much more true of the North than the South. The position of young people in the labour market should improve during the nineteen nineties due to demographic factors (see p. 460).

It is debatable whether there is a single theoretical approach which fully and satisfactorily explains the labour market position of women, black people and youth. Both women and black people have been variously seen as a 'reserve army of labour' or as peripheral workers (pp. 182–3). The

Figure 11.4
▼

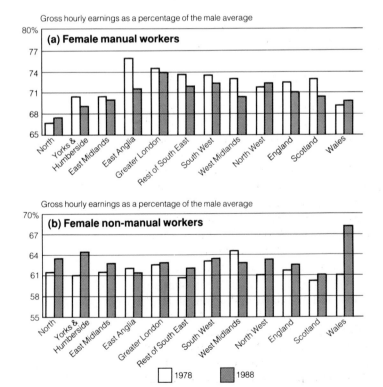

Gross hourly earnings as a percentage of the male average

(a) Female manual workers

80%, 77, 74, 71, 68, 65

North; Yorks & Humberside; East Midlands; East Anglia; Greater London; Rest of South East; South West; West Midlands; North West; England; Scotland; Wales

Gross hourly earnings as a percentage of the male average

(b) Female non-manual workers

70%, 67, 64, 61, 58, 55

North; Yorks & Humberside; East Midlands; East Anglia; Greater London; Rest of South East; South West; West Midlands; North West; England; Scotland; Wales

☐ 1978   ■ 1988

(Source: New Earnings Survey)

problem with the latter approaches is that they fail to explain why significant numbers of women and increasing numbers of black people, especially of Asian origin, do achieve occupations of middle class status. Marxists argue that it is particularly working class women, black people and youth that experience problems both in obtaining work and when they are in work. They do not deny that gender, 'race', and age play a part in disadvantage and discrimination but argue that this should be contextualised in the broader context of class conflict and exploitation.

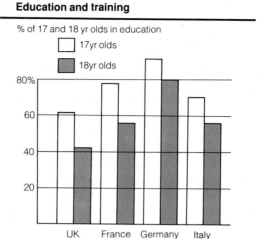

Education and training

% of 17 and 18 yr olds in education

Figure 11.5

Source: DES, (1986)

The Experience of Work

Broadly, there are three possible responses to work: alienation, neutrality and satisfaction, and we study these below. Beyond mere satisfaction lies the prospect of genuine fulfilment at work and we also consider what this might mean.

1 ALIENATION

MARX AND WEBER Two accounts of alienation must be distinguished. First is that of Marx: he considered that workers in capitalist society are alienated from work because they own neither what they produce nor the means by which they produce it.

He is quite clear about this:

Finally, the alienated character of work for the worker appears in the fact that it is not his work but work for someone else, that in work he does not belong to himself but to another person.

A further aspect of alienation is apparent in the quotation. Because of the need to sell 'his' labour, the worker loses his independence in work; he becomes alienated from his own activity and thus from himself. The contemporary Marxists, Bowles and Gintis, have attempted to relate the nature of the division of labour in capitalist society to the need of the ruling class to maintain control over the workforce. By daily repeating the same limited task(s), workers are prevented from understanding the whole of the process of production. What they do not understand they can hardly aspire to control. Bowles and Gintis do not, of course, regard the capitalist mode of production and the resultant alienation and mystification of the workforce as inevitable.

A second analysis of alienation is widely adopted. To understand it we must first briefly describe what bureaucracy is. Bureaucracy is a form of organisational structure characterised by a variety of roles, some of which have more authority and status than others. Nearly all large-scale organisations in modern societies are organised in this way and we are so familiar with this form of organisational structure that we tend to think (wrongly) that it is the only type possible (for alternatives see the next chapter). This approach to understanding alienation rests on the work of Weber, although he himself did not employ the term. In this approach, alienation is seen as caused by the effect on the work situation of the bureaucratic division of labour. Weber considered that working particularly at the lower levels of bureaucracy, such as in a factory or an office, is alienating for two basic reasons. Firstly, doing the same thing over and over again, say, filing invoices, is boring to most people. Secondly, bureaucratic employees have little control over their work situation, and this is unsatisfying. Woodward, Touraine and Blauner have applied Weberian-type analysis specifically to industrial work and we examine their conclusions below. Weber himself was probably the first sociologist to appreciate that lack of identity and control, and a sense of meaninglessness – in short alienation – can equally affect the clerk, the typist, the soldier or anyone who fulfils a small role in a large, bureaucratic organisation. He stressed that alienation can occur as easily in state bureaucracies as in privately owned ones. Indeed, he anticipated that alienation would be a particular problem in socialist societies because of their inevitably (in his view) bureaucratic nature.

Despite the above major differences, Marx and Weber described the psychological consequences of alienation very similarly. The phrase 'feelings of alienation' refers to the same human experience for both. Writing of the industrial labourer, Marx says:

He does not fulfil himself in his work but denies himself, has a feeling a misery, not of well-being, does not develop freely a physical and mental energy, but is physically exhausted and mentally debased.

Etzioni summarises Weber's view and usefully links it with that of Marx:

... the worker, soldier, and researcher – and by implication all employees of all organisations – are frustrated, unhappy ... When asked, 'all said and done, how satisfied are you with your work?' about 80 per cent of American blue-collar workers answered 'not satisfied'. Alienation is a concept that stands for this sentiment and the analysis of its source in Marxian-Weberian terms.
   (Etzioni, 1964)

Despite their common understanding of what it means 'to feel alienated', Marx and Weber's difference over the origin of alienation is highly significant. Differing diagnoses lead to differing prescriptions. For Marx, the ultimate solution to inequality and alienation at work is to abolish capitalism and establish a communist system in which the means of production and what is produced are the common property. What is produced is then distributed on the basis of need, not purchasing power. This is a road down which Weber had no wish to travel – as we have noted, he anticipated that, whatever the theoretical ideal, communist societies would be very bureaucratic. He offered no solution to bureaucratic alienation, but regarded the march of 'rationality' as inevitable in all modern societies whether capitalist or socialist. He saw practical advantages in bureaucracy but feared its potential to alienate. Perhaps this accounts for the occasional pessimism and faint sense of regret for more romantic and less 'rational' times past in Weber's work.

BLAUNER, TOURAINE, WOODWARD AND THEIR CRITICS About the early nineteen sixties, a succession of books appeared which examined the relationship between technology and work satisfaction. Notable among these were works by Touraine, Blauner and Woodward. The findings they presented were very much in accord. The French sociologist, Touraine, summarised three recent historical stages in production technology and worker involvement: flexible machines/craftworkers; standard machines/unsuperintendents. He associated the first and third of these with relatively higher levels of satisfaction. Blauner's typology is similar though slightly more complex.

Blauner's model is virtually self-explanatory. Machine-minding is usually required in batch production which is technically less efficient than assembly line mass production, but usually involves the worker in a slightly more varied way. Although the empirical basis of his work has been criticised as not very adequate, his conclusions find support not only from other sociologists but from common experience. Many artists have preferred the creativity and fulfilment of craft-work to the humdrum security and financial rewards of a safe but boring job. At the other end of the satisfaction-alienation spectrum is assembly line work. Of course, as we shall see, workers find ways of surviving and coping, but the phantoms of monotony, repetition and sheer tedium are never far away. In process work, by contrast, the worker is 'freed' from the machine. S/he oversees much, if not all, of the process of production and therefore has a closer involvement and identity with the whole. The brutal fracturing of the division of labour is partly healed.

Woodward's terms – unit, batch, mass and process production – cover the same area as Blauner's typology – craft, machine, assembly-line and process production. Like Blauner, she sees mechanisation as causing an increase in alienation until the onset of process production, which would show on a graph as the upside-down 'U curve' of alienation, takes a steep plunge. She also notes that in unit and process production, the dividing line between workers and technical and supervisory staff tends to be more blurred than in the case of batch and mass production. The situation was closer to what Burns and Stalker call the organic model of organisation involving more communication and democratic decision making. Thus, less alienation occurred through powerlessness.

Blauner's optimistic view of the effect of automation on work satisfaction has been sharply criticised by Duncan Gallie. He notes pointedly that the size of Blauner's sample of process workers was only 99, of which 78 were sampled in 1947 and 21 in 1961. Gallie himself, however, did not choose a sample survey method. Instead he made four detailed case studies of workers in automated oil refineries, two in France and two in Britain. The point of this was to supply a comparative cultural frame of reference which he felt was missing in Blauner's work. In both cases Gallie found that indifference, not satisfaction, was the most frequently expressed attitude to work. On a whole range of other matters mainly affecting industrial relations, however, he found substantial differences between the French and British workers. He concluded that broad generalisations about workers' attitudes and about industrial relations, should consider variables relative to given cultures and not simply technological change. We can accept this basic point of Gallie's but it should be said that other work, including that of Wedderburn and Crompton, tends to support Blauner, Woodward and Touraine's conclusion that automated labour is in itself relatively more satisfying than other forms of mechanised labour.

We earlier made an important distinction between Marx's and Weber's understanding of the major cause of alienation. Blauner, Woodward and Touraine are closer to Weber

Technology and Alienation

Type of Work →	Craft	Machine Minding	Assembly Line	Process
	↓	↓	↓	
Type of Production/ Product →	No Standardised Product	Mechanisation and standard-isation	Rationalis-ation Standardised Product	Rationalis-ation Uniform Product
Level of Skill →	High	Low	Low	Responsi-bility & under-standing needed
Level of Alienation →	Low	High	Highest	Low

▲

Table 11.4

in that they analyse alienation in terms of the technical organisation of production rather than in terms of the private ownership of the means of production. Blauner suggests four dimensions of alienation, which he contrasts with four non-alienative states:

	Alienated States	Non-Alienative States
1	Powerlessness	Control
2	Meaninglessness	Purpose
3	Isolation	Social Integration
4	Self-estrangement	Self-involvement.

There is no need to explain the use of these terms at length. A little thought will make it clear why a fragmented, partial relationship to production tends to lead to alienation, and a fuller one to a more satisfied set of responses. 'Self-estrangement' can be regarded as the final stage of alienation in which the individual begins to lose self-respect and motivation. Blauner's list is a useful summary of what has already been said or implied about the psychology of alienation.

One point of Blauner's can usefully be taken further here. It is the contrasting conceptual pair of self-estrangement and self-involvement. The notion that work can alienate people from themselves is common to both Marxist and Weberian inspired literature on alienation. The idea presupposes that there does exist a self to be alienated from. The humanist psychologist Abraham Maslow has attempted to define broadly what the fundamental, common properties of human nature are. He argues that whereas practically all jobs provide the means to satisfy basic social needs (food, shelter), fewer satisfy egoistic needs (status), and fewer still allow for relatively full self-actualisation (self-fulfilment, creativity). Others have elaborated on Maslow's simple scheme, but as a clear statement of the root social-psychological cause of alienation it is difficult to improve. Alienation is the frustration of human potential as a result of unfulfilling work.

MARX REVISITED: THE 'DESKILLING' DEBATE: HARRY BRAVERMAN AND HIS CRITICS

Harry Braverman's *Labor and Monopoly Capital: The Degradation of Work in the Twentieth Century* (Monthly Review Press, 1974) has perhaps been the most influential book on the nature and experience of the labour process in the last quarter of a century. Braverman argues that in capitalist society the organisation and experience of work is the product of managerial control rather than of 'rationalisation' required by technology in itself. To the extent that Braverman sees alienation as the product of social relations (i.e. between capitalist-management and workers), he is in the tradition of Marx himself.

As the title of his book suggests, Braverman considers that the quality of work has been 'degraded' during this century. He argues that degradation has taken place because management has sought increasingly to control workers partly by deskilling the labour process. The bulk of his analysis is of manufacturing industry but he applies his thesis equally to clerical workers and personal service and retail trade workers. As he puts it:

The giant mass of workers who are relatively homogeneous as to lack of developed skills, low pay, and interchangeability of person and function (although heterogeneous in such particulars as the site and nature of the work they perform) is not limited to offices and factories. Another high concentration is to be found in the so-called service occupations and in retail trade.

(Braverman, 1974, 359).

According to Braverman, the main organisational strategy adopted by management to control and exploit labour is labour specialisation. Braverman's particular target is F W Taylor's theory of scientific management (see p. 272). Briefly, Taylor argued that if management divided the labour process up into small functions both increased efficiency and greater control over the labour force would result. Organising labour in this way would lessen the chance of workers understanding the whole process of production and enable the appointment of less intelligent workers. Taylor is quite frank on the last point, stating that the full possibilities of his system 'will not have been realised until almost all of the machines … are run by men who are of smaller calibre and attainments, and who are therefore cheaper than those required under the old system' (Braverman 1974: 118).

Conveniently, in view of our previous analysis of the Fordist/post-Fordist debate, Braverman gives the mass production of the Model T Ford as an early example of the degradation and deskilling of manufacturing work. It is worth quoting his description and comments at some length:

The key element of the new organisation of labour was the endless conveyor chain upon which car assemblies were carried past fixed stations where men performed simple operations as they passed. This system was first put into operation for various subassemblies, beginning around the same time that the Model T was launched, and developed through the next half-dozen years until it culminated in January 1914 with the inauguration of the first endless-chain conveyor for final assembly at Ford's Highland Park plant. Within three months, the assembly time for the Model T had been reduced to one-tenth the time formerly needed, and by 1925 an organisation had been created which produced almost as many cars in a single day as had been produced, early in the history of the Model T, in an entire year.

The quickening rate of production in this case depended not only upon the change in the organisation of labour, but upon the control which management, at a single stroke, attained over the pace of assembly, so that it could now double and triple the rate at which operations had to be performed and thus subject its workers to an extraordinary intensity of labour.

(Braverman, 1974: 147–8)

Braverman also amply illustrates how – as he sees it – the labour process has become increasingly controlled through timing, simplification and routinisation in office work. Indeed, he claims that 'management experts of the second and third generations after Taylor erased the distinction between work in factories and work in offices' (319). He cites the time standards for various clerical activities suggested in a handbook widely used in American companies. The examples given here are 'drawer' and 'chair' 'activities':

Open and close	Minutes
File drawer, open and close, no selection	.04
Folder, open or close flaps	.04
Desk drawer, open side drawer of standard desk	.014
Open center drawer	.026
Close side	.015
Close center	.027
Chair activity	
Get up from chair	.033
Sit down in chair	.033
Turn in swivel chair	.009
Move in chair to adjoining desk or file (4 ft. maximum)	.050
(Cited Braverman, 321)	

Braverman goes on to mention that the handbook gives the time value for 'Cut with scissors' as .44, with '.30 for each additional snip'.

Braverman is aware that other approaches to the organisation of capitalist labour than Taylorism occur. However, he dismisses them as of relatively little importance. Thus, he considers human relations theory – which pays specific attention to the human needs of workers – as merely concerned with the adjustment of the worker to the ongoing production 'as that process was designed by the industrial engineer' i.e. 'Taylorites' (87).

CRITICS OF BRAVERMAN A number of commentators on Braverman – both Marxist and liberal – have contended that he underestimates the extent of class conflict in general and specifically industrial conflict resulting from workers' struggle. They further argue that control strategies have been affected by worker power and resistance. Richard Edwards, himself sympathetic to Marxism, and Andy

Friedman have both made these points. Edwards argues that not one but several types of control have been adopted by capitalists over workers. Initially, in the nineteenth century, 'simple control' (direct and personal control) was typically used by capitalists (or their foremen or managers) whereas later 'technical control' (i.e. control by machinery) and then 'bureaucratic control' (i.e. control by hierarchical organisational systems) became dominant. Like Edwards, Andy Friedman distinguishes between the types of control adopted by management. What he refers to as 'direct control' involves the explicit exercise of managerial authority whereas 'responsible autonomy' allows workers some freedom in the work process provided they operate within the framework of company goals. Stephen Wood succinctly describes Friedman's view that workers' efforts have forced management to adopt more 'liberal' (or, what Paul Thompson refers to elsewhere as, more 'consensual' managerial strategies):

Both Friedman (1977) and Edwards (1979), who emphasise the importance of resistance by workers, for example to Taylorism, in relation to managerial behaviour illustrate . . . arguments. In the twentieth century, managements have had to come to terms with resistance, especially in times of full employment. As a result, they have had to adopt more liberal methods than Taylorism: what Friedman terms 'responsible autonomy' strategies. Methods such as the gang system, human relations, job re-design, are all treated by Friedman as genuine alternatives to Taylorist methods, or 'direct control' strategies, as he prefers to call them. In certain circumstances management has to come to terms with human needs and potential recalcitrance of workers, by building real autonomy and discretion into jobs or by allowing groups of workers to run themselves. This contrasts with Braverman's position, according to which such methods merely represent an alternative style of management rather than a genuine change in the position of the worker. For Friedman, the collective organised strength of work groups can force management to

adopt strategies other than direct control, or Taylorism.

(Stephen Wood, in R Deem and G Salaman eds., 1985: 81–2).

Feminist perspective has provided a second standard of criticism of Braverman. It is suggested that Braverman underestimates the level of skill involved in much of the work done mainly by women in capitalist society. In this way, he himself reflects the patriarchal assumptions of capitalist society. Thus, as Veronica Beechey argues, the skill involved in a wide range of occupations, such as sewing, cooking and apparently routine office work may be much greater than the low status and rewards associated with them. Further, work in which females tend to be concentrated has frequently been classified as less skilled than male-dominated occupations in order legally to maintain the sex pay differential. This strategy was sometimes adopted to avoid the consequences of the Equal Pay Act (1975).

A research project funded by the Economic and Social Research Council, throws some empirical light on the deskilling issue. A survey of employees was conducted to find out what their own subjective views on their skill range might be. Over half of the respondents felt that they had acquired more skills over the previous five years. This was true of respondents in both the manufacturing and service sectors which, of course, runs counter to Braverman's degradation thesis. However, this data does not comprehensively disprove Braverman's case – though it does damage it. First, what people think has happened and what has happened on the basis of more objective criteria may be very different. To find out the latter would require a different kind of survey. Second, the survey does suggest that whereas the skills of those who already possessed high level skills tended to increase, those with lower level skills – notably part-time female workers – tended to experience a decrease in their skill levels.

2 A SOCIAL ACTION APPROACH TO THE EXPERIENCE OF WORK: GOLDTHORPE AND LOCKWOOD

Both Marxist and technological theories of alienation have been rejected by Goldthorpe and Lockwood who adopt a social action approach to this issue in which they give prime consideration to workers' own meanings. They point out that many of the workers in their sample did not have high expectations of work and were not therefore disappointed by their experience of it. They worked not for satisfaction, still less for fulfilment, but for money. Goldthorpe and Lockwood call this an instrumental orientation to work (the term orientation is preferred to attitude): it is used as a means or instrument to get something else – money. Their sample was mainly of young married workers who, mindful of family commitments, may have been particularly 'money conscious', but other research bears out and extends this finding. Dubin shows that, for many industrial and white collar employees, work is not a major area of interest and self-expression. In a generally more representative sample of the male manual workforce than Goldthorpe and Lockwood's, Wedderburn and Crompton nevertheless confirm the latters' findings. The cumulative implication of these findings is that the workers are neither consciously alienated from, nor satisfied with, work but accept it neutrally as a means to an end. They work largely to finance their family and leisure life which does have personal meaning to them.

Another way of explaining this is to distinguish between intrinsic and extrinsic orientations to work. A person who works for intrinsic reasons does so for the satisfaction the job gives. Such people include craftsmen or vocationally motivated nurses. In this context, extrinsic means the same as instrumental. Most people appear to work for predominantly extrinsic reasons, and to have low expectations of what the job offers in itself. If dissatisfaction is the difference between expectation and experience, then, most are not dissatisfied, because they expect little in the first place. Thus surveys suggest that women in routine office work are more satisfied than men doing work of a similar level of skill. A possible reason for this is that work is less of a central life interest for them than for men and so they are more easily 'satisfied' with it.

We seem then to have two almost contradictory perspectives on work experience: on the one hand, certain kinds of work are considered alienating and, on the other, the people who do these kinds of work may regard them as a neutral but not alienating experience. We can easily reconcile the two views if we extend our understanding of alienation. Alienation is not just a description of subjective (personally experienced) feelings of many workers; it is also a more objective (more widely generalisable) statement about the waste of human potential that certain kinds of routine work, both manual and white collar, involve. In this sense, alienation is about lack of fulfilment, not just actual feelings of misery. It is quite possible to have many unfulfilled capacities without knowing it. Such a grossly unfulfilled person is alienated from his or her true potential. Marx argued that fulfilment at work is generally possible in socialist, but not in capitalist society. Weber thought fulfilment at work for the majority was incompatible with the extreme division of labour of large scale organisation, whether in capitalist or socialist societies. We need to look at the concept of fulfilment in greater detail because its use does imply the value judgement that some kinds of activity, including varieties of work, are more or less better (in the sense of more fulfilling) than others.

3 FULFILMENT IN WORK

Abraham Maslow's theory of human needs can be usefully applied to the concept of fulfilment at work. Nearly everybody will expect to meet their basic needs of food and shelter through work, and most will hope for some pleasant social interaction while at work. Fewer will acquire substantial esteem or prestige for the work they do though only the most humble will be outside the positive status hierarchy altogether. Only a tiny minority achieve self-actualisation or self-fulfilment through work. Very few are allowed to perform at a level of personal excellence that brings their best creative skills and abilities into play. Examples of some who can are people at the very top of our occupational elites, such as managing directors of large companies, star sportsmen and entertainers, and creative academics. Many others are perhaps haunted by what Gouldner calls 'the unemployed self' – a sense of potential underdeveloped and a life wasted in senseless work.

We have noted that Marx did not consider fulfilling, non-alienating work to be generally possible in capitalist society. Some Marxists regard with suspicion the limited industrial participation or power-sharing schemes involving workers, which have been adopted in Germany and Sweden, but others consider them a step on the road to a more socialist and less alienating society. Those who, unlike Marx, see alienation primarily as the result of technological and/or organisational factors, naturally look for solutions within these terms (we exclude of course, those who ignore the problem or believe it to be insoluble). We examine a variety of attempts to achieve relatively more 'human' systems of organisation and technology both later in this chapter and in chapter 12.

INFORMAL ATTEMPTS TO DEAL WITH ALIENATION: AN INTERACTIONIST PERSPECTIVE

Reform and revolution aside, those who have to work in boring jobs are faced with the day-to-day need of 'getting by'. Here are some of the ways they use to do so.

The interactionist concept of managing self and others provides a helpful perspective on the many people who 'survive' monotony at work (and school). Apart from snatched conversational exchanges, day-dreaming is perhaps the most universal 'strategy', as Jason Ditton remarks in his participant study of work in a factory bakery:

> *Although the workers looked as if they were doing the work automatically, one man, who had worked for twelve hours a day for two years in the 'dough' ... pointed out that, underneath this, the mind never stops. Though giving the impression of working without thinking, he said that 'you think of a hundred subjects a day' ...*
> *(Ditton, 1972)*

Doubtless his 'hundred subjects a day' cover a similar range of musings as those in which you and I indulge.

Next to 'escaping into your head', the most common way of dealing with stress and monotony is probably by humour – 'having a laff'. In his authentic description of nineteen fifties working class life in Nottingham, *Saturday Night and Sunday Morning*, Alan Sillitoe gives us more than a few examples of 'laffs' through the actions of the novel's anti-hero, Arthur. Here is one:

At a piecework rate of four-and-six a hundred you could make your money if you knocked-up fourteen hundred a day – possible without grabbing too much – and if you went all out for a thousand in the morning you could dawdle through the afternoon and lark about with the women and talk to your mates now and again. Such leisure often brought him near to trouble, for some weeks ago he stunned a mouse – that the overfed factory cats had missed – and laid it beneath a woman's drill, and Robboe the gaffer ran out of his office when he heard her screaming blue-murder, thinking that some bloody silly woman had gone and got her hair caught in a belt (big notices said that women must wear hair-nets, but who could tell with women?) and Robboe was glad that it was nothing more than a dead mouse she was kicking up such a fuss about. But he paced up and down the gangways asking who was responsible for the stunned mouse, and when he came to Arthur, who denied having anything to do with it, he said: 'I'll bet you did it, you young bogger!' 'Me, Mr. Robboe?' Arthur said, the picture of innocence, standing up tall with offended pride. 'I've got so much work to do I can't move from my lathe'.

(Sillitoe, 1958)

A tough sense of the ridiculous is at the heart of traditional working class life. In part, it is a way of coping with the absurdity and tyranny of work. We discussed working class humour and other cultural attitudes earlier (chapter 6).

The ultimate escape at work is going to sleep. Quite often, night-shift workers are 'allowed' an informal 'kip' after they have finished their quota, but the British Leyland worker who was dismissed after bringing a bed to work was obviously considered to be taking things too much for granted. Apart from such arrangements, many workers have some recollection of occasionally going to sleep while working, either through monotony or fatigue, just as most students do.

An experienced foreman or sympathetic floor manager will not attempt to stop harmless attempts by workers to 'kill time' or, at least, make it pass more quickly. He may even extend a tea-break or stop to chat with an obviously tired, sick or stressed worker when the occasion seems to demand it.

All the daydreams, 'laffs', 'kips', and 'tea and sympathy', however, cannot make fundamentally boring work interesting. As we shall see, alienation is arguably the underlying cause of much industrial conflict and discontent as well as the milder, improvised 'escape attempts' described above.

The real escape, though, is leisure time. It is then that workers, starved of meaning and expression at work, can hope to 'do their own thing'. If, to use C Wright Mills' image, people sell little pieces of themselves for money during week-days, they attempt to reclaim themselves in the evenings and at weekends with the coin of fun. Mills' tart irony rightly suggests that the problems of personal freedom, pleasure and leisure are more complicated than this simple division of time into 'work and fun' suggests. We examine these issues after the following section on industrial interest groups and conflict.

Unemployment

Unemployment is an issue that has never been far from national concern from the late nineteen seventies, going into the nineteen nineties. This is because it has either been increasing rapidly or for three years in the late nineteen eighties declining rapidly. In the early nineteen seventies unemployment was somewhat less than one million, by 1985 it was three million, by early 1990 it was 1.6 million, and by 1992 it was over 2.5 million again. In the first four post-war decades, it was the conventional political wisdom that no government could survive unemployment at over one million, yet the Conservatives have three times won elections when the figure was well over 2 million. Was the conventional wisdom wrong, or has the nature of unemployment changed, or perhaps people's perception of it?

Figure 11.6

(a) Unemployment: United Kingdom

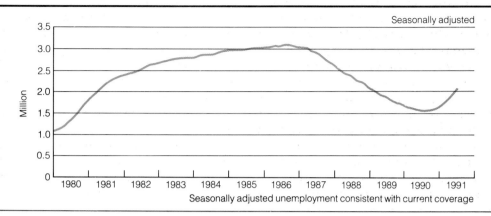

Seasonally adjusted unemployment consistent with current coverage

(b) Jobcenter vacancies: United Kingdom

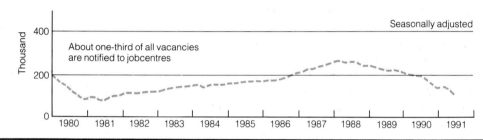

(Source: *Employment Gazette* June 1991)

MEASURING UNEMPLOYMENT The official definition of unemployment is a tight one:

"People claiming benefit – that is, Unemployment Benefit, Income Support or National Insurance Credits – at Unemployment benefit offices on the day of the monthly count, who say on that day they are unemployed and that they satisfy the conditions for claiming benefit."
(Department of Employment, cited Employment Gazette, Jan. 1991)

During the period that the Conservatives have been in office, there have been about 30 changes in the way unemployment is measured which together have substantially reduced the official total (see table 11.5). Thus, unemployed men over 60 have been re-classified as retired. Other groups not included in the official figures are those out of work who do not claim benefit, and those on government training schemes. The Unemployment Unit argues that compared to the old basis of calculation, the official figures underestimate unemployment by about one million (1991). Others claim that overall official figures probably overestimate

unemployment. Thus, the voluntarily early retired who may have no intention of taking employment can appear in the figures.

EXPERIENCING UNEMPLOYMENT Probably all commentators on unemployment recognise that it is a complex phenomenon. Crudely, it is not the same for everyone. However, there is still a difference, at least in emphasis, between those who generally see unemployment as a social evil and those who consider that its impact may vary greatly from group to group and from individual to individual. We will refer to the former as universalists and the latter as relativists.

Andrew Sinfield may be counted among the universalists in that he points out that historically unemployment has tended to hit hardest those least able to cope with it:

It is important to emphasise that the most likely to be unemployed are people in low-paying and insecure jobs, the very young and the oldest in the labour force, people from ethnic or racial minorities, people from among the disabled and the handicapped, and generally those with

	Change	Estimated alteration
1986		
*Two week delay introduced into announcement of statistics		−50,000
New method of calculating unemployment %		−1.4%
Abolition of part-rate unemployment benefit		−30,000
Voluntary unemployment disqualification extended to 13 weeks		−9,000
Restart and availability for work tests toughened		−300,000
1988		
Voluntary unemployment disqualification extended to 26 weeks		−12,000
Definition of part-time work toughened		No estimate
New denominator used to calculate 5 unemployment		No estimate
*16 and 17 year olds barred from benefit		−120,000 (−90,000)
Unemployment benefit contributions tests toughened		−38,000
Some 55–60 year olds paid pensions instead of benefits		−30,000
1989		
*Ex-miners not required to register		−26,000 (−15500)
Claimants required to prove they are looking for work		−25,000
Low wage levels no longer good reason for refusing a job		−25,000
Tightening of regulations to requalify for benefit		−350
Change to the way earnings affect right to benefit		−30,000

*Employment department agree change in counting methods alter unemployment figures. Department figures in brackets

Source: The Unemployment Unit, (The Times., Friday April 19, 1991:2)

Table 11.5

Changes in

unemployment

counting methods

between 1986–89

Table 11.6

Unemployed

claimants: by duration,

sex and age, 1989

the least skills and living in the most depressed areas. Unemployment strikes, and strikes most harshly and frequently, those who are among the poorest and least powerful in the labour force and in society as a whole.

(Sinfield, 1981)

More relativistic approaches to unemployment stress that a variety of individuals in a variety of situations become unemployed. Thus, the type of job a person does, marital status (including whether there are dependents), and age may affect the experience of unemployment. Ken Roberts highlights the age and dependents factors in the following quotation:

... spells on the dole appear far less devastating for school leavers than working class adults with family responsibilities, like life-long steelmen and dockers, who have anchored their identities in these occupations.

(Roberts, 1982)

Long term unemployment correlates strongly with age as table 11.6 shows. In the case of males the percentage of the unemployed who have been out of work over 104 up to 156 weeks rises with each age group until that of 60 and over. The pattern is similar if slightly less consistent for women. In particular, generally fewer are

United Kingdom   **Percentages and thousands**

	Duration of unemployment (percentages)						
	Up to 13 weeks	Over 13 up to 26 weeks	Over 26 up to 52 weeks	Over 52 up to 104 weeks	Over 104 up to 156 weeks	Total Over 156 weeks	(=100%) (thousands)
Males aged:							
16[1]–19	46.6	20.1	20.2	8.7	3.5	0.9	85.0
20–24	37.5	16.9	20.3	14.0	4.7	6.6	255.2
25–34	27.1	15.9	18.7	14.7	6.3	17.3	338.7
35–49	22.0	13.3	15.3	13.4	6.9	29.0	306.4
50–59	13.4	9.0	12.1	12.7	10.8	42.0	244.3
60 and over	26.5	19.0	31.6	11.2	2.6	9.1	32.1
All males aged 16 and over	26.6	14.5	17.4	13.4	6.7	21.4	1,261.6
Females aged:							
16[1]–19	49.7	18.8	19.3	7.7	3.6	0.9	54.3
20–24	45.3	16.4	19.0	10.4	3.3	5.6	127.4
25–34	34.0	19.6	25.0	11.3	2.9	7.1	128.8
35–49	30.1	16.6	19.5	14.6	9.6	36.7	89.1
50 and over	15.0	10.1	14.0	14.6	9.6	36.7	89.1
All females aged 16 and over	34.3	16.4	19.8	12.0	4.9	12.6	509.8

[1] at July. (Source: Social trends 1990)

unemployed between ages 25 and 34 because they are more likely to be out of the employment market.

In general, unemployment becomes progressively more likely from the 'top' to the 'bottom' of the occupational scale (see table 11.7). However, there are variations within and between each sex. Male professionals/employers and managers are a slightly smaller percentage of the unemployed than intermediate/junior non manual and skilled and semi-skilled/unskilled manual also make up roughly the same percentage.

In contrast, in the case of females, 85 per cent of unemployment (1988), is concentrated in the intermediate/junior non-manual (48 per cent) and semi-skilled/ unskilled manual (36 per cent). These figures vividly reflect the concentration of women in jobs of lower socio-economic status.

As employment becomes increasingly concentrated in the service sector, it is inevitable that relatively more employees in the service sector than in the manufacturing sector will be unemployed. This trend was particularly apparent in the recession of the early nineteen nineties. One indicator of this was that in early 1991 over half the reduction in vacancies at Job Centres was in managerial, clerical and service sector jobs – indicating a sharp contraction in these areas.

Great Britain						Percentages
	Male		Female		All	
	1984	1988	1984	1988	1984	1988
Socio-economic group[1] Professional/employers and managers	9	10	6	6	8	8
Intermediate/junior non-manual	10	13	47	48	24	27
Skilled manual	41	39	8	9	29	27
Semi skilled/unskilled manual	39	39	39	36	39	38

[1] Those who did not know or inadequately explained their status prior to unemployment; armed forces; those who have never been in employment or have been unemployed for 3 years or more are excluded from the percentage.

(Source: Labour Force Survey, Department of Employment).

▲

Table 11.7

The unemployed: by sex and socio-economic group, 1984 and 1988

Industrial Interest Groups and Conflict

Industrial interest groups are formal organisations concerned with the interests of their members. There are two broad types, employers' associations and, for employees, trade unions and professional associations. In practice, employees make much more use of formal interest group organisations than employers. This is partly because employers are supposed to be in competition with each other, and indeed the law discourages cooperation that might restrain trade or raise prices artificially. It is also because it is often easier and more convenient for employers to consult informally and in private. Both employers and trade unions are represented by national bodies, the Confederation of British Industry (CBI) and Trades Union Congress (TUC) respectively.

THE GROWTH AND 'RETREAT' OF UNIONISM

Whilst union membership grew from 7.83 million in 1945 to a peak of 13.4 million in 1979, it was only just over 10 million in 1990. The number of unions has declined from 186 unions affiliated to the TUC in 1951, to less than 80 in 1991. As Jenkins and Sherman point out this trend to 'concentration and enlargement' matches the same process in industry itself.

The traditional and still the main purpose of trade unions is to protect and improve the pay and working conditions of their members. Issues of job security, participation in management and even environmental and social policy issues can also fall within their range of concern.

THE GROWTH OF UNIONISM TO 1979 Apart from the recessionary nineteen twenties and early thirties, union membership grew steadily throughout the twentieth century from two million in 1900 to over six times that figure in 1979. The reasons for this were straightforward enough: unions provided a means of negotiating and protecting pay and conditions for workers and the legislative framework was favourable to their growth.

In retrospect, the nineteen sixties and seventies appear to have been the heyday of union power (though matters could change again). In the corporate economy of Harold Wilson, top union officials often worked alongside government and business leaders in the decision making process, particularly in economic and industrial policy but also in social policy. The social contract between the TUC and the Callaghan government (1976–1979) involved an agreement by the unions to exercise industrial restraint in return for improved social programmes. Its breakup presaged a long period of Conservative government.

For most of the nineteen sixties and seventies business seemed quite ready to accept and cooperate with a powerful union movement. No doubt some saw this as simply an unfortunate necessity but others considered that a degree of partnership and shared responsibility was a sound basis on which to run British industry. It was often easier to deal with established union leaders than more directly with the sometimes more radical demands of shopfloor workers. In particular, employers sought to by-pass the powerful grassroots shopstewards movement by negotiating with higher level officials. Generally, larger employers readily accepted the closed shop (i.e. where union membership is made compulsory for all employees) – again, because this seemed to facilitate management and especially the negotiating process.

The shift in the British economy from the manufacturing to the service sector would have brought about a decline in overall union membership much earlier than 1980 had it not been for the rise of white collar unionism in the nineteen sixties and seventies. For instance, during these decades membership of the mainly white collar National Union of Public Employees and Civil and Public Services Association rapidly increased while that of the National Union of Miners and National Union of Railwaymen rapidly declined. However, between 1979 and 1987, the period of the first two Thatcher admini-strations, membership of all these four unions rapidly declined although some whitecollar unions did manage to continue membership expansion during the nineteen eighties.

The 'Retreat' of Unionism, 1979–? There was just over a 3 million drop in union membership between 1979 and 1988. Union density (the percentage of the workforce unionised) also dropped from over 50 per cent in 1979 to under 40 per cent in 1988.

Is the 'retreat' of unionism during the nineteen eighties likely to continue or can it be reversed? The opinions of commentators vary on this issue. J Kelly argues that the unions coped well with the recession of the early nineteen eighties (1988). Union membership declined over a period of about fifteen years during the nineteen twenties and early thirties and then revived sharply. Against Kelly, it has to be pointed out that no such revival occurred during the boom of the late nineteen eighties. Moreoever, it is likely that the recession of the early nineteen nineties will have the effect of further reducing union membership. In 1990, more company collapses occurred than in any previous year and according to a union survey 33,000 jobs in manufacturing were lost in the first six weeks of 1991. There were also heavy job losses in the service sector during this period. This seems more like a recipe for a further setback for the trade union movement rather than a revival though Kelly, of course, could not have been aware of it.

Ken Coates and Tony Topham argue that there has not only been a numerical decline in union membership but a substantial

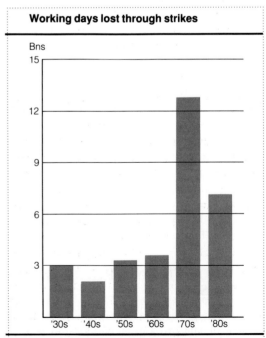

Working days lost through strikes

(Source: *The Guardian* 25th February 1991)

Figure 11.7

(Far right)

reduction in their power, influence and functions (1986). This has occurred both within the context of industrial relations in which they are now much more constrained by law and in the wider context of government policy and decision making in which, as far as Conservative governments are concerned, they are largely ignored.

It is arguable that Thatcherite employment legislation has introduced a new system of industrial relations into Britain (see p. 259). Four Employment Acts and a Trade Union Act (1984) were aimed at achieving three broad goals:

1 The closed shop was undermined and then abolished (1990) – the closed shop is a requirement at a given place of work that an employee be a union member.

2 Strike activity was restricted in a number of ways. Secondary (or supportive strike action by those not directly involved in an industrial dispute) was first restricted and then made illegal (1990). Unions became required to hold secret ballots before strike action can be taken (1984).

3 Union power has been reduced and in certain respects unions have been democratised (see 2). The 1990 Employment Act made it possible to sue unions if they fail quickly and formally to repudiate unofficial calls for strike action.

It cannot be assumed that changes in the law – even major changes such as those discussed above – can inevitably or alone cause a fundamental change in a society's system of industrial relations. It is too early to say whether the reduction in strike activity of the nineteen eighties (apart from 1984) and early nineties will prove the beginning of a new era. However, the 'retreat' of the unions does appear to be linked with long term structural changes in the economy and employment such as post-Fordist 'flexible' labour processes and 'Japanisation' of management technique (see pp. 238–41).

Richard Hyman points out that a variety of circumstances coincided with the Thatcher reforms to change the balance of power in industrial relations ('What is Happening to the Unions', *Social Studies Review*, March 1989). Most of these such as the decline in manufacturing industry, we have already discussed above. Hyman also mentions as relevant that 'the attitudes of employers have also been altering'. There has been a shift away from quasi-partnership concepts of industrial relations to notions of 'human resource management' in which employees are viewed in terms of the skills they can offer. This approach tends to be more hierarchical and directive in nature.

A shift in public opinion against the unions in the late nineteen seventies also smoothed the way for the employment legislation of the nineteen eighties. However, public opinion and socio-economic circumstances could change again. It is always dangerous to declare that a new historical epoch has commenced in any area!

Industrial Conflict: Types of Industrial Conflict

There are numerous types of industrial conflict, of varying degrees of severity. The most important is the strike. Associated with striking is picketing – trying, within the limits of law, to persuade other workers to join a strike. Another form of action often used as an alternative to the strike weapon in industrial conflict is 'working to rule'. The sit-in involves the occupation or take-over of a factory by workers and is often a reaction to large-scale redundancies or closure. It usually occurs as a last resort but sometimes leads to a positive attempt by the workers to save the factory themselves.

Another type of conflict, industrial sabotage, can occur for a variety of reasons, from personal boredom or malice to opposition to management policies or even the capitalist system in general. Minor acts of sabotage sometimes have a comical aspect which helps to release tedium and frustration, as when a distinguished foreign client was delivered a new Mercedes complete with six Coca-Cola bottles clanking deep within its bonnet. Huw Beynon tells of the response of a line worker, who was prone to absenteeism, to the question of what it felt like to come into work on a fine, bright Monday morning. The answer was that he didn't know! The implication is, of course, that the worker found better things to do than work on fine, bright Monday mornings. Certainly, children 'bunk off' school because they find it 'boring' and 'a drag'. (see Chapter four). Presumably some of 'the dads of the lads' indulge in similar practices for much the same reasons. Beynon also gives a number of examples of industrial sabotage which contain a serious message to perhaps otherwise inattentive management. Thus, workers who felt they were undermined or expected to work too quickly sometimes sabotaged cars to make their objection known. As Taylor and Walton imply, sabotage is a somewhat primitive method of communication, and it has been largely, though not entirely, superseded by trade union negotiation. Absenteeism is a form of escapism or even of rejection, rather than conflict. It mostly occurs in industries which take a severe physical and mental toll.

STRIKES

The damage that strikes do or do not do to the economy of Britain is a matter of recurrent controversy in this country. This often bitter debate is frequently conducted with only scant attention to relevant facts. The diagram on p. 254 presents some data on strikes which we can use as a basis of our own discussion.

The graph shows that the general level of strike activity in the nineteen seventies was much higher than in any period since the last war. Between the wars only the short period between 1919–22 produced a higher average level. It was the length not the number of strikes that had increased. However, the graph also puts the 'turbulent seventies' into perspective. Apart from the seventies and 1984 – the year of the miner's strike – the number of working days lost through strikes has tended to be fairly modest. The reduction both in working days lost through strikes and in work stoppages in the Thatcher years compared to the nineteen seventies, looks typical rather than exceptional in the longer perspective.

Compared with other industrialised Western societies, Britain's recent strike record is moderate rather than exceptional. Between 1968–77 the average number of working days lost in Britain was 452 per 1000 workers, compared with 1187 per 1000 in Australia, 1893 in Canada and 1500 in the United States. Some of Britain's more immediate competitors did lose markedly less: West Germany, 24; Sweden, 18 and Holland, 36.

Why, then, were the nineteen seventies such a relatively strike-prone period? W W Daniel and N Millward's Workplace and Industrial Relations in Britain (Heinemann, 1983), gives several indications. They report the findings of a survey of about 2000 workplaces of all sizes which enquired into the frequency and type of industrial action (not just strikes) in each one between mid 1979 and mid 1980. Their findings seem particularly revealing given what we now know of trends in industrial conflict, particularly strike activity, during the nineteen eighties. They found that workplaces that were unionised were more likely to take strike action than those that were not. Among unionised establishments, several factors were associated with greater strike activity: a higher proportion of union membership; a higher proportion of manual workers; a greater proportion of male workers; a greater proportion of full-time employees; and, finally, strikes were more likely to occur in establishments which were the main place of collective bargaining.

A 'stereotype' picture of the late seventies striker is, therefore, a unionised, male, full-time, manual worker. In the nineteen eighties this stereotype was in numerical decline. Union membership substantially declined, female workers increased in proportion to male workers, part-time workers increased in proportion to full-time workers, and service sector workers increased in proportion to manual workers. Given, therefore, that the type of people more likely to strike were becoming a smaller proportion of the labour-force, logically fewer strikes might be expected. This was, in fact, the tendency during the nineteen eighties and early nineties. It is true that the other factor associated with strike activity did not decrease during the nineteen eighties. Localised collective bargaining became more, not less, common but it did so in the context of a weaker union movement, higher unemployment and with the support of the Conservative government and much of management. In general, as Richard

Hyman argues, the extent to which the decline in the factors associated with strikes was the conscious result of government policy and Thatcherite ideology should not be underestimated.

In a work published in 1984 (*Strikes* third edition, Fontana), Richard Hyman divides the period from 1974 to 1983 into three 'phases' in terms of industrial relations. The first was 1974–76 – the phase of the 'Social Contract' between the Labour government and the unions – which was a time of relative cooperation and lower industrial conflict. The second was 1977–79 – a phase of increased industrial conflict ending in the notorious, strike-riven, 'winter of discontent' of 1979. The third phase 1979–?, has been what Hyman calls one of 'coercive pacification' in which the law (including its physical enforcement) and other means were used to weaken and control the unions.

It may be that as the post-Thatcher era emerges the 'coercive' aspect of this 'pacification' will become less obvious, particularly as the sobering effect of a second recession and higher unemployment tends to dampen down industrial conflict anyway.

FACTORS ASSOCIATED WITH STRIKES

The previous section will have made it clear that the factors associated with industrial conflict vary in impact and relative importance over time. At a surface level, it may seem that the economic motive – the first factor discussed below – is likely to be dominant in the majority of cases but Marxists and other conflict theorists argue that tension about control and independence (and, to that extent, alienation) at work often underlie conflict about pay and conditions.

THE ECONOMIC MOTIVE The most commonly stated motive for striking is to improve pay and this is often linked with demands to improve working conditions and reduce hours – broadly material factors. Beween 1965–74, 56.1 per cent of disputes and over 80 per cent of working days lost were the result of conflicts over pay. Most of the strikes during the so-called 'winter of discontent' of 1978–79 were mainly about pay, and were all the more intense as a result

of the previous period of voluntary wage restraint. Between 1965–74, 80 per cent of stoppages were about economic issues, and these involved 90 per cent of the days lost. Even the steelworkers strike of 1980 was superficially about pay; relatively little was said about the British Steel Corporation's plan to reduce its workforce by approximately a third over a period of years – a strategy that might have been expected to result in industrial action. Sometimes strikes also concern working conditions or other matters affecting workers' welfare. The miners threatened to strike in early 1977 if the National Coal Board refused to implement early retirement plans for them.

Two key strikes of the mid nineteen eighties – the miner's strike of 1984 and the teachers strike of 1985 – were partly about pay but illustrate the frequent complexity of major strikes. Some of the leadership in both cases was motivated by political opposition to the government and again in both occupations there was widespread concern that government plans involved a decrease in security and autonomy at work.

STRUCTURAL CONFLICT BETWEEN CAPITAL AND LABOUR Conflict theorists argue that there is a 'in-built' conflict between capital and labour. Hyman makes the general point: the confrontation within the workplace of two bases of control provides a constant source of instability and conflict.

Given that owners and management on the one hand and the labour force on the other want as large a share as possible of the profit of their mutual toil, disagreement and friction is virtually inevitable. Even the most optimistic personnel manager would hardly expect to do more than 'regulate' it in the context of modern large-scale industry. It is because they too see a day-to-day conflict of interest between capital and labour, that Lane and Roberts claim that strikes should be seen as 'normal' rather than labelled a 'problem' (once the public is presented with a 'problem' the next stage is often to look for the 'culprit' – not the most fruitful approach in industrial relations).

Marxists see a final solution to class conflict in industry only in the introduction of a socialist society. Others see a functional need to make the capitalist system operate more effectively. Thus, human relations theorists, Scott and Homans, argue that better communications between management and workers – for instance, through trained personnel managers – can provide a more constructive atmosphere and reduce disruption. Marxists consider this approach to be biased towards management and manipulative of workers. At worst it passes off deep problems of structural conflict and exploitation as personal or even psychological difficulties.

UNDERLYING ISSUES OF CONTROL AND INDEPENDENCE Alvin Gouldner's *Wildcat Strike* (1957) finds that a strike for higher wages was just one event in a long chain of conflict between workers and management. The conflict stemmed from a change in management at the plant. Traditionally, worker-management relations were informal, friendly and based on trust. The new manager, an outsider, introduced new machinery and attempted to 'rationalise' the administration of the plant. This limited the independence and offended the pride of the workers, particularly the miners. The relationship between workers and management was redefined in terms of conflicting interests, rather than a sense of mutual understanding and interest. It was in this context that the wildcat strike 'for higher wages' occurred, but to see it simply in terms of money would be sociologically unsubtle.

The argument that some strikes are about control and independence in the workplace is compatible with the Marxist view that there is a fundamental conflict between capital and labour in which labour is alienated – whether it knows it or not. However, relatively few strikes are overtly political (to some extent the first half of the eighties was an exception – see below). It is possible to accept Gouldner's point without agreeing with broader Marxist analysis.

MULTIPLE MOTIVATIONS FOR STRIKES: WORKERS' MEANINGS The major stated motive for strikes is the economic one. We have also suggested a range of other important contributory factors. As Hyman points out, however, it is a false dichotomy to assume that the causes of a given dispute must be either economic or non-economic. He adds that the relative importance of the various causes that contribute to the start of a strike may change as it goes on, and new

reasons for continuing it may appear. The sheet determination 'not to lose' may increase as a strike goes on. Lane and Roberts point out that strikes can snow-ball. New grievances may become apparent as the strike continues and support may come from the previously uncommitted at the prospect of a good settlement. As the interactionist Silverman succinctly puts it, industrial relations must be seen as a changing process and not merely in structural terms. We must also reiterate that the broad social, political and legal structure within which a strike occurs (or is prevented from occurring) is of fundamental importance in comparing the strike profiles of different countries.

Hyman is emphatic that there is no single, over-arching explanation for strikes in general. He points out that the strike records of firms in the same industry using the same technology can vary greatly. This is true of the steel industry which has a militant history in South Wales and a harmonious one in North-East England. He refers ultimately to historical accident, cultural variation and the particular meanings different employees attach to similar circumstances to 'explain' the varied and impredictable pattern of strike activity.

CAUSES RELATED TO SPECIFIC INDUSTRIES: HEAVY INDUSTRY; TECHNOLOGY; COMMUNITY So far, we have talked about the general causes of strikes. The extent to which strikes occur, however, varies between industries (as well as between societies). We now attempt to account for variations within different industries. James Cronin found that highly unionised workers in industries crucial to the national economy, which tend to use incentive schemes to increase production, and which are subject to economic fluctuation, tend to be prone to strike. A nineteen seventies study showed that, on average, miners, dockers, car workers, shipbuilders and iron and steel workers accounted for a quarter of strikes and a third of working days lost, even though they only cover about six per cent of employees. However, these industries now represent a much smaller proportion of the labour force and in the second half of the nineteen eighties white collar employees such as teachers and nurses were relatively more likely to be involved in strike activity.

On the basis of her study of a variety of production systems, Woodward has argued that 'the face of industrial relations ... seemed to be closely related to ... technology' (*Management and Technology*, HMSO 1958). Again, this relates particularly to heavy industry such as car manufacture and steel production. However, Hyman and, more recently Woodward herself, have argued that technology is only one factor of varying relevance in explaining strike activity (Hyman, 1984). There is considerable international variation in strike activity in both the car and steel industries.

Large-scale industries in areas with strong working class communities are or were particularly associated with strike activity. Union strength and militancy and class solidarity are often the norm in such occupational communities. In some respects, however, this picture of the typical strike-prone industry is out of date. Firstly, these kinds of communities are now in decline, and some of the workers involved in these industries conform more closely to the 'privatised' pattern of living observed by Goldthorpe and Lockwood, rather than the more open community life-style of the traditional working class. Secondly, as we have already discussed, strike activity now occurs more widely across a variety of occupational groups although overall activity is currently at a lower rate than in the nineteen seventies.

STRIKES AS 'NORMAL' Roberts and Lane argue that strike activity is a normal part of industrial relations – even where those relations are generally good (1971). In their own case study of a strike at Pilkington's glassworks, they found that a strike occurred at the end of a period of quite good industrial relations in which most workers expressed no major grievances about pay or other matters. A strike also occurred in similar circumstances at the Vauxhall car assembly-line plant at Luton shortly after Goldthorpe and Lockwood completed their 'affluent worker' study. Lane and Roberts conclude that strikes should be regarded as 'normal', in the sense that they are an accepted 'weapon' in the bargaining process between management and labour.

Tom Keenoy adopts and extends the argument that strikes are a normal part of the bargaining process in his *Invitation to Industrial Relations* (Blackwell, 1985). In doing so, he seeks to refute 'the myth' of trade unionists as industrial spoilers and points out that management itself can sometimes be responsible for a strike.

COMPARATIVE INDUSTRIAL RELATIONS SYSTEMS ANALYSIS: THE 'THATCHER' SYSTEM We will conclude this consideration of the causes of strikes with a comparison of the British system of Industrial relations under Mrs Thatcher with that of some other European countries. Although industrial relations systems analysis particularly reflects the sociological perspective of Talcott Parsons, its basic principles are more generally applicable, and need not embody his own conservative values. This approach links the particular factory or industry to the wider society. Strikes are seen in the context of the total national system of industrial relations, including workers and unions; management and government agencies especially concerned with the work place; the work community and, finally, the tradition of industrial relations in a given society. Industrial law is an important part of the 'environment' of industrial relations in most advanced countries and has often been a cause of dispute between labour and government in Britain. In the space of two years, between 1969 and 1971, both major parties attempted to introduce substantial legal changes in the position of the unions. Both failed, mainly because of the strength and effectiveness of union opposition.

Between 1980 and 1990, the legal framework of industrial relations in Britain was radically changed. Mrs Thatcher came to government in 1979, following a period of substantial strike activity and with the clear intention of curbing union power (see p. 255 for development of this issue). Whether Britain's previously largely collectivist system of industrial relations has been replaced by a largely individualistic one remains to be seen.

Germany's extensive legal framework of codetermined (i.e. between capital and employees) industrial relations appears to have contributed to the greater industrial harmony experienced there in the post-war period than in Britain. Germany's system is both more participatory and more protective in relation to workers. In the old Soviet Union, despite some economic liberalisation, industrial 'harmony' was mainly achieved by legal compulsion – a generally unpopular means in the West. Theirs was a system of industrial relations in which power was concentrated in the Government's hands. The opposite approach would be to adopt a system of real industrial democracy, that is, union participation or control. We consider this option in the next chapter (pp. 280–3), and that section canbe regarded as a continuation of this discussion.

The Professions

The expansion of professions is a further feature of the growth of the service sector characteristic of modern societies. In addition to managers and administrators, professionals make up a large proportion of what Halsey refers to as the 'service class'. Higher professionals include lawyers, scientists, engineers, doctors and dentists. Their market position is significantly stronger than that of lower professionals such as teachers, social workers and nurses and this shows in the much higher salaries they tend to command. Most lower professionals work for the government. Among higher professionals, private practice is becoming more rare and employment in the service of industry or the government increasingly common. This change in the market position of professionals has increased the possibility of conflict with other groups.

Until quite recently, sociological writings on the professions tended to assume both their high social status and that the contribution or 'service' of professionals to the community was qualitatively superior to that of 'lower' status workers. Marxists are an exception to this, as they have always placed the highest value on manual labour. Current analysis of the professions is much more inclined to use the concept of conflict in interpreting their relationship to society. This is apparent in two main ways. First, no necessary 'community of interest' is assumed between client and professional. On the contrary, their interests tend to be seen to be in structural conflict, regardless of the 'goodwill' of individual professionals. Secondly, because most professionals are now paid employees, their relationship to their employers is also regarded as a potential source of conflict similar to that experienced by other employees. Both are part of the general process by which work has become increasingly bureaucratised.

THE FUNCTIONALIST APPROACH AND 'TRAIT' ANALYSIS APPROACH

The work of functionalists such as Bernard Barber and Talcott Parsons, typifies traditional sociological analysis of the professions. Quite simply, this perspective sees the professions as fulfilling useful social functions. They provide necessary medical, legal, architectural or religious advice and service based on specialised knowledge and competence. The key attribute of professions is considered to be a primary commitment to community rather than self-interest. Terence Johnson distinguishes between functionalist analysis of professions and 'trait' analysis though the two approaches are highly compatible. 'Trait' analysis is based on an attempt to list the basic characteristics of professions. 'Trait' analysis has proved to be something of a blind alley. On the basis of his own survey of the relevant literature, Millerson points out that no two authorities agree precisely on what the basic traits of a profession are. The following, however, are frequently mentioned: professional authority (over the 'layman'); the sanction by the community of the power and privilege of professionals; the confidential nature of the professional client relationship; a code of ethics (rules) regulating the profession; a theory of knowledge underlying the practice of the profession (such as medical research/ theory); and the existence of a professional culture. A professional culture involves broad consensus about how to behave as a professional, and is said to be passed on to new recruits. Even today, barristers can still participate in a quite ritualised common culture.

The 'trait' approach is so uncritical of official professional ideology (the views professionals hold of themselves) that it is almost 'pre-sociological'. Client response is assumed automatically to 'fit in' with the expert's view and the possibility of conflict between professionals and other individuals and groups is unexplored. The functionalist approach is hardly more sophisticated. Johnson charges that they do not examine the historical development of professions and so fail to appreciate that professional practice is deeply involved with power relations in society, including those based mainly on money. Consistently enough, he illustrates his argument by reference to various historical stages in the development of professions, and in particular stresses changes in the professional-client relationship. In the sixteenth and seventeenth centuries, professionals were typically answerable to wealthy patrons. The professional's freedom was limited by this dependence and he certainly did not serve the majority of the community. Industrial-isation changed the status of the professions. Their members and independence increased. The technical expertise of, for instance, engineers and specialist lawyers, was formidable and professionals achieved new status and power. Leading professions were able to persuade the general public of their own ideology – their own assessment of their skill and importance. It was at this time that professions developed into self-regulating organisations which were able to control their specialist areas of work, including the standard of entry to them. Control of entry enabled them to regulate the supply and therefore the price of professional services. Obviously, this was a very desirable position for professionals to be in. Medieval craftsmen similarly attempted to regulate occupational entry and the supply and price of services. No doubt members of most occupations would wish to do the same. The difference between professions and other occupations is that they have succeeded in convincing the public of their special skills and importance and of their need for corresponding privileges, whereas others have not.

NEO-WEBERIAN PERSPECTIVE ON THE PROFESSIONS

The common theme of much recent neo-Weberian analysis of the professions is that they organise and operate primarily on the basis of self-interest largely by controlling their own market position. Thus, professions are seen as seeking to control entry, public access to services, and, especially, the price of services. Frank Parkin (1979) and Parry and Parry (1977) exemplify this approach.

Parkin employs the concept of 'closure' to describe how professional group self-interest operates. There are two main types of closure: usurpation and exclusion. Usurpation involves taking power from a dominant group and exclusion involves preventing lower status groups from accessing one's own position. It is the concept of exclusion that Parkin applies to professions. They achieve exclusion mainly by 'credentialism' which controls entry. Credentialism is the requirement of a period of training and assessment which, if successful, results in certification. Interestingly, in 1990, the government made a limited attempt to by-pass the usual qualificatory route for teachers by introducing a licensed teachers scheme which allowed certain candidates for teaching to train in schools rather than in higher education.

Noel and José Parry regard a profession as an occupational group which has successfully established control in the market for the services it produces. It is characterised by a self-governing association of formally equal colleagues which controls recruitment, regulates professional conduct, and determines who can practice. On this basis, they regard medicine as a profession but not teaching. Teachers are seen both as having less occupational autonomy and as less able to command a high level of reward than doctors. In the fifteen or so years since the Parry's published, substantial differences in power (of self-regulation), status and rewards between doctors and teachers have remained. However, the National Health Service, including doctors as well as the teaching 'profession' has been subject to considerable change by government including a new, centrally proscribed managerial regime. It can be argued that in a day-to-day operational context, NHS doctors have lost some autonomy.

Some neo-Weberians specifically relate the ability to maintain exclusive professional control to the knowledge and technical base of professional work. Thus, Johnson argues that, for instance, lawyers and doctors are in a better position than clients to define what clients 'need' and how best their needs can be met. Unsurprisingly, professional closure both in terms of other groups and other knowledge does not go unchallenged.

COMMENT ON NEO-WEBERIAN PERSPEC-
TIVE Neo-Weberians fully recognise that professional control is open to challenge. However, they may somewhat exaggerate the extent to which the higher professions have achieved independence. The main sources of pressure and alternative bases of control are the public, including clients, management, government and business.

Ivan Illich is a celebrated champion of the client and critic of 'professionalised knowledge'. He considers that often professional ideology functions primarily in the interests of professionals despite its supposed concern with standards and quality of service. He reacts against the wrapping up of knowledge in parcels labelled 'expert' because this produces a passive and even timid attitude to learning and makes the client unnecessarily dependent on the professional. He believes in as much open access to information as possible whether it be about medicine, the law or whatever. Underlying his suggestions is a belief that education, formal and informal, should be an active process in which the teacher or expert advises rather than dictates, participates rather than controls.

There has been an increase in public interest in finding alternative routes to meeting needs than those supplied by professionals. Thus, there are 'simple' kits available to do one's own conveyancing and a range of alternative approaches to medicine (see p. 379). Stewart Clegg and David Dunkerly suggest that organisational and technical developments have reduced the authority and exclusivity of professionals:

Increasing standardisation has taken place in the legal and accounting professions. The popularity of 'do-it-yourself' house purchase and divorce is evidence of such routinisation; accountancy, largely through the effects of computers, has become more and more codified, standardised and routinised. In other words, not only clerical work but professional activities as well appear to be subject to an increasing division of labour characterised by routinisation.
(Clegg and Dunkerly, 1980: 363)

Weber left relatively unexplored the relationship between professionals and managers. This relationship frequently occurs when professionals are employed either by the state, such as town-planners, or by business, such as lawyers, accountants, scientists and engineers.

The professional in this situation loses the freedom associated with independent practice and, sometimes, the opportunity to employ a broad range of expertise. S/he tends to do highly specialised work (in a sub-branch of law or accountancy) and, although professional judgement is usually accepted within a limited area, has to submit to the overall authority of management. In general, professionals are better qualified than management but have less authority within organisations. As Burns and Stalker point out, some managers deal with this situation by adopting more flexible, open-ended and democratic modes of decision-making. They use the term 'organic' to describe this tendency. A large-scale empirical study of the same issue led Peter Blau to conclude that this is, indeed, often the approach taken by management who have well qualified professionals on their staff. As Etzioni points out, however, professional and management functions are different, and the possibility of conflict cannot be entirely removed. In ideal-type terms, professionals make recommendations on the basis of what seems 'right' by professional principles, whereas managers look for solutions that 'work' in terms of the rules and goals of the organisation.

A body of legislation passed during the nineteen eighties changed the relationship between management and professionals in education, including higher education. For instance, the collegiate (collective professional) power of academics in the running of higher educational institutions tended to be reduced while that of managers, reflecting government legislation and goals, increased. Thus, management was required to ensure the introduction of plans for appraisal and performance related pay – subject to the government withholding part of the annual salary award to academics.

MARXIST PERSPECTIVE ON THE PROFESSIONS

Whereas Weberians commence analysis with the market position of professionals, Marxists start with their relation to the means of production. It is the relationship to, and functioning within, the total class structure of the professions that Marxists are primarily interested in.

Marxist analysis of managerial, administrative and professional groups, unlike Weberian, does not present these groups as rather independent, would-be self-determining groups. On the contrary, they are typically seen as occupying an ambiguous class position. This perspective is partly the product of the general Marxist framework of class analysis which presents all classes in relation to the capitalist/working class polarity. We have already seen that the very top individuals in these groups – roughly, those wealthy enough to make substantial independent investments in the companies with which they are associated – are generally considered by Marxists as part of the (ruling) upper class. Otherwise, both Eric Olin Wright and Harry Braverman locate these occupational groups within a contradictory class location between the bourgeoisie and the proleteriat. This means that they have certain characteristics in common with capitalists and others in common with the working class. Examples of the former are greater independence and status at work and, often, authority over others. Examples of the latter are that many have to 'sell' their labour either to capitalists or the 'capitalist state' and, in Marxists terms, are therefore in an alienating situation.

It is particularly in respect to the functions they perform for the capitalist system that Marxists see managerial, administrative and professional employees as close to the capitalist class. These include legal and financial functions, and also managerial and administrative functions in relation to the work force. Thus, Vicente Navarro considers that the National Health Service in advanced capitalist societies is a ruling class dominated sector within which management and professionals carry out the task of servicing working class people who have been physically and mentally undermined by life in capitalist society (p. 395). Similarly, Marxists such as Althusser argue that teachers function largely as agents of social control and as reproducers of the class system. In contradiction to Parkin's neo-Weberian view of the professions as quasi-autonomous, Marxists tend to see them as agencies of capitalism functioning within the overall structure of the capitalist system.

Braverman's 'deskilling' and 'proletarianisation' thesis, discussed earlier (pp. 246–8), is relevant to our consideration of the functioning of professions and their place within the class structure. Braverman argues that as professionals are increasingly brought into the service of the capitalist state and business, so their work is increasingly organised and routinised by capitalist management. The need of capitalism for efficient professional service both through the state (e.g. education and training) and within business corporations (e.g. efficient accounting and legal advice) means that professionals are in a working context in which the demands of capital dominate. Professional independence tends to be eroded in the face of targets, deadlines and delivery patterns stipulated by management. Thus, scientific research in industry is routinely driven by a company's practical and competitive needs and within education, courses are increasingly assessed on the basis of 'skills' (some of which are suggested or even stipulated by industry) rather than on the basis of subject content.

Barbara and John Ehrenreich (1979) also consider that professionals contribute to the functioning of capitalism, but argue that they occupy a distinct upper middle class position rather than a 'contradictory' position between capital and labour. The Ehrenreichs classify professionals alongside management in a professional-managerial class whose main function is to reproduce capitalist culture and facilitate (or manage) class relations. This analysis of the functioning of professionals is not dissimilar to that of other Marxists, such as Althusser, but the Ehrenreich's are unusual in allocating a specific class location to them.

Work and Non-Work

The division of existence into work and non-work time is very basic. However, these are better categories than work and leisure because much non-work time may be devoted to activities other than leisure. A number of attempts to develop the work/non-work categorisation have been made. Stanley Parker (1976) makes the following divisions: work; work obligations; existence time; non-work obligations; and leisure.

Parker defines work as earning a living – broadly, employment. Work obligations include activities done outside normal working hours which are associated with the job but beyond what is necessary to achieve a minimum level of performance; voluntary overtime and second jobs. The remaining three categories are, to a progressive extent, leisure categories. The third category, existence time, is the satisfaction of physiological needs such as 'sleep, eating, washing, eliminating'. Non-work obligations refers mainly to domestic duties. Finally, leisure is 'time free from obligations either to self or to others – time to do as one chooses'.

Elias and Dunning's categorisation of work/non-work can be matched fairly closely with Parker's scheme: private work and family management; rest; catering for biological needs; sociability; and 'mimetic' or play activities.

These types of categorisations are useful when considering the lives of males in full-time employment. They give a fair sense of the daily experience of necessity and pleasure. However, they are inadequate for understanding the work/non-work experience of those mainly involved in domestic labour, still overwhelmingly women. Sue McIntosh and her colleagues have criticised Parker sharply on this point. She takes each of Parker's categories in turn and shows their inadequacy when applied to housewives. First, she points out that in defining work as 'activity involved in earning a living', women in full-time housework are automatically excluded from Parker's framework. She observes that the work (domestic) activities of the housewife tend to overlap with and undermine the quality of her leisure. She gives a contemporary, feminist's slant to the old saying 'A woman's work is never done'. Again, she describes the distinction Parker makes in his category work

and work obligations as 'fairly meaningless' for housewives. McIntosh's comment on the functions of existence time – eating, excretion, etc. – is that housewives often help others meet them – work, indeed! On the fourth category, 'the domestic part of work obligations', she observes that this is a large part of her total work in the home. She asks, 'Is women's work therefore to be equated with male "semi-leisure"?' About leisure itself, she states, 'Women have very little of this time.' Even the time a woman has may be defined by the choices her husband makes and she may be deterred from doing things on her own because of his possessiveness.

McIntosh, then, presents a typical work-leisure model of the housewife. The central feature of it is that domestic activity or concern virtually never ceases: there are few total 'escapes' into leisure, little real 'free time'. She pointedly raises the question of how women can gain more genuine leisure time and we will return to this later.

There are other variables besides gender which Parker's model does not adequately encompass. These include age, unemployment and race/ethnicity. Parker's view that work is the major influence on leisure is also of limited usefulness when applied to groups not in full-time work. In fairness, however, we ought to consider the group to which Parker's model best applies: people in full-time employment (mainly males).

Before presenting his own theory of work and leisure, Parker reviews existing work in the field. He classifies this into two schools of thought, segmentalists and holists. The former believe that work is separated from leisure and the latter that there is a tendency towards a fusion of work and leisure. Parker suggests that both approaches are too generalised and selective in their use of evidence. His own survey data found that both perspectives were relevant in relation to different, specific occupations. Consequently elements of these approaches appear in his own categorisation of the typical ways in which people relate their work and leisure:

1 the extension (holist) pattern;
2 the neutrality pattern;
3 the opposition (segmentalist) pattern.

According to Parker:

1 The extension pattern consists of having leisure activities that are often similar in content to one's working activities, making no distinction between what is considered work and what is considered leisure, and having one's central life interest in work rather than in family or leisure spheres.

He gives as examples of occupations in which this pattern is most likely to occur: 'successful businessmen, doctors, teachers, some skilled manual workers and social workers'.

Parker's observation about successful businessmen finds support from Young and Willmott's data on the work and family life of 190 managing directors. Work tended to dominate their lives and even leisure activities were shared with (usually) male business associates rather than with their families. Given the mainly instrumental attitude of many middle and lower level employees to their work, it is doubtful whether this pattern will diffuse down through the occupational system as Young and Willmott thought it might. However, it is worth speculating that as a result of the increase in high income earners in both Britain and the United States in the first half of the nineteen eighties, the extension pattern may become more common among higher social groups. Against this is the trend for more high income families to depend on a double income (indeed, particularly in the United States, children at school or college also often work part-time and thus add to the total income). Where women contribute substantially to the family income, they may be less willing to take total responsibility for the domestic side or to 'lose' their husbands to work and work-oriented pursuits to the same extent.

2 Parker describes the neutrality pattern as having leisure activities that are somewhat different from work, making a distinction between work and leisure, and having one's central life interest in family or leisure rather than in the work sphere.

He gives the following occupations as typically associated with this pattern: 'clerical workers, semi-skilled manual workers, and minor professionals other than social workers'. These occupations offer only low or medium autonomy at work, limited intrinsic satisfaction, but provide substantial leisure time for relaxation.

3 Opposition pattern leisure activities involve a sharp demarcation between work and leisure, and central life interest in the non-work sphere.

This pattern is 'to some extent exhibited by routine clerical workers' but 'seems more typical of unskilled manual workers, and those occupations such as mining and distant-water fishing'. The associated work factors are instrumental motivation, low autonomy in the work situation, limited opportunities for expression of abilities, and alienative attitudes.

Parker's analysis of the opposition pattern is based largely on two studies of extreme occupations: Denis, Henriques and Slaughter's Coal is our life (1956) and Jeremy Tunstall's (1962) The fishermen. For workers in these occupations leisure is recuperative and even escapist. Heavy drinking helps obliterate memories of harsh work and lowers inhibitions. Pleasure takes the form of release of pent-up energy in fun and macho fooling about and fantasy.

It is interesting to apply Abraham Maslow's model of human needs (see p. 249 to Parker's analysis. Only those working in occupations associated with the extension pattern appear to have jobs which will greatly engage them in the process of self-actualisation (the achievement and expression of their highest needs). The neutrality and opposition patterns are associated with jobs unlikely to meet more than certain deficit needs. Some might provide such low status and public recognition that they might not even fully meet the need for self-esteem. Further, some work appears either so exhausting or intellectually blunting as to make the achievement of high levels of self-expression in leisure unlikely.

This trend of thought easily reconciles with Marxist analysis of the alienating nature of wage labour in capitalist society. Marx argued that the worker in capitalist society is alienated from her/himself and her/his species (human) being. In Maslow's terms her/his human potential is frustrated. However, Parker does not link his analysis of work and leisure to a critique of capitalism and Marxists would regard this as a criticism of his work. For them, both the production and consumption of leisure goods and services are alienated under capitalism. In particular, Bero Rigauer argues that the professional production of sport fragments and bureaucratises the experience of participants just as industrial production does that of workers. Similarly, the audience for commercialised sport may be distracted both from their exploitation and from a more active expression and development of their own talents – including, sometimes, sporting.

THE FUTURE OF WORK AND LEISURE

Technological progress has not yet 'liberated' people from work and introduced the 'new age of leisure' some had predicted. Of course, most people do have much more leisure time than they did 150 years ago but not very much more than they did 50 years ago. Work, paid and/or domestic still dominates the weekdays of the majority of adults aged 16–65 and still provides most of them with their core identity. It is as though we have looked at the possibility of a world dominated by leisure and turned back from it. At times it seems as though technology – household, office, business – drives us rather than we it. Perhaps we like it that way – preferring the familiar and secure rhythm of work to vistas of leisure time. Filling that time might require creativity, imagination and effort. At a practical level, as long as money is distributed primarily through work people will be highly motivated to compete against each other economically. Yet, the wealth to provide a basis for human fulfilment, as Marx and Maslow envisaged it, is increasingly available.

SUMMARY

1   The British economy is increasingly influenced by global factors. The flow of investment, already becoming more international, became rapidly more so after the deregulation of the stock market in 1986. Increasingly, the fate of British firms and employees is affected by wider factors.

2   Piore and Sabel (1984) argue that capitalist firms have moved from a Fordist to post-Fordist model of production in which labour and technology are used more flexibly. Among the many comments on this analysis is the Marxist observation that whether or not this adaptation has occurred, the relationship between capital and labour remains basically the same.

3   Economic and employment market changes have impacted strongly on women, ethnic minorities and the young. Details about each group are given in relevant chapters – respectively 8, 9 and 10.

4   Various attempts to theorise the experience of work are presented.

Several theories of alienation are discussed and these are contrasted with Goldthorpe and Lockwood's social action approach who find that their sample of manual workers works for instrumental (money) motives and that alienation does not greatly figure in their considerations. A discussion of the concept of fulfilment in work concludes this section.

5   Unemployment resurfaced as a major issue of the nineteen eighties and early nineteen nineties. The universalist approach – that unemployment is invariably and almost equally a disaster – is contrasted with the relativist approach which sees it as a more variable experience.

6   The growth of unionism in the nineteen fifties, sixties and seventies is explained largely in terms of the representation and protection offered to members by unions and by the positive acceptance of them by government and employers. The 'retreat' of unionism in the nineteen eighties is explained largely by recession and government policy.

7   There are a variety of types of industrial conflict of which strikes are

the main one. Factors associated with strikes vary from explanations arguing an 'in-built' conflict between capital and labour to causes related to specific industries such as those experiencing difficult and dirty working conditions. Some strike activity may be regarded as 'normal'.

8   There are three main approaches to analysing the professions. 'Trait' analysis presents supposed key characteristics of the professions such as service to the community and self-regulation. Neo-Weberian analysis sees the professions as motivated mainly by group-interest including a desire to 'close' others out of their rewards and status. Marxists variously place the professions within the class structure although their precise position tends to be seen as 'ambiguous'.

9   Work is contrasted to non-work because much of non-work time is not, in fact, leisure. This is especially true of people primarily involved in domestic work who rarely experience a 'five o'clock release'.

10   Stanley Parker's model of work-leisure assumes that a person's work greatly influences the nature of their leisure. Marxists tend to see capitalism as dominating the structure of both work and leisure time.

RESEARCH AND COURSEWORK

Many students have part-time jobs and 'doing research' into a place of work is a convenient possibility. However, there is a danger that such a study will be over-descriptive and anecdotal ('gossipy') and lack theoretical perspective and objective analysis. It would be better to do a well-planned study of an unfamiliar place of work than, say, a participant observational study of a familiar one that is highly participant and poorly observed.

The following are some research issues:

1 Alienation (the operationalisation/ measurement of the concept is a key problem).

2 The extent to which a particular organisation is 'post-Fordist' in character (this would require establishing criteria for assessing the extent of post-Fordism and perhaps comparing two occupational groups in the organisation to determine whether they fitted the primary/secondary labour force model.

3 An unusual project would be an examination of the industrial relations record of a particular organisation (probably over a brief historical period). It would be important to provide sociological explanations for the findings.

4 A replication of Parker's study into the relationship between work and leisure could be highly interesting. A close preliminary examination of his methodology would be required.

FURTHER READING

There is a need for collections of readings which cover current debates such as 'post-Fordism' and 'deskilling'. Two are Stephen Wood ed., *The Transformation of Work* (Unwin Hyman, 1989) and Kenneth Thompson ed., *Work: Past, Present and Future* (Open University Press, 1984). Two 'topic books' written specifically for 'A' level students are John Horne *Work and Unemployment* (Longman, 1987) and Rosemary Deem *Work, Unemployment and Leisure* (Routledge, 1988).

QUESTIONS

1 Examine either, Marx's use of the concept of 'alienation' or, Durkheim's use of the concept 'anomie'. (Oxford, 1988)

2 Examine the similarities and differences between trade unions and professional associations. Illustrate your answer with examples. (AEB 1989).

3 Assess the different sociological explanations of strikes and other forms of industrial conflict. (AEB 1990)

12 Organisations, Class & Power

Organisations are a personal issue as well as a public reality. The problem is, people often fail to see the personal importance of organisations. Students often profess boredom at the thought of studying them; yet, no topic has more to offer in the way of practical understanding. Most of us will spend our working lives with large or medium-size organisations and if we do not learn to 'manage' them, they will certainly manage us. Perhaps the feelings of alienation that many students experience at the very thought of studying organisations is a symptom of the fact that they can only conceive of being controlled and manipulated by them, and not vice-versa. This quiet desperation was given a voice by the nineteen sixties student radical, Mario Savio, when he urged fellow rebels at Berkeley, California, to stop the bureaucratic machine of the university by 'laying' their bodies on it. Partly to combat this pessimism, we will examine not only the structure and functioning of organisations but who has power and control within them, and also whether more democratic organisational systems are possible.

Both Weber and Marx were fully aware of the importance of the concepts of power and control in analysing organisation. They agreed that organisations are the instruments which 'run' modern life but disagreed about which groups had real control of them. Weber's organisational theory is linked closely to his analysis of the 'new class'. He had no doubt that top organisational officials had great power both in private industry and government departments. He anticipated the dictatorship not of the proletariat, but of the official. He felt that as bureaucracies expanded they would develop vested interests, and argued that even a democratically elected parliament would have problems in controlling top civil servants and their departments (although he believed it should try). Marx, however, contended that in capitalist society the capitalist class controls the bureaucrats and uses them for its own ends. He argued that this was true not only of the salaried officials of private industry but, ultimately, of state bureaucrats as well, because he considered that the capitalist class also controlled the state. We have already met a modern version of this argument in the work of Dahrendorf and Giddens (chapter 6, pp. 134–6) and will return again to it in this chapter.

Durkheim was not primarily interested in class control of organisations: rather, he took it for granted, as natural. He was more concerned with how a society, made up of complex organisations and characterised by an advanced division of labour, could *hold together*. As we have seen, he believed that this was possible because of organic solidarity – the interdependence of people and organisations in modern societies (see chapter 19). Durkheim's point was a general one: later sociologists have had much more specific interests in the field of the sociology of organisations than he did.

Formal and Informal Organisations: A Preliminary Distinction

Formal organisations are operated on the basis of established rules by appointed personnel, to achieve specific goals. Practically all the large organisations of modern society such as factories, office complexes, super-markets and schools, are formal structures. Their respective officials, rules and goals are familiar to us all. Although formal organisations are a particular feature of urban, industrial societies, certain examples such as armies and monasteries have existed for centuries. To an extent, formal organisations in modern societies have taken over or supplemented functions previously performed by family, kinship and community groups (see chapter 3, pp. 61–3). Thus, state welfare as well as family help is available to the sick and needy through various organisational channels.

Informal organisations develop within all formal organisations. Informal organisations are freely created social group relationships outside or inside formal organisations. It is difficult to imagine that even the most rigidly run prison or concentration camp does not have some form of 'underground' system of communication. The achievement of formal goals may depend on whether informal groups operate 'for' or 'against' the formal organisation. To put it in functionalist terms, they may be functional or dysfunctional. Thus, anti-school peer-groups are an example of informal organisations which are dysfunctional to the achievement of formal educational goals.

It would be misleading to leave the impression that informal organisations exist only within formal structures: friendship groups of peers and gangs occur outside them. Typically, perhaps, people find more meaning in their informal relationships than in their formal ones. The reservation widely felt about the 'over-organised' quality of modern life is partly based on the feeling that formal organisations seem to be intruding more and more into the private area of life. Even though more leisure time exists, it is largely 'organised' for us by the mass media rather than used imaginatively and intelligently. Obviously, this view is controversial and we assess it critically in chapter 18, pp. 420–2.

Theoretical Perspectives on Organisations

Although there are many organisational theories that the student might come across, we can conveniently divide them into four main groups. These are the bureaucratic or mechanistic; systems theories – particularly organic systems theory; theories based on the concept of interaction; and conflict theory. Although these perspectives are frequently contrasted they are by no means wholly exclusive in all respects. Indeed, we will consider the bureaucratic and organic approaches together as much to show their complementary as their contradictory aspects.

We make no analytical distinction between industrial and other kinds of formal organisations in this section. The types of organisational structures described below can occur in both the industrial and non-industrial sectors such as central and local government departments.

1 BUREAUCRATIC AND SYSTEMS THEORIES

BUREAUCRATIC OR MECHANISTIC THEORY

Max Weber laid down the classical or bureaucratic model of organisational theory. His model is a functionalist one. He maintained that bureaucracy is the most functionally efficient form of organisation, even though it can sometimes operate in a rather 'inhuman' way. Bureaucracies are formal organisations generally recognisable by certain characteristics. He constructed an ideal type of bureaucracy to show what these characteristics are. We can summarise them as follows:

1 The existence of different offices (or positions) governed by rules the purpose of which is to fulfil a specific, given function or functions

2 The hierarchical organisation of offices – that is, some positions have more authority and status than others

3 Management based on files and records used with the assistance of office staff

4 The appointment of trained personnel to occupy roles in the bureaucracy

Weber saw the growth of bureaucratic organisation as a major example of the application of rational thought to practical problems. He regarded the triumph of rationality as a characteristic feature of the modern world. Another of its manifestations was the massive development of science and technology. Weber also described the nature of an official bureaucratic position. Above all, it involves a commitment to performing the functions the official is appointed to do and not to any powerful person or patron who might wish to interfere with the official's course of duty. It was necessary for Weber to make this point because, in the middle ages, this principle did not apply. When a king or lord appointed someone to a high position of service within his household, he expected his appointee to be loyal to him personally rather than merely to perform pre-determined and agreed functions. By contrast, a modern bureaucratic official is expected to do the job described in the terms of his contract. The contract defines the duties, establishes the salary scale and gives security of tenure subject to an agreed period of notice and good conduct. Most people reading this book will eventually take up a position of this kind. We live in a bureaucratic world! A classic example of a modern bureaucracy is the civil service. A pupil leaving school with a clutch of GCSEs may begin as a clerical officer. In time, he or she becomes an Executive Officer and then, perhaps, a Senior Executive Officer: more remotely, the office of Principal Secretary beckons. Each office has its own functions and the further one progresses up the hierarchy, the more power and status accrue.

Criticisms of Weber's bureaucratic model will become apparent as we examine alternative organisational theories, and some dysfunctions of bureaucracy. One point is worth making immediately, however. There is an implicit contradiction in Weber's bureaucratic functionalism, and his more usual emphasis on conflict. Oddly, Weber did not fully develop the perspective that as well as fulfilling useful functions, organisations are also frequently the focus of conflict between groups. We develop this issue later in this chapter.

ORGANIC SYSTEMS THEORY The organisational type that most obviously contrasts with the bureaucratic is what Burns and Stalker (1961) termed the organic system. They contrast organic systems with what they call mechanistic systems but, as the latter are in no way distinguishable from bureaucracies, this need not detain us.

Organic systems are characterised by a less rigid division of labour than mechanistic ones; they are less rule-bound, less hierarchical and more open to the influence of the informal group. The last point is crucial. The skill and experience of the individual can be communicated laterally (sideways) across the network of those involved in the task. The team as a whole shares power and responsibility. Overall, the organic approach shows a more subtle awareness of the complex nature and effects of interaction, formal and informal, than does the bureaucratic. Such an approach is often considered appropriate for relatively high level technical or scientific employees in, say, the electronics industry – for example, a team of computer programmers. Nevertheless, it has also been successfully tried with manual workers. At their Kalmar plant, Volvo broke down assembly work into twenty sets of functions. Each set is performed by a team of fifteen or twenty workers. The cars pass from team to team on

trolleys, allowing the worker considerable freedom of movement. The teams are not hierarchically organised, and solutions to problems are supposed to be reached through cooperation and not by authoritarianism.

Although the bureaucratic or mechanistic and the organic systems models of organisations are, to some extent, in competition with each other, there are circumstances in which one model may be more appropriate that the other. Burns and Stalker suggest that bureaucracy is often suitable for the pursuit of clear goals in stable conditions, such as producing a commodity for a safe and established market, and that an organic system is appropriate to less stable conditions in which precise goals may still be developing, such as electronics research.

SCIENTIFIC MANAGEMENT THEORY Frederick W Taylor's theory of scientific management reflects the same principles as Weber's bureaucratic theory, and, to a lesser extent, human relations theory and socio-technical theory bear comparison with organic systems theory.

Taylor, an American contemporary of Weber, reached his conclusions independently of the Austrian social scientist. Taylor was specifically interested in industrial organisations and particularly in developing ways to improve production. What he said about the role and function of the industrial worker was comparable with Weber's comments on the lower level white collar employee. Further, both recognised that higher level bureaucrats and managers had relatively more power. Like Weber, Taylor decided that efficiency was best obtained by task specialisation and standardisation, and the centralisation of decision making power at the top of the hierarchy. He argued that all mental work should be removed from the workshop, and put in the hands of management. He presented his ideas in a book entitled *Scientific Management*. An explicit guiding principle was actually to treat the worker as an extension of the machine or organisation and, indeed, this notion is, more or less, implicit in all bureaucratic structures. Among the advice he offered was that 'the two hands should begin and complete their motions simultaneously' and that 'proper illumination increases production'. In addition, he recommended that pay levels be closely tied to productivity. It seems appropriate that Taylor's approach is often referred to as mechanical or mechanistic theory.

HUMAN RELATIONS THEORY Human relations theory originated as a reaction against Taylor's scientific management theory. From 1927 to 1932, a series of studies was mounted into worker productivity at the Hawthorne Works of the Western Electricity Company in Chicago. Initially, the researchers, led by Elton Mayo, were positively influenced by Taylor and their area of enquiry was actually suggested by his work. They wanted to find out the optimum level of illumination and other environmental factors to maximise production. There is more than a touch of comedy about the way they arrived at the 'results' of their research. They 'found' that the relation between the variables of illumination and production was virtually non-existent. In one of the studies in which the workers were placed in a control room in lighting conditions equivalent to moonlight, they still maintained a reasonable level of production: it fell off only when illumination was so reduced that they could not see properly!

Ultimately, the Hawthorne experiments were of outstanding importance both because of the new theory of industrial relations they suggested, and by virtue of their contribution to a better understanding of social scientific method, specifically that of observation. We have already discussed the second of these, the effect of the researcher on the behaviour of the subject of research, in chapter two. We concentrate now on the first, the content of their findings. To put it simply, they found that the productive performance of the workers was affected by social factors, as well as material ones such as the level of illumination. The social factor at work in this case was the interest of the research team in the workers. Unexpectedly, this seemed to stimulate them to greater efforts than otherwise. The presence of researchers in a factory is, however, rare.

Follow-up studies by the Mayo team showed that the informal relationships of the workers themselves constitute the most important social variable affecting production. The role of informal groups was established by the notable Western Electric Company Bank wiring room experiment involving the wiring of switchboards. A group of fourteen workers was set up separately and observed for six months. It was found that, although they were paid on the basis of a productivity bonus scheme, the men did not respond to this by individually trying to maximise their production, but established their own production norms as a group. Group disapproval was equally the fate of those who produced either more or less than the agreed norm.

Underlying the human relations approach is a more complex and more humanistic theory of human needs than that implied by classical theory. The latter assumes that individuals will work harder in improved material conditions and if they are given higher material rewards for more work. Human relations theory argues that people also need the security, companionship, identity and guidance of the informal peer group. These psychological needs are only capable of fulfilment with others. Taylor's attempt to treat the work force as isolated individuals was based on the misleading fiction that workers are, in fact, isolated. In modern, large-scale organisations, work is a collective experience.

SOCIO-TECHNICAL SYSTEMS THEORY The socio-technical systems theory attempts to combine both the technical and social factors affecting work so as to bring about the most effective overall performance. Mary Weir summarises three major points suggested by socio-technical system theorists to achieve this end: the individual must have some power to control and regulate her or his work; s/he should be able to adapt her or his own standards of work both to the expectations and demands of others and to the changing work situation generally; and the job should be both varied and have a coherent pattern. Finally, it should be linked meaningfully to the rest of the production process. It should also provide the worker with status in the community.

Both the human relations and socio-technical systems approaches have been criticised as merely 'making exploitation more bearable'. In a challenging critique of management theories the Marxist, Harry Braverman, attacks both Taylor's theory, and human relations and similar schools. He suggests that Taylorism did not last because it was too obviously crude and insensitive. The 'softer' theories provided the necessary ideological fig leaves to cover the still basically exploitative nature of capitalist production. But they fail to confront the private ownership and control of industry which Marxists traditionally regard as the root of alienation. Even given Braverman's premise, however, there remains the argument that it is better to be exploited in comfort than discomfort! (Aspects of Braverman's analysis are discussed in greater detail on pp. 246–8.)

THE DYSFUNCTIONS OF BUREAUCRATIC ORGANISATION: BREAKING THE RULES The arguments in favour of bureaucracy are considerable. Firstly, the bureaucratic division of labour combined with technological innovation has greatly increased the production of goods and services: to that extent it is efficient. Secondly, a bureaucracy usually ensures a degree of predictability: production quotas are pre-determined, people know how they are likely to be treated. Thirdly, partly because of its very impersonality, bureaucracy is often a condition of fairness. People are appointed to offices on the basis of qualifications and merit rather than patronage. Further, clients are dealt with by bureaucrats on the basis of equality and need, not favouritism. That, at any rate, is the theory, although several sociologists have criticised and modified it.

Arguing within a functionalist framework, Robert Merton points to several dysfunctions of bureaucracy which can lead to inefficiency. First, rigid adherence to bureaucratic rules may prevent an official from improvising a necessary response to unexpected circumstances. Thus, to offer our own example, a secretary in a production company, in the absence of superiors, may happen one day to find herself having to deal with an important client. Conceivably, by retreating behind her official role – 'I'm sorry, I'm only the secretary. I don't have the authority to deal with business matters' – vital orders may be jeopardised or, at a minimum, the client may feel he or she has not been well treated. In such a case, initiative, confidence and some imagination are needed. Bureaucracy does not always teach these qualities and can actually smother them. The results can be 'passing the buck'. Secondly, there is a danger that those rigidly trained to obey rules rather than to consciously achieve goals will become what Merton calls ritualistic. This means that they attach more importance to observing rules and procedures than to achieving the purpose for which they exist: this is referred to as goal displacement. As lower level bureaucrats are often not kept informed about general organisational goals, ritualism must be considered a potential fault of bureaucracy, rather than an individual failing. Merton classifies ritualism as a form of anomie (see pp. 302–3). Finally, Merton argues that the sometimes alienating effect of bureaucracy on both bureaucrats and the public with whom they deal can be dysfunctional. Bureaucratic or ritualistic characters are not the most adaptable and efficient of people, and clients who have to submit to long bureaucratic procedure before, say, they can receive needed social security are unlikely to be very cooperative.

Merton argues within functionalist assumptions but, as we have seen, Burns and Stalker suggest that in certain circumstances it is more efficient to break with the bureaucratic method of organisation altogether. Broadly, this is when cooperative and organic rather than competitive and hierarchical structures are more suitable to organisation goal attainment. Arguing along similar lines, Peter Blau gives a number of examples in which formal bureaucracy proved inappropriate. One such instance occurred in an isolated American navy island base. Virtually cut off from external control, the formal organisation of the base broke down and natural leaders, who worked effectively but within an informal framework emerged. A better known study by Blau is of an American state employment agency. He compared two groups of job placement interviewers who operated on different organisational principles, the one highly bureaucratic, the other much more informal and cooperative. On balance, the second approach proved more effective in placing clients in jobs. Blau did not over-generalise from this case-study to the point of concluding that informal organisation is more efficient. Indeed, he found evidence to suggest that it sometimes operated in a biased manner as there were fewer bureaucratic checks to prevent officials favouring some clients at the expense of others. Rather, he suggested that what is often needed is balance, varying with circumstances, between formal and informal methods.

It is worth recalling two studies that we have already met which point to the limits of a rigidly bureaucratic approach. First is the pioneering Hawthorne study presented earlier in this chapter which established the importance of the informal social group in production. Second is Alvin Gouldner's case-study of a wildcat strike which showed that unrest can occur when workers, used to informality, responsibility and independence, have a bureaucratic regime imposed upon them.

Finally, there can be no clearer demonstration of the limited effectiveness of rigid rule-following in achieving goals than the fact that workers use the strategy of 'working to rule' (doing all tasks by the book) in the industrial bargaining process.

Refusing to work overtime is a common example. The result is often inconvenience to the public. Thus, transport workers can make chaos out of timetable schedules merely by working a 'normal' day. Strict and time-consuming adherence to safety check rules or a rigid refusal to allow more people on a bus than is officially stipulated can also be used as pinpricks in industrial campaigning. Put negatively, working to rule can be presented as a 'withdrawal of goodwill'. The National Union of Teachers (NUT) adopted this approach in their industrial action of 1979. In particular, lunch-time supervision of children was suspended. This was hardly lethal in its effect but it did result in a number of 'mad hatter's dinner parties' here and there. Clearly, then, relationships and goodwill, as well as rules are a part of organisation.

TALCOTT PARSONS' FUNCTIONAL-SYSTEMS THEORY

Parsons' organisational theory is interesting in that it combines elements of Weberian functionalism with those of systems theory. He retains the notion that organisations have goals, but describes them as potentially much more flexible and capable of adaptation than does Weber.

Parsons treats organisations virtually as though they are small-scale societies, and his organisational analysis strongly recalls his social systems theory (see chapter 22, pp. 499–501). The various parts of organisations are seen as interdependent; they have certain needs that have to be met for survival; they have goals; the whole is something more than the sum of all the individuals who are members of the organisation. The organic analogy is clearly apparent in all this; even so, there is nothing so far mentioned that adds substantially to Weber's analysis of bureaucracy. Parsons, however, goes beyond Weber in two important ways. Firstly, he pays more attention to the capacity of organisations to interact with one another and with the environment in general. The notion that, in order to function effectively, organisations must adapt their structure and goals to changes in the environment has certainly been of influence in modern management. In a fast-changing age the possibility of 'being left behind' is ever-present. An organisation that cannot adapt is not likely to survive. An example of an organisation that has adapted to change is the House of Commons, a very different body now from that of several hundred years ago. British Leyland was an example of an organisation that found adaptation – particularly in its response to foreign competition and new technology – a struggle, to which it eventually succumbed.

Secondly, Parsons recognises that organisations must, in some way, meet man's expressive as well as his instrumental needs. Even so, it is clear that he considers these needs are to be accommodated within the terms of the organisation's pre-set goals and certainly not as ends in themselves. This seems a deterministic and unconvincing way of reconciling personal needs with rational organisational goals. In reality, the individuals and groups that make up organisations often disagree much more than Parsons is willing to concede.

A well known application of functionalist systems theory is Peter Selznick's analysis of the Tennessee Valley Authority, set up in 1933 by President Roosevelt to help the region combat the effects of the depression. The Authority was set up with the intention of involving local people in policy making. In practice, this did not happen and instead powerful local farmers were the major effective interest group consulted by the

Authority's officials. Selznick suggests that the reason why this occurred was that for the organisation to 'survive' and its officials to retain their jobs, compromise had to be made with the major local power group. This may have been so but it is just as easy to see these developments in terms of interest group or class conflict as organisational survival.

2 SOCIAL ACTION AND INTERACTIONIST THEORIES

SOCIAL ACTION THEORY David Silverman describes the meanings that individuals attach to, and find in, organisations, to be the major concern of action theory. People, not organisations, have goals. He is, however, appreciative of Parsons' attempt to conceive of organisations in terms of change and development, and he himself contextualises action within a wider institutional and social environment. He cites the previously mentioned study of Gouldner as an excellent example of an analysis that combines a sense of historical and institutional context with an understanding of the meaning actors attach to their behaviour (see chapter 11, p. 258).

Another excellent example of the importance of understanding how human behaviour, particularly in its emotional rather than its rational aspects, can affect organisations, is given by Ralph Glasser. In a television documentary (1980), Glasser tells how the olive producers of the Italian rural village of San Georgio refused to use a cooperative olive press – even though there existed good 'rational' economic arguments for doing so. Instead, they preferred to take their olives for pressing to the owners of private presses who were usually wealthy. Glasser suggests that the olive farmers acted in this way because they had a traditional relationship, based on established expectation and *fiducia* (trust) with the private press operators. By contrast, as Glasser points out, 'You can't have a relationship with a cooperative'. In fairness, it should be said that cooperatives do sometimes work well, and people do have relationships within them. Nevertheless, it is obvious that the producers did not feel that they could relate to the new situation. This feeling became the major operative factor in the above situation and accounts for the

failure of the cooperative. Glasser indulges in some conservative romanticism, but underlying this is a wise awareness of the texture of relationships and feelings woven over time, and a fear of what the brutal blade of technology and bureaucracy might do to them in the name of progress and rationality.

A better known example of a piece of research utilising action perspective, is Goldthorpe and Lockwood's affluent worker study. It will be recalled that they studiously avoided attributing motives to the workers but took the trouble to ask them what their motives were. It turned out that a majority had an instrumental orientation to work, or, simply, they worked for money, not satisfaction (chapter 11, pp. 248–9).

TOTAL INSTITUTIONS: INTERACTIONIST ANALYSIS OF THE 'ULTIMATE' IN BUREAUCRACY Social action theory and symbolic interactionism are compatible theoretical approaches, but whereas the former has been developed mainly in Europe, the latter was founded in the USA, and has its own characteristic concepts and vocabulary.

We may live in an increasingly bureaucratic world, but most of us can escape from it into our private lives and personal relationships. Most of us think of these 'escapes' as necessary to a balanced life and even to sanity itself. There are, however, some who live all the time, and for a long period, in highly bureaucratic organisations, in total institutions. How does the self – to use the interactionist term – adjust to omnipresent and 'permanent' bureaucracy? Before answering this question, we must briefly examine some different types of total organisations.

A major distinction between different types of total organisations is whether membership is voluntary or compulsory. Monasteries are an example of the former, prisons of the latter. Whether members belong to an organisation by choice or not will tend greatly to affect the quality of life within it – as a brief consideration of the difference between a monastery and prison should show. The voluntary-compulsory membership distinction does not, however, apply in every case: the members of some institutions, old people's homes and mental hospitals, for instance, may contain both types. A further way of categorising total institutions is simply in terms of the purposes they serve. Thus, goals may be custodial (prisons), protective (mental hospitals), retreatist (monasteries), or task-oriented (armies, boarding schools). Often a total institution may serve several purposes, for example, prisons protect the public and, sometimes, seek to reform their inmates.

Erving Goffman's *Asylums*, based on a field study carried out in a hospital in Washington in 1955–56, remains the best known study of a total institution. In order to see at first hand the personal and psychological effects on the patients of life in an asylum, Goffman undertook a participant observational study, playing the role of an assistant to the athletic director. We can divide what Goffman refers to as the career of the mental patient into two stages, the breaking down of the old self and the construction of a new self. Part of the second stage is the adoption of modes of adjustment which enable the individual to 'get by' on a day-to-day basis and perhaps to salvage some of his sense of individuality.

The first blow to a person's old or established sense of identity is when someone – often a close relative – complains of 'abnormality'. Identity is further broken down during the in-patient phase. Not all mental hospitals are equally bureaucratic, but the admission procedures Goffman mentions include photographing, finger-printing, number assigning, listing personal possessions for storage, and undressing. Not surprisingly, he refers to this as the process of 'mortification' of the self. In the second stage referred to above, the inmate attempts to build a new self centred on the institution. The system of privileges and rewards operated by the institution in return for obedience or, perhaps, for doing work around the hospital, focus the individual's attention and energy, and may give a sense of meaning and purpose and so help to reintegrate the personality. Despite the fact that total institutions are geared to standardise behaviour, inmates manage to adopt individual modes of adjustment. Withdrawal or retreatism is an extreme and often irreversible adjustment. Two forms of adjustment in which the institution tends to 'take over' the inmate are conversion and colonisation. Conversion is when the inmate accepts the institution's definition of himself

as, say, 'emotionally immature' and tries to conform to the pattern of 'perfect inmate'; colonisation occurs when the institutional regime so engulfs the individual that it comes to seem preferable to the world outside. Prisoners, as well as mental patients, who prefer to have their lives 'run for them' sometimes adopt this mode of adjustment. Goffman uses the term, playing it cool, to describe a general posture of strategic adjustment. The mental patient may adjust to the bureaucratic power structure, and to other inmates largely as an attempt to improve his chances of discharge. In prisons, a similar adjustment is often rewarded with a remission of sentence. Goffman considers playing it cool to be the most common form of adjustment.

Some inmates rebel or, to use Goffman's precise term, take an 'intransigent line' rather than genuinely adjust, although he says relatively little of this possibility. The film *One Flew Over The Cuckoo's Nest*, based on a novel by Ken Kesey, was a dramatised version of the rebellion of McMurphy, a patient in a mental hospital. McMurphy simply refused to accept the total planning and routinisation of his life. For him, the officially pre-programmed and controlled time-table – meal times, basket-ball games, television watching, lights out and, above all, day trips – provide opportunities for anarchic self-assertion. One episode in the film in which a bus-load of mental patients, led by McMurphy, take over a ship is a classic of comic absurdity. Finally, McMurphy ends up subdued by a brain lobotomy – the ultimate form of control. Lobotomies may be rare but electric shock treatment, the use of drugs, and manipulation of privileges, rewards and punishments to achieve conformity are common. The film does not moralise but, in the end, McMurphy's madness compares well with official thought and personality control. We are reminded that when 'society' defines someone as deviant, the consequent loss of that individual's freedom, and the tools used in reforging acceptable behaviour are formidable. Still, the film ends optimistically with McMurphy's friend, a previously subdued Indian, breaking out of the hospital in a bid for freedom.

A book very much in Goffman's style (although not uncritical of him) is *Psychological Survival: The Experience of Long-*

Term Imprisonment, by Stanley Cohen and Laurie Taylor (1972). The authors frankly proclaim that one of their purposes is to provide a 'manual of survival' for long-term prisoners. Accordingly, they devote one chapter to 'making out and fighting back'. They find much more evidence of resistance in Durham prison – where they did their research – than Goffman did among patients in the Washington hospital. Accordingly, they write of modes of resistance rather than adjustment. They list five types of resistance: self-protection, campaigning, escaping, striking and confronting. Self-protection and campaigning are individual types of resistance. Cohen and Taylor spend little time on the material side of self-protection, for example getting more and better food. They concentrate on the protecting of self-image. They stress how prisoners reject the most damning 'labels' – 'killer', 'thug', 'brutal psychopath', – sometimes humorously and sometimes in anger. Campaigning, the most popular form of which was sending letters to MPs, was more often done as a way of 'getting back' at authority, rather than in any real hope of progress on given issues. Escaping, striking and confronting all involve a high degree of collective effort or connivance. The term 'confronting' needs to be explained. It describes any major collective effort to force the prison authorities, and sometimes a wider audience, to listen to the prisoners' complaints and opinions. There could hardly be a more conspicuous example of trying to draw public attention to grievances than, for instance, occupying a prison roof for a period – as has sometimes happened.

Cohen and Taylor show typical interactionist awareness that the differences between 'normals' and 'deviants' is generally one of degree rather than of kind. In a later book, *Escape Attempts: The Theory and Practice of Resistance to Everyday Life* (1976), they extend their concept of resistance to more conventional, as distinct from totally bureaucratic, situations. We have already seen how, at work and in schools, people attempt to 'manage' their own situations, despite the constraints imposed by the organised environment. Chapters 13 and 15 examine further the tension between the demands of society for order and conformity, and the frequent tendency of individuals not to 'fit in'.

3 CONFLICT THEORIES

This section should be regarded as a direct continuation of the opening part of this chapter, in which the conflict perspectives on organisations of Marx and Weber were introduced. Whereas Parsons tends to see power as being used for 'necessary' purposes in the common interest, for example, in maintaining law and order. Marx and, to some extent Weber, sees it as being used by groups or classes mainly in their own interests. Thus, Weber feared the abuse of power by bureaucrats on their own behalf, and Marx on behalf of the capitalist class.

Clegg and Dunkerley remind us of what should really be obvious – that the reason for the existence of most organisations is the need to organise the labour process, and that this involves the control of workers by employers. Like Bowles and Gintis, they regard the extreme fragmentation of the labour process in industrial and office work as one means of controlling the work-force, because it prevents them from understanding the nature of the whole production process. They differentiate not only between buyers and sellers of labour but also between working groups of different power in the market. Thus, they explain at length the reasons for the particular exploitation of female labour, as we also did in chapter 8. Their discussion leads naturally to the question of different forms of organisational control (see next section), and to whom the product of labour rightly belongs, and how it should be shared. As they point out, their perspective is pertinent to organisations in both communist and capitalist societies. The most obvious difference between organisations today and in Marx's time is that many are now operated by the state. They show that a 'them and us' feeling in the workforce can occur in undemocratically run state enterprises such as those in the former Soviet Union, as well as in capitalist ones. A state that simply gathers in profit or surplus value and redistributes it unequally is hardly likely to be perceived as any improvement on a capitalist entrepreneur.

Wallerstein's comments on organisations are comparable with those of Clegg and Dunkerley. He gives the broadest dimension possible to organisational analysis. He suggests that national societies are inadequate units for economic and social analysis and that they should be seen as only one organisational level within the capitalist world economy. Specific organisations, like the nation state or multi-national corporations, operate within the capitalist world system (see chapter 21 p. 469).

One matter on which Clegg and Dunkerley say relatively little is how private troubles arising in organisations can be related to 'public issues'. An obvious example is how a corporation's policy of plant closures or cut-backs – perhaps the result of recession – can cause the personal misery of unemployment (chapters 7 and 11). There is need for much more analysis of how individual and, indeed, national experience is formed by organisations operating in an unpredictable world system.

A number of liberal structural sociologists have applied Weber's concepts in a way that emphasises the functional aspect of organisations but shows an awareness of conflict. We have already seen that Weber considered that socialist societies were likely to become as bureaucratic, if not more so, than capitalist ones. More recently, this view has been presented as part of the broader, more controversial convergence thesis. In this context, convergence means that the economic and organisational structure of advanced societies, whether capitalist or socialist, are becoming increasingly similar. The view that such societies need central economic planning and large governmental bureaucracies to implement decisions is crucial to this idea. Another aspect of this thesis appears in the work of Daniel Bell and Ralf Dahrendorf. They argue that the complex problems of advanced societies require advanced management techniques. Political argument will not solve essentially technical problems, and may make them worse. Thus, national investment in energy may need to be planned years ahead, regardless of which government is in power. In their view, top managers and their technical advisers are vital in giving long-term continuity in both advanced capitalist and socialist societies. Dahrendorf, and, particularly, Bell, consider this new class of experts to be a highly influential elite (see chapter 21, pp. 473–4 and this chapter). They see potential for conflict between this high status and well paid elite and the less privileged and well-off. Nevertheless, they consider this inequality to be inevitable and as much a feature of communist as of capitalist societies.

As we have seen, Marxists do not consider that managers have as much power as Bell and Dahrendorf suggest. In the West there is also the power of capital to consider and, we must add, in the Soviet Union, that of top communist politicians. Nevertheless, the massive extent of bureaucracy and the power of top management to use bureaucracy as their instrument are noteworthy and quite recent features of modern society.

Marxists can certainly learn from Weberian-inspired organisational analysis. Two points are apparent. Firstly, the 'new managerial class' is both highly paid and relatively powerful. In their eagerness to establish the primacy of capitalist power, Marxists tend to disregard this even though it is a fact that can be easily accommodated to Marxist theory and policy. Arguably, managerial power increased substantially during the nineteen eighties (see pp. 285–8). Secondly, as Weber realised, the power of large organisations to control and alienate is immense because of their very size and of the remoteness of those who control them. The novelist, Kafka, caught the sense of how in modern societies organisations seem to 'run people's lives' almost without personal direction – especially, in his view in the (then) communist societies of Eastern Europe. Clegg and Dunkerley appear to have integrated this important insight into an essentially Marxist framework. They recognise that bureaucratically run organisations tend to produce alienation not only among lower level workers but even among professional employees as well. Crucially, however, they insist that it is still necessary to locate and analyse the major source of control behind organisations, whether it be capital or a political elite. Only then does it become possible adequately to relate organisational analysis to the issues of inequality of power and wealth. The basic question remains 'in whose interest is this organisation run?'

CONTROL AND INVOLVEMENT, OLIGARCHY AND DEMOCRACY IN ORGANISATIONS We have already seen that Weber considered that modern organisations are best run along bureaucratic lines. For him, bureaucracy meant hierarchy and hierarchy meant oligarchy, that is, that power and control are concentrated at the top. More recent theorists have examined the issues of control and involvement in organisations and, as we shall see, have produced a more complex picture. The organic systems theory, mentioned above, has already introduced the notion that organisations can be run on somewhat more democratic lines than the bureaucratic model suggests. We now examine this matter more directly.

Etzioni takes three of Weber's major concepts, power, authority and legitimation, and applies them to the understanding of the way organisations work. Etzioni starts with the basic problem of how the majority of people, workers and employees, can be persuaded or forced to do what they might not freely chose to do – work for others. To understand Etzioni's answer, we must first know what Weber's three terms mean: power is the ability to impose one's will (for example by brute force); legitimation is the acceptance of power because it is considered to be rightly exercised (for example that of a king); and authority is legitimate power. Weber offered a three-part ideal-type model of authority: traditional, charismatic, and rational-legal. Traditional authority is 'hallowed with time', like that of a king, an established dynasty or a pope. Charismatic authority is generated by the personality of the individual, like that of Hitler or Martin Luther King. Rational-legal authority is established in law or written regulations. We have already said that it is this type of authority that characterises modern bureaucratic organisations.

Why is it that individuals accept the control and power of organisations and, specifically, of top organisational officials over their lives? Etzioni presents in turn, an explanatory typology of control: coercive, utilitarian and normative or social. Coercive power is control based on physical means, such as brute force. Utilitarian power is based on the use of material means, such as money payments: it embodies an element of positive incentive to conform, in the form of a reward. Normative power is based on morality and social conscience. When people conform for normative reasons they do so because they believe they ought to. Normative power and conformity are associated with legitimation because they occur when people accept that a given power is legitimate. Thus, a Roman Catholic

who accepts the authority of the Pope does so out of normative conviction. A citizen may obey the law from normative conviction although, for others, the threat of coercion may be necessary. Likewise, employees in an organisation, say a commercial one, may feel normatively disposed to accept its authority even though they originally joined it for utilitarian reasons (to make a living). Bureaucracies are largely based on rules and often create an atmosphere of normative conformity. A little thought will make it clear that in many types of organisations, such as schools, two or even three kinds of control operate.

Etzioni matches three types of involvement with his typology of control. Coercion tends to produce alienation, utilitarian control is based on calculative commitment, and normative control on moral commitment. Calculative and moral commitment have, in effect, already been explained. Alienation is the opposite of commitment: it is the rejection by the spirit of what the body has to do, such as to serve a life-sentence in prison or to do endlessly repetitive and boring work. In part, Etzioni sees it as a leadership problem to decide what kinds of incentives are necessary to involve members in the organisation's goals. He also recognises, however, that workers and employees are likely to have their own ideas about the nature of their involvement, and that these will affect the running of the organisation. As we shall now see, there is perhaps more to this issue than Etzioni himself allows.

IS DEMOCRACY IN ORGANISATIONS POSSIBLE? The most uncompromising statement of the inevitability of managerial elites is the so-called 'iron law of oligarchy' of Robert Michels (1949). With the German Socialist Party chiefly in mind, he argues that popularly representative parties and unions, whose aim is to replace autocracy with democracy, are forced by necessity to develop a 'vast and solid' bureaucratic organisational structure themselves. In due course, the party bureaucracy itself becomes centralised and undemocratic. The vested interest of the organisation's elite rather than the needs of the people at large effectively becomes the most important consideration, despite professed democratic and socialist ideals. Ordinary people acquire no more power or control as a result of these movements. One set of masters replaces another. In that sense, Michels' 'law' is similar to Pareto's theory of circulating elites.

Alvin Gouldner criticises Michels' account as unbalanced. Michels emphasises only the ways in which organisational needs work against democratic possibilities. Tellingly, Gouldner suggests another need – ignored by Michels – that of the consent of the governed (or employees), to their governors. He sees a certain recurrent tension between the need for central leadership and authority and the desire of many people for more power, satisfaction and involvement at work than a rigid bureaucratic regime might allow. He says, with some poetic finesse:

'if oligarchical waves repeatedly wash away the bridge of democracy, this eternal recurrence can happen only because men doggedly rebuild them after each inundation' (1971).

The recent 'democratic revolution' in the Soviet Union seems to provide a particular instance of the resilience of democracy referred to by Gouldner.

Gouldner's thoughts conveniently bring us to the nub of the debate about organisational oligarchy and democracy. Both democracy and oligarchy are possible in organisations and, for that matter, in political systems. What people get depends on what they want, and their power to obtain it balanced against that of others. Power-conflict is a process not an outcome. Thomas Jefferson, the second American President, counselled the people to be ever vigilant in the protection of their democratic rights, lest they be whittled away by central government. 'God forbid' he said 'that we should be twenty years without a rebellion'.

Gouldner has rough words for Selznick as well as Michels. He refers to Selznick's 'dismal' catalogue of organisational needs. These are 'needs' for security; stable lines of authority; stable relationships, and homogeneity (similarity of parts). Gouldner, maintaining his emphasis on democracy, juxtaposes what he sees as an equally important set of needs: needs for challenge, for lateral communication, for creative tension, for heterogeneity (diversity) and the consent of the led. We return to the oligarchy-democracy debate shortly in the context of union organisation.

Gouldner, therefore, sees neither oligarchy nor democracy as 'inevitable' but as alternatives to be championed and contested. Similarly, Rensis Likert offers a model of control-involvement which is more representative of the full range of possible management-worker structures than is Etzioni's. He identifies four important systems of organisation: exploitative/ authoritative; benevolent/authoritative; consultative and participative group management. We can add a fifth: the democratic/egalitarian system of management favoured by some contemporary socialists but probably not fully achieved in any socialist regime.

In exploitative/authoritative systems, power and control are centralised and workers are treated exclusively in terms of their productive capacity. In the early stages of industrialisation in both Britain and America, powerful industrial moguls, such as Ford and Rockefeller, ran their industrial empires in this way. Frequently, this pattern became modified to the extent that the entrepreneur did begin to develop an interest in the general welfare of his workforce – the benevolent-authoritative pattern. Often this was for ulterior motives: a healthy workforce was a better workforce and, in any case, entrepreneurs often wanted to 'spike the guns' of unions which built up on the basis of working class discontent. Frederick Taylor was the theoretical philosopher of authoritative or, perhaps more accurately, authoritarian style of management. The consultative approach recognises that the workforce may have something to offer the management, at least in certain areas, in the way of experience and advice. Even where regular consultative meetings are established, however, ultimate decisions remain in the hands of ownership or management. Again, this system can become little more than decorative diplomacy. The concept of participative group management has had considerable support and success in parts of Europe in the post-war period. In Germany, workers have the legal right to 50 per cent representation on the supervisory boards of companies with more than 2,000 employees. Management is responsible to these boards. An employer is quoted as commenting that: 'Codetermination has really forced both sides to understand the other side better' (The Guardian, 9 October 1990). Similar systems at representation operate in Scandinavian countries. In Britain, the Bullock report of the late nineteen seventies recommended that the nationalised industries should implement a similar system of participation. The report's recommendations were rather complicated and their partial application to British Leyland and the Post Office petered out. The participation 'debate' continues, however, and the Social Charter proposed for adoption across the European Economic Community would harmonise workers' rights, including those of industrial representation. There has been little support for this among the leadership of the CBI.

The democratic-egalitarian model goes beyond the concept of the participation of 'both sides of industry' to that of abolishing the notion of 'sides' altogether. For a Marxist, this would first involve the abolition of class inequality. This does not, of course, mean that separate roles, such as manager or production worker, will cease to exist; rather, it is a question of making management democratic. Perhaps managers could be elected for a term of some years, as MP's are now, and positions on the board could rotate (as the American presidency does in the sense that it can only be held for two four-year terms – for good democratic reasons!). To be genuinely egalitarian, this system would also involve a reduction, if not the abolition, of the differences in reward and status betweeen management and workers. Obviously, this model would be barely acceptable within the limits of capitalist economic and social belief. The implementation of a democratic-egalitarian

system would probably require socialism. We discussed this matter in some detail in chapter 7, pp. 164–5.

It is appropriate at this point briefly to discuss whether, regardless of their capacity to participate in industrial democracy, unions can be successfully democratic themselves. This returns us to Michels' thesis. Lipset, Trow and Coleman (1956), on the basis of a study of a printers' union in the United States, found that in certain circumstances democracy is possible. The printers' union had a thriving two party system. They put this down to the fact that the long and odd hours worked by the printers produced work-connected leisure organisations which, in turn, provided a basis of communication for, and involvement in, union politics, But Lipset's broader conclusion is more pessimistic. In most industries, the majority of workers quickly leave work for home, and it is only a minority which actively involves itself in union politics. This is so in Britain, where, prior to postal ballots, seldom more than a third of workers voted when given the opportunity. Allen, however, points out that the formal machinery of union democracy is time-consuming and cumbersome to operate. In practice, the way union leaders are kept in check is more simple. If the workers disapprove of what they are doing, membership declines. Allen's argument is not entirely convincing. As early as 1949, C Wright Mills pointed to the communication gap beween national union officials and branch officials and between both these groups and the mass membership. These problems are by no means resolved today.

Gouldner perceives oligarchy and democracy as matters of preference and

▶

Figure 12.1

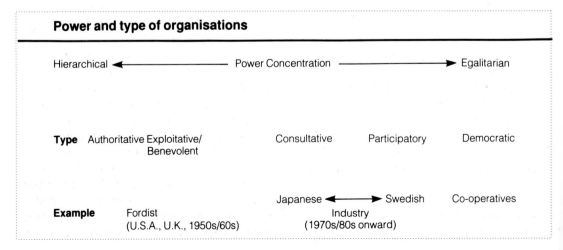

Power and type of organisations

Hierarchical ◀——————— Power Concentration ———————▶ Egalitarian

| **Type** | Authoritative | Exploitative/ Benevolent | | Consultative | Participatory | Democratic |

| **Example** | Fordist (U.S.A., U.K., 1950s/60s) | | | Japanese ◀——▶ Swedish Industry (1970s/80s onward) | | Co-operatives |

belief rather than 'inevitabilities'. This is not to deny that certain circumstances tend to promote oligarchy and others democracy. Professor Schumacher's book, *Small is Beautiful* (1974), made the point that large organisations tend to require centralised power and that smaller ones can be democratically run. Nevertheless, given the intent, a measure of democracy is possible even in large organisations. At root, preference for organisational oligarchy or democracy depends on a view of human nature. Those who consider that people work best in a highly regulated structure will prefer classical or bureaucratic models: those who consider that people best express themselves in freer contexts will tend to support more democratic organisational structures. Even where democratic systems may be more time-consuming and less efficient, they may still be preferred, for human and moral reasons. But to leave the matter thus would be to mislead. Might, not right or need, usually determines the way organisations operate. Historically, there are almost no examples of democracy being achieved without struggle.

ORGANISATIONS IN THE 'POST-FORDIST' ERA: DOES MORE FLEXIBILITY MEAN MORE DEMOCRACY?

Post-Fordism has been critically presented in the previous chapter (pp. 240–1). The key concept of post-Fordism is flexibility. Industrial organisations are seen as needing to be flexibly organised so as to be able effectively to respond to and even mould market conditions. Thus, the 'core' labour force is required to adapt and innovate quickly and the 'peripheral' labour force can be easily employed, re-deployed or laid-off as necessary (this is especially true in Britain where part-time employees have fewer rights than in most other European countries). Similarly, productive technology is designed to be easily and swiftly reprogrammed and otherwise adapted to meet the variety and extent of market demand. How far the post-Fordist model is actually being implemented is debated (see pp. 239–41).

EMPLOYEES Granted that post-Fordist methods of employee organisation are more flexible than Fordist ones, how far are they also more democratic? In other words has the distribution of power changed in organisations which adopt post-Fordist organisational methods. On the issue of prime importance – that of ownership – the answer is 'no'. Ownership remains out of the hands of employees – a reality which employee share ownership schemes barely affect. The tendency for top management to hold shares in the company for which they are employed was established prior to post-Fordism and is distinct from it.

There is more room for debate about whether post-Fordist organisational approaches promote more democracy in *the process of production*. In dealing with this issue, it is essential to differentiate between at least three groups: first, management, professional scientific and research staff; second, skilled manual or white collar employees; third, 'peripheral' employees. At the first level, there is evidence from companies such as ICI and IBM that 'networking' or working in teams in a fairly autonomous way in order to 'problem solve' has become more common. In rapidly changing, highly competitive economic conditions, autonomous teams working within a given framework can often reach solutions more quickly, efficiently and inexpensively than the same number of individuals working more or less in isolation. At the second level – skilled employees – similar principles have also been applied, initially by the Japanese and more recently by their imitators, including some British companies. 'Quality circles' provide an example of this. These are meetings of employees, usually directly involved in production, the purpose of which is to improve production and the product by pooling and discussing ideas. The meetings are attended by or report back to management. Other means of achieving employee feedback – some as simple as providing a 'suggestions' sheet or 'post-box' – have also been widely adopted in industry during the nineteen eighties and nineties.

It can, then, be argued that flexibility has or, certainly, can involve full-time, 'permanent', employees at all levels in more consultation and even participation in the process of production. In general, the higher status the employee is, the stronger this tendency is likely to be. Clearly, part-time and/or temporary employees are likely only to be marginally affected by these tendencies even in employment contexts in which they are well established. Limited experience of and commitment to 'the firm' is likely to limit any effective feedback. For many in their situation, the sharper realities are the need to make money conveniently and the possibility of losing their jobs.

It must be stressed that even for the 'core' labour force, flexibility may involve greater democracy only in the process of production and not in ownership. The power, resources and security that come from ownership are not extended to employees. Indeed, during the recession of the late nineteen eighties/early nineties, tens of thousands of highly qualified employees were 'flexibly' removed from industry, particularly such service industries as banking and finance. Although flexibility may increase satisfaction and involvement in the workplace, it is ultimately a strategy for making production more efficient. As such, it implies a more flexible hiring and firing of the workforce. 'Democracy' in the context of flexibility is a secondary and perhaps even incidental issue.

Another group that experienced a 'boom' in the middle nineteen eighties but struggled during the recession was small business. The 'autonomy' and 'freedom' many small businesses enjoy in fact depends increasingly on supplying big business. When big business contracted, so did sub-contracting which demonstrates that the apparent independence of the small business sector can mask structural dependency.

The strengthening of managerial power during the nineteen eighties to some extent ran counter to the potential employee involvement brought about by 'flexibility'. This trend is discussed in detail below, but needs to be mentioned here in the context of organisational democracy. It is particularly in the public sector – notably in health, education and social work – that the power of management has been increased by government at the expense of that of professionals – doctors, teachers, and social workers. Led more or less directly by government, management is required to set targets, specify and limit costs, and often to stipulate how a service should be 'delivered' to the 'customer' (no longer referred to, in the traditional professional jargon, as the 'client'). This organisational framework as so

far described is hierarchical and probably even less democratic than the more professionally controlled system which preceded it. In fairness, however, the new managerialism is also related to a new (or revived) concept of customer power and it is to this issue we now turn.

'CUSTOMERS' AND CITIZENS The concept of customer or consumer power has been central to notions of broadening economic democracy in contemporary society. In recent debate, consumer power has usefully been linked with the goal of 'quality' in the production and delivery of goods and services. Recently also consumer theory has been linked to citizenship theory by the three major political parties.

Two views of the relationship between consumption and quality can be distinguished here. First, is the laissez-faire liberal approach now associated in its more uncompromising versions with the political right. In this view, the choice of the consumer in the market place forces the producer to meet the consumer's requirements – or risk losing business. This approach can be referred to as consumerism. A second approach to consumer power has been developed particularly in relation to the consumption of public services. In this view, the consumer has a democratic right as a citizen to influence the quality of the goods or services s/he consumes. This approach can be referred to as participatory democracy or, simply, the democratic approach.

The consumerist approach was 'repackaged' in the nineteen eighties by linking it to a new managerialist emphasis on quality control. One of the 'gurus' of management theory, Philip Crossby, defined quality as 'meeting the customer's requirements' (a very different definition from traditional ones which define quality in terms of characteristics of inherent excellence). A means of achieving the goal of 'total quality' is for employees in the same firm to treat each other as 'internal customers'. Critics of the consumerist approach suggest that it is as much motivated by the desire to persuade employees to work harder as by any real concern for the consumer. The competitions, prizes and awards associated with the 'total quality' movement are seen as ways of obtaining cheap publicity. However, the existence of such motives does not necessarily preclude the achievement of greater product quality.

Following the logic of nineteen eighties consumer rhetoric, John Major's Conservative government has attempted to extend the concept of consumer rights to the public services in the form of a 'Citizens' Charter'. By 1992, this approach had received its fullest application to education in the form of the document *The Parent's Charter: You and Your child's Education* (DES, 1991). The heavily consumerist emphasis of the charter is underlined on the second page where five key documents which parents are entitled to receive are listed:

- **A report about your child**
- **Regular reports from independent inspectors**
- **Performance tables for all your local schools**
- **A prospectus or brochure about individual schools**
- **An annual report from your school's governors**

The main purpose of the charter appears to be to ensure that parents (consumers) have enough information effectively to pressure schools to raise standards (quality).

Noami Pfeffer and Anna Coote explore what they refer to as the 'democratic' approach to quality in *Is Quality Good For You? A Critical Review of Quality Assurance in Welfare Services* (1991). As Labour Party policy experts, they are at pains to stress the difference between their 'democratic' approach and a purely consumerist one. They contend that the right merely to be a competitive individual consumer is insufficient in relation to the public services. In the context of education, welfare and social security, it is in the general interest that everybody's needs are equally met and that services are universally maintained at a high standard (as far as resources allow). The right to information about and representation within public services is to achieve more effective cooperation rather than competition. Citizenship is linked to and underpinned by both a commitment to meeting basic needs and to the right to a substantial democratic involvement in how needs are met. Both these principles are well-expressed in a check-list for action to combat poverty presented by Peter Beresford and Ruth Lister (*The Guardian*, 17 July 1991:23):

- **It's best to build from a local level, although local campaigns aren't always the easiest.**
- **It's important to start where people are.**
- **Involving people takes time, support and resources.**
- **It works best by word of mouth.**
- **Education and training have an important part to play in gaining confidence and skills.**
- **Much can be learnt from disability and other self-advocacy movements.**
- **Poor people have allies in professional agencies who will help.**

They stress, however, that the right to democratic participation is complemented by 'the human and civil rights' to housing, income and education.

It is possible that the political debate for the nineteen nineties will substantially focus on defining and delivering some version of consumer or citizens' rights. The way these rights are implemented organisationally – democratically or otherwise – will be crucial to their effective attainment.

Organisational Change Under Thatcherism

Thatcherism demonstrated that government can play a significant role in setting the ideological and political conditions within which organisations operate. The impact of government policy on public sector institutions was partly decentralising but in other respects centralising.

Two main complementary motives behind Thatcherism were the desire to extend the free market and to reverse what were seen as the centralising and bureaucratic tendencies of socialism. In pursuit of these goals, Thatcherism had a major impact on the organisational structure of much of Britain's institutional life. The impact was most direct and obvious in the public sector for which the government had immediate authority. In education, for example, the free market element was strongly apparent in the open enrolment and opting out policies (see p. 107). These policies considerably reduced the power of local education authorities. On the other hand, a centralised national curriculum was established and local educational inspectorates strengthened partly in order to oversee its enforcement. Within schools and other teaching institutions the power, pay and status of senior management was increased relative to that of teachers.

A similar policy pattern occurred in relation to health. Hospitals and General Medical Practitioners were able to apply to 'opt out' of the control of district health authorities (see pp. 388–9). On the other hand, throughout the NHS, the power of management was increased at the expense of professionals, and particularly within hospitals, at the expense of consultants. There was a shift from management by committee and consensus towards management by individual managers. Management itself became more responsible to central government for the achievement of prescribed 'goals' and 'targets' (points on the way to goals). While, therefore, there was considerable institutional decentralisation under Thatcherism, certain threads of control remained with central government and were even strengthened at the expense of local control. Further, within particular organisations, management tended to become more not less hierarchical.

Two key characteristics of management trends under Thatcherism require specifying. First, more power, responsibility and control was put into the hands of management, particularly senior management. While the power and control of management tended to be strengthened at all levels, direct lines of responsibility through senior, middle and junior management were strengthened and clarified. Thus, the overall effect has been to intensify hierarchy. Once strengthened, management was expected to achieve greater productive and cost efficiency i.e. more and better education, health or broadcasting at an economic rate. Whether or not this has happened is, of course, one of the key issues on which Thatcherism will be judged.

A second characteristic of managerial change under Thatcherism, was the requirement that organisations more clearly establish goals and targets and that individuals be held accountable for their part in achieving these goals. Thus, within education, five year plans became the order of the day (ironically reflecting the Bolshevik model!). Senior management was primarily responsible for ensuring that goals were achieved.

In education and health, considerable new tension developed between management and professionals. The latter felt that power, control, prestige (and sometimes, rewards) had shifted away from them towards management. Indeed, they

Figure 12.2

A Manager's Charter?

Conservative reforms

were popular among

managers if not

among NHS

professionals ...

Managers 'put care second'

TRUST managers are putting business before patient care and failing to consult doctors on the running of an internal market, consultants said yesterday (Jill Sherman writes).

At a meeting of the British Medical Association's consultants committee, doctors complained that managers were seen as "an alien occupying force". Although ministers had made clear that NHS reforms would work only if doctors were fully consulted, members of the 80-strong committee said their views had been largely ignored.

Dr Jim Johnson, a consultant in Merseyside, said managers at Broadgreen Hospital Trust, Liverpool, refused to provide x-ray facilities when its own x-ray department ran into difficulties.

Whiston Hospital, which is directly managed, put together a package to assist Broadgreen, but Dr Johnson claimed that the chief executive refused it. "Looking after sick people is about co-operation not competition," Dr Johnson said.

(Source: *The Times*)

NHS MANAGERS' ATTITUDE TO REFORMS

85%
8%
2%
4%
1%
Mostly disapprove
Thoroughly disapprove
Enthusiastic
Mostly approve
Other

themselves felt more controlled within the above 'managerial' frameworks and, particularly, by techniques such as appraisal which could take the form of a detailed self-account of performance by a professional to a manager. Underlying this tension were two different models of organisational control. One is the functional and hierarchical model described above and the other is a more consensual model of professional control described elsewhere (see pp. 260–2).

COMMENT ON ORGANISATIONAL CHANGE UNDER THATCHERISM

There are two levels on which comment on the Thatcher organisational reforms of the public services can be made. First, has it been successful in its own terms? Second, probing more deeply, how worthwhile are the more fundamental purposes of the above reforms and who are their prime beneficiaries? To address the first point, then, are the public services in Britain more efficient as a result of Thatcherism? The only fair answer to this question at the time of writing (1992), is that the jury is still out – although there is no shortage of provisional judgements. A reasonable comment might be, however, that these reforms would have to be quite clearly successful in achieving efficiency gains to convince critics that the concern and disruption they provoked was worthwhile.

The second issue, concerning the fundamental purposes of Thatcherism is one on which people legitimately take different views. The Thatcher governments were strongly, almost militantly, pro-capitalist and made no secret of their intention of reducing the relative cost of the public sector to the private, capitalist sector. Marxists such as Claus Offe argue that Thatcherism was precisely about creating an institutional context and cultural climate favourable to capital and, in particular, rescuing British capitalism from a crisis of profitability (see pp. 369–70). Indeed, Offe has argued that the social democratic Labour government of James Callaghan was attempting to do exactly this prior to the 1979 general election defeat. However, most Labour and other politicians of the centre-left, while agreeing on the need for a successful private sector would also want greatly to distance themselves from Thatcherism. In particular, they argue that they would allocate relatively more resources to public services and implement policy in a different way and through different means than did Mrs Thatcher.

'Ways and means' relate to the issue of 'organisation'. Any serious aspiration to implement 'democratic socialism' – the professed aim of the Labour Party – would promote more democracy in organisations in both the private and public sector. As described earlier in this chapter a number of Britain's European partners have implemented more industrial democracy than Britain and this is a policy favoured by Labour. On the issue of professional involvement and responsibility, it is Labour's policy to establish a Teachers' Council which may initiate a greater share of power and prestige for teachers. To many, however, Labour's commitment to extending organisational democracy still appears lukewarm. The extension of democracy has long been the neglected part of the agenda of social democracy yet the history of socialism suggests that the achievement of greater material equality without achieving greater democracy fails ultimately to satisfy the people.

Finally, although this section concentrates on organisational issues within the public sector, the interplay between Thatcherism and organisational ideology and practice within capitalist enterprise is important. It will be clear from reading the sections on post-Fordism (pp. 238–41) and Thatcherite industrial policy (pp. 259–60) that Mrs Thatcher introduced elements of post-Fordism into the public sector with perhaps more robustness and determination than occurred in the private sector. It remains to be seen whether John Major will pursue similar policies following the Conservative general election victory of 1992.

Conclusion: Organisational Theory: Towards Unification or Fragmentation?

Michael Reed's review article *Scripting Scenarios For a New Organisational Theory and Practice* (1991) raises the possibilities that organisational theory may become either more unified or more fragmentary.

The possibility of a more unified approach to organisational theory is not new. Writing over a quarter of a century ago, Amitai Etzioni considered that the conflict structural approach which he adopted embodied the essential elements of both the classical and human relations perspectives. He clearly considers these to be two sides of the same coin – the rational and the personal-social. He also observes that conflict is a normal and, sometimes, a useful, feature of organisational life. For instance, a strike involves conflict, but it can lead to a settlement of differences and to a new period of organisational stability.

Etzioni is pursuing a promising approach in bringing together conflict-structuralism and micro-level sociology. However, Clegg and Dunkerley's more recent work, *Organization, Class and Control* (1981), is a still more impressive attempt at synthesis. Whereas Etzioni draws mainly from Weber in presenting structural-conflict, Clegg and Dunkerley lean heavily towards Marx. They see class domination and conflict as endemic in both capitalist enterprise and state bureaucracy. They considered that the state bureaucracy in the Soviet Union was even more repressive than the state in capitalist society, and in this analysis Weber's understanding of the oppressive burden of state bureaucracy is apparent. Yet they avoid

implying, as the structural-functionalists do, that the men and women who occupy small roles in large organisations are for that reason powerless. They stress that workers interpret and respond to their conditions and sometimes organise to change them. In this way conflict-structural theory and interactionism seem to complement each other in their work. Of course, Marxists appreciate with functionalists that organisations can function without conflict for long periods and sometimes almost indefinitely. The difference is that Marxists consider that structural division and, therefore, potential conflict is a permanent feature of capitalist society, whereas functionalists consider basic harmony and consensus as more normal. For Marxists such consensus is the result of the ideological conditioning of the working class to conform to a social and organisational order that exploits them and drastically limits their self-expression.

Reed is challenging on the issue of fragmentation in organisational analysis. He writes of a powerful contemporary intellectual undercurrent which suggests that the time may be ripe to abandon the concept of organisation as the core concept of the area. Organisations are not a single coherent category of entities but vary vastly and have different significance to different people. It might be more fruitful if, instead of 'seeing' organisations as structures, we envisage them as processes created by people in consensus or in conflict which they construct or deconstruct continuously.

SUMMARY

1 A preliminary distinction is made between formal and informal organisations. Formal organisations are operated on the basis of established rules by appointed personnel to achieve specific goals. Informal organisations are freely created social group relationships outside or inside formal organisations.

2 Bureaucratic organisations are operated hierarchically by trained personnel on the basis of specified rules and with the help of formal records.

3 Organic systems are organisations which operate on less formal, less bureaucratic lines in which members 'network' (communicate quite freely) with each other.

4 Several organisational theories tend to reflect either bureaucratic or organic theories. However, social action/ interactionist theories and conflict theories do offer distinctive alternative perspective although they are not necessarily or wholly incompatible with the previous two approaches.

5 Traditional organisational theory can be contrasted as follows:

Bureaucratic
(Mechanistic)
Scientific management

Functional systems theory
Organic
Human relations theory
Socio-technical systems theory

6 Social action and interactionist theories argue that within organisations people seek to make their roles and activities meaningful. Erving Goffman's classic study illustrates this in relation to an asylum.

7 Conflict theories raise issues of power, control, domination, exploitation and legitimation and various forms of conflict including interest group and class conflict as these affect organisations. They also explore how organisations may be made more democratic.

8 Thatcherism attempted to introduce elements of the free-market into the public sector and strengthened management at the expense of professionals. Arguably, there is some tension between these two policy aspects.

9 Organisational theory currently manifests both a tendency to 'unification' and to a kind of creative fragmentation.

RESEARCH AND COURSEWORK

You have probably realised by now that the term organisation can be applied to a vast variety of contexts, formal or informal, in which people relate in a more or less structured way over time. This gives a wide choice for research of types of organisation and situations of cooperation, conflict or negotiation within organisations. Whatever organisation or organisational situation you may choose to research, it is essential to retain an overall theoretical perspective.

Theoretical questions asked about organisations are:

■ What are the functions/purposes of the organisation and how are these achieved?

■ Do informal groups within the organisation contribute positively or negatively to the achievement of its goals?

■ How meaningful/alienating are the organisations purposes and processes to its members?

■ Is the organisation characterised by consensus or conflict?

■ Does the organisation operate on behalf of one group or class at the expense of another?

If you find your research is not addressing questions of the above scope, it is probably weighted too much towards description and too little towards theoretical enquiry and analysis.

FURTHER READING

A useful general introduction to the area is Glenn Morgan's *Organisations in Society* (Macmillan, 1990). Erving Goffman's *Asylums* (Penguin, 1968) is an interactionist classic and offers inspiration in an area of notoriously lethal literature.

QUESTIONS

1   Critically assess Michel's assertion that, 'who says organisation, says oligarchy' (AEB, 1985)

2   'Studies of formal organisations that neglect organisational cultures and informal social processes are self-defeating'. Discuss. (London, 1989)

3   What are 'total institutions' and how do people adapt and survive within them?

13 Deviance

This chapter begins by considering issues concerning the data on which theories of deviance are based, particularly in relation to official criminal statistics. Problems concerning official statistics and class, gender, race and age are considered.

There follows a major theoretical section on social order, control and deviance. Of the theories discussed, only functionalism and Marxism and to a lesser extent interactionism offer developed theories of order and control as well as of deviance. However, other theories of deviance are also presented. The chapter concludes with a discussion of suicide – a topic which raises again some of the problems in relation to official statistics and sociological theory and method analysed in the first section of this chapter.

Official Statistics and Their Limitations

The data on crime and suicide given in official statistics represent only one measure. The most widely used measure of crime is based on crimes known to the police and officially recorded. Similarly, the official measure of suicide is based on verdicts of coroners. The analyses of criminal and suicide statistics in this chapter raise important questions about how these are compiled as well as key issues of sociological theory and method.

Table 13.1 gives the number of notifiable offences recorded by the police for the years 1971, 1989 and 1990 for England and Wales, Scotland, and Northern Ireland respectively. Because of differences in the way the statistics were compiled, those of Scotland are not precisely comparable to the others nor are the statistics for 1971 precisely comparable to those of 1989 and 1990. However, general trends can be approximately located.

On the basis of these figures, there was a high increase in all categories of crime between 1971 and 1989 and quite a sharp increase in most categories of crime between 1989 and 1990. Figure 13.1 presents the change in recorded offences between (and including) 1980 and 1990, and shows a steady but by no means unbroken cumulative increase. There was a particularly sharp overall increase in 1990.

The steady and sometimes sharp increase in most categories of crime – particularly those involving violence against the person and burglary/theft (especially car-related) – is now almost a perennial matter of official and public concern. However, there is consistent and convincing evidence that figures based on crimes notified to the police substantially understate the amount of crime committed.

One source of such evidence is the Home Office's *British Crime Survey*. Its findings are based on questions to the general public

Table 13.1

Notifiable offences recorded by the police: by type of offence

▼

England & Wales, Scotland and Northern Ireland									Thousands
	England & Wales			Scotland			Northern Ireland		
	1971	1989	1990	1971	1989	1990	1971	1989	1990
Notifiable offences recorded									
Violence against the person	47.0	177.0	184.7	5.0	14.0	13.6	1.4	3.3	3.4
Sexual offences	23.6	29.7	29.0	2.6	3.1	3.2	0.2	0.9	0.8
of which, rape and attempted rape	. .	3.3	3.4	0.2	0.5	0.5	. .	0.1	0.1
Burglary	451.5	825.9	1,006.8	59.2	93.7	101.7	10.6	14.7	14.8
Robbery	7.5	33.2	36.2	2.3	4.4	4.7	0.6	1.7	1.6
Drugs trafficking	. .	9.2	10.0	. .	2.1	2.8	. .	–	–
Theft and handling stolen goods	1,003.7	2,012.8	2,374.4	104.6	234.7	255.2	8.6	27.1	29.3
of which, theft of vehicles	167.6	393.4	494.2	17.1	29.1	36.1	. .	6.4	7.0
Fraud and forgery	99.8	134.5	147.9	9.4	24.1	25.0	1.5	4.4	4.2
Criminal damage	27.0	465.6	553.5	22.0	79.1	86.4	7.4	2.0	2.2
Other notifiable offences	5.6	18.5	21.1	5.0	40.3	46.0	0.5	1.0	1.0
Total notifiable offences	1,665.7	3,706.2	4,363.6	211.0	493.4	535.8	30.8[7]	55.1	57.2

(Source: Social Trends, 1992)

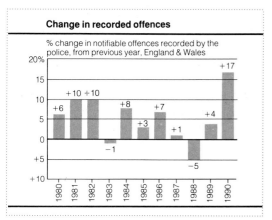

Change in recorded offences

% change in notifiable offences recorded by the police, from previous year, England & Wales

Figure 13.1 (Far left)

males were seven times more likely to become victims of violent street crime than women over 61, yet the latter group was much more fearful of such crime (but see below).

The *Islington Crime Survey* (No. 2, 1990) also provides information on the amount, nature and experience of crime unavailable in official police statistics. The survey is based on detailed interviews of a demographically representative sample of 1,600 people living in Islington, London. Many of its findings are generalisable to other inner urban neighbourhoods. In order to provide a further rough measure of the amount of crime, respondents were asked if they knew people who had committed given crimes. Thirty eight per cent knew someone who had stolen from a shop, 53.5 per cent knew a cannabis smoker, and 13.5 per cent knew a burglar.

The ICS gives a different and perhaps more sympathetic analysis of public fear of crime, particularly among females. The survey found that 30 per cent of respondents had been victims or knew victims of street robbery in the previous year. Fear of crime greatly affects the behaviour of many women in inner urban areas. 26 per cent of women aged between 16–24, 27 per cent aged between 25–54, and 68 per cent aged over 55 never go out alone at night. Further, 74 per cent of women compared to 40 per cent of men stay in very or fairly often and when they do go out are more likely to restrict their movements as a precaution

about their knowledge of, and feelings about, crime, including experience of being a victim. In all categories of crime shown in figure 13.2 there is a massive difference – in most cases of several hundred per cent – between recorded crime and the aggregated figure of the three categories – recorded, reported, but unrecorded, and unreported crime (the so-called 'dark figure'). If these figures are even approximately accurate, the number of notifiable offences recorded by the police grossly underestimates the amount of crime.

The *British Crime Survey* provides a range of other data which can be used to clarify the understanding of crime of both criminologists and the public. Thus, it may surprise some that as well as being the most likely perpetrators of crime, young males are by far the most likely of any age/sex group to be victims of it. The BCS showed that young

Figure 13.2

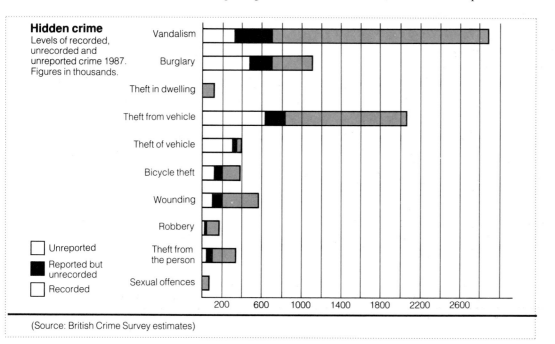

Hidden crime
Levels of recorded, unrecorded and unreported crime 1987. Figures in thousands.

Vandalism
Burglary
Theft in dwelling
Theft from vehicle
Theft of vehicle
Bicycle theft
Wounding
Robbery
Theft from the person
Sexual offences

☐ Unreported
■ Reported but unrecorded
☐ Recorded

200   600   1000   1400   1800   2200   2600

(Source: British Crime Survey estimates)

against crime. This can include avoiding certain streets or public transport. The survey states that 'It is not an exaggeration to conclude that many women in inner city areas live in a state of virtual curfew'. Thus, crime appears to be a further area in which mainly male behaviour largely controls female behaviour.

METHODS OF ACQUIRING CRIME DATA OTHER THAN OFFICIAL STATISTICS: VICTIM SURVEYS; SELF-REPORT; EXPERIMENT

As was indicated above, the British Crime Survey and the Islington Crime Survey employed a variety of questions to establish more information about crime and its impact. These included asking respondents if they had been victims rather than perpetrators of crime (the latter question invariably produces a lower figure than the former – as you can probably discover by putting both to any group of people). A victim survey, then, involves researchers asking respondents if they have been victims of given crimes. The difference between recorded crime and crime claimed by victims to have occurred is high in some categories – such as vandalism – and much less in others – such as bicycle theft and motor vehicle theft. It is generally true that more serious offences are reported to the police and appear in their statistics.

It would be a mistake to assume that the results of victim surveys provide the 'real' measure of crime. Victims do not always realise when a crime has been committed against them. In fact, such a large proportion of white collar crimes – such as offences against the Trade Descriptions Act – may go unnoticed that victim surveys are probably an inadequate instrument for measuring such crime. Indeed, white collar crime is, in general, particularly difficult to measure.

Another technique for measuring crime rates is the self-report study. A self-report study seeks voluntary information from respondents about whether or not they have committed crime. In general, such studies show that a large majority have committed criminal acts at some point in their lives, although only a minority have acquired a criminal record. In a number of self-report studies of young people, the ratio of working class to middle class delinquent activity drops

from the five or six to one of official statistics to about 1.5 to one. Again, typical images of criminals partly depend on how particular sets of criminal statistics are compiled.

Experimentation offers a third means by which the information and stereotypes purveyed in official criminal statistics can be tested. Farrington and Kidd (1980) left apparently genuine letters enclosing money in various public places. The letters varied in the amount of money they obtained and in certain other key respects. The individuals who picked up the letters were observed and a check was effected on whether they kept them or posted them on. Women proved as likely to steal as men except where larger sums were involved, when about a quarter of the women and half the men stole. Despite the latter finding, the experiment as a whole suggests that, contrary to what might be argued from official statistics, females are scarcely less 'naturally' prone to theft than males when given the opportunity. Unlike the other two techniques of enquiry, however, this one refers not to crime committed in 'natural' social circumstances but in 'unnatural' experimental conditions.

CRIME STATISTICS AND STEREOTYPING: CLASS; SEX; AGE AND RACIAL STEREOTYPES

Official statistics influence popular stereotypes of 'the typical criminal'. The classic criminal stereotype is working class, male, young, and more recently black. Of course, not all of these stereotypes always occur together. For instance, organised, large-scale crime is associated with older rather than younger males. Nevertheless, there is a tendency for these stereotypes to reinforce each other. Figure 13.3 represents the likelihood of going to prison dependent on class, gender, race and age (the figure is based on American data but the trends are similar throughout the Western world). The data in the figure appears to support popular stereotypes of criminals but how far is this data and data which appears to show similar trends the result of the existence of stereotypes in the first place? To what extent do the police and courts look for what they expect to find, and so create self-fulfilling prophecies in relation to 'the typical' criminal? We will briefly examine the class,

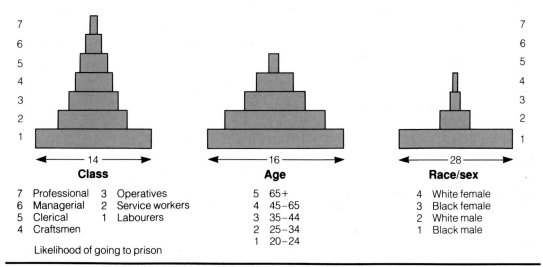

Class		Age		Race/sex	
7	Professional	5	65+	4	White female
6	Managerial	4	45–65	3	Black female
5	Clerical	3	35–44	2	White male
4	Craftsmen	2	25–34	1	Black male
3	Operatives	1	20–24		
2	Service workers				
1	Labourers				

Likelihood of going to prison

(From: J. Lea and J. Yang *What is to be done about law and order?* Penguin, 1984: 98)

CLASS AND CRIME Is the stereotype that working class people commit more crime than middle class people correct? Broadly, it is only accurate in relation to certain types of crime, particularly, 'street crime' and burglary. These types of crime tend to be obvious and likely to be recorded whereas white collar crime is more likely to be both under-detected, under-recorded and, arguably, underpunished. We have already cited a range of studies by both interactionists and Marxists which seek to demonstrate an in-built (though not necessarily always conscious) bias of the social and legal systems in favour of the upper and middle classes and against the working class. As early as 1940, Edwin Sutherland produced evidence that white collar crime might be substantially under-estimated in official statistics. He found that often the petty crimes of pilfering or major crimes of bribery passed unnoticed or were dealt with 'within the firm'. Even the flouting of commercial and industrial law was more likely to be the subject of governmental reprimand than legal action. A study by W S Carson of 200 firms in south-east England some 25 years later, similarly found that only 1.5 per cent of officially detected breaches of factory legislation were prosecuted. To these we must add the more far-reaching allegations, made by Marxists , of crime involving local ruling elites and, internationally, large corporations (pp. 305–6).

It should be stressed, however, that as Britain becomes more a service society and less a manufacturing society, and there is a corresponding decrease in the size of the traditional working class and increase in the number of white collar employees, the types of crime committed and the perception of crime are beginning to change. Computer crime and business and financial fraud have increased alongside burglary and car-related theft. In turn, more attention has been given to white collar crime both by government and law enforcement agencies, which affects statistics and perception in relation to this type of crime. In the late nineteen eighties and early nineteen nineties, there was a spate of major fraud trials in both Britain and the United States including the Guinness share price fixing case and the multi-billion dollar swindles of Ivan Boesky and Donald Milken. Both the potential for this type of crime and the surveillance of it has increased. However, in all these cases the penalties appeared comparatively lenient.

Ethnomethodologist Aaron Cicourel's *The Social Organisation of Juvenile Justice* (1976) indicates how misleading statistics might be compiled about crime among young, middle and working class males. He examines how two towns, with almost identical populations, experience quite different rates of juvenile crime as recorded in official statistics. He gives two explanations: the

sex, age and 'race' stereotypes in turn. Much evidence in relation to these stereotypes will shortly be discussed in other sections of this chapter and will, therefore, be only summarily referred to here.

▶

Figure 13.4 (Far right)

Gender, age and

crime

different organisational policies pursued by the police in the two towns, and the different way police policy towards delinquency was interpreted 'via the background expectancies' of officers dealing directly with juveniles. In the first town, a loose attitude to recording delinquent acts and an informal approach to dealing with delinquents made the problem appear small, and vice-versa in the other town where much 'tighter' practices and stricter assumptions prevailed. In the first case what came to be regarded as a small problem seemed to require progressively fewer officers to deal with it, whereas in the second case the problem became amplified and so more manpower and resources were deployed to 'solve' it. All this, of course, affected the statistics of delinquency in the two towns in opposite ways, decreasing them in the first instance, and increasing them in the second. Cicourel's general conclusion for sociological research is:

> *A researcher utilising official materials cannot interpret them unless he possesses or invents a theory that includes how background expectancies render everyday activities recognisable and intelligible.*
> *(Cicourel, 1976)*

GENDER, AGE AND CRIME Figure 13.4 gives the comparative number of cautions and convictions for indictable offences for males and females under 21 for three years: 1961, 1971 and 1989. While the rate of increase of crime for young females has been slightly greater, the total amount of crime committed by young males was still recorded as about six times greater than that committed by young females in 1989. Similar differences between the sexes occur at other age stages but the 14 to 21 age stage is the peak period in the life-cycle for criminal activity. One third of all crimes known to the police are committed by people of seventeen years of age or under. Given that a large majority of youthful offenders are not convicted of crime as adults, it is difficult to avoid the view that their crimes are transitional learning experiences – which most decide not to repeat.

The work of Anne Campbell on female juvenile delinquency goes some way

Offenders aged under 21 found guilty of, or cautioned for, indictable offences: by sex and age

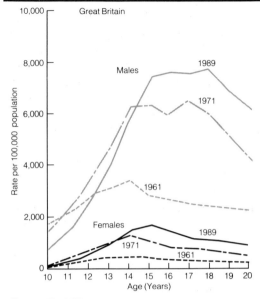

(Source: Social Trends 1991)

Number and age of victims assaulted in Bristol over six month period

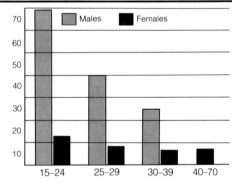

towards undermining the statistical basis for the view that far more males commit crimes than females. Official statistics put the ratio of male to female crime at about six to one – the precise ratio varying with age groups. In a self-report study of 105 adolescent girls, Campbell found that in an overall average of offences, the male to female self-admission rate was 1.12 to one. She attributes this to paternalism on the part of the police who favour what they consider to be 'the gentle sex' in matters of law enforcement. As a result, they issue far more informal and unrecorded cautions to females than males. Campbell's research cannot be considered conclusive, although Farrington and Kidd's evidence (p. 294) also suggests that female crime is under-represented in official statistics. A further consideration is that crimes of violence against the person and property – which males are more likely to commit – are difficult for the police to ignore, whereas it is easier to disregard a crime such as publicly soliciting for sexual purposes – which females are more likely to commit. Certainly, the view that men are 'naturally more aggressive' than women and, consequently, more prone to crime needs to be treated with caution. As more women have moved into the labour force and have received 'tougher' socialisation, the ratio of female to male crime has tended slightly to narrow – even as measured by official statistics.

'RACE' AND CRIME Both official crime statistics and most scholarly studies tend to show a comparatively high rate of 'street crime' among Afro-Caribbeans, especially among the 15–24 year old age group. There are various interpretations of why this is so but the two extreme opposing positions are:

1 Young inner-urban blacks actually do have a higher rate of street crime and
2 Police activity (broadly, 'labelling' blacks as criminal) results in the difference in the general crime rate, although there is little or no real difference.

The police themselves tend to take the first position. For instance, the London Metropolitan Police have used victim surveys giving evidence on the colour of attackers as well as criminal statistics broken down by ethnicity to support their case that the rate of 'street crime' (e.g. assault, robbery, drug-selling) – among young blacks is particularly high. While many police accept that some racism exists among them, racist labelling is seldom cited as a significant factor explaining black crime statistics.

Stuart Hall et al. present a complex analysis of black crime in *Policing the Crisis* (1979) in which they see the oppressive role of the police as part of an oppressive society. They describe inner-urban areas with large concentrated Afro-Caribbean populations as 'colonies' which respond to exploitation by developing their own alternative consciousness and way of life. Hall and his co-authors see crime or 'hustling' as part of this way of life or subculture. For many it offers a better life than drifting between

unemployment and dead-end jobs – with 'mainstream' opportunity closed by racism. Even so, it is only the most successful hustler who can avoid paid-work altogether. Hall refers to the activities of these subcultures as 'cultural resistance' because their members generally reject racial and economic exploitation.

Hall does not consider that the 'high crime rate' of black youth is simply a result of police labelling. Rather, society's racism has 'marginalised' many young blacks and it falls to the police to deal with the resulting 'problem' of social control. As a result of these processes, a significant number of young blacks become 'criminalised'. Hall argues that in the early and mid seventies blacks were scapegoated for, among other things, the cause of white unemployment and of the 'rise in crime'. In particular, young blacks were often seen as potential 'muggers' – a perception certainly shared by numerous police, according to Hall.

John Solomos's observations on crime and the Afro-Caribbean community in *Race and Racism in Contemporary Britain* are compatible with those of Hall. Solomos considers that the way in which young blacks have been presented by much of the media and some agencies of social control as a 'problem' and even as 'the enemy within' (Solomos's phrase) is part of the racialisation of British public life in the nineteen seventies and eighties. They rather than the difficult social and economic conditions they experience, become the object of blame.

John Lea and Jock Young offer an alternative explanation of the role of black crime to what they term as the 'colonial' approach of Hall and others. They describe their own perspective as 'a subcultural approach to race and crime'. They consider that young 'Afro-Caribbean people are more likely to be involved in certain types of crime but also that police stereotyping occurs. These two factors create a vicious circle which has the effect of worsening relations between the police and the black community – a major factor in several urban disorders. Among some young black people an alienated subculture has developed within which crime plays a significant part.

Social Order, Control and Deviance

TERMINOLOGY AND BASIC CONCEPTS The concepts of order, deviance and control describe some of the most basic realities of social life. Order is a state in which social life – actions and interactions – can be conducted without major disruption. The basis of social order is conformity to social norms or rules. Norms may be formal – such as laws – or informal, such as who 'normally' sits where in a common room.

When a society is functioning in an orderly way, most people will generally be observing most norms. Deviance occurs when norms are broken. Deviance can vary from political terrorism – a challenge to social order itself – to failing to observe accepted eating habits. The control of deviant behaviour may be formal or informal. The main formal means of control include the police, the courts, the prison and probation systems and, ultimately, the army. Informal control often takes the form of a look, nudge or frown which says 'behave yourself' or 'get into line'.

Although order is necessary for social life, it is not in itself morally 'good' or 'bad'. How order is achieved in a given regime is a key issue. This can vary from dictatorship to democracy. The purposes to which order is put is also important. Hitler achieved a high degree of order but some of the purposes to which he put it prompted Churchill to refer to Nazism as 'the most wicked and monstrous tyranny that has ever corroded the human breast'.

Concern with the issue of social order long pre-dates the emergence of sociology as a distinct discipline. The political philosophers Hobbes (1588–1679) and Locke (1632–1704) produced work on the themes of power, order and control which is still relevant. Broadly, Hobbes believed that the only way to ensure order was for people to agree to the existence of a single sovereign and absolute governing power – preferably, in his view, monarchy. In contrast, Locke believed that people have natural rights which they cannot sign away and that government must therefore be by consent – this implies that governments which grossly abuse natural rights can be removed (which Hobbes did not accept). The tension between the need for order and the liberties and rights of human beings is expressed widely within sociology and political science.

HISTORICAL PHASES IN DEVIANCY CONTROL The control of deviant behaviour varies considerably between historical periods. Stanley Cohen has examined both the philosophy and practice of deviancy control in three periods: the pre-eighteenth century; the nineteenth and first half of the twentieth century; and the contemporary period from the mid twentieth century (*Visions of Social Control: Crime, Punishment and Classification* (Polity Press, 1985)).

Cohen's historical analysis is very useful to set against the more static picture of deviance presented by the various perspectives discussed below. Cohen describes the control and definitions of

▶

Table 13.2

Two phases of deviancy definition/control

	Nineteenth-Century Transformation	1960s: Counter Ideologies/Destructuring Movements
Trends away from the State	(1) Centralised state control	Decentralisation, deformalisation, decriminalisation, diversion, divestment, information, non-intervention
the Expert	(2) Categorisation, separate knowledge systems, expertise, professionalisation – e.g. social workers, probation officers	Deprofessionalisation, demedicalisation, delegalisation, anti-psychiatry, self-help, removal of stigma and labels
the Institution	(3) Segregation: victory of the asylum/prison	Decarceration, deinstitutionalisation, community control
'the Mind' (i.e., 'Mind Control')	(4) Positivist theory: move from body to mind – treatment, cure of 'causes'	Back to justice, neo-classicism, behaviourism

(Source: Adapted from S. Cohen, 1985:17)

deviant behaviour as culturally dynamic and shifting, reflecting changes in the economic, social and political areas. Table 13.2 deals only with the 'transformation' from nineteenth century principles and practice in relation to deviance to contemporary ones – but it is very illuminating. Cohen sees a movement away from state control of deviance, from unquestioned acceptance of 'expert' opinion, from segregating deviants from the rest of the community, and from a simplistic belief that the causes of deviance could be established by research and treated by science.

Theories of Social Order, Control and Deviance

Of the perspectives discussed below, only functionalism, Marxism and, perhaps, interactionism give full theoretical accounts of social order and control as well as of deviance. Two of the perspectives discussed – the psychological and the ecological – concentrate mainly on deviance. The concluding perspective – the 'rational choice' approach – does consider the issue of control but within too narrow a framework to qualify as a fully evolved social theory.

PSYCHOLOGICAL PERSPECTIVES

The view that some individuals are psychologically predisposed to crime as a result of their biological inheritance is not, of course, sociological, although sociologists must consider its validity against sociological explanations. The recent origins of this view are traceable, in crude form, to Cesare Lombroso, an Italian doctor whose ideas were influential around the turn of the last century. Lombroso believed that certain 'primitive' physical characteristics, including large jaws, acute sight and a love of orgies(!) indicated a criminal type, but empirical research by Charles Goring established no such correlations. More recently, it has been suggested that men possessing an extra male sex chromosome (Y) are more likely to commit violent crime than others. This is so, but such men still account for a very small proportion of all violent crime.

Hans Eysenck is the champion of the hereditarian argument in this as in other fields. He claims to have established a link between certain genetically based personality traits, such as extroversion, and criminal behaviour, although he prudently describes this as a predisposition, not a necessarily causal factor. Sociologists tend to react sceptically to such arguments. It can never be finally proved that a given action is primarily the 'result' of genetic predisposition rather than either the influence of social environment or individual choice. Sociologists are, however, more favourably inclined to psychological arguments which explain behaviour as a response to social or, for that matter, physical environment, rather than heredity. Thus, the Chicago school of sociologists, whose work we discuss later, appreciated that the material deprivation, physical decay and tough cultural environment of the inner city influenced children in such areas towards delinquency. Sociologists also accept that extreme conditions of this kind might produce mental illness, including criminal pathology (acute material or psychological deprivation, or both, could make someone criminally insane). Nevertheless, few sociologists, if any, see such unusual circumstances as the basis of a general explanation of crime. What they do accept is that certain social conditions might produce a given kind of response, such as delinquency, but such resultant activity is certainly not regarded as mentally abnormal. Some sociologists are occasionally accused of being sympathetic to deviants. If true, this is perhaps less dangerous than regarding them as mentally aberrant, for what solutions to crime does this explanation lead to? Drug treatment? Brain surgery? A course of behaviourist psychotherapy? To some, these treatments seem more insane or, to be consistent, more criminal than the behaviour they seek to control.

FUNCTIONALISM: THE NEED FOR ORDER AND CONTROL

Functionalists stress that order is necessary for effective social life. The complex functioning of what Parsons describes as the four sub-systems – the economy, politics, kinship and community, and cultural organisations – requires social order.

Order is achieved partly through socialising members of society into the accepted values and norms. Socialisation is the means by which value consensus (agreement) is brought about. In other words, the basic values members learn in a given society will generally lead them to conform and therefore behave in an orderly way. Those who are not successfully socialised and become 'deviant' may be controlled by more coercive means – such as the police.

Durkheim emphasised the importance of values (though he used the term 'morals') in controlling disruptive individual passions:

> *The totality of moral rules truly forms about each person an imaginary wall, at the foot of which the flood of human passions dies without being able to go further ... if at any point this barrier weakens, (these) previously restrained human forces pour tumultously through the open breach; once loosened they find no limits where they can stop.*
>
> **(E Durkheim quoted in Giddens, 1972)**

Durkheim also stressed the positive as well as the controlling aspects of moral values in that they can enable individuals to feel that they are part of something bigger than themselves (in this case, society). The following quotation from a more recent functionalist, Edward Shils, makes the same point. The second part of the quotation moves on from describing the unifying effect of values to that of symbols which are representations of something 'larger' (thus, the reverence which may be inspired by a national flag occurs because it symbolises a nation).

> *The existence of a central value system rests, in a fundamental way, on the need which human beings have for incorporation into something which transcends and transfigures their concrete individual existence. They have a need to be in contact with symbols of an order which is larger than their own bodies and more central in the 'ultimate' structure of reality than is their routine everyday life.*
>
> **(E Shils quoted in Worsley, 1972)**

The main values of a society – what Shils calls 'the central value system' – are, then, seen as essential in creating conformity and order.

Two familiar criticisms of functionalism in general can be applied to the above analysis of social order. These are that it overstates the degree of value consensus in many societies, and underestimates the amount of conflict. In fairness, the functionalist model of society does allow for considerable conflict within the system and also acknowledges that systems can break down. However, functionalists disagree with Marxists that conflict is at the very heart of society, neither do they accept that order operates primarily in the interests of 'the ruling class'.

FUNCTIONALIST THEORY OF DEVIANCE

DURKHEIM: THE CHARACTERISTICS OF DEVIANCE Durkheim was perhaps the first to analyse deviance, or 'social pathology' as he called it, in terms of broad sociological theory. He argued that deviance is universal (and normal), relative, and functional. We will discuss these characteristics in turn.

DEVIANCE: UNIVERSAL (AND NORMAL) Durkheim argued that in every society some people deviate from the norms and that deviance is therefore universal. However, he stressed that although certain types of deviance may occur normally in a given society, levels can reach abnormal proportions.

Sociologists agree about the universality and normality of deviance in the above limited sense. While the idea of a normal 'level' of deviance is now little used, sociologists certainly do seek to explain major changes in the rate (or level) of particular types of deviance – such as child abuse or theft.

DEVIANCE: RELATIVE In saying deviance is relative, Durkheim meant that what is defined as deviant varies, because different cultural groups have different norms (although there may be some overlap between groups). Thus, to consume alcohol would be deviant in an orthodox Muslim community, but not in most Christian ones. A further illustration of the relative nature of deviance is that what is considered deviant can change historically within a given culture. Thus, divorce used to be generally considered deviant in British society but is now commonly accepted as within the bounds of normal behaviour.

Because of the relative nature of deviance, Durkheim argued that people should completely abandon the still-too-widespread habit of judging an institution, a practice or a moral standard as if it were good or bad in itself, for all social types indiscriminately.

DEVIANCE: FUNCTIONAL Durkheim argued that deviance can be functional to society providing it does not reach excessive proportions (for that society). Thus, he wrote that 'crime is, then necessary' because it contributes 'to the normal evolution (development) of morality and law'. Deviance makes this contribution by stimulating social disapproval and thus causing normally acceptable behaviour to be affirmed. Durkheim referred to this as a 'boundary-maintaining' function – by drawing the line between 'them' (deviants) and 'us' ('normals'), and by punishing the former, 'society' emphasises what is and is not acceptable conduct.

Durkheim also believed that occasionally deviant behaviour can be functional by contributing to social change. Although he did not use the example, the illegal actions of the suffragettes in their campaign for voting rights for women would be regarded as an illustration of this point.

There is clearly some truth in Durkheim's arguments about the functional nature of deviance. However, it is equally arguable that most deviance is generally more damaging (or dysfunctional) to society (and individuals) than functional. Thus, the functions of murder and theft hardly seem to outweigh the damage they do.

DEVIANCE AS 'SOCIAL PATHOLOGY' While probably all sociologists would agree with Durkheim that deviance is both relative and universal, and the majority would accept that it is, in some sense, functional, many query his characterisation of deviance as 'social pathology'. In making this equation, Durkheim seems influenced by his analogy of society with a biological organism – the organic analogy. He was in no doubt that social pathology tended to increase during times of great social change. In such times people are often left without clear rules or

normative guidelines, and so become more prone to deviance. In particular, the decline of religious certainties could undermine security and confidence in traditional morality. Durkheim referred to this state of 'normlessness' as 'anomie'. We analyse his detailed application of this concept to suicide later in this chapter. He considered that the rapid changes of the late nineteenth century generated a climate of anomie characterised by increasing rates of suicide, homicide, drunkenness and other signs of pathological desperation. He believed that the major problem in modern society is to find a new basis of moral solidarity. He did not believe that mutual self-interest, the basis of organic solidarity, was quite enough.

DURKHEIM: CONCLUSION Durkheim was not content merely to theorise about deviance. His empirical study, *Suicide* (1897), was a deliberate attempt to test some of his main ideas through research and we examine this work later (see pp. 314–16). His influence on the sociology of order and deviance has been immense and even those who have disagreed with him have generally fallen into dialogue with his ideas.

URBAN ECOLOGY AND CRIME

The inner city is the major location of crime associated with deprivation, and the Chicago school attempted to establish links between environment, deprivation and crime, both theoretically and empirically. Mainly by the use of official statistics, they attempted to demonstrate empirical correlation between high rates of crime, numerous other forms of deviancy, such as alcoholism, mental illness, prostitution and suicide, and the conditions of life prevailing in what Burgess called the 'zone of transition' of the urban area. Both the transience of the inner urban population (that is, its unsettled, mobile nature) and the physical decay of the environment were conditions conducive to deviance. The Chicago sociologists, when referring specifically to the physical environment, tended to use the terms 'zone of deterioration' or 'twilight zone' and when referring to population mobility, 'zone of transition'. Decaying conditions helped to create stress on the family, to weaken community relationships, and to isolate the individual, thus giving rise to anomie. Such circumstances could predispose individuals towards deviant behaviour. The fact that these areas were already generously populated by more than their share of assorted crooks, pimps and conmen made the possibility of 'picking up' a criminal 'trade' all the more likely.

The Chicago theorists, like Durkheim before them, contrasted the high crime rates of the inner city with the much lower crime rates of rural and suburban areas. They found an explanation for this, to some extent, in the thinking of Durkheim and Tönnies on the break up of traditional community and the growth of anomie. Small, rural communities can 'police and protect' their own, but in cities, both property and people become impersonal. Cars and luggage, for example, can be stolen in full view of the public who may have no idea of what is going on. Related to this is the vast growth in the amount of property, both personal and public, during this century and particularly since the war. When 'nobody' seems to own, say, a lamp-post or a telephone kiosk, it becomes, psychologically, easier to hurl a brick at it. A further point is that the sheer mass and variety of conflicting interests in the city makes community control difficult, and generates friction conducive to crime.

An overview of studies of delinquency in Britain by John Barron Mays seems to support the conclusions of American research. Studies in Liverpool dockland, in Croydon, in a mining town in the Midlands, and in old and new areas of Bristol all appear to agree that delinquency is a larger part of the way of life of such areas than elsewhere, and has survived the coming of greater prosperity. Mays' work, however, is more recent by some 30 years than that of the Chicago school, and he considers more recent explanations of deviance in the urban context. The Chicago school itself mainly developed that part of Durkheim's anomie theory dealing with social disorganisation in modern urban society.

ROBERT MERTON: SOCIAL STRUCTURE, ANOMIE AND NONCONFORMITY

Functionalist, Robert Merton, greatly modified Durkheim's analysis of deviance. He dropped any notion of deviance as social 'pathology' (illness) and instead conceptualised it as the product of 'strain' between individual goals and the means provided by society for achieving these goals. Where such strain existed, individuals would be more likely to adopt deviant means to achieve their goals. In developing this theory, Merton modified Durkheim's concept of anomie. Durkheim had argued that deviance is likely to increase in circumstances of anomie, i.e. circumstances in which social norms are no longer clear and people are morally adrift. Merton used the term anomie to describe the strain which occurs when individuals experience conflict between their pursuit of society's goals and the means society provides to achieve them (see table 13.3). Merton's theory is sometimes referred to as 'structural' because like Durkheim's, it contextualises deviance or nonconformity within the total social structure.

Merton contrasted conformity with four types of non-conformity (deviance) – see table 13.3. Non-conformity occurs as a result of strain due to anomie.

Table 13.3 (Far right)

	Culture goals	Institutionalised means
1 Conformity	+	+
2 Innovation	+	−
3 Ritualism	−	+
4 Retreatism	−	−
V. Rebellion*	±	±

* This fifth alternative is on a plane clearly different from that of the others. It represents a *transitional* response which seeks to *institutionalise* new procedure-orientated toward revamped culture goals shared by members of the society. It thus involves efforts to *change* the existing structure rather than to perform accommodative actions *within* this structure, and introduces additional problems with which we are not at the moment concerned.
(Source: Taken from Peter Worlsey, ed, *Modern Sociology*, 1978:619.)

For him, conformity lies in accepting the 'culture goals' of society – material success is such a 'culture goal' in the USA – and in pursuing them by legitimate 'institutionalised means' – that is, within the limits of normative and legal acceptability. Correspondingly, three of the four forms of adjustment lie in rejecting either or both culture goals and the institutionalised means by which they can be pursued. The fourth, rebellion, involves both a rejection of the goals and means of the old order (−) and an attempt to assert new ones (+).

There is much to question in Merton's model, as we shall see when we examine his analysis of 'innovation' (his major concern) as applied to criminal deviancy, but he does map out the chief areas of deviancy in a way that is interesting and suggestive of possibilities for further research. Merton himself has developed the concept of ritualism as applied to bureaucratic work. He points out that people involved in such work can become so dominated by rules of procedure and routine that they lose sight of the purpose of their work. Thus, to suggest a contemporary example, a social security official who delays urgently needed assistance until every bureaucratic check has been made on a client is indulging in ritualistic behaviour. Merton feared that such 'bureaucratic characters' might become something of a plague in large-scale, highly organised modern societies.

Merton describes retreatists as those who can succeed neither by legitimate nor deviant means. These 'drop-outs' include 'psychotics, autists, pariahs, outcasts, vagrants, vagabonds, tramps, chronic drunkards and drug addicts'. However, there is a wide range of explanations as to why such people might become retreatist or otherwise nonconformist, which Merton's rather schematic model does not even hint at. Generally, his plus and minus signs tend to oversimplify the complexity of real life, although his model has some value as a starting point for classifying types of deviance.

SUBCULTURAL EXPLANATIONS OF DEVIANCE

The work of Albert Cohen (1955) and Cloward and Ohlin (1961) moves the focus of analysis to the nature of deviant subcultures. A key concept in Cohen's explanation of young working class male delinquency is 'reaction formation'. He describes these delinquents as reacting in a hostile way to middle class or 'college boy' values but at the same time recognising the status and legitimacy that these values bring. The reactive nature of their delinquency maintains the link with middle class values. Part of the reason why a minority of working-class boys become delinquent is that they find it hard to cope with the 'middle class world' – including schools. Delinquency is an adjustment to this problem – though not the only possible one. It is partly anger and frustration which drive the delinquent to pursue values which are in opposition to, or to use Cohen's phrase the very antithesis of, middle class values. The delinquent way of life, then, provides alternative ways of achieving status. Cohen stresses that the most convenient and supportive context in which to pursue delinquency is to join a group or gang. Despite this, Cohen suggests that most delinquents still feel a lingering attachment to the more respectable world they have 'lost'.

Cloward and Ohlin offer a useful typology of deviant subcultures (which clearly owes something to Merton's typology of nonconformity). Whereas Merton highlights that access to legitimate opportunity is unequal, they point out that the same applies to illegitimate opportunity. As a result, the forms deviant subcultures take vary.

They describe three types:

(i) **Criminal subcultures.** These are fairly well organised and hierarchical criminal groups in stable lower class areas. They are run by adults who keep control over potentially erratic younger criminals partly by offering a criminal career structure of possible advancement.

(ii) **Conflict subcultures.** These occur in more disorganised, less stable neighbourhoods. Crime is not controlled by an adult hierarchy and street violence, including gang warfare, among young males typically occurs.

(iii) **Retreatist subcultures.** These occur among lower class youths who have failed to enter either criminal or conflict subcultures. These members typically withdraw into drugs.

Walter Miller (1962), unlike Cohen, does not see lower class delinquency as a reaction against middle class values. Instead, he presents the behaviour as part of the 'distinctive' culture of the lower class as a whole. The lower class way of life is characterised by certain 'focal concerns', among which are a liking for trouble, toughness and masculinity, smartness, excitement, a belief in luck, and a liking for freedom coupled with a dislike of authority.

Two further aspects of Miller's analysis are worth stressing. First, delinquent boys learn their delinquent behaviour within their own subculture. In principle, therefore, learning delinquent behaviour is the same as learning to conform. If delinquency is learnt, then it is not biological or psychological in origin. Second, lower class 'focal concerns' become magnified among adolescents because of the importance of peer group conformity and particularly the need for peer group status among adolescents.

COMMENT AND CRITICISM: STRUCTURAL AND SUBCULTURAL THEORY

Both Merton's structural theory of nonconformity and the various subcultural theories explain deviance in terms of a sharp difference between the mainstream and the deviant. In the former case, criminal behaviour is seen as due to difference in legitimate opportunity (i.e. lack of it on the part of the criminal) and in the latter cultural differences between the mainstream and deviant subcultures are stressed. Both these explanations have achieved wide, if qualified, acceptance in deviancy theory. Further, the views that lack of opportunity and/or cultural environment can 'push people' towards crime have considerable popular credibility.

David Matza (1964) finds structural and subcultural theory mechanistic and deterministic. First, he argues that there is less difference between conformists and deviants than subcultural theorists propose. Most deviants want what most people want. They also share with other people conventional moral values as well as what Matza refers to as 'subterranean' or hidden values of excitement, pleasure and gratification (see p. 223). Unlike others, however, deviants express the latter values illegitimately, i.e. in a deviant way. They are able to do this by 'neutralising' or suspending moral controls. Often this involves a justification of the deviant act. Thus, victimising a member of a minority group may be seen as a contribution to 'cleaning up' society. Matza considers that once moral neutralisation has occurred a person may more easily 'drift' into crime. His second point is complementary. Despite the complex circumstances that may contribute to the committing of a crime, he still allows for an element of individual choice. He regards structural and subcultural theory as over-deterministic in their emphasis on 'external' social factors in explaining crime.

SUBCULTURAL PERSPECTIVE AND BRITISH DEVIANCY THEORY

As might be expected, the concepts of social structure (including norms and values) and subculture figure prominently in British deviancy theory. Thus, we saw that the concept of pupil subculture was widely used in the context of education (pp. 87–8) and earlier in this chapter in relation to youth (pp. 303–4). However, the concepts tend to be used somewhat differently than in American theory.

First, the highly structured gang is regarded as less typically a British phenomenon. Both Downes (1966) and Corrigan (1981) present descriptions of delinquent 'lads' in which the latter kick against authority in a fairly disorganised way. Downes sees delinquency as providing the most exciting leisure opportunities available to the boys and similarly, Corrigan sees them as mainly motivated by the search for 'kicks' and 'fun'. Second, class cultural analysis tends to take a different form in British deviancy theory. This is because it is mainly influenced by Marxist and interactionist theory rather than functionalist/subcultural theory. Thus, Paul Willis does not see a rigid contrast between 'the lads' and 'dominant society' so much as a highly complex relationship within which the lads are ensnared. Willis conveys the subtleties of this relationship by use of such originally interactionist concepts as labelling (pp. 79–80). To a considerable extent, Willis and others echo some of the qualifications made by Matza in analysing cultural aspects of deviancy.

Granted the above comments, there is a broad similarity between American subcultural theory and the British theory referred to above. Stanley Cohen, sees relatively little fundamental difference between the two. Both groups of theorists describe structural 'strain' between the 'deviant' minority and the majority which comes to be expressed in cultural and behavioural terms (Preface to Folk Devils and Moral Panics (Robertson, 1980)).

MARXISM: POWER, ORDER AND CLASS RULE

Marxists recognise that for a society to function efficiently, social order is necessary. However, apart from communist societies, they consider that in all societies one class – the ruling class – gains far more from society than other classes. Because of these benefits, the ruling class seeks to maintain or impose social order – by a variety of means.

Marxists agree with functionalists that socialisation plays a crucial part in promoting conformity and order. However, unlike the latter, they are highly critical of the ideas, values and norms of capitalist society which they term 'capitalist ideology'. Modern Marxists particularly point to education and the media as socialising agencies which delude or 'mystify' the working class into conforming to a social order which works against its 'real' interests. Althusser refers to these agencies as the 'ideological state apparatus'. Nevertheless, most Marxists believe that the working class may come to question dominant ideas and challenge social order which enforces their own inequality. N Abercrombie, N Hill, and B Turner argue that the working class's own collective experience of oppression at work and elsewhere provides them with a possible alternative basis of values and ideology (1980).

If ideology is the 'soft edge' of social control, the hard edge is the army, police, courts and custodial system – what Althusser calls the 'repressive state apparatus'. Marxists suggest that these come increasingly into play when the capitalist system is seriously challenged.

Despite attempts by the ruling class to maintain order in class-divided society, Marxists argue that conflict not consensus is the fundamental social reality. However, they believe that the effective way of combating oppression and inequality is through political organisation and action rather than through acts of deviance. Some Marxists see high rates of crime and other forms of deviance as signs of the weakness of the capitalist system but few consider that such behaviour contributes significantly to the achievement of a new social order.

MARXIST THEORY OF DEVIANCE

Marxist theory makes two main points about deviance. First, deviance is partly the product of unequal power relations and inequality in general. For example, in a capitalist society the rules (e.g. laws) operate broadly in favour of capitalism and the capitalist class and to the disadvantage of the working class. Because of this 'bias' working class people are more likely to become classified as deviant. This is especially true of the poor who may be driven by necessity into crime. Second, despite the fact that 'the rules' operate broadly in favour of the dominant class, some of its members often break and 'bend' the rules for their own gain.

Let us look at these two points in more detail. Marxist analysis of power relations in capitalist society leads them to take the view that the basic legal framework of capitalist society and the way the law is enforced tend to support capitalist society. On the question of the content of the law, they see individual property rights as much more securely established in law than the collective rights of, for instance, trade unions. The latter are seen as insecurely established and likely to be whittled down as they were during the Thatcher administrations of the nineteen eighties. For instance, the closed shop is shortly to be abolished and union membership to be left entirely to the individual.

Marxists argue that not only does the law protect inequality but that, depending on class, people have unequal access to the law. Having money to hire a good lawyer can mean the difference between being found innocent or guilty. At a more subtle level, the ability to present a respectable image in court might appeal favourably to the sentiments of predominantly middle class magistrates, judges and jurors. These points may well explain why there is some evidence to suggest that working class people are more likely to be found guilty than middle class people for the same offence (see pp. 310–11 for data supporting these arguments).

By citing such examples, and there are plenty of them, Marxists are able to throw back the ideals of liberal justice at those who profess them. Does freedom under law simply mean freedom to be unequal? Can freedom exist without a much greater degree of equality? Does equality under the law really exist when the content and operation of the law seem to favour the middle class?

Of course, these are Marxist questions based on controversial Marxist assumptions, but they merit consideration.

We now turn to the second main aspect of Marxist theory of deviance – the crimes committed by the rich and powerful.

In *Crimes of the Powerful* (1976), Frank Pearce offers a critique of upper class crime. He outlines and in part empirically illustrates a full Marxist theory of the law, crime and power of what Marxists call the ruling class. Central to his argument is the concept of 'ideology' which he treats, in traditional Marxist terms, as the ideas of the ruling class (which are sometimes also believed in by sections of the working class). To a large extent, the idea of 'law and order' in capitalist society is regarded by Marxists as simply an ideological tool of the ruling class, intended to make sure that the working class conform. Public moral concern with lower class crime and the money, time and energy spent on controlling it diverts attention from the exploitative activities of the ruling capitalist class, whose leading representatives would not creditably survive close legal scrutiny of their own business or professional lives. Generally, they have the wealth and power to ensure that such examination seldom occurs, but gradually a body of research on upper class crime is being produced. Pearce himself quotes an American Federal Trade Commission estimate that detectable business frauds in that country accounted for over fifteen times as much money as robbery.

William Chambliss' detailed study (1976) of organised crime in Seattle, Washington, reaches the conclusion that leading figures in the business, political and law enforcement fields made up the city's major crime syndicate and worked together for massive criminal gain in gambling, prostitution and drug trafficking. Much illegally made profit was then ploughed back into legitimate business. Chambliss contends that crime occurs among all classes, but that the types of crime committed and the extent to which the law is enforced varies between classes. The crimes of the powerful are likely to be more lucrative and to escape prosecution. It is important to get Chambliss' work in perspective. He does not show that the majority of the local upper class in Seattle is criminally corrupt, and still less that the majority of the upper class in the United States is corrupt. Nor does he or any Marxist have to do so to prove that capitalists control the capitalist system. They do this, according to Marxists, whether they break the law or not. If the 'rules of the game' are weighted in their favour, they may not need to break them. Perhaps the point of Pearce's and Chambliss' research is that if the needs or convenience of the upper class require them to commit crime, some of them do. Robert Maxwell is a spectacular case in point and it cannot be *assumed* he is *wholly* exceptional

Marxists believe that there is a need for the general public to be more precisely informed about the 'crimes of the powerful' and particularly about the relationship between powerful economic interests, the law and political power. The Watergate scandal and aspects of the Westland affair, concerning the relationship between business and politics, hardly fill the public with confidence. Similarly, the large sums shown to have been illegally paid by many international companies to help create favourable trading relations with given countries make petty theft look very petty indeed. To what extent do these cases, however extreme, throw light on what is typical? Here is a tangled but fascinating web for researchers to trace and explain.

Just as Marxists do not accept the law in capitalist society at face value, neither do they accept the categories of crime and deviance as fair or objective. On the contrary, many so-called criminals and deviants in capitalist society are seen as 'victims of the system'. Yet the plight of the lower class criminal and deviant has never concerned Marxists to the extent that it has liberals. This is because Marxists see the hope for social change in a revolutionary movement of the 'solid' working class, certainly not in the criminal fraternity.

COMMENT ON MARXIST THEORY OF DEVIANCE: 'IDEALISM' AND 'REALISM'

Although there is considerable empirical data to support some aspects of Marxist analysis of deviance described above (particularly in relation to the 'crimes of the powerful'), the sheer scope of the overall theoretical framework is perhaps so broad as to be impossible to prove or disprove conclusively. This seems especially true of the central Marxist point that in capitalist society the law and its enforcement basically favours the capitalist class rather than the majority of the public.

Recently some Marxist and Marxist-influenced criminologists have argued that legal justice is more complex than 'idealistic' Marxism suggests. Notable among these is Jock Young whose more recent work we referred to above, p. 297). Young, John Lea and others describe themselves as 'left realists' and distinguish themselves from 'left idealists' whom they see as tending to romanticise working class crime. First, they have begun to pay more attention to the victims of crime – and have acknowledged that often –probably most often – the main victims of 'working class' criminals are working class people. Second, and relatedly, Marxist-influenced criminologists have, in practice, accepted that democracy and the law in capitalist society can be used to improve the protection of working people against crime and criminals. Thus, former sixties radicals such as Young have joined other criminologists in seeking adequately to survey and more effectively to control crime (however they sharply distinguish themselves from those they see as 'right realists' (see pp. 311–12).

INTERACTIONISM: IMPOSED AND NEGOTIATED ORDER

Interactionism does not provide a 'grand theory' of order in society but focuses on small or medium scale social interaction. Groups and individuals are presented as trying to impose their will on others or, more democratically, to negotiate with them.

Howard Becker, perhaps the most influential interactionist theorist of deviance, frequently stresses the extent to which people use power to get their own way:

People are in fact always forcing their rules on others, applying them more or less against the will and without the consent of those others.

In various studies, Becker presents groups and individuals as seeking to impose their order – indeed, their view of 'reality' – on others. Thus, he argues that the law banning the use of marijuana for social purposes in the United States was largely the result of a publicity campaign by the Federal Bureau of Investigation which manipulated the media and Congress. At a smaller scale level, Becker cites evidence that teachers are able to affect the attainment levels of pupils by the force of their own expectations – which can function as 'self-fulfilling prophecies'.

Interactionists consider that in most situations total power is not in the hands of one group or individual. They employ the term 'negotiation' to describe the bargaining process by which order is 'worked out' in contexts as varied as the courts, the classroom and the home. Aaron Cicourel gives an example of negotiation in his book, *The Social Organization of Juvenile Justice (1976)* in which he researches responses *to* juvenile delinquency in two Californian cities. One finding was that after arrest, middle class juveniles were less likely than working class juveniles to be charged with an offence. Ultimately, this affects both criminal statistics – in which working class juveniles 'appear' more prone to crime – and the public's 'image' of the kind of person who is most likely to threaten 'law and order'. The power to 'negotiate', therefore, can have substantial social consequences.

INTERACTIONIST THEORY OF DEVIANCE

LABELLING: HOWARD BECKER

Becker argues that the 'central fact about deviance' is that 'it is created by society'. This seems to turn the 'commonsense' notion of deviance on its head. Society, not the deviant, is being held responsible for deviance. What does Becker mean by this?

I mean ... that social groups create deviance by making the rules where infraction constitutes deviance, and by applying those rules to particular people and labelling them as outsiders. (1966:8)

Becker goes on to give his famous definition of deviance: 'deviant behaviour is behaviour that people so label'. Much of Becker's analysis of deviance concentrates on how and why some people are labelled as deviant and the effect this can have on them. Once a label such as 'troublemaker' or criminal has been given, it can be difficult to get rid of.

Becker does not present the deviant as merely passive. He stresses that much deviant activity is learnt and that learning often has an active aspect to it. The idea that deviant behaviour is learnt is implied in the title of Becker's key essay 'Becoming a marijuana user', and is consistent with Mead's theory of socialisation. Becker points out that to smoke marijuana and find it enjoyable, the technique has first to be learnt; then it is necessary to learn how to perceive the drug's effects and, finally, the user has to learn to enjoy them. It perhaps needs to be explained that, without this learning process, taking the drug can be both unpleasant and seemingly without effect. (We gave a fuller account of the meaning of psychedelic drug use in pleasure-seeking sub-cultures in chapter 10.) Learning and meaning are linked in Becker's analysis. People only voluntarily learn what seems meaningful to them. Like Mead, Becker fully allows for the influence of 'significant others', (in this case dance musicians who use marijuana), on the individual. Using it is part of their way of life; it fits in with their style and they naturally offer 'established newcomers' the opportunity to try it. Becker notes that the individual is likely to drop or cut back on marijuana smoking when he or she leaves this environment, and the habit ceases to have much cultural meaning.

There is some tension between the concepts that society 'creates' deviance and that individuals act in ways that are meaningful to them. Several concepts used by Becker embody both notions. Thus, the concept of negotiation implies that the individual has some power over his or her situation, including perhaps whether a deviant label is successfully applied in the first place. On the other hand, the concepts of deviant career and career contingencies tend to stress the influence of factors outside the power of the individual. Like any 'career', that of a deviant is affected by a variety of unpredictable factors which Becker refers to as career contingencies. For instance, happening to come into contact with a deviant individual or group may be crucial in turning a person's 'career' in a given direction.

PRIMARY AND SECONDARY DEVIANCE: EDWIN LEMERT

Whereas functionalists stress normative consensus, interactionists argue that modern societies are characterised by a great variety or plurality of values and norms. This diversity of attitude exists in most areas of human activity, including religion, sex, politics and race. Conformity to the law is seen not as a product of moral consensus but either as the ability of some groups to impose rules, or as a matter of practical necessity.

Interactionists do not, then, analyse deviance simply as rule breaking, but equally in terms of how and to whom the rules are applied. This is the basis of Lemert's distinction between primary and secondary deviance. According to him, primary deviance is the initial commission of a deviant act. Secondary deviance is the effect that 'societal reaction' has on the conduct of the deviant subsequent to the commission of the initial deviant act. 'Societal reaction' means the reaction of society, or specifically of any group within society, such as the police, the courts, the family and acquaintances of the deviant, the media and, through the media, the public. Lemert's relative silence on primary deviance is a matter we will return to, critically, later.

Lemert and other interactionists have overwhelmingly given their attention to secondary deviance. If, as Howard Becker claims, 'an act is deviant when it is so defined', (an act is deviant when societal reaction declares it to be), then it is what happens in the life of the deviant after the social definition has been made that is the focus of interactionist analysis. We can illustrate the distinction between primary and secondary deviance in schematic form (see table 13.4).

STANLEY COHEN: DEVIANCY AMPLIFICATION, MORAL PANICS AND BOUNDARY CRISES

The insight that deviance is 'constructed' by a combination of individual action and

Table 13.4

Primary and Secondary Deviance

▼

Primary Deviance	Label	Secondary Deviance
(Rule Breaking) for example, Speeding →	(Societal Reaction) Charge, Conviction ↓ or No Label for example Ignored, Not Noticed Rationalised (Seen as a 'Mistake') →	That is, Deviant Status In this case, 'Traffic Offender' (Minor Criminal)

societal reaction is central to interactionism. We use Stanley Cohen's book, *Folk Devils and Moral Panics* to provide a detailed analysis of this process which rests squarely on Lemert's concept of secondary deviance.

Interactionists frequently argue that societal reaction can actually increase or 'amplify' the deviant behaviour of the labelled individual or group. Stanley Cohen has used the example of the rival 'Mod' and 'Rocker' youth factions of the mid nineteen sixties to illustrate the point. The dramatic pre-publicity given to their expected confrontations almost certainly attracted many more young people than might otherwise have been present. In this way, the media helped to create the events it anticipated, or as Cohen says, 'these predictions played the role of the classic self-fulfilling prophecy'. Similarly, over-reporting of what did (or did not) happen at a confrontation could help attract more people on another occasion (don't we all like 'being in the papers'?) In turn, over-reporting could provoke excessive public reaction. Once a 'spiral of amplification' of this kind is generated, it can acquire an artificial momentum of its own: when this happens, what is 'real' and what is imagined is not easy to disentangle (see pp. 425–6).

Given that the media does not consciously seek to popularise deviant activity, why does this over-reporting take place? There is, of course, the sound commercial reason that deviancy stories make good copy and sell newspapers. A more sociological explanation is offered by Cohen. It is suggested in the title of the book itself: *Folk Devils and Moral Panics:The Creation of the Mods and Rockers*. In what sense, then, were the Mods and Rockers 'devils' and what was the nature of the 'moral panic' they precipitated? To answer this question, Cohen uses the concept of 'boundary crisis'. Post-war Britain was relatively affluent, but the majority had not yet adjusted psychologically to the new prosperity. The frank pleasure-seeking and instrumental attitude to work of some groups of young people seemed to undermine the work ethic in a dangerous and uncomfortable way. Although most people had experienced a shift in the balance between work and leisure in their own lives, commitment to the values of hard work and self-discipline prevented them from entering the newly-discovered pleasure gardens with the abandon of the Mods and Rockers. The activities of the latter could be tolerated to a greater degree than would have been imaginable in the thirties, but even so morality dictated that 'there had to be limits'. The press presented 'the need for limits' as 'self-evident' and a matter for 'common sense', but such terms should not be taken at face value by the sociologist. Whatever their moral validity, their effect is to tend to close down a debate in favour of the dominant consensus. No doubt this is partly because an open discussion on some of the issues raised by the behaviour of the Mods and Rockers, including attitudes towards drugs and sex, would by definition bring into question majority consensus on such matters.

COURTS AND 'COMMONSENSE': PAT CARLEN; HAROLD GARFINKEL

Pat Carlen examines the labelling process in relation to the judicial system (1976). Carlen's study, like a number of other interactionist and ethnomethodological ones, concentrates on the actors in the courtroom drama itself, usually with due attention to what happens 'behind the scenes'. The variety of accidental contingencies that can affect the outcome of a trial is striking. The kind of support a defendant gets from key figures, such as probation officers and social workers, can often greatly influence and even determine the nature of a sentence. If, for instance, a probation officer decides that a client has finally 'gone too far' (admittedly a crudely unprofessional response) and makes this clear in his report to the court, a harsher judgement may be likely. The 'plea-bargaining' system, prevalent both in Britain and the United States, is a practice which would seem to lend itself to abuse. Plea-bargaining involves the accused obtaining more favourable treatment in return for an admission of guilt. Firstly, the interrogation of suspects in police custody can involve 'deals' in which, say, a lesser charge is 'traded-off' for a statement admitting an offence. Secondly, judicial officials sometimes give more lenient sentences in return for guilty pleas. When justice is put into the market place like this, the possibility of a 'bad deal' for the poor and less well-informed seems correspondingly greater. Needless to say, this trade-off process can facilitate police and court business and sometimes gains prestige for the police and prosecution: that is, presumably, the justification for it.

The kind of detailed, closely observed study we have been describing is frequently favoured by the ethnomethodologists, although such an approach is by no means their monopoly. Harold Garfinkel (1967), one of their chief exponents, was led to his conclusions partly by his attempts to analyse the deliberations of a group of jurors. In the following taped comment, he appears to be saying that the jurors used their own commonsense knowledge of society to arrive at what seemed to them a fair verdict:

> *What I mean is that it was for them a matter that somehow or other in their dealings with each other they managed, if you will permit me now to use it [commonsense], to see.*

Garfinkel further suggests that it is the job of sociologists to describe and understand what this commonsense knowledge is and how it is applied in a particular context. The application of this view to control theory is that jurors arrive at verdicts not merely on the basis of legal considerations but by calling upon a much wider fund of general knowledge, including an acquired idea of justice. Functionalists tend to consider that the process of legal enforcement is relatively unbiased. Ethnomethodologists make the point that even though people are, to some extent, guided by mutually accepted standards of conduct, behaviour is diverse, different and not wholly predictable. This includes the process of normative and legal enforcement. To put the matter extremely, in a given case justice can be what jurors and judges decide it is, rather than something more objective.

COMMENT ON INTERACTIONIST THEORY OF DEVIANCE

Two major criticisms of the interactionist approach can be made. Firstly, it does not offer an explanation of primary deviance. Secondly, it is said, particularly by Marxists, that it fails to explain adequately the relationship between power, especially class

power, and deviance. We take these points in order. Even Lemert hurries past primary deviance on his way to analysing secondary deviance, which is clearly his main interest. Becker, with engaging frankness, agrees that 'stick-up men' do not 'stick people up' simply because somebody has labelled them 'stick-up men', but he still leaves unexplained why some men and women behave in this way whilst others do not. It is true that interactionists do not claim fully to explain why deviance occurs in the first place, but this does result in certain weaknesses in their general theory. In particular, the notion that certain social environments – perhaps those which are in some way 'deprived' – may be associated with certain sorts of deviant behaviour is, apparently, of little interest to them. Yet this view is not necessarily incompatible with the interactionist perspective and, if it were explored by interactionists, might even be found complementary to it.

We now turn to the second criticism commonly made – that it deals inadequately with the relationship between power and deviance. More precisely, this is a specifically Marxist criticism that most interactionists do not sufficiently link their analysis of law and deviance to class theory. In the Marxist view the law and the state ultimately operate in favour of the ruling class. Marxist sociology of deviance is, therefore, concerned with showing how this is so. Many interactionists do not subscribe to a Marxist class conflict theory of society. Rather, they see the power structure in terms of a contest between all sorts of groups – including ethnic, religious, feminist – as well as classes which seek to establish their own interests and moral values. Becker's own case study of the interests behind The Marijuana Tax Act of 1937 (aimed at stamping out use of the drug) does not mention class at all, but concludes that the Federal Bureau of Narcotics was the major influence or 'entrepreneur' in getting the Act passed.

The above Marxist-interactionist disagreement in no way invalidates basic interactionist labelling theory nor its associated concepts. Indeed, many Marxists freely use interactionist concepts and notably so in the area of sub-cultural analysis. We have already come across examples of this in the work of Paul Willis. Further, when interactionists deal with class and power, they often reach conclusions compatible with Marxism. Thus, the proposition that white collar crime might be under-recorded in official statistics because of police and judical bias in favour of the middle class is commonly found in Marxist and interactionist literature.

RATIONAL CHOICE AND SITUATIONAL EXPLANATIONS OF DEVIANCE: CONTROL THEORY; RIGHT REALISM

Rational choice and situational explanations of crime and the current emphasis on making it more difficult to commit crime (control) are closely related developments in the field of criminology. Rational choice interpretation is based on the simple premise that people choose to commit crime or not by weighing the possible benefits against the risks. Clearly, possible benefits and risks depend largely on the situation in which a crime may be committed. Thus, forcing the door of a wealthy house may offer more 'benefits' than that of a poor house – though if the door of the latter is actually open, the risks may be so reduced that a criminal will choose to rob it rather than the less accessible wealthy house. On the basis of such logic – supported by research – some criminologists have suggested that the best way to reduce crime is not to try to change the criminal but to take practical measures of prevention, i.e. to control it.

Writing in the late nineteen sixties in, respectively, the United States and Britain, Travis Hirschi and Steven Box have suggested the situations in which people are more or less likely to choose to commit crime. Hirschi gives four elements which make the choice of crime less likely – all of which relate to the strength of the bond between the individual and society:

- **Attachment,**
- **Commitment,**
- **Involvement,**
- **Belief.**

Thus, people in regular work or school attendance, with busy home lives who believe they should obey the law are less likely to commit crime than those less involved with mainstream society. The latter have more opportunity and 'reason' to deviate. For example, several studies show

that when school truancy is reduced the day-time crime rate in the relevant area tends to drop. Steven Box further develops the idea that it is those in situations of less commitment to society and therefore of less social restraint that are more likely to commit crime and deviance. The following factors can be conducive to crime:

- **Secrecy (chances of concealing deviance),**
- **Skills (having the ability to commit the deviant act),**
- **Supply (of the means to commit the act),**
- **Social support (peer approval),**
- **Symbolic support (e.g. indicating high status).**

Control theories have tended to develop in a policy-orientated context. It was at the Home Office Research and Planning Unit that Clarke, Cornish and Mayhew developed this approach. On the basis of situational theory, they devised policies which would create situations in which potential criminals would be less likely to choose to commit crime. Thus, crime might be able to be controlled by making it situationally more difficult to commit. Two examples of this approach are target hardening (such as strengthening telephone coin-boxes) and surveillance (such as designing built environments so that people can see what happens within them – including criminal activity).

The percentage of incidents in which alcohol is involved

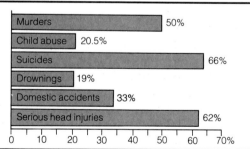

(Source: *The Guardian*, 21st June 1988: 20)

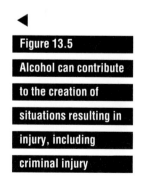

Figure 13.5

Alcohol can contribute to the creation of situations resulting in injury, including criminal injury

Clarke, Cornish and Mayhew saw situational theory as an approach to crime which might lead to practical ways of combating it. They were disillusioned with highly theoretical explanations of crime – of the kind discussed in previous sections of this chapter – which saw the causes of crime either within the individual's psychology, biology or within the social environment. They were scathing that these theories had not produced any effective solutions to crime during a period when the crime rate was rapidly rising. They pursued their work, therefore, with a highly practical intent.

Jock Young has characterised control theorists as 'right realists' and has been highly critical of what he sees as punitive, 'law and order' types of solution to crime. However, his own 'left realism' is pragmatic enough to support more technical aspects of crime control such as improving police deployment and 'target hardening'.

COMMENT ON RATIONAL CHOICE THEORY OF DEVIANCE

Rational choice and situational explanations of crime and control theory have undoubtedly made a contribution to understanding and controlling crime. However, their long term effectiveness in controlling and reducing crime remains to be proven. If, in fact, potential criminals are often merely diverted from more to less well defended 'targets' or if, in time, they develop more effective means of dealing with them, criminologists may again be forced to prioritise the question of why certain people tend to commit certain sorts of crime.

Two further comments can be offered about these theories. First, control methods may have unintended consequences that may be problematic in themselves. It may be that the cost of controlling crime will result in an 'armoured society' or, at least, a society in which the richer social groups feel the need to 'armour' their possessions against criminals. This has, perhaps, already occurred in certain areas in the United States, particularly in wealthy, urban districts adjacent to much poorer ones. In such areas, houses, hotels and business premises are often fortified with locks and chains, burglar alarms, bars, walls, guards, dogs and double-doors. There is more than a touch of Orwellian 1984 about all this!

The second comment is that in societies in which the social extremes are growing more unequal (e.g. in the United States and Britain), expensive investment in protecting the life 'situations' of the wealthy may separate them even further from the lives of the less well off. This may or may not be considered to matter, but it is an observation of some sociological interest.

The discussion in the previous paragraph leads back to wider theoretical considerations about the causes of crime, notwithstanding the reluctance of some control theorists to probe them. In fact, the earlier rational choice theories of Hirschi and Box do recognise that the wider social experience of individuals affects the likelihood of their becoming deviant. In effect, both suggest that those with less of a material or psychological stake in society are more likely to commit certain kinds of crime. If so, it remains necessary to consider the social context of the deviant in explaining deviance and, perhaps, to direct policy towards it. For instance, if it is true that the poor are more likely to rob the rich than vice-versa, then policies to improve the situation of the poor may yet reduce crime. Of course, 'throwing money' at so-called 'social problems' is now a discredited way of dealing with them but ignoring their wider social causes may, in the end, prove even less effective.

Indeed, recent research from the Home Office establishes a long-term correlation between increases in personal spending power and decreases in the growth of property crime and vice-versa (*Trends in Crime and Their Interpretation*), Home Office Research Study 119). The study was completed before the large increase in property crime in 1990 occurred. However, the fact that the increase coincided with the beginnings of a recession provides further evidence for the link between spending power and crime. Thus, this research gives a more sophisticated basis for the old adage: 'poverty breeds crime'.

MAKING SENSE OF DEVIANCY THEORY

The various theoretical approaches to social order and deviance are often presented as mutually exclusive. Certainly, it would be ludicrous to imagine that 'sticking them all together' would somehow result in a complete theory satisfactory to all parties. Nevertheless, in some ways the major theories can be seen as complementary rather than contradictory. Further, in some instances, differences in terminology obscure a larger measure of agreement than might at first be apparent.

Even on the subject of social order, control and integration, it is possible to uncover elements of agreement between the two major structural theories about how society functions. Functionalists argue that conformity and consensus are necessary for the orderly functioning of society, but Marxists, too, need to explain why, in many capitalist societies, the majority accept the system, and appear to have no taste for revolution. Marxists believe that the many working class people who accept and even support the capitalist system have been deluded by 'bourgeois ideology' into a state of 'false consciousness'. Both theories are describing the same phenomenon: what differs is the terminology and the underlying political values: functionalists tend to support and want to conserve bourgeois, liberal society, whereas Marxists do not. Not surprisingly, these preferences often seep into their theoretical analyses.

There is also a considerable measure of unstated agreement between Marxism and functionalism about social deviance. Merton thought of criminal behaviour as a result of exclusion from the legitimate opportunity structure of society, and strain theorists examined what this meant in terms of economic and status deprivation. There is a clear implication in all this that 'society' bears at least some responsibility for crime simply because the gateways to legitimate achievement are wide open for some and almost closed for others. Marxists observe the same unequal access to material and status reward hierarchies but condemn it more comprehensively. To them, theft is just the distorted mirror image of capitalism's already ugly face. The convergence between the two perspectives is even apparent sometimes at the level of moral evaluation. The Marxist 'what can you expect?' response to the high crime rate in Western Europe and the USA expresses a sentiment comparable with that of the liberal Daniel Bell, when he refers to crime as 'part of the American way of life'.

The major achievement of interactionism has been to rediscover for sociology the notion that the central social reality is individual meaning and experience. In view of the tendencies towards determinism within both structural theories, this is a crucial contribution. As an account of how people behave in everyday life in relation to the legal and normative order, interactionism seems closer to what actually happens than the functionalist conformity-deviance model. Life is more complex than the functionalists allow. Marxists argue, however, that interactionism is inadequate in its analysis of how the power of institutions and the class interests behind them affect and even control individual lives. The laws, rules or norms of institutions are powerful means of regulating behaviour, and this is notably true of the institutions that constitute the 'bourgeois' state. Moreover, institutional frameworks often survive the coming and going of individuals. In their different ways, Marxists and functionalists appreciate better than interactionists that it is the institutional structure of society that both limits and provides opportunities for individual and group action.

Perhaps interactionism would be more effective if, as well as concerning itself with individual meaning, its protagonists also attempted to develop it more vigorously as a 'linking theory' between the concept of the 'creative' individual, and the 'formative' institutional structure of society. We have already noted some efforts in this direction, though these have been more a matter of Marxists using the interactionist perspective than the other way around. Despite the limits of the interactionist approach, many would feel that amidst such abstract concepts as order, social control and deviance, individual meaning and reality should be retained. If that makes sociological generalisations more difficult, then so be it.

Suicide

The study of suicide has become a sociological classic. This is because major studies of suicide so well illustrate theoretical and related methodological debate within sociology. In particular, they illustrate the main differences between positivism/

Figure 13.6 (Far right)

▶ quantitative methods and interpretism/ qualitative methods.

DURKHEIM AND POSITIVISM

Durkheim argued that even in the case of apparently so individual an act as suicide, the suicide rate or 'social suicide rate' as he termed it, is the product of social 'forces' external to the individual:

There is, therefore, for each people a collective force of a definite amount of energy, impelling men to self-destruction. The victim's acts which at first seem to express only his personal temperament are really the supplement and prolongation of a social condition which they express externally.

(Durkheim, 1970:299)

Durkheim presents a model of four types of suicide – altruistic, fatalistic, anomic and egoistic – and relates each one to the degree of 'integration' ('connectedness') of the suicide with society.

Altruistic suicide is the result of the over-integration of the individual into the social group. The individual sacrifices himself or herself to the 'greater good' of society. A spectacular example of altruistic suicide was the action of Japanese pilots who dived their planes into enemy shipping, thus committing Kamikaze. Durkheim associated altruistic suicide with traditional societies which are characterised by mechanical solidarity (see pp. 432–3). He considered individuality to be less developed in such societies and that members would observe even self-destructive norms. Another example was the ritual self-immolation on their husband's funeral pyres of widows in certain parts of India.

Fatalistic suicide is also the product of the over-regulation of the individual by society. In this case, the individual feels powerless before 'society' or 'fate' – and simply 'gives up'. Durkheim did not much refer to this category.

Anomic suicide occurs when lack of social regulation causes low social integration. Thus, Durkheim considered that 'anomic' social conditions (i.e. conditions of great and rapid change in which people tend to become morally and normatively confused) produced an increase in 'anomic suicide'. Anomie, then, is part of the 'collective force'

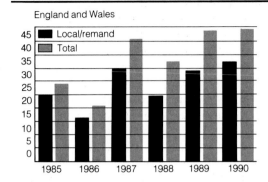

Self inflicted deaths in prison

England and Wales

in society 'impelling' people to suicide. We can illustrate the point by taking an example which, again, occurred after Durkheim's own death in 1917. The Wall Street crash of 1929 caused an outbreak of suicide among the American rich or, more precisely, the previously rich. It can be argued that they were driven to suicide not only by material loss but also because of stress in the face of the psychological and normative adjustment to the different life style that loss demanded. Durkheim's own nineteenth century research substantiated the view that economic change, whether for better or worse, tended to increase the suicide rate.

Egoistic suicide arises because an individual's links to the social group become weakened or broken. Durkheim argued that the greater personal and moral freedom allowed by Protestant countries explained why they tended to have a higher suicide rate than Catholic ones which were more likely to be morally integrated communities.

Durkheim found that although the social suicide rate varies between societies, it tends to be 'regular' over time in a given society. He considered that this demonstrated that there are indeed consistent social forces which determine the suicide rate within a given society. Perhaps few sociologists would now make such a claim – without considerable qualification – and probably fewer still would set out to prove it. Durkheim's great work is a reminder of the original aim of sociology to establish correlations and, if possible, causal relationships between 'social facts' – usually by use of statistics. Although this enterprise has been made more complex by advances in statistical techniques and sociological theory, for many it remains a central aim of the discipline.

A number of criticisms have been made of

Durkheim's study from those who share his broadly positivist approach (see pp. 8–9). M Halbwachs was an early commentator (1930), suggesting that the key variable explaining the difference in the suicide rate between Protestants and Catholics was probably their respectively predominantly urban and rural locations, rather than their religions. More recently, Gibbs and Martin (1964), have argued that Durkheim did not define the concept of social integration in a way that could be adequately operationalised (see p. 29 for an explanation of this term). Inevitably this would adversely affect the quality of his empirical analysis.

THE INTERPRETIST CRITIQUES OF DURKHEIM

Durkheim's study, *Suicide*, has been extensively criticised by two interpretists, J D Douglas (1967) and J M Atkinson (1978). As is indicated by the title of Douglas's book, the core of their criticism is Durkheim's failure to consider the different meanings given to suicide by different people and within different cultures. This results in two major mistakes. First, the statistical basis of Durkheim's study is inaccurate. Second, in assuming all suicides to be 'the same', he fails adequately to categorise the phenomenon. Let us take these two related points separately.

Both Douglas and Atkinson give many examples of potential statistical problems resulting from Durkheim's failure to address the issue of meaning. They both criticise Durkheim for apparently assuming that all coroners used the same criteria in deciding what was or was not suicide. They are easily able to give evidence to the contrary. Douglas points out the example of one coroner who would decide that suicide had occurred only if the evidence of a suicide note could be produced. Other coroners accepted less conclusive evidence. Ultimately, this meant that different coroners were contributing a different range of 'facts' to the 'same' statistical category, with the result that 'statistical reality' could be imprecise and misleading. Let us take a further example of this point: the issue of the statistical basis supporting Durkheim's claims about the distribution of egoistic suicide. Durkheim explains the relatively 'low' rate of suicide in Catholic societies as

compared to Protestant ones, in terms of the greater integration of the former. But another explanation can be given for the differences in the recorded rates of suicide between the two types of society. The Catholic religion condemns suicide as a mortal sin, something which merits eternal damnation. In many cases this cultural attitude towards suicide might very well influence coroners to return a verdict other than suicide. Pressure of this kind would not generally be put on coroners in Protestant societies where moral condemnation of suicide tended to be less. In view of this, uncritical acceptance of official suicide statistics for the purposes of comparative social analysis would be poor methodology.

Douglas forcefully argues that despite dismissing the stated intentions and commonsense interpretations of others, Durkheim himself used his own version of commonsense.

Both Douglas and Atkinson argue that a more precise and valid approach to the study of suicide should involve the study of particular cases. However, whereas Douglas argues that different types of suicide can be usefully categorised and compared according to social meaning, Atkinson considers that each case of suicide is unique and must be considered as such. Thus, Douglas suggests that in Western societies one classificatory category might be 'revenge' suicides (i.e. on a person or people who have hurt the suicide) and in some traditional societies religious categorisations such as 'transformation of the soul' might be appropriate. For Atkinson the purpose of sociology is to study the unique meaning of the individual case.

In his commentary on interpretist critiques of the use of official statistics, Barry Hindess is sharply critical of the 'strong' position adopted by Atkinson but finds the 'weak' position, such as that adopted by Douglas, uncontroversial. In refuting the 'strong' position, he suggests that a standard of certainty is implicitly being demanded which is unavailable in any walk of life. Sociologists, like the practitioners of other disciplines, must simply make sure that, as far as possible, their data, including statistical data, are representative and internally consistent (that is, that each unit that is supposed to refer to a given phenomenon actually does so). Admittedly, this is more easily said than done, but it must be done if sociology is to be practised at all. The second or 'weak' version of the interactionist position as construed by Hindess is that because the 'everyday understandings' of police, magistrates and others help to 'create' official statistics, these must be taken into consideration when evaluating and interpreting a given set of statistics. Hindess agrees with this but considers it to be a statement of the obvious. In effect, it is the position he himself takes in refuting the first, and in his view more typical, version of the interactionist position. In putting forward the view that the 'everyday misunderstandings' of those who create statistics must be considered in this way, Hindess also refutes the simplistic positivistic position: that official statistics can be used unquestioningly to 'prove' a given case.

SUMMARY

1 There was a substantial and steady increase in most categories of recorded offences between 1971 and 1990. However, recorded offences underestimate the extent of crime by several hundred percent in most categories. Victim surveys, self-report studies and even experiment suggest a much higher rate of crime.

2 Both the general public and agencies of law enforcement are affected by stereotypes of criminals. Class (working class), sex (male), age (young) and 'race' (black) are stereotypical characteristics frequently associated with criminals. There is a substantial body of detailed research which suggests that stereotyping of criminals tends to be misleading. More qualified and measured statements are more accurate.

3 Of the theories discussed in the remainder of the chapter, only the functionalist, Marxist and interactionist can be considered to offer fully developed perspectives on social order, control and deviance.

4 Early psychological explanations of criminal behaviour are now generally discredited. Sociologists tend to be sceptical of attempts to demonstrate a genetic basis of criminal behaviour and rather explain it as behaviour, learnt within the context of a particular social environment.

5 Much of Durkheim's analysis of deviance remains fundamental and, even when opposed, of continuing influence. Durkheim stated that deviance is universal (it occurs in all societies), relative (it takes different forms in different societies, and functional (it focuses and reinforces communal morality). Abnormally high rates of deviance indicate that social solidarity (order/cohesion) is under strain – thus, Durkheim's analysis of deviance is part of a total understanding of social functioning.

6 Merton, like Durkheim, explains deviance or 'nonconformity' as he calls it, in terms of the total social structure. In his case, he explains crime as the pursuit of society's 'goals' by illegal 'means'.

7 As the term implies, the subcultural theorists explain deviance in group or subcultural rather than in individual terms. There is some disagreement among subcultural theorists about the origin of the values and behaviour of members of deviant subcultures: Albert Cohen considers that they imitate mainstream culture – albeit in deviant ways – whereas Miller thinks they are indigenous to working class culture. In describing deviant subcultures in terms of hierarchies which broadly mirror those in mainstream society, Cloward and Ohlin are closer to Cohen. British subcultural theories of deviance variously reflect Marxist and interactionist influence and overall appear more complex than American theories.

8 Marxist theories explain deviance firmly within the context of capitalist society. Emphasis is put on the frequently 'hidden' crimes of the powerful and on the disadvantaged and 'oppressive' conditions which may promote deviancy among the working class.

9 Interactionists define deviance as behaviour which is labelled as such. Secondary deviance occurs once a deviant label has effectively been attached to someone. Stereotyping by agencies of social control can greatly affect who is labelled 'deviant'. Class, sex, age and 'race' can be the basis of stereotyping.

10 Rational choice and situational theories of deviance explain criminal behaviour as deliberate action in pursuit of self-interest which takes circumstances (situations) into consideration. Despite the appealing 'commonsense' of this approach, it has recently come under criticism from researchers who demonstrate an apparent link between economic recession and the crime rate.

11 It is possible to find many complementary aspects between the major structural theories of deviance – functionalism and Marxism – and the major interpretist theory – interactionism. In particular, Marxism and interactionism have frequently been blended to create a more complete approach.

12 Durkheim's *Suicide* and Atkinson's and Douglas's reply now have the status of a classic set-piece illustration of the contrast between positivism and interpretism.

RESEARCH AND COURSEWORK

A problem with doing first-hand research into deviance is that it could take you into places and situations you should not sensibly be in. This topic could provide an opportunity for a piece of coursework based on existing literature.

Students often find the interactionist perspective on deviance particularly interesting. An intensive and critical study of a single book – such as Goffman's *Asylum* (Penguin, 1968) or Cohen's *Folk Devils and Moral Panics* (Martin Robertson, 1981) could be made. Such a study might concentrate on the use and development of a number of key interactionist concepts such as 'labelling' and 'stigma' in Goffman's book or 'amplification' and 'moral panic' in Cohen's. Reference is likely to be made to the use of these concepts in other works – although in less detail. Critical perspectives could be achieved by using other theoretical approaches to assess the effectiveness of the concepts used.

A piece of original work that could be attempted is the analysis of a deviant youth subcultural group. You will need to develop a theoretical perspective and to do this reading relevant studies such as S Hall and T Jefferson eds., *Resistance through Rituals* (Hutchinson, 1979) or, again, Cohen's classic would be helpful. A key decision for the fieldwork is likely to be whether to research covertly or overtly. Another study could be a comparison of official crime statistics with crime as reported on the media. More locally oriented research could explore a local 'moral panic' or a victim survey could provide the basis of a piece of research.

FURTHER READING

In addition to the books referred to under 'Guide to Coursework' J Lea and J Young's readable, accessible and wide-ranging *What Is To Be Done About Law and Order?* (Penguin, 1984) can be recommended. Steve Taylor's *Suicide* (Longman, 1988) raises theoretical and methodological issues at a level suitable to 'A' level students. Laurie Taylor's *In the Underworld* (Hodder and Stoughton, 1985) is a typically good read and highly informative about London's criminal underworld.

QUESTIONS

1 Either (a) What is a subculture? (5)
(b) How useful is the concept in explaining juvenile delinquency? (20)
or
(a) Why have studies of criminal behaviour begun to survey the victims of crime? (12)
(b) Why do estimates of the level of crime obtained from victim surveys differ from official statistics? (13). (Oxford, 1989)
2 Assess the contribution made by labelling theory to an explanation of deviance (AEB 1990)
3 'Durkheim did not produce an adequate account of suicide'. Discuss. (AEB, November 1989)

Power and Systems of Government

POWER, AUTHORITY AND POLITICS: WEBER AND MARX

Politically, to be 'in power' is to have control of certain resources with which to 'get things done'. Weber and Marx's analyses of political power differed in important respects and in this, as in other matters, they have bequeathed distinct traditions.

According to Max Weber, power is 'the probability that one actor within a social relationship will be in a position to carry out his own will despite resistance, regardless of the basis on which this probability rests'. In more ordinary language, power is the ability to get one's way – even if it is based on bluff.

Although we think of power as being associated particularly with politics it is, in fact, an aspect of all, or nearly all, social relationships. As Weber writes, positions of power can 'emerge from social relations in a drawing room as well as in the market, from the rostrum of a lecture hall as well as the command post of a regiment, from an erotic or charitable relationship as well as from scholarly discussion or athletics'. We can add that power plays a part in family and school relationships also. If Weber's sociology has a single central concept, it is that of power. He considered that economic and social goals as well as political ones are achieved through power-conflict. People compete for limited resources and status: for every one who achieves fortune and fame, there are thousands who do not. Nevertheless, it was characteristic of Weber that he stressed the importance of the political sphere. Political decisions, such as changes in taxation or educational policy, could be taken, and these could have great effect on the economic and social life of a country.

Weber distinguished authority from power. Authority may be thought of as *legitimate power* (power that is accepted as being rightfully exercised). He divided authority into three broad types: traditional, charismatic and rational-legal. We have already examined authority in the context of organisations. Here, our interest in it is as a form of political power: accordingly, we choose our examples from the political sphere. The sense of the inevitability of traditional political authority is well illustrated by an established dynasty, such as the centuries-old Hapsburgs of Austria. By contrast, charismatic authority is generated by personality and the myths that surround it. Hitler, Martin Luther King and the Cuban revolutionary leader, Ché Guevara, are all examples of charismatic leaders. The fact that they are all recent figures shows that charismatic authority is still a feature of modern politics. In advanced industrial countries, however, rational-legal authority tends to be the predominant type and has, in particular, replaced traditional authority. Rational-legal political authority is established in law. The American system of government provides the best example of it because, unlike Britain, it has a written constitution (articles of government). This establishes the relationship between the legislature (which passes laws), the judiciary (which can determine if these laws are constitutionally allowable), and the executive (which, under the law, runs day-to-day government). Britain is often considered to have an 'unwritten' constitution but this has never been codified in a single, rational-legal document.

Weber's commitment to 'liberal democracy' was largely on the basis that he considered it to be based on rational-legal principles. Power is obtained and used within a framework of rules and part of the rules are that power can be 'lost'. Thus, democracy ensures against the 'raw' and easily abused power of dictatorship – it is safer if not always more efficient.

Marx emphasised the origin as much as the use of power and this led him to a different view than Weber on the nature of liberal democracy. For Marx, the basis of power lies in the relations of a group (or class) to the means of production. In any age, the ruling class – the class 'in power' – is the class that owns the means of production. He did not consider that liberal democracy – which he sometimes referred to as 'bourgeois democracy' – changed the basis of power in capitalist society. He argued that the economic power of the capitalist class gives them a political power greater than 'the vote' gives the rest of the people.

This fundamental difference between Weber and Marx provides the central theme of this chapter although many others 'cross' the debate with a variety of contributions and developments.

POWER AND SYSTEMS OF GOVERNMENT

Politics is about power and purposes. It is the struggle to achieve the means to do certain things or, more precisely, to implement policies. Sometimes, what politicians want to do becomes obscured in the struggle to get the power to do it, but we must recognise, at least analytically, both these aspects of political activity.

Firstly, we deal with the means of power. The major means of political power is government and we can conveniently discuss the chief types of government here: democracy, oligarchy and dictatorship. We will consider each in turn.

DEMOCRACY: REPRESENTATIVE, PARTICIPATORY AND DELEGATORY Democratic systems can be divided into three broad types: representative or indirect democracy; participatory or direct democracy, and delegatory democracy. In representative democracy, the people do not rule directly but elect representatives to rule for them. Representative democracy is associated with parliamentary institutions to such an extent that it is often referred to simply as parliamentary democracy: Britain and America are major examples. In addition, representative democracies tend to be characterised by what are termed civil liberties. These include freedom to organise politically, freedom of speech and of the press, and the equal status of citizens under the law. In practice, these freedoms – except arguably the last – are not absolute. They are established in, and limited by law. Thus, freedom of the press in Britain is limited by the laws of libel and contempt (which cover what can legally be written about other people), and the Official Secrets Act. In the USA the comparable legislation is less strict and, to that extent, it has a freer press than Britain. The principle that freedom, like anything else, has to be balanced against other principles, applies in both countries.

The crux of our concern with democracy is the debate between liberals and Marxists about the nature of democracy in advanced capitalist countries. Liberals consider that, for instance, Britain, West Germany, Italy, Australia and the United States are genuinely democratic. Marxists disagree: they argue that, at best, these countries are 'bourgeois democracies' which deny 'real' freedom to the majority of their population. For Marxists, 'real' freedom depends on greater equality. For instance, freedom under the law may not seem very meaningful to someone who cannot afford a lawyer. This liberal-Marxist debate is the main recurrent theme of this chapter.

Participatory or direct democracy strictly means that people represent themselves and take their own decisions. The term 'participatory', however, is often used to mean some degree of personal involvement in decision making, short of direct democratic control. It has been in small communities, such as ancient Athens and medieval Geneva, that something approaching direct democratic self-government has proved most feasible. Nevertheless, in modern Tanzania, popular involvement in day-to-day affairs has been found possible at the local or village level. However, this has not replaced central government and bureaucracy (such as the civil service), often of a rather authoritarian kind, at the national level. The Russian revolutionary Lenin hoped and believed that a socialist revolution would replace the capitalist state with a proletarian state largely run by, or at least answerable to, direct democratic institutions called soviets or communes. At first, there were some signs that this might happen during and after the revolution of 1917. The fact that it did not, and that an authoritarian government developed instead, poses problems for modern socialists, who continue to seek more direct forms of democracy than are common in parliamentary democracies.

Delegatory democracy is a form of 'half-way house' between direct and indirect democracy. Delegates are mandated (told) by those who elect them to carry out specific orders and are, therefore, much more 'tied' to the wishes of their constitutents than are undelegated representatives. In the late nineteen seventies and early eighties there was a fierce debate in the Labour Party which focused on the extent to which MPs should be representatives or delegates.

OLIGARCHY Oligarchy is government by the few: the term is usually used to describe government by an unrepresentative few. Frequently, the basis of oligarchical power is military. Thus Greece, the ancient home of democracy, was ruled by a junta (group) of colonels for several years. Although it is theoretically possible to talk of representative oligarchy, different terms are usually preferred. Liberal political theorists use the terms 'representative elite' or 'democratic elite'. Marxists deny that what liberals call democratic elites are, in fact, genuinely democratic; instead, they use the term 'ruling class'.

DICTATORSHIP Dictatorship is government by a single individual responsible only to himself or herself. Hitler and Stalin were dictators, each man professing different political ideologies, Fascism and Communism respectively. Yet it is for the similar way in which they both concentrated total power in their own hands, and the great inhumanity with which they exercised it, that they are remembered, rather than for their ideological differences. The term 'totalitarianism' is often associated with dictatorship, but has a rather wider usage. Totalitarian regimes are those in which power is wholly concentrated in the hands of a few people or of a single person.

THE MODERN STATE AND THE PEOPLE

Central to any analysis of political sociology must be an understanding of the modern state. It will be helpful first to give a brief organisational or descriptive definition of the state and, then drawing on Patrick Dunleavy and Brendan O'Leary, present a more abstract definition of its key characteristics.

Governments, whether democratic, oligarchical or dictatorial, generally exercise power through the state. The state includes the government itself – of whatever kind – both in its capacity as the maker of law and of policy. It also includes the civil service – a vast bureaucracy of many thousands of people. The judiciary and magistracy are also part of the state. Local government is, by definition, not part of the central state apparatus but is often greatly influenced and, in some respects controlled, by central government. Local government can, therefore, sometimes be a powerful arm of central government. (The Labour governments of the nineteen sixties and seventies persuaded most local authorities to accept and implement some form of comprehensive education.) In addition, local governments have their own bureaucracies.

Dunleavy and O'Leary suggest that the modern state has the following five characteristics:

1 The state is a recognisably separate institution or set of institutions, so differentiated from the rest of its society as to create identifiable public and private spheres.
2 The state is sovereign, or the supreme power, within its territory, and by definition the ultimate authority for all law, i.e. binding rules supported by coercive sanctions. Public law is made by state officials and backed by a formal monopoly of force.
3 The state's sovereignty extends to all the individuals within a given territory, and applies equally, even to those in formal positions of government or rule-making. Thus sovereignty is distinct from the personnel who at any given time occupy a particular role within the state.
4 The modern state's personnel are mostly recruited and trained for management in a bureaucratic manner.
5 The state has the capacity to extract monetary revenues (taxation) to finance its activities from its subject population.
(Dunleavy and O'Leary, 1987: 2)

The first point describes how the modern state has created a distinct sphere within which the struggle for and exercise of (public) power and authority occurs. Other matters such as family and leisure life remain apart from the state. Secondly, within modern societies, the state is the supreme authority (not, for instance, a religious figure or outside political body – although on the latter point, membership of the European community raises important issues of sovereignty). The authority of the state can be enforced by a variety of sanctions. Thirdly, in a modern society no individual is outside the sovereignty of state. The fourth point emphasises the bureaucratic way in which modern states are run and the fifth states that they have the crucial power to raise revenue.

It is impossible not to be impressed by the power of the modern state. It is worth recalling that in democracies the state is supposed to represent and serve the people. How and to what degree this is the reality in practice will be discussed later. The main means by which national politicians are made accountable is the general election. We discuss the matter of voting next.

Voting Behaviour: Three Models

Until the mid nineteen seventies one model explaining voting behaviour was overwhelmingly dominant: the class model. In general elections between 1931 and 1970 the percentage of the total vote of the Labour and Conservative vote added together was between 84.2 (1945) and 96.8 (1951). It seemed to be a fact of political life that the vast majority voted for either the Labour or the Conservative Parties and, generally, it was the working class who voted for the former and the middle class who voted for the latter. In the two general elections of 1974, however, the share of the vote of the two main parties was almost precisely 75 per cent on each occasion – a substantial drop on

▶

Figure 14.1

Voting trends 1945–87: The fate of the parties

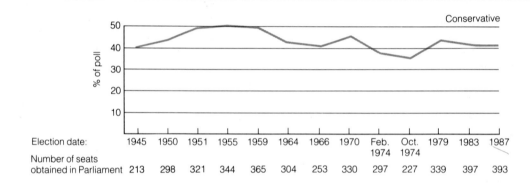

Election date:	1945	1950	1951	1955	1959	1964	1966	1970	Feb. 1974	Oct. 1974	1979	1983	1987
Number of seats obtained in Parliament	213	298	321	344	365	304	253	330	297	227	339	397	393

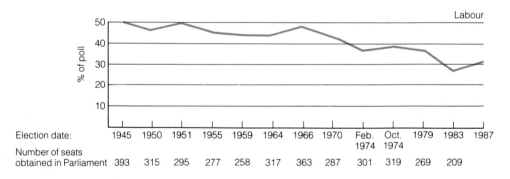

Election date:	1945	1950	1951	1955	1959	1964	1966	1970	Feb. 1974	Oct. 1974	1979	1983	1987
Number of seats obtained in Parliament	393	315	295	277	258	317	363	287	301	319	269	209	

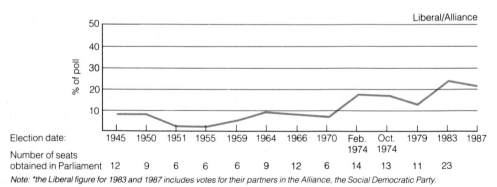

Election date:	1945	1950	1951	1955	1959	1964	1966	1970	Feb. 1974	Oct. 1974	1979	1983	1987
Number of seats obtained in Parliament	12	9	6	6	6	9	12	6	14	13	11	23	

*Note: *the Liberal figure for 1983 and 1987 includes votes for their partners in the Alliance, the Social Democratic Party.*

what had been the norm. In contrast, the Liberal vote had leapt from 7.5 per cent in 1970 to 19.3 per cent in the first election of 1974. These trends did not reverse. Something appeared to have changed.

The picture painted by the facts given above is misleadingly simple. The trends underlying the shifts in voting behaviour since 1970 are a matter of dispute as are the explanations of them. Two models of voting behaviour have emerged to challenge the class model – the rational choice or consumer model and the radical model. The three models will be discussed under the following headings:

1 The party identification and social class model
2 The rational choice model
3 The radical model

The Party Identification and Social Class Model

David Butler and Donald Stokes were influential in putting forward this interpretation, particularly during the nineteen sixties. They argue that social class factors resulted in a large majority of voters developing a long-term attachment and loyalty to a particular political party (party identification). In interviews, they found that over 90 per cent of respondents expressed such an attachment (*Political Change in Britain*, 1969). In general elections the majority of middle class voters voted Conservative (70 per cent in 1955) and the majority of working class voters voted Labour (69 per cent in 1966). Data from Tapper and Bowles comparing the class percentages voting Labour and Conservative between 1945–58 do show a very strong link between class and voting behaviour during this period (see table 14.1).

	AB	C1	C2	DE
Conservative	85	70	35	30
Labour	10	25	60	65

(Source: Tapper and Bowles in L Robins ed., 1982: 175)

Theorists adopting the class model of voting behaviour invariably distinguish between objective and subjective class. Objective class is based on a generally accepted definition of class, such as the Registrar General's used in table 14.1. Subjective class is the class to which a person thinks s/he belongs.

The relationship between subjective class and voting behaviour is even stronger than that between objective class and voting behaviour. Evidence from a number of sources, including Butler and Stokes, has shown that about 80 per cent of those who are both objectively and subjectively working class vote Labour, whereas the objective working class vote as a whole never rose above 69 per cent between 1952 and 1962. The strength of subjective class image and voting patterns is further illustrated by the behaviour of the minority of unskilled workers who think of themselves as middle class. According to Butler and Stoke's data, 55 per cent of this group voted Conservative in 1959. The tendency for those at the top of the occupational hierarchy who see themselves as working class to vote Labour is not quite as marked, but is still statistically very significant.

CLASS VOTING AND SOCIALISATION

Socialisation is the 'mechanism' by which most people come to identify with a particular party. Working class homes 'breed' Labour voters and middle class homes 'Conservative' voters. Socialisation is stronger if both parents support a given party. Neighbourhood schools tend to reflect the class of the children who attend them and this reinforces class/party identification. Similarly, children of middle class origins are more likely to get middle class jobs than working class children and vice-versa – again reinforcing class experience and identification. Where continuity of class experience is broken – say, by social mobility, there is an increased chance of a change of party allegiance. Otherwise, the class model of voting behaviour, presents party preference and, therefore, attitudes on a range of political matters, as well

◀

Table 14.1 (Far left)

Class percentages

voting Labour and

Conservative 1945–58

established from a young age and likely to 'become more set as a person gets older'.

Frank Parkin offers an interesting explanation of the strength of traditional working class identification with Labour during the nineteen fifties and sixties (1972). He suggests that, given the generally Conservative nature of British society, what is surprising is that a majority of the working class consistently voted Labour. He contends that the traditionally dominant institutions of our society – the established church, the monarchy, the military, legal and civil service elites, the public schools and ancient universities, the institutions of private property and the media – embody values which are both middle class and closely in accord with conservatism. Conservatives have for a long time appealed to communal values, such as nationalism, monarchy, religion and imperialism to 'unify' the country. It would seem almost inevitable that this powerful and pervasive conservative influence would encompass all classes. How is it, then, that a majority of the working class resist its full import? Simply, various 'shields' or 'barriers' exist against it, which allow socialist values to be fostered. These protective barriers are formed by working class sub-cultures which generate different values from the dominant culture. The major source of these values is the work-place. There, working people may experience both the collective strength of their peers, and possible conflict with employers. Thus, the work-place is the cradle of socialist values. Parkin also sees the traditional working class community as an additional basis of working class and socialist solidarity. Where occupational communities such as mining towns and dock areas exist, solidarity is likely to be especially strong. These areas, however, are on the decline (see chapter 11, pp. 236–7).

Goldthorpe and Lockwood in their *Affluent Worker* study (1968) recognise the influence of class socialisation but also, importantly, observe that more individualistic attitudes to social and, potentially, political life may have been developing among some workers. They divide the working class into three groups:

1 'Proletarian' traditionalist.
2 'Deferential' traditionalist.
3 'Privatised' worker/Instrumental Collectivist.

The proletarian traditionalists are those who have internalised the traditional and historic values of the working class community such as collectivism and solidarity. Deferential traditionalists are those who have succumbed to the powerful conservative influences in society (indicated by Parkin) and accept 'their place in the hierarchy'.

The privatised workers/instrumental collectivists (see p. 143) are, however, of immediate interest. These are workers who are committed to a collective approach to unions and the Labour party not out of loyalty or solidarity, but because of what they can get out of them. In a quota survey that is now almost thirty years old, Goldthorpe and Lockwood found that affluent workers tended to support Labour to an even greater extent than the working class as a whole, for precisely these instrumental reasons. This analysis does, however, allow for the possibility that instrumentally motivated workers will switch their vote if it seems in their interest to do so. More recent evidence argues that this may, indeed, be what some of them do.

'CONFORMIST' AND 'DEVIANT' VOTING IN THE CLASS MODEL

In the class model of voting behaviour, those who vote according to their class status are considered 'conformist' voters, and those who do not 'deviant'. We will in turn look at explanations of middle and working class 'deviant' voters.

1 MIDDLE CLASS 'DEVIANT' VOTERS

Consistently in general elections there are fewer middle than working class 'deviant' voters. Three types of middle class 'deviant' voters are described in the literature. These can be termed:

1 The 'intellectual' left.
2 The 'status deprived' left.
3 The 'recently upwardly mobile' middle class.

The first group tends to contain many with considerable experience of higher education: these can be referred to as the 'intellectual left'. They include, particularly, some academics, journalists and 'media people' and members of vocational or 'helping' professions, such as social work or teaching.

Slightly controversially perhaps, it can be argued that the wide education and knowledge of these people enables them to see beyond their own interest and to sympathise with the disadvantaged. They vote Labour because they see it as the party which better represents the disadvantaged.

The second group is those with low status within the middle class. Unlike the first group, they do not vote Labour for idealistic reasons, but more out of pique and insecurity. Typically, they rank higher in education and qualifications than in social status: they find outlets for the resulting resentment in radical politics. (It is worth noting that the analysis of radicalism in terms of status deprivation has been influential in recent American sociology and history, where it has been criticised as both conservative and speculative.) Certainly, this approach employs a highly cynical interpretation of motive. In refuting it, Frank Parkin argues that low status jobs are a result of radical ideals and not vice-versa. He suggests that the political attitudes of middle class radicals are formed before they start work, and that they choose work which is most compatible with their radical values. This tends to be vocational and of relatively low pay and status. However, Parkin's analysis could equally apply to higher status middle class radicals. What both have in common is a concern for the welfare of others as well as themselves.

The third group for consideration are numbers of first generation white collar employees, or 'the sons of affluent workers' as John Goldthorpe calls them. It seems that some of these continue to support the Labour Party even after their rise in socio-economic status. No doubt this partly reflects loyalty to their 'roots' but it also suggests that, as the traditional working class shrinks, the Labour Party may have succeeded in presenting policies that potentially widen its basis of support.

2 WORKING CLASS 'DEVIANT' VOTERS: 'DEFERENCE' AND 'SECULAR' VOTERS The most convincing explanation of the large working class Tory vote, and one which is echoed in most writings on the subject, is that the dominant institutions of British society embody conservative and middle class values. As a result, the working class as well as the middle class becomes socialised into conservative values unless more radical socialisation cuts across this central flow of influence (see Parkin, above). In functionalist terms, this simply means that a 'consensus around the central value system' is created by institutions such as the monarchy and the church, which exist partly for that purpose. Marxists agree, but consider that this process misleads or 'mystifies' the working class into conforming, sometimes enthusiastically, to a social system that exploits them.

Detailed study of the working class Conservative vote supports the above analysis. As we have seen, Goldthorpe and Lockwood have given the term deferential traditionalists to one group of working class Tories. Referring to the same group, McKenzie and Silver use the term 'deference voters'. These are people who prefer ascribed 'socially superior' leaders to those who have risen by their own efforts. McKenzie and Silver found these attitudes among some of the urban proletariat, although they are more usually associated with farm labourers. Often it seems that isolated, individual workers, such as caretakers of prestige, private establishments or personal and domestic employees of the wealthy, adopt deferential attitudes.

McKenzie and Silver suggested that what they term 'secular voters' may be superseding deferential voters as the major working class basis of Conservative support. Compared to deference voters, secular voters are young and well-paid. In general secular voters seems to describe the group re-ferred to by Goldthorpe and Lockwood as instrumentalists. The latter, of course, deny that this group is tending to become more Conservative and, in doing so, refute the embourgeoisement hypothesis. Nevertheless, the strong swing (11.5) of affluent workers from Labour to the Conservatives in the 1979 election suggested that the embourgeoisement hypothesis or something like it might have more long-term mileage in it than Goldthorpe and Lockwood suspected. In any case, they themselves pointed out that instrumentalists are more likely than traditionalists to change their voting habits to suit their perceived interests – a point also made by McKenzie and Silver. The latter also pointed out that instrumentalists tend to be less attracted to Labour by socialist values than of the

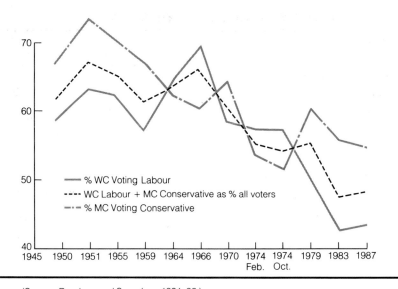

(Source: Dearlove and Saunders, 1991: 93)

▲

Figure 14.2

benefits of practical policies. If such benefits are not apparent they might decide to vote for another party (see also p. 143).

HAS THERE BEEN A DECLINE IN THE CLASS BASIS OF VOTING SINCE 1974? CREWE VERSUS HEATH ET AL.

Ivor Crewe has argued that both party or partisan dealignment and class dealignment have been occurring in Britain since around the early to mid nineteen seventies. Party dealignment refers to a tendency for fewer voters to feel attached to the Labour and Conservative Parties. Class dealignment refers to the tendency for class based voting to decline.

The evidence in favour of party dealignment is quite strong and is related to the rise of the Liberals, now Liberal Democrats. From the nineteen fifties to the nineteen eighties the third party vote increased by about 15 per cent and the total vote for the two largest parties decreased by a similar percentage although up to and including the 1987 general election, the decrease was greater in the Labour vote. Further, party membership of both major parties decreased steadily from the mid-nineteen fifties. Conservative membership more than halved during that period (to 1.2 million) and Labour membership dropped five-fold (to 300,000). Similarly, party identification has weakened. In 1964, 81 per cent identified with the two main parties, 40

per cent very strongly, whereas in 1987, 67 per cent and 24 per cent were the respective figures: a substantial drop.

The evidence for class dealignment is more disputed. It is clear that in absolute terms Labour's share of the total working class vote has fallen and the Conservative's share of the total middle class vote has fallen. Figure 14.2 shows these trends very clearly.

It is particularly notable that in 1983 and 1987, the working class Labour and middle class Conservative votes added together were less than 50 per cent of all votes. This was largely due to the strength of the third party during these elections which attracted both middle and working class votes as well as the working class 'Tory' and middle class Labour votes.

Ivor Crewe argues that the 1987 election showed a politically divided middle and working class. In that election, the university educated and those working in the public sector swung away from the Conservatives compared to 1983 whereas those working in the private sector voted overwhelmingly for them in both elections (64 per cent in 1983 and 65 per cent in 1987). Crewe contends that the 'Conservatives' vote only held steady because they made further inroads into the affluent working class'. They gained 36 per cent of the manual workers' vote, the largest percentage for any postwar election. However, the gains were exclusively among the skilled manual; the Conservatives lost support slightly among semi-skilled and unskilled manual workers and substantially among the unemployed. Whereas 43 per cent of skilled manual workers voted Conservative only 34 per cent voted Labour.

Heath, Jowell and Curtice (1985) oppose the view that the class basis of voting is weakening. In their analysis of the 1983 general election, they argue that the Labour vote declined among both the middle and working classes and that relatively the decline was much the same in both groups. They point out that such an overall decline is normal for the party which loses a general election. If and when the fortunes of Labour substantially revived, then a relative increase in both its working and middle class support could be anticipated. In fact, briefly in April 1990, an opinion poll taken when the Conservative government was extremely unpopular gave Labour a lead of 62 per cent to 20 per cent among skilled manual workers which does suggest that what goes down can come up!

COMMENT ON THE SOCIAL CLASS MODEL OF VOTING BEHAVIOUR It is common to suggest that the social class model of party identification 'works well' up to and including the 1970 general election but less well and perhaps increasingly less well after that. However, as we shall see, others do not consider that a sharp shift from 'old' to 'new' explanations of voting behaviour is justified. The class model already accommodates considerable variation from the 'norm' of voting according to social class – particularly if Parkin and Goldthorpe and Lockwood's analyses are considered as constructive amendments to it. It contains a recognition that various cross-currents of socialisation can disrupt party identification built-up through early class socialisation. Thus, deferential working class voters may be particularly strongly exposed to conservative social and economic influences, and Parkin, in any case, sees these as generally a strong counter-influence to radicalism.

Nevertheless, there was a substantial change in voting patterns from 1974, however it is interpreted. Figure 14.1 illustrates this in terms of the percentage of votes cast for the three main parties. It is to the economic and social developments that underlie this and other changes in political behaviour that we now turn.

INFLUENCES ON VOTING BEHAVIOUR OTHER THAN CLASS: REGIONAL, GENDER, AGE, ETHNIC AND RELIGIOUS

A problem with discussing several of the factors other than class which may affect voting behaviour is that, on closer examination, they tend to 'dissolve' into class. This is particularly true of the geographical-spatial factor. Here we briefly examine the geographical-spatial, gender, age, ethnic and religious factors.

In recent elections up to and including that of 1987, there has been an increasing tendency for 'the South' to vote Conservative and 'the North' to vote Labour. Clearly, it is unlikely that there is anything about the geography or climate of these regions that turn people one or other political direction! Underlying the spatial factor, then, must be

a) CONSTITUENCIES WITH HIGHEST UNEMPLOYMENT

Constituency	% of men	% of women	Total %
Liverpool Riverside (Lab)	31.7	12.2	23.4
Manchester Central (Lab)	27.6	9.2	19.9
Glasgow Provan (Lab)	25.8	10.5	19.5
Glasgow Springburn (Lab)	24.5	9.9	18.2
Birmingham Smallheath (Lab)	23.5	9.9	18.2

b) CONSTITUENCIES WITH LOWEST UNEMPLOYMENT

Constituency	% of men	% of women	Total %
Henley (Con)	1.5	1.0	1.3
Mole Valley (Con)	1.7	0.8	1.3
Wokingham (Con)	1.6	1.1	1.4
Surrey North West (Con)	1.7	1.1	1.4
Mid-Sussex (Con)	1.8	0.9	1.4

▲ Table 14.2

something more fundamental. The deeper factor is probably the economic. The greater development of manufacturing industry in the North and service industry in the South means that the spatial distribution of classes is skewed accordingly. Further, economic expansion has favoured the 'middle class' South, whereas recession has tended to hit hardest in the 'working class' North. This appears to have had the effect of intensifying regional support for the two largest parties. In 1990, the 20 constituencies with highest unemployment were all Labour-held and the 20 constituencies with the lowest unemployment were all Conservative held. The former were overwhelmingly in the North and the latter in the South. Table 14.2 gives details of the five constituencies with the highest and lowest unemployment respectively.

Support for a party in a particular region, if well established, can be cumulative. Party policy comes to reflect a region's needs, and local socialisation tends to reinforce existing political attitudes.

There used to be a greater tendency for women than men to vote Conservative but this has been reduced to negligible proportions since the 1979 election. The slightly higher percentage vote among women for the Conservatives in 1987 (see table 14.3) is better explained by the age than the gender factor. Women tend to live longer than men and the elderly are slightly more likely than other age groups to vote

Gender and voting behaviour				
	Con	Lab	Lib/SDP	Others
ALL	43.3 (−0.2)	31.6 (+3.3)	23.1 (−2.9)	2.0 (−0.2)
Sex: MEN	41 (0)	33 (+3)	23 (−3)	3 (−1)
WOMEN	43 (−1)	31 (+3)	23 (−3)	3 (+1)

(Figures in percentages; changes since 1983 in brackets. Source: ITN/Harris exit poll)

▲

Table 14.3

Conservative. However, the age factor, too, appears to be of diminishing effect. In the 1987 general election, the Conservative vote was slightly less among the under 21 than among other age groups, but even in this case ran ahead of Labour.

There is a strong tendency for members of black ethnic minorities to vote Labour. This is partly due to Labour's policies on immigration and race relations which are perceived as more sympathetic. However, again, the class factor may be the most influential one as most members of black minorities are working class. There are some signs of a slightly greater tendency to vote Conservative among upwardly mobile Asian-Britains.

It used to be said that the Church of England is 'the Tory Party at prayer'. However, with few people participating in formal prayer at all, this epigram has lost its relevance. In a secular society, religion appears less and less significant in explaining voting behaviour but as a general factor in politics there are signs of a modest revival in its importance (see pp. 405–6).

The Rational-Choice Model of Voting Behaviour

The rational-choice model of voting behaviour sees the voter as a thinking individual who is able to take a view on political issues and vote accordingly. It rejects the notion that voting behaviour is largely determined by class socialisation. Rather, this logic is reversed and those who vote for 'the party of their class' – a diminishing number – are regarded as doing so because it serves their interests and meets their views on particular issues.

At a theoretical level, the rational choice model of voting behaviour neatly dovetails with Thatcherite notions of economic rationality in which rational behaviour is seen as the pursuit of self-interest in the market. Anthony Downs develops this parallel in *An Economic Theory of Democracy* (1957) in which political parties are compared to firms supplying products (policies) to individual consumers (Voters). Voters do not 'belong' to parties but may change if it suits them to do so.

The main piece of empirical research reflecting the rational-choice model approach is Himmelweit et al. How voters decide (1987). A small sample of men from the Greater London area were repeatedly interviewed between 1959–74. They find that the strongest influence on voting behaviour is the individual's own response to the issues of a particular election which, of course, change to a greater or lesser extent from election to election. Two 'weaker' influences are also observed to affect voting behaviour. These are the habit of voting for a particular party and the example of significant others. Again, the comparison with market activity is made, party loyalty being compared to brand loyalty, and the influence of spouses, friends and others on voting behaviour is compared to the influence such people may have on an individual making a purchase.

Himmelweit et al. recognise limits in the parallel between the economic and political:

While the analogy between purchasing a party and purchasing goods is a useful one, there are aspects which make choosing a party that much harder. In the case of voting, options are few and the policies on offer are those generated by the parties, not the voter. The timetable too is fixed by government. De facto, there are few opportunities for the ordinary voter, only moderately interested in politics, to hear the parties' claims seriously challenged, except by the other parties' counter claims. There is also no Trade Description Act to limit the claims of the parties, nor is there a consumer guide like 'Which?' to assess their realism. Relative costs and incompatibility of policies are rarely mentioned; for example, that it would be difficult to reduce government expenditure while improving the lot of the needy, health and education services, as well as provide help for the developing countries. Yet all parties claim these as their objectives.

Is it any wonder that there are wide fluctuations in the opinion polls and that the voter is particularly critical of the party for which he had voted last time or the one he tried 'for size' in the pre-election period?

(Himmelweit et al. 1987: 210)

As the concluding sentence of the above extract indicates, Himmelweit et al. see the world of political support and voting behaviour as one of considerable and perhaps increasing flux.

COMMENT ON THE RATIONAL-CHOICE MODEL OF VOTING BEHAVIOUR Two main criticisms of Himmelweit et al.'s research can be offered. First, the interview sample was small and unrepresentative and became more so as the research continued. Of the original sample of 600, only 178 took part in every stage of the interviews and of those who did the large majority were upper middle or middle class. This almost certainly skewed the findings in the individualistic direction that, as it happens, coincided with the authors' bias. Second, whereas the Butler and Stokes model is structural and almost anti-individualistic, Himmelweit et al. make the reverse emphasis. As Dearlove and Saunders succinctly express it:

(t)his individualistic perspective on voting behaviour fails to provide an account of the origins of the political attitudes of those interviewed' (1990: 101).

What, then, appears still to be needed is detailed work on the links between the political attitudes of individuals and the social background variables that must influence them.

The Radical Approach to Voting Behaviour

In *British Democracy at the Crossroads*, P Dunleavy and C Husbands argue a third and radical interpretation of voting behaviour. They regard the class-based model as outdated and insufficiently complex to explain contemporary developments and consider that the rational choice model inadequately addresses the new social structural issues that influence voting.

Dunleavy and Husbands argue that two main sources of influence structure political alignments in contemporary Britain:

1 Sectoral cleavages which separate people into groups with different interests and priorities – e.g. public sector employees; private sector employees; those dependent on public services; those dependent on the private sector. Dunleavy and Husbands particularly emphasise the importance of public/private sector cleavages which result from the involvement of the state in production and consumption (see below).

2 Dominant Ideological Messages which are conveyed mainly through the media and which form 'political consciousness'. In Dunleavy and Husbands' view consciousness is directed away from more fundamental issues of class cleavage towards more superficial but immediate issues such as the management and delivery of education or health.

The political parties compete and people's political attitudes are formed within the context of the above two influences. Again, it needs to be emphasised, this is at the expense of the presentation, appreciation and debate of deeper class issues.

Dunleavy and Husbands present the two main aspects of their analysis as part of a total framework of explanation. It is because voters are ideologically confused about their deeper class interests and identities that they become so focused on more limited sectoral issues. However, it is their analysis of sectoral cleavages that has had the widest influence. For instance, Ivor Crewe's views on the divided middle and working class votes draws directly from data on sectoral cleavage within both classes. Both table 14.4 and figure 14.3 explore elements of sector cleavage in relation to the working and middle classes and in the case of the former geographical data on voting patterns is also given.

Table 14.4 shows cleavages formed in the work place (i.e. at the point of production) and household status which is a consumption cleavage. It is quite clear that working class people who work or live in the private sector are more likely to vote Conservative than those who work or live in the public sector. However, it is worth noting that even in the 1987 election the tendency for the latter groups to vote Labour was still considerably stronger than for the former groups to vote Conservative. A revival of Labour's fortunes would probably see big changes in these figures.

university educated were more likely to vote Labour than the non-university educated middle class. However, there was a greater swing towards the Liberal/SDP Alliance than to Labour among both middle class public sector employees and the university educated in 1987. It may be that both other parties will benefit as groups such as teachers and, more latterly doctors perhaps begin to feel disenchanted with the Conservative policies towards, respectively, public education and health. Again, it is necessary to put these still quite short term trends in context. The Conservatives' support among the 'self-made' in the private sector slightly strengthened in 1987 to 65 per cent and even among public sector employees it was 44 per cent.

▶

Figure 14.3

The new division

in the middle

classes (%)

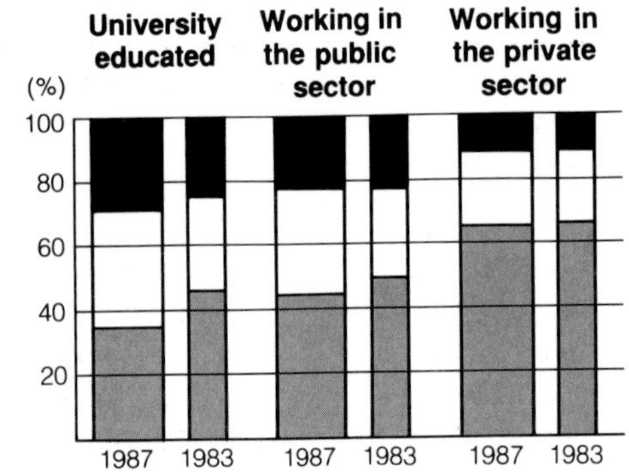

Note: The figures show the parties' shares of the three-party vote; the columns do not always add up to 100% as the figures have been rounded to the nearest whole number.

Conservative / Lib/SDP Alliance / Labour

(Source: *Social Studies Review* September 1987, p.5)

Table 14.4

The Working Class

Vote, 1987: Sectoral

and Geographical

Cleavages

▼

The middle class vote in 1983 and 1987 showed a greater tendency for those working in the public than the private sector to vote Labour and vice-versa. Similarly, the

COMMENT ON THE RADICAL MODEL OF VOTING BEHAVIOUR Dunleavy and Husbands convincingly present what had often previously been referred to as the 'deviant' working and middle class votes in a significantly new context: that of sectoral cleavages. Their approach is likely to influence other models although it is unlikely to replace them. They themselves contend that there are deeper divisions than sectoral ones and in their view, these are class divisions – a familiar and traditional view. The aspect of their analysis which remains relatively untested and the point on which many disagree with them is that much of the working class fails to appreciate its true interests because of the strength of the dominant capitalist ideology.

A possible 'solution' to the problem of competing models of voting behaviour would be to try to construct a composite

Party	Geography	Consumption	Production	Production	Geography	Consumption	Production	Production
	Lives in South	Owner Occupier	Non-union member	Works in private sector	Lives in Scotland or North	Council tenant	Union member	Works in public sector
Conservative	46	44	40	38	29	25	30	32
Labour	28	32	38	39	57	57	48	49
Lib/SDP Alliance	26	24	22	23	15	18	22	19
Conservative or Labour majority in 1987	Con +18	Con +12	Con +2	Lab +1	Lab +28	Lab +32	Lab +18	Lab +17
Conservative or Labour majority in 1983	Con +16	Con +22	Con +6	Lab +1	Lab +10	Lab +38	Lab +21	Lab +17
Category as percentage of all manual workers	40	57	66	68	37	31	34	1
Change since 1983	+4	+3	+7	+2	−1	−4	−7	−

Note: Figures have been rounded to the nearest whole number, so totals do not always add up to 100%.

(Source: *Social Studies Review*, Vol. 3 No 1, September 1987: Adapted)

model from the three. In fact, commentators do acknowledge and use elements in each other's models. Few adopt an unreconstructed class-based model of voting but whereas some still work within such a model, others find it increasingly inadequate to explain recent voting patterns in general elections. However, although the rational-choice model has restored the importance of political issues and personalities to consideration, it is widely seen as part of rather than the total explanation of voting behaviour. The radical model of sectoral cleavage might appear to explain the more fragmented pattern of contemporary voting but Dunleavy and Husbands themselves are residual class model theorists! Class is not out of the picture. It may be significant, however, that the Liberal Democrats seem to have survived the chaos of the centre parties in the late nineteen eighties and again have support comparable to that of the Alliance in the mid-nineteen eighties. If the relative strength of the centre party or parties (if the Greens maintain their 1989 form), is the incontrovertible new factor since the mid nineteen seventies, then, the least that can be said is that more voters are opting out of the Conservative/Labour option than in the previous period. Whether the introduction of proportional representation in place of the present 'first past the post' system would further break the mould of traditional voting patterns is an hypothesis not yet tested.

CONCLUSION: THE GENERAL ELECTION OF 1992

The general election of 1992 confirmed most of the trends referred to above. Labour decisively lost the middle class vote but gained a larger percentage of the AB vote than historically. Labour failed even to reverse the fact that since 1979 more skilled manual workers (C2s) have voted for the Conservatives. The Labour vote among the partly skilled and unskilled (DEs) was strong but those groups are numerically declining and do not provide an adequate basis for electoral victory. The gender, age and regional voting trends were broadly in

%	Con	Lab	Lib Dem	Other
All voters	43	35	18	5
Men	42	37	17	5
Women	43	34	19	3
Aged 18–24	36	37	21	6
Aged 25–34	40	38	17	5
Aged 35–54	44	34	18	4
Aged 55+	45	35	17	2
AB	59	20	19	2
C1	52	24	20	5
C2	41	38	17	5
DE	29	50	17	4
Owner-occupied	53	27	18	2
Council rented	22	53	18	6
Scotland	25	39	11	24
North	38	44	16	1
Midlands	42	41	15	2
South	50	26	23	2

Figures rounded up; therefore, do not always add up to 100%
(Source: NOP)

Figure 14.4

How Britain Voted in 1992 by Gender, Class, Housing and Region.

line with those of recent elections as was voting according to the type of housing occupied. Although the Liberal Democrats did not do as well as the Alliance in 1983 or 1987, they did well enough to suggest that third party politics and the issue of proportional representation are here to stay.

Arguably, Labour did just well enough in the 1992 election to suggest that it can win an election. What is less clear is *how* it can win. Can it widen its appeal to the middle and upper working classes without losing support among the rest of the working class? Does Labour need new ideals or new policies or both? Does Labour need a charismatic, accomplished media-performer as leader? Should the party negotiate a Lib-Lab pact for the next election? As Labour looks for answers, Britain or, rather, England is being moulded by a Conservative Party kept in power partly by people whose parents voted Labour. Unless Labour finds a blend of idealism and pragmatism which enables it to appeal to them as it once did to their parents, the party is likely to be condemned to even longer-term and more frustrating opposition.

Liberal Model of the Democratic Society

Those who contend that liberal democracy 'works' argue that parties and pressure groups effectively represent people and influence government. Further, they believe that political government, reflecting the will of the people, is the supreme state power. The civil service is seen as the 'servant' of government: the judiciary is regarded as independent of government, but is not expected to concern itself with political matters. The liberal model of democracy is examined below. In addition to the term 'liberal democracy', that of 'liberal pluralist' or, simply, 'pluralist' is often used. Pluralist refers to the many groups – notably parties and pressure groups – that liberals believe participate meaningfully in democratic politics.

PARTIES, POLITICAL ELITES AND THE STATE

Political parties existed in Britain well before universal suffrage (that is, the right of all people to vote). Parties, therefore, predate democracy. Nevertheless, the party system has adapted well to the demands of liberal democracy. The major parties attempt to appeal consistently to certain broad groups of people. The Labour Party seeks support mainly from the working class and certain sections of the middle class, such as members of the new professions. The Conservative Party is traditionally the party of the middle and upper classes. There is, however, as we have seen, much overlap in the class basis of party support and, in particular, among the upper working and lower middle classes. Even so, a major party seems to require a solid base of class support to achieve power. The Liberal Party rapidly declined as a major party when it ceased to appeal to an identifiable section of society. The compatibility of the two party system with liberal democracy is further suggested by the American example. Two competing parties quickly established themselves after the Americans had won their independence from Britain. In time, these developed into the present day Democratic and Republican parties. Like the chief British parties, these also tend to represent major sectional interests, although not to the same extent.

Political parties have ideologies or certain principles and beliefs which usually reflect quite closely the values and material interests of those groups and classes from which they draw most of their support. The British Conservative Party is strongly committed to capitalism, whereas the Labour Party believes in socialism – although the majority in the party support the 'mixed' nature of the economy. It is still probably true that the Conservative Party is the party of tradition, whereas the Labour Party identifies with progressive change and reform. For liberal-democratic theorists these are very significantly different ideological positions, but Marxists argue that, rhetoric aside, the two major parties actually behave rather similarly when in government. By contrast, liberal-democratic theorists consider that philosophical differences can lead to practical policy differences. Thus, various measures of the Labour government of 1945–50 would be considered distinctly socialist, and in sharp contrast to the clearly free-enterprise policies of the Thatcher government elected in 1979. In fairness, this example is selected to suit the argument and most Labour and Conservative governments have been more similar to one another than this. In any case, it is a tacit assumption of liberalism that no major party will seek to overthrow the basic social and political 'consensus'.

Liberal democracy is, in part, a theory about the relationship between the majority of the people and their leaders, the political elite. This relationship has balancing elements: the elite is representative, and yet it also leads. We will deal with these two aspects separately.

Historically, elite theory has tended to be undemocratic. Of the two major early twentieth century elite theorists, Pareto and Mosca, it was the latter who argued that the political elite could be generally representative of the people or 'masses', to use the term preferred by elite theorists. The party system, free elections and pressure group activity were means to ensure representativeness.

An important related issue to the representative nature of elites is the extent to which, once elected, they remain under democratic control. Is democracy 'real' only once every five years when people cast their vote? Robert Dahl believes that elections play an important part in controlling government and he also cites a second major means by which leaders are made answerable to the people:

The election process is one of two fundamental methods of social control which, operating together, make governmental leaders so responsive to non-leaders that the distinction between democracy and dictatorship still makes sense. The other method of social control is continuous political competition among individuals, parties or both. Elections and political competition ... vastly increase the size, number and variety of minorities whose preferences must be taken into account by leaders in making policy choices. (1968:18)

Above all, elections, or the certainty that an election must come, means that a governing party must always conduct itself in a way that will ultimately appeal to the majority of the electorate. There is evidence that widespread retrospective voting does occur: many voters do remember major features in the overall performance of administration and this acts as a check upon it. As Dahl points out, however, many particular policies may be concerned with the interest only of a minority, such as farm subsidies for the agricultural interest, though this does not necessarily mean that they therefore alienate the rest of the electorate. Many policies which please a minority are non-contentious to the majority. When the election comes, nevertheless, the government knows that, to win, it must have the backing of a 'majority of minorities'. This, according to Dahl, keeps it in check.

Liberal elite theorists have stressed the necessity of leadership by the political elite almost as much as its representative nature. In large societies, only a minority can be involved in leadership. Further, competitive political selection should ensure that the elite leads on merit. The prime general function of leadership is to create social consensus and establish social order. Edward Shils believes that, in doing this, the elite protects its own interest, as well as those of

the majority. Whilst agreeing that the process of consensus production does occur, Marxists deny that in capitalist society it works for the common good. On the contrary, it merely misleads the working class. Class conflict tends not to be stressed by democratic elite theorists. The alternative term to classes, 'masses' – which obscures classes and class conflict – sounds too contemptuous to modern ears to be used by liberal theorists. Instead, they stress the need for the political elite to lead the public towards a workable consensus.

We can link Dahl's democratic theory with the functionalist view put forward by Talcott Parsons of how power operates in a democracy. Parsons argues that leaders use power for the general good or, more precisely, for collective goals. Leaders are 'honest brokers' in power. Defence of the country and maintenance of law and order are two examples of the necessary use of power for the general good. It is crucial to Parsons' theory that how much power political leaders use ultimately depends on the will of the people. In war-time, the representative of the people in Congress or Parliament may sanction the use of greater powers by the government. Emergencies aside, the use of power is controlled by the processes described by Dahl. Parsons, therefore, conceives of power rather as some economists think of money: more or less can be created as the situation demands.

THE LIBERAL VIEW OF THE STATE

Liberal theorists tend to regard the relationship between government and the rest of the state as relatively unproblematic. The government rules and the civil service implements its policies. The Marxist idea that the capitalist class is the 'real' controller of the state is simply not taken seriously. Weber, however, raised an important question in relation to the civil service. He considered that, like all bureaucracies it created its own vested interests and tended to be slow-moving. Civil servants, for reasons of their own, may give partial advice to ministers or take too long in producing it. Weber regarded a powerful Parliament as the best protector against an oppressive civil service bureaucracy.

	Sectional Groups	Promotional Groups
Permanent	Trades Union Congress	Child Poverty Action Group
Ad Hoc	Archway Road Campaign	Band Aid

▲

Table 14.5

PRESSURE GROUPS

Pressure groups, as well as parties, are parts of the liberal-democratic model. If parties are the bulwarks of democracy, pressure groups are the supports and buttresses. They are an essential part of the pluralist vision in which power is seen as widely shared and exercised. Like parties, pressure groups predate democracy but like them they have become part of liberal democracy. Jean Blondel, who shares the pluralist perspective, sees parties and pressure groups as equally involved in the democratic process, although in different ways:

Interest groups differ from political parties by their aim, which is not to take power but only to exert pressure. They differ from parties by their objects, which are usually limited in scope. They differ from parties by the nature of their membership, which is often limited to one section in society. (1969: 160)

There have always been groups sharing a common interest which have collectively pressed their case to the powerful. The Wolfenden Report states that in the period since the war the number of pressure groups has increased considerably. From the liberal point of view, pressure groups provide a necessary means of limited conflict on specific issues but this takes place within a context of fundamental consensus.

We can classify pressure groups into two broad types: sectional (or protective) and promotional. Sectional groups are those whose membership has some common factor, such as occupation. It is to defend the common interest of their membership that such groups exist. Trade Unions and professional associations provide the best known examples of sectional pressure groups. The biggest union is the Transport and General Worker's Union (TGWU), and a well known professional association is the British Medical Association (BMA). Sectional groups are usually economic but can also reflect for instance, religious or ethnic interests. The Islamic Society for

Racial Tolerance and the Indian Workers' Associations are examples.

Promotional groups seek to promote a cause. One example is Amnesty International which seeks to aid and assist political prisoners throughout the world. Political prisoners are prisoners of conscience as opposed to criminals. Amnesty International is an organisation for which there is likely to be a long-term need. By contrast, other promotional groups achieve their aim, and can then disband. For example, a variety of anti-Vietnam War groups sprang up in the nineteen-sixties but dissolved when the war came to an end.

We need to distinguish between pressure groups in terms of the time-span of their existence, as well as on the basis of their interests or the causes they champion. The anti-Vietnam War groups were examples of ad hoc groups, formed to contest a specific issue, whereas Amnesty International and, still more obviously, the Trades Union Congress (TUC) are permanent groups (see table 14.5). Blondel also makes the important point that certain organisations which are not strictly speaking interest groups may occasionally use their influence in the political process. Thus, the Catholic Church makes its official (though not necessarily representative), opinion felt on such matters as divorce and abortion legislation.

Pressure groups use a variety of means to influence public opinion, such as advertisements, demonstrations and meetings. Sometimes they focus more directly on Parliament or the executive government. Often this means lobbying a powerful or influential individual such as an MP. Our interest, however, is less in the detail of the methods of pressure group activity than in whether or not the results of this pressure are effective. Pluralists would say that they are, Marxists that they are not. At least, that is the essence of the argument, although both positions require some qualification. Christopher Hewitt has attempted to test which of these two cases is more correct by reference to empirical data. He examines the roles of a variety of interest groups in relation to twenty four major post-war crisis issues which cover the area of foreign, economic, welfare and social policy. The issues he analyses include the debate and struggles over the Suez crisis, the nationalisation of steel, the National Health

Service Act and the Commonwealth Immigration Act of 1962. He includes interest groups from all major sections of national life in his study, including trade unions (blue and white collar); business organisations; religious organisations; local government bodies; research organisations and various promotional groups. He concludes that policy making in Britain is not elitist in the sense that any single elite or interest is dominant, but that different interests succeed at different times. Statistically, the unions were particularly successful in that issues were most frequently resolved as they wished. The Marxist response to this argument is that issues dealt with in national politics are within the national consensus and that genuinely alternative (Marxist) principles and policies are not discussed. This view is examined in the next section.

There are other arguments put forward by liberal democrats in support of the pressure group system. Pressure groups provide an accessible, day-to-day means by which popular opinion and influence can be expressed. They act upon political parties but are not necessarily part of the party system. In practice, however, the two major industrial interest groups tend to be tied into the party system. The unions and the TUC, and business and the CBI tend overwhelmingly to support, respectively, the Labour Party and the Conservative Party. It is significant, although seldom stressed by pluralists, that in a society noted for its class system, the two major parties and the two major interest groups should divide along class lines. Nevertheless, the major groups which support and, in part, finance the political parties exact a 'price' for loyalty: in return, they expect their interests to be protected and advanced. If, in their opinion, this does not occur, then, on a given issue, they may oppose the party they normally favour. Thus, the proposals to change the legal position of the unions, put forward by the Labour government of 1966–1970, were opposed with great determination by the union movement.

A further criticism of interest group politics, in addition to that put forward by Marxists referred to above, is that it tends to leave out, or at least to leave behind, those who are least able to organise themselves: these people are found in the overlapping categories of the poor, the old, and the chronically sick and disabled. Immigrant groups also have tended to be less organised than their needs require. This is partly because they are financially and materially disadvantaged, and therefore have difficulty in affording the cost of organisation, and partly because it takes time for a group to accumulate the knowledge and experience to deal with the complex structure of institutionalised power in this country. It was a feature of British and American politics that, in the nineteen sixties and seventies, the disadvantaged became increasingly organised and vociferous. Instead of assuming that the welfare state would 'take care of them', the disadvantaged formed groups such as Claimants Unions (concerned with supplementary benefits) and Tenants Associations aimed at obtaining what they saw as their rights. Even pensioners were seen to converge on Parliament Square to lobby MPs. Often the disadvantaged were assisted in pursuing their interests by community social workers or radical professional people and, occasionally, students. Sometimes this link took an institutional form. Des Wilson and Frank Field, the charismatic former directors of Shelter (the pressure group concerned with housing) and The Child Poverty Action Group, respectively, exemplify this kind of alliance. Of course, the involvement and concern of radical intellectuals with the poor is by no means new, but it did receive fresh stimulus in the nineteen sixties, and there are signs of revived concern in the early nineteen nineties. The large number of pressure groups, particularly involved with the disadvantaged, may suggest that pluralism works; equally, however, the continuing need for these pressure groups may indicate that the way liberal capitalism functions fails to satisfy the wants of large numbers of people. Arguably, the emergence of a so-called 'underclass' indicates the failure of pressure group politics as far as they are concerned.

It is not easy for people living in a Western democracy to evaluate the extent and quality of the political and civil 'freedom' that liberals claim exists in these countries. This freedom is manifestly not absolute. Freedom of speech and freedom of the press is limited by law. The party-pressure group political system seems to favour the loudest voices: certainly political rights have not led to a radical reduction in material inequality. But it would be very foolish to undervalue the freedom that does exist. Within broadly defined limits, people can speak their minds, even if some have far easier access to a public audience than others. People are able to organise for a cause even though some, by virtue of greater knowledge, wealth or influence, can do so more easily than others. Private lives are largely left private by the State – in their own homes, at least, people can 'be themselves'. These freedoms might not seem so substantial or so precious if we did not have before us the bloody alternatives of totalitarianism practised in Germany and the Soviet Union in the nineteen thirties. Perhaps the major argument in favour of liberal democracy is that attempts to improve on it have usually resulted in something much worse and in the reduction of political, civil and personal freedom. In the post-Second World War period a cautionary, even defensive, note has characterised liberal statements about democracy. Ageing liberals remember pre-war Germany and Russia as far worse than any liberal regime and are now inclined to settle for and defend what they know and value rather than radically to experiment. By contrast, socialists and Marxists argue that a fundamentally freer, more equal and more just society than exists in liberal democracies is possible. While legitimately disagreeing with liberals, they can learn from them that creating such a society is fraught with dangers and that, if the attempt fails, far more may be lost than gained. To regard liberal warnings of this kind as 'mere moralism' is to show a gross ignorance of the failures and cruelties of recent European history.

Marxist/Liberal Debate: Ruling Class or Representative Political Elite

MARXIST PERSPECTIVES ON THE 'CAPITALIST STATE'

Most Marxists would deny that the model of democracy described in the previous section represents 'real' democracy. For them, it is merely 'bourgeois democracy', a smoke-screen behind which the capitalist class pursues its own interests. Parliament and political government are not considered to be the major source of power. Capitalists make the important decisions and control politicians. Although many contemporary Marxists would modify this view, some also retain a firm commitment to it in its classic form.

We have discussed in sufficient detail already Marx's view of society as fundamentally divided by class conflict. Of more relevance here is the issue of how Marxists consider that the ruling class rules. Both Tom Bottomore and Anthony Giddens make the point that, if capitalists do rule, they do so indirectly. They cannot do so directly as they are in a minority, both in the legislature and the executive in most capitalist countries. In feudal society, there was a much more precise correspondence between economic and political power. The feudal lords were the ruling class in the sense that they occupied the major political as well as economic positions. The landed nobility fulfilled the most important positions in central and local government. That is not true of capitalists today, although they are well represented in politics. If capitalists rule at all, therefore, they do so indirectly. Because of this, Marxist attempts to 'prove' the existence of a ruling class have often tended to be either circumstantial (relying on suggestive rather than conclusive evidence), or rather abstract and theoretical. Ralph Miliband's book, *The State in Capitalist Society* (1969), appears to fall into the first group, although Miliband himself would claim that he more than demonstrates his case. As the title of his book suggests, he is concerned with the control and operation of the state in capitalist society. He considers the state to be made up of the following institutions: the government, the administration (the civil service), the judiciary and parliamentary assemblies. State power lies in these institutions. In addition to what Miliband says, it is useful to bear in mind Althusser's concept of state apparatuses. The capacity of the state to control the armed forces and police as well as the major means of communication, notably the media, is crucial to its power. This control is open to challenge and, in any case, it is fiercely argued between liberals and Marxists precisely how much power the state in capitalist societies has over the ideological state apparatus. Obviously, the relationship between the government and media differs somewhat in different capitalist countries but, generally, Marxists argue that there is relatively limited freedom of expression, whereas liberals take the opposite view.

THE UPPER CLASS BACKGROUND OF OCCUPATIONAL ELITES

A major part of Miliband's book examines two related questions whose answers, taken together, determine whether or not there is a ruling class in British and other European capitalist societies. Firstly, is the state actually operated by people from the same upper class social background? Secondly, if so, do these people run the state in their own interest and at the expense of other classes? Miliband's answer to both questions is 'yes', although he has an easier time answering the first than the second. On the common social background and experience of those who dominate the command positions of the state, Miliband is unequivocal:

What the evidence conclusively suggests is that in terms of social origin, education and class situation, the men who have manned all command positions in the state system have largely, and in many cases, overwhelmingly, been drawn from the world of business or property, or from the professional middle classes. Here, as in every other field, men and women born into the subordinate classes, which form of course the vast majority of the population, have fared very poorly ...
(Miliband, 1969: 61)

Although Miliband is primarily concerned with Britain, he cites considerable empirical evidence to show that the same situation prevails in other Western European 'democracies'.

Miliband's book was published in 1969, but substantially the same argument was presented in 1979 by the non-Marxist Anthony Giddens who, in fact, makes a broader claim than Miliband – that there is no major institutional sector in Britain where less than half of those in top positions

are of public school background, and, by implication, also of upper or upper middle class background. (For details, see chapter 6.) Drawing on a study of elites carried out at Cambridge, Giddens concludes that over 80 per cent of Anglican bishops, of principal judges and of army officers over the rank of major-general were from public schools, as were 60 per cent of chief secretaries in the civil service, and 76 per cent of Conservative MPs (1951–70). In contrast, only 26 per cent of Labour MPs had a public school background.

Giddens emphasises especially the upper class dominance of industry, which, from the Marxist point of view, is particularly important because the economy is seen as the ultimate basis of power. In a sample taken from the Cambridge survey, 73 per cent of the directors of the industrial corporations and 80 per cent of the directors of financial firms proved to be of public school background.

Giddens cites other work which shows that directors of industrial and, especially, financial companies very often have kin 'within the trade'. The phenomenon of interlocking directorships is a point emphasised in both British and American literature on industrial elites. The term 'industrial elites' refers to the way in which various individuals hold directorships in more than one company so that the same individuals may sit together on several different boards. Accordingly, they may influence and even co-ordinate the policy of two or more companies: indeed, this is often precisely the intention of interlocking directorships. The Cambridge study showed an increase in directional connection between large companies. At the beginning of the century, fewer than half of the 85 corporations studied were linked by shared directorships, whereas in 1970, 73 out of 85 organisations studied appeared in the network of connections. Potentially, this provides an impressive basis for control of industry.

IS THE UPPER CLASS ALSO A RULING CLASS?

We come now to Miliband's second area of enquiry. Does the upper class rule in its own interest, and at the expense of others? As Miliband and Giddens are well aware, to demonstrate upper class dominance of major elites does not prove either that the upper class is the 'real source of political power' or, still less, that it rules in its own interest. In particular, the powerful position of the upper class in industry does not automatically mean that it can control the political process or that, 'in the last resort', its economic power is more decisive than the political power of government. These issues require further examination.

In attempting to determine whether the upper class is also a ruling class, it is helpful to establish what links exist between business and politics. If these are considerable, we can conclude that there is at least the potential for business to influence the political process and, perhaps, even to control it in its own interest. A study by Roth and Kerbey shows that, between 1960 and 1966, MPs held, in total, 770 directorships and 324 positions as chairmen, vice-chairmen or managing directors. It is highly significant that 90 per cent of these positions were held by Conservative MPs. In so far as the economic-political flow of influence does express itself through personal links of this kind, it is, therefore, far more likely to be found in the Conservative Party than in the Labour Party. The upper class is well represented in both industry and the Conservative Party. As we have seen 76 per cent of Conservative MPs over the period 1951–70 went to public school, a major purveyor of upper class culture, compared with only 26 per cent of Labour MPs. Few Marxists, however, regard the Labour Party as the likely means by which capitalism will be abolished and socialism established. Why is this so?

Marx himself held out little hope that socialism could be successfully introduced through Parliament, although there is evidence that he thought that the arrival of universal male suffrage (voting rights) might make the system more responsive to socialist demands. In the event, Marxists are able to point out that, despite seventeen years of Labour government since 1945, the fundamental facts of inequality have not changed very much. Everybody has become better off, but the relativities have not changed significantly. Marxists tend to consider that the welfare state has partly 'humanised' but not fundamentally changed the position of the working class and the poor. Writing in the late nineteen-sixties, but expressing a perennial mood among Marxists, Miliband says:

Social-democratic parties [Labour parties] or rather social-democratic leaders, have long ceased to suggest to anyone but their most credulous followers [and the more stupid among their opponents] that they were concerned in any sense whatever with the business of bringing about a socialist society.
(Miliband, 1968: 244)

In qualification of Miliband's remark, it should be said that there is still a sizeable socialist, if not Marxist-inclined, group within the Labour Party, which continues to work for fundamental change through the parliamentary system, despite its dissatisfaction with the performances of the Labour government of the nineteen sixties and seventies.

NICOS POULANTZAS

Further analysis of the role of the ruling class in capitalist society is presented by Nicos Poulantzas, a French Marxist. In a celebrated exchange with Miliband, Poulantzas criticises him for concentrating too much on details about the social background of various occupational elites and of the ruling class as a whole. For Poulantzas, these factors are not particularly crucial. In his view, it would be possible for large numbers, even a majority, of people of quite humble social background to administer capitalist society – but it would still be capitalist society and therefore run in the interests of the capitalist class and not the proletariat. This brings us to Poulantzas's central point and the one on which he considers that he differs, at least in emphasis, from Miliband. Poulantzas contends that it is the structure of the capitalist system and not the social background of the various elites which is the major factor for Marxists to consider when analysing the state. According to him, what matters is the relationship of the parts, including the state, to the social totality (the whole of society). Thus, it comes as no surprise to Poulantzas that socialist parties with a wide basis of popular support and even, perhaps, with leaders of working class origins, should find it difficult to implement socialism when, supposedly, 'in power'. The British Labour Party might be elected 'to power' but what it can actually do is limited by the rest of the system. It would almost certainly be afraid to introduce policies that would lose the confidence of international financiers and stock exchange investors. To do so would probably cause a major economic crisis. There might even be the possibility that radical policies would turn the military against the government. This threat, however, is most easily demonstrated in relation to underdeveloped countries. Thus, the popularly elected (although not with an absolute majority) president Allende of Chile, a Marxist, was overthrown by a conspiracy involving some of the parliamentary opposition, members of the armed forces and the American Central Intelligence Agency. The implication is that when legality fails to protect the interests of capital, then illegal means may be used.

The above does not mean that Poulantzas dismisses the state as unimportant – far from it! Some years after his debate with Miliband, he wrote: 'The state plays a decisive role in the relations of production and the class struggle'. But Poulantzas warns that what a socialist party could actually do with state power, if it were to obtain it, would be conditioned by the relationship of the state to the rest of the system at that time. This would include such matters as the strength of capital and the extent of socialist support among the working class.

There is an element of 'shadow boxing' about Miliband's and Poulantzas's disagreement, because the former insists that his work is a structural critique of the state in capitalist society and not just a collection of loosely interpreted empirical data. In any case, Poulantzas's point that an adequate theory of the state must relate coherently to the rest of the social system is valid.

It is worth briefly exploring the wider implications of Poulantzas's remark that 'the state plays a decisive role in the relations of production and the class struggle'. In saying this, he is rejecting the deterministic interpretations of Marx's base-superstructure model of society. He denies that capitalism will inevitably collapse as a result of its inherent economic 'contradictions' as some Marxists still believe. (Whether Marx himself ever believed this, in any simplistic sense, is debatable.) For Poulantzas, the capitalist nature of society and class relations arising from relations to the means of production do structure class conflict – both in the economic and political context – but they do not pre-determine its outcome: socialism has to be achieved through political struggle. With some reservations, the American Marxist sociologist Erik Wright supports this position in his book, *Class, Crisis and the State*. In particular, he offers a sensitive discussion of the issue of whether socialism can be achieved through the 'bourgeois' democratic system or whether it requires violent revolution. We have already referred to some of the problems of the former approach: the difficulties in relation to the second are perhaps greater. Firstly, the human cost of violent revolution needs to be profoundly considered. Can it be justified? Secondly, modern governments have at their disposal such powerful and centrally controlled arsenals of destruction that they seem virtually unassailable (although several communist regimes were overthrown from below during the nineteen eighties).

IDEOLOGY AND POWER

A crucial question that Marxists need to explain is why the majority, who are not the prime beneficiaries of capitalism, do not oppose the system more vehemently, Miliband and Poulantzas are agreed that the dominant ideology plays a vital role in securing the compliance of the majority to the power and position of the ruling class. We have already discussed how the educational system can teach people to conform – even to a society in which they have relatively little material stake – and the role of the mass media in this respect is worthy of much more space than we can give it here. For the moment, a single quotation from Miliband will serve to represent the Marxist perspective:

> *Given the economic and political context in which the mass media functions, they cannot fail to be, predominantly, agencies for the dissemination of idea and values which affirm rather than challenge existing patterns of power and privilege, and thus be weapons in the arsenal of class domination.*
> *(Miliband, 1969: 211)*

Ideological control involves power over people's minds. As Bachrach and Baratz point out, an aspect of this is the ability to decide which issues should be allowed to become publicly debated and which should not be, for instance, control of the press. Steven Lukes takes this point further by frankly recognising that the values, attitudes, and even wants of the majority can be moulded by the power of a few. Marxists are unimpressed by exercises such as that carried out by Hewitt (discussed earlier) which seem to support a pluralist model of power, because they argue that the issues that really matter are seldom discussed publicly, anyway. For Marxists, such issues would include whether a society based on private property (including that of the ruling class) can be socially just, whether violence is necessary to destroy the capitalist system and what a 'liberated' socialist culture might be like. The limits of the political debate are reflected in decisions taken and not taken (for example, issues of pollution and poverty may be disregarded and defence/law and order and immigration policy vigorously pursued). Marxists, then, agree with functionalists that ideological consensus can be achieved in capitalist society: the difference is their evaluation of it. Functionalists see it as necessary; Marxists regard it as an element in class exploitation. For them, there is no more telling illustration of the power of the ruling class than their ability to persuade the working class to accept and even morally approve of their own subjection.

POWER ELITE VERSUS RULING CLASS THEORY: A RADICAL DISAGREEMENT: CHARLES WRIGHT MILLS

Before summarising the merits of the pluralist and Marxist views of democracy, we must briefly analyse the power elite theory of the American radical sociologist, C Wright Mills. Mills was a conflict theorist but was much less of a Marxist than the other authors so far discussed in this section. He probably owed more to Weber than to Marx. He was a severe critic of post-Second World War American society. His fierce but measured language broke across the bland face of functionalist orthodoxy like a fire-cracker. A startled Talcott Parsons compared him to a gun-happy outlaw, free with the trigger but not very accurate in his aim. It is true that Mills began more than he was able to finish, but by the time of his death in 1962, he had sown the seeds of a radical

revival in American sociological scholarship, and provided an intellectual starting point for the emerging political radicalism of the American new left. His best known and most influential work is 'The power elite', first published in 1956. It is typical of Mills's intellectual inventiveness that he reworked traditionally conservative elite theory within a radical perspective. He argued that there are three unrepresentative elites at the top of American society: the political elite, the military elite and the industrial elite. Together, these made up the power elite. The relative power of the three elites could vary. In his own time, when the Cold War was at its height, he believed that the military was the most powerful of the three. He insisted, however, that members of the elites shared common material interests as well as, frequently, a common upper class background. Individuals such as President Eisenhower moved easily between the elites, and thus helped to fuse more closely identity of ideology and interest. Mills was in no doubt that the power elite 'ran' America to its own benefit and against that of the majority of people. He considered that the American Congress operated only at the middle level of power and was unable to check the power elite. It was influential mainly on those issues that did not fundamentally affect the structure of society or the essential interests of the power elite. Thus, it might legislate for a little more or a little less welfare aid but not for a fundamental redistribution of wealth. Below the power elite was what Mills did not hesitate to describe as 'the masses'. They comprised the middle and working classes and the poor. He regarded the middle class as fragmented and generally concerned with its own various sectional interests, and the working class as sufficiently 'well-fed' to be thoroughly deradicalised and uninterested in change. Mills's comments on the working class had plausibility in relation to the relatively unorganised and non-socialist American labour force but they were rejected by European Marxists as much less applicable to that continent. The poor consisted of such groups as the unemployed, the old and disproportionate numbers of coloured minorities. Mills saw little prospect that this group would become an effective agency for change, but he did refer, in passing, to the 'moral idea of a counter-elite' and to 'images of the poor, the exploited, and the oppressed as the truly virtuous, the wise and the blessed'.

As we shall shortly describe, this notion had considerable appeal to the young American radicals of the nineteen sixties to whom Mills became something of a folk hero and intellectual father figure. In turn, Mills regarded young, radical intellectuals as the best, if still unlikely, chance for change in America.

LIBERAL PLURALIST AND MARXIST THEORY: SUMMARY

Pluralist theorists take liberal democracy more or less 'at face value'. They believe it works, and consider that political parties and interest groups adequately represent the people. Marxists present a variety of arguments to demonstrate that pluralist claims are incorrect and that power in capitalist societies is, in reality, in the hands of the ruling class. They point to the dominance of the upper class in various major elites and, in particular, to the overlap between Parliament and industry. Even Labour governments have been seen to pose only a minimal threat to the ruling class and to have made no fundamental change in inequalities of power, wealth and prestige. The power of the ruling class in the area of ideological control helps to explain, for Marxists, the acquiescence of large sections of the working class in their own 'exploitation'. Mills's mixed legacy defies categorisation, but he caught the ascendant mood of the emerging American and European New Left of the nineteen sixties. The popular slogan of that decade 'power to the people,' is not so distant an echo of Mills's inspirational rhetoric.

PEOPLE AND POWER: PARTICIPATORY DEMOCRACY

Pluralist democratic assumptions, as well as being attacked from a Marxist point of view, have received criticism from another perspective. The phrase 'participatory democracy' describes this perspective which was presented particularly forcefully by radical American activists in the nineteen sixties and seventies, although the concept has deeper roots both in America and Europe. The terms 'position' and 'perspective' perhaps suggest more precision and sophistication than actually existed in the thinking of those who supported participatory democracy in the sixties. The concept represented a commitment to the idea that people should have some control and involvement in the organisations and decisions that affect their lives. It was as much a matter of sentiment as of ideology, of action as of theory. In the late nineteen fifties and early sixties a strong feeling had grown up among some students and intellectuals, both in Europe and America, that power had become remote from ordinary people who typically played out their working lives in small roles within large organisations run by the powerful few. Groups of young radicals began to try to change this state of affairs by working with the poor and deprived in various community action projects. The concept of participatory democracy was influential among younger radicals in Britain, particularly in the community development movement. However, in Britain it tended to be absorbed into socialism or find expression through the local politics of the Liberal Party. (The issue of popular participation and power is again on the agenda in the early nineteen nineties, see pp. 348–9.)

Although the new radicals were not very precise about their own theoretical position, they were able to articulate their criticism of pluralism. Firstly, they regarded power and inequality as issues that went far beyond merely formal political processes and institutions into every part of social life. They wanted to make participatory democracy real in every major institutional system from education to welfare organisations. Secondly, they considered that the poor were handicapped within competitive, pluralist democracy, as they have fewer resources and less knowledge than other groups to publicise and achieve their aims. Therefore, they needed help in these matters.

The practical expression of the new radical sentiment took the form of a 'return to the people'. An American student organisation, Students for a Democratic Society, established several community development projects in a number of depressed urban areas. It was hoped that, with help, the poor would begin to control the organisations that presently controlled them. The immediate purpose was to educate the poor in dealing with the power structure as well as to win specific 'battles' over such matters as welfare claims, housing conditions and official 'neglect' of the environment. In Britain, two officially funded ventures, the Community Development Project and the Young Volunteer Force, to a certain extent pursued a similar philosophy to the SDS.

Many of those involved in such schemes soon began to feel that their effectiveness was likely to be very limited. They realised, too, that in trying to help the poor in this way they were tacitly accepting the pluralist assumption that the poor really can compete successfully with other groups even in unequal, capitalist society. They began to appreciate that, in practice, their efforts were likely to make little difference to the fundamental causes of inequality and powerlessness. John Benington of the Coventry CDP expresses an opinion commonly arrived at by radical community organisers in Britain and America:

> *A growing awareness of 'the flaw in the pluralist heaven' has forced a number of the CDPs towards a structural class-conflict model of social change. This is based on the assumption that social problems arise from a fundamental conflict of interests between groups or classes in society. The problems are defined mainly in terms of inequalities in the distribution of power and the focus of change is thus on the centres of organised power (both private and public).*
>
> *(Benington in Raynor and Harris eds., 1977:218)*

Benington's emphasis on fundamental as opposed to reconcilable conflict puts him firmly in the socialist camp. Indeed, the concept of popular participation, especially in industry, has long been a theme in socialist thought. Because of this, some critics, such as Tom Bottomore, did not regard participatory democracy as a new

idea at all and would certainly deny that it provides the basis for a new political ideology. The fact that the principle of participation was also enthusiastically accepted by the British Liberal Party as well as by many socialists, indicates that Bottomore is correct in regarding it as an inadequate basis for a distinctive political philosophy. Equally, it might be argued that any political philosophy that does not encourage and develop participation is itself inadequate. There is an increased awareness of this point among contemporary Western Marxists. Genuinely democratic socialism will not suddenly appear in the absence of democratic practice within socialist organisations. There is a growing consensus among Marxists and socialists that greater equality can only be securely achieved in the context of greater democracy (see pp. 503–4).

To a limited extent and, often, grudgingly, the principle of participation has gradually gained more acceptance in British society. In the past twenty five years, participation in education, planning, housing, transport and, marginally, in industrial decision making has tended to increase. The process, however, is slow and uncertain. Raymond Williams was right when he wrote of the emergence of democracy as 'the long revolution'. For this 'revolution' to be successfully established, democratic participation and (to accept the full logic of democracy) control, must exist in all major areas of social life. This includes the economic and social as well as the political. Democracy at work will probably affect the daily lives of people much more profoundly than do present political rights. Indeed, democracy cannot be properly understood in merely political terms. Families, peer groups and relationships can be more or less democratic. We saw earlier that power exists in virtually all social interactions. Democracy means sharing power by popular involvement and, by involvement, generating meaning and identity.

The New Right: Forward to the Past

However defined, the new right was the dominant influence in British politics during the nineteen eighties. This is certainly true in terms of ideas and probably true in terms of policies – although in the latter case the need

to compromise frequently resulted in a dilution of ideological purity. One of the big questions of the nineteen nineties – perhaps the big question of domestic politics – is whether the removal of Mrs Thatcher from a position of political dominance also means that the ideas she stood for will decline in influence. What does seem irreversible in the foreseeable future is the shift of the political debate to the right that Thatcherism bought about. It may be that in the long term, 'the Thatcher revolution' will be more significant in the areas of ideas than in the precise policies introduced between 1979 and 1990.

THE IDEOLOGY OF THE NEW RIGHT

Ideology is used here in two senses. First, it is used simply to describe the ideas and values – roughly, the philosophy – of the new right. Secondly, and more briefly, it is used in the specifically Marxist sense of self-interested or class-interested ideas, i.e. ideas which may be presented as fair and objective but which, on closer analysis, can be shown to reflect personal or class interests.

In Britain, for a time, the new right became equated with 'Thatcherism' and in the United States with 'Reaganism'. However, there is an underlying body of ideas associated with the new right which transcends the comings and goings of Mrs Thatcher and Mr Reagan. These ideas will be described in detail in the broader context of world development/under-development (pp. 481–2) and several practical applications of them are given in this book (see pp. 107–9 and pp. 365–9). As Dunleavy and O'Leary state, the 'core value' of the new right is 'freedom, concerned as an argument that individuals should be free from the inappropriate coercion of others' (1979:93). Freedom, then, is virtually synonymous with radical individualism. There are economic, political and moral aspects to new right ideology. The fundamental context in which freedom occurs is the economic market. According to both the European Hayek and the American Friedman, individuals must be allowed to buy and sell in the market. Friedman considers that this freedom is a precondition of democracy (see p. 482). Hayek particularly stresses the role of the market as a source of information about what people want and do not want and therefore of the value of goods and services and of what should be made and provided.

Both Hayek and Friedman wish to see political power limited. They recognise that the state has certain specific functions but they also regard it as the potential enemy of economic freedom. In particular, they oppose socialist economic planning, attempts to redistribute wealth and to provide (social) services to the general public (i.e. on a universalistic basis – see pp. 364–5). Friedman describes the legitimate areas of government concern as defence, law and order, the provision of necessary public works not provided by the market and the protection of those who cannot protect themselves.

The moral aspect of new right philosophy is largely based on the perception of economic activity as productive and useful and attempts to control and exploit it (e.g. through taxation) as parasitical and destructive of the 'engine of wealth'. As will become clear below, many other moral overtones became attached to new right ideology during the nineteen seventies and eighties.

New right ideology has the same legitimate status as other political and social ideologies. In the nineteen eighties, it appeared to be the ideology 'whose time had come' and it remains dynamic and developing in the nineteen nineties. But whose interest does new right ideology most represent? Undoubtedly, it is a capitalist ideology and has had great appeal to business people and the wealthy. However, new right ideas have reached far beyond the upper class, not only to the middle but also to large sections of the working class. What has been the basis of this appeal?

THE RISE OF THE NEW RIGHT

So far I have described what the new right stands for. However, it is largely because what the new right opposed to was in such disarray in the late nineteen seventies, that Mrs Thatcher was elected in 1979. This was true in both an immediate and longer term sense. Immediately, the Labour government of Jim Callaghan (1976–79) had become somewhat discredited. The government was partly blamed for the strike-torn 'winter of discontent' of 1978–79 and there was also a feeling that after a long period in power from 1964, broken only by the Heath administration of 1970–74, Labour was beginning to 'lose its way'. Before the 1979 election, Callaghan rather fatalistically observed what he thought was a 'sea change' in the political climate – destined to bring Mrs Thatcher to power. More profoundly, what was changing ran deeper than politics and had begun to gather momentum at least several years earlier. It was a growing reaction against the progressive and 'permissive' culture associated with the nineteen sixties. Politically, this progressive period was represented by a series of reforms including in the areas of divorce, abortion, and 'race' and gender. Culturally, it was reflected in less formal life-style and apparently freer sexual morality.

The concept of 'boundary crisis', introduced by Durkheim, is useful in understanding the rise of Thatcherism. Mrs Thatcher was able to exploit a feeling – which she no doubt sympathised with – that 'things had gone too far'. The country could plausibly be presented as economically and socially in disarray, and, generally, in decline. Both personally and ideologically Mrs Thatcher appealed greatly to those who felt this supposed decline most – the 'respectable' middle class. To varying degrees they felt uneasy or appalled by the developments of the nineteen sixties and seventies. To that extent, the progressive and permissive epoch had left them dispossessed. They were almost without a spokesperson – except Mrs Whitehouse who could easily be presented as a joke. 'Cometh the hour, cometh the woman'. Mrs Thatcher articulated the sentiments and won the affection of much of 'middle class' England who helped to return her to power on an unprecedented three occasions.

Thatcherism appeared to offer the hope of a return to traditional standards and even to national greatness. The economic and increasingly the political reality had been one of steady relative national decline in the post-war period. The facts suggest that Thatcherism did not reverse this decline but for some the illusion of national revival was created. Mrs Thatcher's style of leadership grew in confidence and robustness as the decade progressed. Her popularity soared after the Falklands war – although in retrospect the war looks like a last venture of imperialist irrelevance (whatever its specific rights and wrongs). She became a genuinely charismatic leader, embodying the energy and enterprise she insisted the nation needed. Stuart Hall has used the term 'authoritarian populism' to describe her political style. She offered strength and direction (Hall would say, the wrong direction) to the 'masses' (her appeal to 'the nation' crossed class lines), where previously there had been a sense of muddle and drift.

Frequently, national revivalism is associated with a tendency to locate a scapegoat or scapegoats who bear the blame for national decline. Mrs Thatcher found a number of groups 'in need' of this kind of castigation and correction. In the 1979 election she highlighted two: black immigrants and the trade unions. She referred to the former as people of 'a different culture' who might 'swamp' Britain if allowed to do so. Most of the popular press endorsed this negative attitude to black people blaming them for a variety of ills, including 'mugging', taking 'white people's' jobs, and being social security 'scroungers'. It is perhaps not surprising that a sinister backdrop to Thatcherism was a high level of racism, including brutal street violence. The trade unions were blamed (along with 'socialism' and the Labour Party) for Britain's economic decline. By the end of her period as Prime Minister their powers had been greatly reduced.

THE POLICIES AND VALUES OF THE NEW RIGHT

Although there was considerable continuity of values and objectives throughout the Thatcher governments, there were substantial developments and changes in how these were to be achieved, i.e. in policy.

The main themes in domestic policies during the first two Thatcher administrations (1979–87) were 'clearing away' the apparatus of 'socialism'; privatisation; and creating a 'vibrant', free enterprise economy (which required controlling inflation and making tax cuts). The dismantling of aspects of socialist planning such as the abolition of the Prices Commission and the National Enterprise Board (i.e. government funded not private enterprises) and the steady trimming of union power were pushed through with little lasting objection. Nevertheless, the deep recession of the early nineteen eighties resulted in equally deep government unpopularity from which it might never have recovered had it not been for the Falklands war. Even in the traditional mid-term dips in government electoral support of the next two administrations, such unpopularity was never plumbed again.

The second Thatcher administration was the main period of privatisation and apparently the beginning of the promised long term economic recovery. Privatisation involved selling publicly owned industries such as British Airways, British Telecom, and British Gas by inviting offers for shares both from institutions (e.g. insurance companies) and individuals. Privatisation was appreciated – at least by participants – as something of a bonanza as shares in privatised companies invariably increased substantially in value as soon as they were quoted on the stock exchange. However, the beneficiaries of privatisation were generally Conservative supporters. A shrewder move in terms of potentially gaining new support for the Conservative Party was the sale of hundreds of thousands of council housing units through-out the Thatcher years. Again, this was appreciated by those who benefited from the policy but this clearly did not include those on the waiting list for council accommodation who suffered from the diminishing stock of houses and flats. Critics of privatisation argued that public assets were being sold cheaply – 'selling-off the family silver-ware' in the words of former Conservative Prime Minister, Harold Macmillan. The reduction in public housing and the growth in homelessness became a major issue in the emerging debate about 'uncaring' Thatcherism.

Crucial to the Conservative election victory of 1987, was apparent economic recovery and growing prosperity for the majority (but not for a 'new underclass' of about twenty per cent of the population – see pp. 144–5). Economic optimism almost became euphoria following the Nigel Lawson 'give away' budget of 1988 when he reduced the top rate of income tax from 60 to 40 per cent and basic rate from 27 to 25 per cent. However, even before the 'miracle' evaporated into a 'mirage' and the second severe recession in a decade developed, the seeds of possible disaffection from Thatcherism were apparent. Indeed, in retrospect, the hard basis of support for Thatcherite values and policies may have been a good deal less than the powerful performance and unwavering confidence of the lady made it seem.

In June 1988, the *Sunday Times* published the details of a Mori poll into the political values and opinions of the electorate. With the benefit of hindsight, the answers to the following questions are particularly revealing: 'Do you support or oppose the government adopting the following policies?' (see table 14.6.)

A decisive majority opposed the privatisation of electricity and water (seven and nine). Yet the government went ahead and privatised these industries despite clear signs that public support for such measures was beginning to fade. Responses to question six are perhaps the most telling of all. A two to one majority opposed the introduction of what became widely known as the poll tax. Again, Mrs Thatcher went ahead with this measure and perhaps more than anything it brought about her downfall.

Significantly, whereas the privatisation measures of the previous Thatcher administrations had benefited substantial minorities and superficially appeared not directly to damage the majority, the policies she introduced after the 1987 election victory immediately confronted the material interests of the majority. The poll-tax was the single major domestic issue which 'broke' Mrs Thatcher. Perhaps even more important in the long run were the areas of education and health. Privatisation and even cuts in welfare directly affected only a minority, but these two public services are at the core of the Welfare State and both are

Do you support or oppose the government adopting the following policies?

		Support %	Oppose %
1	Giving legal protection to trade union members who refuse to join a strike, even if a majority of members have voted in favour	64	27
2	Selling British Rail to private shareholders	40	52
3	Withdrawing state benefit from anybody who is unemployed and refuses to take a low paid job	39	52
4	Giving people who contribute towards private health insurance a tax allowance because they are less likely to use the NHS	38	57
5	Replacing student grants with loans	30	60
6	Replacing the system of domestic rates with a fixed charge paid by people in each household aged over 18 (the 'poll tax')	31	61
7	Selling the electricity industry to private shareholders	30	63
8	Introducing a system in the National Health Service whereby people could pay extra to get treatment more quickly	30	66
9	Selling the water authorities to private shareholders	25	66

(Source: Mori)

▲

Table 14.6

The Shape of Things to Come? 1988

used by well over 90 per cent of the population. Education and health emerged as even more important issues in the post-Thatcher era but they began to loom larger on the agenda prior to her downfall.

The Conservatives wanted to bring 'the disciplines of the market' to education and health as they had done with the nationalised industries. However, there was little public support for privatising these basic public services. To have done so would have been political suicide. Aided by a battery of think-tanks and advisors, Mrs Thatcher came up with alternative solutions. The 1988 Educational Reform Act introduced a free market package of local management of schools, open enrolment and opting out – in addition to the National Curriculum (see p. 109). For health, the market mechanism was to allow General Practitioners to opt out and administer their own budgets, and to allow hospitals to opt out and to sell their services to the highest bidders (among GPs) (see pp. 389–90). In both cases, the main criticism has been that a two tier system will be created. In education, opted out schools have been presented as likely havens of privilege – generously funded by central government – whereas schools remaining within local authorities are seen as likely to have to educate the less privileged with less funds. In health, the two tier is seen as created by the ability of GPs with budgets to bid ahead and, therefore, jump the queue in front of GPs without their own budgets whose patients are then disadvantaged and whose health may suffer.

The Thatcher agenda developed in such a way that the simpler and more popular measures were introduced early or relatively so in her period of office and the more difficult and controversial measures came later. It was in these deeper, choppier waters that she floundered. The determination and confrontationalism that had apparently helped to carry her policies through before 1987, rebounded against her later. The headline in the 1988 Sunday Times piece referred to above was perceptive: 'So far so good, but now proceed with caution'. Caution was not Mrs Thatcher's way and she paid the price. With the additional problem of an emerging second recession, the three-time winner began to look like a probable fourth-time loser and she was unceremoniously ditched by her leading party colleagues.

THE THATCHER LEGACY?

Many of the key issues for Britain in the nineteen nineties have been posed by Mrs Thatcher even if she herself will not personally resolve them. Will education and health be primarily concerned with equality of public access or will they be 'driven' by competitive internal markets? Will there be a return to greater planning and partnership in industrial policy, perhaps involving some participation by the trade unions as well as more formal consultation between government and industrial leaders? In foreign policy, will a 'little England' nationalism prevail or will a mood of internationalism embracing Europe and the 'new' emerging world prevail?

John Smith or John Major or another may seek different answers to these questions than would Mrs Thatcher, but in fairness, their answers are likely to be different simply because of the fact that Mrs Thatcher was around.

THE SOCIOLOGY OF THATCHERISM

The above analysis of the new right, particularly the Thatcherite version, weaves sociological concepts into a broad historical backcloth. Here, we stand back somewhat and examine what light the larger theoretical perspective of sociology throws onto Thatcherism and vice-versa.

The 'Thatcher phenomenon' raises interesting problems in relation to personality and social structure. Was Thatcherism a product of circumstances or a product of Mrs Thatcher? Or, put another way, was the reaction against the nineteen sixties and seventies so 'inevitable' that someone else would have played the role Mrs Thatcher played, if she had not played it – as, indeed, Ronald Reagan played a similar role in the United States. Was the stage set and the script written so that who played the main part was almost incidental?

The above view is a deterministic one – that 'events are in the saddle and ride humankind'. Max Weber's concept of 'congruence' offers a more qualified alternative analysis. He suggests that sometimes circumstances are 'ripe for' or 'congruent with' particular ideas (and ideologues). By 1979, British social democracy had, for the time being, completed its agenda and had become associated with certain problems, such as industrial unrest, welfare bureaucracy and even, in a vague way, cultural permissiveness. Mrs Thatcher offered an alternative to social democracy and an antidote to some of the problems for which it was blamed. However, there is no basis for seeing the details of her policies as predetermined. In fact, some of these seemed rather improvised.

Marxists frequently explain Thatcherism in terms of a structural crisis of capitalism. With the support of capitalists, Mrs Thatcher attempted to restore conditions of greater profitability for the capitalist system. In this perspective, she and her ideology are seen more as symptoms than causes of the revival of capitalism that occurred during her period of office. Thus, she is seen as part of a wider capitalistic movement rather than as a uniquely innovative individual.

In the end, Margaret Thatcher perhaps did overestimate her own uniqueness and power. Circumstances had moved against her and she had changed circumstances rather less than she thought. Certain charismatic leaders develop an almost symbiotic relationship with their 'times' and with 'the people' but if they lose their 'touch', the fall from grace can be swift and complete.

CONCLUSION: TOWARDS CITIZENS' POWER?

The nineteen eighties was an unusually ideological decade. Thatcherism represented a revival of radical right thinking and policy that was almost wholly unpredicted. By the nineteen nineties, the ideology had not only lost its leader but also much of its revivalist spirit. Thatcherism continues but, for the moment, it is mediated by more pragmatic and compromising people.

In the Labour Party, pragmatism triumphed some years earlier. The Militant tendency was more or less driven completely out of the party and in 1991 an official Labour candidate and a Militant Labour candidate opposed each other in a Liverpool by-election. Meanwhile, the strength of 'Bennite socialism' subsided within the Parliamentary Labour Party. Benn himself was ill and the 1983 general election loss – when the left was in the ascendancy –

loomed like nemesis over the party. For many the lesson seemed to be 'do that once more and risk political oblivion'.

John Major and John Smith seem to be battling over the middle ground which is not to say there is no difference between them. It used to be said in the nineteen sixties and seventies that there was little difference between the two parties. In retrospect, however, the Wilson years do have a distinct character of liberal, social democratic reform – apparently different from what Mr Heath was briefly offering and certainly very different from what Mrs Thatcher did offer. Politics in the nineties will be dismal if the battle for power turns out to be over the right to make cuts in health or education. In any case, things could change quickly. As Harold Wilson himself said 'a week is a long time in politics' and in the year until this book is published much might happen to make the above paragraph redundant.

Is it possible that beneath the current struggle for the centre ground, under the eagle's eye, something else is stirring? If there is vitality, it probably lies in the continuing interest in popular democracy and institutional and professional accountability which has straddled the decades since the nineteen sixties without ever quite coming top of any party's agenda once in power. In the nineteen sixties participatory democracy was a 'bottom upwards' movement aimed at rendering welfare and capitalist bureaucracies more directly accountable to 'the people'. It would be too dismissive to say the movement had no effect but it became so diffuse that it was superseded by stronger currents – ultimately Thatcherism. Perhaps, it is the central failure of the post-war Labour party that, apart from a flirtation with industrial democracy, it has never seriously addressed the issue of democratising the framework of British institutional life. Ironically, the Thatcher governments arguably did move in this respect in the drive to empower the consumer. However, this has been so deeply associated with free market philosophy that it has produced great inequalities – some health, educational and industrial 'consumers' consuming more and better than others. Indeed, part of the premise of Thatcherism is the production of inequality.

Within a number of local Labour parties there has developed the concept of a 'citizens' charter'. These take the form of rights – such as health and education to be delivered in a quantifiable way by the relevant agency. Agencies that fail to meet targets can be brought to account and perhaps made to render compensation. Both major parties have begun to adopt this approach at national level. Whatever, the merits of the 'charter' idea, it may be the harbinger of a more sustained commitment to popular power. It seems clear now that the 'free market' empowers some but disposes and disempowers others. It is also clear that while the Welfare State may achieve greater equality of resources it, again, often disempowers its 'clients' or 'consumers'. A countervailing sentiment may be emerging for an extension of democracy both in the economic and welfare frameworks of British life.

SUMMARY

1 A distinction must be made between power and authority. Power is the ability to achieve one's own will. Authority is legitimate power. Weber considered that liberal democracies exercise legitimate power on a rational-legal basis but Marx challenged the legitimacy of liberal democracy arguing that, in relaity, capitalists 'rule'.

2 There are three main models of voting behaviour:

i) The party Identification and social class model.

ii) The rational-choice model.

iii) The radical model.

3 The party identification and social class model argues that both historically and in contemporary Britain, the main factor explaining voting behaviour is social class. The mechanism through which this occurs is class socialisation. 'Conformist' voters are considered to be those who vote according to their class and 'deviant' voters are those who do not.

4 The rational-choice model argues that people vote mainly on the basis of self-interest in relation to the issues presented to them by the political parties. The notion of the voter as 'consumer' has a parallel in free-market economics.

5 The radical model argues that sectoral cleavages (e.g. whether people work in or consume in mainly the private or public sector) explain some major trends in contemporary voting behaviour. These distract people from the deeper cleavages of class which still remain.

6 The liberal model of democratic society argues that in a liberal society the state is and should be answerable to the people who organise mainly through political parties and pressure groups. Liberal theorists state that democratic political elites are representative of the people and are ultimately accountable to them at general elections.

7 Marx considered that in liberal capitalist democracies, the capitalist class rules, not the people (the majority of whom are working class). There is a debate within Marxism between Miliband and Poulantzas about how capitalist power is exercised. Miliband argues that class power operates partly through personal contact and shared experience among capitalists, whereas Poulantzas contends that the institutional structure of capitalism would function in favour of the capitalist system whoever 'operates' it.

8 Elite theorists offer another model of modern government. Elites may be either representative (democratic) or unrepresentative (undemocratic). C Wright Mills argued that the United States is ruled by a power elite made up of three subsidiary elites – the military, business, and political. Representative democracy functions at a level of power below that of the power elite.

9 Participatory democracy argues that people have the right and should have the means to be effectively involved in the decisions which affect their lives. This ideology had some influence in the nineteen sixties and seventies but this receded under the impact of Thatcherism in the nineteen eighties.

10 New right ideology is founded on the view that the free market provides a basis for freedom in other aspects of life. The new right has never satisfactorily dealt with the inequalities that the free market also creates. It was this ideology which characterised 'Thatcherism'.

RESEARCH AND COURSEWORK

It is unlikely that a project focusing on national politics could involve much original research. What this topic does provide is the opportunity to address some interesting issues relating to the theory and practice of political power. What is the evidence for the Marxist view that Britain is (still) governed by a 'ruling class'? Or is Mills' power elite theory applicable to Britain as he attempted to apply it to the United States? A demanding area of enquiry would be the role that ideology played in the rise and 'reign' of Thatcherism – does a detailed examination of the history of 'the Thatcher decade' tend to support the view that her success depended on the appeal of her ideas? Clearly, an examination of these quite theoretical areas would require a careful review of the relevant literature and perhaps accessing press and/or periodical coverage of key events of the period.

A more concrete topic would be to examine the functioning and effect of a pressure group. National pressure groups such as 'Friends of the Earth' have regional offices and/or representatives which provide the opportunity for interviews and material.

FURTHER READING

For sociologists, a useful recent survey of politics and social policy is P Dunleavy et al., eds., *Developments in British Politics* (Macmillan, 1990). Introductory volumes to political sociology as such are hard to come by but a wideranging if partial book, with substantial political content, is Ralph

Miliband, *Divided Societies Class Struggle in contemporary Capitalism* (Oxford Paperbacks, 1991).

QUESTIONS

1 Assess the strengths and limitations of pluralist theories of the nature and distribution of political power. (AEB, 1989)

2 Compare and contrast two different sociological accounts of voting behaviour since 1974. (London, 1989)

3 Examine Marx's view that the State is 'a committee for managing the common affairs of the bourgeoisie'. (AEB, 1990)

15 Social 'Problems' & Deviance: Social Policy & the Welfare State

Sociology and Social Problems

Many people study sociology because they expect the subject will give them a better understanding of social problems. This expectation is often not quickly met and is sometimes not met at all. The relevance of the subject to practical issues can get lost in a welter of theory. However, I believe sociology can deliver its promise to provide insight into social problems and inform the policies designed to solve them. I will set aside the issue of definition until later and for the moment simply regard a social problem as a matter perceived by the general public or by a given group as causing difficulty.

The first way in which sociology can illuminate social problems is by clarifying the link between social structure and personal experience. This connection has been most eloquently expressed by Charles Wright Mills:

Perhaps the most fruitful distinction with which the sociological imagination works is between 'the personal troubles of milieu' and 'the public issues of social structure ...'

Troubles occur within the character of the individual and within the range of his immediate relations with others; they have to do with his self and with those limited areas of social life of which he is directly and personally aware ...

Issues ['problems' in the terms of this chapter] have to do with matters that transcend these local environments of the individual and the range of his inner life ... An issue is a public matter: some value cherished by publics [organised groups] is felt to be threatened.

(Mills, 1959:8)

Having distinguished between personal troubles and public issues, Mills then goes on to argue that very often they both have a social structural dimension. Major social events and changes such as high unemployment, war and urban decay are public issues but they are, of course, experienced in a personal way by many individuals. The fundamental causes of these problems cannot be dealt with by personal adjustments but must be tackled by major public response.

A second contribution sociology can make to the understanding of social problems is to demonstrate the problematic but hidden consequences of certain social practices and conditions. Robert Merton calls this making manifest (public) latent (hidden) social problems. By way of illustration, he refers to the body of research which has increased awareness of the human, economic and social cost of sexual and racial discrimination. Writing in almost Millsian language, Merton states:

Sociologists who demonstrate the waste of socially prized talent that results from great inequalities of opportunity bring to focus what was diffusely experienced by many as only involving personal troubles rather than constituting a problem of society.
(Merton and Nisbet, 1976:12)

Indeed, Merton's point is really a particular application of Mills' analysis.

A third contribution of sociology to the study of social problems is that it can show how certain matters come to be defined as social problems and can locate the assumptions made by interested parties. The key concept here is power – the power to identify and promote (or suppress) a given matter as a social problem. Both Marxists and interactionists have made notable contributions to our understanding of this process. Marxists argue that the wealthy and powerful are generally more able to define social problems and affect policy towards them than the poor and less powerful. In the area of social problems, Marxist class analysis is complemented by the middle and micro range perspectives of interactionists who have examined how professions and interest groups such as the police and the judiciary have affected public perception of social problems. We can take drugs as an example. Marxists typically point to the commercial and advertising interests which seek to romanticise the public's image of cigarette smoking and to inhibit more robust policies of control. The interactionist, Howard Becker, has studied the contrasting case of marijuana – a drug seemingly no more dangerous than tobacco. The use of marijuana was legal in the United States until the passage of the Marijuana Stamp Tax Act of 1937. Becker argues that the Federal Bureau of Narcotics campaigned to make marijuana use illegal partly to expand its own social and organisational power. In 'getting the rules changed' on marijuana, it succeeded in doing this. Separately, but particularly taken together, Marxist and interactionist perspectives make a major contribution to our understanding of public attitudes and policy towards drug use. Functionalists also readily accept the element of group conflict in social problem definition and policy formation. As Robert Merton puts it, 'one group's problem can be another group's solution'. Nevertheless, the focus of functionalism typically remains on those problems about which there is a broad consensus of concern and which seem to them to be dysfunctional to the operation of society.

Fourthly, by helping to explain the causes, context and perception of social problems, sociology can inform the humanistic concern that many people feel about issues such as poverty, unemployment and violence within the family. As Becker puts it, sociology helps to discover strategic points of intervention in the social structures and processes that produce the problems. The Head Start programme was one such strategic intervention supported by sociological analysis (see chapter 4). Informed by structural perspective, many workers in the 'helping' professions take up political positions in support of, for instance, more resources for the poor, more jobs and policies to reduce stress on the family.

What sociology cannot do is give an absolute definition of the content of a social problem or provide a comprehensive list of social problems. With few exceptions, sociologists would agree with Howard Becker that 'social problems are what people say they are'. We have to decide for ourselves, in the light of our values and understanding, what we regard as social problems and what, if anything, we are going to do about them. But sociology can provide the perspective and data to sustain alternative moral points of view to those widely supported and publicised.

SOCIAL PROBLEMS AND DEVIANCE Merton very usefully divides social problems into problems of deviance and problems of disorganisation (see below p. 355). He defines social problems of deviance as those involving rule breaking (or assumed rule breaking). Social problems involving disorganisation result from some malfunctioning of society or part of society, i.e. 'the system'. An example of the former is theft and an example of the latter is pollution from car exhausts.

Social Problems: Definitions and Perspectives

SOCIAL PROBLEMS SEEN AS INDIVIDUAL DEVIANCE: CONSERVATIVE PERSPECTIVE

From this perspective, the cause of a person's problems is seen as lying within the individual who then tends to be characterised as deviant. The cause might be perceived as moral failure or even biological deficiency (see p. 299). This approach has already been fully discussed in relation to poverty (pp. 157–8). It occurs again in the context of new right approaches to welfare. In fairness, individualistic explanations of social problems are only one and not necessarily the most important explanation that occurs in new right thinking.

THE FUNCTIONS AND DYSFUNCTIONS OF SOCIAL PROBLEMS: FUNCTIONALIST PERSPECTIVE

THE INFLUENCE OF DURKHEIM The major contemporary statement of functionalist perspective on social problems is probably Robert Merton's introduction to *Contemporary Social Problems* edited by himself and Robert Nisbet (1976). Like much functionalist theory, Merton's piece greatly reflects the thinking of Emile Durkheim. The latter's analysis of deviance has deeply influenced the functionalist approach to social problems. The basic characteristics Durkheim associates with deviance were given earlier (pp. 300–1). Functionalists define many social problems as deviant and for that reason the concept of deviance is prominent in this section.

We can now briefly summarise the influence of Durkheim on functionalist perspectives on social problems. First, Durkheim's analysis of social problems of deviance is structural-functional; major changes in the social structure can produce social problems and these problems and people's response to them can feed back into the social system (or parts of it). Second, Durkheim sought to demonstrate that the functional consequences of social problems are not always apparent (or manifest) – a point given central importance by Robert Merton. Third, the concept of anomie has been widely used in functionalist analysis of social problems – again, notably in modified form by Merton. Fourth, Durkheim introduces the concept of social equilibrium. He links this to the concepts of normal and abnormal social states. Abnormally high rates of deviance (and perhaps, by extension, other social problems) are associated with lack of equilibrium (or disequilibrium). Some functionalists have treated this group of concepts cautiously but they have had a powerful influence on the work of Talcott Parsons. Fifth, like Durkheim, many functionalists regard modern society as particularly prone to generate social problems because of the extent and rapidity of change. Sixth, Durkheim considered that social problems of deviance could be functional in that they increased moral solidarity by focusing communal disapproval. However, like later functionalists, he appreciated that 'abnormally' high rates of deviance were likely to be socially disruptive.

ROBERT MERTON

We now turn to Robert Merton's work on social problems. First, Merton locates his analysis of social problems within the total structure and functioning of society. The very way society is institutionalised and organised is likely to produce particular kinds of problem:

The same social structure and culture that in the main make for conforming and organised behaviour also generate tendencies towards distinctive kinds of deviant behaviour and potentials of social disorganisation. In this sense, the problems current in a society register the social costs of a particular organisation of social life....

(Merton and Nisbet, 1976:26)

To suggest an example, perhaps the pressures to respectability and moral behaviour in Victorian Britain created the need for a deviant underworld of indulgence and promiscuity.

As the quotation indicates, Merton divides social problems into two main categories, those caused by social disorganisation and those caused by deviance. These will be examined separately after Merton's general analysis of social problems.

OBJECTIVE AND SUBJECTIVE ASPECTS OF SOCIAL PROBLEMS Like most sociologists in this field, Merton distinguishes between the objective and subjective aspects of social problems. The former is the social condition itself – poverty, unemployment or whatever – and the latter is the perception of it as a problem. Like the interactionist Howard Becker, Merton points out that people do not always agree about what is a social problem. However, he seeks to emphasise the objective rather than subjective aspect. He counters the interactionist wisdom that 'if men define situations as real, they are real in their consequences' with the caution that 'if people do not define real situations as real, they are nevertheless real in their consequences'. He insists that subjective failure to define real conditions such as inferior housing and overpopulation as problems may result in 'dysfunctional' consequences for society. He argues that sociologists have a special role in revealing the 'latent dysfunctions' of given situations, including those unintentionally caused by government policy. To give an example, sociological research might establish that social security cuts aimed at reducing public expenditure have the unforeseen consequence of undermining the health of certain groups and so raise health costs. Such a finding could influence future policy formation.

SOCIAL PROBLEMS OF (I) DISORGANISATION AND OF (II) DEVIANCE To return to Merton's division of social problems into problems of disorganisation and problems of deviance, these are broad groupings and we have already devoted a chapter to one of them, deviance (chapter 13). Accordingly, we will concentrate on 'problems' of 'disorganisation' here. Merton states that social disorganisation 'refers to inadequacies in a social system that keeps people's collective and individual purposes from being as fully realised as they could be'. So, Merton sees any failure of social organisation which frustrates goal achievement as a problem. This seems uncontroversial. But Merton's view of the major sources of social disorganisation suggests a conservative drift in his functionalist model. Thus, he regards conflicting interests and values and faulty socialisation as major sources of disorganisation. As an example of the former, he describes as disorganised a society which does not provide an effective way of settling the disputes of management, workers and stockholders. His argument illustrates the familiar functionalist concern with consensus. By contrast, Marxists consider such institutionalised attempts to deal with industrial conflict as little more than a papering over the cracks of class antagonisms.

Merton also categorises deviance as a major form of social problem. He states that deviant behaviour 'involves significant departures from norms socially assigned to various status and roles' and that it usually constitutes a social problem (see pp. 302–3).

Another aspect of Merton's 1976 version of his essay on social problems is his attempt to take into consideration certain criticisms of previous versions and of functionalist perspective generally. This applies particularly to his treatment of deviance. Thus, as indicated above, he finds labelling theory helpful in understanding the subjective side of social problems and in analysing secondary deviance (see p. 355). He attempts to reconcile functionalist anomie theory with labelling theory by arguing that the former tries to explain the social origins of deviant behaviour whereas the latter focuses on how stigmatisation can perpetuate it. More broadly still, he argues that differential association, anomie, labelling and conflict theories 'have a potential for being complementary' partly because they apply to different aspects of social deviance. However, he does not then go on to offer even in outline a unified theory of deviance to support his claim.

CRITICISMS OF MERTON'S APPROACH TO SOCIAL PROBLEMS Despite Merton's attempt to embrace concepts and insights from other perspectives, his analysis remains classically functionalist and is therefore open to the classic criticisms of functionalism. First, from social action and interactionist perspective, his analysis envisages social problems in terms of systems rather than people. It can be argued that the

'dysfunctions' of systems are often better seen as the problems caused by some for others (e.g. by polluters for those polluted). To focus on people as the producers and victims of social problems means writing about the topic in a different way from that of Merton and the functionalists: it involves stressing the intentions and purposes of people rather than the functions and goals of systems. Second, the limitations of Merton's aspirations to theoretical synthesis are shown in his scant analysis of radical conflict and social problems. For him, social problems are the dysfunctions of a given social system. Nowhere does he engage the possibility that a social system might be fundamentally problematic, i.e. prone to conflict rather than harmony. To do this would draw him into a discussion of social legitimacy and change of the kind that functionalists tend to avoid.

THE SOCIAL CONSTRUCTION OF SOCIAL PROBLEMS: INTERACTIONIST PERSPECTIVE

In a memorably simple statement, Howard Becker defines social problem as follows: 'Social problems are what people think they are.' This definition parallels the one he gives for deviance: 'deviant behaviour is behaviour that people so label'.

Becker, like Merton, recognises that there is an objective and a subjective aspect to social problems: the former being the condition or behaviour itself, the latter being the definition of it as a problem. Whereas Merton's emphasis is on the objective aspect, Becker is more concerned with the subjective which for him is the starting point of any understanding of social processes, problematic or otherwise. Becker scrutinises the notion of objectivity as closely as Merton does that of subjectivity. He stresses that the moral and political concern that often surrounds social problems means that sociologists must carefully establish details about objective conditions and indeed check whether these exist at all. He points out that 'People … can define non-existent conditions as a social problem.' He gives the witch hunt at Salem as an example of when many members of the community imagined that they were infested with witches and 'took stern measures to deal with the supposed social problem'. Such moral panics can of course do great damage to their victims.

THE 'HISTORY' OF SOCIAL PROBLEMS

Becker develops the interesting concept of the 'natural history' or 'career' of a social problem first introduced by Fullers and Myers. They describe three stages in this history: awareness, policy determination and reform. Becker illustrates these stages in the case of his own detailed study of the rise of marijuana as a social problem (see p. 308). According to his account, the Federal Bureau of Investigation played a major role in moulding initial awareness of the issue. The FBI was also prominent in the debate and policy determination phase, as was the media, which Becker argues tended to take an alarmist line about the drug. The emotively titled film *Reefer Madness* (1937) was a near propaganda piece of the period. The reform stage, when a 'solution' becomes institutionalised, occurred with the passage of the Marijuana Stamp Act of 1937 which made the drug illegal in the United States for the first time. History does not stop at this point of course, and the marijuana issue came to the fore again in the nineteen sixties. The current situation is that it is illegal but very widely used.

It is thought-provoking to compare the histories of marijuana and tobacco use in the United States (and Britain) and to speculate on why one is illegal and the other not. In this respect, Jack Douglas and Frances Waksler suggest that part of the opposition to legalising marijuana is based on a dislike of the bohemian, pleasure-seeking lifestyle still vaguely associated with it. By contrast, tobacco smoking is 'acceptably' associated with the work ethic, either as an aid to concentration or as legitimate and earned relaxation.

The interest of interactionists in how people come to perceive and define 'problems' has resulted in a body of work analysing how the media 'construct' and even 'create' social problems. Several of these studies have already been referred to here, including Stanley Cohen's now classic *Folk Devils and Moral Panics: The Creation of Mods and Rockers* (1980), which describes how news reporters and processors, various 'moral entrepreneurs', and the Mods and Rockers themselves, created what was largely a media event (see pp. 425–6). More recently, Marxists have employed interactionist concepts to analyse media presentation of 'problems' of racial and industrial conflict and have attempted to relate media bias to the structure of racial and class inequality and domination (see pp. 422–3).

CRITICISMS OF INTERACTIONIST PERSPECTIVE ON SOCIAL PROBLEMS

Two criticisms of interactionist perspective on social problems may be considered. First, the approach is sometimes thought to exaggerate the subjective element in social problems at the expense of the objective. Merton, for instance, denies that 'social problems exist only if many people declare them to exist' because they may be latent but real and damaging. However, my own view favours Becker who argues that research may be required to identify a given condition but 'its problematic character would arise from how people defined its consequences'. A second criticism of interactionist social problem theory tends to be made by Marxists. They criticise interactionists for adopting a pluralist model of power conflict in explaining the emergence, definition and solution of social problems. Marxists argue the need for class analysis and there have in fact been several Marxist studies of social problems/conflict synthesising interactionist concepts with class perspective, including those referred to below.

THE 'SYSTEM' AS THE PROBLEM: RADICAL STRUCTURAL AND MARXIST PERSPECTIVES

As understood here, radical structural and Marxist perspectives agree on one central point: that capitalism produces fundamental social problems. The classic free enterprise system, so praised by the new right is seen as bound to produce losers – people with 'social problems' as well as winners. This criticism goes far deeper than Merton's analysis that social problems result in part through 'disorganisation' within the system. Radical structural and Marxist theorists find an inherent contradiction in the (capitalist) system itself i.e. the capitalist market inevitably produces a highly unequal distribution of wealth. In other words it produces great inequality and poverty. This analysis and the distinction between radical structural and Marxist theorists is fully discussed on pages 160–5.

Social Policy

DEFINITIONS

As Michael Hill suggests at the beginning of his book *Understanding Social Policy*, one way to answer the question 'What is social policy?' is to list the areas of public policy included under the heading. The areas that Hill himself deals with are social security, the personal social services, the health service, education, employment services and housing. Together these constitute the substance of the British Welfare State. However, as Hill emphasises, this simple definition of social policy will not suffice. Nor, any longer, will T H Marshall's classic statement that 'the avowed objective of twentieth century social policy is welfare'. Marxists and others argue that the objective of certain social policy measures is to control disaffected groups in the population rather than to act out of concern for their welfare. Indeed, the whole subject of social policy has been 'blown open' in that it is now widely accepted that social policy is generated through political conflict and debate and that its study must encompass this. Social policy analysis, therefore, must consider political ideology and the effect on social policy of other policy areas, especially economic (since economic factors greatly influence social policy). Hill suggests three points for consideration in defining social policy: first, that social policy may not only be concerned with welfare; second, that other policies (such as economic) may affect welfare more than social policy; third, that public policy should be seen as a whole and that social policy is related to other policies.

Finally, Hill does not give a single, brief definition of social policy. However, the following statement by Peter Townsend summarises the broad view of social policy now widely adopted:

If social policy is conceived of as the institutional control of services, agencies and organisations to maintain or change social structure or values, then what is at stake is not just the social division of welfare or the management of public, fiscal and private welfare, but the allocation of wealth, the organisation of employment, the management of the wage system and the creation of styles of living.

(Townsend, 1981:26)

In short, social policy is about the kind of society people want to create and what they do to create it.

Social administration refers to the means by which social policy is implemented. Given that analysis of policy goals involves political issues, then so must analysis of administrative means. Naturally social policy makers seek to shape their administrative machinery – say the social or education services – to their purposes. There are, of course, a variety of administrative skills but in so far as we are directly concerned with administration, it is as a tool of policy. Administrators may intentionally or unintentionally hamper the goals of policy makers and this is a relevant point to study in policy outcome analysis. Indeed, the civil service is often criticised in this respect not least in the celebrated television series ironically titled *Yes, Minister*.

The Welfare State

Although the emphasis is now changing somewhat, much modern social policy analysis has focused on the Welfare State. Debates have ranged from fundamental matters of ideology to practical issues of cost and efficiency. Asa Briggs defines a welfare state as one which modifies the effects of market forces to provide citizens with a minimum income, to protect them against a range of problems such as sickness and homelessness, and to ensure equal access to a range of services such as education. Of course, what this comes down to in practice is a matter of public intent and political decision. As A N Rees points out, it can be far more difficult and humiliating to be 'on welfare' when the consensus is moving against welfare than when it is more favourable. A welfare state securing the citizen's accepted right to certain minimum provisions cannot be assumed. The reader might find it useful to consider how much of

Briggs' definition of the welfare state remains intact in the light of Conservative government policies since the mid-nineteen eighties which are discussed below (pp.365–70).

The British Welfare State was largely established by the Labour government of 1945 to 1950. The major exception was Butler's 1944 Education Act. The mood in support of social reform to achieve greater security and opportunity for the majority developed strongly as a result of wartime experience. Many felt that they had earned a fairer society by virtue of their efforts and deprivation over the war years. In addition, war often has a somewhat egalitarian effect by throwing the social classes together in a common cause. Personal value, including one's own, can become more important than status and wealth. Politicians recognised the new climate of opinion and a variety of government reports on a number of social issues were carried out during the war. The most important of these was the Beveridge Report (1942) often thought of as the blueprint for the Welfare State.

Beveridge proposed an attack on the five giant evils of want, disease, ignorance, squalor and idleness. It helps to group these five evils into a triad of (i) ignorance (ii) disease and (iii) want, idleness and squalor. Ignorance was attacked by the Education Act (1944) and disease by the National Health Act (1946) although it was the Conservative, Butler, and the socialist, Bevan, rather than the Liberal Beveridge, who were respectively most responsible for them. Beveridge's name is associated with the National Insurance Act (1946) which (along with the National Insurance Act of 1944) established a compulsory flat-rate system of contributions covering basic social needs, primarily sickness, injury, unemployment and old age pensions. Beveridge, then, led the attack on want. A M Rees refers to the above three pieces of legislation as the 'three pillars of the British Welfare State'. A fourth could be added in the form of the National Assistance Act of 1948 which was also inspired by Beveridge. This provided assistance for special cases who slipped through the national insurance safety net. Both the National Insurance Act and the National Assistance Act have been superseded by later legislation. Insurance contributions and major benefits now have an earnings related element and national assistance has been replaced by income support and family credit (1988).

Idleness in the sense of unemployment, and squalor in the sense of inadequate housing, are forms of want. It was part of Beveridge's thinking that the government would take economic planning measures to ensure a very high (if not full) level of employment. This view reflected the Keynesian consensus of the period which followed John Keynes' view that the government could 'fine-tune' the economy to achieve a buoyant labour market. In part, the government used its control of the nationalised industries to do this. The Thatcher administrations from 1979 broke with the Keynesian consensus, believing that job creation occurs as a result of the expansion of the private sector. In reality, however, it intervened with a series of schemes and subsidies to stimulate the private sector comparable to those adopted by previous governments to assist both the public and private sectors. Beveridge's fifth evil 'squalor' is usally taken to refer to housing and, more recently, to the environment. Squalor was attacked by both the Labour and Conservative Parties with substantial programmes of house building, programmes which were severely cut back during the nineteen seventies and eighties, particularly by the Thatcher governments. The New Towns Act (1946) was aimed at providing new and thriving environments for the inhabitants of deprived and decaying inner city areas (see pp. 437–8). The Act is characterised by a sensitivity to environmental issues perhaps ahead of its time.

HAS THE WELFARE STATE INCREASED SOCIAL EQUALITY?

Beveridge was no revolutionary and the welfare measures of the war coalition and post-war Labour government did not amount to revolution. Rather, they represented the height of a long evolution of liberal or social democratic reform. Each of the major areas of reform – education, health and welfare – was characterised by a long period of increasing government involvement. The nature of capitalist industrial society stimulated this concern, raising as it does problems of inequality and insecurity, and of social order and control. Education to the age of ten years was made compulsory in 1880 although a national infrastructure of elementary education had been established ten years previously. The Public Health Act of 1875 was a legislative landmark, establishing a national system of local health authorities, yet, typically of the British reformist tradition, it codified and developed existing tendencies rather than established an entirely new system. Lloyd George's National Insurance Act of 1911 first established a contributory system of national insurance against unemployment and sickness. Prior to this the poor had been variously treated as objects of charity or control, depending on whether humanitarian or punitive sentiments were uppermost. The Victorian workhouse reflected a tough, almost penal attitude to the poor, who, in the individualistic ideology of the period, were often blamed for their own condition. More recently, something of the same attitude was widely expressed in sections of the media and public opinion in the anti-'social security scrounger' campaign of the first Thatcher administration (see p. 157). The National Insurance Acts of 1944 and 1946 greatly expanded the application of insurance which Beveridge envisaged as a citizen's right. Similarly, the liberal policy analyst, Thomas H Marshall wrote of the three rights of modern citizenship: political, civil and social. Within the liberal/social democratic tradition, Beveridge is considered to have made a major contribution to establishing social rights.

So far, the immediate post-war years have been the most productive period of welfare reform. However, many developments have since been introduced including some quite radical and controversial ones in the nineteen eighties. Changes in the national health and education systems are described elsewhere (chapters 4 and 16). Perhaps the most significant change in National Insurance has been the introduction of an earnings related element, initially by the Conservatives (1959) and extended by Labour (1966). In itself, this is less egalitarian than Beveridge's original scheme, involving only an equal contribution and equal benefits dependent upon need, but for many it removed the incentive to join private insurance schemes.

To what extent has the welfare state brought about greater equality in Britain? Again, this point is discussed in relation to education and health elsewhere (pp. 76–86). In brief, in respect to education, formal equality of opportunity does not compensate for class, gender or ethnic disadvantage and the result is that increasing inequality of outcome occurs from primary to higher education. As far as the NHS is concerned, a relatively high degree of equality of class access has not resulted in the outcome of equal health across the classes (see pp. 386–8). This is largely because members of the middle class use the NHS more effectively and adopt healthier lifestyles – partly because they can afford to.

The contribution of the rest of welfare to social equality is a complex matter. Most commentators agree that the relatively small component of the welfare state involving cash transfers – such as rent rebates and one parent family allowances – are broadly redistributive. The charge that the welfare state is inegalitarian is generally aimed at the universal services, i.e. those subsidies and services available to all. These include public transport, public libraries, tax relief to owner-occupiers (as well as most of the NHS and educational systems). Summarising his own work on the matter, Julian Le Grand states that 'the better off almost invariably used such services to a greater extent than the poor, and ... such services have failed to achieve equality, however defined'.

Arguably, the attack on housing squalor and inadequacy has been the most successful aspect of welfare state policy since the war although since the mid-nineteen eighties major problems have again developed. As Donnison and Ungerson point out, there is now greater equality of housing accessed by most basic standards of measurement. Thus, there are more houses per number of households, more rooms per person, and a higher proportion of baths and toilets per person than in 1945. The basic housing of the majority has greatly improved. Ironically, however, for a significant minority of people, one of the great areas of welfare progress – better housing – is now under threat. First, the relative position of those in rented council and private property in relation to owner-occupiers has worsened since the early nineteen eighties. The Conservatives' taxation and 'economic' rent policies have reduced housing benefit whilst the substantial system of tax concessions for mortgage holders remains intact. Alan Murie argues that a highly polarised and segregated housing market is the most likely consequence of continuing failure to develop housing policies other than the encouragement of owner-occupation. Second, the policy of selling council houses has reduced both the number and quality of public housing stock. Third, and related to the last point, the number of homeless families and families on council waiting lists has been increasing. This may be another indication of the development of a growing underclass or, in Marxist terms, lower working class, substantially worse off than the rest of the working class. However, in qualification of the above, some owner occupiers also experienced major housing problems in the early nineteen nineties – victims of a house-price boom and slump.

If the attack on squalor is now a tarnished success story of the British Welfare State, the ideal of full employment has become its Cinderella. The widespread belief that the levels of unemployment seen in the nineteen thirties would never be approached again has proved an illusion. In 1985 the number of unemployed (as conservatively measured by the government) exceeded the peak of the nineteen thirties although the percentage figure (thirteen per cent) was still lower. International economic factors certainly played a part in this, and throughout Europe governments of a variety of political complexions struggled to stem the rising tide of unemployment. However, in Britain what was new in 1979 was a government which disclaimed primary responsibility for reducing unemployment, and which by its monetarist policies, was widely considered to have exacerbated it. In any case, the British unemployment rate became the second highest in Europe. In 1991 unemployment again rose towards 3 million apparently confirming that such high figures are part of a new economic 'reality'.

In assessing how egalitarian is the Welfare State, we need to consider who pays for it as well as who benefits. This involves a brief review of the British taxation system and particularly the extent to which it is progressive, i.e. taxes the rich more, or regressive, i.e. taxes the poor relatively more. Two recent developments have made the British tax system more regressive. First, the proportion of income on which tax is paid has been increasing steadily during the post-war period. In other words, the tax threshold – the point at which people start paying income tax – has got much lower and non-taxable earnings allowances much less (in percentage terms). As a result, quite low paid employees are taxed on more of their income than previously. Second, the introduction of Value Added Tax, and particularly the raising of this to 17.5 per cent in 1991, has proved regressive. A higher percentage of the incomes of the poor than the rich goes in VAT, though, of course, in absolute terms a rich person pays more than a poor person. In addition, there are a great variety of ways in which the better off, and the corporations from which they derive much of their wealth, can avoid taxation. Overall, Westergaard and Resler conclude that, apart from the lowest paid who are taxed relatively less, the British taxation system is barely progressive. So whilst the burden of paying for the Welfare State is relatively evenly shared across the classes, the middle class is the prime beneficiary. Further, government figures show that between 1981–87 the average income (after housing costs) rose by almost 20 per cent whereas that of the bottom tenth of the pay scale rose only two per cent. To put it mildly, this does not amount to a situation remotely suggesting social equality.

The question of whether the Welfare State has increased equality can be applied to gender, particularly to whether it has improved the situation of women. Beveridge's support for family allowances which were adopted during the war had been widely campaigned for by feminists in the inter-war years. However, reflecting the general view of his time, Beveridge did not question the sexual division of labour and by channelling family and other welfare benefits mainly through the male, probably strengthened patriarchy. With Beveridge's traditional family ideals partly in mind, feminist Elizabeth Wilson suggests that his plan 'now reads as deeply conservative'. Many contemporary feminists seek a system – supported by the state – which will secure the individual welfare of women and children, i.e. income and benefits without dependency on males.

The above review clearly indicates that

the Welfare State has not achieved equality of access (availability) or equality of outcome (use) in relation to key services, though the situation varies greatly between them. Neither is the financing of the Welfare State very egalitarian. Growing realisation of

this has brought about what is widely referred to as a Welfare State 'crisis'. There is a variety of views about how to respond to this, each reflecting ideological preferences. It is to these matters of policy and ideology that we now turn.

Social Policy Perspectives on the Welfare State

The three major ideologies underpinning social policy positions are liberalism/social democracy, Conservatism (including the 'new right') and Marxism. I shall also make brief reference to functionalist theory on social policy although this is a sociological perspective rather than a political ideology. These ideologies have already been described in some detail in the context of development/ underdevelopment. The liberal/social democratic view dominated political and public opinion for the 30 years following the war. The liberal consensus involved an acceptance of a mixed economy and of the Welfare State. Most members of both major parties subscribed to this consensus. A portmanteau word – Butskellism – made up of the surnames of a leading Conservative, Butler, and of the leader of the Labour Party, Gaitskell, was sometimes used to describe this approach of moderate reformism.

LIBERALISM/SOCIAL DEMOCRACY: THE ORIGINAL VISION

Nevertheless, significant differences of emphasis existed among both politicians and scholars within this generally liberal approach. A key issue that emerged was the extent to which welfare should be provided universally or selectively. Universalism is based on the principle of providing a service to all citizens as a matter of right. Selectivity involves establishing criteria of acceptability for a given welfare service and means-testing applicants accordingly. A parallel distinction is that between institutional and residual concepts of welfare. In the words of Harold Wilensky and Charles Lebeaux: 'a residual system provides that social welfare institutions should come into play only when the normal structures of supply, the family and the market, break down', whereas an institutional system sees 'the

welfare services as normal, "first line" functions of modern industrial society'. Beveridge recommended a system of national security that was universal and compulsory. Aneurin Bevan set up a national health service free to all. Yet, the principle of universalism has been eroded in both cases and by both parties, in the former case by introducing a two tier system of payments, and in the latter by introducing now quite substantial prescription charges.

We now consider the arguments put forward in favour of a universal/institutional system. First, it provides services on the basis of right and equality and therefore fosters a sense of common community. This amounts to a considerable social vision. Second, social democrats typically considered that a more socially secure society would be a more orderly one – a belief that parallels Smelser's functionalist argument that the development of welfare has promoted social integration. Similarly, a healthier labour force was widely perceived as likely to be more productive. The major argument against universalism is cost – the more comprehensive the system of free services, the higher the taxation. In addition, the related charges of abuse of services, dependency and loss of work incentive are made, mainly from the political right. More broadly supported was the view that emerged of the welfare bureaucracy as too large, inefficient and alienating. Richard Titmuss was committed to a basic 'infrastructure of universalist services' but tried to meet the above criticisms by suggesting that other services might be available only to certain 'categories, groups and territorial areas' on the basis of specific need. In this way, he hoped to avoid the means testing of individuals which had caused great bitterness in the nineteen thirties. In fact, in the post-war period, the drift of the British Welfare State has been away from universalism towards selective means testing. Since Margaret Thatcher came to power in 1979, this drift has been given a sharper sense of direction.

The main argument in favour of the selective/residual model is that it is cheaper and resources go to those who 'really need' them. It is also seen by its supporters as less likely to spawn bureaucracy. Against this is the increase in humiliating means testing and the possibility that once a service is no longer regarded as a universal right it can be qualified and reduced indefinitely. We will return to the universalism versus selectivity debate when dealing with the rise of new right (Conservative) social policy alternatives.

THE IDEOLOGICAL AND INSTITUTIONAL CRISIS OF THE SOCIAL DEMOCRATIC WELFARE STATE: CAN 'CORPORATISM' RISE AGAIN?

The crisis in the British Welfare State preceded by several years the coming to power of Margaret Thatcher in 1979. Underlying the crisis of welfare was (and is) the long relative decline of the country's economy. This endemic problem was intensified in 1974 by the quadrupling of the price of oil following the action of the OPEC cartel. Against a background of world economic recession, the Labour governments of Harold Wilson (1974–76) and James Callaghan (1976–79) struggled to maintain intact the Welfare State and a policy of near full employment. However, the crisis was to test the post-war social democratic compromise between capitalism and socialism – basically accepted by all parties – almost to the limit.

Ten years previously, there was little appreciation of the crisis to come. In his professorial inaugural lecture of 1962, F Lafitte expressed the optimistic orthodoxy that a well-managed mixed economy would supply the wherewithal for a gradual expansion of the Welfare State – particularly its 'communal services'. As late as the mid-nineteen seventies, Ramesh Mishra was still commenting unproblematically on the need for a balance between the values of 'fraternity and collectivity' of the welfare ideal and of 'liberty and individuality' of the free market. In reality, however, the 'balance' or compromise was already under severe stress. This was because the free market itself failed to produce a reliably expanding surplus with which to finance the

Welfare State. Social democrats of all parties were therefore faced with an unpleasant choice which few of them had foreseen: should government policy be directed mainly at taking pressure off the free market by trying to reduce taxation and expenditure, primarily welfare expenditure, or should it continue to support and even expand the Welfare State by squeezing the private sector? On the horns of the dilemma, social democracy split, letting in the Thatcherite new right which, without a qualm or ambiguity, opted for the first solution.

No doubt in response to the ideological and policy turmoil of the late nineteen seventies and eighties, Ramesh Mishra has critically reviewed his own social democratic perspective. In *The Welfare State in Crisis* (1984), he presents a qualified case in favour of a particular form of social democratic Welfare State – the corporatist Welfare State. He believes that this model – relatively successfully practised by Austria and Sweden – more effectively integrates economic and social policy than any other. The corporatist Welfare State retains the mixed economy, with a strong private sector, but is managed by a mixture of Keynesian demand stimulation and supply side economics (often associated with the new right) to encourage production and labour mobility. On the social side, a 'social partnership' of capital and labour is encouraged by government, in which high levels of social welfare and of industrial productivity are pursued as mutually beneficial and compatible goals. As Mishra himself points out, such an approach can only deal with social problems at a national level whereas, in fact, many are now caused at the international level (see chapter 20 pp. 460–1).

THE NEW RIGHT: THATCHERISM AND AFTER

In both Britain and the United States, it was the political right which primarily benefited from the problems of social democracy. In 1979 Margaret Thatcher became Prime Minister for the first time and in 1980 Ronald Reagan was elected President. Both were returned for a second period of office in 1983 and 1984 respectively and they left office within two years of each other in 1990 and 1988 respectively. The ideology of the new right has been described earlier in this chapter (p. 354) and, in detail in chapter 14.

As far as social policy is concerned, it is relevant to divide the Conservative period in office into two parts, 1979–87 and 1987 onwards. The change is less one of rhetoric than of substance – not always the way in politics. What remained consistent throughout the Conservatives time in office was the overall aim of creating a successful, free-market economy. This was seen as requiring both cuts in public expenditure and a reduction in income tax. Cuts in public expenditure were more likely to be made in welfare than in, say, law and order or defence programmes.

SOCIAL POLICY, 1979–87

The 1979–87 period covers the first two Thatcher administrations. Related to the overall goal of reducing expenditure and increasing efficiency in the area of social welfare, three aspects of Conservative policy are noteworthy during this period:

1 A move towards residual and away from universalistic welfare policies;
2 The privatisation of certain aspects of welfare;
3 De-institutionalisation (using 'the community' as a resource).

Taking a broad definition of 'the community', the government's increased emphasis on the voluntary or charitable sector can be regarded as an aspect of this policy.

THE MOVE TO RESIDUALISM Public housing policy illustrates both the move from a universalistic to a more selective/residual model and privatisation. In 1979 government policy was to keep council house rents generally low by means of a general subsidy. In fact, in 1979 council rents were at their lowest post war level. The 1980 Housing Act gave the Secretary of State strong powers to push up rents in areas receiving the central subsidy. Between 1979 and 1982 rents more than doubled. However, for those who met the means test criteria, protection was provided by increased rent rebate and supplementary benefit payments. A problem with such schemes is low take-up, particularly amongst the most needy. Only 50 per cent of eligible

one parent families and 46 per cent of two parent families took up rebates compared to 82 per cent of childless households. To what extent this was due to inadequate publicity of the scheme, too little time on the part of harassed parents, or repugnance at the stigma of means testing, is a matter for speculation. Further, those just above the eligibility line would have been particularly hard hit by the doubling of rents. The above and other aspects of Conservative housing policy lead Alan Murie (from whom the above data is taken) to term it 'a thoroughly residual policy'.

By forcing up council house rents, central government created a climate favourable to the sale of council houses. The impact of this policy was massive both in terms of raising revenue and in extending owner occupation. The 27 billion pounds raised was more than the rest of the privatisations put together up to 1990. Up to the same year, it created about 1.5 million more owner occupiers (see figure 15.1a). Some authorities have suggested that this group has provided a new source of Conservative support but others argue that the evidence is they were inclined to Conservatism prior to buying their properties. As we have seen, critics of council house privatisation, see it as a squandering of a key public asset and as partly responsible for the growth in homelessness in the late nineteen eighties and early nineties (see figure 15.1b). Critics of Conservative government housing policy, such as Peter Ambrose, argue that the mix of 'market' and 'social' (welfare) criteria in housing allocation has become too skewed to the former when compared to more effective policies in some other European countries (*Times Higher Educational Supplement*, 31 June 1991).

There are other examples of the move towards residualism.

In the many cases where means tested schemes already existed in 1979, the Conservatives frequently reduced benefits and/or eligibility. Thus, between 1979 and 1980, about 174,000 children lost entitlement to free school meals for which the government, in any case, gave up responsibility for nutritional quality. However, the number eligible tends to increase during times of high unemployment. It is not easy to quantify the reduction in social security benefits under Thatcherism, let alone to trace their human cost. However, writing of the first administration, Ruth Lister and Paul Wilding refer to the 'cuts, nicks and slices which have in three and a half years taken some £2000 million away from those dependent on social security'.

THE PRIVATISATION OF ASPECTS OF WELFARE The privatisation of welfare was another aspect of the social policy of Reaganism and Thatcherism. Le Grand and Robinson indicate that it applies in three areas: the provision, subsidy and regulation of services. Examples of a reduction in state provision are the closing of local authority residential homes (some of which are now privately run) and the sale of council houses. Examples of state subsidy reduction are the reduction of the general subsidy to council house tenants and the increase in NHS prescription charges. An example of decreasing regulation is the lifting of restrictions on competition between private and public bus companies.

A policy that covers so many situations is not easy to generalise but the main issues are clear and vital. Those in favour of privatisation argue that it is more efficient than the public provision of services.

Research on this point varies from case to case but, on balance, does not sustain this generalisation. Thus, Millward's review of the evidence found that the private collection of refuse tended to be more efficient, but that this was not the case with the provision of water or electricity. By now, the privatisation of several major utilities should give most readers a chance to make their own judgement on this issue. Second, supporters of privatisation tend to argue that it increases liberty both by releasing initiative and increasing choice. However, it is as logical to argue that the Welfare State increases the liberty of the disadvantaged by providing them with the basic means of life, without which they could not make significant choices (whereas private enterprise does not seek to guarantee this). Third, critics of the Welfare State argue that it has failed to produce equality and that a combination of privatisation and income subsidies for the 'truly needy' would be more effective. The key issue here is how big the redistribution of income would be. In the absence of public services, it would have to be very substantial to increase equality. In any case, to do so is not a goal of Conservatives.

Figure 15.1

(a) Stock of dwellings: by tender

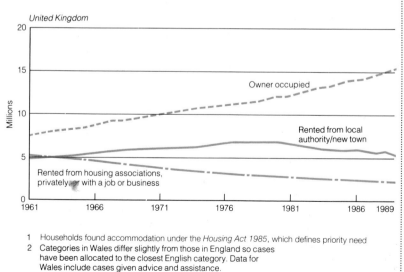

1 Households found accommodation under the *Housing Act 1985*, which defines priority need
2 Categories in Wales differ slightly from those in England so cases have been allocated to the closest English category. Data for Wales include cases given advice and assistance.

(Source: *Social Trends*, 1991, p. 135)

(b) Homeless households found accommodation by local authorities: by reasons[2] for homelessness, 1981 and 1989

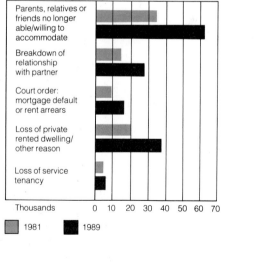

(Source: *Social Trends*, 1991, p. 141)

DE-INSTITUTIONALISATION (USING THE COMMUNITY AS A RESOURCE) The policy of de-institutionalisation, pursued by both the Reagan and Thatcher governments, provides an interesting example of the dovetailing of economic expediency with ideology. It simultaneously reduced public expenditure and large-scale welfare bureaucracy. De-institutionalisation means directing certain dependent groups out of public institutions and into the family and community. It has been practised mainly in relation to the mentally ill and handicapped but also in relation to the old. The policy has potential advantages, but for it to work, substantial support for the concerned families and communities (however that term may be defined) must be provided. Without this, two groups tend to suffer – as has been apparent in the de-institutionalisation of many of the mentally ill. First, are those who traditionally carry the burden of care – overwhelmingly women, often with many other commitments. Second, are members of the dependent groups – as was seen by the apparently increased numbers of mentally ill people wandering the streets in the mid-eighties. In a review of community care policy the Audit Commission estimated that over 40,000 inmates of mental hospitals had 'disappeared' from the records of health and welfare agencies. To attempt to save money at the risk of 'dumping', say, a middle aged,

long-institutionalised psychotic on his elderly mother is the kind of sad consequence that can result from under-financing de-institutionalisation. Yet, it is in these 'small' corners of human misery that the cost of cuts must be sought.

THE 1988 SOCIAL SECURITY ACT Although the 1988 Social Security Act only came into force early during the third Thatcher administration, it was fashioned during the second. It illustrates that there was substantial continuity between the Conservative administrations before and after 1987 as well as the major differences referred to shortly. Although trumpeted by some as the most radical restructuring of social welfare since Beveridge, in retrospect the Fowler Act appears to have nothing like the vision and scope that inspired Beveridge's reforms. Indeed, critics see the 1988 Act as little more than a grandiose exercise in cutting public expenditure – at the expense of the poor. The main measures introduced by the Act are as follows:

Income Support
Income support is the main means tested benefit for the unemployed. Calculation of it varies according to certain commitments of the claimants.

Family Credit
Family credit supplements or 'tops up' the income of low paid workers with children.

The Social Fund
The Social Fund replaces grants formerly available through social security with loans (although a very limited number of grants are still made).

Housing Benefit
Claimants have to be responsible for paying rent and rates to be eligible and to have a low income.

COMMENT ON THE SOCIAL SECURITY ACT
At the time the Act was introduced there was widespread debate about which groups would gain or lose under the Act and the extent to which this would be so. Broadly, the government claimed there would be more gainers than losers and its critics vice-versa. In June 1990, The Guardian published research by the Child Poverty Action Group into the first two years of the Act's operation. Even if the figures given below somewhat overestimate the degree to which groups have lost income, it still seems highly likely that the government reduced per

Figure 15.2

A victim of 'Community Care' policy?

▼

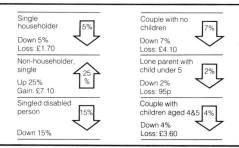

Changes in social security
In real terms (1990 prices) since 1987

Single householder	
Down 5% Loss: £1.70	5% ⬇

Couple with no children	
Down 7% Loss: £4.10	7% ⬇

Non-householder, single	
Up 25% Gain: £7.10	25% ⬆

Lone parent with child under 5	
Down 2% Loss: 95p	2% ⬇

Singled disabled person	
Down 15%	15% ⬇

Couple with children aged 4&5	
Down 4% Loss: £3.60	4% ⬇

(Source: *The Guardian*, 4th June 1990)

capita spending on the poor as a result of its Social Security Act.

Perhaps one reform in particular illustrates the cost-cutting spirit of the Act: the change from a grants-based system through social security to a loans-based Social Fund as a means of last resort for the poor. This involved two important changes of principle. First, the social security grants were intended as a 'safety-net' – people would get them if (subject to means testing) they needed them. In contrast, the Social Fund budget is relatively small and limited and sometimes 'needy' applicants do not receive a loan. Second, the principle that those in most extreme or urgent need should pay back what they received from public assistance was introduced. In conclusion, this 'reform' did achieve considerable savings which have been more precisely accounted than their human cost.

THE COST OF SOCIAL POLICY: 1979–87
Figure 15.4a shows the cost of social welfare in Britain between 1959 and 1984 according to the main areas of expenditure. Figure 15.4b puts Britain's expenditure in comparative perspective and shows that the percentage of gross domestic product spent on welfare in Britain is much closer to that of the United States – the bastion of private enterprise – than social democratic Sweden.

The most notable point that emerges from figure 15.4a is that no marked changes in trends emerge after 1979. Perhaps the clearest change is the increase in social security expenditure caused by the rapid and large rise in unemployment during the early nineteen eighties (a similar rise has occurred as a result of the recession of the early nineteen nineties). Even the very sharp drop in expenditure on housing began in the mid nineteen seventies although many would

argue that it has continued too long and been too steep. Only in the area of education is it clear that the Conservatives even slowed the rate of increase in expenditure.

Yet, government expenditure as a percentage of gross domestic product (GDP) did fall steadily between 1981 and 1984 (and continued to do so until 1989). The main reasons for this were that privatisation revenue is subtracted from government expenditure thus significantly 'reducing' it, oil revenue greatly increased during these years, and economic recovery boosted GDP in the years between the two recessions. However, as we have seen, expenditure on the major public services increased in real terms. In this respect, government policy failed during the early nineteen eighties.

(a) How UK spending on social welfare divides up

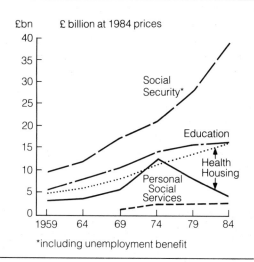

*including unemployment benefit

(b) How spending on social welfare programmes has grown

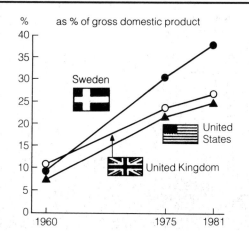

◄

Figure 15.3 (Far left)

◄

Figure 15.4

367

COMMENT Given the high rate of expenditure on the public services in the early nineteen eighties, it is arguable that the first and second Thatcher administrations made no radical break with the recent past on social policy. The Welfare State was maintained albeit trimmed in places. However, Thatcherites still criticised the Welfare State as costly and inefficient while acknowledging that the first two Thatcher administrations had not succeeded in solving these problems. After 1987, they set about dealing with these issues in a different way and in doing so found means which matched their radical rhetoric.

THE WELFARE STATE AND 'QUASI-MARKETS' 1988–1992

Something of a watershed in Conservative social policy occurred in 1988–89. The goal of increasing efficiency and cutting costs (i.e. of improving productivity) remained, but a new 'mechanism' was introduced to achieve it. This 'mechanism' – a term used by the Minister of State for Health, William Waldegrave – is the 'quasi-market' or 'internal market' as Ministers tended to call it.

A 'quasi-market' is a partial approximation in the public sector to the free-market situation that supposedly exists 'normally' in the private sector. This requires that means be found to ensure that the public sector is operated on the basis of supply and demand, competition, and the resulting success or failure of institutions (i.e. schools or hospitals would be subject to the same market disciplines as businesses). The assumption of advocates of this view is that this would increase the efficiency of public services by requiring them to respond to the demands of the 'consumer'.

Prior to the attempt to introduce quasi-markets, the public services operated on the principle of meeting public need on the basis of equal access among individuals. Increases in demand for, say, education or health provision would be met (mainly) out of the public purse (taxation) and efficiencies would be achieved by management and professionals operating on behalf of the public (members of which sat as school governors or on health boards). We will leave aside, for the moment, criticism both of the quasi-market and public needs driven systems, and instead describe some examples of the former.

Major examples of quasi-markets occur within the education and health services and both these are discussed in detail elsewhere. Only a brief description is needed here. In primary and secondary education the two systems of open enrolment/local management of schools and opting out effectively puts schools in competition with each other. If parents/pupils do not like what they are getting, they can go elsewhere (see pp. 107–9). Funding follows pupil numbers. Similarly, in higher education there are built-in financial incentives to encourage institutions to expand. Those that expand are rewarded and those that do not are less well funded and risk 'going under'. A more radical system would be the introduction of student vouchers which students could 'spend' at the institution of their choice – subject to their qualifications. The National Health Service increasingly operates in a similar way with some hospitals opted out of local authority control and others increasingly subject to competitive pressures (see pp. 388–90).

Attempts have also been made to introduce quasi-market elements into housing and personal social services. Thus, council tenants now have the right to choose a landlord other than the local authority. In the area of residential accommodation for the elderly, local authorities have increasingly used private residential homes. Case-managers operate on behalf of elderly clients in this context, rather as parents do for pupils in education and General Practitioners who have their own budget do for patients – at least, this is the theory.

COMMENT It is too early to assess how effective quasi-markets might be, or on the other hand how much damage they might do. However, the arguments on both sides of the question are vociferous – understandably, given what is at stake. Those who support the quasi-market mechanism contend that it will increase 'consumer' choice, improve efficiency, and ultimately be fairer by improving the quality of welfare services. Those who oppose quasi-markets argue that the cost-cutting is likely to reduce the quality and scale of services. A second criticism has been that the managements and inspectorates which, respectively, control and police the new welfare systems, may become oppressive and expensive. There has been tension between teachers and management in education, and between hospital doctors and management in the NHS. A third criticism is made strongly by the Labour Party. It contends that the changes discussed above are having the effect of creating a two tier system in both health and education, thus contradicting the principle of an equal service for all. Fourthly, and most fundamentally, it is argued that access to basic needs such as health and education is the equal right of all citizens and should be equally provided through public services rather than through the inevitably unequal mechanism of the market.

The notion that markets enhance consumer or client choice has had considerable appeal across political lines. Suggestions from the political left include child care vouchers and health vouchers (to be 'spent' at a doctor of one's own choice). Julian Le Grand has pointed out that such vouchers will increase inequality unless the less well off get vouchers of greater value than the rich. He refers to these as positive discrimination vouchers. Whether such schemes to increase consumer freedom are compatible with producing a fair and efficient welfare service may fall to a future Labour government to discover.

MARXIST PERSPECTIVES ON SOCIAL POLICY

Marxists have always faced a dilemma in relation to the liberal Welfare State. On the one hand, elements of the Welfare State benefit the working class and have been won partly by the efforts of the trade union movement, the Labour Party and other predominantly working class organisations. On the other, Marxists commonly view the Welfare State as a means developed by the ruling class of reducing working class militancy and demand for socialism. This conflict has produced some ambivalence in Marxist perspectives on the Welfare State.

One of the most influential recent Marxist works is James O' Connor's *The Fiscal Crisis of the State* (1973). The crisis to which he refers lies in a contradiction between what he describes as the two main functions of the state: accumulation (of wealth through capitalist enterprise) and legitimisation (partly through the pacificatory effects of the welfare state referred to above). The crisis is that the cost of legitimisation is becoming more than private enterprise can support – hence the budget deficit. In commenting on O' Connor's work, Ramesh Mishra concedes that O' Connor focuses on a potentially contradictory tendency in liberal capitalism. However, Mishra argues that it is only a tendency and that, in general, the Welfare State supports rather than weakens capitalism. Whatever the general merits of Mishra's observation, there is no doubt of the current relevance of O' Connor's analysis when most social democracies do appear to be struggling with the contradiction he indicates.

Whereas O' Connor concentrates on the fiscal crisis of capitalism, more recent writings by Ian Gough and other Marxists analyse in addition the broader aspects of the economic crisis of the seventies and particularly its consequences for the working class. These writings agreed that capital would try to make labour pay the price of this crisis in lower wages and reduced welfare. Nevertheless, Ian Gough in *The Political Economy of the Welfare State* (1979) argues that working class organisations should continue to press for reform. The state of the political left in the nineteen eighties was one of much greater disarray than Gough anticipated but his contention that socialists must distinguish between reforms that promote 'welfare capitalism' and those that promote 'welfare socialism' continues to generate interest and controversy. Ramesh Mishra's response is that, in practice, such a distinction is not possible: the aim of many social reforms is both to improve conditions (socialist-inclined) and to adjust beneficiaries to 'the system' (capitalist-inclined). My own view favours Gough because any political movement must struggle to bend change in its own preferred direction. In fact, several Thatcherite and post-Thatcherite initiatives require carefully discriminating response: examples are community versus institutional care, and the various attempts to empower the consumer and render the professional accountable in education, health and the social services (see p. 365). More broadly, Gough sees potential for such groups as the Claimants' Union and Women's Aid, supported by the trade union movement, to defend and ultimately extend the more socialist aspects of the Welfare State.

Whatever the room for manoeuvre of the kind Gough indicates, Marxists consider that no major party has yet attempted to introduce a genuinely socialist Welfare State in Britain. Similarly, they point out that the Labour government preceding the first Thatcher administration had already begun to make cuts in welfare – largely to defend the capitalist economy. Accordingly, in *Public Opinion, Ideology and State Welfare* (1985), Peter Taylor-Gooby, argues that 'the view that the Welfare State is currently the victim of a sudden attack by the new right is somewhat misleading'. In support of Taylor-Gooby, it is arguable that even before 1979, the British Welfare State was barely better than minimal, certainly when compared to those of the Scandinavian countries. In practice, Thatcher found it difficult to cut 'fat' without flesh and has made most of her savings through privatising nationalised industries rather than reducing welfare expenditure. Even so, whatever the long-term estimates of the Thatcherite cuts, it is worth recalling Harold Wilson's comment on unemployment, and applying it to social welfare reductions: 'If it happens to you, it's a hundred per cent.' Taylor-Gooby goes on to state:

> **The vision of the history of the Welfare State as a decline from the golden age tends to mask the conflicts and continuities that have always existed in policy. The contemporary problems of the Welfare State arise from the failures of policy to meet the demands of changing circumstances – from inertia rather than the radical development of policy.**
>
> **(Taylor-Gooby, 1985)**

The 'radical development of policy' Taylor-Gooby considers necessary is, of course, socialist. However, publishing in 1985, he was well aware that few, even of the working class, are Marxist (indeed, in the 1983 and 1987 general elections the majority of them did not even vote Labour!). Norman Ginsburg in *Class, Capital and Social Policy* examines the wider problem of why the consciousness of the working class is not more socialist. He considers that it is seduced by capitalist commodities into obsessive consumption (commodity fetishism) – a behaviour which is strongly expressed and regenerated within the family. Partly as a result, class solidarity is fragmented. Patriarchy is also obscured by commodity fetishism and by the individualisation of collective family concerns into 'accepted' roles. The Welfare State is widely presented and perceived as another mechanism for distributing commodities rather than as a potential instrument of socialism. Interestingly, the social democrat, Ramesh Mishra, argues that Marxists uselessly lament the consumer tendencies, or applying O'Connor's term to workers as well as capitalists, accumulative tendencies of the working class. Its members merely share these desires with other classes and Marxism must provide for them if it is to have political appeal. Whilst Mishra's point may be valid, it is worth commenting that socialism is not merely concerned with material consumption, but with the quality of human relations and culture. Thus, in theory, consumption as well as production would be organised and experienced differently under socialism than capitalism.

While Gough cautiously draws attention to the socialist potential of the Welfare State, Taylor-Gooby and Ginsburg tend to stress its limits and, indeed, its services to capitalism. One conclusion from this is that any Marxist or socialist party needs to be quite clear on what it can realistically expect to achieve through the Welfare State, given a situation of influence or power. Clarity of vision would be especially necessary in a situation of transition towards socialism.

GENDER AND SOCIAL POLICY (WITH PARTICULAR REFERENCE TO THE FAMILY)

The Marxist/socialist 'wing' of the contemporary feminist movement appears to have reached a generally clear analysis of female oppression within capitalism and a clear programme of change. The purpose of this section is critically to present the latter, but it will help first to recall how they conceptualise women's oppression. Mary McIntosh's article *The State and the Oppression of Women* argues that in capitalist society the family household has two basic functions – 'it serves (though inadequately) for the reproduction of the working class and for the maintenance of women as a reserve army of labour, low-paid when they are in jobs and often unemployed.' The point is that women's labour is made cheap in capitalist society: domestic labour is unpaid except by grace of the husband and their paid work is more poorly rewarded and more easily expended with than men's.

McIntosh argues that within capitalism the family household has been 'importantly structured and constrained by state policies' to ensure that it achieves its functions. The form of marriage encouraged by the state has involved a 'dependent-breadwinner' structure. This family structure provides unpaid maintenance of male labour (the reproduction of labour) and systematises biological reproduction. Family policy in particular, and welfare policy in general, such as unemployment and supplementary benefit, support this situation (see pp. 68–70). Women who do not fit into the system may suffer as a result. Women living with their husbands or lovers, and school leavers cannot claim supplementary benefit and can only claim unemployment benefit if they have paid full contributions. McIntosh suggests that policy towards one parent families has provided the means to survive, whilst seeking to avoid encouraging the practice. McIntosh is aware of the 'Marxist functionalist' nature of the argument but strongly differentiates it from classical functionalist perspective by insisting on the 'contradictions' between the family and state within capitalist society and within the family itself. A central contradiction is that the role of women as cheap reproducers of (male) labour and as a reserve army of labour themselves can conflict – thus forcing substantial direct state intervention in the supposedly 'private sphere' of the family, as notably occurred, for instance, during the second world war.

C C Harris sharply criticises the kind of Marxist functionalist arguments used by McIntosh on the grounds that they may explain how but not why institutions function in a given way. Thus, no historical explanation is offered as to why women rather than men perform domestic labour (though see pp. 48–9). Harris also seems to regard the focus on oppression as emotive and unscientific. However, it is hardly surprising that women should focus on this matter and suggest policies to relieve it.

Anna Coote's article *Labour: The Feminist Touch* assumes that women have been domestically oppressed and that the main strategy for dealing with this is for women increasingly to penetrate the labour market and to achieve equality within it and otherwise. Publishing in 1985 seven years after McIntosh, she suggests that the number of women in paid work (60 per cent) 'suggest that we are no longer a "reserve army of labour"; we are regulars'. What remains to be done, however, is for women to gain equality at work whilst the needs of children and people (men or women) doing domestic work are met. The programme she offers is bold but perhaps no bolder than is necessary to achieve the end she seeks:

> *The strategy focuses on the spheres of reproduction and production, but starts with the former, on the grounds that this is the primary sphere, from which production springs.*
>
> *The strategy would give priority to breaking down the traditional division of paid and unpaid labour, so that responsibility for children would be shared equally among men and women, and between home-based parental care and community-based collective care. It would mean a much shorter working week for men and women, vastly improved child-care provision outside the home, and a restructuring of family income, by increasing female earning power and child benefit, and improving the 'social wage'.*
>
> *(Coote, 1985:14)*

The shorter working week Coote refers to is to provide more jobs for women and more time for men to do domestic work (including caring for their children). She also suggests extended parental leave, on an equal basis for men and women. To protect low-paid workers, a disproportionate number of whom are women, she emphasises the need for a statutory minimum wage.

How does the socialist feminism of McIntosh and Coote relate to other strands in the feminist movement? Neither appear to want to be at odds with the libertarian wing of the movement as represented by, for instance, the Americans, Leghorn and Parker (see pp. 484–6). However, they clearly consider that the localised, network-based activities of feminists must be complemented and supported by central government action. Neither McIntosh nor Coote seek to improve the situation of women by attacking only patriarchy. Coote's programme blends an attack on patriarchy with an attack on certain main aspects of capitalism. While recognising that men are unlikely voluntarily to relinquish power, she nevertheless attempts to make a feminist-sensitive programme of social reform appealing to them (e.g. in its job creation and leisure aspects). Nothing as specific or coherent as this has emerged from those feminists who regard patriarchy as the sole source of female oppression (referred to as radical feminists). Indeed, arguably the equality package of the mid-seventies has largely established the framework that they want for fair and open competition between the sexes (see pp. 184–5). McIntosh and Coote seek a framework of equality and cooperation founded on mutual independence between the sexes, rather than competition.

To summarise, the socialist feminist programme seeks to restructure the family household both in terms of functions and roles. Families will continue to reproduce children but the rearing of them will be shared more equally between the sexes and much better public child-care facilities will be established. All modern movements to release women from domestic bondage – from the kibbutz to Soviet socialism – have attempted to find means other than the mother to rear children. Britain has not seriously done so. Even progressive local authorities such as Camden in London have only a small number of publicly provided nursery places relative to need. For instance, the children of many single parent families are not provided with places – virtually making it impossible for their mothers to work. Coote argues that better nursery and pre-school facilities and more male involvement in child rearing would better enable women to achieve the equality that decently paid work brings. Thus, the era in which women are 'second bested' at home and in paid work could begin to draw to a close.

CITIZENSHIP AND WELFARE

The issue of citizens rights and responsibilities was raised in chapter 14. The concept of citizenship has an obvious application to the area of welfare although this has not yet been fully developed. In theory, welfare claimants could be guaranteed the delivery of services to a certain level of quality, where

appropriate by a certain date. Failing this, they could have the right of redress, including, perhaps, financial compensation. Such rights might be a powerful weapon against the impersonality and unresponsiveness often associated with Welfare State bureaucracy. However, I am not aware of any serious attempts to find out the priorities of welfare recipients let alone establish rights of redress.

The application of the concept of citizenship to welfare recipients might empower groups in danger of becoming marginal and dispossessed. Some single parent families, young ethnic unemployed, and the long term unemployed, might just regain a sense of civic dignity and power by such means.

SOCIAL PROBLEMS AND POLICY: CONCLUSION

High unemployment, poverty, racial and gender disadvantage, urban disorder – these are social problems by almost anybody's definition and Britain has its share of them. There is limited agreement between the major ideological/policy perspectives discussed above on how to deal with these problems, although supporters of each have increasingly come to stress that wealth has to be produced before it can be distributed. There is also potential for overlap between radical social democrats and Marxists. It is quite possible that given favourable circumstances, each of the above approaches could be made to work effectively and to improve social conditions – at least, within the terms of its own frame of reference. When we choose to support a particular approach to social policy, we are making a statement of value as well as of practicality. Of course, policies must be workable. Passionate statements of value and goals are useless unless related to effective solutions. Currently, we are perhaps moving into an era of greater openness and discussion in relation to means. Some of the problems of both universalist and selective solutions are now much more obvious. Positive alternatives and compromises are hard to find but lively efforts to do so both among politicians and theorists are certainly occurring.

1 Sociology can throw light on social problems in the following ways:

(i) By clarifying the link between social structure and personal experience;

(ii) By demonstrating the hidden consequences of certain social practices and conditions;

(iii) By showing how certain matters come to be defined as social problems and by clarifying the reasons why certain people define them as problematic;

(iv) By explaining the causes and contexts of social problems, sociology can inform people's humanistic concern about them.

2 There are several sociological perspectives on social problems.
First, social problems are seen as individual deviance, i.e. as caused by individual moral failure or biological deficiency.

3 Second, the functionalist perspective divides social problems into problems of deviance and problems of disorganisation. Problems of deviance may be functional or dysfunctional to society but problems of disorganisation are more generally dysfunctional.

4 Third, Howard Becker provides a classically interactionist definition of social problems: 'Social problems are what people say they are'. Inter-actionist emphasis on the subjective aspect of social problems contrasts with functionalist stress on the objective reality of problems such as poverty and unemployment both to those who experience them and in their effects on society.

5 Fourth, radical structural and Marxist perspectives argue that in capitalist society many social problems are the product of the workings of the capitalist system which inevitably produces 'losers' as well as 'winners'.

6 Social policy is now generally perceived as an area of ideological and political contest and debate. If defining something as a social problem causes debate, prescribing a policy to deal with it can be even more contentious.

SUMMARY

7 Beveridge helped to consolidate and expand the Welfare State in order to combat the 'five giant evils of ignorance, disease, want, idleness and squalor'. Yet, it is debated whether the Welfare State has brought about greater equality.

8 There are a number of political/social policy perspectives on the Welfare State.
Liberalism/social democracy aspired to create a Welfare State which provided basic public services universally and equally although there have always been some politicians in the post-war period that have preferred a more selective and, therefore, means tested system of welfare. The more universalist approach experienced a crisis from about the mid-nineteen seventies and increasingly the new right developed a new model of welfare.

9 The new right considerably influenced the social welfare policies of the Thatcher administrations. Welfare policy under Mrs Thatcher can be divided into two periods: 1979-87 and 1987-90 (the latter period perhaps continuing into the nineteen nineties). The first period was characterised by:

■ Cost-cutting;
■ A move to residualism;
■ Privatisation;
■ De-institutionalisation.

The second period has been one in which 'quasi-markets' (as near as possible, 'free markets') have been increasingly introduced into the Welfare State.

10 Marxist analysis tends to see the Welfare State, in part, as a defensive achievement of working class pressure and, in part, a liberal compromise to take off the edge of working class militancy. Thatcherite policies are seen by O'Connor as an attempt to revive the profitability of capitalist enterprise by reducing the burden of taxation spent on welfare.

11 Much feminist social policy

analysis, particularly Marxist, seeks to remedy the oppression of women both in the area of reproduction and production. In the former area childcare needs to be better publicly financed and shared and in the latter a range of equalising measures are suggested.

RESEARCH AND COURSEWORK

See also chapter 14, p. 351.

The problem to avoid in this area is to assume that either the concept of 'social problem' or 'social policy' is unproblematic. In fact, the selection and exploration of a social problem gives the opportunity to apply some of the rich theoretical insights and perspectives presented in this chapter. These are some of the questions you would need to address in analysing a social problem:

Who says it is a problem?

Who is it a problem to?

Who gains from the fact that it is defined as a problem?

Does any group regard it as not a problem?

What is the wider structural context of the problem?

Are the policies (if any) adopted to deal with the problem a matter of broad consensus or are they debated?

'It', the problem, might be anything from cigarette smoking to the rising suicide rate among young males. Adequate contextualisation and definition is the crucial thing! Given proper theorisation, the primary research into a social 'problem' could be locally based. Many areas have been 'hit' by, for instance, unemployment and housing shortage and both these matters ought to provide an opportunity to relate 'personal troubles' to 'public issues'.

More specifically social policy oriented research equally ought to recognise the ideological and political nature of policy. Again, however, empirical material might be gathered locally.

FURTHER READING

Michael Hill's *Understanding Social Policy* (Basil Blackwell and Martin Robertson, 1987) is a standard introductory text. Ramesh Mishra's *The Welfare State in Crisis: Social Thought and Social Change* (Open University, Harvester Press, 1984) fairly presents a number of perspectives, including Mishra's own corporatist one. Patrick Dunleavy et al., eds., *Developments in British Politics* (Macmillan, 1990) contains several contributions which usefully address policy issues in the later stages of Thatcherism.

QUESTIONS

1   Discuss either unemployment or poverty as a 'social problem'.

2   Distinguish between social problems and sociological problems, and discuss their relationship to social policy. (London, 1989)

3   Discuss the relationship between political ideology and social policy during Mrs. Thatcher's premiership.

16 The Sociology of Health & Health Policy

Themes and Definitions

There are two main and recurrent themes in this chapter. The first is that there are different paradigms or frameworks for perceiving and organising health. Cultural anthropology is the discipline best suited to exploring these different frameworks. Accordingly, the chapter begins with a survey of cultural paradigms of health and illness: magical, religious (briefly), modern scientific, and holistic medicine. A particularly narrow form of scientific medicine – 'mechanistic' or positivistic – is subject to criticism from a more humanistic medical perspective (of which holistic medicine is an example). Mechanistic and humanistic approaches to medicine are also contrasted in the sections on mental health and illness and on gender and health. The sociology of knowledge examines the relationship between paradigms and social factors and, along with the later section on the sociology of educational knowledge, our examination of health paradigms is a main example of the sociology of knowledge in this book. The second major theme is the unequal distribution of health, and it explicitly or implicitly occupies most of the chapter. It includes an analysis of health inequalities in relation to gender and the Third World as well as social class. The chapter concludes with a review of sociological perspectives on health and relates these to social policy perspectives.

Webster's Dictionary gives a commonly accepted definition of health: it is 'the condition of being sound in body, mind or soul; esp: freedom from physical disease or pain' (1965). The constitution of the World Health Organisation presents health as more than freedom from disease but in addition as 'a state of complete physical, mental and social well-being': a quality of life as well as a material issue. Such generalities aside, understanding of health and illness, perhaps especially mental illness, varies significantly from culture to culture and even within cultures. The terms illness and disease will be used interchangeably here although a useful distinction is sometimes made between them.

L G Moore et al. (1980) present disease as 'a reflection of failure to adapt to the environment ... usually manifested by abnormalities in the structure and function of body, organs and systems'. Illness, however, relates to the 'experience' of such abnormal conditions and 'thus includes those social psychological aspects of disease that not only affect the ill person, but may also affect the person's family and friends'. How we experience disease is an important aspect of being ill. Figure 16.1 is intended to stimulate consideration of the relationships between illness and disease. Disease reads down and illness reads across.

►
Figure 16.1
Dimensions of
illness and disease

	Disease	
	Yes	**No**
Illness **Yes**	Influenza	Mental illness
No	Undiagnosed cancer	Good 'health'

Cultural Paradigms of Health

A paradigm is 'the entire constellation of beliefs, values, techniques, and so on shared by members of a given community' (Kuhn, 1970). Without using the term, James Frazer, in effect, presented the evolution of human knowledge in terms of the paradigms of magic, religion and science (*The Golden Bough*, 1922). More recent research has shown Frazer's scheme to be over-simple, but he does usefully indicate the major cultural paradigms of explanation and belief.

MAGICAL AND RELIGIOUS PARADIGMS OF HEALTH AND ILLNESS

Health and illness can usefully be understood within wider cultural paradigms or belief systems, particularly those of magic, religion and science. Magic involves the manipulation and control of the natural world by certain individuals such as witches, sorcerers and shamans. These powerful figures were considered able to cause or alleviate much misfortune, including illness.

Two forms of magic are witchcraft and sorcery. Witchcraft is generally regarded as an in-born ability to generate misfortune, whereas sorcery requires conscious effort and often involves the ritual manipulation of items belonging to the object of the sorcery.

Edward Evans-Pritchard carried out an anthropological study of the African Azande, including their understanding of death and illness as a result of witchcraft and sorcery (1937). Whereas disease is generally regarded as a materialistic phenomenon in the West, for the Azande it is generated psychically and spiritually. The Azande believe that witchcraft is a substance in the bodies of witches, the 'soul' of which may leave the witch and take possession of the victim at any time but especially at night. The 'resulting' illness is seen as the production of witchcraft and often a witch hunt follows.

Accusation plays a key role in the response to witchcraft. From the perspective of the Azande and cultural groups with similar beliefs, accusation is part of the process of explanation and reparation. From a more detached sociological perspective, we can see that the practical affirmation of the belief system strengthens social solidarity. Accusation is the vehicle for this as it labels and stigmatises deviant behaviour. In Durkheim's terms, accusation helps to redraw normative boundaries. Conflict theorists point out, however, that certain groups may benefit more than others from ritual reaffirmation of the social status quo. Andre Singer and Brian V Street adopt this approach in Zande themes. They note that the beneficiaries of witchcraft are invariably the wealthy and powerful. Members of the princely class are not accused of witchcraft but by successfully accusing others they can acquire forfeits and thus extend their wealth and power.

Not all examples of witchcraft and sorcery lend themselves so easily to explanations of self-interest or social systems maintenance (solidarity). In any case, respect is due to magical belief systems simply because they may in certain ways be true and powerful. This is the impression left by Carlos Castaneda's long and continuing study of the magico-religious beliefs of the Yacqui Indians and of M J Harner's research on the Jivaro Indians of the Ecuadorian Amazon. Even the anthropological detachment of Evans-Pritchard seemed on one occasion to falter into affirmation of magic when he became a 'witness' himself: 'I have only once seen witchcraft on its path....'

I will deal very briefly with the relationship between religion and health and illness because what has been said about magic applies equally to religion. Frazer's key and still useful distinction between magic and religion is that the former is controlled by human beings and the latter by God or spirits. In practice, this distinction is not always so clear. For example, powerful religious intermediaries have something in common with shamans or benevolent sorcerers, especially in their roles as healers and interceders with the divine. More fundamentally, despite the fact that they are different systems of knowledge, both magic and religion are non-scientific (though not illogical in their own terms). Just as magic explains illness in terms of witchcraft and sorcery, so many religions explain it at least partly in terms of 'God's will'. Like magic, religion is sometimes used as ideology to justify self or group interest (see pp. 401–2). There is a potential, but not inevitable conflict between the religious and scientific explanation of illness.

MODERN SCIENTIFIC MEDICINE

Lorna G Moore et al. present two major defining assumptions of modern scientific medicine: first is the germ theory of disease and the need to cure infection to restore health; second, is the efficacy of preventive medicine. The two arms of modern scientific medicine are, then, the curative and the preventive. All scientific theory depends on the empirical demonstration of causal relationships and it was the work of Louis Pasteur on germ theory, particularly germ contagion, in the mid to late nineteenth century that established the basis of modern medicine. Criticisms of modern scientific medicine tend to focus on (a) a limited approach to curative medicine that has developed, based on drugs and surgery, (b) a corresponding failure adequately to emphasise the role of prevention and (c) a tendency to undervalue subjective feeling states. Few, however, would oppose the use of science in medicine, it is the abuse that is criticised.

The advantage of Moore's broad definition is that it highlights the common assumptions underlying certain traditions of treatment within scientific medicine. Moore states that allopathy, homeopathy and naturopathy share the two core assumptions mentioned above. There are also significant differences between them. Allopathic medicine is based on the principle of finding a means to counteract disease. Drugs are the main counteractive agents used. Because of the successful use of drugs in combating germs, Western medicine is often identified with allopathic medicine to the neglect of other systems of treatment. Homeopathic medicine is based on the principle that a particular sickness can be treated by administering minute doses of a remedy that produces the same symptoms as the disease. The homeopath regards symptoms of disease as an attempt by the body to restore homeostasis (balance), a process which treatment seeks to stimulate. Reactions to disease vary and individuals rather than diseases are treated. In so far as homeopathy reaches out to the whole person, it shares the principles of holistic medicine (see pp. 379–80). Naturopathy is based on the principle that a natural, mainly fruit and vegetable diet, provides the body with the ingredients it needs to avoid disease. Similarly, herbal remedies are used when disease does occur. Naturopathy can also include regular exercise, a healthy environment, avoidance of and techniques to deal with stress.

Although allopathic medicine remains dominant in the West and is increasing in influence elsewhere, serious criticisms of the way it is practised are now widely made. The essence of these criticisms is that a machine-like, dehumanising model of health and illness has come to dominate allopathic medicine and there is, in addition, too much dependence on surgery and 'high-tech' medicine. Elliot Mishler refers to this approach as the biomedical model and he identifies four assumptions which underlie it. First, disease is seen as deviation from normal biological functioning. A criticism of this assumption is that effective biological functioning varies somewhat from person to person. Second is the doctrine of specific aetiology or causation, i.e. a specific germ causes a given disease. A problem here is that individuals do not respond to germs in the same way so that other factors in disease causation must exist – presumably related to

the individual's health and ability to maintain health. Third is the assumption of generic diseases which means that the same kinds of diseases occur in all human societies. Despite its analytical usefulness, this perspective tends to ignore the variety of cultural interpretation given to disease. Fourth is the assumption that medicine is scientifically neutral. In fact, as we shall see, the practice of medicine has profound personal and social implications which the attitude of scientific 'objectivity' can obscure.

In essence, the above criticism of the biomedical paradigm is that it is too mechanistic (sometimes it is referred to as the bio-mechanical model) and fails to take account of either individual variety and need, or of cultural diversity. A particularly sharp critique of the bio-medical model is given in *The Machine Metaphor in Medicine* by Samuel Osherson and Lorna Amara Sigham which appears in Elliot Mishler's edited volume *Social Contexts of Health, Illness and Patient Care*. I shall use their discussion of the influence of the mechanical metaphor on the management of death to illustrate their main points. They present three dimensions of a machine metaphor which they find expressed in contemporary medicine.

	1978 (%)	1988 (%)
25–34	4	1
35–44	13	4
45–54	32	17
55–64	56	37
65–74	79*	57
75+	79*	80

* 1978 figure is average for both age groups

As a result of mechanistic thinking, hospitals rarely provide the atmosphere and rituals in which the individual's spiritual and emotional feelings about death can be freely and fully expressed and discussed. Medics and paramedics do not see this as their 'job': they are not trained and sensitised to help deal with this 'side' of death. Thus, this is one nurse's idea of role-appropriate behaviour at the impending death of a patient, quoted by Glaser and Strauss (1981):

▶

Table 16.1

Percentage lacking their own teeth (UK, by age group) – one measure of the effectiveness of scientific medicine.

A stern face, you don't have to communicate very much verbally, you put things short and formal. ... Yes, very much the nurse.

(Mishler, 1981: 241)

Osherson and Amara Singham's primary message is that 'to understand medicine truly, we must look beyond it'. Personal and cultural meaning and context are relevant to the consideration of health, illness and death. They are certainly not opposed to scientific medicine or even to all applications of mechanistic medicine, but they see a need for a broader perspective. There are, of course, others who are opposed in principle to the major forms of treatment of 'mechanistic' medicine, drugs and surgery. However, complete rejection of the biomedical paradigm is not the only response to the critique of it presented in this section.

IVAN ILLICH'S CRITIQUE OF MODERN SCIENTIFIC MEDICINE Although sometimes couched in obscure rhetoric and jargon, the brunt of Illich's critique against modern medicine is clear enough. Based in the Third World, in Mexico, the immediate object of his attack in *Limits to Medicine* (1975) is the medical establishment of the industrialised countries. Illich pitches his critique widely. He argues that medical iatrogenesis (illness caused by medicine itself) extends beyond the clinical, such as ill-advised drug use, to the social and cultural. Social iatrogenesis refers to the injury – much of it psychological – caused by the bureaucratic and impersonal way in which modern medicine is organised: it occurs when the language in which people could experience their bodies is turned into bureaucratic gobbledegook; or 'when suffering, mourning, and healing outside the patient role are labelled a form of deviance'. Cultural iatrogenesis describes the widespread acceptance of 'managed health' and failure to accept personal responsibility for one's own health. Illich also adopts the concept of 'medicalisation'. This term describes how even minor problems such as a headache or a depressive mood which individuals could often cope with, alone or with friends' help, have been 'taken over' by medical professionals.

As the Marxist Vicente Navarro acutely observes (1976), Illich's critique of modern bureaucracy in *Limits to Medicine* and other

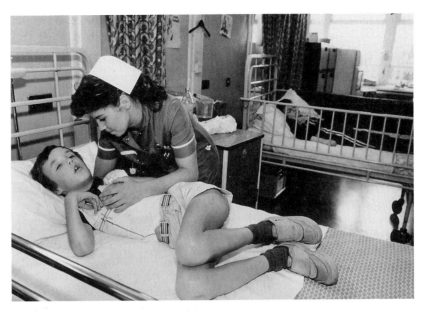

▲

Figure 16.2

works is based on a disillusionment with industrial society. Illich echoes the scepticism of Tönnies and Simmel about the 'bigness' and impersonality of modern society which they saw as undermining individual and local power and involvement in many aspects of life. These populist sentiments were revived in the nineteen sixties and early seventies when not surprisingly Illich became something of a cult figure among radical activists. From his own socialist perspective, Navarro suggests that Illich offers no real alternative principle of social organisation to capitalism. Illich's reply might well be that most socialist systems are as open to his criticisms as capitalism: democracy and participation are readily found in socialist theory and authoritarianism and bureaucracy more easily in practice.

HOLISTIC MEDICINE: A HUMANISTIC ALTERNATIVE

Holistic medicine understands health and illness not merely in biomedical terms but in total personal and cultural terms as well. Moore et al. refer to holistic medicine as a biocultural (which embraces personal/social factors) rather than simply a biomedical approach. There is wide agreement in the literature about the nature and goals of holistic medicine. The following comments by Kenneth R Pelletier define holistic attitudes to health and illness and express the humanistic emphasis of holistic medicine. By emphasising the integration of mind and body, he rejects the dualism of the bio-medical model:

Holistic medicine recognises the inextricable interaction between the person and his psychosocial environment. Mind and body function as an integrated unit, and health exists when they are in harmony, while illness results when stress and conflict disrupt this process. These approaches are essentially humanistic and re-establish an emphasis on the patient rather than upon medical technology. Modern medicine has tended to view man as a machine with interchangeable parts, and has developed sophisticated procedures for repairing, removing, or artificially constructing these parts. ... Consideration of the whole person emphasises the healing process, the maintenance of health, and the prevention of illness rather than the treatment of established disorders.

(Pelletier, 1979: 8)

The title of Pelletier's book is *Mind as Healer, Mind as Slayer: A Holistic Approach to Preventing Stress Disorders.* He contends that stress-induced disorders have substantially replaced infectious disease as the major medical problem of advanced industrial nations. In Western Europe, the United States and Japan, cardiovascular disorders, cancer, arthritis, and respiratory diseases are prime causes of ill-health and death. Pelletier argues that mental processes play a part in the contraction and management of these diseases. In making his case, he conducts an interesting incidental 'dialogue' with the language of scientific medicine in which he attempts to 'rehumanise' it. Thus, he rejects the dominant definition of 'psychosomatic' as a disorder which persists in the absence of clearly diagnosed organic pathology (and which is sometimes thought of by practitioners as 'imaginary'.) Instead, he uses the concept 'to convey ... a fundamental interaction between mind and body which is involved in all diseases and all processes affecting health maintenance'.

Pelletier describes a number of techniques for controlling stress, including meditation and biofeedback. An important aspect of both is the active involvement of the individual in maintaining his/her own health. Yet, Pelletier emphasises that it is possible to measure scientifically the effectiveness of this subjective involvement. He refers to '(n)umerous research projects (which) have demonstrated that meditation is psychologically and physiologically more refreshing and energy restoring than deep sleep'. Among the measurable indications of this in an experiment with Indian Yogis are the extreme slowing of respiration to four to six breaths per minute and a predominance of alpha brain-wave activity (associated with the absence of stress). Biofeedback is the monitoring of bodily functions to establish the effect of given factors on them. Pelletier refers to research and clinical practice which show that a large range of bodily functions normally thought to be involuntary can be brought under conscious control. These include heart rate, muscle tension, body temperature, and more experimentally, stomach acidity and white blood cells. The potential here for taking personal responsibility and action for one's own health is obvious.

There is today a wider awareness than say 30 years ago of the importance of a range of factors in health and illness among people, many of whom have barely heard of holistic medicine. This awareness gained impetus from the humanistic and naturalistic movements of the sixties. There is now greater understanding of the importance of exercise, as illustrated by the popularity of jogging, aerobics and various other workouts. The same is true of diet and stress-control. Pelletier, writing soon after the sixties, speculated that a 'profound transformation of human consciousness' was fuelling these developments. In the tough, 'realistic' nineties, it is not easy to feel that this is still so, but there has certainly emerged a lively health movement that looks beyond 'mechanistic' medicine to a more caring, humanistic approach to health (see also p. 391).

Political Economy and Health Policy

How health services are organised in a society is a central issue of social policy. Disagreements about the organisation of health services reflect differences of political and economic ideology and values, hence the title of this section. I have already described principles of conservatism, Marxism, and social democracy in the context of social policy and these same principles underlie health policy. It might be helpful to note that some of the standard texts on social and health policy use somewhat different terminology to refer to these ideologies. Thus, G Room in *The Sociology of Welfare* refers to what I call conservatism as market-liberalism, a term which reflects the roots of the ideology in eighteenth/nineteenth century laissez-faire capitalist thought. Marxism he refers to as neo-Marxism – an acceptable way of indicating that Marxist ideologies differ not only among themselves but sometimes apparently from the views of Marx. His use of the term social democracy to refer to what I sometimes term modern liberalism is common practice.

The health systems of different societies naturally reflect varying outcomes in the conflict of health policies and underlying economic and political interests. In Britain, the health services are predominantly, but not exclusively, public – a social democratic compromise. In the United States, health is mainly provided through the private market but with important elements of public involvement. The health service in Marxist China is almost entirely public and reflects elements of traditional as well as Western health care. The point of mentioning these three cases is not to suggest precise, 'ideal types' of given health policies. The outcome of real political struggle and the imperfections of policy implementation is almost always more messy than model descriptions of ideologies, as our detailed discussion of the British system will show.

The British System of Health Care

HISTORICAL

Important improvements in the health of the British people had occurred well before the setting up of the national health system in 1946. Indeed, some of these developments can be traced back to and probably beyond the mid-eighteenth century. Progress in prevention rather than cure accounts for the gradual improvement of the health of Britons up to the time when the use of new curative drugs, (notably antibiotics) became widespread in the mid-twentieth century. All the major infectious diseases – tuberculosis, typhus, measles etc. – were well in decline before antibiotics and immunisation were introduced (see figure 16.3). This was due to improvements in public and private hygiene.

First, improvements in the quality and cleanliness of the environment contributed substantially to health improvement. This was (and remains) a fundamental matter as Disraeli's reference to the need for good 'air, light and water' when speaking for what became the 1872 Public Health Act indicates. This Act codified over a century of fragmented central and local government initiative in the health field and required all local authorities to appoint medical officers of health, and sanitary inspectors. Sewage, drainage, the construction of pavements, roads and housing, street-lighting, and the

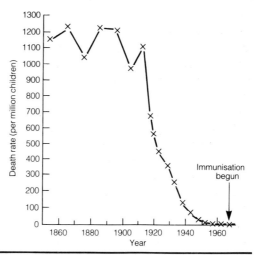

(Source: T. McKeown,
The Modern Rise of Population, 1976)

Figure 16.3

Measles death rates

of children under 15 in

England and Wales.

The decline in deaths

through measles

before immunisation

began was typical of

what happened in the

case of most infectious

diseases.

quality of food production, storage and distribution, all continued to improve. A second factor, improvement in personal and family nutrition and hygiene, is complementary to the first. Clearly the availability of running water and the existence of adequate sewage and drainage helped people to a more hygienic lifestyle. Better quality and availability of cleansing agents and utensils was also a factor as was the contribution of health education in schools, attendance at which became compulsory to the age of ten in 1880.

Third, the government took steps to

improve the quality of professional health care. Thus, in 1858 the Medical Act established a Medical Register administered by the Medical Council with the purpose of establishing and monitoring professional standards among doctors. The Certification of Midwives Act of 1902 did the same for that group and improving standards of midwifery and this no doubt contributed to the fall in child mortality in the immediately ensuing period.

Fourth, the role of government, obvious in points one and three, deserves separate mention. Both Tory and Liberal governments, often against their preferred laissez-faire principles, had repeatedly passed reforming legislation to reduce the rigours and ill-health of industrial, urban life. In the early twentieth century, the (then) major parties were further stimulated in this direction by the rise of the Labour Party. The Liberal government elected in 1905 passed a series of measures which foreshadowed the post-Second World War Welfare State. Acts were passed which used the school system to improve the nutrition (school meals) and health (medical inspections) of children. The National Insurance Act of 1911 was highly significant in the history of popular health provision. It provided financial benefits and free doctor's services for the poor. Government, employers and employees made weekly contributions to pay for the scheme which was run by private insurance companies. The Liberal package made a fundamental contribution to the basic security of the lives of millions of working people but was partly motivated by the hope of buying off socialist revolution and gaining the party working class support.

The decline in the death rate and general improvement in the population's health occurred before the invention and widespread availability of most modern 'wonder' drugs. However, these further improved matters. The infectious diseases that were the main killers before the nineteenth century, such as the 'plague', smallpox and typhus, are now curable. Instead, diseases of physical and mental degeneration such as cancer, which modern medicine has been less successful in treating, increasingly take their toll. Even so, the spread of AIDS in the nineteen eighties and nineties reminds us that new types of infectious diseases which are difficult to cure

can still develop. Again, this emphasises they key role of personal hygiene and the limitations of scientific medicine.

Finally, it is worth noting that the steep decline in infant mortality lagged behind that of adults and older children. This decrease did not occur until the birthrate itself began to drop sharply. The lesson seems to be that fewer children generally get more and better resources and attention. In addition, services for mothers and children expanded rapidly during the first quarter of the twentieth century.

THE NATIONAL HEALTH SERVICE

The National Health Service was established in 1948. It was organised into three separate parts, a 'tripartite' structure: the hospital sector, the executive council sector, and the local health authorities. Hospitals were not run by local authorities but by regional hospital boards on which consultants were strongly represented. Consultants retained the right to do some private as well as National Health Service work. Primary services to individuals and families were to be the responsibility of General Practitioners, dentists, opticians and pharmacists who were answerable to the executive council. The Local Authorities were to take care of a range of remaining health concerns including environmental health, maternity services, home helps and school services. All health services were to be free. In 1974, the tripartite structure was unified into a single hierarchical system: Secretary of State for Social Services; Department of Health and Social Security; Regional Health Authorities and Districts. Unfortunately, the level at which a (rather weak) degree of popular participation was built in – the area level – has proved ineffective and was dropped in 1982. In 1989 the Department of Health and Social Security was divided into two separate Departments.

The National Health Service was introduced to the accompaniment of much idealistic rhetoric. The setting up of the service had been one of the major recommendations of the Beveridge Report of 1942 which had been enthusiastically received by a wide public. Considerable national support for and pride in the NHS remains – making a cool assessment of its achievements difficult. Even many critics of the service's limitations and failures make it clear that they support it in principle. In any case, the achievements of the NHS are substantial. These include a much fairer distribution of General Practitioners and certain other medical services to women on a comparable basis with men – which the 1911 Act had conspicuously failed to implement, and notable comparative cost effectiveness. However, there remain substantial inequalities of health care and the NHS continues to be a highly centralised and undemocratically administered service. Whether the reforms implemented in the early nineteen nineties will improve or worsen these problems is discussed below.

Two issues – the dominance of the hospital sector of the NHS and the continuing role of private medicine – were apparent in the negotiations leading to the setting up of the system. The consultants effectively established their claim to a substantial share of resources, for research as well as practice, and to the right to practise a limited but highly lucrative amount of private medicine within NHS premises. Many consultants, therefore, seem to get the best of both worlds. More broadly, the power and prestige of the hospital sector is a prime example of the triumph of curative rather than preventive medicine in the NHS. The allocation of a large share of resources to high-level, 'scientific' medicine occurs at the expense of preventive medicine and the delivery of mass services. Another important penetration of the NHS by private profit is the operation of the drug companies. Their return on capital has typically been twice as much as that for manufacturing industry as a whole. Doctors are often bombarded with advertising for new products which are in many cases little different from existing lines. Recently, the government has promoted the buying of generic drugs (as opposed to 'brand' names) to cut costs.

After a detailed review of opinion and debate before the NHS was set up, Vivienne Walters concludes that 'the NHS was not so much a response to the difficulties working class patients experienced in obtaining care, as an attempt to rationalise an inefficient health care system and provide it with a stable financial base'. Before 1948 many people were not covered by insurance and frequently could not afford treatment. This, of course, affected the earning potential of

doctors and other medical practitioners. The NHS extended their clientele and guaranteed their income. A second point is that though the NHS functioned to improve the quality of the existing and future labour force, it certainly did not deliver control or extensive participation in the health service to working people. Government, professional, managerial and commercial interests remained dominant. These comments do not seek to detract from the immense personal benefit many, especially women and children, obtained in gaining access to free primary and hospital care for the first time.

Walters does not suggest any elite conspiracy about the way the NHS was set up. Indeed, she emphasises that neither the TUC nor the Labour Party pressed for a genuinely democratic socialist health service but broadly supported the NHS as it was set up. Lesley Doyal who, like Walters, writes from a Marxist perspective, argues that British medicine is best thought of as 'nationalised' rather than 'socialised'. She suggests that the NHS represents a definition of health by the state largely in terms of access to care. This approach has been at the expense of a more thorough exploration of 'the links between health, the organisation and delivery of health care and the nature of class relations in British society'. Echoing Althusser, she goes on to say that '(t)his suggests that the state has served an ideological function in so far as it has legitimised medical definition of health and failed to address class inequalities in health and the political bases of these'.

Doyal argues that a socialist system of health care will not be achieved in the absence of powerful working class demand and organisation for it. As it stands, the NHS is a social democratic compromise in which the state mediates the interaction of classes and interest groups in the health field within the framework of a mixed economy.

CONTINUING INEQUALITIES IN BRITISH HEALTH CARE: SECTORAL, REGIONAL AND SOCIAL CLASS

Lesley Doyal examines three aspects of NHS resource allocation – between different sectors of the NHS, between geographical regions and, most importantly, between social classes. I will follow her analysis, occasionally supplementing it with data and comment from the government commissioned report *Inequalities in Health* (1979) and other sources.

SECTORAL As was mentioned above, the hospital sector is the dominant one within the NHS. In 1948 it accounted for 55 per cent of total NHS expenditure and in 1974, 65 per cent. This inequality is increased in the case of those teaching hospitals which have private endorsements. Resource allocation between different medical specialities shows a complementary pattern. More resources are available for the acute sick, the major client population of such hospitals, and less for the chronic sick, particularly the mentally ill and handicapped, who are typically treated in non-teaching hospitals (which also receive relatively fewer resources for acute patients).

REGIONAL As far as geographical differences in resource allocation are concerned, the south fares better than the north and the richer areas better than the poorer. Despite this, matters have improved since 1948 and, according to the Inequalities in Health report, England has a more even regional distribution of doctors than other industrialised Western countries. However, the rough correspondence between the unequal geographical distribution of health resources and social inequality generally, leads Julian Tudor Hart to suggest the 'inverse care law': the more a social group has need for medical resources, the less likely it is to find them locally available.

SOCIAL CLASS AND HEALTH INEQUALITY The facts of health inequality between the social classes are well-documented. Mortality and morbidity rates are higher among the working class, especially social class V, than among the middle class. As Vivienne Walters points out, infant mortality rates 'are among the more sensitive indicators of class inequalities in health' and '(s)tatistics published since the turn of the century have consistently shown higher death rates for lower social classes and though the rates for all classes have declined, the differences between them have not narrowed'. Figure 16.5 illustrates this point.

As Lesley Doyal remarks, these continuing differences in mortality arise both from the greater incidence of 'new' diseases such as lung cancer and of 'older' diseases such as TB and bronchitis which are 'traditionally associated with poverty'. Not surprisingly, class patterns of sickness or morbidity follow the same trend as the mortality rate.

Lesley Doyal's comment after analysing much of the relevant data on morbidity and mortality has fundamental, indeed, revolutionary implications for health care:

> *These class differences in morbidity and mortality, ... provide strong evidence to support the argument that social and economic factors remain extremely important in determining the ways in which people live and die.*
>
> *(Doyal, 1979: 65)*

Relative ill-health, then, seems largely to be a product of socio-economic inequality and could be reduced with the reduction of inequality.

EXPLANATIONS OF CLASS-BASED HEALTH INEQUALITIES

What is it about social class that generates the health inequalities presented above? The *Inequalities in Health* report identifies poverty and the relatively poor access of lower social-economic groups to the knowledge and

Figure 16.4

Regional variations

in perimortality

▼

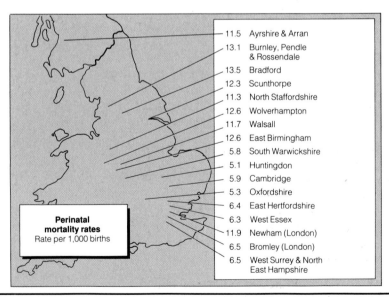

11.5	Ayrshire & Arran
13.1	Burnley, Pendle & Rossendale
13.5	Bradford
12.3	Scunthorpe
11.3	North Staffordshire
12.6	Wolverhampton
11.7	Walsall
12.6	East Birmingham
5.8	South Warwickshire
5.1	Huntingdon
5.9	Cambridge
5.3	Oxfordshire
6.4	East Hertfordshire
6.3	West Essex
11.9	Newham (London)
6.5	Bromley (London)
6.5	West Surrey & North East Hampshire

Perinatal mortality rates
Rate per 1,000 births

Note: The variation in perinatal mortality rates between London's affluent Bramley and less well off Newham indicate that social factors are more important than regional ones in explaining inequalities.

(Source: *The Times*, 23rd March, 1990)

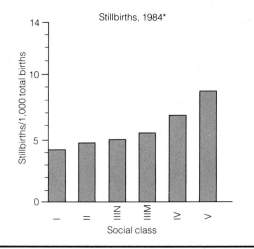

Stillbirths, 1984*

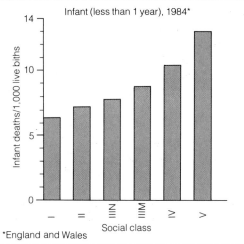

Infant (less than 1 year), 1984*

*England and Wales

(Source: OPCS in *Inequalities in Health* 1988: 229)

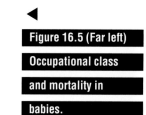

inequality in the values, attitudes and behaviour of the lower class which are passed on from generation to generation (see pp. 158–9).

MARXIST PERSPECTIVES ON CLASS-BASED HEALTH INEQUALITIES

Marxists, such as Doyal, consider that health inequality is reproduced throughout the major institutional areas of capitalist society. The system of private profit generates this inequality and she traces health inequality through the processes of production and consumption. She shows that health inequality does, indeed, begin at the point of production. Industrial accidents and disease tend to occur more often in traditional working class occupational areas such as mining, construction and railways. In part, this is due to the nature of heavy manual work but more could be done to secure a safer working environment. For instance, in 1975–76, 59 miners were killed at work, 538 seriously injured, and 52,946 injured and off work for more than three days. The toll of industrial disease among miners is particularly high. About 30,000 still suffer to some degree from lung disease and in 1973, 367 deaths were officially declared to be caused by the lung disease pneumoconiosis. Doyal argues that the two major potential defenders of the working class – trade unions and the state – have not been very effective in achieving adequate enforcement of industrial health and safety legal regulations. For example, there are still very few factory inspectors for all the workplaces to be visited and even when successful prosecutions do occur, penalties are often very light.

Doyal states the problem of the production/consumption of unhealthy items sharply:

Commodities are being produced for sale and consumed at an ever-increasing rate, and a great many of these products are not 'useful' according to any commonsense definition of the term. More than this, they may actually damage the health of consumers. ·
(Doyal, 1979: 80)

For discussion of the issue of consumption I will adopt Doyal's examples of tobacco and certain processed foods, though I am responsible for the detailed commentary. Despite the known correlation between

resources which help to maintain health. So both the cultural and material disadvantages of the working class are indicated as causal factors, with the latter considered to be the more fundamental. Health inequality is simply a function of basic social inequality. The health of the working class, particularly the lower working class, would improve if it had 'sufficient household income, a safe, uncrowded and unpolluted home, warmth and hygiene, and means of rapid communication with the outside world'.

There are potentially as many explanations of the poorer health of the working class and of solutions to it as there are of poverty itself. The *Inequalities in Health* report itself takes a radical social democratic line, arguing for a significant increase in income, resources and services (including health services) for the needy and especially for children. The most fatalistic is the Conservative version of the culture of poverty thesis, which locates the causes of tobacco smoking and lung cancer, the government allows a situation in which the public is overwhelmingly encouraged rather than discouraged to smoke (for instance, in 1975 between £50–70 million was spent on the former, and £1 million on the latter). It is not only the massive quantity of tobacco, particularly cigarette advertising, but the insidious nature of it that seems to be effective. Appeals are variously made to status, masculinity, femininity, and 'cool-ness' depending on the brand and the 'bright ideas' of the 'creative' (advertising) depart-ment. Members of the public sometimes claim that they are 'not affected' by such advertising beyond being amused or enter-tained in passing. One wonders, however, whether if the proportion spent on encouraging and discouraging tobacco smoking were reversed tobacco consumption would remain stable.

There are social class and gender dimensions to tobacco consumption. As information has spread to the public about the unhealthy effects of tobacco, rates of consumption have fallen among higher socio-economic groups but not among lower. Speculatively, it may be that working class people are more aware of and affected by pro-tobacco television advertising than even the popularised versions of scientific evidence on its harmful effects. It may also be that 'having a smoke' or 'a fag' is more deeply embedded in the culture of working class relaxation. Smoking may be felt as a necessary release from the stress of hard, physical work (even though, in fact, it increases stress in the long run). The rapid growth in tobacco consumption among working class women may also be related to the increasing number who work in the occupational as well as the domestic economy. Smoking may be experienced as a crutch against the pressures of dual roles.

A variety of reasons are cited for the government's tolerance of the above situation. First, the government relies for a significant part of its tax revenue on the sale of tobacco – rather less than five per cent in 1975. Second, the tobacco industry is a powerful and well organised lobby. It has presented an appearance of compromise such as developing 'safer' cigarettes and acquiescing in the banning of cigarette advertising in cinemas whilst managing to

retain the bulk of its commercial freedom. Third, Britain is predominantly a capitalist society and to control an established area of free enterprise may be ideologically repugnant to some and seem to set an undesirable precedent. Finally, perhaps a society as well as an individual can become addicted to a bad habit. Apparently, the collective will to 'kick it' is not yet here.

There have been several significant changes in dietary patterns in Britain over the last 150 years. Whilst food is more abundant and usually more sanitary, there is often cause for concern about its content – or lack of certain content. Between 1860 and 1960, it is estimated that the average annual consumption of refined sugar doubled, while that of fat increased by 50 per cent whereas the consumption of fibre decreased by 90 per cent. Increasingly, dietary experts regard these developments as unhealthy especially where there is little balancing intake of fresh vegetables and fruit which is more likely to be the case among the working class. The processing of food is a significant feature in the above trends. Processing creates homogenous (consistent) and long-lasting products, i.e. the product always tastes the same and has a long shelf-life. Processing also forms and even stimulates taste and consumption by, for instance, adding sugar or other sweeteners. There is obvious commercial advantage in all this. This is achieved mainly by chemical and other additives but what is taken out of many natural products must also be considered. Thus, refined sugar and processed bread lose many natural nutrients (which may or may not be artificially replaced). Sometimes, what is removed is sold as a separate product to increase profit.

CRITICISMS OF MARXIST PERSPEC-TIVES: NICKY HART Nicky Hart uses the comparative method to criticise Doyal's linkage of ill-health to the capitalist system of production and consumption. She cites data which show that the rates for death caused by industrial accidents were somewhat higher in the (then) socialist societies of Czechoslovakia and Hungary than in Britain, and that whilst lung cancer caused a higher proportion of deaths in Britain the rate for circulatory disease was rather lower. Hart argues that the 'drive for industrialisation' and the lack of workers' freedom to protect themselves may account for these rather higher rates. She also observes that a substantial improvement in the general level of health has occurred in Britain under capitalism. Recent figures on the percentages of people in various age-groups now keeping their own teeth provide an effective, if mundane, illustration of Hart's point. (See table 16.1, p. 378).

SOCIAL CLASS: NEGOTIATING HEALTH

As Doyal notes, ever since the inception of the NHS, there has been a continuing debate about whether working or middle class patients use it most. Simplifying somewhat, it seems that the working class use curative services more than the middle class but not to the extent that their need implies, given their higher morbidity and mortality rates. However, the middle class use a broader range of services particularly of a preventive kind such as mass miniature radiography, cervical cytology, and antenatal and postnatal care. On the issue of quality as distinct from quantity of service, the middle class appear to be at an advantage. This is largely because facilities and availability of services tend to be better in middle class areas.

The comparative quality of social relationships requires consideration as well as the material and technical quality of health care. Interactionist as well as structural perspective is helpful here. Structural perspective suggests that middle class patients may come to medical practitioners with a number of cultural advantages such as language skills and greater self-assurance. As David Tuckett puts it, the absence of these in working class patients 'may hinder a relationship of mutual participation', leaving power and decision-making entirely in the practitioner's hands. Interactionist perspective is helpful in understanding the detail of the doctor-patient relationship, particularly in the matter of negotiation or lack of it. Negative labelling may occur for a variety of reasons in addition to social class. Irving Zola gives an interesting example of the negative labelling of Italians resulting in the self-fulfilling prophecy of illness in a comparative study of the treatment of various ethnic groups in Boston. He found that in cases where no organic basis for illness was discovered, Italians were consistently diagnosed as having some psychological difficulty such as personality disorder or tension headaches, whereas Irish and Anglo-Saxon were usually diagnosed as having nothing wrong with them. Zola suggests that doctors were able to prise symptoms out of the more voluble and dramatic behaviour of the Italians in a situation in which illness was being looked for. I am not aware of any comparable study of the possible labelling of ethnic groups in the NHS but the much higher diagnosed rates of mental illness among the Afro-Caribbean community suggests that the issue might be worth researching in that context.

Conservative Health Policy, 1979-92

Great controversy surrounded the Conservative government's health reforms introduced in the late nineteen eighties and implemented in the early nineteen nineties. These reforms made radical changes in the NHS but the aims behind them were consistent with those of the first two Thatcher governments in relation to health policy.

In the early nineteen eighties, government ministers frequently emphasised the need for efficiency and value for money in the public services, including health. This was a change from previous prime concern with inequalities of health. The government was acutely conscious of the increased demands an ageing population would continue to put on the NHS. Several policies had a major cost-cutting element about them including a sharp reduction in the amount of time patients spent in hospital, a reduction of 25 per cent in the number of hospital beds between 1977 and 1989, and the community care policy (see p. 366). Nevertheless, overall spending on the NHS more or less kept pace with the rise in gross domestic product during the nineteen eighties (see figure 16.6). This was partly because short-stay hospital visits greatly increased in numbers.

By the late nineteen eighties, the government was looking for new ways to increase efficiency (or productivity) and keep costs down in the NHS. As described in the previous chapter, it was during this period that the strategy of introducing quasi-

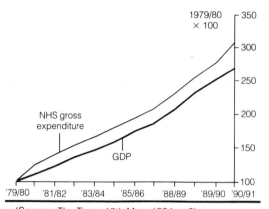

NHS gross expenditure

GDP

1979/80 × 100

(Source: *The Times* 10th May, 1991, p.2)

Figure 16.6
NHS spending
compared to GDP.

Figure 16.8 (Far right)
Health markets
within the NHS

Figure 16.7
Organisation of the
NHS in England, 1990.

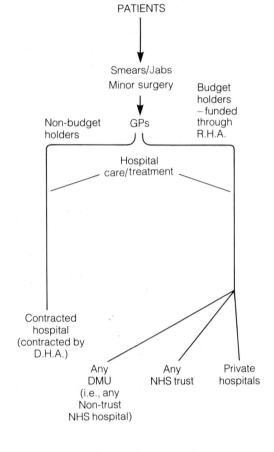

markets into the public services was adopted (see pp. 368–9). A quasi-market is an attempt to introduce the conditions of the free-market into the public sector, including public services. Quasi markets in the public sector are often referred to as internal markets. Before examining how this strategy has been applied to health it is necessary to be clear about the organisational structure of the NHS (see figure 16.7).

In outline, the structure of the NHS in 1990 was not fundamentally different from what it had been since it was set up in 1948 (see p. 382). The Secretary of State for Health is at the top of the managerial chain and is responsible to Parliament. The fourteen Regional Authorities are responsible for

planning the development of services within national guidelines. They allocate resources to and monitor the performance of District Health Authorities and Family Health Services Authorities. The 189 District Health Authorities are responsible for purchasing hospital and community health services for their residents. The DHAs work closely with Family Health Services Authorities which manage the 'grassroots' services of general medical practitioners, general dental practitioners, retail pharmacists, and opticians. Hospitals which have opted for the new trust status (see figure 16.8) are not contractually tied to DHAs to deliver hospital services to the local area, as other hospitals are. They can deliver their services 'in the market' – to any DHA or private individual (in the latter case they cannot use NHS funds although some access to NHS facilities and equipment is allowed). Briefly, Special Health Authorities have very particular purposes, such as overseeing medical training. The Community Health Councils

SECRETARY OF STATE FOR HEALTH

Department of Health
Policy Board
NHS Management Executive

Special Health Authorites

Regional Health Authorities

NHS Trusts ('opted out' hospitals)

District Health Authorities

Family Health Services Authorities

Community Health Councils

are advisory bodies representing the public interest which are outside the NHS management chain.

Some further description is required in order to clarify how a quasi-market has been introduced into the NHS. The quasi-market operates mainly through NHS Hospital Trusts, described above, and through those General Medical Practitioners (local doctors) who have been given their own budgets to administer (about seven per cent of the total by 1991). In both cases, funding comes from central government. Unlike other doctors, budget holding doctors are not contracted to hospitals managed by DHAs but can buy hospital services for their patients wherever they choose – from trusts, private hospitals, or the directly managed units (hospitals) of the District Health Authorities. Figure 16.8 compares and contrasts the situation of non-budget and budget holding GPs.

THE CONSERVATIVE HEALTH REFORMS: FOR AND AGAINST

The aim of the above reforms is to limit the cost of health services without cutting patient care or, put simply, to increase productivity in the provision of health services. The mechanism for doing this is to introduce an element of competition by creating a limited medical marketplace. Only time will establish whether effectiveness and fairness is achieved by the reforms.

Was there need for the above changes or are they more the product of a stubborn commitment to right-wing ideology? The Conservative government has not been able to claim that the National Health Service has been expensive compared to the cost of 'delivering' health in other advanced countries. As table 16.2 shows, spending on health as a percentage of the gross national product is exceptionally low. Moreover, it is clear that this economy has been achieved overwhelmingly within the public sector as the private health sector in Britain, although steadily expanding, is still relatively small.

Such seemingly impressive figures to the NHS do not mean that greater improvement is impossible. The Conservatives have pointed to the fact that considerable differences between districts in the length of waiting lists and, more controversially, success in specific treatments. Table 16.3 illustrates the more extreme differences in

relation to waiting lists for general surgery.

The assumption behind the reforms is that under the new competitive regime within the NHS there will be an all-round improvement in the performance of hospitals and particularly of the less efficient ones.

The most common criticism of the reforms made by opposing politicians is that they have created a 'two tier health service'. GP budget holders are able to buy 'the best' whereas non-budget holders are contracted to a specific hospital. In the early days of the reform, budget holders were able to 'jump queues' on behalf of their patients and it is not clear whether this will continue or not.

Spending on Health as a Percentage of GDP, 1989		Total Health Spending, 1987	
		PUBLIC	PRIVATE
8.7	France	74.7	25.3
8.2	Germany	78.4	21.6
6.7	Japan	72.9	27.1
8.3	Netherlands	73.8	26.2
6.3	Spain	71	29
8.8	Sweden	90.8	9.2
5.8	UK	86.4	13.6
11.8	US	41.4	58.6

(Source: OECD)

▲

Table 16.2

District	Patients on list	% waiting over a year
East Cumbria	1,262	42
Hull	1,515	51
North Herts	1,415	46
West Essex	2,332	45
Brentwood	2,363	44
West Lambeth	872	72
NE Hants	903	52
Salisbury	969	51
Bristol	2,296	52
Oldham	1,661	45
St Helens	237	0
Halton	115	1
NW Durham	113	1
East Yorks	293	0
Bassetlaw	82	0
Cambridge	361	3
SW Herts	267	0
West Dorset	471	7
Southmead	58	19
Bromsgrove	263	0

(Source: The Guardian, August 2, 1990:2).

◄

Table 16.3

Health districts with some of the longest and shortest waiting lists for general surgery (March 1989)

Underlying the 'two tier' accusation, is a perhaps even more serious one: that both the principle of equal treatment on the basis of need and the means of achieving it are in danger of being discarded. On the issue of principle, it does appear that some patients can obtain preferential treatment on the basis of the budget holding system ('some are more equal than others'). Historically, the means of achieving equality of access and treatment based on need have been the District Health Authorities. Rather like local education authorities in relation to 'opted out' schools, the DHAs now can no longer plan the health services of all NHS patients within their areas with power to use full,

available resources or expertise (because 'opted out' hospitals and budget-holding GPs are independent of them).

A major criticism of the NHS prior to the above reforms was that inequalities in meeting health needs occurred because of relative inefficiencies within the system. A major criticism of the NHS after the introduction of these reforms is that it is in danger of becoming, if it has not already become, a system which is basically unequal in the way it delivers treatment and care. How this matter develops or is perceived by the electorate to develop may well remain one of the top two or three political issues of the nineteen nineties.

Gender and Health

This section examines gender and health in the context of the power and status of women within the health professions and in relation to the 'medicalisation of childbirth'. Further, discussion of the issue of fertility occurs in chapter 20, pp. 460–2. The important work which women do as informal and largely unpaid providers of health care was discussed in chapter 15, pp. 370–2.

The dimension of gender cuts through health as it does through other aspects of life. In general, health services are managed by men and 'manned' at the lower levels by women. According to figures published in 1975, women occupied only eight seats out of 253 on the major committees of the British Medical Association and only four out of 46 members of the General Medical Council were women. Although nearly 80 per cent of employees in medical and other health and veterinary services are female (1983) only about 25 per cent of doctors are female – well reflecting the 'doctors and nurses' stereo-typing of childhood. Yet there is nothing 'natural' in these figures as comparative data show. In the USA women make up 8 per cent of doctors, in Finland 24 per cent, in Poland 46 per cent and in the former USSR 74 per cent. In the Eastern European socialist societies childcare and health are associated areas, heavily supported by the state, which present women with a wide range of career choices. Even though women are much less well represented at the policy-making level in the socialist societies, the general pattern in

the health professions is much less patriarchal than in Britain and the United States.

We now consider the quality of care provided by the health services and, in particular, what Ann Oakley refers to as the 'medicalisation' of childbirth. Health care can intrude into what is normally regarded as core personal space – the body (and, in the case of mental health, the mind). Quite obviously, sex differences can play a major part in the dispensing and experience of health care. Female fertility is the key differentiating factor. A pregnant female, whether she gives birth or terminates, embarks upon a series of experiences unavailable to the male. Yet, it is usually males who attempt to manage these experiences. Let us take the case of childbirth. In *Women Confined: Towards a Sociology of Childbirth* (1980), Ann Oakley identifies five features of what she refers to as the 'medical frame of reference' which she describes as 'a qualitatively different way of looking at the nature, context and management of reproduction' from that of mothers. These are the five features:

a) the definition of reproduction as a specialist subject in which only doctors are experts in the entire symptomatology of childbearing;

b) the associated definition of reproduction as a medical subject, as exactly analogous to other pathological processes as topics of medical knowledge and intervention;

c) the selection of limited criteria of reproductive success, i.e. perinatal and maternal mortality rates;

d) the divorce of reproduction from its social context, pregnant parenthood being seen as women's only relevant status;

e) the restriction of women to maternity – their derived typification as 'by nature' maternal, domesticated, family-oriented people.

After an extensive critique of the above 'medicalised' model of childbirth, Oakley tries to establish the subjective reality of childbirth. It is a complex human experience, involving losses and gains and often unmet expectations. Her proposals for changes in the management of birth indicate the direction of her argument: an end to unnecessary medical intervention in childbirth, the re-domestication of birth, a return to female-controlled childbirth and the provision of therapeutic support for women after childbirth. (It will be clear from the above that as well as attacking the medical framework of childbirth, she also seeks to demolish popular romantic conceptualisations of childbirth and motherhood.)

Significantly, Oakley's arguments are applicable to the general paradigm of 'mechanistic' medicine as well as to the particular case of medicalised childbirth. (See also chapter 8 pp. 170–1 for further analysis of scientific medicine and gender.) Male domination and scientific domination (though not science itself) are presented as twin partners in the repression of not only womankind, but of humankind. Accordingly, her proposals for change extend beyond birth to the bringing up of children and to the wider social context. These proposals have much in common with those offered in Anna Coote's social policy package described in the previous chapter (pp. 370–2).

Health in the Third World

For far more people in the Third World than in the West, health is an urgent matter of life and death. As we will see, the people most at risk are children (see pp. 458–63). It was probably the death and threat of death to children, particularly, that sparked the worldwide response to famine in Ethiopia in 1985. I have attempted to cover the main policy issues concerning the health of Third World children in chapter 20: here the emphasis is on the broader theories linking development or underdevelopment with health.

Modernisation theory provides limited insight into this matter and a better starting point is the free-market theory of Peter Bauer and the new Conservatism. His comments on birth control and population are pertinent to health. He criticises internationally-funded birth control programmes in the same terms that he criticises international aid – they interfere with the processes of choice and with the real limitations of circumstances which for him define socio-economic life. A first criticism of Bauer is that many (probably millions) of preventable deaths will occur if what he regards as natural forces are left to work themselves out. The chances of wage and subsistence economies sustaining the population of poorer 'developing' countries, particularly in sub-Saharan Africa, are remote. Second, there is nothing essentially natural in the economic and social relations of the developed and undeveloped world. The contrary is equally arguable. The impact of the West on many primitive and traditional societies has been chaotic and often destructive, as well as sometimes beneficial (see below). Third, it is entirely subjective (though germane to his theory) to regard help organised by governments and international agencies as somehow unnatural and interfering.

What differentiates liberal social-democrats from Bauer and his ilk is the acceptance of the last thee points. The Brandt Report, for instance, takes a broadly capitalist world economy for granted but seeks to modify the negative effects of its distortions and failings. Thus, it advocates help for those exploited by or struggling within the capitalist world economy – ultimately as a matter of 'mutual interest' (see pp. 483–4). Clearly these arguments apply rather more urgently to health than many other matters. On the matter of hunger and food, Brandt says simply: 'there must be an end to mass hunger and malnutrition': mainly by a combination of improving the food producing capacity of developing countries and by increasing food aid.

Marxist scholars argue that historical and contemporary capitalism has grossly exploited the health as well as the labour of the peoples of the Third World. Authors such as Teresa Hayter and Lesley Doyal amply illustrate that the spread of disease, slaughter and massive social and psychological disruption were typical products of European expansion. The slave trade is perhaps the most vivid example, although it was not only the enslaved whose lives and health were threatened through contact with Europeans. In the nineteenth and early twentieth century, the migrant labour system in sub-Saharan Africa resulted, in Lesley Doyal's assessment, in a deterioration in the health of the workers involved. Contact with Europeans and European diseases, the unhealthy living and working conditions imposed on the labour force, and the disruption of the traditional rural economy undermined the health of men, women and children. The argument that the economic interest of employers favoured a healthy labour force hardly applied – a common pattern was to send unhealthy workers back to their villages and simply recruit more. The break-up of families and communities, the isolation of males in labour compounds and the frequent poverty of women and children, resulted in an increase in alcoholism and prostitution. Ironically, some colonialists saw the poor and unhealthy life they had created for Africans as proof of black inferiority.

Although Marxists welcome the achievement of political independence by colonial nations, they stress that in the 'post-colonial era', the economic dependency of much of the Third World continues. Vicente Navarro's *Medicine Under Capitalism* (1976) is a study of health inequality in the Third World which complements Gunder Frank's broader theory of underdevelopment. Like Frank, he takes Latin America as his area for detailed study. In countries such as Colombia, Peru and El Salvador, he typically finds urban enclaves of privileged bourgeois consumption and largely poor and exploited rural areas. In health terms, this translates into the consumption of largely private, curative medicine for the urban rich and a lack of investment in preventative measures, such as water and sewage projects that would benefit the rural majority. Nor is the wider development that might ultimately benefit the standard of living and health of the majority occurring:

The industrial sector ... is controlled by and functions for the lumpen-bourgeoisie and its foreign counterparts, not for the benefit of the development of the whole of the individual country.
(Navarro, 1976: 41)

Communist China provides an interesting example of a socialist solution to the health problems of a developing nation. When the communists came to power in 1949, they were faced with widespread famine and disease and a broken-down and inadequate system of medical care. Emphasis was put on sanitation and other forms of prevention such as inoculation and the Chinese also developed a tiered medical system which has been an influential model to other developing socialist societies. The base of the system is made up of the tens of thousands of 'barefoot' doctors who provide a basic medical service designed to reach all the peasantry. They receive a maximum of eighteen months training which combines Western medicine with traditional Chinese medicine, particularly herbal treatment and acupuncture. In addition, the doctors stress the role of personal and communal responsibility for health. A similar system of grassroots medical care operates in urban areas, but here more developed and professional facilities are usually available. Medical problems that cannot be treated by a 'barefoot' doctor can be referred to more fully trained doctors and nurses. Hospitalisation is also possible where necessary. Part of the cost of the Chinese health system is financed by individual payments or insurance, nevertheless, it seems broadly egalitarian and effective.

Mental Health and Illness

PSYCHIATRY

The biomedical model of medicine is perhaps most sternly tested in its application to mental illness. The classic example of this model in mental health is the psychiatric hospital which commonly relies on drug-based treatments. First, the organic basis, if any, of a mental illness is much harder to establish than in physical illness. Thus, chemical changes in the brain seem to accompany schizophrenia, but precisely what relationship these have to the values, attitudes and behaviours of schizophrenia is quite unclear. Second, partly because the etiology (causes) of mental illness are so unclear, effective scientific treatments of mental illnesses have proved particularly difficult to develop. Third, the very label mental illness has been called into question in a way that reference to physical illness could hardly be questioned (see below). Fourth, there is evidence that those who claim to be able to recognise scientifically (diagnose) the symptoms of mental illness cannot do so reliably.

The last point requires substantiation as it implies scepticism of a body of 'expert' opinion which is widely, though far from universally, accepted. D L Rosenhan's *On Being Sane in Insane Places* (1978) reports two experiments which test the claims of scientific psychiatry on its own traditional territory, the psychiatric hospital. The first experiment describes how eight sane people gained secret admission to twelve different hospitals. Apart from alleging certain symptoms, and falsifying name, vocation and employment, no further alterations were made. After admission – which was gained in every case – the pseudopatient ceased simulating any symptoms of abnormality. Despite their normal behaviour following admission, none of the pseudopatients were detected. All, apart from one, were admitted with the diagnosis of schizophrenia, and each was discharged, not as wrongly diagnosed, but with a diagnosis of schizophrenia 'in remission'. Length of hospitalisations ranged from seven to 52 days, with an average of nineteen. Rosenhan comments:

The label 'in remission' should in no way be dismissed as a formality, for at no time during any hospitalisation had any question been raised about any pseudopatient's simulation. Nor are there any indications in the hospital records that the pseudopatient's status was suspect. Rather, the evidence is strong that, once labelled schizophrenic, the pseudopatient was stuck with that label.

(Rosenhan, 1978)

As Rosenhan observes, whereas labels of physical illness are not commonly pejorative, psychiatric labels are. The failure of the psychiatrists to change their diagnosis contrasts vividly with the observations of many ward patients that the pseudopatients were normal (35 out of 118 patients made comments to this effect on the first three cases, when accurate counts were kept).

The reports of the pseudopatients also provide data on the experience of being in a psychiatric hospital. The fact that patients appear to have made more accurate observations than psychiatrists on the conditions of the pseudopatients indicates that their experience in relation to the hospital power structure was profoundly de-personalising. In this respect, the findings complement those of Erving Goffman's study *Asylum* to which Rosenhan sympathetically refers (see pp. 276–7).

In critically scrutinising his own findings, Rosenhan raises the possibility that there may be a tendency in psychiatry, as in medicine, to diagnose illness rather than health – 'to be on the safe side' (referred to by statisticians as the type two error – a false positive). An experiment was therefore arranged to test the reverse tendency – to diagnose the (supposedly) insane as sane. The staff at a research and teaching hospital were told that in the course of the next three months, one or more pseudopatients would attempt to gain admittance. Staff were asked to rate each patient according to likelihood of pseudopatient status on a scale of one to ten, with one and two reflecting high confidence that the person was a pseudopatient. Judgements were obtained on 193 patients from all staff with whom they had contact – attendants, nurses, psychiatrists, physicians and psychologists.

Forty-one were considered with high confidence to be pseudopatients by at least one member of staff. 23 judged suspect by at least one psychiatrist, and nineteen suspected by one psychiatrist and one member of staff. In fact, no pseudopatients from Rosenhan's group presented themselves during this period. Rosenhan comments:

The experiment is instructive. It indicates that the tendency to designate sane people as insane can be reversed when the stakes (in this case, prestige and diagnostic acumen) are high. But what can be said of the nineteen people who were suspected of being 'sane' by one psychiatrist and another staff member? Were these people truly 'sane', or was it rather the case that in the course of avoiding the type two error the staff tended to make more errors of the first sort – calling the crazy 'sane'? There is no way of knowing. But one thing is certain: any diagnostic process that lends itself so readily to massive errors of this sort cannot be a very reliable one.

(Rosenhan, 1978)

PSYCHOANALYSIS

In his two books, *The Myth of Mental Illness* (1960) and *The Myth of Psychotherapy* (1985), Thomas Szasz rejects altogether the labels mental illness (and the accompanying stigma) and psychotherapy (and the accompanying mystery of cure). He replaces them with the proposition that people have problems in living about which they may have conversations (i.e. seek solutions). In rejecting the biomedical model of mental illness, he insists that complexities of behaviour and communication should not be reduced to the organic level. He argues that the label mental illness obscures what in fact is a normative judgement: people call others mad when they do not like them or when they disagree with their behaviour. In his view, normative disagreements should be stated and resolved not in medical terms but in social, legal and ethical ones. Thus chronic hostility should not be seen as a mental problem but as an ethical and social one. In surveying the vast and various range of 'psychotherapies' in his more recent book, Szasz argues that most of them are of no more than some help in solving problems,

rather than the comprehensive cure-alls some claim to be. At worst, some of these therapies are bogus 'rip-offs' as well as confusing and confused 'mumbo-jumbo'.

In comment, Szasz's work leaves more than a doubt that there are certain conditions and related behaviours for which the term mental illness may still be appropriate, viz. those for which no apparent rational explanation exists. Thus, the notion of mental illness could be relevant in the case of a 'schizophrenic' who murders his mother for no apparently 'rational' motive, whereas it would not apply to an otherwise 'normal' person who murders his mother for a comprehensible motive such as to speed his inheritance. Of course, to take this view, is to make a judgement about what is rational, which Szasz would consider subjective. Szasz's own argument attempts to restore to normality a huge range of problems frequently regarded as instances of mental illness – depression, chronic hostility and repression. He attacks the almost religious mystique that has developed around therapy, at the centre of which is the psychotherapist as priest or guru – the only one with sacred access to the temple of psychic mysteries. Instead, he suggests that people talk about their problems – to friends or to others who may help, including, sometimes, psychotherapists.

Michel Foucault's 'archaeological' approach to the 'history of madness' in *Madness and Civilization* also treats mental illness in a non-judgemental way. Foucault's method is to ignore current and recent writings on madness in the past and to immerse himself in primary sources. Just as an archaeologist reassembles artifacts from the past, so Foucault reassembles cultural attitudes and ideas. He deliberately avoids defining madness because what is regarded as mad and reactions to madness vary from period to period. Thus, the medieval world maintained an uncertain but persistent dialogue with madness. Madness was not without meaning as the influential figure of the court 'fool' indicates. The 'Age of Reason' incarcerated the mad and madness as the unwanted opposite of its own rationality. Foucalt extended his scepticism to what he takes to be a positivist approach to mental illness in our own time. Madness becomes the alienated object of science with which there is no meaningful discourse.

The view that contemporary treatments of mental illness may be subject to cultural limitations is sometimes seen as radical. Certainly, the above perspectives suggest that the claims to expert status and reliable knowledge of psychiatrists and psycho-therapists merit close examination. Drugs and gurus may provide temporary escape, but finding answers to problems requires a more demanding personal and social inquiry.

Sociological and Social Policy Perspectives on Health: A Review

The emphasis of this chapter has been on health policy. As a result, the political perspectives of free-market conservatism, liberal social-democracy, and Marxism have been more prominent than sociological ones. The second major emphasis of the chapter – on paradigms of health – was presented mainly in comparative historical and cultural terms rather than on a sociological perspectives basis. It might be helpful, therefore, to summarise the various sociological perspectives on health.

MARXISM

In the case of Marxism, political and sociological perspective are closely related: The analysis of what 'ought to be' is implicit in the analysis of what 'is'. Marxist analysis of health begins, as with other matters, with the economic system and particularly relations to the means of production. Thus, Lesley Doyal explains the poorer health of the working class in historical and contemporary capitalist society by reference to the exploitation of their labour. Both she and Vivienne Walters then analyse the whole complex of working class health and ill-health – including the workplace, housing, the environment, commodity consumption, use of and access to health facilities – in terms of social class inequality. In her analysis of British colonial Africa, Doyal shows how the exploitation of labour and resources led to a disruption of local cultural and environmental stability, leading to widespread ill-health. In the post-colonial period, the multi-national company is seen by both Doyal and Vicente Navarro as the main agent of Western domination of the Third World. Navarro, in particular, argues that the structure of health inequality in the Third World (Latin America is his example) is a product of underdevelopment. Foreign and domestic capitalists and the upper middle class consume quality health care whereas the peasantry and the poorest elements in the urban population suffer scarcity. Neither foreign nor domestic capitalists are primarily committed to development which would benefit the majority. The former seek resources and cheap labour but their products are sold mainly in the advanced countries whereas the latter are more concerned with their own consumption than developing mass domestic production and markets. Thus, underdevelopment, including health underdevelopment, occurs. According to Navarro, Rostow's 'take-off' stage of development which requires mass domestic consumption and would improve the general quality of life, including the level of health, is hampered by the economic domination of the multinationals.

Navarro's disagreement with modern-isation theory extends even to a sharp critique of the radical populist, Ivan Illich. Problems that the latter attributes to modern science and organisation, Navarro attributes to capitalist control of these areas.

FUNCTIONALISM

Functionalist perspective on social welfare indicates that the 'mass' health policies of modern societies represents 'adjustments' to popular pressure for an improved environment and health facilities and also serve the function of maintaining a healthy labour force. However, it is Talcott Parsons' analysis of the sick role that has been the seminal functionalist work of the post-war period in this field.

He defines sickness as a form of deviant behaviour which, like crime, requires a social response (1951). He presents four cultural expectations which he felt the sick person typically understands and accepts when adopting the sick role:

1 relief from normal duties;
2 non-responsibility for own condition and cure;
3 that the condition is undesirable and the patient must want to get well;
4 medical help should be sought.

By structuring the sick role in this way, society asserts control over and copes with sickness. Left to themselves, the sick might be a considerable source of havoc and hamper the well functioning of society. Acceptance of the sick role contains the problem and implies an intent to 'get back to normal'.

Parsons' concept of the sick role has generated much research and comment. He himself observed that not all ill people accept that they are sick. Some 'fight it', literally until they drop, and such behaviour can obviously cause problems. Various studies have examined whether all 'sick' people do, in fact, accept the four expectations. Thus, the notion that the sick person must want to get better (3) does not appear to be accepted in the case of those with chronic afflictions. Similarly, reliance on others for cure (2 and 4) has limited applicability to those seeking psychoanalysis because most analysts require clients to participate in their own recovery. Arguably, this expectation is becoming more widespread in most branches of medicine and to that extent Parsons' model of the sick role is beginning to date.

Two further criticisms can be made of Parsons' model. First, his tendency to describe the sick role as rather helpless and dependent on the medical 'expert' lays him open to the now familiar criticisms of over-scientific medicine. Second, in presenting the social structuring of the sick role primarily in terms of society's need for maintaining order and stability, he fails to explore the links between capitalism and ill-health. Rather, he assumes that the relationship between (capitalist) development and health is positive. As we have seen conflict theorists provide contrary analysis and evidence.

INTERACTIONISM

The premise of interactionism is that people create meaning through symbolic communication. This perspective is helpful in understanding the various paradigms of health presented in the first section of this chapter. Thus, the magical and scientific paradigms of health describe two very different, but internally consistent, frameworks of thinking and action. Interactionists explore the idea that people create their own reality at the micro level of interaction as well as at the macro-cultural level. As this chapter has illustrated, concepts such as negotiation, labelling and self-fulfilling prophecy illuminate the doctor-patient relationship as much as, for instance, the teacher-student one. Analysis of negotiational dynamics is most effective when important variables such as the class, gender and ethnicity of the participants are considered.

Despite the insight interactionism provides into cultural processes it is not a fully developed theory of social structure. This is because it does not adequately address the issue of power. Often, interactionists are a little vague about who has power and how it is used or, they adopt liberal-pluralist, functionalist or marxist theories of power. In the area of health and health policy, as in others, interactionist can supplement (and sometimes humanise) the major structural perspectives.

LIBERAL REFORMISM AND FREE MARKET LIBERALISM

Much of this chapter has been devoted to discussing these two forms of liberal perspective in relation to health. Liberal reformism or social democratic reformism was the dominant philosophy underlying the NHS from its founding in 1948 to the late nineteen seventies. Few doubted that the driving motivation behind the NHS was to provide equal access to equal health services on the basis of need.

The policy of quasi- or internal markets has introduced into the NHS a principle of competition which appears to have an inherent aspect of inequality – 'winners' and 'losers' are produced, i.e. some patients systematically get quicker and/or better health care than others. The purpose of introducing competition is to achieve greater efficiency in terms of cost and delivery (although the NHS was already relatively efficient in cost terms prior to the introduction of the reforms). The reforms themselves had by mid-1991 cost £2 billion. Critics argue that this money could have been better spent increasing NHS resources.

Indeed, social democrats tend to see the problems of the NHS mainly in terms of inadequate resources to meet growing demands and regard the new reforms as a wasteful diversion of funds. The verdict of the electorate in 1992 appears to have determined the future of Britain's health service in favour of the market approach.

SUMMARY

1 A distinction is made between illness and disease. Illness is a subjectively felt state of ill-health whereas disease is socially defined, usually by experts such as doctors.

2 There are several broad cultural paradigms or perspectives of health. Among these are:

■ Magical and Religious;
■ Modern Scientific;
■ Holistic.

3 Magical explanations of ill-health explain it in terms of witchcraft or sorcery. Purely religious explanations do so in terms of divine intervention. Modern scientific theory of health and disease is based on the premise that the latter is caused by an outside agency (usually a germ). Holistic medicine understands health and illness not merely in biomedical terms but in a total personal and cultural context.

4 The National Health Service was established to improve the health of the British people. However inequalities of health remain reflecting the following factors:

1 Sectoral differences within the NHS;
2 Regional differences in resourcing and in standards of health;
3 Class;
4 Gender;
5 Ethnic differences.

5 There is overwhelming evidence of a correlation between class factors and ill health. Marxists argue that the inequalities and exploitation of the capitalist system cause ill-health. Others point out that these inequalities have not been reduced in so-called communist societies.

6 The health policy of the Conservative governments was less concerned with inequalities in health than with achieving cost efficient delivery of health care. The attempt to do this was based on the introduction of elements of the free market within the NHS and by strengthening management.

7 The important issue of women as providers of informal and largely unpaid (health) care and the price they pay for doing this work is dealt with in other sections of this book (pp. 170–1). In this chapter, the issues of the medicalisation of childbirth and, briefly, the lack of power of women within the medical profession are dealt with.

8 The important issue of mortality rates in undeveloped countries is dealt with in chapter 20. In this chapter free-market, social democratic and Marxist on the relationship between development and health are discussed. One free-market view is that attempts to 'help' the undeveloped world simply hinder the 'natural' processes by which people flourish or not. It is precisely the processes of the capitalist world market that Marxists see as injurious to people in the undeveloped world. Social democrats argue that a combination of aid and market adjustment can contribute to improvements in health.

9 The debates within mental health and illness echo those within the area of health as a whole. The traditional psychiatric model of mental illness seeks physical causes and solutions to 'the problem'. Within psychoanalysis more social and humanistic approaches occur.

10 Among the main sociological approaches to health are:

■ Marxist;
■ Functionalist;
■ Interactionist;
■ Liberal Reformist and Free Market.

The Marxist approach has been summarised in point 7. Functionalist perspective sees 'mass' health policies as functional in maintaining the labour force and as adaptation to popular pressure. Interactionist perspective stresses that outcomes in treatment and health are partly the product of negotiation between medical personnel and patients. Liberal reformist and free market liberal approaches differ in the way in which they consider health resources should be distributed.

RESEARCH AND COURSEWORK

This topic offers possibilities for both micro and macro level research – and for linking the two. At a micro level a comparison could be made between the informal caring done by an appropriately matched middle aged woman and man (possibly two or three pairs). The research could be carried out by interview, perhaps observation, and some element of quantification of care might be introduced. Another area appropriate to small-scale research is the interaction/negotiation between doctor/patient or nurse/patient.

At a macro level, the 'politics of health' offer possibilities for theoretical-historical analysis. Particularly interesting is the relationship between the health ideologies of various political parties and their policies when in office.

FURTHER READING

Two readers in the sociology of health can be recommended: S Osherson and E Mishler eds., *Social Contexts of Health, Illness and Patient Care* (Cambridge University Press, 1981) and D Tuckett ed., *An Introduction to Medical Sociology* (Tavistock, 1976). A simple, non-sociological introduction to recent (1980s/90s) changes in the NHS is Chris Ham *The New National Health Service* (Radcliffe Medical Press, 1991).

QUESTIONS

1 What explanations have sociologists offered for the variations in health and illness between different sections of the population? (AEB 1988)

2 'Decisions regarding the provision of health and welfare are essentially ideological'. How far do you agree with this statement?
(London, 1989) (See also chapter 15)

3 Assess the view that the power of the medical profession is the main but not the only factor in the continuation of health inequalities. (AEB 1991)

17 Religion & Meaning

INTRODUCTION: THE SOCIAL RELEVANCE OF RELIGION

Sociologists cannot decide between the competing claims of religions nor should they try to do so. Religious belief is based on the view that there is a spiritual reality in addition to material reality. Sociologists have no access to 'divinely revealed truth' but must seek to reveal their own 'truth'. This is concerned with the relationships between social phemomena, including the meanings people have and the consequences of these meanings for themselves and others.

Religious and other beliefs have social consequences and it is these that sociology studies. The following are the kind of questions addressed by sociologists of religion. Is it true that Protestants are more likely to commit suicide than Catholics and, if so, why? Why are a disproportionate number of young people attracted to religious sects and cults? What is the effect on a person's way of life of being an 'untouchable'? Is there something in the belief-systems of Muslims and Western liberals which means that tension and conflict between them is likely or even inevitable?

The Social Effects of Religion: The Classic Theorists

RELIGION AND SOCIAL SOLIDARITY: EMILE DURKHEIM

Durkheim argues that religion functions to reinforce the collective unity or social solidarity of a group:

There can be no society which does not feel the need of upholding and reaffirming at regular intervals the collective sentiment and the collective ideals which make its unity and its personality.
(Durkheim extracted in Bocock and Thompson, 1985:54)

One way in which a society can express its shared identity and unity is through religious worship and ritual.

Durkheim stated that traditionally people divide phenomena into the sacred and the profane or the religious and the secular. The category of the sacred is concerned with those matters and forces which seem beyond everyday experience and explanation. Durkheim compares religious sentiment to the feelings of awe which people may have towards royalty or the famous.

Symbol and ritual are crucial to Durkheim's analysis of the social function of religion. Symbols – such as the ancient totem or Christian cross – provide a focus of emotion and belief. Rituals – such as animal sacrifice or the Catholic mass – bring people together and bind them in shared experience. In social terms, Durkheim is clear that what people are 'worshipping' is society. In reference to clan worship,

Durkheim says that it awakens 'within its members the idea that outside of them there exist forces which dominate them and at the same time sustain them ...' He considers that public rituals – whether religious or secular – in modern societies function in the same way.

Moral remaking cannot be achieved except by the means of reunions, assemblies and meetings where the individuals, being closely united to one another, reaffirm in common their common sentiments; hence come ceremonies which do not differ from regular religious ceremonies, either in their object, the results which they produce, or the processes employed to attain these results. What essential difference is there between an assembly of Christians celebrating the principal dates of the life of Christ, or the Jews remembering the exodus from Egypt or the promulgation of the decalogue, and a reunion of citizens commemorating the promulgation of a new moral or legal system or some great event in the national life?
(Durkeim extracted in Bocock and Thompson 1985:54–5)

RELIGION AND IDEOLOGY: KARL MARX

Marx considered religion to be a form of alienation – both emotional and intellectual. Religion serves as a poor substitute for social justice and happiness in the present world, and offers even poorer explanations as to why these are 'unobtainable'. Marx considered that religion stood in the way of the emotional and intellectual development of the working class and prevented them from developing a non-alienated society in the 'real' world. He referred to religion as the 'opiate of the masses' and some latterday Marxists have pilloried it as 'pie in the sky when you die'. Marx believed that once it had thrown off the 'illusion' of religion, the creative potential of working class people might express itself in work, art, and intellectual life.

Marx regarded religion as a form of ideology. It both developed 'false consciousness' and conformity among the oppressed (an aspect of alienation) and justified the behaviour of the powerful to themselves and others. Marx's analysis of tribal religion goes straight to the heart of what he regarded as its ideologically exploitative nature. Priests and witch-doctors conspired to relieve ordinary tribal members of their surplus wealth by claiming that they needed to be supported in order to practise magic and to communicate with the gods. Often contributions were such that they were able to do so in some style. He considered that working people in nineteenth century Britain were equally the victims of religion. He urged them to shake off the 'chain' of religion and 'call the living flower' of social justice in the 'real' world:

The task of history, therefore, once the world beyond the truth has disappeared, is to establish the truth of this world. The immediate task of philosophy, which is at the service of history, once the saintly form of human self-alienation has been unmasked, is to unmask self-alienation in its unholy forms. Thus the criticism of heaven turns into the criticism of the earth, the criticism of religion into the criticism of right and the criticism of theology into the criticism of politics.

(Marx and Engels, extracted in Bocock and Thompson, 1985:10–11)

Marx also considered that religion could be used as ideological justification by dominant groups and cited the role of Protestantism in justifying capitalism.

He argued that merchants and industrialists of the sixteenth century and later, preferred the Protestant to the Catholic religion because the former satisfied their commercial requirements more than the latter. Whereas Catholicism forbade usury (lending money at exorbitant rates), it was acceptable under Protestantism. Whereas Catholic theologians regarded great interest in acquiring wealth as greedy, Protestants, and particularly Calvinists (members of a Protestant sect) looked upon material success as a sign of God's grace and favour. Protestant philosophy offered a further bonus to practical minded capitalists. Hard work and industry were at the core of Protestant moral practice and these virtues applied as much to the working class as to the bourgeoisie. Credit in the heavenly bank account rather than a hefty wage-packet was to be the reward of labour. This view had much to commend it to industrialists concerned with profit, accumulation and investment rather than the standard of living of the working class.

FREUD AND MARCUSE

Freud considered that human beings are driven by powerful instincts of aggression (thanatos) and love (eros). 'Love' includes sexual needs as Freud understood it. He believed that in order to achieve 'civilisation', society had to control these instincts – otherwise they would wreak havoc. He argued that historically religion had played a major role in directing surplus and unexpressed instinctual energy, particularly 'erotic'. He referred to the displacement of love from people to spirits, saints or God as sublimation. In this way, he believed that religion functions as a form of social control. However, like the other major 'turn-of-the-century' social scientists to which we have referred, he was inclined to think that religion would lose its credibility in the face of the rise of science and rational explanation.

Marcuse attempted a neo-Marxist blend of the thought of Marx and Freud. He argued that historically some members of the working class had been misled into misplacing their intelligence, creativity and much of their capacity for pleasure and fun. He borrowed the concept of ideological (intellectual) repression from Marx and that of emotional repression from Freud. He argued that a thoroughly repressed working class offered little threat to the capitalist system. However, Marcuse did not consider that the rise of science and reason would necessarily liberate working people. Rather, he believed that capitalism had created a new 'god' of consumerism through the media and advertising.

MAX WEBER

(I) RELIGION AND SOCIAL CHANGE
In one of the most celebrated of historical-sociological encounters, Max Weber took issue with Marx on his analysis of religion as ideology. Superficially, the debate is about a question of empirical fact, but at a deeper level it concerns the cause and nature of historical change. The factual issue is itself profound enough: was Protestantism primarily the product of capitalism, or did it on the contrary help to produce capitalism? Marx takes the former view, Weber the latter. Marx's position has, in effect, already been explained. He argued that, like other forms of religious ideology, Protestantism helped to justify certain social relations – in this case the exploitation of the proletariat by the bourgeoisie. For Weber, the matter was less simple. He argued that Calvinism, a particular form of Protestantism, had played a major role in creating a cultural climate in which the capitalistic spirit could thrive. It would be too crude to say that Weber thought that Calvinism 'caused' capitalism, but he did consider that there was a certain correspondence between Calvinist ideas and the qualities required to be a successful capitalist. Calvinism provided favourable conditions for the development of capitalism. For instance, Calvinism preached hard work and frugality, the Protestant ethic – very useful virtues to a businessman. Weber cited many examples of Calvinists who became businessmen while, however, fully recognising that factors other than the spiritual content of Calvinism contributed to the rise of capitalism. An important one was the development of new machine technology which massively increased production potential.

Weber's major theoretical point is that ideas can change history, and in so doing can contribute to changes in the material context of life. It will be remembered that the whole trend of Marx's analysis of religious ideas is in the opposite direction. He sees them primarily as justifying existing social and economic circumstances, and certainly not as providing a major source of historical change. On the contrary, religion was an ideological pall intended to obscure new and different ideas. But Marx did recognise that new ideas could be developed. Human consciousness is able to react thoughtfully and creatively to experience, particularly everyday work experience. Socialism itself had to be 'thought of' before it could become a reality. However, for Marx, ideas are formed within, and structured by, socio-economic material reality. Socialism only becomes possible or practically 'thinkable' when society is economically and socially developed to the point where socialist ideas are seen to be realistic.

Weber's studies of religion are also important from the methodological point of view. As an exercise in comparative sociology, they rank alongside Durkheim's study of suicide. Weber drew his examples of the relationship of religion and society from worldwide. His conclusion was that the relationship is one of variety. Religion can help to cause change or impede it; it might be used to support the status quo or against it.

(II) SECULARISATION: DESACRILISATION, 'DISENCHANTMENT' AND RATIONALISATION
Like Durkheim, Weber considered that it is a feature of modern life that the supernatural is little used to explain events and behaviour. A process of 'desacrilisation' has occurred.

The medieval world in which God was Creator, 'His' mother a virgin, and in which spirits, good or evil, were believed to intervene in everyday life must have been perceived in a qualitatively different way from that in which most people see the world today. Belief in mystery and miracle has largely gone, apart from the imaginings of children. 'Disenchantment', to use Weber's term for this, has set in. The triumph of science and reason has been at the cost of myth, fable and spiritual romanticism. This is part of the process of secularisation which is defined and discussed in the next main section.

For Weber, secularisation was an aspect of the wider process of rationalisation. He considered that the underlying principle behind modernisation is rational, scientific thought. Applied to technology and to organisation, rational thought has restructured the social world. Equally to the point, applied to the human race's understanding of itself and its place in the universe, rational thought has undermined religion and replaced it with various secular and, largely, materialistic explanations of our existence and relationship to nature. Darwin, Freud and Marx were also major contributors to the replacement of religious explanations of human behaviour by scientific ones. Loss of intellectual authority and status helped to erode the moral authority of the church.

RELIGIOUS AND OTHER SYSTEMS OF MEANING: BERGER AND LUCKMANN

Berger and Luckmann argue that people routinely try to make sense of or construct meaning out of their experience. Religion is one type of meaning system. Religion is a particularly effective type of explanation because it encompasses the whole of 'reality' – spiritual as well as temporal.

There are, however, a wide variety of non-religious philosophies by which their adherents seek to construct a meaningful interpretation of existence. Thus, secular humanists argue that their concern for the welfare of fellow human beings needs no added religious motive to be effective and vital. Marxism is another belief system. It has frequently been argued that Marxism emerged as an alternative belief-system to religion and, in fact, has many religious characteristics.

The Secularisation Debate

The thesis that British society has become more secular – the secularisation thesis – is easy to grasp in outline but complex to define and demonstrate in detail. Broadly, the secularisation thesis proposes that religious belief and practice have declined and that science and rationality have increased in importance. Duncan Mitchell emphasises the former in the following definition:

Secularisation (or the secularisation process) is the term popularly used to depict a situation in which the beliefs and sanctions of religion become – or are in the process of becoming – increasingly discounted in society as guides to conduct or to decision-making.

(Dictionary of Sociology, 1979)

This proposition is of obvious importance. If correct, the secularisation thesis describes a radical and fundamental change in the cultural and institutional foundation of society. If 'God is dead' or generally believed to be, then, the life of human beings is likely to be very different as a result.

Despite its apparent importance, the very notion of the secularisation thesis has received severe criticism. David Martin contends that the concept is 'an intellectual hold-all' made up of a variety of unconnected arguments (1979). More recently, Michael Prowse has suggested that the secularisation thesis is 'out of date' – so great, in his view, is the evidence of the continuing vitality of religion (Changing Patterns in the Search for Faith, *Financial Times*, April 1 1990).

Given the importance of the secularisation debate, it is no doubt better to define secularisation precisely rather than dispose of the concept altogether. Various aspects of possible secularisation have been identified. Both leading proponents of secularisation, such as Bryan Wilson, and leading opponents, such as David Martin, commonly accept three areas as relevant: formal religious practice; the influence of the church as an institution on other areas of society; and individual 'consciousness' of religion. Glock and Stark (1970) tease out several dimensions of what they term 'religiousness'. In addition to religious practice, they define belief, experience, knowledge and the consequences on daily life of these four aspects as 'core dimensions' of religion. It is easier to measure formal religious practice than the other dimensions and it is to this issue we first turn.

SECULARISATION: FORMAL RELIGIOUS PRACTICE

There is widespread agreement among students of secularisation that there has been a steady general decline in formal religious observance among the Trinitarian churches during the post-war period (the Trinitarian churches are those that believe in the union of the Blessed Trinity in one God). Table 17.1 gives details of the decline in adult membership of the major Trinitarian religions between 1975 and 1990 which is estimated at seventeen per cent overall. A comparable decline occurred in participation in the rites of passage – baptism, confirmation, and church marriage. Table 17.2 shows that the number of civil as opposed to church marriages in Great Britain rose from 40 per cent in 1971 to 48 per cent in 1988 although this is still a majority in the former category.

Figure 17.1 (Far right)

Active church membership in selected European countries

Table 17.1

Church membership, ministers and buildings: estimates

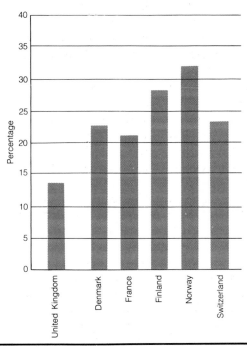

(Source: *Social Trends*, 1991)

United Kingdom					Millions and thousands	
	Adult members (millions)		Ministers (thousands)		Buildings (thousands)	
	1975	1990	1975	1990	1975	1990
Trinitarian Churches						
Anglican	2.27	1.84	15.9	14.1	19.8	18.3
Presbyterian	1.65	1.29	3.8	3.1	6.4	5.6
Methodist	0.61	0.48	4.2	2.3	9.1	7.5
Baptist	0.27	0.24	2.4	2.9	3.6	3.4
Other Protestant Churches	0.53	0.70	7.1	9.0	8.0	9.9
Roman Catholic	2.53	1.95	8.0	7.6	4.1	4.6
Orthodox	0.20	0.27	0.1	0.2	0.1	0.2
Total	8.06	6.70	41.6	39.3	51.2	49.8

(Source: Social Trends, 1992)

Great Britain				Thousands and percentages
	1971		1988	
	All marriages	First marriages[1]	Second or subsequent[2]	All marriages
England and Wales	41	31	78	48
Scotland	31	29	70	42
Great Britain	40	31	77	48

1 First marriage for both partners.
2 Remarriage for one or both partners. (Source: Social Trends, 1991)
(Office of Population Censuses and Surveys: General Register Office (Scotland))

Table 17.2

Civil marriages as a percentage of all marriages

Britain's reputation as 'the most secular nation in Europe' is supported by figure 17.1 which shows active church membership in Britain clearly lower than that of five other European countries.

David Martin does not disagree that a decline in formal religious practice occurred during the post-war period. However, he does question whether certain previous periods were such 'golden' eras of religion as is sometimes assumed. There is evidence of considerable religious scepticism and non-observance in the middle ages. Martin also suggests that the high church attendance rate of the Victorian middle class may have reflected their concern with respectability rather than religious commitment! In addition to Martin's comments, the relative flourishing of major non-Trinitarian churches and the recent growth of world religions such as Islam, in Britain (discussed below) must also be considered to qualify the argument that formal religious observance has generally declined.

SECULARISATION: THE INSTITUTIONAL INFLUENCE OF THE CHURCH

Writing in 1977, Bryan Wilson argued that the 'content of the message that the churches seek to promote, and the attitudes and values that it tries to encourage, no longer inform much of our national life' (How Religious Are We? in *New Society*, 27 October 1977).

A disengagement of church and state into separate domains has replaced their near unity in the middle ages. He sees the role of religion in school and at the workplace as now almost negligible. Religious instruction in schools has often become a travesty: many teachers using the periods for current affairs. He suggests that the workplace is perhaps the environment 'most alien' to religious values. Mechanical principles of organisation, whether in factory or office, seem almost the antithesis of religious myth and values. The remoteness of contemporary religion from political life is worth more space than Wilson gives it. In the reign of Henry II, the major political opponent of the King was the Archbishop of Canterbury. It is difficult to imagine the contemporary church ever being more than an irritant to its political 'masters'.

Nevertheless, there was certainly an increase in political and social comment during the nineteen eighties on the part of the church, both as a body and by individuals. Most famously there was the report, *Faith in the City* (1985) published by a commission set up by the Archbishop of Canterbury. The report criticised the effect of government policies in the inner city for 'making the plight of some classes of citizens actually worse'. This was strong and specific comment and may even have had some effect. In 1987 Mrs Thatcher declared that a main goal of her new administration was to revive the inner cities. Arguably, however, the moral agenda and tone of the nineteen eighties was set by Mrs Thatcher and her supporters rather than by her critics. After her election victory of 1979, she quoted St Francis of Assisi on the steps of 10 Downing Street and subsequently frequently stated or implied a moral basis for her policies. Philosophically, Thatcherism represented a moral backlash against the 'permissivism' and social reformism of the nineteen sixties and seventies in favour of traditional morality and individual effort. Undoubtedly, this meant 'losers' as well as 'winners' economically. The bishops' report was concerned for the 'losers' but it was answering to the dictates of Thatcherism.

Even the radical Bishop of Durham, David Jenkins, opposed Thatcherism from a largely defensive posture. In particular, he was concerned with the closure of coal pits and the resulting effect on mining communities. However, in his book written with Rebecca Jenkins, *Free to Believe* (1991), he reached beyond reaction politics to outline the basis of a new political consensus in which national and global problems – poverty, the environment, war – might be dealt with in a renewed spirit of international collective understanding and cooperation. This coincided with a post Gulf War reinvigorated United Nations – the most likely practical agency for such a movement.

In opposing the secularisation thesis, David Martin does not deny that there has been a long term decline in the influence of the church on national life. However, he turns the argument on its head and suggests that the church may be more effective and purer by concentrating on its own chief concerns, the spiritual and moral. To others this might seem like condemning the church to practical irrelevance – rendering to 'Caesar what is Caesar's and to God what is God's' could leave the latter in danger of seeeming irrelevant to modern society! In any case, church leaders have continued to comment on political and social matters. In 1991, the recently appointed Archbishop of Canterbury, Dr Carey, argued that urban disorder, specifically that in Tyneside, was 'inextricably linked to social and economic conditions.

SECULARISATION: INFORMAL, PERSONAL RELIGION

Religion as a source of personal meaning and fulfilment survives much more widely and with greater vitality than institutional religion. Interestingly, Thomas Luckman considers that the primary function of religion is to give personal meaning to life. Although few in Britain go regularly to church, the vast majority believe in 'something', even if no more than a vague force behind the universe. What is more, according to David Hay, 'well over a third of all women and just under a third of all men in Great Britain claim to have had some sort of religious experience'. To use Hay's own terms, almost half of these 'wouldn't touch the church with a bargepole'. It is worth giving a brief extract from one of the examples of 'mystical' experience cited by Hay:

Then it happened. 'I lost all sense of time, of my own body and 'ego'; it was as if I became one with the natural world ... for an unthought passage of time I was filled with the certainty and knowledge of

405

*the meaning of life'. Previously he'd been
cynical about religion ...*
(New Society, 12/4/79)

No doubt many who would not claim
anything resembling a mystical experience
routinely pray or 'talk to God in their own
way'. For them neither belief in science
nor in humanity has been quite enough to
make them feel complete. The secularisation
thesis is, therefore, less applicable to
personal religion of this kind than to formal
religion.

SECULARISATION: CHURCHES AND SECTS

The constant rise and fall of religious sects is
often cited as evidence that religion is not
slowly dying. Ernst Troeltsch first made the
distinction between churches and sects in
the early nineteen thirties (1981). Churches
are large religious organisations. They tend
to support the state and generally to be
conservative. In contrast, sects are typically
smaller religious organisations and often
oppose the secular and ecclesiastical
establishment. Whereas churches represent
orthodoxy in teaching and ritual, sects are
frequently innovative and even spontaneous
in these matters. In addition to churches and
sects, Bryan Wilson has suggested the term
denomination to describe religious organisations which do not have the status, power
and perhaps size of membership of a church
but which have a stable and settled
existence. Examples in Britain are the
Roman Catholic and Methodist denomi-
nations.

Roy Wallis has suggested that there are
three main types of sects: world rejecting,

world accommodating and world affirming.
Just as the 'church, denomination, sect'
typology should be regarded as an ideal type
rather than a framework into which every
religious organisation fits, so should Wallis'
typology of sects. World-affirming sects
accept the world as it is and members seek to
deal with problems and to find fulfilment
through spiritual means. An example of
such a movement is Transcendental
Meditation (TM). TM had its origin in the
Hindu religion. It offered spiritual solutions
and experience without requiring its
members to give up worldly pursuits. It has
attracted, in particular, middle class young
people who may have been materially
satisfied but spiritually deprived.

World-accommodating sects neither
accept nor reject wordly pursuits but seek
vital spiritual expression as a priority. They
are often break-aways from churches which
are considered to have 'lost touch with true
spirituality'. The Pentecostalists believe that
the Holy Spirit is in direct communion with
them whereas the ritual and formalism of
other churches impedes such communication. World-rejecting sects separate
themselves from what they see as a corrupt
world, sometimes to prepare for an
anticipated second coming. One of the best
known contemporary sects of this kind is the
'Unification Church' or 'Moonies' led by the
Reverend Moon.

Although accurate statistics on the growth
of sects are notoriously difficult to produce, it
seems that the increase in popularity of sects
which began in the nineteen sixties, is
continuing into the nineties. Although the
membership in Britain of the Church of
Scientology increased between 1970 and
1990, its own claim of a tenfold increase to
50,000 ought to be treated with scepticism.
Table 17.3 gives more reliable information on
the overall growth of fundamental Christian
'sects' between 1975–1990 and while this is
substantial, it is not quite spectacular.

Whereas in the nineteen sixties cults
tended to develop as splinters from major
religions, such as the Jesus People and TM
(Hinduism), in the nineteen nineties,
paganism and the occult re-emerged as
additional influences. The 'new age movement' is an umbrella term covering such cults
but also ecological and environmental groups.

What accounts for the recurrent and
perhaps currently growing popularity of

Table 17.3

Church membership, ministers and buildings: estimates

United Kingdom					Millions and thousands	
	Adult members (millions)		Ministers (thousands)		Buildings (thousands)	
Non-Trinitarian Churches	1975	1990	1975	1990	1975	1990
Mormons	0.10	0.15	5.3	9.8	0.2	0.4
Jehovah's Witnesses	0.08	0.12	7.1	12.7	0.6	1.4
Spiritualists	0.06	0.06	0.2	0.4	0.6	0.6
Other Non-Trinitarian	0.09	0.13	0.9	1.5	1.1	1.0
Total	0.33	0.46	13.5	24.4	2.5	3.4

(Source: Social Trends, 1992)

sects? First, a reason often given by members of sects themselves seems highly convincing. They claim to find formal religions cluttered with 'empty' ritual and lacking in the immediate spiritual experience for which they crave. This interpretation is compatible with Troeltsch's analysis that established churches tend to become like other organisations in society – hierarchical, bureaucratic and often impersonal. A second explanation for the appeal of sects, given by Max Weber, is still of relevance. He suggests that 'marginal' social groups may find compensation and explanation for their lack of privilege and status in the life of a sect. To a considerable extent, the nineteenth century Methodists drew on the working class for its membership. If the Church of England was 'the Conservative Party at prayer' the Methodists often had a more radical political as well as religious hue. In the post-war world, black people have sometimes lifted their sense of oppression by joining a religious sect. In addition to fundamental Christianity, the Rastafarian religion in Jamaica and Britain and the Black Muslim religion in America have attracted sizeable membership.

Young middle class people are sometimes associated with sectarian activity. This can hardly be explained by social marginality. Roy Wallis has suggested, however, that they may feel emotionally alienated from society and seek more meaningful experience and a sense of community in a sect. The Moonies, Scientologists, and the neo-hippy Children of God appear to offer a total package of emotional, religious and even intellectual security not available elsewhere. However, the youthful search for community does not exclusively take a religious form. In the nineteen sixties, 'the counterculture' (see pp. 222–4) and today an array of 'new age' groups provide closeness and purpose of a non-religious kind. Sometimes alternative secular movements and the religious impulse converge as when psychedelic drugs are taken to achieve a 'short-cut' to mystical experience.

Bryan Wilson associated the growth of sects with social change. As old orders crumble or appear to, people seek new answers and reassurance. Methodism waxed at a time of considerable social and economic change and the current appeal of sects may reflect the need for explanation and solution to an array of seemingly overwhelming global problems. The uneasy sense, as we approach the millennum, that the human species may be evolving on a course to self-destruction prompts some to find a different way of life.

Liberal intellectuals frequently criticised the radical activity – religious and non-religious – of young people in the nineteen sixties as naive and sometimes dangerous. Contemporary concern frequently focuses on the vulnerability of young people drawn into sects and away from previous family and other ties. The 'dark side' of sectarianism is perhaps less in bizarre belief but in the ability of some sects to deprive members of their possessions, their previous friends and relations, and their independence of thought.

SECULARISATION: THE STRENGTH OF WORLD RELIGIONS IN BRITAIN

The growth of non-Christian world religions in Britain, particularly Islam (the Muslim religion), has revitalised religious debate in Britain. Their expansion (see figure 17.2) has occurred primarily because of post-war immigration from the new Commonwealth and Pakistan (see pp. 194–5).

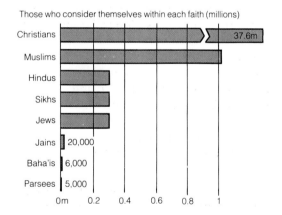

Those who consider themselves within each faith (millions)

Christians	37.6m
Muslims	
Hindus	
Sikhs	
Jews	
Jains	20,000
Baha'is	6,000
Parsees	5,000

0m   0.2   0.4   0.6   0.8   1

Figure 17.2

World religions

in the UK

These religions are central to the lives of relevant minority groups and are a fundamental element of multicultural Britain. They bring difference, diversity and interest into a society in which the Christian religion had perhaps been drifting into irrelevance. The members of these religions differ from most professed Christians in that they regularly observe formal ritual and practice. Inhabitants and citizens of a 'modern' society, many remain traditional in their religious and moral outlook. For some this means that religious authority and principle overrides that of secular law.

The religious and moral strength of communities based on traditional world religions other than Christianity has both helped and hindered their adjustment to life in Britain. Crime, drug abuse, marital and family break-up tend to be substantially lower than the national average in these communities. However, on certain points of principle, their religions have bought them into conflict with majority opinion. An early example of tension occurred when male Seikhs felt morally unable to wear crash helmets when riding motor-bikes because of their religious custom of always wearing a turban in public. The Rushdie matter has already been discussed (see p. 197). One of the most important points that it underlined was the potential conflict among some Muslims of their commitment to Islam and their commitment to observe British law when the two appeared to clash. On the one hand is the principle of free expression enshrined in law and on the other is the injunction by the highest Islamic authority to punish blasphemy. The Gulf War further tested the allegiance of some British Muslims although the 'Muslim world' itself was divided on the issue.

Despite the complexity and tensions of the above events and despite the provocation of substantial racism, the British Muslim community has, on the whole, remained peaceful and law abiding. Yet, the example of entrenched and bloody religious/political strife in Northern Ireland, suggests that there can be no comfortable assumption that something similar could not happen on the British mainland. The further example of the Lebanon, long torn by sectarian-inspired civil war, is another caution. Those stricken landscapes ought to stimulate a creative meeting of minds and cultures in mainland Britain.

Finally, it is not surprising that religion is strong among immigrants to Britain from traditional societies. This is largely what secularisation theorists, as well as others, would expect. It is the impact of 'modernity' that secularisation theorists regard as likely to erode religion. Sociologists will be in a better position in twenty or so years time to see if formal religious practice among these recent immigrant groups declines as a result

▶

Figure 17.3

of living in a 'modern' society.

THE UNITED STATES: A COUNTER-EXAMPLE TO THE SECULARISATION OF MODERN STATES?

Church membership and attendance are much higher in the United States than in Britain, being on average about 50 per cent and 40 per cent in recent decades. This seems to provide substantial evidence against the view that secularisation tends to occur in 'modern' societies.

However, several observers have noted that religious practice in the main churches in America, the Protestant, Catholic, and Jewish, is typically of a social and secular kind. Will Herberg sees it as denoting community membership – both ethnic and of wider American society. Seymour Martin Lipset qualifies this analysis with the observation that religion has historically been of this character in the United States. The United States in its modern form has been created partly by religious refugees for whom freedom to practise their religion is a reaffirmation of a wider freedom. It is perhaps perverse of Herberg to regard religious practice of this kind as 'secular'.

The Secularisation Thesis: For and Against: A summary

FOR

1. **Formal religious practice** in Britain has tended steadily to decline in the post-war era.

2. The **institutional influence** of the church has tended to decline over several centuries.

AGAINST

1. **Personal religion** – in terms of a belief in the spiritual and as a source of meaning – appears to thrive (although precise measurement is difficult).

2. The vitality of **religious sects** runs counter to the secularisation thesis.

3. The growing strength in Britain of several of the great **world religions**, at the least, complicates the secularisation thesis.

4. A **comparison** of religion in Britain with that of another 'modern' society – **the United States** – appears partially to refute the secularisation thesis.

Note: A 'for and against' summary inevitably over-simplifies. Qualifications and counter-arguments to each point can be found in the main text.

In the nineteen seventies and eighties evangelical movements – which seek more immediate spiritual experience and communication – grew in popularity in the United States and to a lesser extent in Britain. Their rise survived even the well-publicised sexual and financial scandals that some of their leaders became involved in. Evangelism, like sectarianism, is one answer to the desire for religion with 'heart and soul'.

SECULARISATION: CONCLUSION

Secularisation has occurred in Britain to the extent that there has been a decline in formal religious observance and in the institutional influence of the church. On the other hand, in a less formal sense, 'there is a lot of religion about' – personal, sectarian and evangelical. The growth of the great world religions in Britain has interrupted any smooth flow towards secularisation even in the area of formal religion. It may be that the secularisation thesis needs to be reformulated to apply only to the major Christian churches and perhaps not to all of these. Secularisation in the sense of the triumph of science and reason over religion and the spiritual has not occurred.

Comparative Religion: The Global Picture

On the basis of his own massive comparative survey, Weber concluded that the effects of religion on society are unpredictable and varied. Sometimes religion might have a conservative effect, whereas in other cases it might contribute to social change. Thus, he thought Buddhism militated against the development of capitalism in China, whereas in Northern Europe, Calvinism had the opposite effect (see p. 504).

An overview of religion in the contemporary world similarly shows a pattern of variety and often unpredicted development. With the opening up of the Soviet bloc, it appears that traditional religions, particularly Catholicism and Islam, have remained much stronger in parts of Eastern Europe and the southern Soviet republics than many had suspected. In the United States, the dominant Western nation, religion has remained a much more visibly buoyant part of national life than in Britain. World-wide, 'Eastern' religions flow west and Christianity is well established in nearly all areas of the world.

LIBERALISM, FUNDAMENTALISM AND SECULARISATION

A distinction must be introduced here between liberalism and fundamentalism. Liberalism is associated with Western democracies and is based on mutual toleration of differences between groups (i.e. it is pluralistic). Fundamentalism is associated with opposition to liberalism and

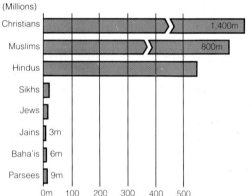

(Millions)

Figure 17.4

World religions

a militant and sometimes violent attitude to enforcing 'moral purity' (as defined by the fundamentalist). Frequently, fundamentalists seek to use the state to establish and enforce what they see as morality. In origin, the term fundamentalist applied to Christians who believed that social morality should literally be based on the bible. More recently, it has also been used by Western academics and the media to describe more militant Muslim societies and individuals, but not all Muslims. Liberal and fundamentalist approaches occur in both religion and politics and more widely.

The distinction between liberalism and fundamentalism is relevant to the concept of secularisation applied to the global context. Secularisation has occurred in the west in the particular and crucial sense that a division is made between the authority of the church and state. In Islam such a distinction is not established and, indeed, the general assumption is that Islamic law should govern civil as well as religious life. The term theocracy can be used to describe societies ruled by a single version of 'God's law' applied to both public and private life. Despite tendencies to theocracy, a degree of religious and political pluralism occurs in most Muslim states. Nevertheless, theocracy and liberalism are ultimately contradictory.

THE RISE OF ISLAM, WORLDWIDE AND IN BRITAIN

The Islamic religion has been a particularly powerful and dynamic force both globally and in Britain for the past two decades. The immediate reason for this was the quadrupling of the oil price in 1974 which made several Muslim nations highly wealthy and greatly increased their importance in global investment and development. The money to finance a Muslim revival was available. Historically, Islam has been an expansionist religion, and new economic power coincided with a feeling among many in the Muslim world that they had suffered from Western 'exploitation and arrogance' for long enough. These sentiments were notably strong in Iran and Iraq whereas the 'West' managed to maintain more friendly relations with the neo-feudal regimes in Saudi Arabia and Kuwait.

In 1984, the Shah of Iran was overthrown in a revolution that was partly inspired by Muslim clerics. The Shah had previously been enthroned as a result of a coup inspired by the United States Central Intelligence Agency (CIA). The so-called 'rule of the mullahs' (clerics) led by Ayatollah Khomeini followed the Shah's overthrow. Internally, Iran became governed on more strictly Islamic principles and externally its relations with the West deteriorated. It was during this period that Western hostages were taken and the notorious fatwa against Salman Rushdie was issued (see p. 408). With the death of Ayatollah Khomeini in 1989 and the rise of Rafsanjani, the Iranian leadership adopted a more pragmatic style, but the influence of Muslim clerics remained strong.

The recent history of Iraq provides another example of the influence of the Islamic religion both in the internal affairs of a country and more widely. Prior to the Gulf War of 1991, Saddam Hussein had seemed a relatively 'modern-minded', dictatorial and violent leader, in the sense that he appeared to distinguish between the political and religious areas of power. However, during the early stages of the war, he did play the 'religion card' by declaring the war to be a 'jihad' (holy war) against the infidel. In fact, this did not have the effect of uniting the Muslim world against the coalition but, according to press coverage of the war, it seems that Hussein had more support among the Arab masses than among their leaders.

Undoubtedly, religion is a major element in Muslim opposition to and resentment of 'the West'. However, whether it is a cause or a justification – or both – is debatable. In the following extract, Martin Woollacott first describes the anger of one individual, Sheikh Tamimi, against 'the West', and then broadens his description to suggest that the Sheikh's views are widely shared in 'the Arab' or, more precisely, parts of the Arab Muslim world.

Sheikh Tamimi is not sure whether Bush is best compared to Charlemagne or Richard the Lionheart, but he is sure that the West is engaged in a new crusade against Islam. 'It is not our holy war against you, but your holy war against us,' says the Sheikh. 'Saddam Hussein has become an agent of God and he has had to face the West and the whole world of the unbelievers.'

The Sheikh is one of scores of such fundamentalist leaders through the Arab world today. They differ in theology, in ability, in sophistication and in political visibility but they share one common characteristic. They see themselves as the inheritors of a pure tradition which compromising and sometimes evil politicians have sullied, and they see themselves as having the right to influence political leaders if not to replace them. This is the great opposition movement – anti-Western, anti-Israeli, anti-modern, and anti-rational – which is waiting in the wings in the Middle East and whose day may come if the Arabs and the West do not learn the right lessons from the disastrous war which has just ended. [ie: the Gulf War]

(Martin Woollacott, The Guardian, 1991:25)

The Muslim religion is a reference point in many countries outside the Middle East for those who feel dispossessed by the West. Arguably, the Muslim religion is now a more popular vehicle for opposition to the West than Marxism. For instance, during the early nineteen nineties a rising tide of Muslim fundamentalism occurred in Nigeria. One of its leaders, Mallam Zakzaky, made great emphasis of the complete nature of the Islamic system which, in his view, offers a total political, economic and social programme unlike the Christian religion which he sees as practically irrelevant. It is precisely this failure to separate matters ecclesiastical from matters secular that his critics find threatening.

To what extent does Britain's Muslim population feel a conflict of allegiance between commitment to the Muslim faith and loyalty to Britain? The first point to make is that the evidence to answer this question is not available. The second point is that British Muslims vary immensely both in their interpretation of the Muslim faith and of their duties towards Britain. Some find no conflict between their faith and their commitment to British law whereas others seem prepared to obey external Muslim authority even if it conflicts with British law. Vivck Chaudhary and Dave Hill comment interestingly on such differences:

The sheer diversity of British Muslims makes the gelling of a cohesive, grass-roots British Muslim identity still seem a long way off. In trying to see the future, it would also be naive to regard Muslims as functioning in isolation from the enduring social mechanisms of Britain as a whole. Social class and economic climate permeate the lives of Muslims as they do everybody else. Islamic culture will no more evolve in a vacuum in Britain than it does in Saudi Arabia.

(V Chaudhary and D Hill, The Guardian, 3 May 1991:19)

Thirdly, however, the years between 1988 and 1991 saw a series of situations arise which sorely tested the judgement of members of the Muslim community. Matters were made worse by a continuing tide of racism against Asian Britons (see p. 193). Again, Chaudhary and Hill express the position well:

But the last three years have seen Britain's Muslim communities embroiled in major convulsions of identity, going right to the heart of their role in British life and in the wider world. The Rushdie affair, arguments about Islamic schools and political parties and, most recently, the Gulf War, have dragged abstract issues of social and spiritual identity down from the stratosphere and set them firmly in the discourse of everyday life. The full implications are, as yet, uncertain. But the debate has been loud: and with it have come shifting sensibilities for uncomfortable times.

(V Chaudhary and D. Hill, The Guardian, 2 May 1991:19)

CONCLUSION: CLASSIC SOCIOLOGY AND CONTEMPORARY RELIGION

Collectively, the works of Marx, Durkheim, Weber and Freud convey a sense that the credibility of religion as a type of explanation of 'reality' was being seriously challenged by the discoveries of science and reason. They appeared to think that religion would not 'stand up' against the onslaught of rationality and the achievements of 'modernity'. Their own work could largely be interpreted as drawing back the cloak of religious 'illusion' and revealing it as the frail handmaiden of social function and personal projection. In one sense they were right about decline – or, at least, right so far. In the West, formal religious practice has been in long term decline. With increasing leisure and material wealth, most people tend to do other things with their time than go to church.

On the other hand, the need for spiritual experience and religious explanation strongly persists. Informal religion thrives, at the personal and sectarian level and in the form of evangelism within mainstream churches. World-wide, religion remains the most popular of belief systems with Marxism trailing perhaps a poor second.

Social science cannot comment on the competing claims to truth of the various religions. What analysis of historical and contemporary religion does demonstrate is that without mutual tolerance religious and other ideologies are likely to add to human misery rather than comfort and joy – which presumably is not part of their members' intentions.

SUMMARY

1 Major sociologists offer a number of key analyses of religion:

Durkheim argues that religion functions to reinforce the collective unity or social solidarity of a group.

Marx considered religion to be:

(i) a form of alienation – from 'real' happiness in the present world;

(ii) a form of ideology which developed 'false consciousness' among the oppressed. Freud considered that religion helps to control potentially socially disruptive instincts through sublimation.

Marcuse, drawing on both Marx and Freud, describes both religion and the capitalist media as forms of ideological and emotional repression of the working class.

Weber analysed religion both in terms of:

(i) its varied contribution to social change and maintaining the status quo;

(ii) the process of desacrilisation which he perceived as a move from super-natural to rational explanation.

Berger and Luckmann argue that religion is only one way in which people try to construct meaning out of their experience.

2 The secularisation thesis proposes that religious belief and practice have declined and that science and rationality have increased in importance.

3 Two main points were discussed which seem broadly to support the secularisation thesis:

(i) Formal religious practice in Britain, as measured by church attendance and observance of the rites of passage, has declined;

(ii) The institutional influence of the church on other areas of national life has tended to wane.

4 Four main points were discussed which broadly seem to argue against the secularisation thesis:

(i) Personal belief in the spiritual still appears widespread;

(ii) The ebb and flow of religious sects continues apace;

(iii) There has been a growth of membership in several world religions in Britain;

(iv) The view that secularisation tends to occur in 'modern' societies is severely questioned by the example of the United States.

5 The secularisation thesis was not intended to apply to traditional societies, and certainly world-wide the great religions show few signs of overall decline.

6 There is a fundamental difference between the more secular, liberal, Western societies and those societies in which church and state are scarcely, if at all, differentiated (theocracies). Officially, liberal states are committed to religious and ideological tolerance and pluralism, whereas theocracies, such as Khomeini's Iran, are not. On the contrary, 'true believers' in theocracies are often militantly intolerant of 'non-believers'. This difference of principle is a recipe for great tension and potential conflict. It is a difference which recurs internationally between liberals and religious fundamentalists, including in Britain.

7 Despite the great tensions created by the Rushdie matter and the Gulf War, the overwhelming majority of British Muslims observe both British law and their normal religious practices. Nevertheless, a surge of racism against Muslims during this period (1989–91) and fundamentalist and uncompromising utterances by some Muslims indicated that elements of much greater civil strife existed.

8 Whether right or wrong about secularisation, the classic sociologists and some more recent ones offered an array of analyses and insights into religion which remain challenging and provocative. Sociology cannot determine the truth of any religion. What it can offer is the empirical observation that religious belief without religious tolerance is likely to lead to civil tension, if not disorder and bloodshed.

Of the many possible areas of study under this topic, the relationship of religion and community could be particularly interesting. You may select an area for study in which one religion predominates. If so, what effect does this have on the community. Does it greatly increase community solidarity as, following Durkheim, one might hypothesise? Is religious leadership in the community dominated by a particular age group, class or sex? What is the experience of those who cease religious practice in a strong religious community? To what extent does the church deal with local social problems?

On the other hand, you may select an area for study in which several religions are practised. Do patterns of leisure sociability tend to be affected by membership of a given church? Are there religious-based rivalries within

RESEARCH AND COURSEWORK

the locality? Again, are particular religions associated with a given class, ethnic group or even age group (it is unlikely that gender will be a significant variable in this context)? How do you explain these relationships?

A starting point for the type of enquiry suggested above might be a church notice-board and/or calendar of events. These may indicate who leading and active church members are. Prior to examining the links between church and social relationships and activities the issue of whether to proceed in an overt (possibly using interviews) or covert (possibly, using participant observation) way will have to be resolved.

FURTHER READING

R Bocock and K Thompson eds., *Religion and Ideology* (Manchester University Press, 1985) is a very useful reader. Ian Thompson's *Religion* (Longman, 1987) is written for 'A' level students. A recent book by a protagonist of the secularisation thesis, Bryan Wilson, is *Religion in Sociological*

Perspective (OUP, Oxford, 1982) and, on the other side, is D Martin *A General Theory of Secularisation* (Blackwell, 1978).

QUESTIONS

1 Has there been a universal decline in the importance of religion during the last 25 years? (London, 1989)
2 'The main function of religion is to integrate individuals into society'. Examine this view. (AEB, November 1989)

3 'The weight of statistical evidence suggests that Britain is now a secular society.' Examine this view.

18 The Media

Structure and Ownership

The media in Britain are divided into a public and a private sector. The public sector is concerned only with broadcasting, whereas the private sector covers the whole range of media.

PUBLIC SECTOR MEDIA The British Broadcasting Corporation was set up as a public company in 1926. It is currently financed by a licence fee and run, not for profit, but in the public interest. It was responsible for all radio broadcasting and, from 1932, television broadcasting as well. The BBC is run by a Board of Governors which is constituted as independent of the government. However, there is a continuing lively debate about whether the BBC is, in practice, fully independent of government (see pp. 420–1). In the era of privatisation, the rumour that the BBC might be 'broken up' and largely privatised has occasionally surfaced.

PRIVATE SECTOR MEDIA The press is wholly commercially owned in Britain and there is also a trend towards greater commercialisation in relation to broadcasting. Commercial television started in 1955 and commercial radio in 1973. The Broadcasting Act of 1990 greatly extended the potential scope of commercial television. In addition to the two existing commercial channels, three and four, provisions were made to set up several more. The Independent Television Commission was set up with the intention that it would regulate television with a 'lighter touch' than its predecessor, the Independent Broadcasting Authority.

The international satellite companies, SKY and British Satellite Broadcasting company offered multiple channel viewing – at a price – and came on the air in 1989 and 1990 respectively. Like the other commercial channels, the two satellite companies planned to finance themselves from advertising revenue. However, in early 1990 SKY was losing 2 million pounds per week, and BSB also ran at a loss. It was little surprise when the two companies merged. Cable television, though not yet widespread in Britain, offers potential for commercial development.

MEDIA OWNERSHIP: CONCENTRATION AND CONGLOMERATION Two main trends characterise media ownership in Britain: concentration and conglomeration. Concentration refers to businesses in a given area – in this case in the media – merging so that ownership becomes concentrated in fewer hands. This has notably occurred in relation to the national press. In 1948, the three biggest press groups commanded 48 per cent of total circulation whereas the figure for 1985 was 74.8 per cent. The tendency to concentration has affected local newspapers, many of which are owned by national media companies. Conglomerates form when one company takes over another (or others) in the same or a different line of business. Rupert Murdoch's News International is a massive global multi-media conglomerate and Murdoch also has interests in software, energy and transport. Whether these trends in ownership result in less free media, influence media content, and have an effect on audiences is discussed later. Broadly, liberals argue that, despite these developments, the media in capitalist-democracies remain fundamentally free. Socialists and Marxists vary in the extent to which they consider business interests limit media 'freedom'.

The Pearson Group	
Contributions to Profit	£ million
Book publishing (includes Penguin/Longmans)	57
Lazards merchant bank	33
Financial Times	26
Westminster Press	19
Royal Doulton	17
Oil Services (USA and Europe)	17
Tussaud Group (Madame Tussauds, Chessington Zoo, Warwick Castle)	12
Other publishing (includes Dutch publishing interests)	9

◄

Table 18.1

An example of a

Media-based

Conglomerate

THE EFFECTS OF TECHNOLOGICAL CHANGE ON THE MEDIA The modern media are highly dependent on technology. Technological innovation has always 'driven' the development of the communications media and businesses unable to afford or adapt to it have usually perished. This has been true from the printing press to satellite broadcasting.

Two consequences of technological change in the media should be noted. First, the cost of the technology and the competitive importance of early but sometimes high-risk investment in it, means that large, rich companies tend to control investment. This tends to promote media concentration. Thus Rupert Murdoch was able to invest in high-technology printing at Wapping and eventually recoup his investment through reduced labour costs and greater efficiency. As far as SKY is concerned, he was prepared and able to afford to lose about half a billion pounds before achieving profitability. Few are able to play a 'game' with such high stakes but there must be concern about the effects on the rest of us from those that can.

The second trend in media technology is towards greater access by the general public. This has different and possibly contradictory consequences to the first trend. A large range of media hardware (videos, tape-recorders, computers, including those with desk-top publishing facilities) and software (tapes, computer software) are readily and cheaply available. Undoubtedly, this increases potential choice and creativity (e.g. producing videos, newsheets etc.) both for individuals and groups. Of course, for those who do wish to create their own material for an audience, problems relating to the cost and quality of production and distribution still have to be overcome. In these matters, Rupert Murdoch has something of a start!

Perspectives on the Influence of the Media

The title 'perspectives on the influence of the media' provides a broad umbrella for a variety of approaches to analysing the relationship between the media and society. In fact, these approaches are somewhat different in kind.

Liberal and Marxist perspectives are comprehensive paradigms of how societies operate and should operate. They function at such a broad level of generalisation that it is difficult, if not impossible, finally to prove one or the other 'right' or 'wrong'. However, specific propositions in liberal and Marxist theory are susceptible to empirical proof or disproof. Thus, the Marxist proposition that ownership of the media is concentrated in relatively few hands can be factually examined. Feminist and anti-racist perspectives are more limited in scope than liberal and Marxist ones. They are concerned, respectively, with sexism and racism and either can be integrated into broader perspectives such as liberalism and Marxism (in fact, anti-racist perspective is strongly associated with Marxism) or can stand alone as critical perspectives. The ideological values behind feminist and anti-racist perspectives are obvious – indeed, the perspectives only exist because of opposition to sexism and racism.

Interactionist perspective is less ideolog-ical than the others so far mentioned. This is partly because it is a 'middle range' perspective concerned mainly with how people perceive and create everyday 'reality'. In particular, Marxists have drawn extensively on interactionism in explaining media processes at a more detailed level.

The material presented under the sub-heading 'effects research' is largely positivist in nature. Most of it is based on the behaviourist view that when stimulated by something (e.g. television) people's behaviour will change (effect) and that this effect can be measured and quantified.

LIBERAL PERSPECTIVES

LIBERAL PLURALISM Liberalism – in one or another of its forms – is probably the most widely used perspective in understanding the media in Britain and other liberal-capitalist societies. In so far as most people, including journalists, 'believe in' this approach, it is the 'dominant ideology' or, simply, most popular understanding of the media. There are several main varieties of liberal ideology but all share certain fundamental principles. The basic form of liberalism is liberal pluralism. It is based on the view that for a society to be democratic individuals and groups must be free to compete for political power and influence. It follows from this, that people must also be free to express themselves through the media – otherwise, they would not be able to compete politically. So, political freedom requires free media. Generally, liberal pluralists also believe that for political and media freedom to be achieved, a society's economy must also be 'free' or largely 'free': by which they mean capitalist or mixed.

Liberal pluralists argue that the free market is the main enabling mechanism for a free media. Freedom to own and produce media and freedom to 'consume' media output means that audiences can feedback their opinions on media content to owners and producers who can then respond. In the pluralist model, consumers – the people – ultimately 'rule' because by exercising their right of choice in consumption they can influence and, sometimes determine media content.

There are other significant aspects to liberal pluralist media theory. Traditionally, liberals have taken the view that the potential power of individual media owners is limited by the convention of editorial independence, i.e. the right of the editor to shape, say, a newspaper's opinion stance and to control its day-to-day operation. This convention has perhaps been tarnished by the willingness of owners, not least, Murdoch and Maxwell, to sack editors and by the fact that it has not been generally extended into commercial broadcasting. Finally, most media are open to some direct public access such as letter columns or 'open space' facilities.

Journalists themselves often hold a liberal (or *laissez-faire*) view of their own activities. they see themselves as trying to provide the public with objective facts to which it makes its own response(s). When journalistic opinion is expressed, the convention is that it is clearly indicated as such.

John Whale is a well-known advocate of the liberal pluralist view of the media. In the following extract he unambiguously concludes that readers rather than proprietors (owners) 'ultimately determine' the 'broad shape and nature of the press'.

It is readers who determine the character of newspapers. The Sun illustrates the point in its simplest and saddest form. Until 1964 the Daily Herald, and between 1964 and 1969 the broadsheet Sun, had struggled to interest working people principally through their intellect. The paper had declined inexorably. Murdoch gave up the attempt and went for the baser instincts. Sales soared. By May 1978, selling just under 4 million copies, the Sun was reckoned to have overtaken the Mirror – which had held the lead since winning it from the Express in 1949 – as the biggest selling national daily paper. At the Express, the message was received. The year before, after a struggle between assorted financiers, the Beaverbrook empire had passed to a shipping and property concern named Trafalgar House. The new chairman was Victor Matthews; and in November 1978 Matthews launched, from Manchester, a paper called the Daily Star which extended the Sun formula even further downmarket. At the London Evening Standard (another Beaverbrook paper) Matthew's dismissal of a cultivated editor, Simon Jenkins, in the same month presaged a similar approach there. These were owners' decisions, certainly; but they would have meant nothing without the ratification of readers.

That, in the end, is the answer to the riddle of proprietorial influence. Where it survives at all, it must still defer to the influence of readers. The policy of the Daily Telegraph, its selection and opinion of the news it reports, is decided by the editor and his senior colleagues. But there is a regulatory force which keeps the paper's policy from straying too widely or suddenly from pre-ordained paths; and that force is not the proprietor but the readers. They chose the paper for qualities they expect to see continued.

(Whale, 1977:84)

There are two main criticisms of the liberal pluralist approach. The first is that the theory of the free market does not fully work in practice. In particular, capitalism can produce large conglomerates – including media conglomerates – which may dominate the market, stifling competition and variety (see p. 420). Second, the criticism is frequently made that where the media is used exclusively or even primarily to make profit, quality can seriously suffer. For

▶ example, the highly profitable newspaper The *Sun* is often accused of tasteless, inaccurate and sometimes cruel 'cheque book journalism'.

LIBERAL PATERNALISM The term liberal paternalism is used here to describe liberals who accept the basic principles of liberal-pluralism but who also believe that, in part, the media should reflect high cultural goals and that systematic check, if not control, must be kept on the media to ensure certain general standards and quality. Liberal paternalists are prepared to accept a greater degree of state intervention in the media than pure *laissez-faire* liberals. Many liberal paternalists are strong supporters of public broadcasting, and believe that the BBC has achieved perhaps unequalled high standards.

The first Director General of the BBC, Lord Reith, was a prototype liberal paternalist. He believed in high-quality broadcasting which would inform and educate as well as entertain. Reith had the personal charisma and power to impose his beliefs for many years, and the Reithian tradition has survived in the BBC, particularly in respect of its commitment to quality broadcasting.

By the early nineteen nineties, the issue of media quality concerned many others besides liberal paternalists. There was widespread public revulsion against what were seen as the worst excesses of cheque-book journalism referred to above. Regularly, long-range photography and payment of large fees to ex-wives, lovers and 'friends' to elicit 'revelations' resulted in humiliation and invasion of privacy for the famous and, sometimes, not so famous. Successful libel actions by celebrities such as Elton John (see figure 18.1) and Tessa Sanderson put pressure on the popular press. If anything, the establishment was more incensed than the general public – not least because some of its members were prime victims of tabloid journalism. Judges imposed high fines on publications which broke the libel laws (see figure 18.1) and increasingly politicians began to threaten controlling legislation unless the press quickly 'put its house in order'.

The debate about both moral and cultural standards in the media was given urgency by the rapid expansion of the commercial

Figure 18.1
The Sun edited by Kelvin Mackenzie (bottom) paid £1 million in damages for libelling Elton John (top). Invasion of privacy and misleading reporting became a major issue in relation to the popular press in the late nineteen eighties.

broadcasting media during the late nineteen eighties and early nineteen nineties, including SKY corporation which started broadcasting in 1989. The possibility now presented itself of low-grade programmes beamed in by international satellite some of which might offend against existing norms and laws in Britain governing the portrayal of sex and violence. In 1988 the Broadcasting Standards Authority was set up to monitor sex and violence in broadcasting. Although it has powers to recommend rather than enforce, the possibility that its powers might be strengthened remains. The Broadcasting Act of 1990 was intended to enable the further commercialisation of British Broadcasting but it, too, reflected concern about quality. Companies granted broadcasting franchises had to guarantee to achieve certain quality thresholds (levels). The 1990 Broadcasting Act went some way to satisfying the aspirations of the freemarket lobby in respect to commercial television. Companies which sought franchises were required to bid against each other but any plan accepted by the ITC had to pass a quality threshold. However, critics argued that the auction system would force companies to bid beyond their means and leave them insufficiently funded to achieve high quality production. Some felt justified in their concern when Thames Television was outbid in the first auction of 1991.

Concern about media standards, then, extends far beyond liberal paternalists. Groups ranging from Marxists to traditional religions expressed similar opinion – though, of course, they put it in different ideological context. Nevertheless, it is significant that a highly pro free-market government should have been sufficiently concerned about a threatened decline in broadcasting standards to implement even the limited measures outlined above. The Labour Party favoured rather more guarantees of quality. The tradition of protective liberal paternalism has by no means been destroyed by free-market liberalism.

FREE-MARKET LIBERALISM: THE NEW RIGHT

The free-market liberals of the new right have a particularly strong commitment to the free-market and a corresponding objection to 'unnecessary' state interference in its operation. Ideologically, they are close to pre-welfare state nineteenth century liberalism. Norman Tebbitt and Rupert Murdoch are powerful exponents of this ideology.

Like the populist, Tebbitt, Murdoch is scathingly critical of those intellectuals whom he sees as interfering with audience freedom of choice by trying to impose so-called 'quality' media. In 1989 he made a rare formal statement of his views at the Edinburgh Television Festival. In his lecture, he attacked the BBC as elitist and slow to adapt, and held up American broadcasting as the model for the future. He contended that the BBC typically produces dull programmes, is obsessed with class and the past, is wary of the commercial spirit and wealth, and allows itself to be brow-beaten by government.

John Birt, deputy director-general of the BBC responded by claiming that the BBC had shown itself capable of achieving both quality and popularity. He cited Ben Elton's comedy and Tony Harrison's celebrated drama-documentary of the Salman Rushdie issue, 'Blasphemors' Banquet', as then current examples. He was perhaps implying that, though Murdoch's output usually achieved 'popularity' as measured by sales, its quality was open to criticism. By 1991, it had become arguable that, even popularity might not be achieved, as SKY and BSB merged, for financial reasons, into BSKYB.

The main criticism of the new right's media populism (attempt to appeal to a wide popular audience), is that it threatens the quality of the media by seeking the lowest – and most profitable – common denominator among the public. This criticism has two main aspects to it: a concern with journalistic quality and a concern with the moral standards expressed in the media. A wide section of public and political opinion has expressed worry on both counts, including the churches and sections of the Conservative party, especially the more traditional.

MARXIST AND SOCIALIST PERSPECTIVES

Marxists argue that the continued existence of capitalist society requires that ideas and values favourable to it are the dominant ones expressed through the media. Liberals largely agree with this, but whereas they believe capitalist ideology is dominant because it has 'won out' in 'the market place of ideas', Marxists believe that the dominance of capitalist ideology reflects capitalist control of the media.

In *The German Ideology*, Marx wrote that: 'The class which has the material means of production at its disposal has control at the same time over the production and distribution of the ideas of their age'. Marx contended that the owners of the media (mainly newspapers in his day) were able to control content. Where owners appointed managers he believed them not to be independent but answerable to the owners. Nor did Marx consider that the spread of share ownership significantly affected the control of major shareholders. Liberal pluralists contradict Marx's analysis. They argue that a 'managerial revolution' has taken place (Burnham, 1943), with the result that the operational control of major industrial (and state) organisations, including media companies, is in the hands of management. Managers are answerable not only to shareholders but to the public – as consumers of their product.

Contemporary Marxists, Murdock and Golding have attempted to refute the managerial argument. First, they argue that the processes of media concentration and conglomeration have increased the control of owners. In *Capitalism, Communication and Class Relations* (1977), they point out that in the early nineteen seventies the top five firms in the following sectors of the media accounted for:

> 71 per cent daily newspaper circulation
> 74 per cent homes with commercial television
> 78 per cent admissions to cinemas
> 70 per cent paperback sales
> 76 per cent record sales

In their more recent work they observe that concentration of ownership is as pronounced in new media fields as in established ones. For instance Robert Maxwell had major holdings in electronic data service companies, was the sole owner of Britain's largest cable TV network, and had a 20 per cent share in a French broadcasting satellite company, TDF-1. As previously noted, Rupert Murdoch's interests in media fields, established and new, are very extensive. A further point which Murdock and Golding attach great importance to is the interconnections between major share-holders of different companies who may appear to be in competition but can actually collude in their mutual interest.

Murdock and Golding's second point is that even those media organisations which may be operated by relatively independent management are also constrained by the need to maximise profits. In the drive for profit they function in a typically capitalist fashion. Thus, newspaper and television seek profitability by running advertisements and in trying to increase audience size. The BBC, too, is forced to compete for audience ratings and, despite public services ideals, is drawn into the ethos of capitalism which typifies its commercial rivals. Here, Murdock and Golding are almost tautological: a capitalist society produces a capitalist media which partly reproduces a capitalist society. In fairness, however, they also stress that the accessibility and variety of much of the new media technology provides the possibility of alternative, radical media:

The possibility of using video as a cheap and flexible campaigning tool and means of expression is already widely accepted. Alternative computer applications are less well developed but potentially even more far-reaching. The scope for radical software is enormous. The possibilities of radical databases are even greater. Picture a continuously updated information store that contained and developed the kinds of materials that Labour Research now publishes monthly. Databases can also help to develop contact networks. In the USA for example, the National Women's Mailing List keeps a file with the names and interests of over 60,000 feminists who have agreed to be listed, making it very much easier for individuals and groups to contact people with similar interests or useful expertise. The word processing facilities of many micro computers can also be used to develop collective writing, since text can be added to, deleted or moved without having to retype. Computer networks can also be a valuable campaign tool. In the spring of 1985, for example, there were large demonstrations on campuses across America to urge university authorities to pull their investments out of companies operating in South Africa. Computer messaging was used extensively to exchange information and coordinate protests ...

(Golding and Murdock, 1986:183)

THE GLASGOW UNIVERSITY MEDIA GROUP: 'BAD NEWS'? *Bad News*, the first major publication of the Glasgow Media group, concentrated on industrial relations. The groups method involved detailed content analysis of news programmes, with interpretations informed by interactionist and Marxist theories. Interactionist approach is apparent in the close analysis of the way media content is selected and framed, and Marxism in the broad class-based framework of analysis adopted. However, the Glasgow group's contention of media bias basically rests on their quantitative analysis of relevant data, i.e. news reports.

The Glasgow group demonstrates its findings on the existence of hidden 'codes' or patterns of assumption tending to favour dominant groups in several ways. First, they point out in *Bad News* that in reporting industrial disputes, the media tends to rely on official management sources. Second, they find that the language used to describe disputes favoured employers and disfavoured employees. Thus, initiatives of the former tended to be termed 'offers' or 'pleas' whereas those of the latter were described as 'demands' or 'threats'. Third, the non-verbal context of reporting similarly tended to favour employers. For instance, employers were more likely to be inter-viewed in orderly, dignified surroundings than employees' representatives. Fourth, the Glasgow group finds examples where the editing (and re-editing) of reports of disputes focuses on the negative role of striking employees (e.g. on the economy) whilst management is less critically treated. They give us an example of how a speech by then Prime Minister Wilson, warning both management and unions of the possible consequences of a strike at the Cowley car production plant, was edited down over a series of news bulletins by BBC1 to read as a warning given specifically to the unions. ITN embraced this view from the outset but BBC2 did represent the speech as critical of both management and workers. Cumulatively, the Glasgow Media group considers that the findings referred to above support their case of hidden ideological bias in television news journalism which sees industrial action primarily in terms of it being disruptive both to the economy and to the public. Such negative assumptions structure the 'agenda' – questions asked – by

journalists when reporting in this area. The Glasgow group argues that in making these assumptions, journalists tend to believe that they are reflecting the consensus of public concern about industrial conflict.

In a later publication, *War and Peace*, the Glasgow group argue that the news about the Falklands War was far more censured than required by the demands of military security (see figure 18.2). In analysing news coverage of the Women's Peace Camp at Greenham Common, they find a similar bias in favour of 'official' interpretations as apparently demonstrated by their earlier work.

There has been considerable criticism of the Glasgow group's conclusions, especially from within the media. Both BBC and ITN have asserted that there is a more objective basis to their news coverage in which they do try to present all relevant parties fairly rather than favour establishment groups such as government or employers. They have received academic support from Martin Harrison whose own analysis of the relevant broadcasts concludes that the Glasgow group itself may be characterised by a bias in selection which favours their own Marxist interpretation.

In their analysis of news production, the Glasgow group frequently refer to Stuart Hall, who reaches similar conclusions to themselves. They quote Hall as follows:

News values appear as a set of neutral, routine practices; but we need also to see formal news values as an ideological structure – to examine these rules as the formalisation and operationalisation of an ideology of news.
(Glasgow University Media Group, 1976:11)

However, both Hall and the Glasgow group believe that such 'official' ideology can be challenged both through the 'main-stream' and 'alternative' media. Hall prefers to use the concept of ideological hegemony rather than dominance (see p. 146). Hegemony, in the context of culture, means a broad power and influence to structure the cultural 'agenda' – but not the power to dictate people's beliefs and values. Alternative ideas can be effectively, if seldom easily, expressed through the media – 'the balance of cultural power' is always in flux. Indeed, Hall's own work, including his televised history of the Caribbean, is a case in point.

Figure 18.2 (Far left)

Falklands War (1982)

Twenty-nine carefully selected British reporters were kept under strict Ministry of Defence control. Reporters, who had to agree to censorship, were told what was happening after the event.
Some reports had to pass through three stages of vetting before they could be released.

(Source: Guardian)

ANTI-RACIST PERSPECTIVE

Anti-racist perspective is opposed to racism

in the media. It is a structural perspective which links racism in the media and culture generally to racism in the main institutional areas of society including the economy. Of course, much cultural activity occurs within organisational structures which, like other institutional areas, tend to be dominated by white middle-class males. However, it is ideological rather than institutional racism that this section mainly explores although in reality the two areas reinforce each other. It is useful to conceptualise anti-racism in terms of Gramsci's concept of hegemony (p. 107). Anti-racism can be thought of as a challenge to the cultural 'grip' (hegemony) of racism although in suggesting this, it is essential to bear in mind that anti-racists regard their attack on racist ideology as part of a wider challenge to institutional racism. The latter is the 'ultimate' target because it is institutions which in a practical way bring about ethnic inequalities of power and resources.

Anti-racists see racism in British culture as bound up with the history and development of the British empire and capitalism. From the late sixteenth century, British explorers regarded blacks as inferior and this supposed inferiority became part of the ideological legitimisation for conquering and enslaving them. Racist beliefs, then, legitimised commercial exploitation, including trade in human beings. James Walvin charts how black people have been caricatured in British culture as indolent, stupid, sexually immoral,

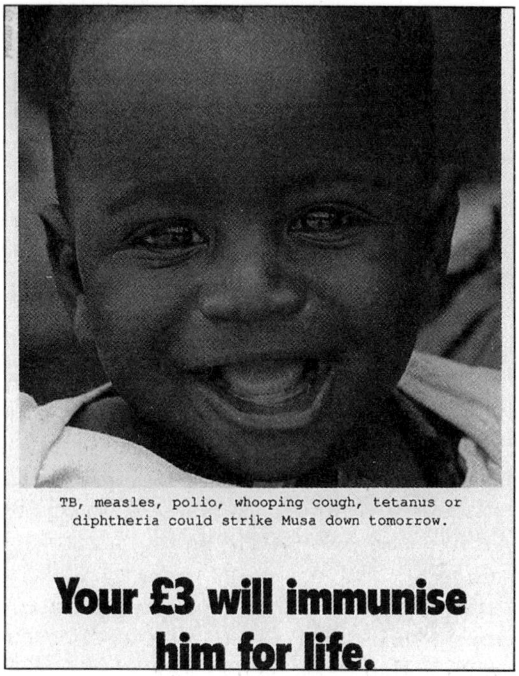

Figure 18.3
A more positive
image of a child
in need?

TB, measles, polio, whooping cough, tetanus or diphtheria could strike Musa down tomorrow.

Your £3 will immunise him for life.

and much else over several hundred years. It is important not to conceptualise such stereotypes merely in individual terms but to link the choice of stereotype with its usefulness to those making it. Walvin suggests that the nature of the stereotype varied according to the convenience of those making it at a given time:

Between the English settlement of the New World and the fumbling attempts to reconstruct the colonial government of the former slave societies, successive generations had to cope with the intricate problems of colonial economics and government. Central to all these problems was the person of the imported Black. To justify his importation, his slavery, his freedom and finally his position as a free man, Englishmen conjured up a variety of stereotype images of the Negro best suited to each particular purpose. Almost without exception these images, which made such an impression on the public at large, bore little resemblance to fact. Caricature rather than truth was the hallmark of the English impression of the Negro.

(in Husbands ed., 1982)

Uncomplimentary stereotypes of blacks were purveyed by leading nineteenth century authors, for example Carlyle and Trollope, and continued to be widespread in literature during the twentieth century. Enid Blyton, the best-selling children's writer, created a character called Sambo who, in one story, is turned white (or 'pink') as a reward for doing a good deed: 'He was a nice looking doll now as good as any other ... No wonder he's happy little pink Sambo.' It is rarer today to find such absurd stereotypes in children's literature and many mainstream publishers now offer children's books which are broadly and positively multicultural. Even so, many children's books still appear to be written and illustrated in the belief that Britain is a wholly white society. Given the importance of childhood socialisation in attitude formation this remains a serious issue.

In contemporary Britain, perhaps the most extreme stereotypes occur in the popular press. Bhikhu Parekh reviewed one such case in *New Society* (7 November 1986). In 1986 the government had imposed visa requirements on visitors from five Commonwealth countries. A relatively small number of those to whom the new requirements were to apply decided to try to 'beat the deadline': Parekh takes up the story:

When around 2500 Asians arrived, the tabloid newspapers were awash with denigratory headlines. 'Asian flood swamps airport', screamed The Express. 3000 Asians flood Britain', shouted The Sun. 'Migrants flood in', echoed The Mail. The Sun, in a six-inch headline, called them 'liars'. Only The Independent and The Guardian agreed that the scenes at Heathrow were a 'disgrace' to Britain.

Shortly after Parekh's article was published, The *Sun* weighed in with another headline: 'Cheating Asians Cost Us £5000 a Week' (27 November 1986).

It is, of course, not possible precisely to quantify the effect that such journalism has on readers. Current models of the media-audience relationship tend to be interactive rather than simple cause/effect. First, individuals select media material which interests them, and second, their attitudes are more likely to be reinforced than changed. Nevertheless, reinforcement of racism makes it more entrenched.

In addition, the media have a more general influence on society than reinforcing individual attitudes. Hartmann and Husband (1974) suggest that the media 'provide people with a picture of the world' which may influence attitude development, particularly when people have no 'situationally based knowledge' (i.e. first-hand experience) of a given phenomenon. In a survey on the media and race, they found that respondents with little or no experience of blacks had broadly more negative impressions than those who had first-hand experience of them. They explained this in terms of the tendency of the media, especially the popular press, to present blacks negatively and in circumstances involving conflict.

Anti-racist perspective, like Marxist class perspective, contextualises the media in the wider society. Thus, racism in the media is seen as ideological reinforcement of structural racial inequalities. Many anti-racists are also Marxist and racism is seen by them as functional to capitalism (see earlier in this section). Thus, John Solomos (1989) argues that in the post-war period new stereotypes were found as needed which had the effect of 'keeping blacks in their place'. Broadly, he argues that initially much of the press (and some politicians) played on the popular fear of whites of being 'swamped' by blacks whereas since the 1970s blacks have more often been presented as the threat from within, and especially as the cause of 'social problems'. Racism can function to create inequality in subtle as well as the crudely obvious ways illustrated above. Thus, Adrian Hart in *Images of the Third World* (1989) points out how even well-meaning whites, such as those who run 'aid' organisations, often present blacks in a state of dependency on whites. Repeated portrayals of blacks as 'in need' and disempowered is arguably another form of negative stereotyping, however well intentioned.

FEMINIST PERSPECTIVE: GENDER STEREOTYPING

Research into representations of women in the media has shifted in emphasis from content analysis to semiotic interpretation (i.e. the 'decoding' of signs/ images/ language/style. In relation to gender and the media, content analysis simply counts or quantifies the number of a given sex portrayed in a particular category, such as domestic or 'boss'. It was the most widely adopted technique in the nineteen fifties and sixties. More recently, qualitative analysis in the form of semiotics (defined above) has become increasingly popular.

In 1978, Gaye Tuchman reviewed gender content analysis across a range of media in *Hearth and Home: Images of Women in the Media*. Her survey of the literature showed that women were portrayed in only two significant roles: the domestic and the sexual (including the romantic). In contrast, males appeared prominently in spheres of employment, family, politics and other areas of social life. Clearly, the media were presenting men as dominant and women as subordinate (and usually as accepting this situation submissively and passively). Tuchman describes this as a 'symbolic annihilation' of women. Strong though this phrase is, many feminists would feel that the 'symbolic annihilation' of women in the media reflects something akin to the 'real annihilation' of women in society.

423

Tuchman argues that the 'symbolic annihilation' of women in the media occurs through their absence, condemnation or trivialisation. They tend to be absent from positions of power, authority and status. They are condemned by such damning stereotypes as 'bitchy', 'catty', 'gossipy' and 'not interested in 'important' (i.e. male dominated) things.' They are trivialised by being presented as mainly interested in romance or by appearing as sex objects or domestic workers. Whilst some media, including the main television channels, now seem less sexist in the way women are presented, in other areas, such as tabloid newspapers and 'teen' magazines, there appears to have been less change.

Angela McRobbie's *Teenage Girls: Jackie, and the Ideology of Adolescent Femininity* is an example of the more qualitative research mentioned earlier by Ross Gill. McRobbie finds that *Jackie* is characterised by a recurrent 'code of romance' in which the ultimate object of a girl is a boy. Frame after frame reiterates this simple message:

Each frame represents a selection from the development of the plot, and is credited with an importance which those intervening moments are not. Thus the train, supermarket, and office have meaning, to the extent that they represent potential meeting-places where the girl could well bump into the prospective boyfriend, who lurks round every corner. It is this which determines their inclusion in the plot; the possibility that everyday life could be transformed into social life.

Within these frames themselves the way the figures look, act, and pose contributes also to the ideology of romance ...

(Angela McRobbie, in Bernard Waites et al, 1983:272)

According to McRobbie, there are two central features of the ideology of adolescent femininity as presented by *Jackie*. First, it sets up 'the personal' as of prime importance to the teenage girl. Secondly, *Jackie* 'presents "romantic individualism", as the ethos ... for the teenage girl.' So, individualism is not contextualised in terms of, say, the pursuit of career or academic excellence but in terms of 'romance' or 'falling in love'. 'In the end' (i.e. according to the 'code' or 'myth' or

'story'), romance overrides everything, including friendship with other girls (who may be both supporters and competitors in 'the search for romance').

What effect does reading material such as *Jackie* have on teenage girls? As McRobbie acknowledges, we do not know and research does not tell us. Perhaps, many girls 'read' it for relaxation or even to laugh at. On the other hand, perhaps the heroines of *Jackie* do offer a role model which is consciously or unconsciously imitated. In general, research at the Centre for Cultural Studies where McRobbie worked indicated a strong link between ideology and social structure. In this case, the romantic and individualistic ideology of adolescent femininity might socialise many girls for life – situations subordinate to males both domestically and in paid work and in society generally. In so far as females do tend to occupy such subordinate positions, there is a 'complementary fit' between ideology and structure.

In contemporary Britain, there are many attempts to counter traditional patterns of gender socialisation in the media by presenting females positively, with a capacity for independence, cooperation, and having varied and demanding goals and the ability to achieve them.

INTERACTIONIST PERSPECTIVE

Interactionist perspective on the media differs from liberal and Marxist in that it is less specifically political. The latter perspectives are based, in part, on theories of how society should be, whereas symbolic interactionism offers middle-range analysis of certain social psychological processes. Thus, 'labelling' and 'stereotyping' were originally interactionist concepts although they are now absorbed into sociology generally, particularly radical sociology.

Three specific applications of interactionist media analysis will be discussed here. First, the production of media content by media professionals; secondly, audience interaction with the media; thirdly, the tendency of the media to reinforce consensus.

The first point – the production of media content – has largely been researched in relation to 'the news'. The news is first selected and then 'framed' within the context of assumptions about what is important (Hall, 1973) and within certain organisational routines and constraints. Howard Becker argues that the news reporters tend to seek the opinions of those with power and status rather than those without them. He refers to this as 'the hierarchy of credibility'. Further, the powerful are able to use their knowledge of the routine of news production by, for instance, exploiting news deadlines in relation to press releases and speeches. So whilst the news media play 'gate-keeping' (decide what is or is not news) and 'agenda-setting' (decide the order of importance of news) roles in relation to the news, they do so under the influence of powerful people and institutions. It will be obvious that this analysis lends itself to Marxist interpretation and, in fact, Stuart Hall has argued that 'news values' reflect much more the interests of capital than of the working class.

It is in the area of audience interaction that interactionists have done some of their most imaginative work. Stan Cohen's *Folk Devils and Moral Panics: The Creation of the Mods and Rockers* remains a classic study of the relationship between the media and deviance. Cohen employs several concepts (as previously used by Howard Becker), which have become standard in media analysis. He argues that the media have the ability to 'amplify' certain forms of behaviour such as youth gang confrontations and soccer hooliganism. Amplification occurs in two forms: first, the media may make an event seem 'bigger' than it was; secondly, media coverage of an event may have 'the effect of triggering off events of a similar order'. Cohen refers to a 'spiral of amplification' by which the Mods' and Rockers' confrontations of the mid-sixties appeared to escalate as they fed off the media.

Cohen's work can also be used to illustrate the consensus-reinforcing role the media can play. He gives a very useful ideal type model of how the process of deviancy selection, condemnation, and consensus-affirmation can occur. He titles the model, the 'signification spiral' (that is, the labelling of deviance) and it is only slightly adapted here:

THE SIGNIFICATION SPIRAL

1 Identification of specific issue: e.g. student political 'extremism'.
2 Identification of culprits: e.g. 'subversive minority', 'lunatic fringe'.
3 Convergence: Linking of issue to other problems: e.g. lack of discipline and control of the young.
4 Notion of thresholds – once they are crossed, further escalation must result – 'slippery slope to anarchy'.
5 Explaining, warning and prophesying – 'Look what happened elsewhere'.
6 Call for firm steps – clamp down hard leads to the effect of reinforcing consensus.

A key part in the process of consensus reinforcement is played by what Cohen refers to as 'moral entrepreneurs' or 'moral crusaders'. These people set themselves up as the conscience of society and orchestrate the 'moral panic' that is often the result of deviancy and/or deviancy amplification by the media. Mrs Mary Whitehouse of the National Viewers' and Listeners Association is one of the best known of these.

In Britain, interactionist analysis of the media has frequently been integrated into broader structural analysis, particularly Marxist, which argues that inequalities present in the media reflect those in society. However, as Jock Young points out, people's social experience by no means always leads them to conform to the consensus and similarly there is scope in the media for the expression of divergent and alternative ideas and values.

Figure 18.5 is largely based on a similar diagram by John Muncie (*Social Studies Review*, November 1987). Muncie suggests that the panics fall roughly into three phases: 'discrete' (1950s/early 60s); more 'diffuse' (1964–70), and 'generalised' (1970s–early 80s). In other words, the tendency to link specific examples ('outbreaks') with a

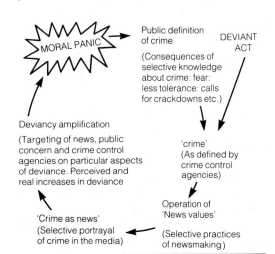

(Source: Social Studies Review, Nov. 1987)

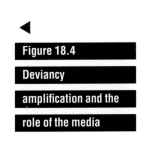

Figure 18.4

Deviancy

amplification and the

role of the media

Examples of Moral Panics)

1950s	Teddy Boys
Early 1960s	Mods and Rockers
Late 1960s	Permissiveness – Drugs, Sexual 'Freedom' Youth Violence – Skinheads, Football Hooliganism Radical Trade Unionism
1970s	'Muggings' (Racial Overtones to 'the panic') Social Security 'Scroungers' Youth Subcultures, e.g. Punks
1980s	Feminist, e.g. Greenham Common Protest Urban Disorder (again, with racial overtones), AIDS (Some scapegoating of homosexuals) Child Abuse Drugs – especially 'crack'

The above diagram is largely based on a similar one by John Muncie (*Social Studies Review*, November 1987). Muncie suggests that the panics fall roughly into three phases: 'discrete' (1950s/early 60s); more 'diffuse' (1964–70), and 'generalised' (1970s–early 80s). In other words, the tendency to link specific examples ('outbreaks') with a supposed wider social 'crisis' has increased. Certainly, this fits in with the view that Thatcherism (and Reaganism) was a response to a 'boundary crisis' in which the limits (boundary) of 'Civilised' moral values were thought to be 'threatened'

Figure 18.5

supposed wider social 'crisis' has increased. Certainly, this fits in with the view that Thatcherism (and Reaganism) was a response to a 'boundary crisis' in which the limits (boundary) of 'civilised' moral values were thought to be 'threatened' (see p. 308).

EFFECTS RESEARCH

To a greater or lesser extent, all the theories so far discussed are concerned with the effects of the media. However, liberal, Marxist and interactionist theory are all, to varying extents, interactive: they assume active involvement on the part of audiences in selecting and, generally, evaluating media content. Further, these theories contextualise the media within the wider society.

From the early part of the century, a rather different model of the relationship between media and audience has persisted. No single name is given to this tradition of research but in so far as it is characterised by an attempt to measure the effect of media 'stimuli' on individuals and conceives of them as reactive rather than interactive, it has much in common with positivism. An early example of this type of approach – still sometimes adopted today – was mass society

theory – sometimes referred to as 'hypodermic needle' theory, in which the masses are seen as 'doped' by the media.

More recent work by Dr William Belson 1980, and by psychologists H J Eysenck and D K Nias 1978 is far more empirical than mass society theory, but resembles the latter in its tendency to see the individual as the rather passive object upon whom the media 'produces effects'. Belson compared the behaviour and viewing habits of 1,565 London boys aged between 13 and 16, between 1959 and 1971. Markedly less violence was admitted by those who watched less television. Of those who had watched a lot of violence on television, 7.5 per cent confessed to having engaged in serious violence themselves. Belson's findings clearly need to be taken seriously, but they are certainly open to criticism. It cannot be proved that watching more violence on television was the factor that 'caused' more violence. Other variables may have been operative. Watching a lot of television is itself associated with lower socio-economic status. Perhaps it is some other factor or factors associated with lower class culture that produces violent behaviour. It is almost impossible to separate the effect of television from other variables affecting behaviour.

Eysenck and Nias, in their own laboratory research into violence and the media, attempt to isolate the effect of violent films on behaviour from that of other factors. Groups – both adult and children – exposed to televised violence consistently behave more aggressively than control groups. If – and they do not show this – these effects were duplicated in real life then they would have proved their case. But before rushing to conclusions, it is prudent to mention some critical comments on Eysenck and Nias' work. As Anthony Smith points out, comparative cultural data complicates the apparently simple truth of their findings. Japan, for example, has a very substantial degree of violence in its television, but a very low level of social violence. It seems that the Japanese emphasise the suffering caused by violence, rather than the aggression that caused it. This observation leads Smith on to a wider point. He suggests, in effect, that society gets the media it deserves. A violent society will tend to produce violence on the media – no doubt many will even want violence on the media. Though Smith does

Who Watches Most

Hours of viewing per person per day, by age. March 1990

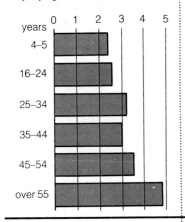

years	0 1 2 3 4 5
4–5	
16–24	
25–34	
35–44	
45–54	
over 55	

(Source: Barr)

Q For how long did you watch television programmes (live or recorded) after school yesterday?

Percentage	1st year (11+)		3rd year (13+)		5th year (15+)	
	Boys	Girls	Boys	Girls	Boys	Girls
None	5.3	6.6	4.9	6.0	6.9	8.1
Less than 1hr	13.6	16.9	12.7	16.5	14.4	19.2
1–2hr	20.4	23.4	18.8	21.7	20.8	22.7
2–3hr	19.4	18.4	21.7	18.4	21.0	20.0
3–4hr	14.6	15.0	18.1	16.7	16.1	14.9
4–5hr	11.3	9.3	9.7	9.8	10.3	7.5
5hrs or longer	15.4	10.4	14.1	10.8	10.3	7.6

(Source: Exeter University)

Figure 18.6

Some commentators express concern about the effects of television on the young, although older age groups watch more. However, a minority of the young watch almost to saturation point.

not say this, he seems to imply that what first needs reducing is real violence, then, perhaps, people will want less violent make-believe. This is not at all the conclusion of Eysenck and Nias, who ask for a degree of censorship of media violence and pornography. In so doing, they have the support of the National Viewers' and Listeners' Association, the 'brainchild' of Mrs Mary Whitehouse. Liberals and radicals alike tend to resist this. If entertainment, even art, can be censored today, who knows how far censorship may go tomorrow? The issue is important enough in itself but, for our more immediate academic purposes, it is worth noting how social scientific research can easily become a part of political and social policy debate. So much for the ivory tower!

CONCLUSION Despite the seemingly unstoppable development and pervasive impact of the media, it is not agreed who controls them. The state, capital, media professionals, and the audience are all suggested candidates for prime controlling agency. Sinister images of the media as the all-seeing eye of government or as the purveyor of trash for profit abound in modern literature. However, there are obvious counter trends to centralised control. Alvin Toffler sees increasing options for the individual both as a consumer of media output and as a potential producer (e.g. of audio and video tapes and material produced through desk-top publishing). Certainly, it now seems more possible for individuals and small groups to create 'alternative' media both by selective use of the increasing range of mass media products and by producing their own. How far this freedom is meaningfully available only to a few – an intellectual elite, perhaps – is a matter for critical consideration.

SUMMARY

1 Media ownership in Britain is characterised by concentration and conglomeration. Concentration refers to the merger of media businesses so that control becomes concentrated in fewer hands. Conglomerates form when one company takes over another (or others) either in the same or in a different line of business.

2 There are a number of perspectives on the influence and effects of the media, including three types of liberal perspective.

3 Liberal pluralism considers that many influences and opinions are expressed through and exerted upon

the media. The media are perceived as democratic.

4 Liberal paternalism modifies a commitment to a democratic media with a concern that the media is required to maintain high cultural standards.

5 Free market liberalism wants a wholly private media responsive to competition and to consumer demand.

6 Marxist and socialist perspectives argue that private control of the media threatens media freedom. To a greater or lesser extent, the media is seen as reproducing and reinforcing capitalist ideoloby.

7 Feminist perspective is opposed to representations of women in the media which continually reinforce negative stereotypes, e.g. women as decorative or compliant. Positively, feminists want women to be presented in the media as creative, assertive and as the equals of men.

8 Anti-racist perspective is opposed to representations of black people in the media which continually reinforce negative stereotypes, e.g. as subordinate to white people or as 'clowns' or 'entertainers'. Positively, anti-racists want black people to be presented in the media as capable of exercising power and authority.

9 Interactionism is mainly a middle-range perspective which explores the two-way flow of influence between the media and audiences (who can sometimes almost 'take over' the media).

10 Effects research reflects the positivist model that the influence of the media on behaviour can be isolated and measured. Effects research particularly concentrated on the effects of media images of sex and violence.

RESEARCH AND COURSEWORK

The media is the graveyard of many a well-intentioned student project or assignment. This is because many media projects attempt to establish what the effects of the media are on behaviour. It is very difficult to establish such effects in any circumstances and particularly so given the limitations of student research. Rather than attempt generalised research suggestions here, it may be better briefly to explore a particular research technique – content analysis. Content analysis can be either purely quantitative or, better, involve both a quantitative and qualitative aspect. Ros Gill suggests five stages in the content analysis of a daily paper but these could apply to other publications, including 'teen' magazines. (It needs to be stressed, however, that content analysis in itself is simply a research technique and would only be part of an adequately theorised piece of work.)

Using sexism as an example, Gill's five stages are:

1 Having *familiarised* yourself with the newspaper, count how many articles feature a woman or women as the main subject. (You may wish to do a comparison with the number featuring men.)

2 *Measure* up how many column inches the articles on women take up as a proportion of the total paper.

3 Decide how to *categorise* or label the articles according to type, e.g. about sportswomen, businesswomen, etc.

4 Analyse more thoroughly two or three articles about women. If you wish to maintain the *quantitative* nature of your research, you could count the number of words or references to, for instance, a woman's physical appearance or to her domestic or familiar role.

5 Stage four takes the research perhaps as far as it can go in a quantitative direction. From here you could move into a more *qualitative* *interpretation* of the words, images and any other 'code carriers' in your material. You may or may not find themes of female subordination (romantic? sexual?) and male dominance. If you do find positive images of females, it may be worth analysing in what context these occur. Do they still appear positive, even after you have examined their context?

FURTHER READING

Brian Dutton's *The Media (Longman, 1986)* and David Barrat's *Media Sociology* (Tavistock, 1986) are good, general introductions to the area. James Curran et al. eds., *Bending Reality: The State of the Media* (Pluto, 1986) is a stimulating collection of readings.

QUESTIONS

1 Assess the extent to which ownership of the mass media can influence the content of the mass media. (AEB, 1988)
2 How have sociological approaches to the study of the mass media changed over the last 40 years? (AEB, 1989)
3 'Reporting of the news tends to be partial, selective and biased'. Discuss. (London, 1990)

From Rural Community to Urban Society

There have, of course, been great changes in Western society in the last two hundred years. Crudely, we can say that Western society has moved from the traditional to the modern. Poorer societies – nearly all of them in the southern hemisphere – are today going through a similar process of change even though many are trying to control, interpret or even resist it in their own way. What we seek, therefore, are concepts and theories that explain and illuminate this near-universal pattern of change.

The shift from traditional to modern is probably the most fundamental development in world history. Raymond Aron, the French sociologist, remarked that it was not until he visited India that he realised that the significant division in the world was not between communism and capitalism but between the modern, industrially-advanced states and those which remained industrially underdeveloped. Over-simplified or not, this comment at least helps to knock aside the cultural blinkers which often obscure the way Westerners see the world.

COMMUNITY DEFINED

It is frequently observed that over the past few centuries there has been a 'loss of community'. This comment is often expressed with the sentiment that, in a human rather than material way, life was better 'then' than 'now'. Before any assessment of the validity of this feeling can be made, we must be clear about what is meant by community. There are three major usages:

1 The term community is employed to describe locality (a given geographical area) as a basis of social organisation. Thus, a traditional rural village where people are born, live and die close to each other fits this usage.

2 Community is used to refer to a local social system or set of relationships that centre upon a given locality. Margaret Stacey suggests that, from a sociological point of view, it is the concentration of relationships, rather than the geographical factor that matters. Stacey would prefer to drop the term community in favour of local social system. She considers that the former term has acquired so many meanings that a precise use of it is almost impossible, whereas the latter term simply indicates relationships in a given locality as the topic for study.

3 Community is also used to describe a type of relationship which produces a strong sense of shared identity. This usage does not depend on physical whereabouts or even on people having met each other. Thus, it is possible to refer to the Catholic or Jewish community in a neighbourhood, town, country or, even, throughout the world. Sometimes a shared threat or triumph can produce or intensify a 'feeling of community'. Thus, people in Britain during the Second World War sometimes claim that there was 'a stronger sense of community' then. As Howard Newby points out it is 'loss of community' in terms of shared identity and accompanying experiences that accounts for much of the usage of the phrase.

We will consider how useful and accurate the notion 'loss of community' is when we have reviewed the literature comparing traditional and modern society. First, however, you might find it helpful to 'test' the above usages of community against your own experience. Usages **1** and/or **2** might apply to your local area whereas usage **3** might apply to some experience you have had.

FERDINAND TÖNNIES AND EMILE DURKHEIM: GEMEINSCHAFT/GESELLSCHAFT AND MECHANICAL/ORGANIC SOLIDARITY

Tönnies and Durkheim sought to understand the change from traditional to modern society. Their major writings on this matter were published before the turn of the century and their focus was European rather than global. Nevertheless, their theories have influenced more recent thinkers, particularly those of a functionalist perspective, who have had a major interest in world development.

Tönnies in *Gemeinschaft and Gesellschaft* (1887), and Durkheim in *The Division of*

Labour (1893), contrast the social life of traditional rural communities with that of rapidly developing, industrial urban areas. On the one hand, they stressed family and community as sources of identity and support and, on the other, their relative weakness in the urban context where a more individualistic and impersonal way of life was developing. Tönnies used the terms gemeinschaft and gesellschaft to describe this broad sweep of social change. Gemeinschaft means community and gesellschaft can be translated either as society or association. He considered gemeinschaft relationships to involve the whole person and to be typical of rural life. Because people related more fully to each other, and not simply in respect of their specific functional roles (shopkeeper, policeman, teacher), greater mutual involvement and caring existed, and so a stronger community was formed. Thus, a policeman was not merely somebody who did a given job, but a friend or at least an acquaintance who had a general concern for the order and welfare of the community. The difference between the two types of relationships is summed up in the admittedly rather exaggerated and idealised contrast between the 'friendly village bobby' and the modern, panda-car policeman.

Gesellschaft relationships are seen as associations or transactions for practical purposes, with little informal content. Dealings with 'modern' professionals such as lawyers or doctors tend to be of this kind. Terms that are virtually interchangeable with the rather cumbersome phrases gemeinschaft and gesellschaft relationships are, respectively, holistic (full) and segmental (partial) relationships. Tönnies used his key terms not only to describe relationships but also organisations. Gemeinschaftlich ('community-like') organisations such as the church are stronger in traditional societies, whereas gesellschaftlich organisations, such as big businesses, are stronger in modern societies. Churches have a moral and emotional influence, whereas businesses predominate in the practical and economic spheres. These examples illustrate the deep change perceived by Tönnies from the moral/emotional quality of traditional life to the practical/rational quality of modern life.

Durkheim's analysis in *The Division of Labour in Society* (1907) concentrated rather more systematically than did Tönnies on the problem of how societies achieve social order and cohesion or, to use his term, social solidarity. Nevertheless, his terms mechanical and organic solidarity overlap and complement Tönnies' gemeinschaft and gesellschaft. He described solidarity in traditional societies as mechanical and in industrial societies as organic. Mechanical solidarity is the product of a uniformly accepted and strictly enforced system of belief and conduct and is facilitated by a small, homogeneous (similar) population. Classically, it occurs in primitive or traditional societies in which everybody shares the same religiously inspired beliefs and habits. In such societies, a person would not think of rejecting the moral consensus: personal fulfilment and identity are gained by identifying with the whole group and not through a separate sense of individuality. A different basis of order and cohesion – organic solidarity – develops as societies become more complex. Organic solidarity is a product not of common beliefs but of shared material interests and practical interdependence. To understand this, we must first describe what Durkheim meant by the division of labour. The division of labour means that work is broken down into specialised tasks performed by different people. It is a particular feature of modern society, and assembly-line production may be considered the prime example of it. Organisationally and humanly, the division of labour divides people but it also makes them more dependent on one another. Thus, a single group of workers, say toolsetters, can bring an assembly-line to a halt by taking disruptive industrial action. Interdependence is broader than this example might imply and encompasses the whole of a modern society – a strike in the gas or electricity industries might bring other forms of industrial production to a halt. Durkheim himself succinctly reconciles the paradox of increased job or role specialisation with increased solidarity:

This (organic) solidarity resembles that which we observe among the higher animals. Each organ, in effect, has its special character and autonomy; and yet the unity of the organism is as great as the individuation of the parts is more marked. Because of this analogy, we propose to call the solidarity which is due to the division of labour, 'organic.' (1947)

Although Durkheim commented on the strength of organic solidarity, he felt that the ultimate stability of modern society depended on finding a new moral basis of solidarity in addition to practical inter-dependence. He argued that without moral and normative consensus in society, people tend to suffer from anomie – a sense of normlessness or lack of moral guidance to behaviour. In such circumstances, deviant activities such as crime and suicide tend to rise. We examine Durkheim's theory of anomie and deviance in greater detail in chapters 13 and 15.

The work of Georg Simmel, (1858–1918), echoes many of the sentiments of Tönnies and Durkheim. More than they, he attributed most that is characteristic of modern life, including 'lack of community', almost solely to the growth of the city. His stress on the impersonality and isolation of city life parallels Durkheim's concern with anomie. Simmel's particular interest in the effect of the urban environment on the individual – eloquently expressed in his essay *The Mind and the Metropolis* – places him as much within the tradition of social psychology as sociology. This essay and his work on dyads (two people) or tryads (three people) have led some to claim him as a founding father of interactionism, which is the sociological perspective that gives most attention to individual psychology.

Yet Simmel also had a strong sense of structure, as his analysis of the characteristics of urban life shows. He designated urban life as rational in the sense that it involves quick, logical and calculating reactions. This is because of the many practical, money-based relationships that city life depends upon. He contrasted this to the slow, habitual quality of rural life. Quite simply, he argued that the mind became more agile in the city through sheet overstimulation. Crudely, we could say that he gives academic clothing to the popular stereotypes of 'city slicker' and 'country bumpkin.' There is no doubt, however, that like Tönnies and Durkheim, Simmel is on the side of what he sees as a receding rural past, rather than the emerging urban present. He regards the blasé and reserved attitudes necessary to cope in the city as poor change for the involvement and community of rural life, despite the greater material wealth and cultural sophistication of the city. Within it, the values of the market-place so predominate that people often treat others as things or mere bearers of commodities and services. Like Durkheim, Simmel had great influence on the Chicago School of urban sociologists, whose work we consider shortly.

COMMENT ON THE 'COMMUNITY/SOCIETY' MODEL

Several comments and criticisms can be made about the community/society model. Firstly, it is suffused with conservative romanticism about the past. As a result, it tends to minimise the repressive nature of traditional community and perhaps exaggerate its satisfying aspects. Secondly, the model largely disregards class conflict, or reduces it to the level of mere 'disequilibrium' in society. There were immense differences in wealth, power, life-style and prestige between people before the industrial revolution, as well as after it. The fact that the privileged position of the nobility was sanctioned by custom, tradition and religion never did convince all the peasantry that such glaring inequalities were either natural or justifiable. Thirdly, a bi-polar or two part model of change is too simple. Durkheim himself constructed a more complex scheme of comparative change but rather than describe this in detail now, we will go on instead to consider more recent and often more complex theories of order and change.

TALCOTT PARSONS' PATTERN VARIABLES

Parsons' attempt to analyse the transition from traditional to modern society owes something to both Durkheim and Weber. His lists of pattern variables (which categorise pairs of contrasting values and norms) can be regarded as an expansion of Durkheim's mechanical-organic axis of comparison. Accordingly, we can present them as follows:

Pattern Variables 'A': characteristic of Traditional Society	Pattern Variables 'B': characteristic of Modern Society
Ascription: The status etc. a person is given at birth, for example, king	*Achievement:* The status a person acquires through her/his own efforts, for example, a pop star

433

(Role) Diffuseness: relationships are broad or gemein-schaftlich (see above)

Particularism: people treat each other in a *personal* way, so a farm-labourer asks 'the squire' to give his son a job

Affectivity: the expression and satisfaction of emotions is felt to be important, e.g. criminals are publicly punished, so the community can express its vengeance

Collective Orientation: shared interests are most important, for example, with the family or community

(Role) Specificity: relationships are for for specific purposes or gesellschaftlich (see above)

Universalism: the same rules, princi-ples or laws apply to everybody equally, as in appointing a person to a post in the civil service

Affective Neutrality: the affective or emo-tional side of people is controlled so that it does not interfere with 'the job in hand', e.g. bereaved people must control their grief in public

Self-Orientation: individual interest is most important, as in the pursuit of personal success even if it distances an individual from her/his family

At this stage, it is enough to read through Parsons' pattern variables paying as much attention to the examples as to Parsons' tongue-twisting terminology itself. Having presented his pattern variables as a contrast between traditional and modern society, we must immediately complicate the picture. First, Parsons fully recognised, as did Tönnies and Durkheim, that there can be considerable overlap between the two types of society. Indeed, it makes sense to think in terms of a graded rural-urban continuum (development) of which pattern variables 'A' and 'B' are the extremes, which, in practice, are more likely to appear together in various 'mixes.' Further, Parsons considered that though modern society is relatively rational and affectively neutral, people do of course have feelings which they need and want to express. These feelings or 'expressive functional imperatives', as Parsons called them, find their main outlet in the kinship and cultural community sub-systems (see chapter 22). However, what we want to emphasise here is the continuity of Parsons' model of societal types with those of

Durkheim and Tönnies. As such, it hardly does more than offer a useful comparative check-list for locating given societies on a traditional-modern continuum. Thus, an Indian tribe would 'score' high under 'A', a modern state high under 'B', and an industrially developing country, such as Saudi Arabia, would show a mix. We will further evaluate Parsons' pattern variable model in the section on development later in this chapter.

THE URBAN AND COMMUNITY STUDIES OF THE CHICAGO SCHOOL OF SOCIOLOGY

The Chicago school of sociology established an international reputation between the two world wars. Durkheim was a major influence on the urban sociology for which the school became renowned. This showed itself in two ways: first, in the clear cut contrast made between rural, 'folk' society and urban society, and also in the use of the organic analogy to describe the processes of urban life.

Louis Wirth followed Durkheim closely in making a firm distinction between rural and urban society. He defined the city in terms of three fundamental features: population size, density and heterogeneity (Wirth, 1938). These characteristics meant that though the city dweller would experience more human contacts than the rural inhabitant, he would also feel more isolated because of their emotionally 'empty' nature. Social interactions typical of the city, those required to obtain goods and services, were seen by Wirth as impersonal, segmental (narrow in scope), superficial, transitory, and usually of a purely practical or instrumental kind. These kinds of interactions were referred to as secondary contacts. Wirth considered that secondary contacts had increased at the expense of primary contacts (which are total relationships involving emotional as well as practical content, such as those within a family). Like Durkheim, Wirth saw a partial solution to individual atomisation in the rise of voluntary associations, representative political institutions, industrial organisations and other collective or corporate organisations. However, he too did not think these provided the quality of emotional self-expression characteristic of primary group relations.

It is in the work of another urban sociologist of the Chicago school, S W Burgess, that we find the most faithful application of functionalist theory to the physical and social development of the city. Burgess describes urban processes 'as a resultant of organisation and disorganisation analogous to the anabolic and catabolic processes of metabolism in the body'. More usually, Burgess draws on plant ecology rather than human biology as a model for understanding urban processes. He writes of 'urban ecology' almost as if it is an impersonal and natural phenomenon, rather than a human creation and susceptible to control.

Burgess presents a model or, as he referred to it, ideal construction, of the tendency of urban areas to expand radially from the central business district. The centre circle of the series of concentric circles in the model is the main business area. Next comes the zone of transition containing the slums and ghettos of the lower working class and immigrant groups. This zone is also characterised by cheap hotels and lodging houses and the easy availability of drink and sex. Other descriptions of this zone used by Chicago sociologists still sometimes employed are 'twilight zone' and 'zone of deterioration'. Later we shall look in some detail at the analysis of 'lower class deviance' within this zone, developed by sociologists at the University of Chicago (chapter 13, pp. 301–2). The next zone contains the homes of more successful and respectable working class people: it is an area of escape from the ghetto. Beyond are the higher class residential areas which make up the next zone. Finally, there is the commuter zone interspersed with countryside and farmland and merging into predominantly rural areas.

In his own day, Burgess' model was far from universally applicable – even in the United States. Since the Second World War, residential patterns have become still further complicated, particularly in countries such as England and Holland, where public housing projects have often been built outside the central urban zones. As a guide to the physical location of particular social groups and as a way of understanding why these groups inhabit particular areas, Burgess's work is inadequate. It does make the point, however, that social groups are cut off from one another both spatially and in their way of life or culture. Other urban sociologists, including Hoyt, have argued that a sectoral model provides a more accurate description of the patterns of neighbourhood layout. More recently, B T Robson's carefully researched study of residential patterns in Sunderland found that Hoyt's model applied closely to the south of the city, and Burgess' somewhat less precisely to the north.

Sociologists now consider other issues to be more important than the relationship between space and residential patterns as such. One such issue is to explain how physical and spatial environments affect people's social and cultural opportunities and the nature and quality of their interactions. We can refer to this type of analysis as socio-spatial. A further sociological concern is to identify the factors that enable some social and ethnic groups to live in 'desirable' neighbourhoods and which force others to live in slums. A major criticism of the sociologists of the Chicago school is that they largely ignored this problem. Their work is descriptive rather than explanatory. Instead of examining how the free-market system in land and property affected socio-spatial systems, they assumed these effects to be 'natural' and therefore did not analyse what caused them. Because they did not adequately examine how the control of wealth and power affects residential patterns and community life, their work can be said to be clearly limited by their own belief in, or ideological commitment to, capitalism. As with Tönnies, Durkheim and Parsons, what they took for granted masks vital issues of social justice both in relation to what might be considered a fair distribution of material resources (property ownership) and in respect of the differential availability of cultural opportunities (educational facilities) between people living in different areas. The Chicago school failed to refine and develop significantly the thinking of their mentor, Durkheim. In addition to the points made above, they underestimate both the survival of the community in the city and the ability of people to develop means of self-expression other than within primary groups. It is to the issue of 'loss of community' that we now turn.

CRITICISMS OF THE 'LOSS OF COMMUNITY' THESIS

The works we have so far discussed have been at the level of 'grand theory'. Perhaps the best way of testing the ideas presented in them is by means of the community study. Of course, it is impossible to go back and examine at first hand what community was once like, but at least the persistent stereotype that community has declined can be measured against real cases. In addition, the world offers many examples of traditional as well as modern communities and these can be studied for comparative purposes. Our first case-study is of just such a kind.

SOME CASE STUDIES In the nineteen thirties, Robert Redfield published a study of social life in Tepoztlan, a Mexican village. He found a stable, well-integrated and harmonious community. In 1949 an account of the same village appeared, written by Oscar Lewis. He discovered a tense, divided and distrustful community. It seems highly probable that some of the apparent 'change' lay in the eyes of the beholder rather than in the social life of the people of Tepoztlan. More precisely, the two researchers approached the village with different expectations and theoretical perspectives: Redfield was predisposed to find community, and Lewis was conscious of the degradation that poverty can produce in traditional societies. Howard Newby, who has a keen eye for the relationship between sociologists' personal values, their choice of theoretical and methodological approach, and their ultimate 'findings', describes the discrepancy between the reports of Redfield and Lewis as 'unnerving'. It reminds us that despite sociologists' impressive battery of research apparatus, they, like others, sometimes end up seeing what they want to see. With due caution, therefore, it can only be said that Lewis further opened up the doubts about the gemeinschaftlich qualities of traditional communities.

Studies of urban life, however, have raised questions about the gesellschaft side of the comparative model. Herbert Gans' *The Urban Villagers* describes the lively, 'village-like' ethnic and working class communities of Boston's West End and New York's Lower East Side. The individual is seldom isolated, but supported by informal groups of family, kin and friends. We have already referred to Willmott and Young's Bethnal Green study which was published in 1957. Some seventy years after Tönnies mourned the passing of community, Willmott and Young found a thriving community in an inner city industrial area. They emphasise especially how 'mum' figures are at the centre of local interactions, functioning as combined information exchanges and transit-depots. The key link in the traditional working class extended family is the relationship between mother and daughter. This continues when the daughter is married because of the likelihood that the newly married couple will live close to the female's family of origin or, in the early days of marriage, actually in her parents' home. Traditionally, men spent much of their leisure time separately from women in pubs and Working Men's or Labour Clubs. This pattern of segregation has long been breaking down, though there are still public bars in some areas where 'respectable' women would not drink, even in male company. Working class children of all ages tend to be left to get on with their own lives much more than middle class children and 'playing out in the backs' or 'on the streets' can be a major activity until well into adolescence, especially for boys. Any 'mischief they get up to' is likely to be met with rougher parental justice than a middle class child would normally expect to receive. Traditional working class community is woven in a web of 'talk' and 'gossip' and in the passing of time together in ways more or less amusing or practically useful. There are reserved areas of personal and family privacy but the whole is or was, relatively open, collective and social.

The waning of the above pattern of life might be regarded as a second phase – and, perhaps, a more genuine one – in 'loss of community'. But the fact that traditional working class community is breaking up does not mean it never existed. Some recent commentators, because they no longer find thriving working class communities of the kind described twenty five years ago by Willmott and Young, seem almost to assume that the whole phenomenon is a romantic fiction. But one of the reasons for chronicling traditional working class life was an awareness of its imminent decline (for more detailed discussion of this issue, see pp. 61–3).

Another development that has undermined any simplistic rural-urban contrast is the fast growth of commuter villages. In *Urbs in Rure (The City in the Countryside)*, R E Pahl draws our attention to the commuter invasion of rural areas. Some villages are almost wholly occupied by people who work elsewhere. Pahl has also written of the culture clash between indigenous village inhabitants and commuters. The irony is that in their search for community, commuters sometimes destroy what they are looking for. Other studies have shown that class division, business rationality and many of the problems of isolation and anomie frequently associated with urban life also occur in rural Britain.

In addition to the above case studies, it is worth recalling that historical enquiry has also thrown doubt on notions of traditional community, at least in so far as they depended on the predominance of the extended family (see chapter 3, pp. 54–6).

SOME GENERAL POINTS OF CRITICISM OF THE 'LOSS OF COMMUNITY' THESIS The empirical data discussed in the previous section provides a tentative basis from which to make some general criticisms of the 'loss of community' thesis.

Firstly, it is an oversimplification. At both 'ends' of the continuum we have found evidence to contradict the model. Secondly, a related point: the model seems to underestimate the capacity of people to rebuild community in new circumstances after the break-up of their old communities. Thirdly, the ideological limits of the model need to be criticised. It is characterised by conservative nostalgia. As a result, it tends to miss or minimise the unpleasant aspects of traditional society. From this limited perspective, a crucial theoretical flaw emerges – which brings us to our fourth point. The model has no use for class or class conflict in the analysis of community life. It takes as a 'given' the capitalist system instead of examining how this system shapes social life. More recent work has sought to rectify this imbalance. Indeed, it has tended to argue that it is precisely what the above critics ignored – capitalism and resultant class divisions – that account for the lack of community which so concerned them.

Before examining these conflict-based approaches, however, we will briefly review the new towns movement in Britain which, among other things, represented a 'search for' better communities than had developed in the urban environment of industrialism.

THE NEW TOWNS: AN ATTEMPT TO CREATE BETTER COMMUNITIES

The new town concept, first popularised around the turn of the century by Ebenezer Howard, was an attempt to plan social idealism into reality. Howard's 'bread and roses' idealism aimed at providing the city dweller with improved housing in less crowded neighbourhoods with conveniently available facilities, but he also advocated sacrosanct agricultural areas around the town, and wanted to erode class barriers by introducing socially mixed neighbourhoods. Welwyn Garden City, one of the early new towns (1920), probably came closest to the fulfilment of Howard's dream but more recent new town developments tend to have been less ambitiously conceived. Notwithstanding the inevitable crop of mistakes and complaints there is no doubt that, in terms of basic amenities provided, the new towns are a vast improvement on what they replaced. One woman in Milton Keynes said: 'It's like being in paradise compared to where I used to live.' There is no doubt, despite her choice of metaphor, that she was thinking in terms of such things as an upstairs bathroom, spacious lounge, perhaps central heating, and having a toilet which belonged to her own house and which worked properly. Against the backcloth of inner city decay (which we examine shortly), the new towns represented a substantial improvement in the standard of life of most who moved to them. Nevertheless, contrary to what is often imagined, only a small percentage of migrants from the inner city have gone to new towns. Crucially, from the point of view of the decline of the inner city, these have often been skilled or semi-skilled workers and their families.

As an attempt to tinker with the class system by introducing 'socially balanced' neighbourhoods, the new towns have been less successful. A useful piece of research in this area is B J Heraud's *Social Class and the*

New Towns – A Detailed Study of Social Class in Crawley. One of Heraud's crucial findings is that movement out of the originally mixed social class areas was usually to social-class defined communities. This was especially true of middle class families. The original balanced areas tended to become socially more working class whereas the middle class moved into the new subsidised housing areas. As Heraud points out, however, the commitment of the town's Urban Development Corporation to social balance seemed to weaken progressively, and it is possible that a more sustained experiment would be more successful.

In the middle nineteen seventies, as the total population went into slight decline and it became clear that the inner cities were, if anything, under- rather than over-populated. New town developments have tended to slow down or be abandoned. Stonehouse, which was to have been near Glasgow, and the planned central Lancashire new town, reputedly to have been named Red Rose, will probably stay on the drawing board. It may be that this slackening in momentum will provide opportunity to adjust to, and improve on, the changes that have already taken place.

The new towns, therefore, have provided materially better communities than elsewhere, but not socially very different ones. In particular, they, too, are characterised by class division. Given that they exist in a predominantly capitalist society, this is probably inevitable.

Confllict-based Models of Urban-rural Analysis: Marxist and Weberian

MARXIST URBAN-RURAL PERSPECTIVES

It is not only Marxist critics who find the ultimate cause of both urban and rural inequality and decay in the nature of capitalism, but the roots of such an analysis are certainly to be found in the writings of Marx and his colleague Engels. Unlike Durkheim and Tönnies, Marx's starting point for understanding society was not community or lack of it, but class. Marx believed that national and international community would be part of a genuinely communist world but he did not consider that such community was possible under capitalism: competition and class conflict prevented it. Only within classes did he consider that community and solidarity (a sense of unity and mutual support) were normal, although he fully recognised that the capitalist ruling class would seek to produce a 'false' sense of national community so as to reduce class conflict and consolidate its own interests (see chapter 5).

The contemporary Marxist, Manuel Castells, contextualises his analysis of urban life within a broad critique of capitalism. Like Marx, he considers that industrial cities in modern capitalist societies developed as a result of the centralisation of production. The early stages of capitalist production required a large, conveniently recruitable labour force. However, Castells regards the capitalist city of the post-Second World War era as increasingly a location of consumption rather than just production which has become increasingly geographically dispersed. Much consumption is public – education, health, transport, social services – as well as private. Castells considers that the working class would be particularly concerned with issues relating to collective consumption i.e. mainly of Welfare State services – although he fully recognises that other social classes may become involved in urban issues (or, equally, rural or suburban issues). He refers to any group which sustains an involvement in an urban issue as an urban social movement and his analysis of this phenomenon is one of his major theoretical contributions.

Stuart Lowe has suggested that there have been three phases in the development of Castell's analysis of urban social movements (1986). In the first phase, Castells stressed that the primary contradiction in capitalist society is that between capital and labour and that urban social movements based on consumption are of secondary importance to the primary class conflict based on work-place relations. In the second phase of his theoretical development Castells describes urban social movements as dealing with 'a new source of inequality' based on consumption rather than production which may be independent both of the class system and established political parties. Thus, local movements concerned with the damage to private or public property of, say, transport 'development' often cross both class and party lines in their 'membership'. In his third phase, Castells describes urban social movements as primary sources of change, independent of class and institutional politics. He describes the core characteristics of urban social movements as a concern with issues of consumption, as drawing on community (i.e. cross-class support), and as seeking a high degree of local democratic autonomy and decentralisation of service provision from the central state. Again, it is possible to suggest at least partial example in the British context in the various locally based movements that opposed central governments cuts in health and other welfare services (and, some would argue, the anti-poll tax campaign).

Several comments can be offered on Castells theory of social movements. First, as he is aware, any given movement is unlikely to survive for more than a few years at most, unless it feeds into the institutionalised political system and, in particular, establishes links with political parties. Given this, what Castells is describing as urban social movements are, in fact, essentially contemporary types of pressure group. Second, movements concerned with matters of consumption are not exclusive to the urban context but can also occur in suburban and rural areas. Castells concentrates on the urban context because it remains the primary location of the capitalist economy and government and of the majority of consumers.

Finally, it is possible to draw out of Castells' urban theory a highly non-Marxist conclusion. Indeed, this appears to have been accomplished by one of Castells' British interpreters, Peter Saunders. Saunders argues that as people become more consumer-oriented – notably, in respect to a preference for private home ownership rather than rented tenancies – they are likely to become less politically radical. However, it is equally possible to argue that social movements that reflect the demands of black people, of women, and of the environmentally concerned can most logically be incorporated into a radical agenda and party. Castells argues that one element of social movements is a concern for meaning and values. Racial justice in, for instance, employment and housing, adequate day-care facilities to allow mothers to do paid work, and an adequately protected environment, are all matters which may require radical policies and actions.

WEBERIAN URBAN-RURAL PERSPECTIVES

According to Weber, the most fundamental and enduring feature of a city is that it functions as a market-place. As he put it: '(t)o constitute a full urban community a settlement must display a relative predominance of trade-commercial relations'. The complexity of urban commercial and other activity requires a local government, administration and law. In other words, like Tönnies, Weber considered that much urban life is directed by associational (rational-functional) and often contractually-based activity. The core urban activity, as Weber saw it, is 'trading-commercial'.

JOHN REX AND ROBERT MOORE: THE HOUSING MARKET AND THE 'UNDERCLASS'

Writing broadly within the Weberian tradition, John Rex and Robert Moore examined the position of black people in relation to housing allocation (*Race, Community and Conflict*, 1967). They consider 'that the basic process underlying urban social interaction is competition for scarce and desired types of housing' (274). They describe two main modes of housing allocation. First, is allocation through the private market by means of which most of the middle and much of the skilled working class acquire housing. Second, is the allocation of public housing through local government bureaucracy. An individual's strength or weakness in relation to housing allocation places her or him in a particular housing class. In the inner-city area of Sparkbrook, Birmingham, Rex and Moore discerned seven housing classes and considered it likely that the same or similar classes occurred in other inner-city areas. These classes are:

Outright owners of large houses in desirable areas;
Mortgagees wholly occupying houses in desirable areas;
Council house tenants;
Council house tenants in slum

**dwellings designated for demolition;
Tenants wholly occupying houses owned by a private landlord;
Owners of houses bought with short-term loans who need to let rooms to meet repayments;
Tenants of rooms in lodging-houses.**

Rex and Moore concluded that in the mid nineteen sixties black immigrants, both Afro-Caribbean and Asian, tended to be disproportionately concentrated in lower housing classes compared to the whole population (with the partial exception of Irish immigrants). A main reason for this which applied to both private and public housing was racial discrimination. This could occur as a result of prejudice by estate agents, vendors, mortgage providers, or public housing officials. What Rex later referred to as institutional racism (p. 193) also played a part in hampering access by black people to public housing. A major example of institutional racism given by Rex is that the length of residency requirement for allocation to council housing automatically prevented recent immigrants from accessing this type of property (although this now applies only to a small percentage of black people).

In a later volume, written with Sally Thompson, Rex argues that it is in the context of neighbourhoods of low-quality housing that a 'black underclass' develops (1979). The other major aspect contributing to this process is the low pay of many black workers, to which racial discrimination is also a factor. The extent to which Rex considers that members of the black 'underclass' are likely collectively to organise to defend and promote their own interests is discussed on pp. 205–6.

Rex and Moore stress that relations to the means of consumption – in this case the consumption of housing – as well as relations to the means of production (i.e. occupation) can structure social relations in the city. Thus, Rex found some evidence that people might organise as housing classes as well as occupational classes, although he thought that this was occurring through existing voluntary organisations such as community associations and churches rather than through new organisations. In his emphasis on consumption and the possibility of social movements arising around consumption issues, Rex is close to the position adopted by Manuel Castells some years later. Some Marxists see this emphasis as a departure from the orthodox Marxist analysis that roots all major social conflict in the relations by social groups to the means of production. Whatever view one takes, it is clear that in an age of increasing consumption, the issue is an urgent one for Marxists to face. Rex and Moore can claim to have grappled with it some years before even Castells.

THE SOCIO-SPATIAL EFFECTS OF CAPITALISM The separation here of the social and socio-spatial effects of capitalism is purely for the purposes of presentation and in recognition of the fact that the use of space has been of particular interest to both Marxist and Weberian sociologists in recent years. Clearly, the amount and quality of space people occupy and otherwise enjoy is a major feature of their social life. The spatial question is, therefore, essentially a social rather than a physical issue as far as we are concerned. 'Space' is rather an abstract word, but what is meant is that identifiably different groups of people occupy different 'bits of territory' within a given society. Thus, as we saw, black immigrants are over-represented in inner-city areas as, for that matter, are poor whites. The middle class predominates in suburbia, although, as Herbert Gans has shown, this is something of an oversimplification as far as the United States is concerned. What sociologists seek to do is to explain why some groups occupy more and better space (both environmentally and in terms of amenities) than others. Put as simply as possible, why do some people live in bigger and better houses and less crowded and more attractive neighbourhoods than others?

The answer given to the above question by the social geographer, David Harvey, is the same as that offered by Castells and by Rex and Moore. The problems associated with the city – housing, environmental decay, poverty, crime – are not caused by the city as such, but by the way the socio-economic system affects the city. In other words, the problems are societal rather than essentially urban in nature. It is the unequal way in which the employment, housing and consumer markets work nationally (and internationally) that is the main cause of these problems. Logically, therefore, these problems can also occur outside the urban environment in places where the capitalist system favours some at the expense of others. As we have seen, R E Pahl's appropriately titled *Urbs in Rure* (1965) makes exactly this point: high-income commuters and 'second-house' weekend visitors introduce new class divisions and material and status inequalities into rural society. Raymond Williams, however, makes the point that class divisions, including the glaring juxtaposition of ostentatious wealth and humiliating poverty, have long been a feature of rural life. He stresses that the capitalistic development of agriculture has often been as hard on the peasantry as industrial development has been on the urban proleteriat. Indeed, originally it was partly because the peasantry were dispossessed of their land by the agricultural revolution that they spilled into the cities in search of work. This sort of systematic socio-economic analysis is far from either the static concentric circles model of Burgess or the simple rural-urban continuum of Tönnies.

LOCALITY, ECONOMIC RESTRUCTURING AND WORLD DEVELOPMENT

It has been a main theme of this section that particular localities or socio-economic areas are fundamentally affected by wider forces largely beyond their control. As Philip Cooke put it much of local life 'is increasingly, controlled by global political and economic forces' (1989:1). Cooke has edited a book, *Localities*, which examines these 'forces' and the responses to them of people in localities in respect to seven local areas: Thanet; Swindon; Cheltenham; south west Birmingham; Liverpool; Lancaster; and Middlesbrough. The key process studied in the book is the 'restructuring' of the British economy. The term restructuring means reshaping, and in part rebuilding of the economy. It is generally considered that Britain underwent a period of economic restructuring from the 1960s in which the economy was changed decisively from being a predominantly manufacturing one (up to the mid 1950s) to being predominantly a service one. This process is not completed and, indeed, economies continuously change, but its main effects are probably now apparent (see figure 19.1).

It is the socio-spatial effects of restructuring that is of primary interest here (the occupational aspects are discussed in chapter 6 and the technological/work-organisation aspects in chapter 11). As Cooke remarks, '(b)y showing detailed patterns of change at locality level it is possible to gain some indication of the spatially uneven distribution of advantage and disadvantage as it has developed'. In going on to discuss some of these changes, Cooke is at pains to point out that people are not necessarily helpless victims of such change but interact with and initiate change themselves:

The most important employment location tendencies in the 1970s were metropolitan deindustrialisation and the urbanisation of the countryside. Substantial shifts of population and employment from cities were in part an effect of the failure by older, city-based UK firms to compete with those from overseas. But movements of this kind may also be an expression of changed preference in residential location, in this case for what may be perceived as a 'rural idyll'. In the past the process of suburbanisation that produced the urban sprawl of the interwar years arose as jobs followed residential development, especially when employers realised that the suburbs contained sizeable pools of relatively cheap, female labour (Hobsbawm, 1968; Mills, 1973; Scott, 1982). As Scott (1982) points out, though, while a multiplicity of 'factors' are at work in the decentralisation process only a few of these can be seen in operation using information about employment change. To be interested in the changing nature of localities as distinct from local economics involves tracing changes in their social composition and, for example, the extent to which private as against public consumption of services, density of white or blue collar occupation, or level of professional qualification may have varied from place to place over time.

(Cooke, 1989:4)

Although Cooke stresses that the seven selected localities are not in any sense statistically representative of the 334 'travel-to-work' areas in the United Kingdom, they were selected to illustrate the restructuring

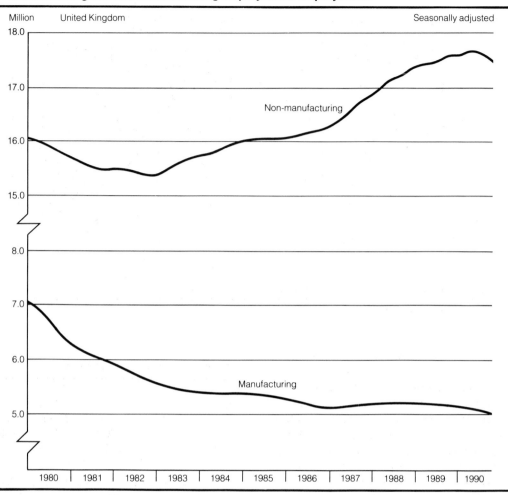

Manufacturing and non-manufacturing employees in employment:

(Source: *Employment Gazette*, June 1991)

process. Overall, the studies show a prospering south, at the core of which is London's financial, governmental, cultural and tourist-attracting capacity and dynamism and a deindustrialised north (i.e. with a substantially reduced manufacturing capacity and concentration of employment in manufacturing). In addition to London, other southern urban areas such as Swindon and Cheltenham have also attracted investment – significantly for manufacturing as well as service development. Cooke explains this partly in terms of the more 'flexible' suppliers and workforces more common in the South and contrasts these with the entrenched union power and traditional labour and managerial styles associated with Northern manufacturing industry. Cooke emphasises that there are variations and exceptions within the contrasting 'North-South' stereotype and that each locality requires specific analysis. Thus, Lancaster in the North

had a much higher growth in producer services than the national average between 1971 and 1981 and Swindon in the South grew rapidly in both manufacturing and services employment between 1981–84.

As a result of the above trends more high paying occupations tend to be in London and the South East and more low paying occupations elsewhere. This results in a marked difference in average pay between the South East and the rest (see figure 19.2 which also shows regional differences in unemployment).

Unequal economic development and inequalities of income and wealth, in turn, cause inequalities of health, educational attainment, and differences in consumption and life-style between regions. These differences are discussed in class, gender, racial and age terms elsewhere in this book, but it is important also to remember that they have a regional and economic developmental

Figure19.2

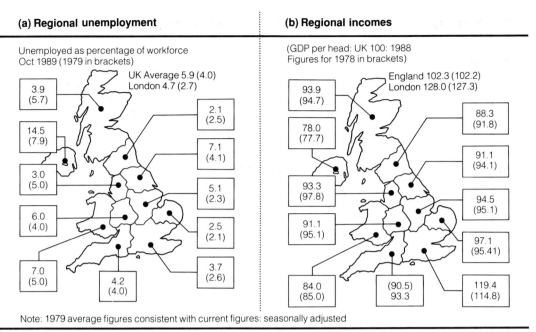

(a) Regional unemployment

Unemployed as percentage of workforce
Oct 1989 (1979 in brackets)

UK Average 5.9 (4.0)
London 4.7 (2.7)

3.9 (5.7)

14.5 (7.9)

3.0 (5.0)

6.0 (4.0)

7.0 (5.0)

4.2 (4.0)

2.1 (2.5)

7.1 (4.1)

5.1 (2.3)

2.5 (2.1)

3.7 (2.6)

(b) Regional incomes

(GDP per head: UK 100: 1988
Figures for 1978 in brackets)

England 102.3 (102.2)
London 128.0 (127.3)

93.9 (94.7)

78.0 (77.7)

93.3 (97.8)

91.1 (95.1)

84.0 (85.0)

(90.5) 93.3

88.3 (91.8)

91.1 (94.1)

94.5 (95.1)

97.1 (95.41)

119.4 (114.8)

Note: 1979 average figures consistent with current figures: seasonally adjusted

(Source: Department of Employment)

dimension. Inequalities between regions are also sharply reflected in the tendency for the South to vote Conservative and the North to vote Labour. An extreme example of this is that the ten constituencies with the highest unemployment all returned Labour MPs in 1987, whereas the ten constituencies with the lowest unemployment all returned Conservative MPs (see chapter 14, p. 332). In the former case all the constituencies were north of the Trent and in the latter case, they were south of it.

Although the general analysis offered in the 'Localities' study is likely to remain relevant to trends in the 1990s, the latest data it draws on are for 1987. Since then there may have been a modest reduction in the differences between North and South. First, there has been an increase in investment (particularly foreign investment) in parts of the North, particularly the North East, and in certain industries in Scotland and Wales (see table 19.1). In the latter case, there has been no revival in the traditional extractive industries but expansion has occurred in electronics and financial services.

It appears that the national economy is becoming increasingly dominated by the service sector. Second, the economic recession of the early 1990s initially affected the South East more than the North. Indeed, the early 1990s recession affected the service perhaps as much as the manufacturing

Table 19.1

Employment changes in Wales

	1978	1990	%
Electronics	13,000	23,000	+77
Financial services	43,000	68,000	+58
Coal	39,000	4,000	−90
Iron and steel	63,000	18,000	−71

sector. The overall effect of the recession may be slightly to reduce inequalities between South and North.

CLASS AND GROUP CONFLICT IN THE URBAN CONTEXT: CAPITAL, POLITICIANS, PLANNERS AND CITIZENS

We now discuss the urban context in terms of groups which have power and those which have little or none. The groups we will consider are business people, politicians, miscellaneous 'gate-keepers' and the citizenship as a whole. Although this section will mainly be descriptive, two conflict theories should be noted. First is the pluralist, rooted in Weber, which regards multi (plural) group conflict as essential to liberal democracy. Second, is the Marxist, which places group conflict in what they consider to be the more profound context of class conflict.

CAPITAL Business people have power to affect the lives of other people. Investment

443

provides work and a basis for prosperity, and lack of it causes unemployment and social hardship. The fact that we tend today to think of business in terms of large national and international companies and institutions may make economic power seem more impersonal, but the effects of it are real enough. When, in 1991, Rolls Royce decided to switch some of its production to Germany, there was relatively little its British employees workers could do about it. It is true that trade unionists are beginning to respond to the international nature of many large companies by organising internationally themselves, but they often lack the resources and experience to do so effectively.

POLITICIANS National and local politicians are a second group whose power affects others. As elected representatives of the people, their policies ought to benefit the public though this does not always seem to happen. Let us look at local government first. Joe Chamberlain, as mayor of Birmingham in the eighteen seventies, was an early urban reformer who successfully sought to improve the public amenities and standard of health of his city. His achievements were a model for other local politicians concerned with the standard of public amenities in their areas and were the prelude to great advances in civic provisions. Not all local authorities, however, have matched what he helped to inspire. Theoretically, government should be 'above' sectional interest and seek to serve the common good. This involves placing checks and controls on the activity of business. There is always a danger, however, that government may favour business 'development' at the expense of others. Sometimes it even happens that the immense revenues controlled by local authorities which are the practical basis of their power and patronage are mis-spent. Much of the design and construction of public works such as the building of roads and houses is contracted out by local authority officials to private companies of builders and architects. Inevitably, this sometimes leads to corruption. An example is the case of T Dan Smith, the leading politician on Newcastle's Labour-dominated Council in the early nineteen seventies. Smith was found guilty of giving contracts to architect John Poulson in return for bribes and favours. Such clear-cut cases of corruption are rarely proven but sometimes Council contracts do seem to favour the interests of commercial developers rather than the public.

In the 1980s, central government partly by-passed local government in the area of urban renewal by setting up Urban Development Corporations. By far the biggest was London's Dockside Corporation. A frequent complaint by local residents was that developers and 'outsider, yuppie' purchasers of property benefited from the development, but that they did not.

PLANNERS A third 'group' which has power in the city is made up of planners, architects, state and local authority bureaucrats, welfare workers, and managers of banks and building societies, 'gate-keepers' as Pahl refers to them. We include them together mainly as a matter of convenience. The important thing that these various people have in common is that their decisions can profoundly affect the lives of ordinary citizens. They can open or close the door to valuable resources such as public housing, social security payments and help from the social services. More than that, some of these agencies have great power to interfere in, and even radically change, the course of people's lives. Payment of social security will often be made dependent on a visit from an investigator who will ask a range of questions that in normal circumstances would be regarded as constituting an invasion of privacy. In some circumstances, investigation can continue in a secret and lengthy manner. Social security 'fiddling' is, understandably, not popular with the majority of the public and so the pryings of officialdom tend to be grudgingly accepted in this area by the tax-paying majority.

Planning policy, by contrast, is an example of bureaucratic power that has frequently provoked widespread condemnation. With the support of the politicians who employ them and who often depend on them for detailed advice, planning officers can make use of wide legal powers to require people to quit their houses which can then be destroyed. A number of key positions which regulate access to various resources controlled by private enterprise ought also to be mentioned here. In particular, money lending institutions of various kinds, notably banks and building societies, can make decisions that affect people's lives radically.

CITIZENS We now discuss the most important group mentioned above, the citizenship as a whole. Actually, the phrase 'citizenship as a whole', like 'the average man', hides more than it reveals. What we really want to talk about are the varied individuals and groups who live or work in urban areas. For many of these people – and this is one of the most important observations in this book – the problems they have faced in the post-war period have caused them to adjust their practical understanding of democracy. Classically, democracy in Britain involves voting for a representative with, perhaps, occasional communications thereafter. Increasingly, people have become more aware of the possible conflict between their own interests and the policies of government and its official representatives. It may be that the new emphasis on citizen's rights will produce mechanisms to enable people to bring government bureaucracies more effectively to account.

Communities are created and recreated in a crucible of power. Decisions taken by business people, politicians and planners affect the lives of individuals and communities. C Wright Mills sought passionately in his writings to make people aware of the relationship between 'private' troubles and 'public' or political issues. It is largely in an attempt to control, or at least to influence and make more accountable, the above powerful groups that community action movements began rapidly to develop in the nineteen sixties. These movements vary widely in kind and purpose. Tenants' Associations are concerned with practical matters of self and group interest such as rents and living conditions. As Castells suggested these movements bear a similar relationship to public consumption as do trade unions to work: they aim to protect the interest of their members. More ad hoc groups may organise around an issue affecting a particular local area at a given time. An example from the provinces is the protest group in Preston's suburb of Ashton, which organised against a plan to drive a road through an avenue of birches in Haslem Park. Where an issue is general rather than local – such as the poll tax – a movement with a wider geographical base of support may develop.

Figure 19.3

An episode in a decade of sporadic violence: was deprivation a factor in these outbreaks?

CITIZENSHIP AND URBAN CRISIS In the nineteen eighties and nineties, a crisis occurred in the public life of many of Britain's urban areas of a kind that citizens – however they organise – cannot easily hope to solve. There are four obvious aspects to this crisis. First, there is the growing inequality between the inner urban 'have nots' and the suburban and county 'haves'. Second, the poorer urban areas can rarely raise the revenue to deal with their problems – a difficulty intensified by the overall reduction in funds provided by central government. Third, the increasing centralisation of economic power in the hands of large, often multi-national companies makes the urban economy very vulnerable to possible disinvestment. Fourth, and not unconnected with the above, a major problem of public order developed in Britain's inner cities in the nineteen eighties and nineties.

In the light of this crisis it is worth considering the viability of the two models of political conflict referred to in an earlier chapter. How realistic a description of current urban politics is the liberal model of pluralist democracy? As far as the city is concerned, particularly the city poor, is liberal democracy working? On the other hand, is there now a basis for an effective traditional, socialist coalition in urban areas? Deindustrialisation, the numerical decline of the manual working class and union membership, and the growth of the lower (under) class are some problems such a coalition would face as, indeed, the Militant-led Liverpool Labour Council did in the mid-nineteen eighties. (For a discussion of liberal, Marxist and Elite political theories, see chapter 14.)

INNER URBAN DEURBANISATION/ URBANISATION OF THE COUNTRYSIDE

Drawing mainly on conflict perspective, this section is about the inner city not as a physical entity but as the focal point of the activity of groups of people, the most powerful of whom are probably businessmen, politicians and top civil servants. Sometimes these groups act in concert and sometimes in conflict, but their major decisions affect the lives of the rest of us. More abstractly, we want to show how the capitalist system operates on the inner city – always bearing in mind that government can try to act as a checking or, to use Galbraith's term, countervailing power to control business as well as to smooth its path.

Since the Second World War the inner city or, more precisely, the inner city ring (the area around the business centre) has been inhabited by low income groups and beset by social problems. Once-thriving manufacturing areas were hit by the decline of such staple industries as docking, shipbuilding, textile production and heavy manufacturing. Manchester, Liverpool, Glasgow, Belfast, Newcastle and Inner London – all large metropolitan areas – developed 'inner city problem areas.' For instance, the break-up of traditional working class community in East London (see above, Willmott and Young) was due to the decline of the docks and the associated service and distribution trades. In addition, advanced technology and large scale industry made the craft industries and other small scale production units of the East End obsolete and uncompetitive. As described earlier in this chapter much new economic development, notably in the service sector occurred outside the old, inner-urban industrial areas. People followed in droves. Between 1961 and 1971, almost 100,000 people left the single borough of Tower Hamlets. Those that remained in Inner London were drawn, disproportionately, from the old, socially disadvantaged, unskilled and semi-skilled workers. They were joined by coloured immigrants who were prepared to do unskilled and semi-skilled work in the inner city of a kind that many whites wished to avoid.

The above processes of economic decline of urban areas and of population movement out of them are referred to collectively as deurbanisation. On the other hand, the 'urbanisation' of many suburban and rural areas occurred. Of course, not all urban areas declined. It is mainly the 'old' industrial cities that have experienced deurbanisation. Many service industry towns such as Southend, Oxford, Swindon and York have undergone a parallel increase in population. Nor is the process of deurbanisation irreversible. Inner London began to regain population in 1983–4 and other traditional industrial areas may do so although it is unlikely their populations will ever be as densely concentrated as in the mid nineteen fifties.

It would be quite misleading to 'blame' individual business people for inner urban decline. Many of them also suffered as a result of the decline of Britain's traditional industrial base. The point to pursue is a quite different one. It is that when capitalism falters or fails – even if only in the process of change rather than collapse – it is incapable of rectifying the resultant adverse social consequences. The capitalist system works on profit, not philanthropy, and when it fails it is left to the sometimes reluctant hand of government to pick up the pieces.

We now look more closely at occupants of the inner city (and in part, the centre city) to show that class factors like income and education mean that people in the same geographical zone lead radically different lives. Inner city occupants can be divided into various disadvantaged groups, immigrants, 'cosmopolites', and some members of the upper class. We have already explained why the disadvantaged and immigrants are disproportionately represented in the inner city (see chapters 7 and 9). 'Cosmopolites', to use Gans' term, include students, artists, writers, musicians, entertainers as well as other intellectuals and professionals. Though some may be quite poor, this is not the definitive feature of life that it is for disadvantaged groups: for them the city is meaningful because it provides opportunity for self-expression and experience. The fact that different social groups can live in close physical proximity, yet socially in different 'worlds', is still better illustrated by reference to the very rich who keep a town residence (often in the centre rather than inner city) as well as a country home. A member of the upper class may live a stone's throw from a poor community but is sealed off from its occupants by wealth, privilege and power. The urban environment may be the physical limits of the poor person's world but the rich person is much more geographically mobile, and can escape to the 'country' or abroad, almost at will. On the whole, the upper class do not live or spend time in the countryside to seek community except in some cosmetic or whimsical sense. Their residences are usually well secluded from those of nearby inhabitants, although traditionally-minded landed aristocrats and gentry may still pride themselves on being 'part of the local community', however cushioned their position may be by privilege and by the deference afforded to them. In fact most of these, like the nouveaux riches who have bought into rural real estate, tend to have friends of similar social status who, in the nature of things, are unlikely to live close by. The upper class, however, can afford to travel and visits and meetings are easily arranged. Friendship networks are likely to be national or international and may seem to have an unreal, 'starry' quality to those outside the charmed circle. Members of the upper class know each other but others only know of them. Recently, upper middle and middle class people have bought property in some previously working class areas in the inner city. This process is sometimes referred to as 'gentrification'. It has added to the jigsaw-like quality of the social patterns of residence of many of Britain's cities. In fairness, it should be added that the collapse in property prices in the late nineteen eighties and early nineties bought significant hardship to many middle class people who had bought near the price peak.

The role of national government in helping to create the above social and demographic (population distribution) patterns is important. In the post-war period, government and industry co-operated to disperse industry and population away from the old industrial areas. The new town movement was part of this policy. The centre and inner city zones were redeveloped as office and service areas. Some of the new housing, including high rise flats and large estates, was of poor quality and design. 'Living in the sky' made community virtually impossible and caused families great practical problems. Even so,

the new housing was generally a material, if not an aesthetic, improvement on what was left undemolished of the old inner city housing stock. Most of this came to be occupied by those groups who, for reasons already mentioned, did not participate in the new 'out of city' expansion. Welfare State expenditure tends to be relatively high in inner city areas although this is a palliative, not a solution to the basic problem. Various government schemes have been adopted to encourage the economic development of these areas. As in similar schemes in the United States, money has tended to disappear without much seeming to happen.

It now seems unlikely that the urban policies of the Thatcher governments (1979–90) will achieve more substantial inner urban revival than those of previous governments, particularly as Britain moved into recession as Mrs Thatcher moved out of office. The basis of the Thatcher approach was to channel more central government money into private enterprise and less through local government and public enterprise. Urban Development Corporations were set up to by-pass local authorities, but where possible to draw together private and public expertise and investment. The construction of residential and commercial property in London's Dockland and less substantial efforts elsewhere do not yet appear a remotely adequate replacement for traditional industry either in terms of productivity or job creation and, in any case, many projects are languishing and underfunded in the early nineties.

◄

Figure 19.4

'If it wasn't for the

'ouses in-between' –

Docklands as seen

from Greenwich

The above account of the inner city is intended to illustrate the inequalities and potential conflict caused by the capitalist system. Whether government is seen as the partner of capitalism or the saviour of its 'victims' or both is a matter for analysis, but what is undeniable is their mutual involvement in inner city processes.

Conclusion: Perspectives, Politics and Policy

Both Marxists, such as Castells, and Weberians, such as Rex, consider that the conditions, for good or ill, of modern Western cities are generated by capitalism rather than industrialisation or urbanisation. Most contemporary conflict theorists consider that only central government can hope to control capital and deal with its social consequences. The gemeinschaft-gesellschaft model of Tönnies and the rural-urban framework of Wirth now seem rather antiquated or, at least, inadequate to deal with contemporary urban issues.

Unemployment, poverty, racial conflict and public disorder, have increased the urgency of the debate on urban policy. This debate is part of a wider disagreement about the kind of economy and society Britain might become. The Conservatives believe that only free enterprise – large-scale and small – can provide a secure basis of jobs and prosperity. To varying degrees social democrats argue that the state must step in where private enterprise fails, and indeed sometimes take initiatives in its own right. They certainly consider the condition of the inner cities as a suitable issue for substantial intervention. Marxists argue that capitalism is inherently inegalitarian and unpredictable in its consequences and seek to attack urban problems along collectivist lines. In any case, few scholars, these days, find it a priority to make elegant comparisons between rural and urban life.

SUMMARY

From rural community to urban society

1 Sociological definitions of community stress that social interaction is an even more important aspect of community than shared geographical location – although generally the two aspects are linked.

2 Several pairs of contrasting concepts were introduced: gemeinschaft/gesellschaft (Tönnies) mechanical/organic solidarity (Durkheim); rural/urban; (Wirth); and traditional/modern society (Parsons). Each of these pairs of concepts contrasts what their authors see as the essence of pre-industrial, largely rural, traditional society with that of industrial, largely urban, modern society.

3 The notion that the transition from 'traditional' to 'modern' society involved a 'loss of community' was critically discussed. A variety of case studies and theoretical analyses establish that a simple notion of 'loss of community' is untenable. The example of the new towns illustrates both the continuing 'search for community' and problems associated with this.

Conflict-based models of urban-rural analysis (4–6)

4 Marxist urban-rural theory is based on the analysis that capitalism is the basic force that structures both urban and rural social and political life. What are seen as simple contrasts between urban and rural life are rejected.

5 The French Marxist Manuel Castells considers that urban areas in capitalist societies developed first as centres of production (centralising capital and labour) and then more as centres of consumption. He argues that a variety of social movements develop in response to issues of mainly public consumption, such as health and welfare and the environment, in capitalist society.

6 Weberian urban-rural perspectives, like Marxist ones, are not based on an assumption of fundamental urban-rural difference. In Weber's case, it is mainly the economic function of providing a market that distinguishes the city and accounts for many of its characteristics, such as density of population and physical environment. Rex and Moore specifically examine the housing market in the inner-city area of Sparkbrook, Birmingham. The disadvantage of black people within this market led Rex on to examine the concept of a 'black underclass'.

7 The theoretical perspective that the formation of social life in both urban, suburban and rural areas is mainly the product of economic forces and people's response to them is desirable from both Marxist and Weberian conflict perspective. This approach is illustrated and expanded in the sections titled 'The socio-spatial effects of capitalism'; 'Locality, Economic Restructuring and World Development'; and 'Class and Group Conflict in the Urban Context'. The inner city is analysed as an example of conflict analysis.

8 Significant political and policy differences exist about how to respond to the problems associated with urban areas. Some consider that only capitalism and the enterprise and investment it generates can revitalise these areas whereas others consider that public investment and planning is essential.

Community, rural and urban issues offer the opportunity of using one's own local area as the subject of research. Issues of homelessness, the social effects of the closure or opening of a place of work, racial conflict or cooperation, the reasons for and effects of changes in residency patterns, the decline or development of a 'community' are all possible topics for research depending on the area one lives in.

The danger in selecting a local issue is that the resulting research may be merely descriptive and even anecdotal. In fact, this topic area is one of the more theoretical ones and this ought to be apparent in any research into it. Take the example of an analysis of changes in residency patterns in a given area. Let us suppose that evidence suggests that the area has become more 'middle class' as more professional, managerial and administrative employees have moved into the area. It then has to be asked why this is so. It may be that new business ventures or government offices have been established in the area. In the case of the former, there may be foreign capital involved or joint

RESEARCH AND COURSEWORK

private-public sector money. Such data and explanation should lead to consideration of relevant theoretical perspectives. In this case, both Marxist and Weberian perspectives seem particularly appropriate for consideration as both directly deal with economic development (and undevelopment) and its social effects (including occupational, class and residential change).

There is no requirement, even in the case of this topic, that research should be locally based (and even if it is, the relationship between the issue as it occurs in the local context to the wider national, and perhaps, international context should be explored). Indeed, two suggestions for studies made by the AEB lend themselves to a wider treatment. The suggestions are: make 'An assessment of government policy and initiatives on inner city development in the 1980s' and make 'A study of ethnic minority groups and housing, e.g. access to location, type'. In the first case presentation and criticism of Thatcherite ideology as applied to urban policy would be expected and in the second a useful starting point might be Rex and Moore's study of housing classes in Sparkbrook referred to above – (although these by no means exhaust the range of theoretical reference).

FURTHER READING

For those who want an overview of tradition rural/urban theory without returning to the original sources, Michael P Smith's *The City and Social Theory* (Basil Blackwell, 1980) is recommended. This book also contains a chapter on capitalism and urban political conflict. Two books which suggest similar processes are at work in the countryside and the city are Howard Newby, *Green and Pleasant Land? Social Change in Rural England* (Penguin Books, 1980) and Raymond Williams, *The Countryside and the City* (Paladin, 1975). More recently, Philip Cooke ed. *Localities* (Unwin Hyman, 1989) is an excellent survey of socio-economic development in seven areas. David Smith's *Divided Britain* (Pelican, 1989) provides a more general overview.

The condition and problems of some of Britain's inner cities is such as to make this topic one of considerable interest and urgency. Andrew Friend and Andy Metcalf's *Slump City: The Politics of Mass Unemployment* (Pluto Press, 1981) does justice to these sentiments. There are a number of readings on urbanisation in the Third World in Hamza Alavi and Teodor Shanin eds, *Introduction to the Sociology of 'Developing Societies'* (Macmillan, 1982). Several readings relevant to urbanisation are given at the end of Chapter 9.

QUESTIONS

1   Either (a) the problems of the inner cities are essentially those of poverty and unemployment; the problems would therefore disappear if poverty and unemployment were eliminated. Discuss. Or (b) What factors determine the pattern of residential segregation in cities? (OLE, 1983)

2   Sociologists frequently talk about 'urban' and 'rural' ways of life. How useful is this distinction? (UCLE, 1990)

3   Most theories of community underestimate the extent of conflict and diversity on rural and urban communities: Examine this view. (AEB 1990)

4   Critically examine sociological contributions to an understanding of the factors which influence access to housing. (AEB, 1991)

20 Comparative Demography: Population & Development

Introduction

The term 'comparative demography' is a rather high-sounding description of the material covered in this chapter. Demography is the study of the statistics of population. As the Shorter Oxford English Dictionary puts it, 'demography … treats of the statistics of births, deaths, diseases, etc. …'

I will not deal here with the methodological problems of the discipline or with the issues relating to the social construction of statistics (for this, see pp. 294–7). The chapter will present demographic data, generally accepted as reliable, and examine some demographic trends. It will focus mainly on comparative population structure and change and particularly analyse birth and death rates (definitions below). How population trends affect education and employment will be examined in chapter 21, as will a number of related policy issues. As Philip Abrams says, population statistics provide 'maps' of certain problems and therefore inform policy discussion: consequently, no 'maps', no coherent discussion.

There should be no need to justify coverage of demographic trends and issues in a global rather than merely a national context. The affluent West has been too parochial and complacent in its response to the problems associated with world population growth and of the linked issue of Third World underdevelopment. As the Brandt Report points out, in a highly interdependent world, even self-interest requires broader understanding and policies.

Terminology

The birth rate and death rate are key determinants of population size. The birth rate is the number of live births per year per 1,000 people and the death rate is the number of deaths per year per 1,000 people. The fertility rate is the number of live births per 1,000 women of child-bearing age (15–44). The infant mortality rate (IMR) is the annual rate of death of infants 0–12 months per 1,000 live births. The IMR varies internationally mainly according to the quality of child care and makes a critical contribution to the overall death rate. The difference between the birth rate and death rate gives the rate of natural population increase and, if we adjust for net immigration and emigration, we get the rate of population growth. The concept of dependent population is very important. It refers to non-producing members of the population. The dependency ratio is arrived at by dividing non-producers by producers.

Population Trends

WORLD POPULATION TRENDS

Figure 20.1 shows the increasing rate of world population growth:

► **Figure 20.1**

The Growth of World

Population

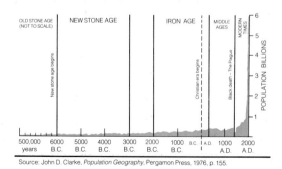

Source: John D. Clarke, *Population Geography*, Pergamon Press, 1976, p. 155.

In many parts of the world, population growth has outstripped available resources. Millions have died through starvation or ill-health caused by malnutrition. Until recently, forecasts suggested that there would continue to be an increase in the rate of population growth. It was feared that the crisis of global over-population would escalate beyond control early in the twenty-first century. However, the *State of World Population Report*, published by the United Nations (1982), indicates that a drop in the rate of population increase has at last occurred and that population will level off at about 10.5 billion in the year 2110. Between

1950 and 1975, the average growth rate was 1.9 per cent a year. By 1978, it had decreased to 1.81 per cent and by 1980 to 1.73 per cent. The decrease is due to an overall fall in the birth rate. In poorer countries this reflects some success in the policy of governments and Third World agencies (see below). In countries at an intermediate level of development, parents themselves often opt for smaller families, largely to secure living standards. In any case, these global figures conceal an average rate of growth of about 2.5 per cent in poorer countries compared to 1 per cent in developed countries.

The report makes the following estimates of the world population at given times:

1950	1980	2000	2110
2.5 billion	4.4	6	10.5

If the current trends are proved correct, the world should be able to maintain its people adequately if resources are developed, distributed and used for this purpose. That is a big 'if'. The exploitation of resources to create private wealth or their diversion into armaments build up are alternatives.

REGIONAL POPULATION TRENDS

The above trends are of concern to the whole species. This section examines briefly specific regional trends.

Population will stop growing and stabilise first in the industrially developed areas of the world. According to the United Nations report, this will happen first in Western Europe in about 2030 when its population will be about 400 million. Next will be North America, levelling off at 320 million, with the former Soviet Union at 380 million.

There has been concern in the European Parliament about the combined effects of a falling birth rate and a low death rate. The danger perceived is that there will not be enough workers to cope with the burden of dependency caused by an ageing population. The population of the ten countries which made up the European Community (1982) was 8.8 per cent of the world total in 1950 but is estimated to be 4.5 per cent in the year 2000 and 2.3 per cent in 2025. European women had an average of 2.79 children each in 1964, and 1.68 in 1982 – well below the population replacement rate of 2.1. A Presidency paper argued that 'this situation is disturbing'.

There are arguments against adopting policies to increase the Community's birthrate. First, Europe, and particularly Britain, is far from employing all of its present population of working age. Secondly, many older people are quite capable of doing productive work should they be required and want to do so. Thirdly, the working population of Europe could be increased indefinitely by changing immigration policies. In view of the continued expansion of population in the Third World, the latter might be a particularly effective policy. In reality, however, more prosperous European nations are increasingly introducing immigration controls designed severely to limit immigration from poorer societies.

Continued population expansion in the Third World contrasts with the situation in Europe. The biggest increase in population will come in the world's poorest continent, Africa. It is the one region in which the rate of population increase is barely slowing down. Africa, where millions already die or are disabled through malnutrition, is expected to quadruple its population by the year 2110. That of South Asia is expected to treble to 4.2 billion, a figure not far short of the present population of the world.

Latin America, which is generally better able to support its people, is also expected to treble its population. East Asia, however, will level off quickly, rising from 1.2 to 1.7 billion. This is largely because of the success of birth control policies adopted in China.

REGIONAL POPULATION AGE STRUCTURES
Table 20.1 gives key demographic data about seven countries from under-developed and developed regions of the world (1978).

Table 20.1
▼

	Birth rate	Death rate	Infant mortaility rate (per 1,000)	% of population under 15	% of population over 64
Tanzania	47	22	167	47	2
Vietnam	41	19	115	41	4
China	22	8	65	33	6
El Salvador	40	8	55	46	3
Australia	17	8	14	28	8
USA	15	9	15	24	11
UK	12	12	14	23	14

(Source: World Health Organisation).

In demographic terms, Tanzania and Vietnam are reasonably representative of the less developed countries of the Third World. The data on both indicate three major problem areas. First, the gap between the birth and death rate shows rapid population growth; second, the infant mortality rate is appallingly high; third, in both countries, over 40 per cent of the population is under the age of 15. This puts a heavy burden of dependency on the adult population, even though many older children in Third World countries contribute to family income. The low death rate in China and El Salvador is a result of success in reducing the rate of infant mortality and to the relatively youthful age structure of their populations. The percentages of the population under 15 are far higher than in advanced industrial countries. However, this situation is rapidly changing in China because of the success of its one child per family policy.

Australia, the USA and the UK are at a similar stage of demographic development. In 1978, the birth and death rates in the UK were actually in balance. The problem of age dependency for Britain and, to a lesser extent, the USA, is with the group 65 or over – the opposite end to where the problem lies for countries such as Tanzania and Vietnam.

Figure 20.2 contrasts the population composition of Mexico, the USA and West Germany. The age structures of South Asia, Latin America and Africa are fairly similar to that of Mexico, and that of the former Soviet Union to the USA. The populations of Western Europe are the oldest, and the region has about five per cent fewer aged 14 or younger than both USA and former USSR. The problem of old age dependency is, therefore, at its most acute in Europe, though it will also be felt sharply in the USA early next century. However, as figure 20.3 suggests, it is the population imbalances within major global regions, that perhaps gives most cause for thought.

BRITISH POPULATION, TRENDS AND AGE STRUCTURE, (COMPARED TO THE THIRD WORLD)

The purpose of this brief section is twofold: first, to establish the historical development of the British population from a demographic point of view; second, to indicate the main demographic issues facing contemporary Britain. Because demography cuts into so many other topics, the reader will be signposted elsewhere in this book for detailed discussion of specific points.

Broadly, the population growth of Britain has followed the pattern indicated in figure 20.4 on p. 456. It is not possible to say precisely when slow population growth gave way to more rapid increase but slow growth, interrupted by occasional natural disasters, occurred throughout the middle ages. More rapid growth preceded the industrial revolution but the improvements in public health and nutrition which underlay the increase became more marked in the nineteenth century, especially the latter part (see pp. 382–3). These improvements reduced the death rate but the birth rate barely fell until the last quarter of the nineteenth century: thus, the rapid population growth for the preceding century. Indeed, a high birth rate was necessary to maintain a stable population in traditional society. Given a very high infant mortality rate, families had to have several children to ensure the survival of two or three. Children functioned as breadwinners and later as protectors of their parents, should the latter reach old age. Fertility was regarded as a blessing and had religious sanction. Similar factors explain the

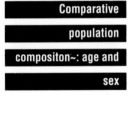

Figure 20.2

Comparative

population

compositon~: age and

sex

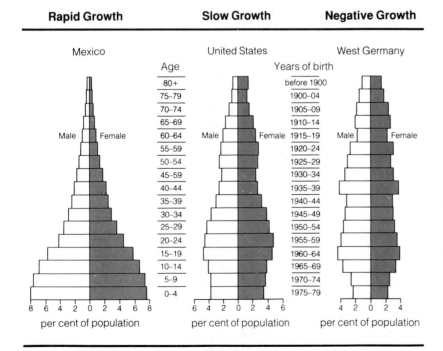

Rapid Growth	Slow Growth	Negative Growth
Mexico	United States	West Germany

per cent of population

(Sources: Censuses of Mexico, The United States and West Germany (The Population Institute, Washington D.C.))

	Developed region	Less developed region
	North America Japan Europe	Latin America China/India Africa
Key Characteristics	Nil/low population growth Low fertility Rich	High population growth High fertility Poor(er)

The main regional pressure to migrate is likely to be from Africa on Europe, although there will continue to be pressure from Latin America on North America. The 15–24 age-group is the one most likely to migrate and the numbers in this group are greatly increasing in Africa.

Numbers in the 15–24 age group (Actual and projected)

	Latin America	Africa
1960	34	52
1980	74	91
2000	170	300 Numbers in millions

Whereas Africa annually produces 15 million more births than needed to replace preceding generations, Europe is 1.2 million short. Migration can, therefore, only be one element in solving Africa's problems. The main solution must be development, including family planning

persistence of high birth rates in the Third World, especially in poorer, more traditional societies. There are two crucial differences, however. First, Britain's period of rapid population growth was supported by and essentially caused by an even greater increase in wealth and resources. Comparable development is not occurring in the Third World. On the contrary, the population boom in the Third World was partly triggered by the entirely artificial factor of Western medicine, particularly in the control of infectious diseases, which destroyed 'natural' population balance. As a result, poor Third World countries with booming populations tend to become highly dependent on the West. Second, and more optimistically, the modern family planning methods, which only became widely available in the West well after its population boom had passed its peak, are currently available to the Third World. Arguably, however, the best stimulus to population control is development itself (see p. 459). The diagram below compares population growth in the developed and underdeveloped world between 1975 and 2000 (projected).

Three main issues present themselves concerning the structure of the British population. Each focuses on a particular generation: the old, the middle-aged and the young.

The elderly have become an issue because of the sheer increase in their numbers which was fivefold between 1901 and 1983 (p. 230). The percentage of people aged 65 or over is expected to remain at about 15 per cent until the end of the century, but within the age group there will be a substantial increase in those aged 85 or over. This will result in heavier demand for health and social services and possibly for care within the family. The latter point raises issues of policy and gender. If a policy of de-institutionalisation of the old is pursued, will sufficient resources be channelled to those who care for them? Will the carers still be overwhelmingly women (often daughters), as they have traditionally been? Already, a woman caring full-time for her senile mother has successfully taken the British government to the European Court and received a ruling requiring it to help pay for her caring work. Beyond the matters of dependency and resources, it is possible that the majority of active and relatively healthy elderly will challenge current negative stereotypes of old age. A Harris poll (1975) of elderly Americans seemed to show that they have much more positive images of themselves than do the general public.

Members of the generational cohort of 1945 (i.e. those born in that year) are now in their

▶

Figure 20.4

Twenty-five years of

world population

growth

In millions

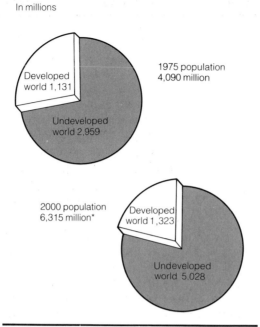

1975 population
4,090 million

Developed world 1,131

Undeveloped world 2,959

2000 population
6,315 million*

Developed world 1,323

Undeveloped world 5,028

Changes in numbers of children and pensioners as a percentage of total population.

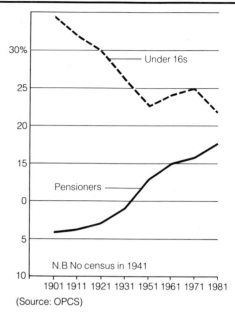

(Source: OPCS)

▶

Figure 20.5 (Far right)

The 'greying' of

Britain – as shown in

successive censuses.

*projected
(Source: The Global 2000 Report to the President, Council on Environmental Quality and the Department of State, USA)

mid to late forties – early middle age. In Britain and the United States the birth rate remained high for an almost unbroken period between 1945 and 1964. One commentator refers to the post-war baby boom phenomenon as 'the pig in the python' – causing problems for itself and others as it moves through the system. In the era of high employment and cultural optimism of the nineteen sixties, the sheer size of the immediate post-war generational cohorts did not appear to constitute a great problem. The educational system was funded to meet their needs and the situations vacant columns offered jobs at every level. However, the recessions of the early nineteen eighties and nineties have bought home the reality of scarcity to the 'lucky' generation.

The younger generation – let us say, those born after the peak year for births, 1964 – are coming to grips with what seems a tougher world than the sixties. First, following the 'pig in the python' must be for many a frustrating experience. The sixties generation, 'beautiful people' and all, are typically clinging to their jobs – like their parents before them. Inevitably this is at the expense of the would-be upwardly mobile young. Second, mass generational unemployment darkens the future of today's young. This situation is not the fault of the now middle-aged, but is caused by factors – international competition, new technology, and arguably government policy – which affect the whole population. However, the young are particularly hard hit and I have devoted a section in chapter 10 to youth and (un)employment (pp. 224–6).

Perspectives on Population Growth

I will review briefly four approaches to population growth and control. The first, that of Thomas Malthus, can fairly be termed a theory on the basis of the historical and comparative evidence he accumulated in support of it. The others concentrate as much on advocating forms of control as on explaining growth and are strongly tinged with ideology. The separation between this section (on perspectives) and the next (on policy) is not precise – there is a particularly large overlap in relation to perspectives (ii) and (iii).

(I) MALTHUS

Malthus (1766–1834) argued that 'population, when unchecked, increases in a geometrical ratio. Subsistence only increases in an arithmetical ratio.' Thus population increases as follows – 1, 2, 4, 8, 16, 32 ... – and food – 1, 2, 3, 4, 5, 6. At the sixth point in this progression, population increase has run ahead of the increase in food production by over 500 per cent. Malthus may not have been precisely correct, but there is no doubt that he observed a general tendency. The one solution he offered to the resultant misery was moral restraint, including postponement of marriage, coupled with pre-marital chastity until the partners could afford to support a family. Malthus's policies of control have not proved popular, but his analysis of population control remains influential. R K Kelsall suggests that as far as many Third World countries are concerned 'the factors in the situation are basically those to which he drew attention', i.e. population growth out-running food supplies. However, the relevant frame of reference has undoubtedly been changed by the development of effective contraception and improvements in agriculture.

(II) NEO-MALTHUSIANISM – FAMILY PLANNING

A second approach is sometimes referred to as Neo-Malthusianism. It broadly accepts Malthus's analysis but argues for the adoption of birth control within marriage. Today, many of those involved in the practical urgencies of population policy advocate birth control whenever necessary with little concern for theoretical reference. Malthus did not adequately anticipate the effect of birth control on population growth, nor did he fully appreciate the extent to which improved crop fertilisation and production could sustain larger populations. In fact, human invention in the fields of birth control, health and nutrition and agriculture has produced a pattern of population growth outlined in the diagram below, rather than repeated cycles of growth and decline back to a stable figure as Malthus indicates.

The theory of population transition presented below (see also Part 1 of figure 20.4 on p. 456), developed at the United Nations, should not be over-generalised. It applies well to most modern societies but it may apply less well to Third World societies if the factors that reduced population growth

Type	Birth rate	Death rate	Population growth
1	High	High	Stable
2	High	High/declining	Slight increase
3	High	Low	Large increase
4	Falling	Falling	Falling
5	Low	Low	Low and stable

▲

Table 20.2

in the West fail to do so there (see Part 2) of figure 20.4 on p. 456).

Type 1 would describe many simple societies unaffected by modern factors and type 5 most modern societies. It should be possible to pick out various types in the chart from the previous section.

In summary, then, the second approach covers those who advocate modern techniques of birth control and improved crop fertilisation to reduce population and improve nutrition in the Third World. (The assumption that technology is the key to progress in population control complements one version of modernisation theory.)

(III) REDISTRIBUTION OF RESOURCES AND POPULATION STABILISATION

We now turn to a third approach. Susan George, in *How the Other Half Dies: The Real Reasons for World Hunger* (1977) sharply attacks attempts to deal with the problems of Third World countries primarily in terms of population control. She states her own position clearly:

> *The first thing to realise when trying to think straight about population/food is that hunger is not caused by population pressure. Both hunger and rapid population growth reflect the same failure of a political and economic system.*
> *(George, 1977:59)*

George finds a grossly unequal distribution of wealth in world and, in most cases, national terms. Hunger and population growth are symptoms – one is not the cause of the other – of this inequality. Couples have many children because only children will protect them against poverty. Population decrease tends to follow decrease in poverty. The abolition of poverty is, therefore, what should come first and the resources are there to achieve it. Belabouring the poor about birth control is to appear to blame them for problems that are not of their own making.

In the following quotation, George summarises some of the evidence for her case:

The Overseas Development Council Population report quotes a 1971 study by William Rich showing that where decrease in birth rates is concerned, variations between UDCs [UDCs is short for Underdeveloped Countries] with similar gross national products per capita result primarily from differences in the distribution of this GNP. In more egalitarian countries, birth rates tend to decline rapidly, and vice versa. These conclusions are also borne out by the comparative figures for five UDCs published by the New Internationalist ...

This [data] shows that if you want to get your natural birth rate from 41 down to 26 (Taiwan) or from 45 to 30 per thousand (Korea), the best way to go about it is not to distribute condoms and IUDs and hope for the best, but to give people effective land reform and more income. They will reward you with fewer babies.

(George, 1977:63)

Very importantly from the point of view of practical policy-making, a study by staff of the World Bank and of the Institute of Development Studies at the University of Sussex came to conclusions similar to those of George. First, they argued that the main goal of development should not merely be growth but 'redistribution with growth'. They noted that growth could occur without the majority benefiting. Instead they argued for development strategies that would meet the needs of the majority. This became known as the 'basic needs approach'. Second, they tended to regard population control as secondary to and dependent on more egalitarian policies of development (see below). Incidentally, this marked a sharp departure from the assumptions of the modernisation theorists who believed that the general population would almost automatically benefit from growth. Consequently, they rarely addressed the issue of the redistribution of resources.

(IV) POPULATION LAISSEZ-FAIRE

A fourth, quite different perspective on world population growth comes from the political right. It reflects the free-market view that became popular in the nineteen seventies and eighties. One example of this approach is a draft position paper prepared in the Presidential White House for the United States delegation to the UN International Conference on Population (August 1984; source, Harford Thomas, *The Guardian*, 3 July 1984, p. 21). It argues that population growth is, in itself, as asset. It became dangerous only because in developing countries 'economic statism' interfered with the natural mechanisms of economic incentives and rewards which would have adjusted population growth to rising living standards. The draft document then goes on to argue that the USA 'does not consider abortion an acceptable element of family planning programmes'.

Although presented as theory, this approach is highly ideological and speculative. Supposing reduced population control results in population increase rather than decrease? Free-market population policies may be no more effective in reducing population than free-market economics has so far been (1984) in reducing unemployment in Britain. Perhaps a free-market 'experiment' in the area of population would be too risky.

My own view favours a policy combining a redistribution of resources (as Susan George argues) and continued efforts to extend birth control (an up-dated version of approach (ii)). Though George's case is well sustained, there is evidence that birth control does have an independent effect in reducing population. In *Human Numbers, Human Needs*, Paul Harrison and John Rowley point out that, in the industrialised world where 70 per cent of couples of reproductive age are using contraception, birth rates are low at 16 per 1,000 whereas in under-developed countries where less than 20 per cent are practising contraception the average birth rate is 34 per 1,000 – twice as high. Estimates suggest that if unwanted births were prevented in Bangladesh, Colombia, Jamaica and several other countries, population growth rates could be halved.

Population Policy and Development

....●

(I) PROBLEMS AND POLICY OVERVIEW: OZZIE SIMMONS

As the previous section suggests, the precise relationship between the rate of population increase and development (and vice-versa) is contentious. Fully aware of this, Ozzie G Simmons, nevertheless, attempts to summarise the relationship between rapid population growth and development in the light of existing research. In his article, *Development Perspectives and Population Change*, he briefly examines this relationship in respect to several key areas: health, education, labour absorption, food and income distribution. Broadly, his perspective reflects the assumptions of (ii) and especially (iii) of the previous section.

On the matter of health, Simmons observes that high fertility rates have a direct effect on the cost of services 'since obstetric and paediatric care constitute a large part of total demand for health services'. However, he emphasises that there are other causes of inadequate health care of comparable importance in the Third World. In most less developed countries (LDCs), health care tends to be concentrated in the urban areas and available mainly to the urban elites and middle class. He argues for a change from expensive, high-technology, hospital-based medicine to a primary care approach carried out by larger numbers of accessible, though less fully and expensively trained, paramedics (for a fuller discussion of this issue, see p. 392).

The provision of education facilities is the factor which Simmons sees as most negatively affected by rapid population increase. Quite simply, an age structure weighted towards children and teenagers tends to raise the cost and decrease the quality of the educational system. On the matter of labour absorption, he considers rapid population growth to exacerbate rather than cause unemployment and under-employment. He advocates meeting the problem by improving the skills and access to productive assets of the majority (a basic needs approach) and through labour intensive development.

The scale of hunger and starvation in the Third World needs to be indicated before we discuss Simmons' comments on food. About 40 million people die each year from hunger, almost half of them children. Of the 122 million children born in 1981 – the International Year of the child – one in ten died within a year, mainly from malnutrition. The Ethiopian famine made world hunger and starvation a major issue of public concern and conscience in 1985. Tens of thousands of personal contributions helped to meet an immediate need though it remains to be seen whether public opinion will pressure national governments and the United Nations to make the fundamental changes necessary substantially to reduce world hunger. As Ozzie Simmons points out, the world can produce enough food to meet foreseeable needs, taking into account estimates of population growth. However, this calculation depends on the food surplus produced by the developed countries (DCs) which is expensive for LDCs to buy. Alternatively and preferably, Simmons suggests that the LDCs should try to achieve the 3.5 per cent to 4 per cent increase in food production required to meet their needs and which is physically, technically and economically possible. He concludes that to be successful, this policy would need to be accompanied by income redistribution which would both enable people to buy food and probably reduce population growth (see George above). In short, he sees the food problem primarily as one of production and distribution rather than as a function of over-population.

Simmons considers that there is a tendency for rapid population increase adversely to affect income distribution in two main ways. First, in the absence of growth, the more people there are, the more thinly resources – health, education, land – tend to be spread. Second, high fertility increases inequality of income between families because the poor tend to have larger families. Despite hazarding these two points, Simmons stresses that the state of research in the area does not support generalisations. He comments that it is 'just as likely' that inequality causes high fertility among poorer, less educated sections of the population as the reverse.

Simmons concludes by arguing that both population control and poverty-focused development strategies are necessary and, carefully pursued, almost certainly complementary. Finally, his emphasis is on eliminating what he refers to as 'the underlying causes of poverty':

The real solution lies in structural change, in changing the distribution of productive wealth and thus the distribution of economic power, and in increasing the participation of the poor in decision-making and thus enabling them to exercise political power. (1983)

He offers no detailed blueprint for population policy or development strategy because the factors involved vary and require different responses in different societies. Similarly, he sees no single political road to change – continued resistance to change, reform and revolution are all possible.

(II) POPULATION POLICY IN THE THIRD WORLD WITH PARTICULAR REFERENCE TO THE YOUNG

Two issues relating to population are discussed below: the reduction of the fertility rate and infant and child mortality and disease, i.e. child health. These issues, particularly the second, are so urgent that they require immediate response. However, in discussing them, the analysis already made in this section needs to be remembered. These are issues not merely of population policy, but of the development and distribution of resources – both within Third World societies and globally. The education and employment of the young of the Third World is discussed in the next chapter (pp.487–9).

(A) THE REDUCTION OF THE FERTILITY RATE

A reduction in the fertility rate is historically a major factor in reducing the rate of population increase. However, a variety of factors make this a more complicated matter than one of contraception education. There is resistance to birth control for both practical and cultural reasons in many Third World societies and, in any case, expert opinion in the West is not certain precisely how key variables such as female education and more equal income distribution affect the fertility rate.

The main practical reason for producing large families in the Third World, is to provide enough workers to run the family's

property and to ensure care and protection for parents in their old age. In the absence of a welfare state this makes sense and even more so given high infant mortality rates among the very poor – three out of ten children die before they reach the age of five. The cultural complement to this is the high status normally associated with having a large family and religious disapproval of 'unnatural' interference with reproduction. For these reasons, it is usually both crude and ineffective for outsiders to impose birth control or to try to bribe people to use it (although China itself seems successfully to have enforced its own one-child per family policy).

A better way is to discover, and where practical to create, the conditions that are associated with a decline in the fertility rate. One commonly found correlation with a decline in the fertility rate is a prior decline in the rate of infant mortality. This relationship occurred in Britain and other European societies as they developed (see p. 454) and in virtually all Third World societies in which the fertility rate has decreased. A decline in infant mortality, then, seems almost a precondition of a decline in the rate of fertility, although the former can occur without the latter. The logic of this correlation appears to be that when there is a high likelihood of children surviving, there is less need to have so many of them. This brings up a second factor associated with fertility decline which is also strongly associated with a decline in the rate of infant mortality: an increase in the income and resources of the poor. Robert Repetto's *Economic Equality and Fertility in Developing Countries* demonstrates that the more equal the total distribution of income in a society, the lower the overall birthrate will tend to be. Again, this appears to establish a crucial link between development and a reduction in the rate of population growth.

According to Ozzie Simmons, the effect of female education on fertility is less certain than is commonly thought. He suggests that '(p)erhaps the most widely accepted generalisation is that of the inverse relationship between education and fertility', i.e. the educated tend to have fewer children. However, in countries with the lowest rates of female literacy, education is likely to increase fertility possibly by simply increasing the ability to have live births. Otherwise, education is associated with a decline in fertility, especially the education of women and particularly in urban areas (see figure 20.5). Simmons also claims that a fourth factor, the paid employment of women, is ambiguous in its effect on fertility. He cites a range of studies of female work status and fertility in Latin America which show no consistent inverse relationship between female employment outside the home and fertility. However, the recent *World Fertility Survey* covering the period from 1972 to the mid-eighties appears to re-establish the general connection between both the education and paid employment of women and low fertility. Three fifths of the world's illiterate are women and this provides an added reason for doing something about it.

Finally, the effect of family planning programmes on fertility remains to be considered. The debate centres on the issue of whether family planning programmes are effective in the absence of development and in the presence of strong cultural resistance to them. The balance of opinion is that such programmes tend to be more effective where at least some development has occurred, but in some cases they may also help independently to reduce fertility. The following example of a successful family planning programme was implemented in a society, Indonesia, which had experienced some development.

With an estimated population of 150 million, Indonesia seems a prime case for an effective planning policy. Its population has been increasing by 2.9 million per year and each year 2 million more jobs are needed. In the face of these trends, Indonesia has achieved a 'success story unrivalled in family planning history', according to demographers Terence and Valerie Hull, and Masri Singarimbun.

The setting up of the National Family Planning Coordination Board in 1970 indicated firm commitment to family planning. Initial funding came from the Indonesian government ($1.3 million) and foreign donors ($3 million). Now the programme's annual budget is over $50 million. The programme has helped to bring down population growth rate from 2.4 per cent in 1964 to around 1.9 per cent in 1981. In the Bali region, for instance, the birth rate fell an astonishing 34 per cent between 1970 and 1975. A lower rate of growth still is the target.

The major reason for the success of the programme is that it has been well organised and implemented. The programme is effective down to the village level. Local part-time field workers and prominent members of the community operate the programme and simple clinics have been established. It is local people, rather than outside experts, who have succeeded in persuading and explaining about birth control. Backing up the field workers are thousands of local volunteers who have helped to set up over 30,000 community family planning posts. Efficient communication between the local administrators and the planning board is crucial. The board evaluates incoming data and advises local workers accordingly.

The success of the above programme goes some way towards undermining the view that there is almost overwhelming cultural resistance to birth control in many traditional societies. Perhaps resistance in the past has been the fault of insensitive administrators, ignorant of local feeling and custom. The Indonesian case suggests that

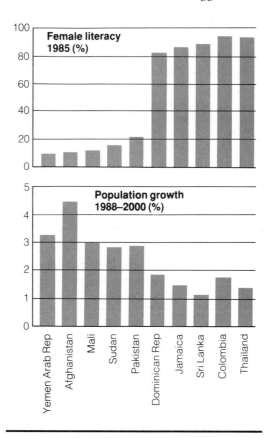

Figure 20.6

The more education people have, the more likely they are to have small families

(Source: UNDP)

▶
Figure 20.7 (Far right)
Fertility trends in the
developing world, by
region

there is another way. Certainly, the case for combining family planning programmes with anti-poverty development strategies seems strong.

(B) REDUCING INFANT AND CHILD MORTALITY AND DISEASE Statistics are not, in themselves, 'appalling' but the misery and deprivation behind the figures of infant and child mortality and disease certainly are. The basic or absolute poverty which underlines them is perhaps the major human and social problem in the world today. Only two other issues of survival – the nuclear and environmental – are of comparable importance. It may help to illuminate the personal experience of childhood poverty and starvation if we concentrate briefly on two aspects of it – mental illness and physical disablement – rather than attempt a global coverage.

It is a myth that mental illness is a 'luxury' of materially rich societies. Different cultures produce different illnesses, but overall, mental illness seems to be as common in the underdeveloped as in the industrialised world. It is not hard to see why. Poverty produces stress and depression; malnutrition can lead to apathy. People in the Third World are more subject to natural disasters, bereavements, rising but often frustrated expectations, enforced migrations and wars than Westerners. All of these are typically emotionally stressful occurrences.

War, of course, causes unequalled physical and emotional damage. The following is a report from Berry Brazleton on a number of Kampuchean children most of whom had been orphaned by war. He is writing about an orphanage in Phnom Penh:

Most infants in these overcrowded orphanages lie around all day, flat on their backs, their heads flattened and the hair worn off the backs of their heads.

The orphans are being physically salvaged in Phnom Penh, but the quality of their future lives is far from assured. We know now that unless a baby is stimulated by his environment to learn and to experience the excitement of learning, he will not be able to learn later. The combination of an undernourished brain coupled with a non-stimulating environment can be critical deprivation to an immature developing child ....

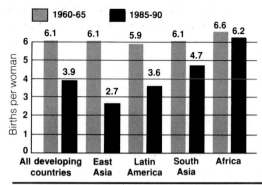

Although fertility rates are falling throughout the developing world, they remain much higher than replacement rates (about two births per woman), except in East Asia.

In Phnom Penh and the Thai border camps the babies are well nourished, but the girls taking care of them have been through too much themselves to be able to respond to the psychological needs of small dependants. Everyone in the orphanages means well and they would institute the same kinds of interactive experiences that I did, but they have not thought of them. Their own lives have been too sparse, and they have barely recovered from a mass depression.

(From Berry Brazleton, Games that Children Play for Survival, The Guardian, 18 December 1981:7)

There are about 200 million disabled children in the world, most of them in underdeveloped countries. Malnutrition is a major cause of disablement in the Third World. For instance, every year 250,000 children become blind through lack of vitamin A. Prevention can cost as little as three or four pence per person. In 1979, a survey in the villages of Camp Tinio and Mananac in the Philippines showed that 119 out of 568 children under the age of six were to some extent disabled – over 20 per cent. Of those impaired, 80 per cent were found to be malnourished. The following is an extract from a report by Teresa Tunay on the low cost community-based care programme that followed the survey. It is particularly worth noting the reasons why she thinks the programme was effective:

Today, only a few months later, 46 per cent of those children have shown very significant improvements.

The original survey also found Josefina, a ten month old baby girl who was a victim of Down's Syndrome. In other words, she was a mongoloid child. When her home was visited by one of the survey team, Josefina was virtually a wilting head of lettuce in her mother's arms. Her body appeared boneless. She could not even hold her head up. Her eyes were lifeless and she responded to neither the sound of a voice nor to a smiling face.

Today only 16 weeks later, Josefina has put on weight, runs around the house in a baby walker, plays enthusiastically with a string of coloured beads, and is just as responsive as any normal child of her age.

Josefina's 'therapy' did not require institutionalisation or gadgetry. Her mother was shown how and where to 'tickle' her baby to exercise the muscles. The treatment progressed through gentle kneading of the child's limbs to a daily ritual of therapeutic exercise. Soon, the child began to make steady and continued progress....

The key to low-cost but dramatic improvements in the lives of the majority of the disabled lies in releasing the care and support which is latent in the family

and the community. And it was from that point that the 'Reaching the Unreached' programme began. Two young researchers, one trained in occupational therapy and the other in pre-school education, went to live in the village, renting a small hut at a nominal rate, from the village or 'barangay' captain.

In discussion with the community, they agreed to concentrate their efforts on children under the age of six, not only because the young child is the most vulnerable, but also because the earlier the help the more potential there is for improvement and the less damage is done to the normal processes of child development.

Village volunteers were trained. Non-technical indicators were listed for the detection of impairments. And the community as a whole was involved in finding impairments in their children, in discussing their attitudes towards it, and in planning and carrying out the rehabilitation programmes themselves.

(From Teresa Tunay, Miracles for the Many, New Internationalist, No. 95:13)

Conclusion: Population Policy and Politics

As the above discussion of world population problems and policy progressed, the political issues that underlay all policy decisions should have become increasingly apparent. As Susan George emphasises, at the centre of the political debate about population is development. Birth control policies may help – international aid helps – but development is essential to solving the problems of the Third

World's people. However, there are deep political and ideological disagreements about how development best occurs. These disagreements are not merely about the 'mechanisms' of development but reflect profound differences of value and preference. At its widest, this debate is about what kind of future world community we will make. To this issue, we now turn.

1 Demography is the study of the statistics of population. This is a topic in which it is essential to understand basic terminology and this is defined in the early pages of this chapter.

2 World population trends are such that only a highly effective development of resources will prevent mass malnutrition and recurrent famine and starvation in the next hundred years.

SUMMARY

In contrast, the population of Europe is projected to increase slowly and to age. Britain's population is unlikely to increase much more and is already relatively aged. While the number of elderly in Britain continues to increase, the number of teenagers will be at a low point throughout the nineteen nineties. These trends raise a number of practical issues discussed in this chapter and in chapter ten.

3 There are four perspectives on population growth:

(i) Malthus argued that, in the absence of sexual restraint, population would expand beyond the point at which it could be sustained.

(ii) Neo-Malthusian approach broadly adopts Malthus's analysis but argues that contraception offers a solution to over-population.

(iii) The Redistributionist approach argues that populations stabilise (stop increasing) when a large majority of their members reach a standard of living beyond subsistence.

(iv) The *laissez-faire* approach to development argues that governments should stop trying to control population growth and leave it to natural economic forces to do so.

4 As Ozzie Simmons argues a population that is growing at a rate that is out of control has substantial negative effects on the society in which this occurs. He demonstrates this in relation to health care, education and agriculture.

5 Whatever the arguments about how they may be solved, two issues are of urgent importance in the undeveloped world:

1) Reduction of the Fertility Rate, and

2) Reduction of Child Mortality and Disease.

6 Attempts to deal with these problems seem to be more effective if they involve the local people and train them in the necessary techniques rather than impose 'solutions' upon them.

7 Population matters in the undeveloped world are fraught with ideological, political and economic issues. These are discussed in the next chapter.

RESEARCH AND COURSEWORK

For demographic/generational issues in relation to Britain see p. 233 and for development issues, see p. 494.

FURTHER READING

R K Kelsall's *Population* (Longman, 1985) is a standard introduction to the topic. Susan George's *How the Other*

Half Dies: The Real Reasons for World Hunger (Penguin, 1977) analyses population as part of the wider issue of development as do several other references given at the end of the next chapter.

QUESTIONS

1 Analyse the cause of any two major demographic changes in any one society you have studied. (London, 1985)

2 Account for differing patterns of disease and mortality between more and less industrialised societies. (Cambridge, 1989)

(See also chapter 16, p. 398)

21 Social Change: Development & Underdevelopment

Terminology

Social change includes development, undevelopment and underdevelopment. Development implies some positive progress in a society's condition whereas undevelopment implies decline or stagnation. Underdevelopment is a term used especially by Marxists to indicate that the operation of international capitalism tends to prevent or retard development in the Third World. What is viewed as development varies somewhat from society to society. The goals of socialist societies are not the same as those of capitalist ones. The former tend to stress egalitarian and communal objectives, whereas the latter put greater emphasis on individuality and personal freedom. Nevertheless, there are some aspects of development on which in practice there is near-universal agreement. These are mainly technological, economic and educational. Nearly all societies seek to improve their technology, increase their wealth and develop the skills of their people. How this should be done and who should most benefit from development are, of course, matters of wide disagreement.

Once we move beyond quantifiable and measurable matters of wealth and technique to consider political and cultural issues, disagreement about what constitutes development becomes more marked. The Western democracies tend to want 'developing' societies eventually to adopt the political and civil liberties common in the West. By contrast, China (and until recently the Soviet Union) looks to the Communist Party – theoretically the organ of the working class or peasantry – as the means of political decision and expression. Even so, a number of 'developing' societies have, at different times, attempted to combine Western-style political institutions and civil liberties with broadly socialist programmes of economic development. Jamaica under Michael Manley's leadership and Chile under Salvador Allende are examples.

There is even less agreement about what constitutes a developed cultural life than about political development. This applies both to the level of popular culture, i.e. the quality of everyday life, and to 'high' culture – literature, music and the rest of the arts. Unsurprisingly, capitalist images of socialism and socialist images of capitalism tend towards the uncomplimentary. In capitalist society, socialism is often depicted as producing mass, wooden conformity from which only a few brave writers and artists successfully break. For their part, socialist societies often present capitalists as greedy and manipulative. Yet, both at the ordinary and exceptional level, there is much successful cultural interchange. Many citizens of the First and 'Second' Worlds seem capable of getting on well with each other and the best of socialist and Western art is appreciated in both cultures. Both at the level of the mundane and the uniquely creative, shared values and concerns exist. If literature and art illuminate the common ideals and hopes of humanity, then they may provide a better guide to developmental goals than the ideological utterances of politicians.

The terminology of social change reflects a variety of ideological perspectives, some of which have been indicated above. The term development tends to reflect an optimistic liberal-capitalist view that world 'progress' is likely, whereas that of underdevelopment has clearly negative overtones. To avoid the polarisation of these terms, some prefer more developed countries (MDCs) and less developed countries (LDCs). As J K Galbraith suggests, the terms rich and poor nations are probably the simplest and truest (see figure 21.1). The widely used terms, First, Second and Third World are useful providing no hierarchy is assumed. The First World is the United States and Western European capitalist democracies, the Second World was until recently thought of as the Soviet Union and its former communist bloc allies (although its status is now in flux), and the Third World is the poor or relatively poor countries.

▶

Figure 21.1

North and South: the

basic inequality

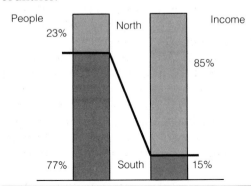

(Source: *The Guardian*, 24th May, 1991)

Not all countries fit neatly into simple categories. Figure 21.2 shows three groups of countries at different levels of development according to income and type of production. A large service sector is usually taken as an indicator of advanced development; such economies, for example the United States, are sometimes referred to as post-industrial or post-modern though Marxists prefer the terms capitalist/socialist/communist. The diagram also gives data about the employed population (usually a smaller proportion of the total population in poorer countries).

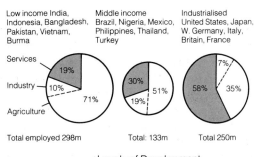

Low income India, Indonesia, Bangladesh, Pakistan, Vietnam, Burma

Middle income Brazil, Nigeria, Mexico, Philippines, Thailand, Turkey

Industrialised United States, Japan, W. Germany, Italy, Britain, France

Services

Industry

Agriculture

Total employed 298m   Total: 133m   Total 250m

Levels of Development

Note. The percentages refer to levels of employment in given economic sectors.

(Source: *The Economist*) February 24, 1979, p. 32

Figure 21.2

Breakdown of

Employment in

Selected Countries

The West and the World: Historical and Contemporary Overview

Many of the problems and issues of the contemporary world are the product of the impact of the Western powers on the rest of the globe. This impact began in the fifteenth century, intensified in the nineteenth and remains very strong. Of course there is nothing new or modern in imperial expansion. The Greeks and Romans established large empires which radically changed the economic, political and cultural lives of their subject peoples. The modern European empires have done no less. The major difference is that between them the Western European powers settled, occupied or subdued virtually the rest of the world. The result is that even today world politics, economics and even cultural relations take place within a framework largely created by Western Europe. On the whole, the societies of what we now call the Third World have been put in a reactive position, few have attained power and influence comparable to that of the Western nations. Put more technically, the causes of change in Western European societies – particularly, Britain – were largely endogamous (generated from within) whereas in the Third World they were and are predominantly exogamous ('imported' or imposed from outside). It would be difficult to exaggerate the shock to many traditional societies as they struggled to re-orientate or even survive (for instance, the American Indians) under the impact of the West.

Three phases of Western influence and domination can be indicated. First, is the period of exploration, trade and conquest beginning in the fifteenth century and which included the 'discovery' of the Americas. Second, is the period of the formal empires – when most European colonies were established – of the nineteenth and first half of the twentieth century. Third, is the post-Second World War period during which the formal European empires were broken up. Politically, the United States and the Soviet Union became the dominant world powers although they have usually tried to avoid (often unsuccessfully) establishing formal occupations of societies they sought to dominate. The world economic power of European corporations (and especially now American) continues, however. The term neo-colonial is widely used to describe a situation in which one country is actually, though not formally, controlled by another (the term can refer to either economic or political control). Finally, during the post-war period, Japan has developed into an economic power of global significance.

What, then for good or ill, has the Western impact of the Third World been? The arguments that surround this question are the substance of the rest of this chapter. Certain key points should be noted here. Economically the issue is whether the West has tended or, at least, tried to stimulate development (economic growth) or whether it has more typically exploited and underdeveloped the Third World. Politically, interest has focused on the struggle between the USSR and the United States and the systems they represented and advocated, and attention has now shifted to the future fate and influence of the Soviet Union. Previously, the European powers had been caught in the contradiction of supporting nationalism and democracy at home but not always in their subject territories. Eventually, however, all of them acquiesced in the political independence of their colonies. Many ex-colonies adopted political systems reflecting the originally European ideologies of liberalism and socialism. The cultural impact of Europe on the rest of the world defies summary. Christianity, liberty and democracy (liberalism), equality (socialism), the idea of linear progress itself, all spread from the West. Currently, the domination of the West, particularly the United States, of the entertainment media raises profound issues of value, and of cultural independence, creativity, quality and taste. The image of members of a Chinese peasant commune avidly watching Western films (shown in the documentary *Heart of the Dragon*) focuses the issue nicely.

CONTEMPORARY CONTEXTS AND ISSUES: GLOBALISATION

It is not possible to make much sense of the development/underdevelopment debate presented below without knowing the basic institutional framework of post-war political and economic life. After the defeat of Germany and Japan, two new power blocs emerged: the North Atlantic Treaty Organisation (NATO) of the United States and most of Western Europe, and the Warsaw Pact which included the Soviet Union and most of the countries of Eastern Europe. The Warsaw Pact was formally disbanded in 1991 following the breakup of the communist bloc. However, on a global scale the independent activities and rivalry of Russia and the United States remain apparent, and to a greater or lesser extent are likely to continue to do so.

The United Nations was established as part of the post-war settlement in an attempt to provide a forum in which international problems and emergencies could be discussed and to some extent acted upon. In practice, the UN was so constituted that the major victorious powers surrendered none of their independence or sovereignty. Nevertheless, the UN is a unique focus of

world opinion and cannot be ignored by the major powers. It has frequently been used by representatives of Third World nations – either individually or in concert. It has also fulfilled important, though, in the total world context, minor functions in such areas as health, education, research and peace-keeping. If these kinds of issues are ever to be tackled primarily through a world agency, then the United Nations and its predecessor, the League of Nations, will be seen as the embryo of this approach.

The post-war world was also divided into two main economic blocs paralleling the political. The General Agreement on Tariffs and Trade (GATT) established the framework of international commerce for most of the world. The Soviet Union opted out and instead introduced Comecon for the Eastern European bloc. In practice, there has been a significant amount of trade between the areas and this has increased with the break-up of Comecon. Many Third World nations argue that GATT favours the manufacturing interests of the First World rather than their own agricultural and extractive industries and have sought changes in the Agreement to accommodate this view.

The monetary system established after the war reflected the emergence of the United States as the world's leading economic power and the relative decline of Britain. The dollar became the world's major reserve currency – because much international trade was now conducted in dollars it became necessary for most countries to keep reserves of dollars if they wanted to buy Western products. The lending institutions related to the United Nations, the World Bank and International Monetary Fund, (IMF) reflected the dominance of the United States and Britain. The role of the World Bank, whose full title is the International Bank for Reconstruction and Development, was to provide loans for development projects in Europe or elsewhere following the destruction of war. In recent years its lending has been concentrated in the so-called Third World developing countries. The International Monetary Fund had a much wider brief to provide loans for countries in major economic difficulty, including balance of payment deficit, (i.e. when the value of imports exceeds exports). Loans are provided at interest and subject to the borrowing recommendations for economic recovery laid down by the Fund.

The countries of the Third World, then, struggle for political, cultural and national identity and for economic development in a world not of their own making. Indeed, some of them, such as Nigeria, were literally put together by Western nations. Others, such as Iran, still cherish aspects of traditional culture as old or older than Western European civilisation. Even apologists for Western imperialism agree that some of the peoples of the Third World have suffered greatly (as well as, in their view, benefited) at the hands of the West. The slave trade alone proves the point. It is hardly surprising that intense and conflicting feelings of hatred and admiration, rejection and imitation, and of disgust and envy are freely expressed about Europe and the United States in the Third World. No doubt, if history had been different, and Western Europe had itself been occupied, its inhabitants would have felt similarly about their conquerors.

It will be obvious from the above survey that economic, political and ideological factors are highly related in the process of world change and development. Few Third World powers have been free from the economic and/or political influence of the Soviet Union or the United States although some, such as India, seek an independent or non-aligned position in relation to the superpowers. Table 21.1 summarises the main economic and political division in the contemporary world.

GLOBALISATION: THE GLOBAL SYSTEM If there is one matter on which the theories of change discussed below agree, it is that in certain crucial respects 'globalisation' is occurring or, put alternatively, a 'global system' is emerging. This means that certain key processes are developing at a

	Developed	Underdeveloped
Communist and formerly communist	USSR EASTERN EUROPE	CHINA, VIETNAM CUBA
Capitalist	NORTH KOREA USA, EEC, JAPAN, AUSTRALIA, SOUTH AFRICA	CAPITALIST THIRD WORLD eg INDIA (non-aligned)

▲
Table 21.1

transnational level which are eroding the independence and 'separateness' of nations and the power of the nation state. Even regional identity – European, Asian – is seen as deeply affected by these developments.

First, the concept of a 'global system' began as an economic theory. It suggested that capitalist economic forces, particularly the major transnational corporations, are creating a situation which challenges and reduces the autonomy and sovereignty of nations. Second, with the continuing collapse of soviet-style communism, some commentators consider that the triumph of liberal-democracy, as well as the capitalist economic system, is likely to be part of a shared global future. There is disagreement about how far socialism might be part of 'the new world order'. Within Europe there is little support for authoritarian-socialism but still substantial support for democratic socialism. Indeed, the European Social Charter contains significant elements of democratic socialism.

There is increasing speculation from both the left and right that global cultural patterns – if not a global culture – are emerging. Most agree that it will be much more varied and individualised than the old 'mass' culture but some fear that style and fashion will be predominantly producer rather than consumer-led. Leslie Sklair (1991) argues that an 'ideology of consumerism' fuelled by advertising and the capitalist dominated media is now dominant throughout most of the globe (see p. 486).

Theories of Change

Neither theorists nor policy-makers agree on why some regions develop and others do not. I have divided the following theoretical section into four parts: development or modernisation theories; Marxist theories; two liberal theories – new conservative

(free-market) theories and social democratic theories; and a feminist account of change. Many important issues are raised within the theoretical discussions but a number of key themes are further analysed in the next section.

Development (Modernisation) Theory

Developmentalists or modernisation theorists argue that the pattern of historical change has been from simple to complex, or modern, societies. They differ in their explanations of change but are in agreement in rejecting the Marxist model (see below). Many developmentalists also subscribe to convergence theory, i.e. they contend that the advanced industrial societies, whether socialist or capitalist, are growing more alike. Again, this differs from Marxists who see socialist and capitalist societies as radically different. Many of the concepts of modernisation theorists can be found in the earlier work of Spencer, Durkheim and Weber.

SPENCER, DURKHEIM AND WEBER ON CHANGE

The view that social development has broadly evolved towards the more complex is apparent in the work of several of the founding fathers of sociology, notably Spencer and Durkheim. Ronald Fletcher usefully distinguishes between the descriptive and explanatory in their work. Thus, Spencer's descriptive criteria were: the simple society; the compound society (clans, tribes); doubly compounded (city states, kingdoms); and trebly compounded (empires, modern nations and federations). His explanatory typology consisted of the military and industrial types of society. He explained the change from the one to the other partly by the very success of military societies in establishing the conditions for the peaceful development of industry and welfare. Durkheim's descriptive criteria are very similar to Spencer's: the horde; the clan; simple polysegmental; polysegmental simply compounded (confederations of tribes); polysegmental doubly compounded (nations and federations). His explanatory typology proposes an increasing differentiation of society from the mechanical to the organic (see pp. 431–3) and has much more currency among contemporary sociologists than the now largely disregarded typology of Spencer.

Both Spencer and Durkheim were influenced by the strong nineteenth century interest in biology and, in particular, the tendency to find parallels between biological and social evolution. Both employed the concept of structural differentiation to indicate that as society develops more functions it becomes structurally more complex. This perspective has been elaborated more recently by Talcott Parsons (see below).

Max Weber's contribution to understanding change does not lie in the development of formal descriptive or explanatory frameworks. Yet, in his 'dialogue with Marx' (see below) he made several observations about the nature of social change which have influenced more recent modernisation theorists and liberal historians. First, Weber stressed the importance of ideas and choice in the process of change (see p. 402). In this respect, Weber is sometimes described as a 'voluntarist'. Second, a related point, he rejected what he took to be Marx's overemphasis on the economic causes of change. Instead of economic 'determinism', he offered a multi-factoral approach to understanding change in which ideas played a major role. Third, he rejected Marx's analysis of class conflict and revolution. Change could be gradual as well as revolutionary and there were other important sources of change than class conflict. Fourth, although he recognised the inequality of capitalist society, he did not attribute it essentially to capitalism. Rather, he thought that large, rational organisations or bureaucracies, including the capitalist corporation, were necessarily hierarchical and unequal. He anticipated that as socialist societies developed large scale industrial and governmental bureaucracies, they would be characterised by inequality. Again, modernisation theorists and liberal thinkers have tended to accept and build on this analysis whilst, in some cases, arguing for the mitigation of the extremes of inequality in their own and other societies. One can see in Weber's analysis of bureaucracy in modern society, the seeds of convergence theory.

DEVELOPMENT (MODERNISATION) THEORY

This section gives examples of modernisation theory. They differ mainly in the extent to which they stress the diffusion (spread) of technology or of ideas as the primary stimulus to development.

Walt Rostow's emphasis is on the role of technology, though not exclusively so. Rostow's influential work *The Stages of Growth* was first published in 1960. He argued that it 'is possible to identify all societies, in their economic dimensions as living within one of five categories'. These are:

1 traditional society
2 preconditions for take-off
3 take-off
4 drive to maturity
5 age of high mass-consumption

There is a broad similarity between Rostow's categories and the descriptive evolutionary frameworks of Spencer and Durkheim. However, he is openly little interested in what he calls traditional societies. He uses the term as a catch-all to describe those societies whose productivity is 'limited by the inaccessibility of modern science'. For Rostow, modern science and its practical application in technology is the key to the 'take-off' into development. In Europe the scientific and technological preconditions for take-offs were developed internally, elsewhere it was the 'intrusion by more advanced societies' which 'shocked the traditional society' and began or hastened its undoing and opened the way for change, especially 'economic progress'. In the take-off phase, growth becomes the 'normal condition'. In traditional society, take-off requires not only the availability of capital and technology but the emergence of a modernising, political elite. The 'drive to maturity' is characterised by a high percentage of national income reinvestment 'to extend modern technology over the whole front of its economic activity'. Once this economic infrastructure is laid down, leading economic sectors 'shift towards durable consumers' goods and services'. Higher personal income and greater leisure time stimulate this process. Rostow also notes that in this stage, money available for welfare expenditure increases.

On the relationship between development and democracy, Rostow acknowledges what in a later publication he refers to as 'an important and painful truth' (1971): that it is possible for development to occur under totalitarian leadership. In *Stages of Growth* he devotes a full chapter to attacking communism although he also refers to the Meiji Restoration in Japan and Ataturk's Turkey as non-communist forms of 'peculiarly inhumane ... political organisation capable of launching and sustaining the growth process'. However, he seems to reveal that his primary concern is with communism rather than totalitarianism as such when he argues the need for a partnership between the Western powers 'in association with the non-communist politicians and peoples' to achieve growth and democracy. To be consistent in opposing totalitarianism, he should have written 'non-totalitarian' rather than 'non-communist'. In fact, it has been a criticism of American post-war international policy that its government has been too ready to work with and support right-wing totalitarian regimes merely to oppose communism, as occurred in the case of the Shah of Iran and President Diem of (formerly) South Vietnam. Frequently, the underlying problem is that there is little or no democratic tradition in Third World countries. This raises the question of whether supporting 'democracy' against communism is a viable basis of political policy in societies in which it has few roots. We return to this controversial and ideologically charged question later.

Talcott Parsons and Bert Hoselitz conceptualise modernisation within a functionalist framework. Following Weber, they stress that the diffusion of ideas and values from the West outwards is the underlying dynamic of modernisation rather than the spread of technology emphasised by Rostow. However, the two approaches are not incompatible. According to Parsons, as society evolves in a more complex direction, so its institutions change and adapt and become more functionally differentiated. Thus, in more modern societies, many of the more formal aspects of socialisation are carried out within the educational system rather than the family. In *Sociological Factors in Economic Development* (1960), Hoselitz draws on Parsons' typology of pattern variables (see p. 498) and uses it as a means to analyse the social factors that contribute to economic growth. He concluded that the values of achievement, universalism and specificity (particularly as applied to the division of labour) are conducive to growth, and those of ascription, particularism and diffuseness to stagnation. Interestingly, he finds that the former three values have accompanied growth in the former Soviet Union as in the West thus indicating some convergence between the two types of society (see below). Finally, he suggests that 'deviant' elites may be more effective agents of modernisation than traditional ones.

The social psychologist David McLelland has also examined the attitudes conducive to development. His work is more empirical than that of Hoselitz. McLelland set out to test whether the need for achievement, or *N*ach as he termed it, is related to development. Using tests he devised for the purpose, he attempted to relate increases in *N*ach in a given culture to increases in the production of certain relevant commodities. His tests included both historical and contemporary societies and seemed to establish the positive correlation he had hypothesised. Since this was so, McLelland recommended greater socialisation in achievement motivation in Third World countries.

McLelland's work is an interesting piece of cross-cultural social psychology but politically naive. To those Third World societies struggling against often acute economic difficulties and, as some of them see it, imperialist exploitation, the advice to take achievement courses must have seemed, if not arrogant, ludicrous. A second criticism is that the correlation he establishes between increases in achievement motivation and production need not be causal. For instance, both could occur as part of a much wider imitation of the West or, in certain cases, both could be imposed by Western powers.

The practical effect of modernisation theory – in so far as it can be gauged – was to underpin a rather simplistic approach to aid and development on the part of the Western powers in the twenty years following the world war. 'Modernisation' turned out to be a much less predictable and neutral and a more political process than these theorists seemed to anticipate.

CRITIQUE OF MODERNISATION THEORY

In retrospect, perhaps the most damaging criticism of modernisation theory is its ethnocentrism, i.e. it assumes the necessity of 'modern' (in effect, American and to a lesser extent Western) values to Third world societies with little consideration of their own cultures. The notion that Third World societies might want to balance modernisation with traditional culture or even reject aspects of modernisation is not adequately appreciated. Instead 'modern man' or rather 'American man' is the presumed ideal goal. What now seems a naive belief in progress supported these chauvinistic attitudes. Second, the grand models of the developmentalists lack the feeling and meaning of historical reality: we are presented with a succession of stages rather than with people acting out of a variety of motives with a variety of results. Third, and related to the second point, modernisation theorists fail to explore the variety of class and national conflicts which radically affect development/ underdevelopment (see section on underdevelopment theory). The issue of inequality has deeply concerned many in the Third World but an appreciation of its profound importance is not apparent in developmentalist writings until the nineteen seventies. Marxists particularly criticise diffusionists for not appreciating that the motive of economic exploitation is the key to understanding capitalist expansion.

Fourth, there is a clear tendency to deterministic thinking in modernisation theory both in its more technological and in its more 'value-functionalist' versions. This tendency is at its strongest in convergency theory which is fully presented in the next section. Weber's original emphasis on values was, of course, intended to give due importance to subjectivity and choice. However, Hoselitz's treatment of values, framed within Parsons' pattern variable pairs, makes them appear prescriptive and restrictive. Ironically, this is probably the oppositive of Weber's intention although he too struggled systematically to reconcile value subjectivity with the objective effects of social institutions.

Finally, mainstream developmentalist thinking both in United Nations development institutions and elsewhere has been steadily moving away from the assumptions of modernisation theory for almost twenty years.

In particular, within the World Bank, it is

no longer taken for granted that economic growth will benefit all social groups within the society it occurs. There is now much more concern to find strategies for development which immediately meet the basic needs of the poor (see p. 459). However, modernisation theory remains of great interest as an example of how social science can play an ideological role – in this case the support and justification of American liberal capitalism – even to the point where, perhaps, social science and ideology appear barely distinguishable.

CONVERGENCE THEORY

Convergence theory is closely related to modernisation theory. It is usually applied to more industrially developed societies which by virtue of certain technological and organisational imperatives (needs) are seen as moving closer together. In particular, the comparison is made of the United States and the Soviet Union. Thus, Raymond Avon, the French sociologist remarked that it was not until he visited India that he realised that the significant division in the world was not between communism and capitalism, but between modern states and those which remained industrially undeveloped. However, the models of development surveyed above imply an assumption of convergence on an even larger scale, which all societies undergo as they 'modernise'.

Convergence theory focused a number of themes in American and, to some extent, European liberal-social democratic thought during the late nineteen fifties/early sixties. Together, these themes cohered into a mood which considerably influenced politicians and policy makers. A key work stimulating this climate of opinion was Ralf Dahrendorf's *Class and Class Conflict in an Industrial Society* (1959). Dahrendorf argues that there has been a decline in the 'old' militant working class and in the 'old' individualistic, capitalist class and in traditional class conflict (see p. 130). He observes instead a managed or organised society in which solutions to social (no longer class) problems are technical rather than ideological in nature. Daniel Bell, who acknowledges Dahrendorf's influence, makes this point the central theme of his *The End of Ideology: On the Exhaustion of Political Ideas in the Fifties* (1961). Bell strongly

contends that ideological and political 'extremism' such as fascism and communism, are not merely redundant but dangerous: their contempt of compromise and intolerance leading almost certainly to inhumanity and bloodshed. He believed he saw a prudent consensus emerging in the West in which the institutions of liberal democracy were accepted as the most mature and realistic means of political expression. With Bell, as with other modernisation thinkers, it can be difficult to disentangle what he believes is happening from what he wants to happen. Although Dahrendorf and Bell's expectations of immediately convergent trends referred mainly to the Western capitalist democracies, it is arguable that the sharply polarised ideological politics of the sixties and eighties (in the West) directly contradict even this limited thesis.

Clark Kerr et al, *Industrialism and Industrial Man* (1959) is probably the most comprehensive statement of convergence theory. Like Dahrendorf he considers that it is the industrial rather than the capitalist nature of modern society which gives it many of its basic characteristics. The same industrial technology produces similar occupational and stratificational systems and in Kerr's view mature industrial society requires higher levels of managerial, technical and labour skills than early industrial society. Both arguments have come in for sharp criticism. John Goldthorpe's view that stratification in socialist 'industrial' societies is produced primarily by political rather than technological or market factors is one noted alternative analysis. The view that advanced industrial society requires a more skilled labour force was refuted in the United States by Harry Braverman and, more recently, in Britain, by Paul Thompson. They argue that 'deskilling' of the industrial labour force has occurred partly because of the deliberate selection by capitalists of forms of technology and organisation that require low levels of worker skills and intelligent participation (and in some forms of production little or no worker involvement at all). No doubt the overall situation is complex. It may be that a highly skilled occupational elite has developed but that the experience of the majority is closer to what Braverman and Thompson suggest.

Kerr envisaged that industrial society

would be marked by increasing wealth and leisure. This trend has occurred but Marxist and many other critics point out that capitalist society does not ensure a growing equality of wealth distribution and that the ability to enjoy leisure is likely to be correspondingly unequal. However, as Kerr assumes that industrial society is hierarchical this presumably is not a problem for him. Like Bell and Dahrendorf, he argues that, contrary to Marx, protest will not increase in later industrial society: 'Rather, turning Marx on his head, protest tends to peak early.' This is partly because increasing general affluence and the welfare state remove the incentive for protest, particularly based on class. In this case, the 25 years since Kerr wrote do not tend to bear him out. Rather, perhaps what has happened is that in Western Europe and the United States, a substantial and growing minority of unemployed and low-paid are not sharing in the now not so general affluence (see Harrington pp. 160–1). Perhaps the urban riots of the nineteen sixties (USA) and eighties (Britain) are a form of protest.

Finally, again echoing Bell, Kerr links industrialism with the development of liberal pluralist democracy and with the consensus about basic values, including a belief in compromise, necessary for it to work. Thus, industrial society 'develops a distinctive consensus which relates individuals and groups to each other and provides a common body of ideas, beliefs and value judgements integrated into a whole'. In comment, whilst a general commitment to liberal democracy and

values persists in the West, the broader liberal consensus of the fifties has been split (pp. 342–8). Social and political life in the West has proved less settled and less easily manageable than Kerr and his liberal contemporaries imagined.

Kerr is somewhat ambiguous in committing himself to the view that either the Soviet Union or countries of the Third World will evolve essentially as the Western industrial democracies have done. Less cautiously, Rostow refers to communism as a 'disease of transition' which popular demand for consumer goods and political freedom (i.e. capitalist democracy) would eventually undermine. The apparent collapse of Soviet communism in 1991–2 makes Rostow's analysis seem less sweeping than it did, but whether convergence will occur throughout the Third World remains an open question.

A most formidable criticism of modernisation/convergence theory has been made by Marxists. They argue that the major impact of the capitalist West on the Third World has not occurred through the diffusion of technology and ideas but through economic and political exploitation. The lack of consideration of this perspective – even in a marginal way – among modernisation theorists does seem a remarkable failure of imagination. That such a viewpoint is widely held, particularly in the socialist Third World, was made forcefully apparent by the North Vietnamese in the nineteen sixties and by the socialist Sandanista government of Nicaragua in the conflict with the Reagan administration in the nineteen eighties.

Marxist Theories

MARX AND LENIN

Like the other founding fathers, Marx attempted to describe and explain historical change. His descriptive categories are primitive communism, the Asiatic mode of production, the ancient form of society, feudalism, capitalism, and communism (with socialism as an intermediary stage between the last two). Primitive communism is a simple form of hunting and gathering society in which goods are held in common and there is no class stratification.

The Asiatic mode of production occurred mainly in Asia and was not a necessary stage in historical change: it was characterised by state exploitation of labour. The ancient form of society emerged out of primitive communism through tribal warfare; successful tribes established cities and enjoyed the surplus produced by conquered slaves. The Greek and Roman empires are examples. A more recent case of a slave society is the plantation society of the southern United States. Feudalism is characterised by control of the land by the minority who exploit the labour of the serfs or peasant majority. Capitalism signals the rise to dominance of the manufacturing middle class over the landed nobility. Marx anticipated that capitalism would be replaced by communism when the urban proletariat overthrew the capitalist class and took over the means of production.

Marx's explanation of historical change is based on class conflict. As he put it, 'the history of all hitherto existing society is the history of class struggle'. He saw class conflict as a 'dialectic' or process which generates change. As the above description indicates, the dominant class is always the one that owns the main means of producing wealth and the exploited class is the one that provides the labour to work these.

Marx was well aware of the role of imperial expansion in causing change. He observed that 'modern industry has established the world market'. He appears to have thought that the impact of capitalism on the non-capitalist world though brutal was necessary to its industrial development. However, his own efforts were directed towards analysing capitalist society rather than capitalism's impact on the world.

In his essay, *Imperialism, The Highest Stage of Capitalism*, Lenin offers a more detailed global analysis. Even so, he is primarily concerned with the internal dynamics of capitalist society which generate imperialism rather than with the detailed effects of imperialism on non-capitalist societies (on, for instance, their class structures). He argues that up to about the last quarter of the nineteenth century, the main purposes of capitalist imperialism were to acquire raw materials and open up markets for manufactured products. From then on – rather earlier for Britain – the nature of imperialism began to change to the extent that a new form – finance imperialism – was already dominant by the First World War. Finance imperialism involved the export and investment of capital in poorer countries. This provided income and cheap labour.

Lenin regarded finance capitalism as an aspect of a new stage in capitalist development, monopoly capitalism. Monopoly capitalism occurs when production is concentrated increasingly into a few, large-scale enterprises. Lenin cited considerable evidence to suggest that the banks control monopoly capital because they finance it –

thus finance capitalism. Much 'surplus capital' is 'exported' abroad where profits are often highest: 'Thus, finance capital almost literally … spreads its net over all countries of the world'. According to Lenin, there develop 'international capitalist monopolies which share the world among themselves'. Supporting this economic 'exploitation' of 'small, or weak nations' is the political activity of 'capitalist' governments who eventually complete the 'territorial division of the whole world'. Lenin referred to the mutual involvement of the state and monopoly capital as 'state monopoly capitalism', and foresaw it as an increasing trend.

In summary, Lenin states: 'If it were necessary to give the briefest definition of imperialism, we should have to say that imperialism is the monopoly stage of capitalism.' Lenin may have under-estimated the continuing need for raw materials and commodity export markets in motivating imperialism but his analysis does accommodate the vital and growing role of the large, international corporation in the world economy – to the extent that he foreshadows the much later commentator, André Gunder Frank.

BARAN AND SWEEZY, AND GUNDER FRANK

Like Lenin, Paul Baran and Paul Sweezy describe monopoly capitalism as a world system of exploitation. In their book, *Monopoly Capitalism*, they state:

> *From its earliest beginnings in the Middle Ages, capitalism has always been an international system. And it has always been a hierarchical system with one or more leading metropolises at the top, completely dependent colonies at the bottom, and many degrees of superordination and subordination in between.*
> *(Baran and Sweezy, 1966)*

They are equally succinct about the purposes of the multinational corporations which dominate American policy:

> *What they want is monopolistic control over foreign sources of supply and foreign markets, enabling them to buy and sell on specially privileged terms, to shift orders from one subsidiary to*

another, to favour this country or that depending on which has the most advantageous tax, labour and other policies – in a word, they want to do business on their own terms and wherever they choose. And for this what they need is not trading partners but 'allies' and clients willing to adjust their laws and policies to the requirements of American big business.

(Baran and Sweezy, 1966)

According to Baran and Sweezy, because of these 'privileged terms' the multinational companies frequently make a much higher profit on investment abroad than in the United States. Accordingly, between 1946 and 1963, foreign direct investments of American corporations increased more than five times. A key concept used by Baran and Sweezy is economic surplus ('the difference between what a society produces and the costs of producing it'). The multinationals make more surplus in foreign than domestic investment, most of which they then repatriate, thus depriving the producing country of its use.

An interesting feature of Baran and Sweezy's analysis is their view that 'the rise of a world socialist system as a rival and alternative to the world capitalist system' has occurred. Twenty five years after they wrote, it is clear that world socialism (by which they mean communism) is less integrated and united than they assume. In particular, deep Sino-Soviet divisions have developed. More recently, the break-up of the Eastern European Communist bloc and the crisis and decline of communism in the Soviet Union itself bring into question whether communism will survive as a substantial 'alternative' global system.

The two major contemporary analysts of capitalism as a world system are Immanuel Wallerstein and André Gunder Frank. Both argue that the 'dependency' produced by world capitalism has typically created 'underdevelopment' in the Third World. 'Development' is a myth which obscures the reality of exploitation: rhetoric aside, the capitalist powers have never seriously intended to give up their economic domination of the Third World. Here I will present only Frank's perspective in detail, occasionally supported by authors of similar views.

Frank's earlier work concentrated on the history of capitalist 'exploitation' – both imperial and neo-colonial – and in laying down the framework of his analysis of contemporary capitalism. As he put it, his 'approach rests on two fundamental pillars, historicity and structural unity', both of which he attributes to Marx. His historical analysis leads him to the conclusion that wherever capitalism impacts, it transforms the local society by forcing it into the capitalist system – in a dependent capacity. Such is the power of capitalism that other forms of social systems such as slave or feudal systems cannot survive independently of it. Thus, following the black Marxist historian, Eric Williams, he rejects the idea that slavery in the South of the United States, the West Indies, and Brazil was pre-feudal and terms it 'capitalist slavery'. He goes on to say:

It extracted immense riches from Africa where the slaves came from, from America where the slave-produced goods came from, and from the slave trade itself, all of which, while serving an undoubtedly important source of the ... accumulation of capital in the metropoli, not only decapitalised the populations of peripheral countries but implanted the social, economic, political and cultural structure of underdevelopment among them.

(Frank, 1975)

Similarly, he wrote of Latin America, his major area of detailed analysis, that whatever previous forms of social organisation existed – primitive or feudal – 'they were turned to the [capitalist] metropolitan outside, produced for the outside and were controlled by the outside'.

Frank's historical analysis indicates the nature of his model of the capitalist world system as a unified structure. The basic system is comprised of the core and the periphery, more usually referred to as the metropolis-satellite relationship. Thus the capitalist metropolis of the United States has many dependent satellites in Latin America, including, for instance, Honduras and Mexico. Within both the metropolis and the satellite, further bi-polar relationships occur. Thus, London is a metropolis for Britain and Mexico City for Mexico. They enjoy a surplus extracted from the rest of the country (see pp. 441–3). This surplus is syphoned up through regional and local metropolitan centres which also take a share of it. For Frank as for Baran and Sweezy, then, accumulating a surplus – crudely, a profit – is the major purpose of capitalism.

Although the key metropolis-satellite relationship is between the capitalist and Third World countries, the role of the major Third World metropolis in facilitating capitalism is also vitally important. The multinational companies seek a relationship with the central political-military and business elites in the satellite country which enables them to enjoy favourable economic conditions. Thus, in order to attract multinational investment some countries, such as Mexico and the Philippines, provide tax-free trade zones. Often, Third World elites become wealthy on the basis of such collaboration. Largely to service the needs of the elite and those of rich foreign nationals, a small urban middle class also develops. The majority – overwhelmingly peasants – remain poor in a situation of 'uneven' development (see pp. 391–2 for health inequality). Frank refers to the total process of Third World 'exploitation' as 'the development of underdevelopment'.

Frank has sometimes been accused of making too rigid a contrast between development and underdevelopment. He goes some way towards meeting this criticism in his twin-volumed study *Crisis: In the World Economy* (1980) and *Crisis: In the Third World* (1981). In the latter volume he introduces a category of 'intermediate, semiperipheral, or subimperialist economies' of Brazil, Mexico, Argentina, India, Saudi Arabia, Iran, Israel and South Africa. Two varying characteristics describe these countries. First, they are generally wealthier than the majority of Third World countries. Most of them practised – with some success – a policy of 'import substitution' by which they replaced First World imports with their own manufactures. Second, these powers sometimes function as control 'intermediaries' between central metropolitan and peripheral areas, such as South Africa on the African continent and Israel in the Middle East. However, Frank emphasises that all these powers are themselves still dependent: several have chronic balance of payment problems, massive debts, or rely on the metropolitan powers for arms – in some cases all three.

The dynamic nature of Frank's analytical framework is further illustrated by his comments on developing relations among the metropolitan powers. He suggests that Japan, Germany and Russia may be seriously challenging the economic and political dominance of the United States. Mindful of Britain's loan under severe conditions from the International Monetary Fund in 1976, he comments: 'The British economy is now threatened by an absolute decline to semi-peripheral or even underdeveloping near-peripheral status.' No doubt the rise of unemployment in Britain from less than one million to over three million since he wrote would help confirm him in his observation.

In *Crisis: In the Third World*, Frank surveys a range of major Third World problems within the above theoretical framework. He examines what he calls the 'super-exploitation' of Third World labour by multinational enterprises, the enormous debts of many Third World countries, 'political-economic' repression and the role of the state, the international arms trade and warfare in the Third World, and the efforts of certain Third World countries to combine in order to maintain the price of exports – as the Organisation of Petroleum Exporting Countries (OPEC) did with oil. Here these points are discussed as an interconnected piece rather than separately.

The common thread behind these themes is in the relentless pursuit of profit by multinational corporations – supported, on occasions, by metropolitan government pressure or military action. Thus, the drive for profit results in the 'superexploitation' of many Third World workers by which Frank means they are paid at less than subsistence level and are kept alive by assistance from relatives and friends who work in the traditional sector of the economy. Profit also accounts for the billions of dollars of arms sold to Third World countries. Sometimes these are used to quell unrest – as in South Africa; sometimes in nationalist wars, which ruin economics and maintain dependency, as in the Iran-Iraq war. Often these arms are sold to states which, far from being democratically representative, need them precisely because they are not.

Thus, to give a recent example, Britain sold arms to Saddam Hussein of Iraq, despite later almost wholesale condemnation of him and his regime. There are many examples of this kind which lead Frank to conclude that profit is a stronger motive than democracy in the capitalist West. On the same issue, Teresa Hayter claims that 'the majority of governments supported by the West are authoritarian, often military regimes of a brutally repressive nature'.

Such is the power of Western capital within the capitalist world system that Frank holds out little hope that OPEC-like strategies could effectively redistribute wealth from the rich to the poor world. He comments that even 'the oil bonanza has been relatively short lived and very localised in a few OPEC countries'. Certainly, in the mid-eighties it is clear that the capitalist countries have been able to diversify or develop their own sources of energy. Further, according to Frank:

The few OPEC countries that have had a balance-of-payments surplus recycled their money to and through the Western banks and financial markets. The deficit counterpart of the first post 1974 'OPEC surplus' was shifted to the non oil-producing Third World countries, where the state and the bourgeoisie obliged the masses to bear the burden of the higher costs of the world's oil.

(Frank, 1981)

In other words, the West raised the money to pay for the increase in the price of oil by lowering the price paid for commodities from poorer, less well-organised Third World countries. Frank suggests that if this was the result of a Third World grouping combining to control the production and marketing of oil – one of the most favourable commodities for such action – the chances of doing better with another commodity are slight. However, he advocates trying.

Two other aspects of Frank's analysis which illustrate the power and pervasiveness of world capitalism require mention. First, in contrast to Baran and Sweezy, he does not see the Soviet Union (or China) as providing the basis of a genuinely alternative socialist world system to capitalism. Indeed, he cites the growing trade links between the First and Second Worlds as evidence of one world market, not two. He further argues that the profit the Soviet Union gains in exporting rather less sophisticated and cheaper manufactured products to the Third World

Figure 21.3 (Far right)

provides it with the capital to buy more sophisticated items from the West – again illustrating the single market system. Second, Frank is pessimistic about the changes of a New International Economic Order (NIEO), demanded by Third World Governments in the United Nations, ever being willingly accepted by or, still less, pressured upon the West. The NIEO would seek to improve the economic and trading situation of the Third World in a variety of ways. However, if anything Frank sees a tendency to First World protectionism rather than an opening up of its markets. In any case, he regards NIEO as an attempt of the Third World bourgeois elites to gain a more secure position in the capitalist world system rather than as a genuinely egalitarian and popular movement.

Frank refers to the huge debts of many Third World countries as 'bondage'. These debts are so enormous that there is no foreseeable prospect of paying them. Indeed, quite frequently debtor nations have to borrow to pay the interest on their debts – as Argentina did in 1985. Some of these debts are owed to international 'development' agencies such as the World Bank but increasingly to private Western banks which charge higher rates of interest. Lenin's concept of finance imperialism would seem applicable here, though Frank does not use it. Frank notes that several of the intermediate level economies have tried to 'grow' their way out of debt dependency by amassing substantial balance of payments surpluses. Several years after Frank wrote, this policy seems to be faltering badly (see figure 21.3).

Debtors' Weakening Trade Balances

Total external debt as of June '85, in billions of dollars		Trade balance, estimated balance of payments basis, billions of dollars at seasonally adjusted annual rates	
Mexico	$98	$12.80 '84	$8.42 '85
Venezuela	37	$8.37 '84	$6.82 '85
Brazil	103	$13.07 '84	$10.50 '85
Argentina	47	$4.3 '84	$3.44 '85

Source: Morgan Guaranty Trust Co and *New York Times*, 13 June, 1985

When, as often happens, Third World countries are unable to pay their debts, they usually turn to the International Monetary Fund to borrow money to do so. In many cases the conditions the IMF imposes for the loan are severe and cause unrest. The left-wing critic, Anthony Sampson, describes the case of the socialist government of Michael Manley in Jamaica:

At first Manley's government kept away from the IMF, but by 1977 they had to ask for help. The fund offered them the biggest loan (per head) in its history, but conditions as usual were strict. After drawing the first loan Jamaica soon failed its 'performance test' and had to negotiate again. The finance minister resigned, the Jamaican dollar was drastically devalued, and in 1978 average wages fell by thirty-five per cent. Wherever their drastic remedies had been applied (one Fund official was quoted as saying) they had either led to the death of democracy or the overthrow of the government. There were riots and demonstrations (or 'social tensions' as the IMF called them), while new disasters visited the island, including floods and the higher oil-price. The only really thriving industry was marijuana. The Government showed no signs of being able to meet its next test, and it had to go back to the Fund....

(Sampson, 1981:339)

In her bitterly titled book, *Aid as Imperialism*, Teresa Hayter makes an analysis of the aid relationship which seems supportive of Frank's perspective on Third World financial dependency. Government aid is usually 'tied' to the purchase of items from the lending country and aid channelled through United Nations institutions is often available only for approved projects which sometimes have more appeal to, for instance, World Bank economic experts than those of recipient countries. Hayter argues that most aid neither reaches the people who really need it nor goes into the kind of projects likely to ensure long-term development. Instead, it sticks in the hands of Third World governmental and business elites to whom it acts as a kind of bribe to pursue policies compatible with the interests of Western multinationals and governments. Even an apparently successful programme

such as the 'green revolution' in India, which greatly improved crop yield, made many rich landowners – some of whom were leading politicians – richer and disenfranchised many poorer peasants from the land.

What solution does Frank advocate to the pessimistic world situation he describes? His answer is socialism, though he finds little to enthuse about in the Soviet model. He is also acutely aware of the danger of socialist societies being incorporated into the capitalist world system. For instance, he believes that in the period following North Vietnam military victory over the United States, the Vietnamese leadership actually sought such economic connection. Which group or groups, then, are the possible agencies of socialist revolution? Here, Frank differs from orthodox Marxists though consistently with his own analysis (see below). He believes that the development of socialist movements in the West does not provide the best model for the Third World. Marx considered the industrial working class to be the agency for change in advanced capitalist societies but in many Third World countries this group is numerically small. Frank argues that capitalism has been imposed on the Third World from the outside and that the peasantry – many of whom are wage workers – are a potentially anti-capitalist revolutionary force. He hints that a world revolutionary alliance between the Third World peasantry and the Western urban proletariat might be possible. He advocates development independent of the world capitalist system to those countries that achieve socialist revolution. He also favours mutual cooperation between socialist societies. At no point does he suggest that any of this is either inevitable or easy. The 'crisis' of capital accumulation (a falling rate of surplus) he considers characterises contemporary capitalism may be resolved as others have been. He offers not prophecy, but struggle.

MODES OF PRODUCTION THEORY (CRITIQUE OF FRANK)

From the point of view of Marxist theory, there is an obvious and major inadequacy in Frank's analysis. In treating capitalism primarily as a market system – a means of exchange – he fails to deal with it systematically as a mode of production. Indeed, the concept of production – fundamental to Marx's theory of change and class structure – is generally of peripheral importance in Frank's work.

An early and perhaps still the most effective critique of Frank along these lines was Ernesto Laclau's essay, *Feudalism and Capitalism in Latin America* (1971). Laclau demonstrates that there are various modes of production existing in Latin America and elsewhere in the Third World. What this means in terms of class structure and for the prospects and strategies for change needs to be examined in detail, case by case. It cannot be taken for granted that the peasantry are a new global revolutionary proletariat. Significantly, however, Laclau agrees with Frank that there is one world capitalist system. What he insists on is that different modes of production occur within this world system and this makes for much more complex analysis both in particular cases and globally than Frank achieves in his over-simplified scheme.

Two more recent works deal further with points raised by Laclau. In *From Modernisation to Modes of Production* (1979), John G Taylor argues that to understand Third World economic systems and social formations (his preferred term to 'societies'), the imposition of the capitalist mode of production on non-capitalist ones is the appropriate framework for analysis. Capitalist imperialism impacting on the non-capitalist world results in economic, social and political effects not found in the West where capitalism developed indigenously. Typically, this produces a highly differentiated, even fragmented, class structure in Third World societies. Thus, the capitalist class is divided into the 'comprador' class supported by multinational money and a 'national' capitalist class seeking more independent development. Sometimes the latter is sufficiently 'progressive' to draw substantial support from the peasantry and urban proletariat. Such a coalition sustained the Christian Democratic government of Edward Frei in Chile between 1964–70. It broke up when the peasantry became sceptical about Frei's proposed land reforms, leading the

way for the formation of Salvador Allende's Marxist minority government in 1970. Laclau's account ends here but we can continue it. Allende was overthrown in 1973 by a military coup led by General Pinochet. According to Nathaniel Davis, US Ambassador to Chile, 1971–73, the United States' Central Intelligence Agency spent at least $6 million on covert operations during Allende's period in office. Pinochet called his regime an 'authoritarian democracy' – an otherwise non-existent term. It was, in fact, a military dictatorship.

As Taylor's example indicates, the complexities of Third World class formations are mirrored in the political and ideological spheres. Instability and unpredictability seem to be a general result of the 'imperial' connection. In a similar vein, Ian Roxborough in *Theories of Underdevelopment* (1979) comments on the weakness of the domestic bourgeoisie in Third World societies. They are generally unable to achieve the bourgeois liberal revolution that the much stronger bourgeoisie brought about in Western societies in the nineteenth century. Instead, Third World societies are vulnerable to the power play of elites which are themselves frequently under pressure from outside forces.

The conclusion of the above debate between Frank and his Marxist critics would seem to be that Third World societies must be analysed in terms of internal and external factors or, in Taylor's terms, the interaction between the two. This brings us rather close to the proposition at the beginning of this chapter that change can be analysed in endogamous and/or exogamous terms. Does this mean that the millions of words written on the 'Frank controversy' were a waste. The answer is 'no' because the theoretical and empirical details that have emerged in the debate have led to a fuller understanding of the complexities and unpredictability of change. Simplistic formulas have crumbled and, amid the ruins, the idea that people make history is discernible. They do not do so in circumstances of their own choosing but nevertheless in circumstances that can be changed.

Two Liberal Theories

1 OLD LIBERALISM: NEW CONSERVATISM

Nineteenth century liberal capitalism has made a revival in the late twentieth century in the new conservatism of Thatcherism and Reaganism and their successors. The label is different but the ideology is essentially the same. Adam Smith's *The Wealth of Nations* (1776) was the most influential early statement of capitalist economics. Milton Friedman, the contemporary American economist, refers to Smith's writings often and enthusiastically in his own work, *Free to choose*. Like Friedman, the British development economist, Peter Bauer has been a significant intellectual influence on the new conservatism. Bauer's book, *Dissent on Development* (1975), is also committed to private enterprise and the free market as the means of development, although he does not return to Smith's classical principles to the extent of Friedman.

Friedman wants (virtually) to exclude government from economic life. He cites four functions for government, the first three of which are given by Adam Smith: defence, law and order, the provision of those necessary public works that private enterprise does not find it profitable to provide, and the protection of members of the community who cannot be regarded as 'responsible' individuals. Bauer sees a wider range of functions for government, including 'the provisions of basic health and education services' but the only economic function he mentions is the 'management of the monetary and fiscal system'. Both regard the production, distribution and exchange of goods and service and investment as best left to private rather than public enterprise. Following Smith, Friedman argues that as long as economic exchange is voluntary both parties can benefit because 'no exchange will take place unless both parties do benefit', i.e. people pursue their own interests. Both Friedman and Bauer seem to believe that this principle operates both between individuals and between nations. In addition to their theoretical arguments, they cite empirical illustrations of the success of the free-market system in stimulating growth. Friedman gives Hong Kong as 'perhaps the best example'. It has no tariffs and virtually no other restraints on international trade and, according to Friedman, the role of government is interpreted rather narrowly within the 'four duties'. Despite the natural disadvantages of small size and dense population, it has one of the highest standards of living in Asia 'second only to Japan and perhaps Singapore'.

Friedman and Bauer's enthusiasm for private enterprise is matched by their opposition to central planning and aid as means to development. Bauer states: 'Comprehensive planning has thus not served to raise general living standards anywhere. There is no analytical reason or empirical evidence for expecting it to do so. And in fact both analytical reasoning and empirical evidence point to the opposite conclusion.' Although this point is made in a typically assertive and authoritative manner by Bauer, it is open to dispute. If we take growth rather than increase in living standards as the basis of assessment, then the Soviet Union achieved some success under central planning in the post-war period when its rate of growth was for a time greater than that of the United States. Much of this growth was in the military sector but there is no theoretical reason why it could not occur in the consumer section of the economy. There are signs that this is beginning to happen. A second example which may be regarded as disproof of Bauer's statement is Sweden – only mentioned once and in passing in Bauer's book. It is not clear whether Sweden represents an example of 'comprehensive planning' as indicated by Bauer but it is certainly one of the more planned mixed economies. In the post-war period, it has had as high if not a higher average living standard than that of the United States. The state also played a major role in the industrialisation of Japan and Germany. One of the most notable features of societies with comparably high living standards to the United States – such as Switzerland, Luxembourg, Japan and West Germany – is the relatively small proportion of the economy devoted to armaments production.

Both Friedman and Bauer are emphatic in their opposition to aid. Aid here refers not to emergency assistance, as in the Ethiopian famine, but aid as a regular strategy for development. They consider it distorts the free market process. As Bauer puts it, if the conditions for a viable development project are present then it will be possible to raise money on the commercial market, if not, the project should not be undertaken. Needless to say, this assertion of freemarket principles would not be considered axiomatic by either socialists or social democrats. A second point made by Bauer is that aid often ends up in the wrong hands and benefits the wealthy rather than the needy. The Marxist Hayter makes the same point. Criticism of aid policies from various quarters suggests a need for radical review. However, there is little support, even among conservatives, for Friedman and Bauer's precise position. Rather, what has happened under President Reagan is that aid has been more closely tied to political goals. Thus, an aid programme for Caribbean countries was made contingent on the political and economic 'suitability' of recipients. Similarly, aid was sent to the Contra rebels in Nicaragua whilst an American trade embargo was set up to undermine the governing socialist party, the Sandinistas. Aid is the carrot, whilst the embargo and, more usually, the activities of the CIA are the stick. In the early nineteen nineties, the policy of linking aid more closely to progress towards democracy was widely discussed. However desirable, such a policy might prove difficult to implement given the complexities of many poorer societies and of United States policy towards them.

Finally, both theorists make a point which demands serious consideration as the core of their socio-economic philosophy. Friedman makes it most succinctly: 'Economic freedom is an essential requisite for political freedom'. Or conversely, comprehensive central planning is a 'sure recipe for tyranny'. Bauer takes to task the Swedish social scientist, Gunnar Myrdal, on the same issue. In his book, *Asian Drama: An Inquiry into the Poverty of Nations* (1968), Myrdal comes out in favour of strong central planning as a means to 'modernisation'. Bauer is able to show that Myrdal at least implies that the price of such policies is likely to be a decrease in political and civil freedom. Smelling the beginnings of the canker of totalitarianism, Bauer severely condemns Myrdal for believing that the conditions for development can or should be imposed. In

comment, it is a major challenge of modern socialism to reconcile equality and freedom much more effectively than, say, the Soviet Union has done. Many social democrats, as well as conservatives such as Bauer and Friedman, make this reservation and consequently choose not to be socialists.

Despite Bauer's criticism of the ideological bias of other development theorists, the conservative-liberal perspective seems equally ideological. Friedman's view that it is human nature to pursue one's interests individually seems neither philosophically nor historically more valid than the view that interests can be pursued collectively. Further, their use of illustrative example is highly selective and both seem to employ the near unprovable generalisation as freely as the Marxists and social democrats they oppose.

2 LIBERAL/SOCIAL DEMOCRATIC PERSPECTIVE ON A 'NEW' WORLD ORDER

Many have long been convinced that the huge gap between the rich and poor countries was both morally wrong and politically dangerous: morally wrong because of the poverty and suffering in the Third World, politically dangerous because poverty makes these countries susceptible to 'extremist' political ideologies. This mixture of humanitarianism and pragmatism is what inspired the liberal reform movements in Britain and other Western European countries earlier in the twentieth century. Just as social reform ameliorated the condition of the working classes in the advanced industrial societies, so now certain adjustments in the world trade, finance and aid could help the Third World. These policies would be implemented within the framework of the world capitalist system of trade and finance which they were partly intended to strengthen. The best known expressions of this spirit of liberal reform are the two reports of the Independent Commission on International Development Issues under the chairmanship of Willy Brandt: *North-South: A Program for Survival* (1980), and *Common Crisis: Cooperation for World Recovery* (1983). It is important to add that many of the recommendations of the 'Brandt Reports' are supported by the politically various 'Group of 77' (now closer to 150) Third World nations established in Algiers in 1967. The view of many in the Group was that the Brandt package, though not ideal, was the best likely to be offered and worth uniting around (see below).

Both 'Brandt Reports' argue that the rich North and the poor South share mutual interests on which to base cooperation. The North needs the raw materials of the South and the South needs the manufactured products of the North. As the South develops more heavy industry, the North can turn more to high technology and services. More 'equitable' prices for Third World products would fuel the ability of the poorer countries to trade with the richer ones. Protectionism would reduce world trade and have a generally damaging effect.

The recommendations of the two Reports are a mixture of idealism and practicality with *Common Crisis* tending more towards the latter. *North-South* states that 'there must be an end to mass hunger and malnutrition' and suggests more international financing of agricultural research and development in the South. Cooperation to avoid the waste of common global resources and of 'irreversible ecological damage' is urged. The Ethiopian famine of 1985 was partly caused by ecological breakdown and underlines the urgency of this issue. Shrewdly, *North-South* recommends both population control and anti-poverty programmes. The report also urges an end to the arms race and a reduction in armaments production. Instead resources should be transferred to production for peaceful purposes including the reduction of world poverty. The peace-keeping role of the United Nations would be increased.

Both Reports make recommendations on industrial development, trade and finance. Finance is perhaps the key issue because without it development is not possible. It is the major focus of *Common Crisis*. Essentially, the detailed suggestion for reforms of the IMF and the World Bank amount to more and easier credit for developing countries. More participation in these institutions for Third World countries is recommended. The hope is expressed that, given a lead, the private banks will follow suit. Aid-giving countries were urged to double their contributions by 1985 (although, in fact, Britain reduced its official aid). Beyond these suggestions, *Common Crisis* indicates that a revision of the post-war settlement of the world trade and financial framework at Breton Woods is required largely with a view to strengthening the currently weak and dependent position of the Third World. The free-trade perspective of the Reports has already been mentioned and the above financial initiatives were perceived as complementing this approach.

In reality, the liberal-conservatism described in the previous section has tended to dominate the world economic scene in the eighties and early nineties rather than the liberal reformism of the Brandt Reports. No consensus has developed among the governments of richer countries to adopt the bulk of the Brandt proposals. The dependency theorist, Wallerstein's comment that capitalism is more dominant at World than national level because of the absence of significant restraining checks, seems increasingly true. The Brandt Reports offered some voluntarily introduced restraints and a marginal redistribution of power and resources. If its major proposals are not adopted, as now seems unlikely, relative global inequalities are likely further to increase.

In 1985 a report was published claiming both to 'defend' and 'extend' the reasoning of the above two reports. It was the report of the Socialist International Committee on Economic Policy, chaired by Michael Manley, titled *Global Challenge: From Crisis to Cooperation: Breaking the North South Stalemate*. Although firmly based on social democratic principles, the Report was more radical than its predecessors. It declared monetarism dead and calls for an application of updated Keynesian principles to tackle the needs of the global economy. In addition it demands 'a major redistribution of resources'. *Global Challenge* is sharply critical both of the failure of the United States to pursue fundamental reforms to deal with the debt crisis of the Third World and of much of the United States' foreign policy. Although the Report's 'main proposal is for a multilateral solution to the North-South' problem, it also suggests that others should proceed without the United States if that country's leaders are unwilling to move ahead. Certainly, one of the Report's most challenging statements will not easily be accepted by any foreseeable United States government: 'Without disarmament there can be no genuine development.'

Gender and Development

The established perspectives on development, including even underdevelopment theories, tend to ignore both the impact of development on women, and the importance of their labour before it. As for strategies for future development, it is only in the area of population control that adequate appreciation of women's role is beginning to occur (p. 462). As Aidan Foster-Carter ironically comments, in development theory, women are 'the satellite that is no-one's metropolis'.

Leghorn and Parker's *Woman's Worth: Sexual Economics and the World of Women* (1981) provides a feminist framework for analysing development. For them the main gender issue is simple:

In virtually all existing cultures, women's work, though usually invisible to the male eye, sustains the economy and subsidises the profits, leisure time and higher standard of living enjoyed by individual men, private corporations, and male dominated governments. In spite of this, women live almost universally without the corresponding economic, political and social control over their lives that such a crucial role should mean. How does this happen?
(Leghorn and Parker, 1981)

An attempt is made to grapple with the issue of why men generally have more power than women (patriarchy) in chapter 8. Here, the question is the relationship between development and gender. Leghorn and Parker provide three categories which they describe as 'an alternative women-centred way of looking at and understanding the economic organisation of cultures throughout the world'. They are:

1 Minimal power. This involves minimal access to crucial resources, low valuation and freedom in reproduction, high violence against them, and few occasions to share experiences, support and resources. Examples are: Ethiopia, Peru, Algeria and Japan.
2 Token power. This is a more variable situation in relation to the areas indicated in (1) and includes 'some freedom to create networks, though these networks may be undermined when they become effective bases of change'. Examples are: USA, Cuba, the USSR and Sweden.

3 Negotiating power. This involves greater access to resources which may be different to men's and enough economic power to provide a bargaining tool, high valuation and support for reproduction and highly developed networks. Examples are: China (post-revolutionary), Ewé and Iroquois cultures.

It may come as a shock to the reader that the modern societies of the USA, the USSR and Sweden appear only in the second category. In this respect, Leghorn and Parker receive some support from Ivan Illich, though their positions require distinguishing. Illich argues in *Gender* that in many pre-industrial societies male and female roles were often complementary in what he refers to as 'the regime of gender'. Development imposes a cruder sexual division of labour in which patriarchal domination increases. Leghorn and Parker are less inclined to romanticise gender relations in pre-industrial societies and show, for instance, that in many such societies women have been physically mutilated (foot-binding in traditional China, infibulation in parts of Africa – a severe form of female circumcision) as well as socially subordinated. They, therefore, discriminate between those pre-industrial societies in which women have more power (3) than in industrial societies and those which have less (1).

Leghorn and Parker offer no grand theory of gender and development. The impact of development on each society varies. They do argue, however, that:

Because women's role was secondary in virtually all cultures before colonialism (whether these assumptions and values were overt or subtle), the existing norms and institutions made it possible for Western-based forms of sexual oppression to be superimposed.
(Leghorn and Parker, 1981)

Thus, the imposition of colonial taxes on indigenous inhabitants would often break up the family, requiring the male to work in the urban-industrial economy and leaving the women to do domestic and agricultural work (including what had been the work of their spouses). The assumption that men are 'naturally' better suited to modern industrial and agricultural work has also reinforced the subordination of women. Thus, whilst women in Africa do 70 per cent of the agricultural work, almost all the agricultural aid has gone to men. Most education and training funds also go to men.

They point out that there are occasions when women's status improves as a result of Western influence. Thus, access to work outside the home in Algeria and Japan broke women's traditional seclusion and improved their chances of acquiring some economic and social independence. In Africa, infibulation, although still widespread, is now typically done in more sanitary conditions. Of course, Western female norms are not always accepted wholesale by traditional societies. For instance, women in Iran have long struggled to balance traditional Muslim belief with what they see as the more desirable aspects of Western female behaviour.

It would be a mistake, in any case, to imagine that liberation, female or otherwise, has been a prime purpose of the Western nations in relation to the Third World. Although not dealt with by Leghorn and Parker, the working conditions of certain women employed by Western corporations illustrates highly patriarchal attitudes. Thus, in the Philippines, Mexico and elsewhere young women are sometimes employed (until they are 'burnt out') in such areas as assembling electronic components or textiles. The personnel manager of one multinational presented the following recruitment criteria:

I choose people with elegant figures and thin hands because they are more agile ... I take physical appearance into account; you can tell if people are aggressive by the way they look, so I try to choose people who seem more docile and can be managed more easily.

A businessman from the United States showed a similar level of enlightenment:

There's no welfare here. You can push Mexican workers. Also there's the 48 hour week. You don't see any horsing around here, no queues for the water-fountain or the bathroom. These girls work.

It is businessmen, remember, along with government and the military, who are mainly responsible for the dealings of the West with the Third World. The people they deal with are usually rich, unrepresentative male elites. As Teresa Hayter says, 'The majority of governments supported by the West are authoritarian.' It is perhaps little wonder that some feminists believe that women would make a better job of running the world than men and that they merit a chance to do so.

The Iroquois cultures of the eighteenth and nineteenth centuries are among those in which Leghorn and Parker consider women have negotiating power. Significantly, women had considerable economic power both in the production and distribution of food. Further, descent was matrilineal and residence upon marriage was the home of the wife's mother. The leading women, the matrons, exercised an indirect political power in selecting the male council of elders. Women worked collectively and had ample opportunity for 'networking' – a process of mutual support which Leghorn and Parker greatly emphasise.

They conclude that despite differences in women's lack of power across cultures, women are a global caste. They record their impression that within each of their three categories, women overwhelmingly carry the burden of family care and receive a comparably limited amount of time and money from their male partners. They urge women to organise on the basis of a matriarchal concept of power, reflecting values of creativity, cooperation and caring. Institutions would reflect those values and would be organised in a decentralised and collective way rather than hierarchically and individualistically.

Strictly, Leghorn and Parker's view of women as a caste is not reconcilable with the socialist view that the primary category of social analysis is class (see pp. 183–4). However, the values and institutional frameworks they advocate are remarkably similar to traditional libertarian socialist ideals and as such are as applicable to men as to women. Leghorn and Parker recognise this but are not prepared to wait for men to act accordingly. In time, perhaps men will change, but in their view, the immediate task is for women to liberate themselves. In the Third World many feminists are, of necessity, less separatist than Leghorn and Parker, and pool their feminist principles in movements of national liberation and socialism. The goals of national independence and combating poverty may take immediate precedence over reforming patriarchal structures within a society, as they did in China. Even so, women often acquire new roles, experience and confidence in these movements and in this practical way the principle of gender equality is asserted.

A Global 'Theory' of the 'Global System': Leslie Sklair

Leslie Sklair's *Sociology of the Global System* (1991) constructively pulls together disparate and apparently contradictory aspects of some of the theories discussed above. He also makes his own substantial contribution to the analysis of social change in global perspective.

The focus of Sklair's analysis is transnational corporations (TNCs) which he sees as a dominant if not *the* dominant global force – the larger ones often transcending the wealth and power of individual nations. He suggests that modernisation/free market theory, on the one hand, and the various Marxist theories, on the other, both fully recognise the central place of TNCs in the global system but evaluate their contribution differently. The former approve – and cite evidence favourable to the TNCs – and the latter disapprove – citing contrary evidence. What this observation usefully does is reduce many of the apparently substantive differences between the theories to ideological differences (i.e. differences of value). Although writing before the fragmentation of the Soviet Union in 1991, Sklair strongly tends to the view that there is a single dominant global system – the capitalist one – and that so far socialism has not seriously upset this dominance.

Sklair explains the global dominance of capitalism not simply in terms of the economic, political and military strength of capitalist societies but also in terms of the appeal of 'the ideology of consumerism'. Advertising and Western-made popular programmes such as 'the soaps' tantalisingly display mainly Western-made consumer items throughout the world, including much of the Third World. These 'modern things' are what most people seem to 'want' (although Sklair considers that much consumption is 'induced' by capitalist display). As Sklair puts it: '"Modernity" becomes what global capitalism has to offer' (230).

Perhaps the most original part of Sklair's analysis is his argument that a 'transnational capitalist class' has now developed. According to Sklair, membership of this class is much wider than the owners of the means of production which make up Marx's 'bourgeoisie'. It is comprised of 'the entrepreneurial elite, managers of firms, senior state functionaries, leading politicians, members of the learned professions, and persons of similar standing in all spheres of society' (62). This mixed group of people is seen as accepting, promoting and benefiting from global capitalism. They often do so at the expense of poorer social groups, whether intentionally or not.

Both the detail and substance of Sklair's analysis will no doubt attract criticism. However, he does pull together a plausible theoretical framework for understanding global capitalism which is likely to be built upon. Sklair accepts the necessity of the productive power and market-choice achieved by capitalism, but also argues that more effective means to redistribute wealth and to effect greater and wider institutional participation are also needed world-wide. What he would like to see is 'democratic feminist socialism'. Some such prescription is more likely to appeal to critics of capitalism than anything that smacks of 'old-fashioned' communism.

Development Themes

Urbanisation, industrialisation, employment and education are key themes in development. Those of health and poverty are given extensive analysis elsewhere (pp. 391–2 and pp. 459–63) and are implicitly further considered here. The themes of change and conflict, inequality and exploitation are, of course, the main content

URBANISATION AND INDUSTRIALISATION

The urban populations of the Third World are expanding much more rapidly than those of the First and Second, where indeed the numbers resident in many major cities are decreasing. By the year 2000, it is likely that only a couple of Western cities will feature in the ten most populous cities of the world. By then, Mexico City may well have over 30 million residents. What has caused this phenomenal increase?

First, it is instructive to note a factor which generally has contributed little to the increase in urban population – industrialisation. This is in stark contrast to what occurred in the developing West, where accelerated urbanisation was largely the result of industrialisation. In the Third World there is usually only a scant industrial base to sustain the expanding urban masses, though this is less true of some countries at an intermediate level of development such as South Korea, Brazil and Argentina. However, most migrants to the city do not get a (relatively) high paying industrial job. Push as well as pull factors account for the move to the cities. First, population increase means fewer jobs to go round in the traditional agricultural sector. Second, where agriculture is modernised an absolute reduction in jobs typically takes place. Of the pull factors, the strongest is the prospect of making a better living than as a rural peasant. Cities, especially international ones, have large formal and informal economies in which the determined or inventive can survive and, in some cases, even prosper. Even begging and the odd official handout are likely to produce a better income in the city. Second, facilities such as clean water and drainage are more likely to be available in the city, as are odd bits of unwanted or 'spare' material with which to build or shelter. Third, is the cultural attraction of the city – the glamour of the 'modern' way of life. John Roberts in *The Triumph of the West* emphasises the fascination and charisma of Western culture and it is in the cities of the world that the artifacts of the West are most temptingly displayed. No doubt what appeals most is Western wealth and lifestyle,

but perhaps, too, there is a deeper desire to 'become' Westernised – to think and feel like us. Modernisation theorists might regard this process as liberating and Marxists as the very trough of ideological dependency, but Roberts is surely right that it is widespread (as, it must be said, is the resistance to it).

Neither governments nor the private housing sector in most Third World countries can hope to house all the people flooding into the city. In any case, many could not afford to rent, still less, buy accommodation. What can work well, is the provision of loans, aid or material by the government or voluntary agencies, for people to build their own houses. In general, however, how people make out in the city, including where they live, depends on what they can earn.

EMPLOYMENT AND EDUCATION

There has been a severe crisis of unemployment in the advanced capitalist countries, especially among the young. Ironically, in Britain this crisis has coincided with policies to make education more vocationally relevant. Unemployment, particularly youth unemployment, in the Third World, is on a far greater scale than in the capitalist West. There are several reasons for this.

Population increase is, of course, a major factor in global unemployment. During the 1970s the size of the labour market in the Third World increased by 200 million. It is estimated that by the year 2000 another 500 million will have joined the labour markets. More than 30 million new jobs per year will be needed to absorb this increase. A second important factor contributing to unemployment is lack of investment in agriculture and industry. Many Third World countries are deeply in debt to Western banks and cannot afford extensive development investment. This observation raises the issue of whether the world trading system is so weighted against the Third World that prospects of significant development and higher employment are remote. We will return to this point shortly. Thirdly, economic development in the Third World, as in the capitalist West, often results in a reduction rather than an increase in employment. This is because some projects are capital rather than labour intensive: machinery replaces people. In such cases, increases in production and profit are likely to benefit the few who own businesses rather than the majority. Frequently, the owners of businesses in the Third World are Western multinational companies who are attracted by the lower wages they can pay, usually unorganised workforces, lack of legal restrictions, and developing markets. Sometimes multi-national companies use Western employees in their Third World operations to avoid the expense of training Third World workers in more technical tasks and to ensure a compliant workforce.

Despite the above difficulties and the fact that employment in the Third World remains overwhelmingly rural, growing opportunities for work exist in the cities, not least in the informal sector:

Many Africans migrating to the cities found themselves without jobs, or unable to get those they aspired to. Some accommodated themselves to a socially disapproved existence as pimps, touts, prostitutes, or thieves, living often at the margins of subsistence or preying, like parasites, on what few pickings a capital city of an impoverished country can offer. Others swelled the ranks of those who staff the industries, small trades and services that blanket the landscape of any African city. This sector of the urban economy, described often nowadays as the 'informal sector', in fact accounts for a considerable degree of urban employment. ... The conditions of employment can be extremely harsh. For three or four years apprentices are bound to their masters in a condition resembling that of servitude. A space on the workshop floor is living accommodation, and pocket money barely covers the means of survival, while the El Dorado to the apprentice, namely a workshop of his own, is difficult to finance and may indeed never materialise.

(Robin Cohen, The emergence of wage labour in Allen and Williams eds., 1982:39).

Tens of millions of people survive in the 'twilight zone' of the informal sector. Uncomfortable though governments may be about the existence of this kind of enterprise, for many it is likely to be the only work available in the foreseeable future. Even in the West, the failure of the formal economy

has forced millions to seek informal means of supplementing their incomes in the so-called 'black economy'. Third World governments and development planners would do better to accommodate the working and living needs of workers in the informal sector rather than viewing them as a temporary phenomenon.

Workers in the informal sector are not the bottom of the urban 'heap' in the Third World. As Robin Cohen puts it, 'there exists a group of genuinely unemployed workers, "job applicants" by self description, but in fact a lumpen-proletariat proper'. A lumpen-proletariat is an ill-defined mass of individuals without any regular employment. One of the major historical causes of the drift to the city in many countries was the seizure of land by white settlers as happened in Kenya and South Africa. Today, rural overpopulation and the hope for material advancement that the city symbolises are important factors.

Increasingly, migration in search of work is not merely internal, but international. The international migrant population of the world is well over 20 million and still increasing. Several millions of these workers are Eastern Europeans who have found temporary jobs in Western European countries. Generally, they receive low pay for doing some of the least attractive work, and do not enjoy the rights of citizenship. In the Third World, migrants across international boundaries frequently do not even find work. Their situation is perilous and many exist in absolute poverty. Their vulnerability was illustrated in Nigeria in 1983. Nigeria is the most prosperous country in West Africa because of its oil and other resources. It attracts many illegal migrant workers. However, it was particularly badly hit by the world recession of the early 1980s because of the drop in the world price of oil. It ordered illegal migrant workers out of the country. As a result, hundreds of thousands had to return to their impoverished homelands.

Many in the Third World see education as the main hope of escaping from the kind of problems we have been discussing. They are probably right, yet the relationship both between education and individual achievement and between education and development is problematic and unclear. First, there is the question of what priority to give to the various sectors of education. There is a strong correlation between development and an extensive primary (and to an extent secondary) system of education. In other words there is a case for concentrating on mass numeracy and literacy, although typically it is secondary and higher education that gets favoured treatment. Second, there is curriculum content and particularly the question of relevance to development needs. In many ex-colonial countries spectacular examples of irrelevance occurred with youngsters becoming more expert in the history and literature of the former colonial power than their own – an example of cultural neo-colonialism and self denigration at the heart of the socialisation process. In higher education, irrelevance has often taken the form of over-concentration on classical subjects and liberal professional training, such as law or medicine, when the greater need was for practically-trained graduates.

Thus, there is a surplus of barristers in the West Indies and of doctors in India but a shortage of trained business people and engineers in both. Curricula can also be over-academic at the secondary level. Thus the promise that all Zimbabwean children would have the opportunity to take 'O' levels came back to haunt the government not only because of its impracticality but because of its irrelevance to the country's economic needs. Third, the principle that 'those who shall get even more' applies as much to education as to other matters. The offspring of the wealthy can buy an education which will equip them for elite membership whilst distancing them from the struggles and feelings of the great majority. Even so, some elite members educated in the West seem responsive to the principles of democracy and social justice for all, while others seem quite resistant to them.

Conclusion: Issues and Future Trends

A character in the science fiction film *Blade Runner* suggested that only three questions 'really' matter: 'Where did we come from? Where are we going? How long have we got?' The social scientific perspective is perhaps not usually consulted to provide answers to these questions but it does have a particular contribution to make. I shall look at the three questions in turn. This chapter has largely been an attempt to answer the first one – in developmental and historical terms. We have come through a period in which the West has indelibly left its imprint on the world. Everywhere one looks, the impact of the West is apparent.

SOUTH AFRICA

Take South Africa, for example. White people are there because their Dutch and British forebears occupied the territory. Over time they established a system of racial domination and segregation – apartheid – only paralleled in modern history by the plantation slavery of the pre-civil war southern states of North America. Despite the ending of the legal framework of apartheid in 1991, most of the social and economic conditions developed under apartheid remain. Nor has a democratic

political system of one person/one vote yet been established (1991). An aspect of apartheid was the setting up of so-called 'homelands' for black people, by which the majority of people are required to reside in a fraction of the country's generally less desirable territory. However, as black labour was (and still is) needed throughout the country a system of residency permits, personal passes and heavy policing and bureaucracy allowed blacks restricted access to 'white' areas. Over a million black workers became migrants within their own land, and remain so despite the welcome abolition of the pass laws and of the 'homelands' separate development system. It is arguable that the most difficult part of achieving black liberation still lies ahead. The African National Congress which clearly appears to have majority black support faces formidable problems. President de Klerk has had the statesmanship to abolish the legal basis of apartheid but the National Party he leads shows no sign of relinquishing government power to the black majority. There are also deep divisions among black people themselves. Nelson Mandela, the ANC's best known leader, is flanked on the right by the mainly Zulu, Inkatha movement and on the left by ANC militants (who threaten to return to armed struggle). So far, he and the ANC leadership have not yet achieved full liberal civil rights for black people, let alone the socialist society they aspire to.

One test of the relevance of the colonial history and theoretical interpretations presented in this chapter is whether they help us understand real issues such as South Africa. First, however, it must be stated that the South African situation is not a typically post-imperial one. In most ex-colonies the newly independent country is taken over by the indigenous majority and the occupying forces, government and administration withdraw and mostly return to their homeland (often the process of withdrawal and achievement of independence is gradual). Sometimes white settlers remain as a minority (Zimbabwe) or, more rarely, as a majority (North America). In South Africa, the difference is that the remaining white minority have retained power, long after Holland and Britain have given up the formal imperial connection. Nevertheless, the problems of South Africa are largely the product of empire even though they are particularly acute and intractable. Both Weberians and Marxists can find support for their theories in South Africa. Weberians can argue that ideas and beliefs – particularly of racial superiority – partly explain apartheid and that South Africa is a caste society in which stratification is based on race rather than class. The former point is illustrated by the use of Calvinist doctrine of predestination by some South Africans of Dutch descent to explain and justify apartheid (though to outsiders a less impressive cause than apartheid for the argument 'God is on our side' may seem hard to imagine). Weber himself does not crudely argue that ideas 'cause' socio-economic systems or vice-versa but that ideas and interests (such as the advantages gained from racial exploitation) can occur concomitantly, i.e. they complement and reinforce each other. Presented in this way, Weber's analysis of the social role of ideas is not incompatible with certain Marxist interpretations of ideology. Marxists stress that racist ideology can obscure economic exploitation and divide the black and white working class: although it is recognised that a simple application of this analysis to South Africa is not appropriate partly because the white working class itself

can be considered in a neo-colonial relationship to blacks and richly enjoys the surplus created by black labour. Marxists universally stress the commercial and financial links of international capital with the South African regime. Whilst many capitalists would prefer to deal with a liberal democracy rather than a racist autocracy in South Africa, historically they have tended to tolerate apartheid. Some, including the pro-capitalist Reagan government, have argued that trading and diplomacy – 'constructive engagement' – could be used to 'soften' apartheid. However, in 1985 a strong Congressional lead persuaded him to accept limited sanctions.

The theoretical debates reflect and illuminate the real circumstances and issues of South Africa. Marxist analysis of oppression and inequality usually leads to support for socialist policies and there are Marxists within the black liberation movement in South Africa just as there were in Angola, Mozambique and Zimbabwe. Thus, the ANC as well as seeking a democratic, non-racist South Africa also intends a redistribution of wealth and the nationalisation of mines, banks, monopolies and land. Indeed, it seems that the longer colonial powers or white settler minorities try to delay national independence, the more likely are the liberation movements to move towards Marxism. Perhaps with these precedents in mind, the capitalist democracies of the West are increasingly urging South Africa to go down the road of liberal reform. Probably all or most of the modernisation theorists, liberal conservatives and liberal social democrats we have mentioned would favour this approach and view with concern the emergence of socialism in South Africa. So behind the central issue of racial struggle, profound political and social issues remain to be resolved in South Africa.

FUTUROLOGY

The second question asked at the beginning of the section was: 'Where are we going?'. It is no job of the sociologist to predict the future, though some have tried. What sociologists can do is establish trends which, other things being equal, may lead in certain directions. This more modest exercise is justified and necessary. It is based on existing statistical data and informs public debate and policy. We have already seen something of the application of demographic trends to policy. Two other sections of this book deal in tentative futurology in relation to work/stratification (Chapter 11, p. 266) and culture (Chapter 18, p. 416). Here I will confine myself to the theme of development/underdevelopment of the last three chapters. The two books chosen to focus our discussion are Alvin Toffler's *The Third Wave* and John Naisbitt's *Megatrends*.

Toffler indicates three 'waves' of historical change: the period of agricultural settlement: the industrial period: and an emerging age of new technologies and social organisation – the third wave. The dynamo behind the third wave is 'accelerating breakthroughs' in areas such as quantum electronics, information theory, molecular biology, oceanics and the space sciences. Currently, we are in a transitional period in which the technologies and social forms of the second and third waves are in collision – with all the gains and losses, triumphs and anxieties that implies. A little more precisely than Toffler, but consistent with him, John Naisbitt argues that post-industrial society is the 'information society'. He cites data to show that nearly all the rapid expansion in the service sector in the United States since the nineteen fifties has been in the information area. In 1950 about 17 per cent worked in information jobs whereas in 1983 more than 65 per cent worked with information as programmers, clerks, teachers, secretaries, accountants, managers, technicians etc. Echoing Toffler, he gives a three-word 'history of the United States' – 'farmer, labourer, clerk'.

As far as the developed societies are concerned, Toffler and Naisbitt present attractive pictures of what is emerging. A constant refrain in both books is how the old centralised, hierarchical, mass society is breaking up into smaller units of production (small business), power (participation/ networking) and individuality (of roles and life-style). Toffler even coins a term – 'prosumer' – to describe a common type of the new age. The central characteristic of the prosumer is self-help and his or her time may be divided between working for someone else and producing independently for personal or market consumption. Utilising the potential of the new technology, the prosumer may do much work at home. In a section titled 'the child-free culture', Toffler implies that, if not always choosing to be

childless, prosumers are likely to be concerned primarily with their own work and leisure. Naisbitt's observations are generally compatible with Toffler's although he is less convinced that the 'cottage-office' will be quite so popular. He believes that people will continue to want to work together and that in medium and higher level occupations, at least, the potential for more communication (networking) and participation in decision making is greater than in the past. Naisbitt also stresses the new political independence of voters whose variety of opinion, lifestyles and interests is no longer reliably reflected in one party or the other. He sees the emergence of a more issue-oriented politics for which more participatory mechanisms such as referenda are necessary.

Two areas receive fairly scant treatment by Toffler and Naisbitt: poverty in the developed countries and the situation of the Third World in relation to the new developments. Toffler recognises that there will be casualties as the second and third waves collide but devotes no space to discussing them. The words 'poor' and 'poverty' are not even listed in Naisbitt's index although it is unlikely that he assumes they will cease to exist in the information society. Both do devote a few pages to the Third World. Naisbitt's position is almost identical with that of the Brandt report which he cites approvingly. He considers that the trend to the information society in the West and Third World industrialisation are complementary and that increased aid should be directed to stimulate this tendency. Toffler concentrates mainly on the issue of what productive technology Third World countries might best adopt, given their frequent need for labour intensiveness and the nature of their social systems. He suggests that decentralised, smaller-scale third wave technology may be less disruptive to these societies than second wave technology has been. Thus, given the new technology, a country like China could become 'industrialised' without most of its population having to urbanise. This is imaginative stuff but overall it is easy to find Toffler's section on the Third World far too vague and cosy.

Quite simply, what is missing in Toffler's and Naisbitt's books is a willingness to face clearly that there will almost certainly be many groups for whom the 'new age' will bring major problems. Peter Hall's article *The social crisis* focuses on the issue. He sees a potentially disastrous consequence in the new technology. He argues that it is possible that the point has now been reached when the loss of jobs due to technological innovation 'is occurring so fast that no amount of further product innovation – the development of new industries – can compensate'. The result would be levels of unemployment more or less permanently as high as they are now in most of Western Europe and, of course, much higher ones in most of the Third World. Some conservative thinkers, such as Milton Friedman, have suggested reducing welfare to force current recipients into low-paid jobs. Indeed, the low paid sector has recently expanded in both the United States and Britain (another factor not considered by Toffler and Naisbitt). Hall cites an alternative approach presented in the Australian Barry Jones' visionary book *Sleepers Wake!* His solutions:

... involve changes in economic measurement to include domestic, informal and DIY work; a vast increase in educational spending to give working class children the same opportunities for higher and further education as their middle class counterparts, with general tertiary education available to everyone; a guaranteed income scheme for all; and legislation to guarantee full and appropriate employment for all those willing and able to work.

(Hall in New Society, 22 November 1985)

Such state intervention is, however, a long way from the liberal capitalism that Toffler and Naisbitt assume.

The potential problems of poverty and starvation in the Third World do not even surface in the two works under discussion. This surely reflects a tunnel vision of the future. The world is not going to be inherited exclusively by the rich and comfortable. To pretend so is not only inhumane, but probably unwise.

HOW LONG IS THE FUTURE? TOWARDS A NEW WORLD ORDER OR SPECIES-DESTRUCTION?

The third question is: 'How long have we got?'. Nobody, of course has the answer to that question. What is new in modern society, however, is that we have the means

to destroy ourselves, and access to those means is spreading. Therein lies probably the greatest danger of a nuclear disaster – that nuclear weapons will finally come into the hands of those willing to use them other than as an option of last resort. Alternatively, and even more horrendously, one of the major nuclear powers may, by intent or accident, actually start a holocaust. It may be that the end of our species is as inevitable as the end of our individual lives but it seems desirable to put it off as long as possible and certainly to avoid self-destruction. For this to be achieved armaments build-up and the global proliferation of nuclear weapons must be checked and reversed. Once agreed, this would involve the setting up of an international inspection system, perhaps under the aegis of the United Nations.

If the energy and intelligence that has been used in the creation and development of nuclear weapons could be released and channelled into economic and social projects, there is no reason why the conditions of poverty and misery described in the last chapters could not be greatly alleviated. We saw an international outpouring of constructive concern over the famine in Ethiopia in 1985. Yet it would take the 'moral equivalent of war' to deal with the problems and hunger and poverty on a global scale. Even Bob Geldoff, the inspiration behind Bandaid, at last complained of 'moral exhaustion' after a period in Africa overseeing the distribution of aid. Something more organised and sustained than an occasional outpouring of charity, however intense, is necessary to meet the problems we have described. It is not for me to suggest an action agenda for the coming generation, but dealing with the nuclear issue and world poverty must surely be close to the top. A third issue of 'survival' is the conservation of the global eco-system.

Disarmament, nuclear and otherwise, and tackling global poverty were central to suggested agendas for a 'new World order' which there was much talk about following liberalisation in the Soviet Union and, particularly, after the Gulf War. The context of a 'new World order' must be a permanent end to the Cold War and to the global rivalry and intrigue that characterised it. Eventually, preferably sooner rather than later, it would mean an end to the massive international trade in armaments which results, quite simply, in slaughter around the world. We must 'turn our swords to ploughshares' or in less metaphorical terms, the technology of destruction must be replaced by the technology of construction. J K Galbraith in his article *The Call of Arms and the Poor Man* describes mass violence and poverty as closely related:

A new world order, if it is to have any meaning or effect, must also go beyond conflict and mass slaughter to their causes. And as to causes the empirical evidence is overwhelming. Violent death is peculiarly the fate of the poor ... The rich and the reasonably comfortable do not take readily to the idea of disciplined military slaughter.

(The Guardian, 27 March 1991:23)

By way of solution, then, Galbraith, argues that 'a new World order must address poverty as the prime source of world disorder. This means a continuing and enlarged flow of resources from the rich countries to the poor'.

The positive role of the United Nations in the Gulf War and in steadfastly attempting to dispose of Iraq's nuclear weapons development and manufacturing capacity after the war, strengthen the hope that it may yet develop as an effective body for promoting and establishing World peace and justice. The political and material means to create a better world are available. What is in question is whether there exists the will and imagination to match them.

SUMMARY

1 Development implies some positive progress in a society's condition whereas undevelopment implies decline or stagnation. Beyond these generalisations, controversy rages around what has caused undevelopment (lack of development) and what might produce development. However, undoubtedly the context of the 'development' debates lies in the historical relationship between the advanced capitalist societies and the rest of the world.

2 In a global context, three main theories of change occur:

- Modernisation Theory;
- Marxism;
- Liberal/Social Democratic.

3 Modernisation theorists argue that the pattern of historical change has been from simple to complex or modern societies. Among the main explanations for development are that adopting 'Western attitudes and values' and/or 'Western' technology can promote development.

4 There are two distinct Marxist theories of underdevelopment. André

Gunder Frank argues that the 'dependency' produced by world capitalism has typically created 'underdevelopment'. He considers that the global economy is a unified world capitalist system. In contradiction, Marxist modes of production theory argues that there remain various non-capitalist modes of production within societies in the 'Third World' and that this is crucial to understanding them economically, politically and socially.

5 The two liberal theories of development have as their common core a commitment to development through the 'free' capitalist market. However, whereas the traditional liberals (often modern Conservatives) want to leave the market essentially unregulated, liberal social democrats argue that governments or international bodies should regulate both the functioning and effects of the free market, including the inequalities it creates.

6 The contribution made by the work of women to development has been frequently ignored. The position of women within patriarchal systems in various societies differs greatly in terms of power and status and is not 'better' in all respects in capitalist societies.

7 What 'true' development 'really' means, particularly in a moral and culture sense, is open to opinion. However, most agree that without improved education and employment opportunities an undeveloped country will not sustain development.

8 South Africa raises, among a welter of complications, the central question of whether one supposed 'race' will finally accept that members of another supposed 'race' have equal rights to full personal social, political and economic development.

9 Nuclear weapons threaten an end to any kind of development for rich and poor alike. Channelling resources to meet real human needs, starting with hunger, shelter and health seems a better way to spend money than on armaments.

RESEARCH AND COURSEWORK

Many find this topic interesting at both the theoretical and the detailed level. The clash of theories is given relevance by the fact that, 'on the ground', in given societies and in relation to specific projects, people are attempting to apply particular theories or combinations of theories. An effective piece of coursework in this area is likely to cover both these aspects. Thus, the theory and practice of development in communist Cuba or in capitalist Hong Kong are possible topic areas. Better still, would be a comparison of the two societies. Sources might be a problem although relevant embassies and overseas development agencies might be able to help. In any case, a retreat into a generalised theoretical piece of coursework is likely to be difficult and less interesting.

FURTHER READING

Two reports produced under the chairmanship of Willy Brandt contain a mass of still useful data and analysis. They are *North-South: A Programme for Survival* (1981) and *Common Crisis: Cooperation for World Recovery* (1983), both published by Pan. See also 'further reading', chapter 20.

QUESTIONS

1 Why are the 'Third World' societies poorer than the more industrialised societies? What role can the industrialised societies play in getting rid of 'Third World' poverty. (Cambridge, 1989)

2 'Many, if not all, of the present problems of the Third World have their origins in Western colonialism and neo-colonialism.' Critically examine the sociological arguments for and against this statement. (AEB, 1991)

3 'All industrially developed societies, due to economic and technological changes, are experiencing convergence in their social, cultural and political structures.' Discuss. (AEB, 1991)

22 Sociological Theory: Paradigm or Paradigms?

This chapter discusses sociological theory at a more advanced level than chapter one. As was the case in chapter one, each of the main perspectives is discussed in turn and here there is in addition a section on phenomenology. The underlying theme of the chapter is whether sociology is moving towards a single unified paradigm or perspective or whether on the contrary, it is destined to reflect many perspectives – as poststructuralists would argue (see pp. 511–12).

Let us begin, however, with some key sociological questions which give focus to the discipline.

KEY QUESTIONS IN SOCIOLOGY

Charles Wright Mills had the work of Marx, Durkheim, Weber and other 'classic' sociologists in mind when he suggested that such thinkers 'have consistently asked three sorts of questions'. Essentially these questions are:

1 What is the structure of this particular society as a whole? (or 'how is a given society made up?).
2 What is the relationship between the individual or self – including particular types of individuals – and this society?
3 Where does this society stand in human history?

Taken together, questions 1 and 2 return us to the relationship between self and society raised in chapter 1. However, let us consider the questions separately as Mills proposes them. Before the question 'what is the structure of a particular society' can be addressed, we need to know what is meant by structure. The structure of society refers to its institutions, particularly major institutional systems such as the economy, the political system and the family. Institutions have a physical aspect, e.g. banks are part of the economy, and a normative and behavioural aspect, i.e. behaviour within given institutional areas is governed by a range of norms, e.g. the professional regulations governing banking. Mills himself uses the term 'components' to describe institutions and emphasises the importance of analysing how they relate to each other and why and to what extent they change. He also stresses that much can be learnt through comparing the social structures of societies.

Mills' second concern, the relationship between the individual and society, is central to sociology. Mills is aware of the power of society to mould individual behaviour (he describes 'human nature' as seemingly 'plastic') but, as we have seen, he also stresses that knowledge and understanding can motivate personal action. Mills also considers it to be an important sociological question why certain types of character – say, fascist or materialistic or idealistic – appear more prominently in certain social circumstances than in others. Here he is raising the issue of the relationship between group character and social structure.

Mills' third question 'where does this society stand in human history' suggests that perspective and a sense of context can be gained on a society by knowing how and why it has changed and how it compares to other societies. Such comparative and historical work has enabled sociologists to categorise societies into types, and thus map out the panorama of human social experience.

Sociological Perspectives: Structural and Interpretive Perspectives

Any adequate sociological perspective must address the relationship between the self and society, particularly social structure, indicated above. However, there is a distinct difference of emphasis within sociology between those perspectives which concentrate mainly on structure and those which concentrate on the interaction of self and others: roughly, the large-scale and the small-scale, respectively. The more structural perspectives are functionalism and Marxism. The collective term used to refer to the other perspectives – interactionism and ethnomethodology – is interpretive. This indicates that they are primarily concerned with how the self (in relation to others) interprets society and finds meaning in doing so. Weber's sociology contains significant elements of both structural and interpretist perspective.

Structural Sociology

Marxist, Tom Bottomore, and functionalist, Robert Nisbet, describe the 'central core of sociological theory' as

...so many attempts to define the fundamental elements of social structure – both those which are universal and those which have particular historical character – and to provide some explanation or interpretation of the unity and persistence of societies, as well as their inner tensions and their potentialities for change.

(Bottomore and Nisbet, 1979:viii)

This nicely sums up the approach of structural sociology which tends to concentrate on questions 1 and 3 proposed by Mills, the structural and historical/comparative.

Bottomore and Nisbet go on to locate the founders of 'sociological structuralism':

It is our view that sociological structuralism arose in the works of Auguste Comte in France and Karl Marx in Germany. In France the pre-eminent sociological structuralist has been Durkheim.

(Bottomore and Nisbet, 559).

Functionalism (Consensus Theory)

Functionalist perspective studies the structure and functioning of society. It is sometimes referred to as structural-functionalism. The concept of structure has already been sufficiently introduced. A function is simply an effect or outcome of the working of a social institution. Thus, a function of the economy is to produce goods and services for consumption. A description is given below of the structure and functioning of society as understood by leading post Second World War function-alist, Talcott Parsons. Functionalism, in general, and Parsons' work in particular emphasises the importance of value consensus (agreement about fundamental values) as a condition for the effective functioning of a society. Both Weber and, especially, Durkheim influenced function-alism but little if any of Marx's thought has been adopted into the perspective.

INFLUENCES ON FUNCTIONALISM: COMTE, DURKHEIM, WEBER

Both Comte and Durkheim distinguished between social statics and social dynamics. Social statics refers to the relatively 'given' structure of society (i.e. norms/rules) whereas social dynamics refers to the active relationships between the various parts of society. This distinction parallels that made by functionalists between structure and functioning. A more general influence of Comte and Durkheim on functionalism is their commitment to produce a science of society comparable in quality to the natural sciences.

Comte and Durkheim left a legacy to functionalism which reflected their view that society has enormous power to form and structure the thought and behaviour of its members. Durkheim argued that sociology is the study of a 'category of facts (which) consists of ways of acting, thinking, and feeling, external to the individual, and endowed with a power of coercion, by reason of which they control him'. So for Durkheim, sociology was largely about establishing what the 'rules or norms of a society are and how behaviour is controlled by them. He considered that the resulting order is essential for society to function well. He acknowledged that individuality exists but stated that it is not the object of sociology to study it. Rather, sociology is the study of the effect of social conditions on behaviour: such as economic crisis on the rate of suicide (see p. 314).

In contrast to Durkheim, his contempo-rary, Max Weber, did not attempt to separate the study of the individual from the study of society. Indeed, he would have considered such a separation impossible because in his view, the individual and society exist not independently but in a state of interaction in which they can change each other. People's values and ideas are influenced by society but they also change society. His theory of social action posits that the starting point of sociology is meaningful action. Weber's study of organisations (pp. 271–2) shows his appreciation of the power of what Durkheim called 'social facts' to structure people's lives, but equally his analysis of charismatic figures such as Luther and Napoleon indicates that he believed individual personality and ideas can have a major impact on society.

TALCOTT PARSONS

Talcot Parsons is the founder of modern functionalism (Durkheim and Weber did not use the term to describe their orientations). His social systems theory attempted to synthesise Durkheim's social structural and Weber's social action perspectives together with the insights of other social scientists, notably Freud. Parsons considered that people learn basic values, norms (rules) and roles through socialisation. He saw the successful internalisation of society's values, norms and roles as a precondition of social

order, and the failure to learn or accept them as a problem of deviance (see pp. 299–300).

The diagram of Parsons' social system model needs explanation. The concept of social system encompasses both structure and functioning. Each of the four subsystems in the model meets a given essential human need. These needs are referred to by Parsons variously as imperatives or prerequisities. The economy meets the imperative of adaption (i.e. material needs); the political sub-systems or polity provides an institutional framework for collective goal attainment; kinship institutions provide pattern maintenance (of accepted ways of behaviour) and tension management (of emotions); and the cultural and community sub-systems provides integration (co-ordination and control of the various parts of the system).

The integrating function of the cultural community sub-system is particularly important in functionalist theory. This is achieved by reinforcing values and socially acceptable behaviour – familiar functions of church and school. These values, of course,

Figure 22.1

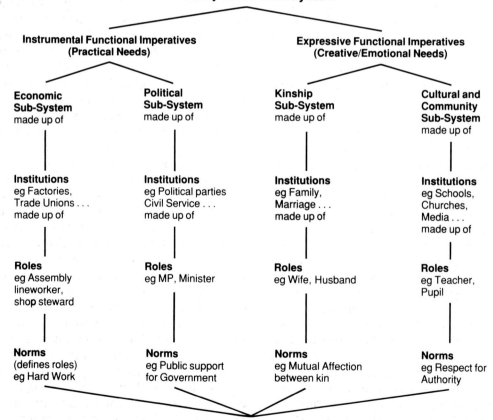

Society as a Social System

Instrumental Functional Imperatives (Practical Needs)

Expressive Functional Imperatives (Creative/Emotional Needs)

Economic Sub-System made up of

Political Sub-System made up of

Kinship Sub-System made up of

Cultural and Community Sub-System made up of

Institutions eg Factories, Trade Unions . . . made up of

Institutions eg Political parties Civil Service . . . made up of

Institutions eg Family, Marriage . . . made up of

Institutions eg Schools, Churches, Media . . . made up of

Roles eg Assembly lineworker, shop steward

Roles eg MP, Minister

Roles eg Wife, Husband

Roles eg Teacher, Pupil

Norms (defines roles) eg Hard Work

Norms eg Public support for Government

Norms eg Mutual Affection between kin

Norms eg Respect for Authority

Norms (and whole system) Supported by Fundamental Values such as Loyalty

permeate the whole system and are the basis of the social consensus that underpins social order. For Parsons, as for Durkheim, society is a moral entity which requires conformity from its members to function effectively. Like his contemporary Edward Shils, Parsons sees a major role for the elite of society to maintain the 'central value system'. Their tendency to equate elite values with society's values has been criticised by conflict theorists who point to class, racial and other opposing values between groups.

HOW ADEQUATE IS THE ORGANIC ANALOGY?

In the first chapter, we introduced the functionalist comparison of society to a biological organism. In later chapters, we examined several applications of the organic analogy. The application examined in greatest detail was the way in which societies are considered to develop from the simple to the complex, just as growing bodies do. This approach stresses the evolutionary aspect of the analogy, and is apparent in the work of Durkheim and Parsons, but can be traced back to the British sociologist, Herbert Spencer (1820–1903), who was substantially influenced by Darwin's theory of biological evolution. We will consider shortly whether the concept of evolution provides an adequate basis for understanding social change.

Apart from applications of the organic analogy based on evolutionary perspective, others reflect the view that society is structured and functions like an organism. This emphasis finds its strongest expression in the writings of the British anthropologist, Radcliffe-Brown, (1881–1955), but it also partly underlies the more sophisticated social systems theory of Talcott Parsons. The basic notion here is that the various parts of society work in relation to one another (see the family-society model, chapter 3, p. 47) and that society can best be understood by analysing these inter-relations (see Parsons' social systems model, p. 498). Functionalists consider that just as some parts of the body are functionally more important than others, so too, must society be hierarchically arranged for functional purposes. This view is apparent in the work of Davis and Moore (chapter 7, pp. 163–4) and Michels (chapter 12, pp. 280–1). Another major functionalist

concept is that of social equilibrium by which society is assumed to seek balance and orderly functioning in the same way that the body does. Consensus on norms and values is considered a necessity for healthy functioning, although the analogy is rarely pursued as literally as this. Deviant behaviour, however, is often compared to physical 'pathology' by functionalists, not least by Durkheim himself.

CRITICISMS OF FUNCTIONALISM (PARTICULARLY THE ORGANIC ANALOGY)

We now turn to a critical appraisal of functionalism. Firstly, in reference to the organic analogy, organs do not think, whereas people do, or to put it more technically, the organic analogy contains no parallel for intentional social action. Biological processes are not generally achieved through the use of will, reason and imagination but mainly take place below the level of conscious awareness. Despite attempting to balance individuality with the effect of social structure, Parsons is widely considered to have produced a model of society which tends much more to the social structuralism of Durkheim than to the social action emphasis of Weber. Whatever his intention, Parsons treats values almost as though they are 'things' socially imposed upon the individual rather than partly the product of his or her own considered choice. As figure 22.1 indicates values are presented predominantly as the property of systems rather than of individuals and groups. (For an example of functionalist analysis of values, see Bert Hoselitz, p. 471). As Anthony Giddens remarks 'recognisably human agents seem to elude the grasp of his scheme: the stage is set, the scripts written, the roles established, but the performers are curiously absent from the scene'. The result of this is that functionalism presents what Dennis Wrong calls an oversocialised conceptualisation of man.

A second criticism frequently made of functionalism is that it exaggerates the role of consensus and underestimates that of conflict in the functioning of society. It should be added that the concepts of consensus and equilibrium are linked, in that functionalists regard the former as a precondition of the latter. This emphasis on stability and order is reflected in the organic analogy itself in that organic bodies, particularly animals, strive to maintain internal balance (partly through an often complex process of homeostasis or adaptation) but there is no proof – indeed, it is most unlikely – that societies as entities are inherently endowed with similar adjustment mechanisms. Social order and equilibrium may be maintained through the conscious action of individuals and groups, but that is a different matter. Although consensus does contribute to social order it, too, must in part be intentionally created and maintained. It certainly cannot be regarded as automatically self-regulating or perpetuating. In other words, social equilibrium and consensus occur in a different way from organic equilibrium. There is no adequate explanatory parallel between the organic and social fields.

To the extent that Parsons does incorporate conflict into his scheme, he tends to assume that 'the system' has the capacity to neutralise it. Thus he allows that 'tension' can arise within society but the fact that he sees this as being 'managed' within the family and kinship sub-system suggests he sees it mainly as an individual problem. Conflict between classes, racial groups, and the two sexes gets scant consideration in his work. Robert Merton, working within the functionalist tradition, has introduced the concept of dysfunction which indicates that a social structure may function in a way that has a negative or maladaptive' effect on society. Thus, it can be argued that means testing the poor is dysfunctional in so far as it puts off some of them from applying for needed social security.

A third criticism of the organic analogy is that it produces a misleading separation of structure (society's parts or institutions) and system (society's functioning). In particular, it leads only to a partial conceptualisation of the problem of social change. By contrast, this division seems to work well in the natural sciences. In biology, it helps to examine the structure of a plant or animal (anatomy) and then to describe how the various parts function in relation to one another and the whole. In a limited descriptive sense, the same approach is useful in sociology although, significantly, society cannot be similarly 'laid out' anatomically for examination. In real life, society 'functions' through the more or less organised actions of individuals and groups, not in the manner of an unreflecting organism. Nor does change occur solely through evolution and adaptation, although it may to some extent. Equally important in the history and development of nations and cultures are revolutions and drastic breaks with the past. Parsons' notion of dynamic equilibrium, by which social balance adjusts to accommodate new phenomena within the system, still stresses continuity at the expense of change and severance. It also woefully underestimates the role of people in making history. For him, systems change and almost 'make' people, not the other way around.

In retrospect, Robert Merton's attempts to use the concept of function to embrace a wide variety of social events looks like the death throes of a theory stretched beyond its inherent capacity. In particular, his concept of manifest function which he uses to describe intended, as opposed to unintended (latent) consequences of institutional functioning does not adequately conceptualise the role of choice in social life. The basic problem is that it is not possible to provide an adequate account of consciously directed action within a framework that takes as its model the unconscious functioning of the organism.

A final criticism of functionalism is that it is teleological, or tautological, as Chris Brown has referred to it. In other words, because functionalists see certain functions being performed by given institutions, they conclude that there must be need for these institutions – that is, they explain causes by their consequences. Actually, many institutions exist, the 'need' for which can be doubted. Inevitably, opinions will differ as to which institutions qualify: some will suggest the class system, others the nuclear family. Further, people create organisations and institutions not only to fulfil social needs but to pursue their own purposes and interests – sometimes at the expense of others.

Finally, although nobody can take exception to a descriptive account of the functions institutions perform, including those many of us may not be aware of, this is only an aspect, and a rather obvious one, of sociological analysis. Who made things as they are, and in whose interest, are equally important questions which functionalists tend to underestimate.

The issue is not whether functionalism is an 'incorrect' perspective but whether it is the most useful and illuminating available. It is certanly helpful as a descriptive, if limited, account of what institutions 'do' – and, as such, it has some appeal to students. Further, the functionalist analysis of socialisation warns us, usefully, of what is 'done' to us individually in order to make us conforming members of society. Both these aspects of sociological analysis, however, are fairly obvious and well dealt with in other perspectives. Functionalism must stand or fall on the fruitfulness of its central concepts as presented in the biological analogy, or in Talcott Parsons' more recent, and, admittedly, more sophisticated systems theory. In either case, it seems to smack too much of evolutionism and not enough of intentionality.

Marxism (Conflict Theory I)

Whereas functionalism is based on the assumption that value consensus and social order are normal to society, Marxists consider that conflict over values and material issues is normal in class divided societies. This is because, in Marx's view, different groups or classes of people have different needs or wants which ultimately brings them into conflict. However, Marxists recognise that even societies divided by classes may remain basically stable and orderly for long periods.

STRUCTURE AND IDEOLOGY

Marx's analysis of the structure of society begins with the issue of human survival: the need to produce goods. The area of society concerned with the production of goods is the economy. Marx referred to the forces of production, the means of production, the social relations of production, and the mode of production. The forces of production are all the factors, including scientific and technological which contribute to production. The means of production are included within the forces of production and are the concrete instruments of production (such as land in feudal societies and factories in capitalist-industrial societies). The social relations of production refers to the way in which production is socially organised – in all non-communist societies, there is a class which owns the means of production and a class which works the means of production. In nineteenth century capitalist society – the society he lived in – Marx described the class which owned the means of production as the capitalist class or bourgeoisie and the class which sold its labour as the working class or proletariat. The mode of production is the most general description of the main type of production in a given society, such as the feudal, capitalist or socialist modes of production.

Considered as a whole, the economy and classes are referred to as the base or infrastructure of society. The other areas of society are collectively termed the superstructure. As presented in figure 5.1, the superstructure covers politics and culture/ideology (see p. 115) – roughly the area of 'ideas'. Marx stated that:

The ideas of the ruling class are in every epoch the ruling ideas: i.e. the class which is the ruling material force of society is at the same time its ruling intellectual force. The class which has the means of material production at its disposal, has control at the same time over the means of mental production.
(The German Ideology, cited in Bottomore and Rubel, 1961:93.)

Marx's phrase 'religion … is the opium of the people' summarises his view that religion has functioned primarily to befuddle dominated or 'exploited' groups and persuade them to believe that they should conform to societies which exploit them. Marx refers to these misguided (in his view) conformist beliefs, as 'false consciousness'. Contemporary Marxists tend to point to education and the media as the main agencies of ideological control. The French Marxist, Althusser, particularly stresses the power of the ruling or dominant class to achieve widespread acceptance of its ideological beliefs among other classes, including the working class. This analysis is referred to as 'the dominant ideology thesis'.

However, other Marxists, including

Nicholas Abercrombie, have stressed another aspect of Marx's analysis of ideology. This is that the working class has the basis of an alternative ideology to the dominant capitalist one, in its own experience of work. Marx argued that their shared experience of 'exploitation' at work could promote working class solidarity and collective action. In short, lead them towards socialism. So, Marx indicates both a potential for ideological conformity and for an alternative ideology among the working class.

CONTRADICTION AND CHANGE

It is important to note, however, that Marx did not consider that ideas alone can fundamentally change a society. He argued that the underlying condition of change in a society exists when a fundamental contradiction or contradictions develop to such a point that the existing social order becomes threatened with break-up. The most basic contradiction a society can develop is when its mode of production and its social relations become antagonistic. By this he meant that the balance of economic power can pass to a new group even though formally the old social order appears intact. Thus, Marx argued that eventually capitalists would become unable to control the system of capitalist production because they would be unable to maintain their domination of the working class (just as the feudal nobility had lost its capacity to control the emerging bourgeoisie). Marx described a complex network of contradictions underlying the basic contradiction described above: these centred upon the falling rate of profit for capitalists, increased competition between them, and increased exploitation (immiseration) of the working class leading to a revolutionary response.

Marx's theory that historical change occurs through the synthesis of contradictions within a system is known as dialectical materialism. It is materialistic in that he sees economic forces and development as providing the dynamic that underlies historical change. Contradictions emerge from the antagonistic economic and social relations of classes.

CRITICISMS OF 'CRUDE' MARXISM

The Marxist heritage is profoundly ambiguous: Marx has left two legacies, although it is unlikely that he intended to do so. The first is based on the belief that class conflict and socialist revolution are historically inevitable, and the other is based on the view that, to achieve a social revolution, it is necessary to work for a change in the consciousness of the working class (as they come to realise the nature of capitalist exploitation, they will surely organise to end it). It is the first of these two legacies of thought which has been the most severely criticised.

The belief that a revolution of the proletariat is inevitable on account of certain economic 'contradictions' in capitalism, has been criticised repeatedly as crudely deterministic. This means that its adherents consider that 'the future is known from the past', and, they state, certain major future events are bound to happen because of 'the laws of history'. We examined Karl Popper's comments on this issue earlier, in chapter 2. Marx's application of dialectical theory to historical change is sometimes cited as an attempt to uncover such laws. The principle of the dialectic is that opposite elements (thesis and antithesis) combine to produce a synthesis (new phenomenon). The concept comes from natural science, but as applied by Marx to recent history, it means that the clash of the capitalist class with the proletariat will produce a new synthesis: the classless society. It is doubtful whether Marx intended this model to be accepted as rigidly inevitable, but if he did, it is, indeed, an example of crude determinism. Perhaps Marx has suffered as much from the ideas of some of his followers as from his critics. No wonder he once said 'I am not a Marxist'. The major refutation of determinism, which modern Marxists do generally accept, is that, within the structural realities of their time, people make their own history and, for that reason, the future cannot be predicted.

A second criticism of Marxism is the reverse of that made against functionalism, that it over-stresses conflict and underestimates the extent of consensus in society. This criticism needs to be qualified. Marx's concept of 'false consciousness' fully recognises that what he would see as a 'false consensus' masking the deeper reality of class conflict, can occur. However, the possibility that many people might consciously and intelligently seek consensus and agreement across class-lines runs counter to his theoretical model. Marx's critics on this point argue that many people quite normally and rationally do act in this way. If they are right, then the basis of Marx's model of society and social change are undermined.

A third criticism of Marxism is that it is idealistic in theory but can frequently be cruel and repressive in practice. When commentators say this they have in mind primarily the example of Soviet totalitarianism and imperialism. They argue that the Soviet record of human rights and foreign policy is not attributable simply to the wickedness of the Soviets, but is a basic feature of Marxist 'dogma' itself. They contend that 'in the real world' it is not possible to combine material equality with a high level of personal freedom and expression. When the state is controlled by an unrepresentative group, it may use its power to repress not only political opposition but also to organise, control or repress a wide range of other activities, not least those of a cultural kind. Many European and American Marxists accept these criticisms, but deny that the former Soviet regime represented a fair picture of Marxism. We now examine some of their ideas on the subject.

RECENT TRENDS IN MARXIST THOUGHT

First is the trend towards Marxist humanism. This aspect of Marxism concentrates on the repression of human potential in capitalist society and the prospect of its release in communist society. The sources of humanism within Marx's own works are his early writings on human potential and his analysis of alienation, discussed in the last chapter. In Britain, Raymond Williams and E P Thompson are major representatives of Marxist humanism, and in the United States C Wright Mills and the German exile, Herbert Marcuse achieved international influence.

At the risk of oversimplification, we include critical theory within the broad trend of Marxist humanism (see pp. 401–2 of chapter 17). Critical theory, as its name suggests, raises the possibility of criticising the way things are from another point of view. Marcuse himself was a critical theorist

until his death in 1979. He attacked capitalist 'reality', particularly from the point of view that it is culturally repressive – especially, although not exclusively, of the working class (see chapter 10, p. 223). Before fleeing to America from Nazi Germany, Marcuse worked at Frankfurt University, the 'home' of critical theorists. Like other philosophers and sociologists of the Frankfurt school, Marcuse was greatly influenced by Freud as well as by Marx, and effected a synthesis of the two that captured the imagination of many student radicals of the nineteen sixties. He took Freud's concept of psychological repression and applied it to capitalist society. He argued that capitalism is not interested in full human expression and development, but primarily in exploiting labour. In doing this, it represses human potential and reduces people to the level of a machine. Because, like Habermas, Marcuse holds out the possibility of more liberated human life, we class him as a Marxist humanist. His work, as well as that of Williams, Thompson and Mills, shows that the interest of Marxist humanists is not narrowly sociological but extends to the whole range of cultural expression.

A second contemporary trend in Marxism is Marxist structuralism, associated particularly with the French Marxists, Althusser and Bourdieu. We discussed their thinking in the context of socialisation, especially education, and referred again to Althusser in chapters 4 and 18. Structuralists tend to see a rather tight fit between the base and the superstructure. In other words, they see culture less as free expression and more as an area in which ideological conformity to capitalist society is created. In this sense they are rather like structural functionalists, although whereas the latter generally approved of conformity to capitalist society, Marxist structuralists certainly do not.

Thirdly, developments in Marxist thought have also been forged in political practice as well as in the studies of academics. Lenin, Mao and the Cuban revolutionary, Che Guevara, were men of action as well as intellectuals. They were all successful revolutionaries and it is not surprising that they emphasised the need for Marxists to organise in order to create the change they wanted rather than to assume that history was inevitably on their side. They stressed the role both of the revolutionary party and of committed leadership in helping to bring about revolution. The danger in this was that the leadership would lose touch with the majority of the people on whose behalf revolution was supposed to take place. Having 'imposed' revolution, post-revolutionary change might also 'have to be' imposed on a population whose 'consciousness' might be far from communist. Marxists differ on whether such imposition is justifiable. The alternative is to seek fundamental change only with mass support, either gradually or through revolution. The difficulty here is that the forces of the system preventing the growth of such support are immense; one way of measuring support is through the ballot box. Zimbabwe has an elected Marxist government, but it remains to be seen whether it can survive the opposition of the powerful countries and international business interests ranged against it. The elected Marxist government of Allende in Chile was prevented from doing this.

It is not easy to classify neatly the theoretical contributions of Marxist activists. The three revolutionaries mentioned above all stressed the need for people to force the historical issue in order to bring about socialist change. To that extent they were humanists.

Whether the violence they used in pursuit of change contradicts their humanism is a point that could long be debated.

Even before the rise of President Gorbachev and the collapse of Eastern European Communism, contemporary Marxism was in a ferment of debate: Some issues are becoming clear. Few Marxists now are historical determinists, although a case could be made that the French structuralists have merely substituted cultural mechanics for economic. Few Western European Marxists support the use of violent means to achieve change in Western Europe (although it is seen as a legitimate means to overthrow unrepresentative and exploitative regimes in the Third World). Most Western Marxists are now democratic in the sense that they no longer support one party rule. These observations prompt the questions – 'Are Marxists with such beliefs *really* Marxists?': 'Are they essentially any different from democratic socialists?' The answer to these questions, upon which the future of Marxism depends, is likely to emerge in the next decade or so. The issue both theoretically and practically is whether there is a distinctly Marxist solution to the inequalities and exploitation produced by capitalism which does not diminish personal and civil freedom.

Max Weber: Social Action Theory (Conflict Theory II)

Max Weber has greatly contributed to both the interpretive and structuralist traditions in sociology. However, according to Weber's own claim, his point of departure and ultimate goal was to analyse the individual person:

Interpretative sociology considers the individual and his action as the basic unit, as its 'atom' ... In this approach, the individual is also the upper limit and sole carrier of meaningful conduct ... In general, for sociology such concepts as 'state', 'association', 'feudalism', and the like, designate certain categories of human interaction. Hence it is the task of sociology to reduce these concepts to 'understandable' action, that is, without exception to the actions of participating individual men.

(Quoted in Gerth and Mills eds., 1970:55)

A clearer commitment to interpretive sociology, a sociology of social action, would be difficult to find. Yet, despite this important statement of principle on

interpretive sociology, Weber's main theoretical contributions to sociology probably lie in the area of structural analysis.

FOUR TYPES OF SOCIAL ACTION

Weber divided social action into four types:

- **Instrumentally rational action (action geared to 'the attainment of the actors own rationally pursued and calculated ends');**
- **Value-rational action (action 'determined by a conscious belief in the value for its own sake of some ethical, aesthetic, religious or other form of behaviour, independently of its prospects of success');**
- **Affectual action ('determined by the actors specific affects and feeling states');**

■ Traditional action (determined by ingrained habituation).

In short, he categorised action as motivated by reason, values, emotion, or tradition – or by some combination of the four. Weber intended his typology of action to cover the range from the rational to the irrational.

Weber's typology of social action appears to be the preliminary to developing a sociology that will have the self at the centre of it. However, both Charles Wright Mills and Alan Dawe have commented that he did not achieve this. Dawe argues that this is because Weber uses his action typology to define particular types of social order, e.g. bureaucratic, religious, rather than to analyse the complexity of subjective (individual) motivation and action. Individuals are categorised as members of particular types of society, institutions or movements rather than in terms of their individual complexity. As Mills implies, Weber's turning away from strictly interpretive to more structural sociology is hardly surprising. No sociologist has yet solved the mammoth task of being 'true to' members of society's subjectivity except, perhaps, in very small-scale research, let alone effectively linking such analysis to broader influences and issues. Perhaps the problem is simply not solvable.

RATIONAL ACTION AND BUREAU-CRACY

Weber considered that the type of action most characteristic of capitalist society is instrumentally rational action, i.e. logically organised action to achieve given goals. He argued that large-scale organisations characterised by a hierarchical and complex division of labour were the main embodiment of rational action in capitalist society. He went further than this, however, and argued that rational action is also the dominant type of action in socialist societies. Indeed, be believed that rational action is characteristic of modern societies themselves. Bureaucracy is the way rational and 'scientific' thinking is expressed in organisational form (see p. 271). Weber considered that religious and traditional thought and action were likely to decline against the relentless march of reason and science. He referred to this process, with a touch of poetic pathos, as disenchantment (see p.402).

Despite his apparent belief in the triumph of bureaucracy, Weber never lost his concern for the individual – even if he sometimes expressed this in a gloomy and even arrogant manner:

This passion for bureaucracy is enough to drive one to despair. It is as if we were deliberately to become men who need order and nothing but order, who become nervous and cowardly if for one moment this order wavers, and helpless if they are torn away from their total incorporation in it. That the world should know no men but these; it is in such an evolution that we are already caught up, and the great question is not how we can promote and hasten it, but what we can oppose to this machinery in order to keep a portion of mankind free from this parcelling-out of the soul, from this supreme mastery of the bureaucratic way of life.

(Cited by Dawe in Bottomore and Nisbet, 1979:391.)

STRUCTURE, PLURALISM AND INDIVID-UALITY

Weber's theory of action and, particularly, his analysis of bureaucracy as institutionalised rational action, never became the rigid dogma that the concept of class has in the hands of some Marxists. The above quotation shows him typically trying to understand the tension and interplay between individuality and social structure – an attempt he never surrendered for a more simplistic approach.

In general, Weber's structural analysis involves consideration of a variety of factors, the precise relationship of which cannot be predicted. As Mills says, his approach to 'social dynamics' (interaction and change) is 'pluralistic'. He sees many (i.e. a plurality of) groups, rather than merely two main classes, as involved in social interaction. Thus, he examines stratification in capitalist society mainly in terms of the relationship between class, status and political groups which he characterises as one of controlled conflict or competition (for this reason Weber is described as a conflict theorist). The precise relationships between the groups varies between capitalist societies: the only way to understand how they relate in a given society is by close and specific analysis. In order to establish and explain patterns of similarity and difference between societies, Weber advocates use of the comparative method (see p. 23) but he also insists that each society or 'case' is in certain respects, historically unique and must be analysed as such.

For Weber, the uniqueness of societies and the complexity of social processes and structures reflects the uniqueness of individuals and groups of individuals. His use of the concept of 'charisma' illustrates his view that the individual may greatly affect society. Literally, charisma means 'gift of grace' and Weber uses it to refer to self-appointed leaders who are seen as extrordinary (sometimes as 'saviours') by their followers. In the contemporary world such leaders as Nelson Mandela and Saddam Hussein appear charismatic. But Weber also considered that more ordinary people could make meaningful choices. Again, his view of society is pluralistic, it reflects the unpredictable conflict of ideas and values. Nor are these merely the reflection of self or class interest as he believed Marx tended to see them but they are partly the product of people's desire to affect and master their own social situations.

COMMENT ON WEBER Whereas other sociological perspectives can be criticised for over-emphasising one or other side of the self/structure relationship, perhaps the more precise criticism of Weber is that he did not achieve the immense task of 'blending' the two aspects together but rather oscillated between them. If anything, as both Mills and Dawe suggest, his practical work tended more towards structural sociology, whereas his statements of intent implied he would attempt to develop a sociology of individual or subjective meaning. A second criticism of Weber is that his perception of the dominance of bureaucracy in modern society underestimated both the relevance and frequency of other organisational forms and the ability of people within bureaucracies to find less formal and often more satisfying and effective ways of working. This is ironic, given his own commitment to understanding individuality. However, paradox is at the heart of Weber's imagination and of his sociology.

Interactionism (and Structural Perspective): Towards a Synthesis?

Since Mead, symbolic interactionism has progressed theoretically as much through practical application as through abstract theorising. Accordingly, we have been able to examine in some detail recent interactionist analyses of work, deviance and organisation. There is no need to review this research now. Instead, we will discuss the criticism frequently made of interactionism – that it lacks a structural dimension. In particular, we will assess Tom Goff's comparison of Mead's sociology to that of Marx. In his book, *Marx and Mead* (1980), Goff attempts to show that the work of Marx and Mead is, essentially, complementary rather than contradictory. To the extent that he is successful, his analysis has profound implications for the theoretical reconstruction of sociology.

Firstly, both Marx and Mead emphasised that the individual is formed in society, and give comparable emphasis to the influence of social structure on people. Mead went into far greater detail about how this takes place and his social psychology has been very useful in much practical interpretist research. Marxists such as Paul Willis appear to have been influenced by it or, at least, by other compatible currents within phenomenology. Secondly, both Marx and Mead describe people as conscious beings with the potential to change and recreate their own social environment. Neither the individual human being nor the group is ever 'reduced' to society. If Mead conveyed much more of the psychology of individual choice and understanding than did Marx, Marx presented a much more urgent message of emancipation from social repression and an alternative and freer way of life. A third point of convergence can be derived from the other two. For both of them, social structure and human creativity are not separate, but dialectically related – that is, people and environment interact and can change each other. This leads to the fourth agreed point – that human thought is located in a social context, and informed by experience. In that sense, it is practical in nature and, for Marx at least, can be directed most rationally towards radically improving the quality of human life.

Goff has indicated Marx's concept of alienation as a major possible area of difference between him and Mead. Certainly, Mead had no particular sense that the division of labour in capitalist society was especially alienating: in fact, he was inclined to argue that the process of productive fragmentation was likely to continue and seemed none too distressed by it. He did, however, have a vivid appreciation of the way social institutions can smother individuality – a sentiment which accords with a Marxist-Weberian notion of alienation (see chapter 11, pp. 243–4). The following quotation shows this:

> **Oppressive, stereotyped and ultra-conservative social institutions – like the church – ... by their more or less rigid and inflexible unprogressiveness crush or blot out individuality or discourage any distinctive or original expressions of thought and behaviour in the individual selves or personalities implicated in and subjected to them ...**
>
> **(Mead, first published 1934, 1962)**

It is not too much to conclude, therefore, that Mead's framework of social analysis can be adapted to accommodate the concept of alienation.

Although the above considerations indicate that Mead's social thought is compatible with, and even complementary to, the structural aspects of Marxist theory, it remains true that the former is more suited to the micro-level of analysis and the latter to the macro-level. It is unquestionable that Mead developed the more detailed conceptual tool-kit for small-scale interaction and Marx the more detailed one for institutional analysis and class conflict, although in so far as these two levels inevitably overlap there is room for synthesis. Even accepting that the two perspectives are most effective at different levels of social analysis, and that theory and research will reflect this, it is inaccurate to present them as radically opposed: the above discussion shows that they need not be.

Phenomenology and Ethnomethodology

PHENOMENOLOGY

Phenomenology was originally a philosophical perspective but it has 'fed into' sociology through ethnomethodology. Edmund Husserl, the most influential philosopher of phenomenology, wanted to develop a philosophy which presented human action in terms of the meanings of actors rather than as the product of 'external' influences. Husserl argued that there is no knowable objective reality 'out there' but that each individual makes her or his own reality by categorising or 'sorting out' their own experience. Thus, what one individual may explain as illness, another may explain as punishment 'by the spirits' and another, still, as just bad luck (see pp. 376–7). It is only when individual or subjective definitions 'agree' that shared meanings or a shared definitions of reality occur.

Husserl considered that it is one of the main purposes of philosophy to establish what meanings a given group might have in common and how these relate to its wider culture. Thus, to refer again to the example given above, an explanation of a particular experience as 'illness' or 'disease' characterises Western, scientific culture whereas an explanation in terms of punishment 'by the spirits' better fits a magical frame of reference (for a fuller analysis of differing perspectives on health, see chapter 16).

Alfred Schütz (1899–1959) applied and developed Husserl's approach in relation to sociology. Like Husserl, Schütz 'bracketed' (set aside) the issue of the nature of objective reality and concentrated on how social actors make sense of and categorise their own experience, including interpreting the actions of others. That for him is the purpose of sociology – not to explain human behaviour as the effect of certain external causes.

Schütz did not consider that actors create and interpret meaning without reference to others. On the contrary, he argued that over time, given groups produce a shared stock of meanings which enable members more or less to understand each other and to anticipate each others' actions. A key concept in understanding the notion of a shared stock of meanings, is typification. A typification is a conceptual category used by a given group to describe phenomena (things) which are perceived as similar enough to be put in the same descriptive grouping. Thus, in British culture most would know who to categorise as a goalkeeper as opposed to a scrum-half or what to typify as a sausage as opposed to a plum-pudding. Different typifications develop in different cultures. Thus, whereas white Americans typify annual seasonal changes into four groupings (typifications), several American Indian tribes describe as many as eighteen changes (one such example is the Abernake Indians of the North Eastern states). Such different typifications reflect a different way of perceiving given phenomena. Typifications shared within a given group enable its members to make sense to each other and create a reasonably orderly social life.

Schütz distinguishes between the naturalistic perspective of the member of a social group and the phenomenological perspective of the outside observer (adopting the phenomenological perspective). The term naturalistic describes the taken-for-granted, 'commonsensical' approach taken by members of a given social group. They regard their way of life as 'normal' and are generally not aware of the extent to which it reflects only their own subjective experience. By contrast, the phenomenologist seeks to describe the way of life of a given group. However, s/he does so from the point of view of the actors involved and not from an external explanatory perspective. This leads to a different choice of methodology from structural sociology. In order 'to get close to' social actors phenomenologists adopt qualitative methods such as observation, rather than more quantitative methods.

Schütz requires comparison with both Weber and the interactionists. He argued that Weber failed to produce a sociological approach fully based on the meanings of social actors. He regarded Weber's types of social action (see pp. 504–6) as too remote from what actors actually think and do to provide the basis of a genuinely interpretive sociology. Similarly, though perhaps more debatably, some recent sociologists influenced by Schütz – the ethnomethodologists also consider that interactionism does not deliver a genuinely inter-subjective sociology i.e. a sociological perspective based

exclusively on how actors create, interpret and share meanings. Schütz himself was a theorist rather than an applied researcher. Whether his own approach successfully provided the basis for an effective interpretive and inter-subjective sociology must be assessed through the contribution of the group of sociologists he influenced most, the ethnomethodologists.

ETHNOMETHODOLOGY

The Californian sociologist, Harold Garfinkel founded ethnomethodology in the late nineteen fifties and early nineteen sixties. It is convenient to think of him as practically applying and developing Schütz's phenomenological approach. Crudely, ethnomethodology is phenomenological sociology.

In the first chapter, ethnomethodology was referred to as an attempt to describe how individuals make sense of, or give explanatory accounts of, their experience. We need to extend this point here before returning to the broader issue of the relationship between ethnomethodology and structural perspective. Two concepts used by ethnomethodologists need to be introduced. Unfortunately, both reflect the extreme verbosity with which ethnomethodology is commonly associated, but they are capable of simple definition and illustration. The terms are the documentary method and indexicality. The documentary method is employed by all of us and involves the assumption that a given event or occasion can be made sense of by seeing it as just one example, or document, of a general type. Thus, to take Cicourel's previously cited study of delinquency, a police officer may see a particular youth with what s/he regards as delinquent characteristics and accordingly place him within the general category of delinquent, that is, s/he reacts to the 'documentary' evidence, perhaps a skinhead haircut and tattooed arms. S/he could, of course, be mistaken. The concept of indexicality means that sense can only be made of any object or event by relating it back to its context, or the circumstances of its occurrence. Thus, the word 'five' makes sense as an anwer to the question, 'What time is it?' but not as an answer to 'How many players are there in a cricket team?' Similarly, to continue with the kind of example that appeals to Harold Garfinkel, the founder of ethnomethodology, a police officer in the outfit of a clown would make sense in the context of a fancy dress ball but not in the context of a drugs raid. We can agree, then, that meaning depends on context. The interrelatedness of meaning and event – almost to the point of equation – is referred to as reflexivity by ethnomethodologists, and is a third key concept of the perspective. Because of their respect for the uniqueness and unpredictability of personal meaning, ethnomethodologists examine social activity with careful reference back to context and the various verbal descriptions (conveyors of meaning) given of it by social actors. Study in this depth of detail has, necessarily, to be on a small scale, as was Cicourel's study of the social organisation of juvenile delinquency, and Atkinson's research into coroners' definitions of suicide.

COMMENT ON ETHNOMETHODOLOGY Three critical comments can be made about ethnomethodology. First, in confining themselves to describing rather than explaining the meanings of social actors, ethnomethodologists are begging an important question i.e. why do members of a particular cultural group reason in the way they do. As the next point illustrates this question becomes even more urgent when put in a comparative context. Second, it is doubtful whether ethnomethodology is quite as original as some of its adherents appear to think. Arguably it is very little different to descriptive cultural anthropology – the careful observation and accounts of the social life of a particular cultural group.

Comparative cultural anthropology inevitably forces the question – a classic sociological one – 'why do cultural groups behave differently?' Ethnomethodologists do not attempt to answer this question because it may involve explanations not shared by members of the cultural groups under examination. Third, despite the commitment of ethnomethodologists to describing social life only in terms of members' subjective and inter-subjective meanings, the concepts of typification and shared meaning bear comparison with the structural ones of norms, values and beliefs. Presumably, the 'external' influence of socialisation is part of the process by which individuals come commonsensibly to accept typifications and shared meanings? Yet, this is another issue which they fail to address.

Both structural perspectives and symbolic interactionism offer theories of social order and structure. For the former, order and structure lie in the institutional framework which constrains members of society, and for the latter order exists through the creation of shared meanings. Ethnomethodologists go a stage further back, as it were, by examining how individuals cope with, and make sense of, existing situations (whether 'orderly' or not). This interest need not, in my view, be incompatible with structural perspective. Presumably, it is not unlikely that the underlying patterns and taken-for-granted assumptions which individuals seek and find reinforced in experience (reflexivity) can be widely shared. If so, this fact structures interaction. Otherwise, there would be chaos.

Sociological Paradigm or Paradigms?

Sociology is often accused of being divided against itself – a discipline whose practitioners share no general theory of society and who consequently spend more time disagreeing with each other than building a solid base of knowledge. It is certainly true that the nineteen sixties and seventies were something of a period of 'warring perspectives' in sociology. Since then, however, what is a perhaps more mature approach has characterised the subject. Three broad trends are discernible.

One is a reversion to empirical work along with a mild cooling of interest in the broad theorising that characterised the earlier period. This trend is particularly noticeable in recent deviancy theory (see pp. 311–12). Secondly, on the other hand, there have been some substantial attempts at theory building which, in their efforts to find common ground between perspectives contrast sharply with earlier fractiousness. A third trend – somewhat at variance with the second – is an acceptance that a variety of paradigms or perspectives are 'inevitable' because the subjective element in enquiry is bound to produce different 'visions' or perspectives. This approach can be thought of as 'poststructuralist' in that it argues that no single 'structure' or perspective can claim to be wholly objective. The concluding pages of this book will examine the second and third of the above trends.

TOWARDS A UNIFIED SOCIOLOGICAL PARADIGM?

Three main points can be made in favour of the view that sociology has an underlying common theoretical grounding. The first point is that the methods of sociology, although highly diverse, can be regarded as a unifying factor in that they are the common property of all practitioners of the subject. The second point is that the major concepts in sociology provide a basic sub-structure to the discipline (Nisbet's term) despite differences in definition and usage within perspectives. The third point is that some trends towards the systematic reconstruction of sociological theory are occurring. Such a reconstruction, however, is likely to be a matter of synthesis rather than complete innovation. Of course, sociologists can and do also use concepts and theories to contradict as well as complement each other's work (this is explored later in this chapter, pp. 511–12).

THEORETICAL AND METHODOLOGICAL PLURALISM The first point can be briefly dealt with. I differ from what still seems to be an assumption of some sociologists that qualitative methods are overwhelmingly associated with interpretist theory and quantitative methods with functionalist theory (and perhaps, too, mere empiricism). Clearly there are substantial links of this kind – some of which we pursued earlier (chapter 2, p. 35). However, I believe that these were stronger, say, twenty five years ago than now. Today, sociologists seem increasingly to use whatever method suits their purpose best, and this is not always 'one or the other type'. Stan Cohen, David Hargreaves and many feminist sociologists have used a wide variety of methods in the course of a single piece of research. As the work of these authors suggests, sociological methods are perhaps better thought of as a varied tool-kit of analysis rather than ideological appendages

of various perspectives. As Newby et al. put it a situation of methodological 'pluralism' characterises contemporary sociology.

CORE CONCEPTS The second point is also relatively simple. It is not difficult to study sociology with the help of a more explicit emphasis on concepts, even though this approach to teaching the discipline appears to have declined in recent years. It might be helpful to list some key concepts which, despite different emphasis between perspectives, are in common sociological usage. These include: self; socialisation; culture; ideology; structure; stratification; power; order; change; agency and community. Some of these concepts were defined and introduced in chapter 1 (and others elsewhere). However, the explanatory power of concepts is only fully tapped when several are used together in the context of theory building. To state that there are certain 'core' sociological concepts, as Nisbet does, indicates a common field of enquiry, but perhaps no more.

THEORY BUILDING The third aspect of a more unified approach to sociology is to adopt a more integrated attitude to theory building. The section on interactionism and structural perspective will suffice as an example of how this can be done (pp. 506–7).

It is interesting that Marxist, Tom Bottomore and functionalist, Robert Nisbet have moved to explore common ground (*A History of Sociological Analysis*, 1979). In a joint essay, they suggest that Marxist sociology can be more positively viewed as a movement within sociology in general, rather than an alternative to it:

> *But there is today no Weberian nor Durkheimian sociology, and even in this case of Marx a considerable gap exists between Marx's own theory of society and the various forms of present-day Marxist sociology, with the development of the latter, we would dare to suggest, embodying advances in, 'sociological' rather than 'Marxist' thought.*
>
> *(Bottomore and Nisbet, 1979:XV)*

Despite the sense that a broad sociological framework does exist, Bottomore and Nisbet recognise that modern sociology contains a variety of different strands of interest, including a vital phenomenology of interaction.

STRUCTURATION THEORY

Anthony Giddens has pointed out a theoretical issue of considerable interest concerning structure, agency and system. He remarks that functionalism tends to collapse the distinction between structure and system to the point where the two terms are used interchangeably. This is the result of regarding the operation of the social system as merely the functionings of social structure (the fundamental functionalist tautology) and, in the process, disregarding the contributions of social actors. It becomes impossible, however, to amalgamate the two if we take the contrary view that people, not institutions or structures, are the dynamic agents of social systems. In order to 'bridge the gap' between structure and system, Giddens proposes that the term structuration be used. He intends to use it to synthesise two elements: (1) that people – individually or in groups – are the active forces in social systems and (2) that they work within structured (or normatively defined) situations. Thus, structure and system meet dynamically at the point of social action. Most illuminatingly, Giddens compares structuration to the process of linguistic communication of meaning (systems operation) and, in the process, it (language) can be changed and expanded (agent activity). It is not difficult to imagine how the concept of structuration could be applied to the analysis of normative structures and creative activity within organisations and social situations. It seems to go some way towards reconciling the two sides of the agency-structure debtate within sociology.

CONCEPTS AND THEORY BUILDING – A QUALIFICATION: MIDDLE RANGE THEORIES

In the previous section a brief exploration was made of how the networking of concepts and building of theories can reduce divisions in sociology. However, concepts and theories can legitimately be used to precisely the opposite effect and this, too, must be demonstrated.

There is a wide range of more or less closely linked concepts particularly associated, respectively, with each of the main perspectives or paradigms. For instance, a comparison of the diagram depicting functionalism (p. 498) with that depicting Marxism (p. 47) includes, in each case, several concepts regularly used only within one or other perspective. Thus, 'instrumental and expressive functional imperatives' are exclusively functionalist concepts whereas 'superstructure and infrastructive' are exclusively Marxist ones. The list of interactionist concepts given below could almost be used as a basis for describing the interactionist perspective. While most of these concepts occur within other perspectives, their total usage within the interactionist perspective is distinctive and largely defines interactionist theory.

Some key concepts within the interactionist paradigm

- Self: significant other: generalised other
- Meaning: interaction: negotiation
- Labelling: stereotyping: self-fulfilling prophecy
- Career: signification: amplification

Robert Merton described the relationship between paradigms and concepts as follows:

(P)aradigms have a notational function. They provide a compact arrangement of the central concepts and their inter-relations that are utilised for description and analysis ... (P)aradigms, by their very arrangement, suggest the systematic cross-tabulation of significant concepts and can thus sensitise the analyst to empirical and theoretical problems which he might otherwise overlook.

(Merton, 1967:70–1)

Merton further argues that sociological research is influenced in its direction by paradigms but is rarely aimed directly at proving a paradigm 'correct' or 'incorrect'. Rather, empirical research is immediately guided by what Merton usefully refers to as 'sociological theories of the middle range'. Such theories are of a sufficiently modest scale that they can actually be tested. Thus, hypotheses about the relationship between social class and voting behaviour; between certain types of work and alienation; and between suicide and social integration; can all be formulated and tested.

POSTSTRUCTURALISM AND SOCIOLOGICAL PERSPECTIVES

Poststructuralist thought appears to contradict

the notion of a unified sociological paradigm.

Poststructuralists argue that all theory – sociological or otherwise – contains an element of the subjective – theory is a 'way of seeing' as well as a description of 'something'. If, then, the nature of understanding (like the nature of physical perception) always involves taking a particular point of view, then, a single agreed version of 'external reality' becomes virtually impossible. Applied to sociology, this translates into an acceptance that a variety of sociological perspectives are inevitable.

Poststructuralism does seem to apply to the state of sociological pluralism briefly described in chapter one and developed throughout this book. In addition to the now familiar structural and interpretive perspectives, feminist, anti-racist, free-market liberal, environmentalist and other perspectives constantly occur. More than that, there are perspectives within these perspectives – feminism, in particular, being characterised by a variety of points of view. If anything, there are a greater variety of perspectives in the early nineteen nineties than when this book was first published in 1981. Yet, debate now is less fractious and more constructive in tone.

The poststructuralist criticism of the structural/interpretist polarisation is, then, all perspectives include *both* poles. Every perception of society involves elements of the observer and the observed – and this is as true of Marxism and functionalism as it is of symbolic interactionism. Although he was a stickler for scientific procedure, Weber himself accepted as much to the extent that he acknowledged that at least in selecting an area for research, the sociologist might be guided by personal preference.

CONCLUSION: NOT 'THROWING OUT THE BABY' Does poststructuralist insight mean that anybody can say anything about society and claim for their comments the status of a sociological perspective of equal status with other perspectives? The answer – fortunately – is 'no'. Sociology is bound by a large body of rules of procedure and method already described in this book. There are ways of doing sociology badly and ways of not doing it at all – just as there are ways of playing chess badly or of engaging with the pieces so ineptly that one cannot be described as actually playing the game at all.

The basic and accepted substructure of sociology is shared with other disciplines – it is what Goldthorpe has referred to as 'the rules of logical discourse'. Sociological work is presented, criticised and improved rationally. Anybody who attempts to achieve these goals irrationally is doing something else. More specifically, the many specific rules and procedures discussed above guide and constrain sociologists.

Poststructuralism should not be regarded as a destruction (or even a deconstruction) of the great tradition of structural sociology began by Durkheim, Marx and Weber and reiterated by Charles Wright Mills and Bottomore and Nisbet. Structural sociology is strengthened (if complicated!) by a better awareness of subjectivity – both the subjectivity of authors and of the people they study. Indeed, it is arguable that such an awareness preceded both the proliferation of perspectives and poststructuralism. In any case, in seeking to move the discipline forward, it is important not to throw out the sociological 'baby' with the philosophical 'bathwater'.

SUMMARY

1   Three key issues focus the central concerns of sociology:
(i) The nature of social structure.
(ii) The relationship between self and society.
(iii) The historical development of society.

2   Functionalism analyses the functions and dysfunctions of society almost as though society is an impersonal organism. Functionalism is criticised for underestimating both intentionality and social conflict.
3   Marxism occurs in a variety of forms all of which are premised on the concept of class conflict. Marxism is criticised for being deterministic and for being superseded by actual

historical developments.

4 Max Weber attempted to develop a sociology which linked social action and institutional formative power. He is criticised for over-emphasising the latter and failing to achieve a convincing synthesis.

5 Interactionism approaches society by attempting to understand the shared meanings of social actors. It can be strongly argued that interactionism and structural sociology are complementary rather than contradictory.

6 Phenomenology and ethnomethodology are related perspectives which analyse society in terms of the attempts of members to create social order. They are criticised for ignoring the formative power of institutions.

7 There are arguments for and against attempting to construct a unified sociological paradigm. On the 'for' side, is the increasingly obvious reality that the sociological perspectives and the variety of sociological methods generally complement rather than contradict each other. 'Against' are the apparently inevitable elements of subjectivity in sociological enquiry which continually contribute to the production of differing sociological models or perspectives.

8 Whatever differences there may be between sociological perspectives, they are all subject to revision through logical criticism and empirical reality.

FURTHER READING

Mary Maynard's *Sociological Theory* (Longman, 1989) is crisp and accessible. E C Cuff and G C F Payne's *Perspectives in Sociology* (Allen and Unwin, 1989) is lengthier and more demanding.

QUESTIONS

'Whilst recognising that theoretical ideas give a guide to research, this does not mean that we should let our preconceived beliefs determine the outcome of research. This brings us to one of the fundamental problems when 'doing sociology', and that is the degree of objectivity that is possible when studying human society.

Earlier sociologists like Auguste Comte were quite certain that all we need do was to borrow the methods of the natural sciences so that we could produce a science of society. By doing so we would be able to gather facts about society that would provide the basis for objective and "value-free" generalisations, i.e. generalisations based on the facts and not on prejudices or ideological assumptions of a subjective nature. However, there are ways in which personal values and beliefs are likely to influence research.'

(Davis and King: *Discovering Society*)

1 (a) The passage refers to borrowing the 'methods of the natural sciences' (line 7). Name the methodological technique most often used in the natural sciences. (1 mark)

(b) What methods do some sociologists use to 'gather facts about society' scientifically? (line 9). (2 marks)

(c) Suggest four reasons why some sociologists believe that the natural sciences should serve as a model for sociological research. (4 marks)

(d) What problems face sociologists in attempting to produce a science of society? (8 marks)

(e) In what ways might sociologists' values and beliefs influence their research? (10 marks)

(AEB, 1987)

Bibliography

ALLEN, C and WILLIAMS, G eds. *Sociology of Developing Societies: Sub-Sarahan Africa* (MACMILLAN, 1982)

ALLEN S. 'Gender, Race and Class in the 1980s', in C Husband *Race in Britain* (HUTCHINSON, 1987)

ANDERSON, A *A Family Structure in Nineteenth Century Lancashire* (CAMBRIDGE UNIVERSITY PRESS, 1971)

ARBER, S 'Class and the Elderly' in *Social Studies Review* VOL. 6, NO. 3, JANUARY 1990

ARIES, P *Centuries of Childhood* (JONATHAN CAPE, 1973)

ARNOT M and WEINER G *Gender and the Politics of Schooling* (HUTCHINSON, 1987)

ATKINSON, J 'The Changing Corporation' in D Clutterbuck ed. *New Patterns of Work* (GOWER, 1985)

BANFIELD, E 'The Imperatives of Class' in J Raynor and E Hams eds. *Urban Education: The City Experience* (WARD LOCK, 1977)

BARAN, P A and SWEEZY , P M *Monopoly Capital* (PENGUIN, 1966)

BAUER P *Dissent on Development* (HARVARD UNIVERSITY PRESS, 1975)

BECKER, H *Outsiders: Studies in the Sociology of Deviance* (MACMILLAN, 1966)

BECKER, H *Social Problems: A Modern Approach* (JOHN WILEY AND SONS, 1966)

BELL, C and NEWBY, H *Community Studies* (ALLEN AND UNWIN, 1971)

BELL, N W and VOGEL, E F eds. *A Modern Introduction to the Family* (THE FREE PRESS, 1968)

BELL, D *The End of Ideology* (THE FREE PRESS, 1960)

BEYNON, H *Working for Ford* (PENGUIN, 1973)

BLAU, P M *On the Nature of Organizations* (JOHN WILEY, 1974)

BLAUNER, R *Alienation and Freedom* (UNIVERSITY OF CHICAGO PRESS, 1964)

BOTT, E *Family and Social Network* (TAVISTOCK, 1957)

BOTTOMORE, T B and RUBEL, M eds. *Karl Marx: Selected Writings in Sociology and Social Philosophy* (PENGUIN, 1961)

BOTTOMORE, T B *Classes in Modern Society* (ALLEN AND UNWIN, 1965)

BOTTOMORE, T B and NISBET, R eds. *A History of Sociological Analysis* (HEINEMANN, 1979)

BOWLES, S and GINTIS, H *Schooling in Capitalist America* (RKP, 1979)

BURNHAM, T *The Managerial Revolution* (PUTNAM, 1943)

BUTLER, D and STOKES, D

BRAVERMAN, H *Labor and Monopoly* (MONTHLY REVIEW PRESS, 1974)

BREUGEL, I 'Sex and Race in the Labour Market' in *Feminist Review*, NO. 32

BRONFENBRENNER, U *Two Worlds of Childhood: USA and USSR* (ALLEN AND UNWIN, 1971)

BROWN, C *Black and White Britain: The Third PSI Survey* (HEINEMANN, 1984)

BURNS, T and STALKER, G *The Management of Innovation* (TAVISTOCK, 1966)

BUTLER, D and STOKES, D *Political Change in Britain* (MACMILLAN, 1974)

CAMPBELL, A *Delinquent Girls* (BASIL BLACKWELL, 1981)

CANNADINE, D *The Decline and Fall of the British Aristocracy* (YALE UNIVERSITY PRESS, 1990)

CASHMORE, E *The World of One Parent Families: Having To* (COUNTERPOINT, 1985)

CASTLES, S and KOSACK, G *Immigrant Workers and Class Structure in Western Europe* (OXFORD UNIVERSITY PRESS, 1973)

CHAMBLISS, W J and MANKOFF, M *Whose Law? What Order?* (JOHN WILEY AND SONS, 1976)

CHODOROW, N *The Reproduction of Mothering* (UNIVERSITY OF CALIFORNIA PRESS, 1978)

CICOUREL, A V *The Social Organisation of Juvenile Justice* (HEINEMANN, 1976)

CLEGG, S and DUNKERLEY, D *Organisation, Class and Control* (RKP, 1980)

CLOWARD, R A and OHLIN, L E *Delinquency and Opportunity* (THE FREE PRESS, 1961)

CLUTTERBUCK, D *New Patterns of Work* (GOWER, 1985) (HEINEMANN, 1976)

COATES, K and SILBURN, R *Poverty: The Forgotten Englishman* (PENGUIN, 1970)

COATES, K and TOPHAM T *Trade Unions and Politics* (BLACKWELL, 1986)

COHEN, A K *Delinquent Boys* (THE FREE PRESS, 1965)

COHEN, S *Folk Devils and Moral Panics* (MARTIN ROBERTSON, 1980)

COHEN, S *Visions of Social Control: Crime, Punishment and Classification* (POLITY PRESS, 1985)

COLES, B 'Gonna Tear Your Play House Down: Towards Reconstructing a Sociology of Youth' in *The Social Science Teacher*, VOL. 15, NO 3.

COOKE, P et al. *Localities* (UNWIN HYMAN, 1989) *Common Crisis: Co-operation for World Recovery* (PAN, 1983)

CORRIGAN, P *Schooling the Smash Street Kids* (MACMILLAN, 1979)

COWGILL, D O and HOLMES, L *Aging and Modernisation* (APPLETON-CENTURY-CROFTS, 1972)

COOTES, A 'Labour: The Feminist Touch,' in *Marxism Today*, VOL 29, NO 22, 1985

CROMPTOM, R and JONES, G *White-Collar Proletariat* (MACMILLAN, 1984)

CREWE, I 'Why Mrs Thatcher was Returned with a Landslide' in *Social Studies Review* VOL 3, NO 1, SEPTEMBER 1987

DAHL, R *A Preface to Political Theory* (UNIVERSITY OF CHICAGO, 1968)

DAHRENDORF, R *Class and Class Conflict in Britain* (RKP, 1959)

DANIEL, W W and MILLWARD, N *Workplace and Industrial Relations in Britain* (HEINEMANN, 1983)

DAVID, HOWARD, H *Beyond Class Images* (GROOM HELM, 1979)

DAVIS, K and MOORE, W E 'Some Principles of Stratification' in R Bendix and S M Lipset *Class, Status and Power* (RKP, 1967)

DEEM, R and SALAMAN, G eds. *Work, Culture and Society* (OPEN UNIVERSITY PRESS, 1985)

DELMAR, R 'Looking Again at Engel's "Origins of the Family, Private Property and the State"' in J Mitchell and A Oakley eds. *The Rights and Wrongs of Women* (PENGUIN, 1977)

DELMAR, R 'What is Feminism' in J Mitchell and A Oakley eds. *What is Feminism* (BASIL BLACKWELL, 1986)

DITTON, J 'Absent at Work: or How to Manage Monotony' in *New Society*, 21 DECEMBER 1972

DOYAL, L and PENNELL, I *The Political Economy of Health* (PLUTO PRESS, 1979)

DREW, D and GRAY, J *The Black-White Gap in Exam Achievement. A Statistical Critique of a Decade's Research* (QQSE RESEARCH GROUP, SHEFFIELD UNIVERSITY)

DUNLEAVY, P and O'LEARY, B *Theories of the State* (MACMILLAN, 1987)

DUNLEAVY, P and HUSBANDS, C T *British Democracy at the Crossroads* (ALLEN AND UNWIN, 1985)

DURKHEIM, E *The Division of Labor in Society* (THE FREE PRESS, 1967)

DURKHEIM, E *Suicide: A Study in Sociology* (RKP, 1970)

EDWARDS, R *Contested Terrain, the Transformation of the Workplace in the Twentieth Century* (HEINEMANN, 1979)

EHRENREICH, B and J 'The Professional – Managerial Class' in P Walker Ed. *Between Capital and Labour* (HARVESTER, 1979)

EISENSTADT, S N *From Generation to Generation: Age Groups and Social Structure* (COLLIER MACMILLAN, 1956)

ENGELS, F *The Origin of the Family, Private Property and the State* (LAWRENCE AND WISHART, 1972)

ERICKSON, E *Childhood and Society* (W W NORTON, 1963)

ETZIONI, A *Modern Organisations* (PRENTICE-HALL, 1963)

EVANS-PRITCHARD, E *Witchcraft, Oracles, and Magic among the Azande* (OXFORD UNIVERSITY PRESS, 1937)

FIRESTONE, S *The Dialectic of Sex* (PALADIN, 1972)

FITZGERALD, M 'Are Blacks an Electoral Liability' in *New Society*, 8 DECEMBER 1983

FLETCHER, R *The Family and Marriage in Britain* (PENGUIN, 1966)

FLETCHER, R *Sociology: The Study of Social Systems* (BATSFORD, 1981)

FRANK, A G *On Capitalist Development* (OXFORD UNIVERSITY PRESS, 1975)

FRANK, A G *Crisis in the World Economy* (HOMES AND MEIER, 1980)

FRANK, A G *Crisis in the Third World* (HOLMES AND MEIER, 1981)

FREEMAN, D *Margaret Mead and Samoa: the Making and Unmaking of an Anthropological Myth* (HARVARD UNIVERSITY PRESS, 1983)

FRIEDMAN, M and FRIEDMAN, R *Free to Choose* (AVON BOOKS, 1981)

FRIEDMAN, A *Industry and Labour: Class Struggle at Work and Contemporary Capitalism* (MACMILLAN, 1977)

FULLER, M 'Young, Female and Black' in E Cashmore and B. Troyna eds. *Black Youth in Crisis* (GEORGE ALLEN AND UNWIN, 1982)

GAILLIE, D *In Search of the New Working Class* (CAMBRIDGE UNIVERSITY PRESS, 1978)

GANS, H *The Urban Villagers* (FREE PRESS, 1962)

GARFINKEL, H *Studies in Ethnomethodology* (PRENTICE-HALL, 1967)

GIDDENS, A 'An Anatomy of the British Ruling Class', in *New Society*, 4 OCTOBER, 1979

GERTH, H H and MILLS, C W *Character and Social Structure* (HARCOURT BRACE, 1953)

GIDDENS, A *New Rules of Sociological Method* (HUTCHINSON, 1976)

GILL, R 'Altered Images: Women in the Media' in *Social Studies Review* SEPTEMBER 1988

GLASGOW UNIVERSITY OF MEDIA GROUP *Bad News* (RKP, 1976)

GLASGOW, D *The Black Underclass* (VINTAGE BOOKS, 1981)

GOFFMAN, E *Asylums* (PENGUIN, 1968)

GOLDING, P and MURDOCK, G *The New Communications Revolution in J Curran Bending Reality: The State of the Media* (PLUTO, 1986)

GOLDTHORPE, J H et al. *The Affluent Worker in the Class Structure* (CAMBRIDGE UNIVERSITY PRESS, 1969)

GOLDTHORPE, J H LLEWELLYN, C, and PAYNE, C *Social Mobility and Class Structure in Britain* (OXFORD UNIVERSITY PRESS, 1980)

GOODE, W J *World Revolution and Family Patterns* (THE FREE PRESS, 1965)

GOULD, J and KOLB, W eds. *A Dictionary of Social Sciences* (TAVISTOCK PUBLICATIONS, 1964)

GOULDNER, A W *Wildcat Strike* (RKP, 1957)

GRIFFIN C *Typical Girls, Young Women From School to the Job Market* (RKP, 1985)

HALL, S and JEFFERSON, T *Resistance through Rituals* (HUTCHINSON, 1976)

HALL, S, CRITCHER, C, JEFFERSON, T, CLARKE, J, and ROBERTS, B *Policing the Crisis* (MACMILLAN, 1979)

HALL, S et al. *The Empire Strikes Back* (HUTCHINSON, 1981)

HALSEY, A H *Change in British Society* (OPEN UNIVERSITY PRESS, 1986)

HARVEY, D *Social Justice and the City* (EDWARD ARNOLD, 1973)

HARGREAVES, D *Social Relations in a Secondary School* (RKP, 1967)

HARRINGTON, M *The Other America* (PENGUIN, 1963)

HARRINGTON, M *The New American Poverty* (RINEHART AND WINSTON, 1984)

HARRIS, C C *The Family and Industrial Society* (ALLEN AND UNWIN, 1983)

HART, A 'Images of the Third World' in *Looking Beyond the Frame* (LINKS PUBLICATIONS, 1989)

HART, N *The Sociology of Health and Medicine* (CAUSEWAY, 1986)

HARTMANN, P and HUSBANDS, C *Racism and the Mass Media* (DAVIS POYNTER, 1974)

HAYTER, T *Aid: Rhetoric and Reality* (PLUTO PRESS, 1985)

HEATH, A, JOWELL, R and CURTICE, J *How Britain Votes* (PERGAMON, 1985)

HEBDIGE, D *Subculture: the Meaning of Style* (METHUEN, 1979)

HIMMELWEIT, H T et al. *How Voters Decide* (ACADEMIC PRESS, 1987)

HUSBANDS, C ed. *Race in Britain: Continuity and Change* (HUTCHINSON, 1982; 2ND EDITION, 1987)

HYMAN, R *Strikes* (FONTANA, 1984)

ILLICH, I *The Limits of Medicine: Medical Nemesis* (CALDER AND BOYARS, 1975)

Inequalities in Health ('The Black Report' and *The Health Divide*) (PENGUIN, 1988)

JOHNSON, T J *Professions and Power* (MACMILLAN, 1972)

JONES, B *The Moving Target: Job Flexibility in Britain* SEMINAR, JOHNS HOPKINS UNIVERSITY, 1988

KEENOY, T *Invitation to Industrial Relations* (BASIL BLACKWELL, 1985)

KELLY, J *Trade Unions and Socialist Politics* (VERSO, 1988)

KINCAID, J C *Poverty and Equality in Britain* (PENGUIN, 1973)

KERR, C et al. *Industrialisation and Industrial Man* (HEINEMANN, 1962)

KUHN, T S *The Structure of Scientific Revolutions* (UNIVERSITY OF CHICAGO PRESS, 1970)

LANE, T and ROBERTS, K *Strikes at Pilkington* (FONTANA, 1971)

LASLETT, P *The World We Have Lost* (METHUEN, 1971)

LEA, J and YOUNG, J *What is To Be Done About Law and Order* (PENGUIN, 1984)

LEGHORN, L and PARKER, K *Women's Worth: Sexual Economics and the World of Women* (RKP, 1981)

LE GRAND, J and ROBINSON, R *Privatisation and the Welfare State* (ALLEN AND UNWIN, 1984)

LENIN, V I in H Christman ed. *Essential Works of Lenin* (BANTAM, 1969)

LEWIS, O *The Children of Sanchez* (RANDOM HOUSE, 1961)

LOCKWOOD, D *The Blackcoated Worker* (ALLEN AND UNWIN, 1958)

LOWE, S *Urban Social Movements* (MACMILLAN, 1986)

MAC AN GHAILL, M *Young, Gifted and Black* (OPEN UNIVERSITY PRESS, 1988)

MACK, J and LANSLEY, S *Poor Britain* (ALLEN AND UNWIN, 1985)

MALINOWSKI, B *The Sexual Life of Savages* (RKP, 1957)

MANNHEIM, K *Essays on the Sociology of Knowledge* (RKP, 1952)

MARCUSE, H *One Dimensional Man* (RKP, 1964)

MARCUSE, H *Eros and Civilisation* (SPHERE, 1969)

MARSHAL, G, NEWBY, H, ROSE, D and VOGLER, C *Social Class in Modern Britain* (HUTCHINSON, 1988)

MARSHALL, G *In Praise of Sociology* (HYMAN, 1990)

MARTIN, D *The Religious and the Secular* (RKP, 1969)

MARTIN, E *The Women in the Body* (OPEN UNIVERSITY PRESS, 1987)

MARX, K and ENGELS, F *The Communist Manifesto* (PENGUIN, 1981)

MASLOW, A 'A Theory of Motivation' in *Psychological Review* VOL. 50

MATZA, D *Delinquency and Drift* (WILEY, 1964)

MAYNARD, M 'Current Trends in Feminist Theory in *Social Studies Review*, VOL 2, NO. 3, JANUARY, 1987

MAYNARD, M 'Contemporary Housework and the Houseworker Role' in Graeme Salaman ed., *Work, Culture and Society* (OPEN UNIVERSITY PRESS, 1988)

MAYNARD, M *Sociological Theory* (LONGMAN, 1989)

McINTOSH, S and work group, 'Work and Leisure' in Alan Tomlinson ed. *Leisure and Social Control* (BRIGHTON POLYTECHNIC, 1981)

McINTOSH, M 'The State and the Oppression of Women' in A Kuhn and A Wolpe eds. *Feminism and Materialism* (RKP, 1978)

McKENZIE, R and SILVER, A *Angels in Marble* (HEINEMANN, 1968)

McROBBIE, A 'Teenage Girls: Jackie and the Ideology of Adolescent Feminity' in B Waites et al. *Popular Culture, Past and Present* (GROOM HELM, 1985)

MEAD, G H *Mind, Self and Society* (THE UNIVERSITY OF CHICAGO PRESS, 1962)

MEAD, M *Coming of Age in Samoa: A Study of Adolescence and Sex in Primitive Societies* (PENGUIN, 1971)

MERTON, R K *On Theoretical Sociology* (THE FREE PRESS, 1967)

MERTON, R K and NISBET, B *Contemporary Social Problems* (HARCOURT, BRACE, JAVANOVICH INC., 1976)

MILES, R *Racism* (ROUTLEDGE, 1989)

MILES, R 'Racism, Ideology and Disadvantage' in *Social Studies Review*, MARCH 1990

MILIBAND, R *The State in Capitalist Society* (WEIDENFELD AND NICOLSON, 1969)

MILLER, W 'Lower Class Culture as a Generating Milieu of Gang Delinquency' in *Journal of Social Issues*, VOL 14

MILLET, K *Sexual Politics* (DOUBLEDAY, 1970)

MILLS, C W *White Collar: the American Middle Classes* (OUP, 1951)

MILLS, C W *The Power Elite* (OXFORD UNIVERSITY PRESS, 1956)

MILLS, C W *The Sociological Imagination* (OXFORD UNIVERSITY PRESS, 1959)

MISHLER, G E *Social Contexts of Health, Illness and Patient Care* (CAMBRIDGE UNIVERSITY PRESS, 1981)

MITCHELL, D A *A New Dictionary of Sociology* (RKP, 1979)

MITCHELL, J *Women's Estate* (PENGUIN, 1971)

MITCHELL, J and OAKLEY, A eds. *What is Feminism* (BLACKWELL, 1986)

MORGAN, D H *Socialisation and the Family: Change and Diversity* in Woodhead, M and McGrath, A eds., (OPEN UNIVERSITY PRESS, 1988)

MOSER, C and KALTON, *Survey Methods in Social Investigation* (HEINEMANN, 1979)

MURDOCK, G and PHELPS, P *Mass Media and the Secondary School* (MACMILLAN, 1973)

MURDOCK, G and GOLDING, G 'Capitalism, Communication and Class Relations' in J Curran et al. *Mass Communication and Society* (EDWARD ARNOLD, 1977)

MURDOCK, G and GOLDING, P 'Ideology and the Mass Media: The Question of Determination' in M Barrett et al., eds., *Ideology and Cultural Production* (CROOM-HELM, 1979)

MURDOCK, G and GOLDING, P 'The New Communications Revolution' in Jo Curran et al, eds. *Bending Reality: The State of the Media* (PLUTO, 1986)

MURDOCK, G P *Social Structure* (MACMILLAN, 1949)

MURRAY, C 'Underlcass: A Disaster in the Making' in *Sunday Times Magazine* NOVEMBER 26, 1989

NAVARRO, V *Medicine Under Capitalism* (PRODIST, 1976)
North-South: A Programme for Survival (PAN, 1981)

OAKLEY, A *The Sociology of Housework* (PANTHEON, 1974)

OAKLEY, A *The Captured Womb* (BLACKWELL, 1984)

O'DONNELL, M *Age and Generation* (TAVISTOCK, 1985)

O'DONNELL M *A New Introductory Reader in Sociology* (NELSON, 1988)

O'DONNELL, M *Race and Ethnicity* (LONGMAN, 1991)

PAHL, J *Private Violence and Public Policy* (RKP, 1985)

PAHL, R *Urbs in Rure* (WEIDENFELD AND NICOLSON, 1965)

PARKER, S *The Sociology of Industry* (ALLEN AND UNWIN, 1972)

PARKIN, F *Class Inequality and the Political Order*

PARKIN, F *Marxism and Class Theory* (TAVISTOCK, 1979)

PARSONS, T *The Social System* (THE FREE PRESS, 1951)

PARSONS, T 'The Family Its Function and Destiny' in R N Ansden ed. *The Social Structure of the Family* (HARPER AND ROW, 1949)

PATRICK, J *A Glasgow Gang Observed* (METHUEN, 1973)

PAXMAN, J *Friends in High Places: Who Runs Britain* (MICHAEL JOSEPH, 1990)

PEACH, C *West Indian Migration to Britain* (OXFORD UNIVERSITY PRESS, 1968)

PELLETIER, K *Mind as Healer, Mind as Slayer* (ALLEN AND UNWIN, 1979)

PHILLIPSON, C *Capitalism and the Construction of Old Age* (MACMILLAN, 1982)

PIORE, M and SABEL, C F *The Second Industrial Divide: Possibilities for Property* (BASIC BOOKS, 1984)

POLLERT, A 'Dismantling Flexibility' in *Capital and Class,* NO. 34, 1988

PRYCE, K *Endless Pressure* (BRISTOL WRITERS PRESS, 1986).

RAYNOR, J and HARRIS, E eds. *The City Experience* (OPEN UNIVERSITY PRESS, 1977)

REICH, C *The Greening of America* (ALLEN LANE, 1970)

RENVOIZE, J *Going Solo: Single Mothers by Choice* (RKP, 1985)

REX, J and TOMLINSON, S *Colonial Immigrants in a British City: A Class Analysis* (RKP, 1979)

REX, J *Race and Ethnicity* (OPEN UNIVERSITY PRESS, 1986)

ROWBOTHAM, S *Women's Consciousness: Man's World* (PENGUIN, 1973)

ROBERTS, K et al. *The Fragmentory Class Structure* (HEINEMANN, 1977)

ROBERTS K *Contemporary Youth Unemployment,* PAPER TO BRITISH ASSOCIATION FOR THE ADVANCEMENT OF SCIENCE, 1982

ROSTOW, W *The Stages of Economic Growth* (CAMBRIDGE UNIVERSITY PRESS, 1960)

RUSTIN, M 'The Politics of Post-Fordism' in *The New Left Review,* NO. 175 (1989)

RUTTER, M
Fifteen Thousand Hours: Secondary Schools and Their Effects on Children (OPEN BOOKS, 1979)

SAMPSON, A *The Money Lenders: Bankers in a Dangerous World* (HODDER AND STOUGHTON, 1981)

SAUNDERS, P *Social Class and Stratification* (TAVISTOCK, 1990)

SCOTT, J *The Upper Classes: Property and Privilege in Britain* (MACMILLAN, 1982)

SEIDLER, V J *Recreating Sexual Politics* (ROUTLEDGE, 1991)

SKLAIR, L *Sociology of the Global System* (HARVESTER WHEATSHEAF, 1991)

SHARPE, S 'The Role of the Family in the Oppression of Women' in *New Edinburgh Review* 1972

SHARPE, S *Just Like a Girl* (PENGUIN, 1976)

SHORTER, E *The Making of the Modern Family* (FONTANA, 1977)

STONE, M *The Education of the Black Child* (FONTANA, 1981)

SIMMONS, O G 'Development Perspectives and Population Change' in *Papers of the East-West Population Institute*, 1983

SILLITOE, A *Saturday Night and Sunday Morning* (ALLEN AND UNWIN, 1958)

SILVERMAN, D *The Theory of Organisations* (HEINEMANN, 1970)

SINFIELD, A *What Unemployment Means* (MARTIN ROBERTSON, 1981)

SIMMEL G 'The Metropolis and Mental Life' in K Wolf ed. *The Sociology of George Simmel* (FREE PRESS, 1950)

SOLOMOS, J *Race and Racism in Contemporary Britain* (MACMILLAN, 1989)

SMITH, D and TOMLINSON, S STANWORTH, M 'Women and Class Analysis: a reply to Goldthorpe' in *Sociology*, 18, 1984, pp. 159–170

STEINBERG, I *The New Lost Generation; The Problems of the Population Boom* (MARTIN ROBERTSON, 1982)

STEWART, A et al. *Social Stratification and Occupations* (MACMILLAN, 1980)

TAYLOR-GOOBY, P *Public Opinion, Ideology and the Welfare State* (TKP, 1985)

TAYLOR, J G *From Modernization to Modes of Production*

TIZZARD, B. et al. *Young Children at School in the Inner City* (LAWRENCE ERLBAUM, 1988)

TONNIES, F *Community and Society* (HARPER AND ROW, 1957)

TUCHMAN, G et al. *Hearth and Home: Images of Women in the Media* (OXFORD UNIVERSITY PRESS, 1978)

TOWNSEND, P *Poverty in the United Kingdom* (PENGUIN, 1979)

TUMIN, M *Social Stratification: The Forms and Functions of Social Inequality* (PRENTICE-HALL, 1967)

WALTERS, V *Class Inequality and Health Care: The Origins and Impact of the National Health* (CROOM HELM, 1980)

WEDDERBURN, D and CROMPTON, R *Workers' Attitudes and Technology* (CAMBRIDGE UNIVERSITY PRESS, 1972)

WESTERGAARD, J and RESLER, H *Class in Capitalist Society* (PENGUIN, 1976)

WHALE, J *The Politics of the Media* (FONTANA, 1977)

WHYTE, W F *Street Corner Society* (UNIVERSITY OF CHICAGO PRESS, 1955)

WILLIS, P *Learning to Labour* (SAXON HOUSE, 1977)

WILLIS, P et al. *Common Culture* (OPEN UNIVERSITY PRESS, 1990)

WILLMOTT, P *Adolescent Boys in East London* (PENGUIN, 1966)

WILLMOTT, P and YOUNG, M *Family and Kinship in East London* (PENGUIN, 1962)

WILLMOTT, P and YOUNG, M *Family and Class in a London Suburb* (RKP, 1960)

WILLMOTT, P and YOUNG, M *The Symmetrical Family* (RKP, 1973)

WILLMOTT, P 'Urban Kinship Past and Present' in *Social Studies Review*, NOVEMBER, 1988

WILSON, B R *Religion in a Sociological Perspective* (OXFORD UNIVERSITY PRESS, 1982)

WIRTH, L 'Urbanism as a Way of Life' in *American Journal of Sociology*, VOL. 44, NO 1

WOOD, S *The Transformation of Work* (UNWIN HYMAN, 1989)

WRIGHT, E O *Classes* (VERSO, 1985)

YULE, V 'Why are parents so tough on children?' in *New Society*, 27 SEPTEMBER 1986

Author index

Subject index